THE ORIGIN OF
ENGLISH SURNAMES

The Origin of
ENGLISH
SURNAMES

by

P. H. REANEY

Readers Union
LONDON

This RU edition was produced in 1969 for sale to its members
only by Readers Union Ltd at 10–13 Bedford Street, London
W.C.2, and at Letchworth Garden City, Herts. Full details of
membership may be obtained from our London address.

Printed in Great Britain by Richard Clay (The Chaucer Press),
Ltd, Bungay, Suffolk. Originally published by Routledge &
Kegan Paul Ltd, London.

CONTENTS

v

CONTENTS

CONTENTS

CONTENTS

CONTENTS

ix

CONTENTS

MAPS

PREFACE

THIS book is not a history of English surnames. That is a task for the future, probably the distant future, for there is a vast accumulation of material still to be studied; many surnames are still undocumented whilst for numerous others the present evidence is unsatisfactory and confusing. To many of my correspondents I have been unable to suggest a satisfactory etymology. For *Mortiboy* I had only a single reference, *Mordeboice* in 1644. The name has been explained as 'dead wood' which implies a place-name, but no example with *de* has yet been discovered and the persistent medial *i* requires explanation. Dr J. R. Greenwood of Windermere has now found examples in Warwickshire from 1461, but these are still too late for anything but guess-work.

For *Tuffin* there is one early example, John *Tuffyn* (1327 SRSf). This is almost certainly from the Scandinavian personal-name *Thor-finnr*, found in the Yorkshire and Northumberland Domesday Book as *Turfin* and still in use in the thirteenth century. But this can hardly be the source of the modern *Tuffin* which a New Zealand correspondent has found in Dorset, Wilts and Hants in the late sixteenth and seventeenth centuries. It occurs, too, occasionally as *Tufften* which suggests a not impossible derivation from a place-name *Tufton*, also a surviving surname. There was a John *Tufton* in Sussex in 1500. *Tufton* (Hants) is *Tochituna* (1086 DB) and Tockington (Glos) is *Tochintune* (DB), both from an Old English personal-name *Tocca*, but the place-name forms so far found throw no light on the development to *Tufton*. Either place may be the source of these southern surnames, and the rare Dorset *Tufften* (1725) may be an isolated example of an earlier form of the name. But there is no certainty here; we need later examples of the place-names and earlier examples of the surnames.

The aim of this book is to give a general account of the development of English surnames, their classification, changes in pronunciation and spelling, and the gradual growth of hereditary family names. Inevitably, the basic material is drawn from my *Dictionary of British Surnames*. Only the compiler knows what a dictionary contains and he is liable to forget. It is a work of reference, one to browse in at leisure, but the mere mass of the material makes it difficult to sort and sift it, to form general opinions and to trace developments. This work, however, is not a mere digest of the dictionary. Whenever possible, fresh examples have been given and various types of surnames have been treated at greater length. To satisfy correspondents, lists have been given of local surnames compounded with prepositions, of others deriving from topographical terms long disused, often surviving only in field-names, and of many from lost and insignificant places difficult to identify. More attention than usual has been paid to the identification of surnames from French and continental places—ignoring those which are not known to survive. The last two chapters treat of the growth of hereditary surnames and the homes of family names. Both are preliminary studies, the latter, in particular, being in need of extension and development.

Most of the material on which the book is based comes from my collection of surnames begun over twenty years ago. For useful information I am deeply indebted to numerous correspondents some of whom are mentioned in the text. My general obligations remain as given in *A Dictionary of British Surnames* and *The Origin of English Place-names*. For permission to quote illustrative extracts, my grateful thanks are due to the following authors and their publishers: E. K. Chambers, *The Medieval Stage* (Clarendon Press); T. R. Glover, *Greek Byways* (Cambridge University Press); G. C. Homans, *English Villagers of the 13th Century* (Harvard University Press); W. G. Hoskins, *The Midland Peasant* (Macmillan); Eric Partridge, *Slang Today and Yesterday* (Routledge and Kegan Paul); L. F. Salzman, *English Life in the Middle Ages* (Clarendon Press); A. R. Wagner, *English Genealogy* (Clarendon Press); R. M. Wilson, *The Lost Literature of Medieval England* (Methuen).

P. H. REANEY

Tunbridge Wells
August, 1966

ABBREVIATIONS

New sources are described in full. For others, see *A Dictionary of British Surnames*.

a	*ante*	Bury	*Feudal Docs. of . . . Bury St Edmunds*
acc.	accusative		
AD	*Catalogue of Ancient Deeds*	BuryS	*Kalendar of Abbot Samson*
Afr	Anglo-French	c	*circa*
Anglo-Scand	Anglo-Scandinavian	C	Cambridgeshire
		Calv	*Calverley Charters*
ArchC	*Archaeologia Cantiana*	CantW	*Canterbury Wills 1396–1558 (KAS, 1920)*
ASC	*Anglo-Saxon Chronicle*		
ASCh	*Anglo-Saxon Charters*	Ch	*Calendar of Charter Rolls*
Ass	Assize Roll (unpublished)	Ch	Cheshire
Ass	*Assize Roll*	Chirk	*Extent of Chirkland*
AssL	*A Lincs Assize Roll for* 1298 (L Rec. Soc. 36, 1944) *Some Sessions of the Peace in Lincs* (L Rec. Soc., 30, 49, 1933, 1955)	ChR	*Rotuli Chartarum*
		ChwWo	*Churchwardens' Accounts of St Michael's, Bredwardine*
		Cl	*Calendar of Close Rolls*
		Clerkenwell	*Clerkenwell Cartulary*
AssW	*Crown Pleas for the Wilts Eyre* (WAS, Rec. Branch XVI, 1961)	CNat	C. N. L. Brooke and M. M. Postan, *Carte Nativorum* (Nth Rec. Soc., XX, 1960)
Barnwell	*Liber Memorandorum . . . de Bernewelle*		
		Co	Cornwall
Bart	Moore, *Hist. St Bartholomew's Hospital*	ColchCt	*Colchester Court Rolls*
		Coram	*Placita coram domino rege*
BCS	Birch, *Cartularium Saxonicum*	Crawford	A. S. Napier and W. H. Stevenson, *The Crawford Collection of Early Charters and Documents* (Oxford, 1895)
Bec	*Documents of the Abbey of Bec*		
Beds	Bedfordshire		
Berks	Berkshire		
Bk	Buckinghamshire	Cu	Cumberland
Boldon	*Boldon Book*	Cur	*Curia Regis Rolls*
Brabourne	*Brabourne MSS*	CurR	*Rotuli curiae Regis*
		D	Devonshire
Building	Salzman, *Building in England*	Db	Derbyshire
Burton	*Burton Chartulary*	DB	*Domesday Book*

xiii

ABBREVIATIONS

DBStP	*Domesday of St Paul's*	Ha	Hampshire
DC	Stenton, *Danelaw Charters*	He	Herefordshire
Do	Dorsetshire	HeCh	D. Walker, *Charters of the*
Du	Durham		*Earldom of Hereford*
Dublin	Gilbert, *Documents of Ire-*		*1095–1201* (Camden
	land		Fourth Ser., I, 1964)
EA	*The East Anglian*	Herts	Hertfordshire
ELPN	Ekwall, *Early London Per-*	Holme	West, *St Benet of Holme*
	sonal-names	HPD	*Hornchurch Priory Docu-*
Ely	B. M., Cott. Claud. C xi		*ments*
ElyA	B. M., Cott. Tib. B ii	HTO	*Hearth Tax Returns, Ox-*
ER	*The Essex Review*		*fordshire, 1665* (Oxfords.
ERO	Unpublished documents in		Rec. Soc., XXI, 1940)
	the Essex Record Office	HTSf	*Suffolk Hearth Tax Returns*
ERY	East Riding of Yorkshire	HTSo	*Somerset Hearth Tax Re-*
Ess	Essex		*turns*
EwenG	*Guide to the origin of British*	Hu	Huntingdonshire
	Surnames	Husting	*Wills in the Court of Husting*
Eynsham	*Eynsham Cartulary*	ICC	*Inquisitio Comitatus Canta-*
f.	feminine		*brigiensis*
FA	*Feudal Aids*	InqEl	*Inquisitio Eliensis*
Fees	*Book of Fees*	Ipm	*Calendar of Inquisitions post*
FeuDu	*Feodarium Prioratus Dunel-*		*mortem*
	mensis	K	Kent
FF	*Feet of Fines*	KentW	*Testamenta Cantiana*
FFSo	*Pedes Finium* (So Rec. Soc..	L	Lincolnshire
	6, 12, 17, 22, 1892–1906)	La	Lancashire
Fine	*Calendar of Fine Rolls*	Lat	Latin
ForSt	*Staffordshire Forest Pleas*	Lei	Leicestershire
France	Round, *Calendar of Docu-*	LeiAS	*Leicestershire Archaeologi-*
	ments preserved in France		*cal Society*
Frides	*Cartulary of the monastery*	LeicBR	*Leicester Borough Records*
	of St Frideswide (Oxford	Lewes	*Lewes Chartulary*
	Hist. Soc., 28, 31, 1895–6)	LG	Low German
FrLeic	*Register of Freeman of*	LLB	*Letter Books of the City of*
	Leicester		*London*
FrNorw	*Freemen of Norwich*	Lo	London
FrY	*Register of the Freemen of*	LoCt	*Early Mayor's Court Rolls*
	York	LondEngl	*A Book of London English*
gen.	genitive	LoPleas	*London Plea and Memoran-*
Gilb	*Gilbertine Charters*		*da Rolls*
GildY	*Guild of Corpus Christi,*	LP	*Letters and Papers of Henry*
	York		*VIII*
Gl	Gloucestershire	m.	masculine
Glapwell	R. R. Darlington, *The*	Malmesbury	
	Glapwell Charters (DbAS,		*Registrum Malmesburiense*
	1957–9)	MD	Middle Dutch
Guisb	*Cartulary of Gyseburne*	ME	Middle English

xiv

ABBREVIATIONS

MESO	Fransson, *ME Surnames of Occupation*
Miller	*The Abbey and Bishopric of Ely*
MinAcctCo	
	Ministers' Accounts of the Earldom of Cornwall
MKS	F. R. H. Du Boulay, *Medieval Kentish Society* (KAS, Recs. Pub. Cte., XVIII, 1964)
modFr	Modern French
MustersSr	
	T. Craib, *Surrey Musters* (Sr Rec. Soc., III, 1914–19)
MW	Middle Welsh
Mx	Middlesex
Nb	Northumberland
NED	*The Oxford English Dictionary*
neut.	neuter
Newark	*Documents relating to the Manor and Soke of Newark-on-Trent* (Thoroton Soc., Rec. Ser., XVI, 1955)
Nf	Norfolk
nom.	nominative
NorwDeeds	
	W. Rye, *Calendar of Norwich Deeds* (Nf and Norw Arch. Soc., 1903, 1915)
NorwDep	
	W. Rye, *Depositions . . . of Norwich* (Nf and Norw Arch. Soc., 1905)
NorwLt	W. Hudson, *Leet Jurisdiction in the City of Norwich* (Selden Soc., V, 1892)
NorwW	*Norwich Wills*
NottBR	*Records of the Borough of Nottingham*
NRY	North Riding of Yorkshire
Nt	Nottinghamshire
Nth	Northamptonshire
NthCh	*Northamptonshire Charters*
O	Oxfordshire

OBret	Old Breton
ODa	Old Danish
ODCN	*Oxford Dictionary of English Christian Names*
OE	Old English
OEByn	Tengvik, *Old English Bynames*
OFr	Old French
OG	Old German
OIr	Old Irish
OLG	Old Low German
ON	Old Norse
ONFr	Old Northern French
Oriel	*Oriel College Records*
OSax	Old Saxon
Oseney	*Cartulary of Oseney Abbey*
OSw	Old Swedish
OW	Old Welsh
Oxon	*Register of the University of Oxford*
P	*Pipe Rolls*
ParlWrits	*Parliamentary Writs*
Pat	*Calendar of Patent Rolls*
Petre	Petre Documents in ERO. Calendared by Canon C. J. Kuypers
Pinchbeck	*Pinchbeck Register*
plur.	plural
PND	*Place-names of Devonshire*
PNDb	*Place-names of Derbyshire*
PNEss	*Place-names of Essex*
PNWRY	*Place-names of the West Riding of Yorkshire*
PNWt	*Place-names of the Isle of Wight*
PopLond	Ekwall, *Population of Medieval London*
PR	*Parish Registers* (Bisham, Denham, Greenwich, Hartland, Horringer, Ledbury, Lewisham, Rothwell, Staplehurst, Stourton)
PrGR	*Preston Guild Rolls*
PromptParv	
	Promptorium Parvulorum
Putnam	*Statutes of Labourers*
R	Rutland

ABBREVIATIONS

Rad	*The Priory of St Radegund*	SRSx	*The Lay Subsidy Rolls for*
Rams	*Ramsey Cartulary*		*Sussex 1524–5* (Sx Rec.
RamsCt	*Court Rolls of the Abbey*		Soc., LVI, 1956)
	of Ramsey	St	Staffordshire
RH	*Rotuli Hundredorum*	StCh	*The Staffordshire Chart-*
Riev	*Cartularium de Rievalle*		*ulary*
RochW	*Rochester Wills*	StP	*Early Charters of St Paul's*
Ronton	*Ronton Cartulary*	St Thomas	
RotDom	*Rotuli de Dominabus*		*Chartulary of the Priory of*
Sa	Shropshire		*St Thomas*
SaG	*The Merchants' Guild of*	Sx	Sussex
	Shrewsbury (SaAS, 2nd	SxAS	*Sussex Archaeological Soc-*
	Ser., vol. VIII, 1896)		*iety*
Seals	*Sir Christopher Hatton's*	Templars	*Records of the Templars*
	Book of Seals	W	Wiltshire
Sf	Suffolk	Wa	Warwickshire
Shef	*Charters in the Jackson*	Wak	*Wakefield Court Rolls*
	Collection	WAM	Westminster Abbey Muni-
ShefA	*Sheffield Manorial Records*		ments
SIA	*Suffolk Institute of Archae-*	We	Westmorland
	ology	Wenlok	B. F. Harvey, *Documents*
Sibton	A. H. Denney, *The Sibton*		*...of Walter de Wenlok*
	Abbey Estates (Sf Recs.		(Camden 4th Ser., II,
	Soc. II, 1960)		1965)
sing.	singular	WhC	*Coucher Book of Whalley*
So	Somerset		*Abbey*
Sr	Surrey	Winton	*Liber Wintoniensis*
SR	Subsidy Rolls (unprinted)	Wo	Worcestershire
SR	*Subsidy Roll*	WRY	West Riding of Yorkshire
SRK	*Kent Lay Subsidy Roll,*	W'stowWills	
	1334–5 (in MKS)		Fry, *Walthamstow Wills*
SRSa	*The Shropshire Lay Subsidy*	Wt	Isle of Wight
	Roll of 1327 (SaAS, 2nd	Y	Yorkshire
	Ser., vols. I, IV, V, VIII,	*	a postulated form
	X, XI; 3rd Ser., vols.		
	V–VII)		

BIBLIOGRAPHY

This is not a full bibliography of the subject. It does not include many books now completely out-of-date. Articles from periodicals are fully described in the footnotes.

ARNOLD-FORSTER, F., *Studies in Church Dedications* (London, 1899).
BARDSLEY, C. W., *A Dictionary of English and Welsh Surnames* (London, 1901).
— *English Surnames* (London, 1875).
BARING-GOULD, S., *Family Names and their Story* (London, 1910).
BAUGH, A. C., *Chaucer's Major Poetry* (London, 1964).
BENNETT, H. S., *Life on the English Manor* (Cambridge, 1938).
BJÖRKMAN, E., *Nordische Personennamen in England* (Halle, 1910).
— *Zur englischen Namenkunde* (Halle, 1912).
BLOCK, K. S., *Ludus Coventriae* (EETS, Extra Ser., CXX, Oxford, 1922).
BOEHLER, M., *Die altenglischen Frauennamen* (Berlin, 1930).
CAMDEN, W., *Remains concerning Britain* (London, 1605).
CAWLEY, A. C., *The Wakefield Pageants in the Towneley Cycle* (Manchester, 1958).
CHAMBERS, E. K., *The Mediaeval Stage* (Oxford, 1925).
CHAMBERS, R. W., *Widsith* (Cambridge, 1912).
DAUZAT, A., *Dictionnaire étymologique des noms de famille et prénoms de France* (Paris, 1951).
— *Les noms de famille de France* (Paris, 1945).
— *Les noms de personnes* (Paris, 1946).
DEIMLING, H., *The Chester Plays* (EETS, Extra Ser., LXII, 1893).
EKWALL, E., *The Concise Oxford Dictionary of English Place-names* (Oxford, 1960).
— *Early London Personal Names* (Lund, 1947).
— *Studies on the Population of Medieval London* (Stockholm, 1956).
— *Two Early London Subsidy Rolls* (Lund, 1951).

BIBLIOGRAPHY

— *Variation in Surnames in Medieval London* (Lund, 1945).

EWEN, C. L'ESTRANGE, *A History of Surnames of the British Isles* (London, 1931).

— *Guide to the Origin of British Surnames* (London, 1938).

FABRICIUS, A., *Danske Minder i Normandiet* (Copenhagen, 1897).

FEILITZEN, O. VON, *The Pre-Conquest Personal Names of Domesday Book* (Uppsala, 1937).

FORSSNER, T., *Continental-Germanic Personal-Names in England in Old and Middle English Times* (Uppsala, 1916).

FÖRSTERMANN, E., *Altdeutsches Namenbuch* (Bonn, 1900–16).

FRANKLYN, J., *A Dictionary of Nicknames* (London, 1962).

FRANSSON, G., *Middle English Surnames of Occupation, 1100–1350* (Lund, 1935).

GLOVER, T. R., *Greek Byways* (Cambridge, 1932).

GODEFROY, F., *Dictionnaire de l'ancienne langue française* (Paris, 1881–1902).

GUPPY, H. B., *The Homes of Family Names* (London, 1890).

HARRISON, H., *Surnames of the United Kingdom* (London, 1912–18).

HOMANS, G. C., *English Villagers of the Thirteenth Century* (Cambridge, Mass., 1942).

HOSKINS, W. G., *The Midland Peasant* (London, 1957).

LEBEL, P., *Les noms de personnes* (Paris, 1946).

LÖFVENBERG, M., *Middle English Local Surnames* (Lund, 1942).

LOWER, M. A., *Patronymica Britannica* (London, 1860).

LOYD, L. C., *The Origins of Some Anglo-Norman Families* (Harl. Soc., 103, Leeds, 1951).

MAWER, A. and STENTON, F. M., *Introduction to the Survey of English Place-names* (Cambridge, 1924).

MICHAËLSSON, K., *Études sur les noms de personne français* (Uppsala, 1927, 1936).

PARTRIDGE, E., *Shakespeare's Bawdy* (London, 1961).

— *Slang Today and Yesterday* (London, 1935).

PINE, L. G., *They came with the Conqueror* (London, 1954).

REANEY, P. H., *A Dictionary of British Surnames* (London, 1961).

— *The Origin of English Place-names* (London, 1964).

REDIN, M., *Uncompounded Personal Names in Old English* (Uppsala, 1919).

ROUND, J. H., *Family Origins* (London, 1930).

— *Feudal England* (London, 1895).

SALZMAN, L. F., *Building in England* (Oxford, 1952).

xviii

— *English Industries in the Middle Ages* (Oxford, 1923).

— *English Life in the Middle Ages* (Oxford, 1950).

SEARLE, W. G., *Onomasticon Anglo-Saxonicum* (Cambridge, 1897).

SMITH, ELSDON C., *The Story of our Names* (New York, 1950).

STENTON, F. M., *Anglo-Saxon England* (Oxford, 1947).

— *Danelaw Charters* (London, 1920).

— *The Danes in England* (Oxford, 1957).

— *The First Century of English Feudalism* (Oxford, 1922).

SWAINSON, C., *Provincial Names and Folklore of British Birds* (English Dialect Society, London, 1885).

SWANN, H. KIRKE, *A Dictionary of English and Folk-names of British Birds* (London, 1913).

TENGVIK, G., *Old English Bynames* (Uppsala, 1938).

THURESSON, B., *Middle English Occupational Terms* (Lund, 1950).

UNWIN, G., *Finance and Trade under Edward III* (Manchester, 1918).

WAGNER, A. R., *English Genealogy* (Oxford, 1960).

WEEKLEY, E., *Jack and Jill* (London, 1948).

— *The Romance of Names* (London, 1922).

— *Surnames* (London, 1936).

— *Words Ancient and Modern* (London, 1946)

WEST, J. R., *St Benet of Holme* (Nf Rec. Soc., II, III, 1932).

WILSON, R. M., *The Lost Literature of Medieval England* (London, 1952).

WITHYCOMBE, E. G., *The Oxford Dictionary of English Christian Names* (Oxford, 1950).

Chapter One

INTRODUCTORY

Most people are interested in names. Articles and paragraphs on the subject appear from time to time in newspapers and periodicals and these are frequently followed by a correspondence of some length. True, the interest is often superficial, taking the form of collections of odd names, especially queer compounds with the christian name, such as Mr Original Bugg and Mr Ephraim Very Ott, both in reserved occupations during the last war, and surnames which appear particularly apt or amusing, Blight, a seller of fruit in Bournemouth, Cakebread, a baker in Chingford, Screech, an Exeter dentist and Tugwell, a hairdresser at St Leonards, or partners like Doolittle and Dalley or Waite and Waite, both house-agents. During the past few years my own correspondence has produced numerous enquiries as to the origin of particular surnames, some which have given me new and valuable information.

This lively interest makes it the more surprising that there are only two books on surnames still in print, my own *Dictionary of British Surnames* (1958) and J. Pennethorn Hughes's *How you got your name* (1959). The latter is a small compilation dealing with about 900 names which 'preserves its necessity to be scholarly rather than purely entertaining', but is often inaccurate and misleading. He describes Weekley's work as 'all of the highest scholarship', but writes

'Mainprice sounds English enough, even in Texas. It is not. It is the Norman name, and so imported, for one who lived by the *mean praz* or stony meadow', an etymology which Weekley had already effectively demolished in 1914, showing its French origin 'taken by hand', used both for a surety and a man out on bail.[1] *Wakeman* was not 'a knocker-up' whose job it was to arouse people. He was the medieval policeman. 'The first Mr Peel lived by a pool, which is what it meant.' He is more likely to have lived in a peel-castle (John *del Pele* 1301 SRY) and his name is certainly not from *pool*. We should like some evidence that a Palmer was a professional tennis-player or coach or a 'palmer' of cards, a cheater, whilst our confidence in the etymologies is not increased when we learn that 'Mann usually means some one from the Isle of Man' and that 'the maternal grandfather of Thomas à Beckett was a full-blooded Turk'.

Other books on the subject can still be consulted in libraries. Some are good, some bad, others good in parts. Bardsley is suffering the inevitable fate of the pioneer. His Dictionary, published post-humously in 1901, embodies the results of 30 years' work. He was the first to lay down the essential principles on which the study of sur-names must be based, the necessity for the collection of numerous early forms of the name, the earlier the better, and from these to deduce an etymology in the light of the known history of the language. In the 60 years since his death a vast accumulation of printed re-cords has become available to which he had no means of access and our knowledge of the history of the English Language has steadily increased. Many of his etymologies, therefore, need revision, but many still stand and much valuable material remains which cannot be ignored.

Weekley pays due tribute to Bardsley, especially as 'he appears to be the only one who knows that there are such things as chronology and evidence'. He accepts Bardsley's method as the only sound one, but it is clear that for many of his etymologies he had no early evidence and based his explanation on the modern form alone. For *Handyside* he suggests ME *hende side* 'gracious custom', 'but the variant *Handaside* suggests a possible nickname of attitude, "hand at side", for a man standing with arms akimbo'. Both are from a Scottish place-name, Handyside near Berwick, the earliest example being Richard *de Hanggandsid* (1398). '*Harkus* is for "hawk-house", as *Harker* is for *Hawker*.' He gives no evidence, but assumes that

[1] *The Romance of Names*, p. 185; *Surnames*, p. 280, n.1.

2

hawk was pronounced *hark*. *Harkus* is obviously local in origin, from Harcarse in Berwickshire as is proved by Adam *of Harcarres* (1216), whilst *Harker* occurs in 1280, Robert *le Herkere*, a derivative of ME *herkien* 'to listen', hence 'a listener, an eavesdropper'. *Spark*, he assumes to be a contraction of *Sparrowhawk*, but it is found as *Sperc* in Lincolnshire as early as 1202 and is clearly a nickname from ON *sparkr* 'lively, sprightly'.

MISLEADING MODERN SPELLINGS

Many modern surnames are identical in form with words in frequent use, but their meaning or origin is different. The common *bullet*, from OFr *boulet*, first recorded in 1557, is a diminutive of *boule* 'ball'. The surname *Bullett* is a nickname, *le Bulet* (1194), a diminutive of OFr *boule* 'round', hence 'the little round one', cognate with the French surnames *Boule* and *Boulet*, explained by Dauzat as 'un individu gros, arrondi'. *Card* is not to be associated with Arnold Bennett's 'Card'. It is from OFr *carde* 'teasel-head, wool-card', and is one of a number of metonymic occupation-names. We still have *Carder* 'one who cards wool', 'a wool-comber', whilst *Cardmaker* was a common medieval name, in use until at least 1550, 'the maker of the card or comb used by the cloth-maker'. *Cattle* has wrongly been identified with *Kettle*, but is a different name, always with the vowel *a*, identical with *Catell* or *Cattell*. It was a christian name as is proved by that of *Cattle* Bagge (1279), a diminutive of *Cat*, a short form of *Catelin* (now *Catlin* or *Catling*), the medieval popular form of OFr *Caterine* (Catharine). *Kettle*, which always has an *e* and is found also as *Kettel*, is a common Scandinavian personal-name, *Ketill* '(sacrificial) cauldron'. It was anglicised as *Cytel* which has given us *Kittle*.

The medieval *Collier* was a charcoal-burner, not a coal-miner, whilst *Coward* was an honourable calling, 'the cow-herd'. *Evening* is from ME *evening* 'an equal, a match', a neighbour in the scriptural sense. *Service* is a phonetic spelling of OFr *cervoise* 'ale', for a seller of ale, a taverner. The medieval *Farmer* was not a farmer in the modern sense. The name derives from AFr *fermer*, from medieval Latin *firmarius*, 'one who undertakes the collection of taxes, revenues, etc., paying a fixed sum for the proceeds'. It was a common medieval practice to let out a manor or estate 'at farm'. The farmer paid a fixed rent; what he could make from the land above this was his profit.

3

OBSOLETE WORDS AND MEANINGS

Students of English are well aware that words are constantly chang-
ing their meaning. The adjective *sad*, for example, had in Old English the meaning 'satiated, full to repletion'. A man who has had his
fill of pleasure loses his restlessness and excitability. He may become
calm and serious, discreet and so trustworthy, the common meaning
of the word in Middle English. Shakespeare uses *sad* as the opposite
of *merry* and by the seventeenth century the word had become
restricted to its modern meaning of 'mournful'. As the surname *Sadd*
is found as early as 1086, it must have one of the two earlier meanings.

Unfortunately, the literature available does not always permit of
the accurate dating of changes of meaning. In fact, it does not always
give us the earliest examples of the word. It is now well known that
both surnames and place-names often prove that a word was in
common use earlier than its first record in the dictionaries, sometimes by as much as two or three centuries. The Oxford English
Dictionary observes that *Wainwright* 'is not found in Middle English, though its existence is attested by the surname'. This is common
and is found in Essex as early as 1237. *Crabtree*, a surname in 1301,
antedates the dictionary record by over a century (c1425), whilst
Boatman is carried back nearly 300 years, from 1513 to 1225. Within
such a period words could change their meaning and it is often
difficult to decide definitely how to interpret a particular surname.
Lemon has more than one origin. It may be from an OE personal-
name *Lēofmann* 'beloved man', or it may be from the common ME
leofman, leman 'lover, sweetheart', whether man or woman. This
later became a term of contempt for a woman of loose character.
As both Chaucer and Langland use the term as an expression of
endearment without any thought of obloquy, this is probably the
usual meaning of the surname. But as the *Promptorium Parvulorum* of
1440 glosses the word *concubina*, and as Chaucer also uses it in the
same sense, we cannot altogether exclude the derogatory meaning.

In some instances, we can be quite certain that the surname has
its medieval meaning. *Moody* is from OE *mōdig* 'bold, impetuous,
brave', *Quarrell* was a name for an arbalester, from OFr *quarel* 'a
short, heavy, square-headed arrow or bolt for a cross-bow', whilst
Pretty and *Prettyman* derive from OE *prættig* 'crafty, cunning'.
Prater is a variant of *Pretor*, from Latin *praetor*, a common medieval

name for a reeve. *Pray* was one who dwelt near a meadow (OFr *pray*, modFr *pré*), whilst *Prayer* is a Norman name from Presles in Calvados. *Simple*, in Old French, meant 'free from duplicity, dissimulation or guile; honest, open, straightforward', a more complimentary name than one would think, but this will not apply to *Best*, which is from OFr *beste* 'a beast', used of a brutal, savage man, in the earlier examples often denoting stupidity or folly.

Arlott is from OFr *herlot, arlot* 'lad, young fellow', found in English as a masculine noun in the thirteenth century in the sense 'vagabond, beggar, rogue'. It was used by Chaucer both as a term of derision 'ye false harlot', and also playfully for a good fellow, 'he was a gentil harlot and a kynde'. In the fourteenth century it was used of an itinerant jester, buffoon or juggler, and also of a male servant, attendant or menial. The surname is found as early as 1193 and is masculine, *le Harlot*, but which of these meanings is the correct one for any particular name cannot be determined. At any rate, it cannot have the modern sense of the word which is not found before the fifteenth century.

Bridewell is from a place-name, 'dweller by a well dedicated to St Bride or near a spring or stream frequented by birds'. There can be no reference to Bridewell as a prison. The London Bridewell was a 'lodging' built by Henry VIII near St Bride's Well and later given by Edward VI as a hospital. The modern meaning arose later, when the hospital was converted into a house of correction. The surname has been noted in 1297.

Champion is from central OFr *champiun* and *Campion* from ONFr *campiun* 'a combatant in the campus or arena', 'one who "does battle" for another in a wager of battle', 'a champion'. In the ordeal by battle, in criminal cases, the accuser and the accused took the field themselves, but in disputes about the ownership of land, the actual parties to the suit were represented by 'champions', in theory their free tenants, but in practice, hired men, professional champions, and very well paid. In 1294 the Dean and Chapter of Southwell incurred a prospective liability of about £750 in modern money in hiring a champion to fight a duel to settle a law-suit about the advowson of a church. A *pugil* or champion was a regular member of the household of more than one medieval bishop, Thomas Cantilupe, Bishop of Hereford (1275–82), paying his champion, Thomas de Bruges, a salary of half a mark a year.

Many of these pugils acted for lesser folk. Originally, the only competent substitutes for principals in an action were witnesses who could swear that they or their fathers saw the seisin, and Bracton cites a case of 1220 in which a certain Elias Pugin was produced as champion for the defendant in a dispute concerning a stolen mare. Elias swore he had sold the animal to the defendant, having acquired it in Wales in payment for fencing lessons. The appellant pleaded that Elias was a hired champion of fertile imagination, a submission proved to the satisfaction of the justices, and the unfortunate Elias was condemned to lose foot and fist. Hence, presumably, such surnames as those of John *Handelesse* (1440 GildY), Roger *Onhond* 'one hand' (1327 SRSf), John *Stelfot* (1301 LLB C) and Roger *Yrenfot* (1251 Rams, Hu), the two latter having mitigated their disability by the acquisition of artificial limbs.

These surnames have not survived, but the French equivalent of *Ironfoot* is well represented today by *Pettifer* with its numerous variants. This is found in the eleventh century in the Latin form *Pedesferri* 'feet of iron' and is common from the twelfth as *Pedefer* or *Piedefer* (OFr *pied de fer*) and *Petifer* in 1327, whence such modern forms as *Pettipher*, *Pettiver* and *Pettiford*. From *Putifer* (1382) we get *Puddifer* and *Puddepha*, from which popular etymology produced *Pottiphar*.

Elias, as we have seen, spent his spare time in giving fencing lessons, a less dangerous occupation than appearing in the lists. It was not uncommon for these champions to fail to appear on the day fixed for the judicial combat. Defaulters were fined and these fines could be paid by instalments, but it is seldom that the account records payment of the final instalment. Very often the last entry reads: 'Et debet xxx*s*. viii*d*. Sed mortuus est.' The champion had succumbed to the occupational hazards of his profession. Even if he survived the combat, he ran the risk of paying for his defeat by hanging.

The Assize of Arms of 1181 defined the weapons which every free Englishman was bound to possess and its provisions were re-enacted in 1285 by the Statute of Winchester. One would, therefore, expect provision to have been made for training men in the use of their weapons so that they would be efficient if and when they were called upon to serve in the army. There is some evidence for this in the early days when trial by combat was still a judicial proceeding. The Pipe Roll for 1181 contains a charge by the Sheriff of Surrey for the equipment of eight approvers and the hire of champions to teach them to fight. Surrey still had a hired champion in 1219 and two contracts for the hire of a champion still survive.[1] The legal authorities leave us in no doubt that not only fencing but even its aristocratic counterpart, the tournament, have always been unlawful. The keeping of fencing-schools was forbidden in the City of London: 'As fools who delight in mischief do learn to fence with buckler and thereby are encouraged in their follies, it is provided that none shall keep school for, nor teach the art of fence within the City of London under pain of imprisonment for forty days.' Fencing-masters were legally denominated as rogues and vagabonds and classed with stage-players, bearwards, gipsies and other undesirable characters. The coupling of 'escole de eskermerye ou de bokeler' in London makes it clear that the modern *Buckler*, often for a maker of buckles (cf. John *Bokelsmyth* 1384), is also metonymic for *bokeler-player* 'fencer' (cf. Nicholas *Bokelereplayere* 1379).

In spite of their proscription, the authorities turned a blind eye on fencing-schools and fencing-masters. From time to time we read of prosecutions as in 1457 when John Cotton admitted that he had taught some of the ringleaders in a riot against the Lombards 'to pleye atte sword', which suggests a possible, specific meaning for the modern surname *Player*. At the same time there appears to have been an unofficial fencers' guild, whilst Henry VIII, by Letters Patent, conferred on certain Masters of Defence the monopoly of teaching arms within his dominions.[2]

The chief proof, however, of the continued existence of the fencing-master throughout the Middle Ages is provided by surnames. From 1154 to 1533 numerous examples are found of men labelled by some form of OFr *escremisseor*, *eskermisor* or *scremisseur* 'fencing-master'. Their profession was not concealed, the surname was used openly and was so common that it has survived in at least 11 different forms. We find it as *Scrimgeour* in Scotland and as *Scrimshaw* and *Skrimshire* in England, with other variants such as *Scrimiger*, *Scriminger* and *Scrymsour*. In addition, we have *Skirmer*, *Skermer* and *Skurmer* from OFr *eskirmir* 'a fencing-master'.

With these names we may take also *Juster*, *Jewster* and *Joester*, from OFr *justeur* 'jouster'. To give young knights practice in deeds of arms and their elders excitement, tournaments or jousts were

[1] *v.* J. H. Round, *Family Origins* (London, 1930), pp. 117–19 (with references).
[2] *v.* J. D. Aylward, *The Medieval Master of Fence* (Notes and Queries, vol. 198 (1953), pp. 230–4.

held. They began in France in the twelfth century and were popular with the Anglo-Norman knights. 'These early tournaments were very rough affairs, in every sense, quite unlike the chivalrous contests of later days; the rival parties fought in groups, and it was considered not only fair, but commendable to hold off until you saw some of your adversaries getting tired and then to join in the attack on them; the object was not to break a lance in the most approved style, but frankly to disable as many opponents as possible for the sake of obtaining their horses, arms and ransoms.' William the Marshal, later Earl of Pembroke and regent of England during the minority of Henry III, the most brilliant jouster of his day, 'made a very good income out of his tournaments'.[1]

Converse is from OFr *convers*, Latin *conversus* 'converted', 'a convert', and has been thought to refer to a converted Jew, but it is more likely to have the common medieval sense of 'one converted from secular to religious life in adult age', 'a lay member of a religious order'. The Augustinian and Cistercian *conversi* were men living according to a rule less strict than that of the canons and monks, engaged chiefly in manual work, with their own living quarters and their own part of the church. They were numerous among the Cistercians in the twelfth and thirteenth centuries (when the surname is found), often outnumbering the monks, and were, by rule, illiterate. These lay-brothers were employed on the monastic manors and granges where they were liable to fall into the sin of owning private property. They acquired a reputation for violence and misbehaviour—at Neath in 1269 they locked the abbot in his bedroom and stole his horses—and they were gradually replaced by more manageable paid servants.

Jenner, with its variants *Jenoure*, *Genner*, *Genower* and *Ginner*, corresponds to the modern *engineer*, but with quite a different meaning. It is from OFr *engigneor*, Lat *ingeniator* 'engineer, maker of military machines', used in the twelfth century of men who combined the duties of master-mason and architect. Ailnoth *ingeniator*, a military architect, was surveyor of the king's buildings at Westminster and the Tower in 1157, and was in charge of building operations at Windsor from 1166 to 1173. He repaired Westminster Abbey after a fire, and superintended the destruction of the castles of Framlingham and Walton.

Horder is from OE *hordere* 'keeper of the hoard or treasure',

[1] L. F. Salzman, *English Life in the Middle Ages* (Oxford, 1950), p. 202.

8

'treasurer', 'keeper of provisions'. Ordric *hordere* was an eleventh-century cellarer of the monastery of Bury St Edmunds. *Hunn* is no reminder of Attila or of the Germans of 1914. It is an East Anglian surname, both a patronymic from OE *Hunna* and a nickname from ON *húnn* 'young bear'. *Lass* and *Less* are from OE *lǽss* 'less, smaller', used, probably, in the sense 'younger'. *Ostridge* is from OFr *ostrice*, *hostrige* 'a hawk', used by metonymy for the common *ostricer* 'a keeper of goshawks', a hawker or falconer.

SOME MUCH DISCUSSED SURNAMES

For quite a number of our surnames no satisfactory etymology can yet be given. To explain others, various theories have been put forward at different times, often unsupported by evidence, and none meeting with general acceptance. With a fuller collection of early forms, it is now possible to propose new and better interpretations, some of which, at least, appear probable.

It is apparently an impossible task to kill an erroneous etymology. In 1860, Lower derived *Sidney* from a French place St Denis, stating that the founder of the family of Sidney of Penshurst was Sir William Sidney, chamberlain of Henry II, who came from Anjou and was buried at Lewes in 1188. This etymology has since been repeated in book after book for a century (to 1966). It is based on three charters at Penshurst which were exposed as forgeries in *Archaeologia* in 1914 and re-examined and rejected in 1925 by C. L. Kingsford who derived the family from John de Sydeneia, a Surrey yeoman in the reign of Edward I. 'The original home of the Sidneys was a farm, which still bears their name, in the parish of Alford, on the borders of Surrey and Sussex, about ten miles south of Guildford.' It was called *La Sydenye* 'the wide, well-watered land', now Sidney Farm. The surname first occurs in 1280.

The Kent surname *Hogben* or *Hogbin* defeated Bardsley who rightly rejected Lower's 'Probably a pigstye, from *hog* and *bin*, a crib or hutch', hence 'a swineherd'. He could find no earlier evidence than 1786 and suggested it might be an immigrant from the Low Countries. Harrison follows Lower, whilst Barber makes the impossible suggestion of derivation from an OE *Hagbeorn* 'clever bear', a personal-name which could never have existed, or a corruption of *Ogbourne*. Examples are still late, but happen to occur in such a sequence as to give the clue to the etymology. All are from Kentish wills: *Huckebone* 1479, *Hugbone* 1549, *Hogben* 1588. The source is clearly the noun *huck-bone* 'the hip-bone or haunch-bone', huckle-bone, found in the Craven dialect as *hug-baan*. The origin of *huck* is obscure, but it is probably from a Teutonic root 'to be bent', found in ON *huka* 'to crouch, sit bent, sit on the haunches', and in the dialectal *huck-backed* 'hump-backed'. This Kent surname is, there-fore, a nickname for a man with a crooked bone, synonymous with the Scottish *Cruickshank* 'crooked leg'. A similar explanation ac-counts for *Huckbody* (Richard *Hugbody* 1396 AssL).

Beveridge has been variously explained as from 'beaver-ridge', Beveridge in Dorset,[1] 'Beverege', an island in the Severn 'beaver-island', or from a personal-name. It is certainly not local in origin. It is never found with *de*, and the final element is certainly not *-ridge* or *-ige* 'island'. There is no personal-name to fit the forms which must be from ME *beuerage*, OFr *bevrege* 'drink, liquor for consumption', also used of a drink or beverage which binds a bar-gain. Bailey in 1721 has '*To pay Beverage*, to give a treat upon the first wearing of a new Suit of Cloths' and Dr Johnson in 1755 '*Beverage*, a treat at first coming into a prison, called also *garnish*'. These must be survivals of a much older custom, for Langland in 1362 has 'Bargeyns and beuerages bigonne to aryse'. At Whitby in 1199 the purchaser of land paid by custom 4*d.* for seisin and 1*d.* to the burgesses *ad beuerege*. At a court of the Abbot of Ramsey in 1275, Thomas de Welles complained that Adam Garsoppe unjustly detained a copper he had previously bought from him for 6*d.* of which he had paid Adam 2*d.* 'et beuerech', and a drink in advance. Later he went and offered to pay the rest, but Adam refused to take it and kept the copper 'to his damage and dishonour 2*s.*'. Adam was fined 6*d.* and pledged his overcoat. The nickname may well have been bestowed on a man who made a practice of getting free drinks for clinching bargains he had no intention of keeping, though it may have a more general sense, referring to a man who sold or was particularly partial to beverages. The custom of *beverage* was an old one on the Continent, where it was called *vin du marché*.

Bardsley, retracting his earlier etymology of *Bunyan* from *Bonjean* 'Good John', adopted that of Lower, from Welsh *ab Enion*, *Benyon*, and was followed by Harrison, Ewen and Weekley, although Dr

[1] There is no such place in A. Fagersten's *Place-names of Dorset* (Uppsala, 1933).

J. Brown in his *Life of John Bunyan* (1885) had solved the problem. Adducing the 1219 form *Buignon* (Bardsley had no form earlier than 1624), he equated it with OFr *beignet* 'fritter' and cited from Godefroy 'Et bon char et granz buignons' with the comment: 'The word signifies a little raised pattie with fruit in the middle.' His only error was to regard this as the original instead of a derived meaning. OFr *bugnon* is a diminutive of *bugne* 'a bile, blane' which survives as *Bunney* and came to be applied to any round knob or bunch, and later to a raised pattie and also to a bunion, first recorded in NED c1718. The surname, which can now be carried back to 1204, Henry *Buniun* (all the early examples come from Bedfordshire), is probably a nickname for one disfigured by a knob, lump or hump. The earlier explanations are ruled out by the early forms. Even if a Welsh surname were possible in Bedfordshire in 1204, *Beynon* and *Benyon* would have taken the form *ab Eynon* which could not have become *Beynon* until about 1450.

The surname *Death* is often pronounced *Deeth* and is so spelled, but many of those so named, anxious to rid themselves of an unpleasant association, have jumped at Burke's derivation of the name from Aeth, a place in Flanders, and have given it the aristocratic form of *D'Eath(e)*, *De Ath*, *De'Ath* or *D'Aeth*. There is just a possibility that the name may occasionally be of topographical origin from Ath in Belgium, but Gerardus *de Athia* is the only example I have found among the many thousands of surnames I have noted. Bardsley obviously distrusted this explanation and derived the name from an unidentified place *Dethe* in Cambridgeshire. But this is obviously a mis-reading or a printer's error for *Deche*, Henry and Alice *de Deche*, who in 1279 lived in Swaffham Prior, near the Devil's Dyke when this was called simply the Ditch or the Great Ditch. Weekley suggests that one origin of *Death* and its variant *Dearth* is a pageant-name. Death was personified in the Chester plays and *Mort* is an English surname paralleled by the French *Lamort*. This might well explain the surname of Robert *Death* who was living in Battle in the reign of Edward I.

The early forms are usually *Deth* or *Deeth* and come from Bedfordshire, Cambridgeshire, Suffolk and Essex, whilst the modern *Deeth* is found in Essex and East Anglia. The clue to its real origin is to be found in a rare Essex occupational-name noted by Fransson in 1297, John *le Dethewright*, from OE *dȳð* 'fuel, tinder', a maker of tinder; which survives as *Deathridge* and *Detheridge*. OE *dȳð* would

11

become Essex *deeth* which survives also in *Deether* and *Deetman* with the same meaning as *Dethridge*.

'*Leapingwell*, evidently from some pool associated with the old ceremony of leaping the well—

"Leaping the well, going through a deep and noisome pool on Alnwick Moor, called the Freemen's Well, a *sine qua non* to the freedom of the borough" (Hall).'

Such is Weekley's explanation of the surname found also as *Leppingwell, Lippingwell* and *Leffingwell*. It is a local surname which appears to have only one place of origin, Leppingwells in Little Maplestead (Essex) from the neighbourhood of which come all the early examples. The place is called *Leffingwelles* in 1561 and owed its name to the possessions here of the family of Robert *de Leffeldewelle* (1302) who is called *Leffingwell* in an Elizabethan transcript of the Court Rolls, a common form of the name in the fifteenth century, which became *Leppingwell* in the sixteenth. It is found as early as 1258 and derives from a lost place *Liffildeuuella* (1086) which may survive in a corrupt form in Levit's Corner in Pebmarsh into which the family lands extended.

Rumbelow, Rumbellow or *Rombulow* is a name which Bardsley, Harrison and Weekley agree in taking as a nickname for a sailor from the meaningless combination of syllables sung as a refrain whilst rowing, an explanation unlikely in itself, as there is no evidence for the use of *rumbelow* as a generic name for a sailor, whilst the nickname seems quite unsuited to the first known bearer of the name, Stephen *Romylowe*, constable of Nottingham Castle in 1347. Of 10 examples of his surname only one contains a *b* (*Rombylou* 1351), whilst two, *de Romylo(u)* (1346, 1363), point clearly to a place-name ending in *-low*. This must be identical in origin with The Rumbelow in Aston (Warwicks), *Rumbelowe* 1461, the home of Richard *de Thrimelow* in 1334. A second example of the same name is Tremelau Hundred in the same county, and a third is *Rumbelow* in Wednesfield (Staffs), *le Thromelowe* 1339, *Romylowe* 1420. All three are from OE *æt þrēom hlāwum* '(dweller) by the three mounds or barrows'.

Prettyjohn or *Prettejohn* has been regarded as a nickname or possibly a corruption of the French *Petit-jean*. In 1219 in Lincolnshire and in 1301 in Yorkshire we find men named simply *Prestreiohan* which is found as a surname in Somerset in 1346. That England was fully abreast of the news of the world is shown by the occurrence of

12

the name *Prestreiohan* borne by a Lincolnshire attorney. Tales of a great priest-king who ruled in central Asia were current in the twelfth century in Europe. He is first mentioned by a western chronicler in the middle of the century when Otto of Friesing tells how Johannes Presbyter won a great victory over the Persians and Medes. Between 1165 and 1177 a forged letter purporting to come from him was circulated in Europe. Some rumour of this must have reached Lincolnshire and caused at least one English child to be christened by the name of this supposititious eastern king.[1] No early example of *Prettyjohn* has been noted. The occurrence of Prestrejohan as a surname in 1346 suggests that this is the real origin. The name can never have been common. The meaning of *Prestre* would be known and the name assimilated to the later French form, becoming *Pretrejohn* and *Pretterjohn*, a form no longer suggesting *Prestrejohn* whose story was probably by then unfamiliar to the bearers of the name and they made it intelligible as *Prettyjohn*.

SOME QUERIES

In the past few years my correspondence has included a number of enquiries as to the origin of various surnames, often of those on which I had no information. Some correspondents have supplied information which has proved useful in solving problems whilst others have called on me to recant. Some few of these names may well be discussed here as they frequently illustrate not only the methods by which such problems can be solved but also the need for relevancy and accuracy.

A lady from Beverley Hills asked for help in tracing the origin of her maiden name *Swezey*. It had arrived in America with John Swasey about 1630 and has been spelled *Swayze* and *Swasse*. I had never met the surname before, but at once said it must come from Swavesey in Cambridgeshire. Later, on a visit to England, the lady discovered two Sweaseys (related) in London and one in Portsmouth, and found the name spelled *Swaiesy* and *Swayse* between 1576 and 1744 at Bridport where one of the name founded a charity. The surname is rare in England and rather uncommon in America except in a few of the eastern states.

A problem of a different kind was that of *Solf*, *Soffe* and *Sofe*, the

---

[1] *v.* Sir Denison Ross in *Travel and Travellers of the Middle Ages*, ed. A. P. Newton (London, 1926), pp. 174–94.

last two both pronounced *Soaf*. It is found in Hampshire between 1541 and 1586 as *Solfe*, as *Sofe* in 1592, *Souf* in 1670, and in 1576 in Wiltshire as *Selfe* and *Sawffe*. It seems to be limited to a small area of the New Forest[1] and must be a variant of *Self*, from OE *Sǣwulf* 'sea-wolf', which occurs in DB as both *Seulf* and *Saulf*, and in 1249 at Chittoe in Wiltshire as *Soylf* (AssW).

Mr A. J. Winsbury propounds an interesting problem when he asks what is the connexion, if any, between the surnames *Mathums* and *Matthews*. The birth of William Matthews on 8 December 1687 is entered in his family Bible. No place is mentioned, but his mother had a dim recollection that they came from Blasted Hill, near Chelmsford, which he could not find on the map. It is now known as Blastford Hill in Little Waltham and in the parish register of Great Waltham the Bible entry appears, but under the name of *Mathums*. He has also found in the Great Tey parish register a record of the marriage of Hannah *Mathams* alias *Mathews*. The tendency is always to make sense of the unintelligible, so that the original name must have been *Mathums* which the clerk or the parson regarded as an error for *Mathews*. Martinfield Green and Martins Wood in Saffron Walden, with Mattins Farm in Radwinter (*Matthams* 1387), owe their name to the family of John *de Matan* or *de Matham* (1248). He came from Mathon in Worcestershire or Herefordshire, probably the latter as the Bohuns, Earls of Hereford, were benefactors of Walden Abbey. Some of the family moved south into the Chelmsford area. In 1945 all the haystacks at Steven's Farm in Chignal were destroyed in a fire which lasted a week. For 61 years, Arthur *Matthams* had worked here and for 40 years had built nearly all the stacks and thatched them; he had been 'Lord of the Harvest', leading the harvest-cutting and setting the pace for other workers.[2] The surname survives also as *Mattam*, *Matham(s)*, *Maddams* and *Maddans*.

Mr Winsbury also gives an interesting example of the survival of a surname. During the 1914–18 war, whilst billeted in the village of Tramecourt, which adjoins the battlefield of Agincourt, a farmer's wife told him she had known a certain Madame *La Tame* whose husband was descended from an English soldier wounded at Agincourt who had been left behind and had married a French woman. As the name did not sound English, he asked her to spell it, which

[1] *Ex inf.* Mr A. D. Williams of Cardiff.
[2] *Sunday Express*, 26 August 1945.

14

she did—*Latham*, a surname deriving from Lathom (Lancs) and surviving also as *Laytham*, *Leatham* and *Lethem*.

For 15 years Mr P. Macqueen has been collecting information
about the name *Marson* which he has found from the sixteenth
century in a group of Midland counties from Worcestershire and
Warwickshire to Cambridgeshire and Lincolnshire. 'Staffordshire is
the Marson country par excellence.' In parish registers the name
varies between *Marson* and *Marston*, with minor variants, including
Marsom (1720) and *Murson* (1622). At Olney (Bucks), Thomas and
Elizabeth *Marson* (1796–8) appear as *Marston* in 1801 and 1804,
whilst their daughter Sophia (baptised 1797, buried 1806) is called
Marson. At Church Leigh (Staffs), William, son of James Marston
(born 1685), was baptised as *Marston* in 1721, but is called *Marson*
on his tombstone (1787), whilst his son was baptised and married as
Marston, but buried as *Marson*, and this has since been the family
name.

Which was the original form, *Marson* or *Marston*? There is a rare
surname *Markson* 'son of Mark', found as *Martson* in 1521, which
might well have become *Marson* later, but there is no evidence for
this or for a similar development in *Marsden*, from places of that
name in Yorkshire and Lancashire. Marston 'marsh-farm' is a common place-name and that in Bedfordshire appears as *Marson* in
1662 and is still so pronounced. The same spelling is also found
occasionally between 1568 and 1670 for the Marstons in Wiltshire,
Hertfordshire and Buckinghamshire. It did not replace the normal
form on the maps which are conservative in their spellings, especially
as *-ton* is frequent in village names. For the surname, *Marson* appears
more natural as a compound of *-son* and tended to persist as it was
dissociated from the place-name. At a later stage, as often, an
intrusive *t* crept in and the name reverted to *Marston* and then see-
sawed between the two forms. Today *Marson* is less common than
Marston and *Marsom* is rare.

From the little Cumberland village of Moresby between White-
haven and Workington, which was not a village until the Middle
Ages—before that it was a locality and even today does not possess
much identity apart from a railway-station, post-office and hall—
sprang what appears to have been a single family. Its name provides
no problems, but its ramifications from Cumberland to Yorkshire
and Durham, Australia and New Zealand, New Guinea and South
Africa, is a fascinating story as revealed by Mr E. Morrisby with

full and careful documentation. Until the fourteenth century the family is found in West Cumberland, then until the eighteenth in East Cumberland and the flanks of the Pennines. About the sixteenth century some families worked their way down the dales into Yorkshire where they first appear in York and south-east of Leeds. Others moved into Durham and later to the south of England. From Yorkshire one branch emigrated to Australia in 1788, from whom sprang Admiral John Moresby (1830–1922) who surveyed and named Port Moresby in New Guinea, whilst others went from Australia to New Zealand, South Africa, Rhodesia and Kenya.

During the early middle ages the most common spelling was *Moresby*, but after the sixteenth century *Morrisby* took over, preserving the pronunciation of the place-name. This was the name of the Australian family though *Moresby* is also found there, deriving from the Durham family. It is still found occasionally in England. In Yorkshire, in the late eighteenth century, the common spelling was *Morrisby*, but within a period of about 20 years this gave way to *Morsby*[1] and finally to *Mosby* and *Moseby* which still survive in Leeds. The surname dates from about 1196.

The rare surname *Nixseaman* is an interesting example of the pitfalls which may lie in wait for the unwary etymologist. My first assumption was that it was one of the common compounds of *-man*, 'servant of a man named *Nixsea*', whatever that might mean, but the Rev. A. J. Nixseaman of Norwich tells me that, by deed poll, he himself eliminated the hyphen in the name he had inherited, *Nix-Seaman*, and that some members of the family have reverted to the original *Seaman*. It is an old Norfolk name (OE *Sǣmann* 'sea-man') borne by ancestors who can be traced back to the seventeenth century. The family lived in India for over four generations and in the days of the old John Company one of them saved the life of a General Nix who ordered his junior officer to adopt his own surname as part of his name, hence *Nix Seaman*.

NAMES OF MULTIPLE ORIGIN

Many of the surnames discussed above make it clear that a name with a single, definite origin may, through the combined effects of change of pronunciation, variation of spelling and the influence of popular

---

[1] Compare *Morse* for *Morrice*: John *Morice*, *Morce* 1382 AssC. 'Maurice' or *le Moreys* 'the swarthy'.

etymology, give rise to a variety of modern surnames, some so much altered that they often appear to be quite distinct names. Conversely, many modern surnames, as a result of similar changes, are found to have more than one origin. A modern *White*, for example, may owe his name ultimately to an ancestor bearing the OE name of *Hwīta*, a nickname from OE *hwīt* 'white', or to one nicknamed 'the white' from his fair hair or complexion (*le white*), or to one who lived by the bend or curve of a river or road (*atte wyte*) as at Great Whyte (Hu), or to a man from White (D), *atte Wayte* 'a look-out post'. The personal-name and the nickname can be definitely distinguished only when the article occurs and these two sources account for the majority of the surnames.

Turner is from OFr *tourneour* 'one who turns or fashions objects of wood, metal, bone, etc., on a lathe' and this is certainly the common source of the occupational-name. Its frequency is due to the variety of objects that could be turned, especially wooden measures for wine and ale, a maker of which was also called *Disher*. Turner was, too, the term used of turnspits, translators and jousters and has absorbed *Turnehare* 'turn hare', a nickname for one so speedy that he could outstrip and turn the hare or, as so often, a derogatory nickname, the antithesis of *Turnbull*, one whose courage was just sufficient to enable him to face and turn aside a hare.

Seller, *Sellers*, etc., have a variety of meanings, including 'sadler' from OFr *seller*, and ME *seller* from OE *sellan* 'to give, hand over,' hence a seller or dealer. Tengvik and Fransson regard the latter as an improbable meaning for the surname. But *Vender* still survives. Sanson *Sellarius* of Yorkshire in 1175 paid five marks into the exchequer as a fine for selling shields to the king's enemies and Walter *Sellarius* of Warwickshire was fined half a mark in 1183 for false description of his wares. Bodo *Sellator* (1175) was a sadler, but this may be a translation of either the French *seller* or the English *sadler*. Philip *le Celler* is also called *le Sadeler* in 1320. ME *celerer* is a form of *cellarer* and equivalent to *atte celer* (*seler*). Ordingus *cellerarius* was the cellarer of the Abbey of Bury St Edmunds in the early twelfth century, and Robert *le Celerer* (1297) and William *Sellerer* (1419) must have held similar, though less exalted, positions. AFr *celer* meant not only 'cellar' but also 'a store-house or store-room for provisions; a granary, buttery or pantry'. Richard *ate Celer* (1308) was a taverner. His surname would become *Seller* to which *celerer* would inevitably become assimilated. In Sussex we find *Seller*

17

parallel with *atte Selle* (Humfrey *ater Selle* 1296 SRSx, John *Seller* 1327 ib.). This is from OE (*ge*)*sell* 'shelter for animals' which survives as *Sell* with the same meaning as *Seller* 'dweller at the herdsmen's hut'.

OFr *Huard* from OG *Hugihard* 'heart-brave' is found in DB as *Huardus* and *Houart*. As *Hugh* appears in ME as both *How* and *Hew*, this is the origin of *Heward*, with its variants *Hewart*, *Huard* and *Huart*, and a source of *Howard*, but there has been confusion with OG *Howard*, the cognate of *Haward* of Norse origin, and also with *Hayward*. In DB, OG *Howard* 'high or chief warden' occurs as *Houardus* and is common thereafter in East Anglia both as a personal-name and as a surname. Even the Norfolk *Howard* has been confused with *Haward*: 'Henry *Hawarde*, Esq., son of Sir Thomas *Hawarde*, Viscount Bindon' who succeeded as 'Viscount *Howard* of Bindon' (1566). Occasionally we have an occupational-name, John *Howeherde* (1348) 'ewe-herd', with inorganic *H*, a rare but contributary source. In parish registers of the seventeenth century *Howard* is often used for *Hayward* and in court rolls for the hayward or marsh-baley, so that some of our Howards were probably once Haywards and others Hawards.

Moore may be a personal-name, *More*, from OFr *Maur* 'swarthy', a nickname *le Mor* 'the swarthy', local from residence in or near a moor, or from a specific place, as Moore (Ch) or More (Sa). *Waller*, too, has more than one origin. It may denote a builder of walls, a salt-weller or salt-boiler, a dweller near a stream, from *wall*, a form of *well* (chiefly West Midland), or it may be the Norman form of OFr *galure*, *gallier* 'a coxcombe, spark' or 'a man of pleasant temper', which itself survives as *Gallear*, *Galler* and *Gallier*. *Powell* may be Welsh *ap Howel* 'son of Howel', for *Pool*, Ralph *ate Powel* 1288 'dweller by the pool', or for *Paul*. On his seal, John *Paul* (1296) is called John *Powel*. *Warner* is sometimes patronymic, from ONFr *Warnier*, corresponding to OFr *Guarnier* (now *Garner*) and sometimes occupational, ONFr *warennier* 'warrener', an officer employed to watch over game in a park or preserve, surviving also as *Warrener* and, with intrusive *d*, as *Warrender*, corresponding to OFr *garennier*, now *Garner*.

Many other examples of the kind are to be found, but we must confine ourselves to one of particular interest. *Forrester* usually means 'an officer in charge of a forest' or one employed there. The name was contracted to *Forster*: Walter *Forster* or *Forester* (1356).

It also appears to be a development of OFr *fustrier* 'saddle-tree maker', which is found as *Furstare* in 1305, and a contraction of *Forseter* from OFr *forcetier* 'maker of scissors, shearer, cutler'. *Forster* then became *Foster*, which, however, may also be from ME *foster* 'foster-parent, nurse'. Occasionally in medieval England a man would give his son to another to foster, the foster-father being granted a piece of land for life in return for his services.[1] It is only occasionally that we can decide the real origin of *Foster*, but one clear case is that of Walter *Forestier* (1371) whose seal bore the legend 'Sigillum Walteri *le Foster*'.

From the examples already discussed, it will be clear that surnames are of various types. We have personal-names like *Edwards* and *Simon*, place-names in *Newbury* and *Smallwood*, occupation-names such as *Carpenter* and *Plowman*, and obvious nicknames in *Redhead*, *Nightingale*, *Sheepshanks*, *Careless*, *Proud*, *Sharp* and *Jolly*. Some names it is difficult to classify, whilst others, like *White*, have more than one origin and belong to more than one class. Where are we to place *Garlick*, *Mustard* and *Pepper*? They are all commodities much in demand in medieval times and for all we have corresponding names for those who sold them, *Garlicker* and *Garlekmonger*, *Mustarder* and *Mustardman*, *Pepperer* and *Peverer*. There seems to have been a common tendency to abandon the longer forms of such names and to call the man by the name of the article he sold or made so that the *Meleman* or *Melemonger* by metonymy becomes *Meale* and the milkman (*Milker*, *Melkberere* 'milk-carrier') is called simply *Milk*, though this may also be a nickname for one with milk-white hair (cf. Hugh *Milkeheved*). These names, in spite of their form should really be classed as occupation-names, just as *Colt* may be used of the keeper of the colts, metonymic for *Colter* and *Coltman*, though it must often be a nickname for one lively and frisky as a colt. Similarly *Kitchen* and *Pantry* must be occupational, denoting the place where the man worked, whilst *Bridge* is local when it means 'dweller by the bridge', but occupational if it refers to the keeper of the bridge and the collector of tolls there.

Surnames, we must always remember, were given spontaneously

[1] G. C. Homans, *English Villagers of the Thirteenth Century* (Cambridge, Mass, 1942), p. 193.

19

and not according to any fixed rule. They were given to distinguish one John or one William from the numerous others of the same name and any distinction served which would satisfy this need. Strictly speaking, all surnames are really nicknames, *ekenames* or additional names, and for what appeared good reasons John *Adam* was distinguished by reference to his father, William *Alis* was named from his mother *Alice*, others from their place of birth or residence, or from their occupation, whilst still others received real nicknames as we understand the term. In fact, in the days before surnames became fixed as hereditary family names, a man usually had more than one surname, e.g. Richard Poche of Preston called le Belleyetere (1315) whose descendants might now be called either *Pouch*, *Preston* or *Billiter*.

All surnames, it will be found, will fall into one or other of four classes:

1. Local Surnames.
2. Surnames of Relationship.
3. Surnames of Occupation or Office.
4. Nicknames.

Within these groups there is considerable overlapping. Local surnames may be occupational. Surnames of office such as *Abbot*, *Bishop* and *King* are often nicknames whilst the last two may also be patronymics. A single modern surname may belong to more than one class. *Low* may be a French nickname from the wolf, a Scandinavian nickname for a small man, a pet-name from Laurence, or a local surname from OE *hlāw* 'hill'. *Mew* may be a patronymic (OE *Mēaw*), a nickname from the sea-mew, or occupational, either metonymic for *Mewer* 'keeper of the hawks', or from a local surname (*atte Mewe*), with the same occupational meaning. The classification must be based on the original meaning, not on the modern form; if the original meaning cannot be definitely decided, any attempt at classification is useless.

'Surnames of Relationship' is used in preference to 'Patronymics' because not all surnames of this type are from the name of the father. Many are from the mother's name, e.g. *Muriel*, *Murrell*, *Merrell*, *Gillian*, *Gellion*, *Jillions*, *Jellings*, from *Juliana*. Other relationships, too, were expressed, though these seldom survive, as Johanna *Jonwyf*, Matilda *Tomelyndoghter*, Adam *Childesfader*, William *Lucebrother*, Thomas *Vicarcosin*, Alice *Prestsyster*, John *le Personesneve* 'nephew', Marjoria *Vicar neys* 'niece' and Gilbert *Fathevedsteppeson* 'Fathead's step-son'. The only names of this type to survive are *Bairnsfather, Dawbarne, Dawborne* 'David's child', *Huban, Huband* 'Hugh's child' and certain compounds of *-magh* 'relative' or 'brother-in-law', which will be discussed later. Here, too, should be included such names as *Cousin(s), Uncle, Eames* and *Neame(s)* 'uncle' and *Neave* 'nephew'.

These latter names Ewen includes under 'Characteristic Surnames', a classification he uses to avoid 'nicknames', a term he loathed. He has to admit numerous nicknames into the various subdivisions of this class, such as *Ballard* 'bald-headed', *Fairfax* 'fair hair', *Sheepshanks, Cruickshanks, Noble, Savage* and *Proud,* but more than once he states categorically that the countless medieval nicknames did not survive and he is frequently driven to desperate straits in his attempt to explain away such modern names as *Shakespeare* and *Turnbull.* He rightly insists that such names should not be derived from nicknames without ample proof, but when he says that 'every practical source in a dozen different languages [should be] thoroughly explored before the origin is assigned to an alternative epithet' we must add that these languages must be known to have been spoken in the district in which the surname is found. William *Hog*, who was living in Huntingdonshire in 1079, is unlikely to have borne a name derived from Gaelic *og* 'the young' nor is that of Thomas *le Hen* of Suffolk (1275) likely to be from Welsh *henn* 'old', still less the personal-name *Hen* found in Nottinghamshire in 1275.

Ewen's etymological efforts are often as varied as they are impossible. There is no personal-name which will account for *Shakespeare, Waghorn* or *Wagstaff* nor has Bickerstaff or Eavestaff any bearing on the local appearance of the latter. *Wagstaff* means what it says, 'wag staff' and may well have been a nickname for a beadle. The *-staff* is original whereas in the place-name it is a corruption of *-stath* 'the staith or landing-place of the bee-keepers' which survives in one form of the surname, *Bickersteth* by the side of *Bickerstaff(e).* *Eastaff* is similarly irrelevant. It probably derives from Eastoft (WRY). Toponymics, which Ewen includes in this same class, should surely be regarded as a particular type of local surname. *Cornwall, Cornwallis* and *Cornish* could interchange. Walter *le Cornewaleys,* sheriff of London in 1277, is called Walter *de Cornwall* in 1280, whilst Adam *le Cornwalais* (1275) is probably identical with Adam *Cornys* (1300).

21

The Distribution of the Classes of Surnames in Middle English

	Date	Total number of persons	Local %	Relation-ship %	Occupa-tional %	Nick-names %
Winchester[1]	1066	243	8	9	13	13
	1115	274	13	6	21	9
	1148	855	13	2	26	10
Kings Lynn[2]	1166	186	14	6	14	16
Newark[3]	c1175	365	7	5	23	9
	1225–31	299	29	7	8	6
Shrews-bury[4]	1209–19	982	8	4	18	7
	1384–1415	511	36	7	11	9
	1450–9	268	37	16	12	12
London[5]	1292	805	42	8	26	15
	1319	1,860	50	7	24	12
	1332	1,631	51	8	18	13
Boldon[6]	1183	284	22	4	17	8
Subsidy Rolls Sussex	1296	7,210	43	9	9	7
	1327	7,243	41	14	12	12
	1332	6,973	40	14·5	11	12·5
Surrey	1332	5,471	42	14	15	10
Kent	1334	11,016	33	20	10	9
Cambs	1327	6,385	23	25	14	12
Suffolk	1327	11,720	26	19	15	14
Somerset	1327	11,100	30	18	11	14
Worcs	1275	6,235	14	14	14	12
	1327	4,644	34	24	14	13
Warwicks	1332	5,457	33	23	15	10
Salop	1327	4,897	31	11	17	9
Yorks	1297	3,402	39	8	16	16
	1301	8,699	37	5	18	8
	1327	3,848	43	5	18	8
Lancs	1332	2,571	49	1	11	8

[1] Liber Winton.   [2] Pipe Roll.
[3] Surveys, the first for the town, the second for the large country manor.
[4] *Shrewsbury Gild Merchant Rolls* (Trans. SaAS, 2nd Ser., VIII (1896), 21–43; 3rd Ser., V (1905), 35–54, 81–100).   [5] Subsidy Rolls.   [6] Boldon Buke.

Statements made about the relative frequency of the different classes of surnames are valueless when based on the modern forms alone for this takes no account of the varied origins of many surnames and, in addition, ignores the thousands of surnames no longer in use. Nor does any analysis of lists of medieval surnames provide really reliable statistics. Many of the documents are in part illegible or defective. Even at this period, many surnames cannot safely be assigned to a particular class, whilst numerous others are at present unexplained and must therefore be excluded. In spite of these limitations the table of percentages on p. 22 gives certain general impressions which are probably correct. The largest class, in town and country alike, is that of local surnames. Surnames of relationship were more numerous in the country than in the towns, occupational names more common in the towns (13–26 per cent), but by no means negligible in the country (9–18 per cent). Nicknames in both varied from 7 to 16 per cent. The London figures are based on the Subsidy Rolls alone, but in other documents many of these men had other surnames of a different type. In Yorkshire and Lancashire a larger proportion of the men than elsewhere had no surname, whilst the numerous Robertsons, Wilsons, etc., of these counties do not appear until about fifty years later.

An interesting comparison is provided by Bardsley's analysis of the first five letters of the alphabet in the London Directory of 1870: Local 11,360; Baptismal 8,203; Occupative and Official 4,388; Nicknames 3,096; Foreign 1,584; Doubtful 1,695; Total 30,326.

Chapter Two

SPELLING
AND PRONUNCIATION

No surer way can be found to annoy some people than to mis-spell or mis-pronounce their name. One *Midgley* could always be roused to fury by spelling his name *Midgeley*, a form others accepted without complaint. I have been severely censured for including *Morrice* in my Dictionary but excluding *Morice*, whilst many Clarkes are touchy if they are deprived of their final *e* and *Smythe* insists on both his particular spelling and pronunciation. But there is nothing aristocratic about the name. It is merely an antiquated spelling dating from the time when *i* and *y* were interchangeable and is identical in origin with the common and honourable name of *Smith*. The correct pronunciation of my own name is *Rainey*, which I seldom hear now. When, more years ago than I care to remember, I corrected the pronunciation *Reeney*, I was told this must be correct as *bean* was pronounced *been*. To which I could only reply that *great* was pronounced *grate*. I could now add that the place-name from which it derives, Ranah Stones in Thurlstone (WRY), was spelled *Reynoe* and *Raynoh* in the seventeenth century. The present spelling of the surname dates from the middle of the sixteenth century.

The man who says his name was always spelled as it is today is talking rank nonsense. The modern form of very many of our surnames is due to the spelling of some sixteenth- or seventeenth-century parson or clerk, or even to one of later date. It is not a matter of illiteracy in our sense of the word. These parsons who kept the parish registers were men of some education. Their ability to read cannot be questioned, but they had no guide to the spelling of names. It was the printing-press which gradually established a recognised system of spelling. That of Tudor and Stuart England was very different from ours, and the spelling of many of our words is not earlier than Dr Johnson's Dictionary. But there was no recognised spelling for names. A great part of the population was illiterate. Their names were written only at birth or marriage or death, or if they happened to come within the clutches of the law. Then they gave their names orally and the clerk put them into writing as best he could. He wrote them down phonetically, using his own system of spelling, sometimes spelling the same name in different ways at different times, and it is this variation in spelling which often gives us the clue to the real origin and meaning of the surname.

In the parish register of Rothwell (Yorks), between 1632 and 1679, Tristram *Farrey* is also called *Farrer* and *Farrah*. This proves that his surname was really *Farrer*, which is identical with *Ferrer* from OFr *ferreor* 'smith', but the final *-er* was being pronounced as *-ah* or *-ey*. This pronunciation had developed some time earlier. It is found in 1559 and was clearly regarded as an incorrect and dialectal pronunciation, similar to that of *barrer* for *barrow*, and was accordingly spelled also *Farrowe* and *Farro*, thus showing that the modern *Farrar, Farrer, Farrah, Farra, Farrey, Farrow* and *Faro* are identical in origin. In Suffolk, in 1674, the name is found as *Pharrow* and *Pharoe*, which by 1760 had become *Pharaoh*, which still survives, along with *Pharro*. In 1835, at Hoxne (Suffolk), Dinah *Farrer* signed the marriage register *Farrow*. Without these varied spellings, what fanciful explanations should we have had for *Faro* and *Pharaoh*?

The 1524 Subsidy Roll for Suffolk, in addition to the frequent *Partriche* for *Partridge*, also spells the name *Parterych, Patrick, Pattrik* and *Patryk*, so that some of our Patricks owe their name to the bird and not to the saint. In the 1674 Hearth Tax for the same county we find a greater variety, *Pattridge, Pattrige, Pateridge, Pattarage, Pattrage* and *Putteridge*, none of which actually survives, though we have *Patriche* and *Patridge*. In the sixteenth century,

25

alternative forms of a single man's surname frequently provide proof of the development of variant forms still found, e.g. in 1509 LP: Andrew *Busby, Busbe, Bushby* or *Bussheby*, from Busby (NRY), a surname still surviving as *Busby* or *Bussby*, with a colloquial pronunciation *Bushby*, whilst *Busbe* is an early example of such modern spellings as *Wetherbee, Chantree*, etc.; Philip *Cokerham* alias *Cockeram* alias *Cockram*, from Cockerham (La), illustrating the development of *Cockerham* to *Cockram* which later became *Cockran* (1756); Robert, *Crauthorn, Craythorn, Cratton, Crawthorn* or *Crathorn*, now found as *Craythorne, Crathorne* and *Crathern*, from Crathorn (NRY).

'Spell it *Cholmondeley* and pronounce it *Chumley*' is not so perverse and absurd a proceeding as is so commonly thought. There are hundreds of similar examples. Cholmondeley is found in DB as *Calmundelei* and was originally *Ceolmundesleah* 'the wood of an Anglo-Saxon named Ceolmund'. The name, as usual, was variously spelled and gradually shortened until it came to be pronounced, as it still is, *Chumley*, but, as so often, the form adopted for the maps was the fuller, medieval form. The family which held the manor took its name from the place and their surname varied with the spelling of the place-name, but ultimately they adopted the map-form as normal, though they used the common pronunciation. In 1502 Sir Richard *Cholmley* is called *Chamley* and his son Roger, *Chomley*. Others born there left the place and their surnames were usually spelled as pronounced, hence the modern variants, *Cholmondeley, Cholmeley, Chomley, Chumley, Chumbley, Chamley* and *Chambley*.

Mainwaring, of which Dugdale is said to have found 130 variants, is pronounced *Mannering*, whilst *Marjoribanks* is *Marchbanks*. In *Knollys* and *Sandys* we have medieval plural forms for *Knowles* and *Sands*, with the same pronunciation. *Streatfeild* preserves old spellings of both *street* and *field* and *Sclater*, that of ME *sclat* from OFr *esclat*. The medieval use of *ff* for *F* is still preserved in *ffrench* and *ffoulkes*. Both *Fry* and *Free* mean 'free', but derive from different forms of the OE word, *frīg* and *frēo*. Some modern surnames preserve ancient old spellings we should expect to have been normalised: *Cartter, Cornner, Goodrham, Kilbuern, Kilbuy, Shortt*. *Brixhe* is for *Brixey* (OE *Brihtsige*), whilst *Hughff* is a variant of *Huff* 'a dweller at a projecting ridge of land' (OE *hōh*, now often *Howe*) or at a place Hough (Ch, Db), pronounced *Huff*. *Proundfoot* is an eccentric form

SPELLING AND PRONUNCIATION

of *Proudfoot*, whilst *Tugwood* is proved by the Bisham parish register to be not a local surname but a corruption of *Toogood*: Hilton *Toogood, Twogood, Tugwood* (1763–5).[1]

PURE SPELLING CHANGES

Some spelling changes are purely orthographic and do not affect the pronunciation. *F* and *Ph* both represent the same sound and frequently interchange: *Fair, Phair; Fear, Phear; Fazackerley, Phizackerley*. Similarly, *c* often has the sound of *s* or of *k*: *Cecil, Saycell* (OW *Seisill*); *Center, Senter* (OFr *ceinture* 'girdle'); *Cely, Seeley* (OE *sælig* 'happy, blessed'); *Sisley* (Cecily); *Sisson, Sisterson* ('son of Ciss or Sissot', pet-forms of Cecily); *Rees, Reece; Diggens, Digance; Styants, Styance; Carslake, Karslake; Cayzer, Kayser; Curtler, Kirtler* 'maker of kirtles' (ME *curtil*). The sound of *ks* may be represented by *x*: *Deeks, Deex; Dickson, Dixon; Wicks, Wix*. Interchange of *i* and *y* is frequent: *Sime, Syme; Sirett, Syrett*.

As a final element, with weak stem and loss of *r*, *-er* was pronounced with a vague, indeterminate vowel which was often expressed by *-ah* or *-a*: *Blackah*, from Blacker (WRY), *Bowrer, Bowrah, Bowra; Bender, Benda; Boneter, Bonetta* 'maker of bonnets'; *Coucher, Coucha; Huller, Hullah; Rayner, Reyna; Shearer, Sheara; Vanner, Vannah*. Occasionally other final elements have the same ending: *Abra, Goulsbra, Stanbra*, from *-bury* or *-borough*; *Brammer, Bramah*, from *Brammall*, or *Bramhall; Boldra*, from *Baldrey. Fella* may be *Feller* 'fell-monger' or 'feller of timber' or from *Fellow* 'companion', the normal medieval form of the modern *Fellowes*.

PHONETIC CHANGES

A full treatment of the phonetic changes which surnames have undergone would be long and tedious and quite out of place here. We shall confine our attention to the more common and limit examples to the minimum.

There is a marked tendency in dialect to prefix an inorganic *s* to words beginning with a consonant as in *scrumple, snaisty* (nasty), *squench* and *scotchneal* (cochineal). It is found also in place-names

[1] The difficulty of identifying many modern English-looking surnames is illustrated by the recent announcement of the engagement of Shell Bror *Youngwall*, son of Mr and Mrs *Ljungwaldh* of Stockholm.

27

SPELLING AND PRONUNCIATION

as in Scaldhurst (Ess) for earlier *Caldhous*, in the local pronunciation *Skringells* for Corringales in the same county, in Sparkinson Spring in Dore, *Parkinson Spring* 1821, from James Parkinson 1667 (PN Db 241) and in *Spillisbiry* alias *Pillesbiry* for Pilsbury (1304 ib.). The same tendency is found also in surnames. We have *Scripps* for *Cripps*, *Sturge* and *Sturgess* for *Turgoose*, from ON *Þorgils* 'Thor's Hostage' and *Spashett* for *Patchett*, whilst *Spearpoint* is probably for *Pierrepoint* which is found also as *Pearpoint*. Other examples are found which have not survived: Herry *Spargiter* 1524 SRSf, for *Pargiter*, Thomas *Sprakley, Prakley* or *Sprakleyn* 1513 LP (Lei), now *Sprackling*; *Tichbourne*, from Tichborne (Ha), is found as *Sticheborne* in 1569 at Cowden in Kent, whilst *Chamberlain* is *Scamberleyn* in a Kent will of 1548. As often, we find also the reverse process in which an initial *S* is lost: *Tacey* for *Stacey* (Eustace), *Pickernell* for *Spickernell* (ME *spigurnel* 'a sealer of writs') and *Trafford* from *Stretford* (La). For *Springett*, we have an 1193 form *Pringet*, whilst *Stockfish* occurs as (Walter) *tocfyssh* (1332 SRSr).

The effect of these changes is well shown in the various modern forms of names from OE *stælwurðe* 'sturdy, robust', now *stalwart* and its derivative *stalworthy*. This latter survives as *Stallworthy, Stolworthy* and *Stollery* and is found in 1765 as *Stolladay*. The former is now *Stallard* and *Stalwood*, and is the first element of *Stolerman*. With loss of the initial consonant, these have become *Tallerman* and *Tolworthy* which, found as *Towlewardie* in 1574, *Towlardy* in 1664, *Towlworthy* in 1672 and *Tilladay* in 1674, now survives also as *Tolladay, Tollady, Tolleday* and *Tolliday*.

S becomes *sh* initially in *Shakesby* for *Saxby*, *Sacheespee* 1183, *Shakespey* 1292, identical with Fr *Sacquépée* 'draw sword', whilst *Shawyer* is probably for *Sawyer*; medially in *Pashley* for *Pasley*, and finally in *Morrish* for *Morris*, *Norrish* for *Norris* and *Parish* for *Paris*.[1]

Loss of *r* is common: *Antcliff*, from Arncliffe (Y), *Basham, Bassam*, from Barsham (Nf, Sf), *Batterham* and *Battram* for *Bartram*, from OFr *Bertran*, *Bastable*, from Barstable or Barnstable, *Funnell* for *Furnell*, *Haberer* for *Harberer* 'lodging-house keeper', *Sattin* for *Sartin* or *Sertin* (OFr *certeyn* 'self-assured, determined'), *Staziker* and *Stezaker*, from Stirzacre (La).

Initial *P* and *B* interchange: *Baskerville, Paskerful, Pasterfield*,

[1] Cf. Simon *Schordewaner, schordewaner* 'cordwainer' 1381 SRSf; *Shercheours* 'searchers' 1423 (R. W. Chambers and M. Daunt, *London English* (Oxford, 1931), p. 150); 'two *shirplices*', i.e. surplices (1604 SaAS, 2nd Ser., I, 279).

28

Pesterfield, from Boscherville; *Blamphin, Plampin* (OFr *blanc pain* 'white bread'); *Blandamore* is from Fr *pleyn d'amour* 'full of love'; (cf. *Fullalove*); *Bullinger, Pullinger* (OFr *boulengier* 'baker'); *Pease-good, Bisgood*, from *Peascod*. In the following, of Welsh origin, the variation is due to that between Welsh *ap* and *ab* 'son': *Binnion, Pinion* (*ab, ap Enniaun*); *Boumphrey, Pumfrey* (*ab, ap Humphrey*); *Brobin, Probin* (*ab, ap Robin*).

A similar interchange of *T* and *D* is generally considered to explain *Tennyson* from *Dennison* 'the son of Denis', but no firm proof is forthcoming, although there is some evidence for this interchange, both early and late. *Dunstall* is a common variation of *Tunstall* and *Tunnicliff* survives by the side of *Dunnicliff*. Tavistock is found as *Davistok* in 1220 (Cur). Peter *Tyson* or *Dyson* occurs in a Canterbury will of 1528, whilst Robert *Dredegold* (1327 SRSo) must have been a *Treadgold* or *Threadgold*. Ekwall has derived Tandridge (Sr) from an original *Denn-hrycg* 'ridge with denns or swine-pastures' and there may be some support for this, though there is a considerable gap in time, in the modern surname *Dandridge* or *Dandrick* which is known from 1688. Early place-names lend further support. Tanfield (NRY) occurs as both *Tanefeld* and *Danefeld* in 1086; Tidenham (Gl) is *Dyddenhamm* in 956 and *Tideham* in 1086, whilst Trimworth (K) is *Dreaman uuyrða* in 824. From surnames the evidence is later. The name of Robert *Disard* (1220 Cur) may well be an early form of *Tizard*, surviving as *Dysart*. Bardsley cites Homfrey *Dandy* 1582 and Homfric *Tandy* 1584 (the same man) and this gives us the parallel of *Dandy* and *Tandy*, from a pet-name of *Andrew*, and suggests that *Dancock(s)* and *Tancock* both derive similarly from *Dan*, a suggestion confirmed by Bardsley's note that *Dannet(t)*, a common name in the Cheshire wills, occurs in 1670 as *Tanet* and in 1674 as *Tannat*, so that the modern *Dannatt, Dannett, Dannit* and *Tannett*, along with *Danks, Dankin* and *Tankins* are diminutives of *Dan*. We may, therefore, accept *Tennyson* as a variant of *Dennison*.

The final *n* of names ending in *-son* sometimes becomes *m*: *Densum* 'the dean's son', *Haysom* 'son of Hay', *Lettsome* 'son of *Lett*' (or Lettice), *Millsome* (Miles), *Poulsom* (Paul), *Ransom* 'son of *Rand*' (Randolph). *Curzon* is found as *Cursham*.

Medieval scribes added or omitted an initial *H* at whim and inserted many a medial inorganic *h*, sometimes with unfortunate results. *Handsaker*, from Handsacre (St), was found by one writer on surnames as *Handeshaker* which he ingenuously explained as a

D   29

nickname, 'hand-shaker'. One result of this instability of the aspirate is that we have a number of doublets in which the *H* is an excrescence, as *Adkins, Hadkins; Askin, Haskin; Arkwright, Hartwright; Earnshaw, Hearnshaw; Evans, Heavens; Oldham, Holdham; Osgood, Hosegood.* In some names the original form has been ousted by that with the inorganic *H*: *Hosker* (OE Ōsgār), *Hoskin* (a compound of *Ōs-*), *Haslock* (ON Áslákr); in Arlott (OFr harlot 'young fellow') and *Elwes* (OFr Heloïs), the aspirate has completely disappeared. *Hexter* is for *Exeter*.

DIALECTAL VARIATIONS

The Middle English dialects each had pronunciations of their own which were reflected in the spelling, so that it is possible for a number of words, place-names and surnames to be assigned to particular broad areas provided we have sufficiently early forms.[1] Generalisations from the modern forms, however, are unreliable as surnames identical with a common noun or adjective have often been assimilated to the standard form.

OE *y*, for example, became in ME *i* in the North and East Midlands, *e* in the south-east and *u* in the West and Central Midlands and the southern counties, excluding Kent. Modern English has standardised different dialectal forms, *ridge* and *hill*, *rush* and *hurst*, *merry* and *knell*. As a surname, we still have all the varieties in *Hurst*, *Hirst* and *Herst*, but *Hill* is now the common form, though it may still survive occasionally in *Hell*, once common in Essex, and in *Hull*; the persistence of these, however, is probably due to personal-names, *Hell* from *Ellis* or *Helen* and *Hull*, a pet-name for *Hugh*. *Ridge* is now more frequent than *Rudge*, whilst *Bridge, Merry* and *Rush* today survive only in the standard form except in the derivative *Risher*.

In East Sussex and the adjoining parts of Kent we find *Hoad* and *Hoath*, with *Hoadley, Hoather* and *Hother* from a dialectal *hōth* corresponding to the normal *Heath*. In the south-east, particularly in Essex, Kent and Sussex, certain words like OE *fenn, wente* 'path, way' and *denu* 'valley' became ME *fann, wante* and *dane* and this *a* survives in *Fann(er), Vann(er), Want* 'dweller by the crossroads',

[1] For place-names, *v.* P. H. Reaney, *Origin of English Place-names* (1960), pp. 43–8.

30

corresponding to the Suffolk *Went*, and *Dane*, often wrongly regarded as a sign of Danish origin.

The west-country *Yea*, *Yeo* and *Atyeo* preserve a dialectal development of OE *ēa* 'stream'. The Anglian and Kentish *wella* 'well, spring, stream' has become *Wells* or *Atwell*; the West Saxon *wiella* survives occasionally in Devon and Somerset as *Will* and *Atwill*, whilst in Dorset it has become *Wooll* and *Attwool*. In the West Midlands, South Lancashire and South-west Yorkshire, the corresponding Mercian *wælla* 'spring' survives as *Wall*, but it is difficult to distinguish this from Anglian *wall* 'wall'.

One broad distinction between north and south was their treatment of the consonants *c, f* and *s*. The northern *cald* 'cold', *calf*, etc., preserved the sound of *k* in *Calf*, *Calvert* 'calf-herd', *Cawker* and such place-names as Calcraft 'cold croft', Caldecot, Caldwell, etc., but the corresponding southern *ceald*, etc., still survives with *ch*, though there has been some assimilation to the standard form: *Chalk(er)*, *Chalcroft*, *Chaldecot*, *Chadwell* 'cold spring'. The southern voicing of *s* is still preserved in *Zeal*, *Zealey*, *Zell* and *Zeller*.

Initial *F* in the south was pronounced *V*, which is now, at times reflected in the spelling: *Venn*, *Fenn*; *Vink* for *Fink*, *Finch*; *Volkes*, *Vokes* for *Folkes*, *Fokes* (from *Fulk*); *Voller*, *Fuller*; *Vowell(s)*, *Vowles* for *Fowle* and *Vowler* for *Fowler*; *Vroome*, *Frome*.

This voicing of *f* has led to some confusion. *Fidler* (OE *fiðelere*), pronounced *Vidler* in Essex and Suffolk, was confused with *Vidlow*, from OFr *vis de leu* 'wolf-face', which survives in Phillow's Farm in Little Baddow (*Videlowes* 1493), and has become Fiddlers Dykes in Norfolk and Fidler's Hall in Suffolk, both once held by Walchelin *Videlu*. The French nickname *le enveise* or *le envoisie* 'playful, wanton' is now found occasionally as *Lenfesty*, but has usually shed its first syllable and now appears in 28 variants in which the normal *Vaisey*, *Voysey* or *Vesey* alternates with *Faizey*, *Foizey* and *Feasey* or *Phaisey*, *Pheysey* and *Pheazey*. Rather surprisingly, the pronunciation of *Vivian* seems to have caused difficulty. In the south the *v* was regarded as the normal southern pronunciation of *f* and was replaced by it, *Fifian*, *Fyvyen*, *Phivien*. Just as the child says *fevver* for *feather* and the dialect-speaker *favver* for *father*, these latter forms were regarded as errors and corrected to *Phythien* and *Fythien* and these, in turn became *Fidian* and also *Vydyan*, which, like the colloquial *Injun* for *Indian*, finally became *Fidgeon* and *Vidgen*. One Essex man had his surname spelled *Fiffeon*, *Phiffion*, *Pfiffian*, *Phithian*

31

and *Fitheon* between 1604 and 1638 and another in 1712–34 as *Phydian, Fython, Pythian* and *Pitheon*. There are at least 13 modern variants, including *Videan, Vidgen, Fiddian, Fidgeon, Phethean* and *Phythian*.

EVIDENCE OF SCANDINAVIAN ORIGIN

Local surnames from places of Scandinavian origin such as Booth, Hanby, Hesketh, Scales or Scholes obviously originated in an area formerly occupied by Scandinavians. So, too, where a surname is a patronymic from a Scandinavian personal-name such as *Allgrim* (ON **Alfgrimr*), *Kettle* (ON *Ketill*) or *Tuckey* (ON *Tóki*), or from a nickname, *Brockless* 'without breeches', *Skarfe* 'cormorant', *Skarth* 'hare-lip' or *Sprackling* 'the man with creaking legs', the name almost certainly comes from the Danelaw, though we must remember that under Canute men of Scandinavian origin obtained lands in the south[1] and, after the Norman Conquest, descendants of theirs, still conscious of their race, may well have borne surnames of Scandinavian origin. Some of these surnames reveal their origin by the preservation of the Scandinavian *k* or *sk* for the English *ch* or *sh*: *Keswick* for *Chiswick, Kirk, Kirby*, and *Carlton* for *Charlton*; *Skirlaugh* for *Shirley* and *Skelton* for *Shelton*.

The Normans, too, were of Scandinavian origin and at the time of the Conquest still used some of their native names and brought them to England, some of them modified by French pronunciation. ON *Ásketill* (now *Ashkettle*) was popular in Normandy as *Anschetill* and *Anketill*, whence the modern *Anketell, Ankettle, Ankill* and *Antell*. It was also used in Normandy in the forms *Anketin, Asketin* and *Astin*, all of which still survive in the surnames *Ankin, Antin, Askin, Astins, Haskins, Haskings* and *Hastins*. ON *Þorsteinn* was common in the Danelaw and has given us *Thurstan, Thurston* and *Thirsting*; in Normandy it was also popular as *Turstin*, whence the modern *Tusten, Tusting, Tutin* and *Tuting*.

ANGLO-FRENCH INFLUENCE

After the Norman Conquest there were difficulties of communication between Normans who knew no English and Englishmen who were

---

[1] One of them, Esgar the staller (ODa *Esger*, ON *Ásgeirr*), a tenant in Lambourn (Berks) in 1066, gave name to East Garston (Berks), formerly *Esgareston*.

ignorant of French. Each had to learn something of the language of the other, and gradually the upper and middle classes became bilingual just at the time when surnames were developing and many of these were formed from christian names, occupational terms and nicknames of French origin. This often resulted in the creation of doublets, surnames of the same meaning, one French, one English, so that we have the French *Carpenter* by the side of the English *Wright* and *Bonifant* with the same meaning as *Goodchild*.

There are other doublets, too, due to the differences of pronunciation in the northern French spoken by the Normans and that of central French. Some few of the land-holders recorded in Domesday Book came from south of the Loire and surnames prove that already in 1086 there were immigrants in England from Paris, the Gâtinais, Poitou and Anjou and their numbers were considerably increased under the Plantagenets. In certain words northern French has initial *C* for the *Ch* of central French. Sometimes only one form survives in the surname, at others both. *Chamberlain* is a central form, though the earliest examples are *Camberlain*. From OFr *chaperon* 'hood' we get the modern *chaperon* which is found occasionally as an early surname but with an entirely different meaning 'maker of hoods', as the modern sense is not earlier than the eighteenth century. The common early form is ONFr *Caperun*, surviving in the northern forms *Capuron*, *Capron* and *Caporn*. Where both northern and central forms survive, there is a curious difference in their relative frequency. In the London Telephone Directory there are only 13 *Candlers* to about 300 *Chandlers* and only 12 *Charters* to about 1,000 *Carters*, whilst *Caplin* (200) is only slightly more common than *Chaplin* (180). Other examples include *Caffin* and *Chaffin*, *Canter* and *Chanter*, *Capel* and *Chapell*.

Galer and *Gayler* are from the Norman–Picard *gaiolere*, *Jailler* from the central French *jaioleur*. This difference in pronunciation accounts for the variation between *Garden* and *Jardine*, but the occupational-name is found only as *Gardener*, *Gardiner* and *Gardner*. In some instances, it is not easy to account for this variation. *Goss* is from OG *Gozzo*, *Gauz*, whilst *Joss*, now often *Joyce*, is from *Jodoc*, the name of a Breton saint, but already in the twelfth century, the same man could be called either *Gosce* or *Joce*. Similarly, at the same period, *Joscelinus* and *Goscelinus* were alternative forms of one man's name. This is OFr *Goscelin* or *Joscelin*, which may be a diminutive of OG *Gautselin*, *Gozelin* or of the Breton *Judoc*, a compound of which, *Judicael,* was common in England and survives as *Jekyll* or *Jeckell* and *Jiggle* or *Giggle.* In Normandy *Gosselin* is still common and we know that there was a strong Breton contingent among the followers of the Conqueror. The names must have been confused at an early period with the result that initial *G* and *J* became interchangeable. *Geoffrey* is the regular spelling of the christian name, but as a surname is rare. The common form is *Jeffery* or *Jefferies,* whilst the early pet-name *Geffe* now survives only as *Jeff(s), Jeffcock* or *Jeffcott.* Similarly, the christian names *Gerald* and *Gerard* are rare as surnames for which we have *Garrould, Garrod, Jarrold* and *Jarrott* by the side of *Garrard* and *Jarrard.* This *ar* has been noted only in the surnames and is late, *Garard* 1412, *Garold* 1524. It must be due to the coalescence of the sounds *er* and *ar* and, once the names were spelled with *Gar-,* a spelling pronunciation must have developed, giving *Garrould, Garard,* etc., whilst in *Jerrold* and *Jerrard* we have merely a spelling variation with the sound of *Gerold* and *Gerard,* just as the common *Gent* and *Gentle* are found occasionally as surnames in the form of *Jent* and *Jentle.*

For a century or so after the Conquest, the most popular name among the Normans was *William,* a name of Germanic origin, which in north-eastern France became *Willelm* and farther south *Guillelm,* now *Guillaume.* It became productive of diminutives and has given us the surnames *Williams, Willmott, Williman,* etc. From *Guillaume* we get *Gilliam, Gillam,* with the diminutives *Gillett, Gillman,* etc., but they are much less frequent than the former.[1] Some of the names may have more than one origin. *Gillard* may be a doublet of the Norman *Willard,* but when pronounced like *Jillard* it is a derivative of *Gille* (Giles). So, too, *Gillett* may be Fr *Guillot,* a doublet of *Willett,* or local, from *del Gilheved* 'dweller at the head of the glen' (ON *gil*), but when it has the pronunciation of *Jillett,* it is a diminutive of either *Gille* (Giles) or of *Jill* (Gillian, Juliana).

Guy is much more common than *Wye,* but *Wyatt* far outnumbers *Guyat.* Only the northern form of *guerre* 'war' survives as *Warr,* with its derivative *Warrior* and in *Wastnidge,* from le Gâtinais, a district south of Paris, but we have both *Gaite* and *Waite* from OFr *guaite,* ONFr *waite* 'watchman'.

The earliest occupational-names and nicknames are preceded by the French definite article, even when the origin is an English word. This is usually lost, but survives in such names as *Larcher* 'the

---

[1] *v.* also p. 156 below.

archer', *Lusher* 'the door-keeper' and *Levick* (*le eveske* 'the bishop') and in the English *Le Good, le Hunte* and *Lemay.* It is often difficult to decide whether modern surnames of this type are old or recent introductions from France. An anglicised form like *Le Pelley* 'bald' or *Lefeaver* is certainly old and so are *Le Fever* and *Lefever* 'smith', a frequent medieval name. But such forms as *Lefebure, Lefebvre* and *Le Feuvre* are French dialectal forms never acclimatised in England. Some of these names are native to the Channel Islands (*Lempriere, Le Patourel, Le Sueur*) and some were introduced by Huguenots (*Labat,* from Provençal *abat* 'abbot', *Lefanu, Lefroy*).

Chapter Three
ENGLISH LOCAL SURNAMES

LOCAL surnames is a convenient term for all surnames derived from a particular locality or place, but these are of more than one type. *Hill, Moore* and *Wood* were names given to men who lived near one of these natural features. Earlier, they appear as Richard *Athill*, Jordan *atte More* and Thomas *Attewode*. Sometimes the preposition was retained, in whole or in part, as in the modern *Athill, Atmore* or *Amoore* and *Attwood*. Many local surnames derive from places still on the map and easily recognisable. In early documents the place-name is usually preceded by *de* and it has been held that such a name as *de Baildon* implies descent from a landowner who was a member of a family which was seated at Baildon (WRY). This is certainly true in many instances. Adam de Cokefeld, the first of this name, held the manor of Cockfield (Sf) of the Abbot of Bury St Edmunds from about 1130 and both land and surname continued in his family for a hundred years or more, whilst the Shirleys took their name from Shirley (Db) which they held before 1165.

But many of these surnames undoubtedly indicate no more than the place of birth or origin. They served as a convenient means of identifying a newcomer. Adam de Bidyk (d. 1302) moved south from Biddick in Durham, became the king's tailor and custodian of the assize of cloths 'both on this side and beyond the seas', and acquired

36

manors in Essex and Middlesex which he bequeathed to his son. Adam de Salesbury, who had tenements in Salisbury, moved to London, where he became a pepperer, was sheriff in 1323–4 and alderman of Cornhill 1325–30. He bought a manor in Walthamstow which was held by his family for nearly a hundred years and is still known as Salisbury Hall. Nor was London the only magnet to attract immigrants from a distance. York, Bristol, Leicester and Norwich all attracted newcomers, though from a smaller radius, and the fact that many of these are described as tradesmen or artisans is a clear proof that they were not land-owners and that their surnames indicate merely the place from which they had come. In Norwich, we find John de Heylesdon le Tanur (1285), Alan de Hedersete, lindraper (1287), Geoffrey de Buthorp le Ceyntrer 'maker of girdles' (1288), Hugh de Denton le Bellgh makere 'bellows-maker' (1289) and Laurence de Worthstedde cook (1289).[1] Such surnames as London, York, Carlisle, Leicester and Worcester could never have arisen from the ownership of these cities. Many surnames from continental places, too, have a similar origin. There was a constant stream of merchants, workmen and others from abroad, named simply from their place of origin: Paris, Roan (Rouen), Arras, Aries (Arras), Bullen (Boulogne), Callis (Calais), Cullen (Cologne), Challen(s) (Chalons), Danvers, Danvis (Antwerp) and Sessions (Soissons).

SURNAMES FROM TOWNS, VILLAGES AND ESTATES

As a surname could arise from any feudal or manorial holding or from any place where men lived, their possible number is legion. The original surname would have the same form as the place-name, but as this changed in spelling and pronunciation, so would the surname. But as the place-name was attached to a particular place, it would in due time acquire a distinctive spelling which would become fixed by official use and its repetition on maps. But the surname could be carried to distant parts of the country where both its spelling and pronunciation were strange and unknown, especially if it derived from some small, insignificant spot. It was a mere name, with no apparent meaning, so that there was nothing to check irregular and eccentric changes of pronunciation and it was at the mercy of mispronunciation and the peculiarities of the phonetic spellings of

[1] From Hellesdon, Hethersett, Bowthorpe, Denton and Worstead respectively, all in Norfolk, surviving in the surnames *Helsdon*, *Bowthorpe* and *Denton*.

parsons and parish clerks. Even after the spelling of the place-name had become fixed, new colloquial pronunciations could develop which were adopted as the correct form of the surname. Hence, it is often impossible, at first sight, to identify the place from which the surname originated.

Colloquial pronunciations and dialectal developments

As Weekley has noted, *Barraclough*, a northern name, has become *Barrowcliff* in Notts and reaches London as *Berrycloth* and *Berecloth*, where it is often pronounced *Barraclow* and *Barraclue*. It has also been corrupted to *Barnaclough*. *Fairclough* 'dweller in the fair hollow', probably of Lancashire origin, similarly survives as *Faircliff* and *Faircloth* and is found also as *Fairtlough*. It occurs as *Farcloe* in 1669 and as *Fear Cloth* in 1655, forms which do not seem to have survived. From Blencarn (Cu) we get *Blenkarne*, *Blenkhorn*, *Blenkiron* and *Blinkhorn*.

Birkenshaw, from a place of that name in Birstall (WRY), now appears in no less than 24 different spellings and others are known which do not seem to exist today. Its earliest form, in 1274, is *del Birkenschawe* 'dweller by the birch-wood'. The medial vowel was weakened and the first syllable spelled *ir*, *er* or *ur*, all representing the same sound: *Birkinshaw*, *Bircumshaw*, *Berkenshaw*, *Burkenshaw*, *Burkinsher*. As often, the medial *k* became *t* before the following *n*: *Birtenshaw*, *Burtinshaw*, *Burtonshaw*; then the *r* was lost and *rt* became *tt*: *Buttanshaw*, *Buttenshaw*, *Buttonshaw*. Metathesis of *r* and voicing of *k* to *g* gave *Briggenshaw* and *Briginshaw*, and finally a combination of popular etymology and phonetic spelling produced *Brockenshaw*, *Brokenshaw*, *Brokensha*, *Brokenshire* and the shortened *Bruckshaw*.

It is obviously impossible to deal with all the surnames in which such changes have occurred. They are numerous and of various kinds and are of more than academic interest, especially to those trying to trace the history of a family. *Mallandain*, *Mallandin*, *Mallendine*, *Mallindine* and *Malidine* are all identical in origin, from Manuden (Ess) which, some 60 years ago, had four local pronunciations: *Mallingden*, *Mallendine*, *Mallentine* and *Marnden*. These the genealogist should be able to trace back without too much difficulty, so far as the spelling is concerned, to the fifteenth-century forms of the place-name, *Mallenden* and *Mawnden*. But beyond that, he needs to know that Manuden itself derives from an earlier *Man-*

ningden which appears in various unexpected forms from 1066 onwards, and for these he will need to consult some reliable book on
place-names.

It is not uncommon for modern surnames to preserve medieval
forms of a place-name, as *Umpleby, Humpleby,* from Anlaby (ERY),
Umlouebi 1086. *Manistre* and *Manisty,* found in Yorkshire in the
fourteenth centuries, derive from Manesty in Borrowdale (Cu) which
occurs as both *Manistie* and *Maynister* in 1564. But these surnames
are found also in Suffolk in 1674 as *Manitre, Manister, Manistre*
and *Mannestey* and these certainly derive from Manningtree on the
Essex side of the Stour. This place-name usually occurs as *Manitre,*
but is found also as *Manystre* in 1291 and 1343. This would appear to
have been preserved as the local pronunciation which has persisted
in the surname. *Carwardine* (now also *Carradine*) is an early form of
Carden (Ch), *Orlebar* of Orlingbury (Nth) and *Wrigglesworth* of
Woodlesford (WRY); with a seventeenth-century loss of the initial
W, this has also given us *Rigglesford* and *Riggulsford,* with which we
may compare *Rigley* and *Wrigley,* from Wrigley Head (La).

The West Riding place-name Womersley is found in 1086 as
Wilmereslege 'Wilmer's forest-clearing' and preserved its *i* for 400
years (*Wymbersley* 1504). For the past 450 years, the stressed vowel
has been *o* (*Wommersley* 1501). In 1509 (LP) both these forms are
found as the surname of John *Wymbersley, Womersley* or *Wymbersla,*
and survive today as *Womersley* and *Wimberley,* the latter deriving
ultimately from a 1250 form *Wilmerley,* without the *s* of the genitive.

Sawbridgeworth (Herts), *Sabrixteworde* 1086 'the farm of
Sæbeorht' had become *Sapsworth* by 1565 and *Sapsforde* by 1568.
Both *Sapsworth* and *Sapsford* are now found as surnames and from
these come *Sapserd* and *Sapsed* and, with intrusive *t, Sapsted* and
Sapstead.

Other interesting developments are found in *Higginbotham* and
Shufflebotham. The first derives from Oakenbottom in Bolton-le-
Moors (La), Alexander *de Akinbothun* 1246 AssLa. The place-name
was probably originally **æcen-botme* 'oaken-valley', becoming
Eakenbottom and *Ickenbottom.* The initial *H* is inorganic and it has
been suggested that the present form is due to association with *hickin*
or *higgin,* a Lancashire and Cheshire dialect word for 'mountain-
ash', but the development may be due entirely to colloquial pronunciation, with an inorganic *H* and the common interchange of *k*
and *g.* There are 11 modern variants, including *Heckingbottom,*

Hickinbotham, Higginbottom, Higenbottam, Higinbothom, Higgenbottom and *Heginbotham*. In 1695 the name is found as *Hickabotham*.

Shufflebotham derives from Shipperbottom in Bury (La): Richard *de Schyppewallebotham* 1285 AssLa, 'the valley with a stream where sheep were washed'. The development of the name may be seen from the forms of the surname, though these do not happen to occur in strictly chronological order: *Shepelbotom* 1569, *Shuplebotom* 1583, *Shepobotham* 1579, *Shippobotham* 1582, *Shifabothom* 1626, *Shufflebotham* 1674. The present-day forms of the surname are: *Shipperbottom, Shufflebotham, Shuflebotam, Shovelbottom, Shoebotham, Shoebottom* and *Shubotham*.

Wolfenden and *Woffendon*, with five similar variants, derive from Wolfenden in Newchurch-in-Rossendale (La). Two other Lancashire surnames reveal almost completely in their modern forms the development of their pronunciation and spelling: *Wolstencroft, Wolstoncroft, Woolstencroft, Worstencroft, Worsencroft, Wosencroft* and *Wozencroft*, from Wolstancroft; and *Wolstanholme, Wolstenholme, Wolstenhulme, Woolstenhulme, Worstenholme, Wostenholm, Woosnam, Wusteman, Woosman* and *Worsman*, from Wolstanholme in Rochdale.

Southcott is a surname meaning 'dweller at the south cottage' or deriving from a place called Southcott, as, for instance, that in Linslade (Bk), spelled *Surcote* in 1826 and now pronounced *Cirket*. There was also a lost Southcott in Stone in the same county (*Sircotes* 1511), whilst the Berkshire Southcott occurs as *Circuitt* c1728. One or other of these Bucks places is the source of the rare Bedfordshire surname *Cirket(t)*, formerly *Surcot* and *Surcoate*, found today as *Circuitt, Serkitt, Sirkett* and *Surkett*. The surname may also occasionally be a nickname from the surcoat: John *Surcote* 1327 SRSf, which, at this date, could not possibly be a form of *Southcote*.

Spalding and *Spaulding* derive from Spalding (L). In the seventeenth century several men of this name were freemen of York and the records of their admission show clearly the development of the name to *Spalton* and *Spolton*:

Henry *Spalding*, carpenter 1633
Mathew *Spaldinge*, carpenter, son of Henry *Spaldinge* 1662
Henry *Spawlden*, son of Henry *Spalden*, carpenter 1672
Marcus *Spaldinge*, carpenter, son of Mathew *Spalton*, carpenter 1689
Mathew *Spalding*, son of Mathew *Spalding*, carpenter 1702
Henry *Spaldon*, son of Henry *Spaldon*, taylor 1713

In granting pardons for outlawry or other offences, extreme care was taken to particularise the individual concerned, an extreme example of 1461 containing 11 different descriptions of the man which take up 12 lines of print. Here there is no doubt as to the actual surname, the only variants being John *Beston* or *Beeston*, but he is called both 'yoman' and 'gentilman' and once 'parker' and is described as 'of' or 'lately of' Framlingham and Ipswich (Sf) and of Hawnes (Beds).[1] In the Pardon Roll of 1509 descriptions are less elaborate, but the forms of the surnames provide interesting examples of variant spellings and colloquial pronunciations and, at times, of unusual developments. John *Huddilston, Hudelston, Hodelston, Hudleston* or *Hurleston* provides us with the ancestors of two of the modern forms of this surname from Huddleston (WRY), *Huddelston* and *Hudleston*. We should not expect this to develop to *Hurleston*, but this is probably the origin of the rare *Hurlestone* found in Bradford by the side of *Huddleston*. The fifteenth-century Cheshire *Hurleston*, however, must derive from Hurlston in Acton in that county. Similarly, of the four modern surnames derived from Bagnall (St), *Bagnall, Bagenal, Bagnell* and *Bagnold*, three alternate in the name of Ralph *Bagnall, Bagnold, Bagenall* alias *Bagnald* (1561 Pat).

At times, these variations provide problems. The modern surnames *Bicknell, Bignall, Bignell* and *Bignold* show the same variation in the second element as in *Bagnall*, etc., but, whereas this was originally *-holt* 'wood' (William *de Bagenholt* 1299 AssSt), in *Bicknell*, etc., it varies between *-hill* and *-hall*, whilst the first element also varies between *Bik-* and *Big-* and the surnames derive from three different places. Thomas *de Bikenhulle* 1214 Cur (Wa) owed his surname to Bickenhill (Wa) which is found as *Bigenhull* in 1354 and was long pronounced *Bignell*. William *de Bigenhull* 1279 RH (O) must have come from Bignell House in Bicester (O) which occurs as *Bigenhull* in 1220, *Bikenhulle* in 1285 and *Bygenhall* about 1377, whilst the surname is also found as *de Bigehille* in 1247. There is also a place Bickenhall in Somerset, *Bichehalle* 1086 and *Bikehilla* 1186, which gave rise to the surname of John *de Bikenhull* in 1327 (SRSo). It is obviously impossible to decide from which of these places the modern surnames derive without tracing back the history of the family until some definite proof is found, especially as these forms are often late and found in counties far from Oxfordshire, Somerset

[1] C. L. Ewen, *History of Surnames of the British Isles* (1931), p. 402.

41

or Warwickshire: William *Bignolle*, John *Bygnold* 1525 SRSx, Robert *Bignall* 1758 FrY.

Arscott may derive from Arscott (Sa), William *de Ardescote* 1255 RH (Sa), or it may be from Arscott in Holsworthy (D), earlier *Asshecote* (1292), where the surname appears as *Esshecote* in 1277 and *Ayshcote* in 1333 (PN D 147). But in 1523 we find a Devon man John *Arscot* who, in 1513 (LP), is called John *Aryscote*, *Addescote*, *Addyscote*, *Adescote* or *Addyscoote*. This, like the 1287 surname *Atherscote*, must come from Addiscott in South Tawton (D), ultimately from *Ædrichescota* (1166), which is found as *Arscott* alias *Addiscott* in 1658 (PN D 448).

The name of Sir Walter Raleigh, like Raleigh House in Pilton (D) from which it derives, is pronounced *Rawley*. The place-name is usually found as *Ralegh*, but occurs as *Rawlegh* in 1535. In 1509 (LP), we find six different forms of the Devon surname referring to the same man: Edmond *Rawley*, *Rayley*, *Raweleygh*, *Raleygh*, *Ralegh* or *Rawlegh* of Exeter and Plymouth. There appear to be no examples of *Rayley* for the place-name, but it was clearly an alternative pronunciation in Devonshire and is the normal pronunciation of Rayleigh (Ess). Early forms of this place-name are usually *Reylegh* or *Rayley*, with an occasional *Raleghe*. A solitary *Rawley* in 1519 points to the development of the same pronunciation in Essex as in Devon. The normal pronunciation and spelling in Essex was *Rayleigh*; in Devonshire the name was usually spelled *Raleigh* but pronounced *Rawley*. Here, too, the modern surnames *Raleigh*, *Raley*, *Ralley*, *Rawley* and *Rayleigh* cannot be definitely assigned to Essex or to Devon without further evidence and recourse to family history.

Even a slight variation in spelling may be disconcerting, as *Wincer* for *Windsor*, *Farnorth* for *Farnworth*, *Waistcoat* for *Westcott*, *Plaster* and *Plaister* for *Plaistow*, *Fidling* or *Fidlin* from Fitling (ERY), *Oxbrow* for *Oxborough* (Nf), *Croasdell* and *Croysdill* for *Crossdale* (Cu) and *Handslip* from Hanslope (Bk).

Among local pronunciations not obvious at first sight we may note: *Aram* and *Arum* for Averham (Nt), *Badgery* for Badgeworthy (Gl), *Brayshaw*, *Brayshay* and *Brashaw* for Bradshaw (Y), *Bustin* for Brislington (So), *Cason* for Cawston (Nf), *Ebsary* for Ebsworthy (D), *Ensor* and *Enzer* for Edensor (Db), *Escreet* for Escrick (ERY), *Essery* for Axworthy (D), *Henningham* and *Heningham* for Hedingham (Ess), *Littler* for Littleover (Db), *Mellanby* for Melmerby (Cu, NRY), *Peareth* for Penrith (Cu), *Sneezum* for Snettisham (Nf), *Startin* for

Staverton (Nth), *Stopford* for Stockport (Ch) and *Wyndham* for Wymondham (Nf).

Many of these surnames are misleading in appearance and do not suggest a place-name origin. Whilst *Slaughter* may be a contraction of *slaughterer* 'a killer of animals', 'a butcher', it is often local in origin, from Upper or Lower Slaughter (Gl) or from residence near a slough or muddy place (OE *slōhtre*). *Trickey* is from a Devonshire village of that name and *Thicknesse* from a place in Staffordshire, whilst *Unthank* is the name of various small places in Cumberland, Northumberland and the North Riding, from OE *unþances* 'without leave', hence 'dweller at a squatter's farm'. *Raspberry* or *Rasbery* is from Ratsbury (D), earlier *Radespree* 'red brushwoodland', whilst *Stirrup* or *Sturrup* is usually from Styrrup (Nt), though, as it is found early in Somerset and Sussex without any sign of a preposition, it must sometimes mean 'stirrup-maker'. *Trollope* is from Troughburn (Nb), formerly *Trolhop* 'troll-valley'. *Courage* may be from ME *corage* used as an adjective 'stout' of body which is equated with *Crask* 'fat or lusty', but it may also be from Cowridge End in Luton, formerly pronounced *Courage*, or a phonetic spelling of *Kerridge* from OE *Cynerīc* 'family-ruler' which has also become *Carriage*.

Barnacle is usually derived from Barnacle (Wa), but this was originally *Bernhangre* and did not reach its modern form before 1547. Hence the surname, which is found as *Bernikel* in 1344, must have some other origin, either from ME *bernacle*, a diminutive of *bernak*, a kind of powerful bit or twitch for the mouth of a horse, used to restrain a restive animal and used also as an instrument of torture. The nickname might have been given to an expert in taming horses or to a torturer, or it might have been given to man of savage, unrestrained temper who needed such restraint. Another possibility is a nickname from the barnacle goose (ME *barnakyll*).

The surname *Brighton* is from Breighton (ERY), which occurs as *Bryghton* from 1298 to 1567. It cannot derive from the Sussex Brighton which is a contracted form of an earlier *Brightelmeston*. This is found as *Brighton* in the reign of Charles I, but did not come into common use until the early nineteenth century. Similarly, *Bristol* is from Burstall (ERY) or Birstal (WRY), both with early forms *Bristal*. Throughout the Middle Ages the west-country port was known as *Bristow*, originally *Brycgstow* 'the place by the bridge' and this gave rise to the surnames *Bristow*, *Bristo* and *Brister* which may sometimes derive from Burstow (Sr).

Some common place-name elements are weakened when final and unstressed and were re-spelled in a way which often disguises their origin; these weakened forms were then often confused and incorrect forms substituted. For instance, the Somerset surnames *Hembra*, *Hembrow*, *Hembry*, *Hembury* and *Hennebry* may derive from Emborough (So), Broadhembury (D), two Devon places called Hembury, or Henbury (Do), all from *burh* 'fort' or from two other Devon places named Henborough, both from *beorh* 'hill'. Both *-hill* and *-well* are often reduced to *-ell*: *Sandhill*, *Sandell; Toothill*, *Tootell*, *Tootle*, *Tothill*, *Tottle*, *Tuthill*, *Tutill* and *Tuttle*, from such places as Toot Hill (Ess), Tothill (L, Mx), Tootle Height (La) or Tuttle Hill (Wa), all 'lookout hill'; *Caldwell*, *Caudell*, *Caudle*, *Caddell* and *Cadel*, from such places as Caldwell (Wa, NRY), Caudle Green (Gl) and Cawdle Fen (C), all 'cold spring or stream'; and *Bradwell*, *Braddle* 'broad stream'.

Common weakenings of this kind are:

-ham becomes *-am*, *-om*, *-um*, *-on*: *Balham*, *Ballam* from Balham (Sr); *Balsom* from Balsham (C); *Barnham* (Nf, Sf, Sx), *Barnum*; *Blunsom*, *Blunsum* from Bluntisham (Hu); *Canham*, *Cannom* from Cavenham (Sf); *Ditcham* (Ha), *Ditchum*; *Haversum*, *Haverson* from Haversham (Bk); *Holtham* (Ha), *Holtom*, *Holttum*, *Holtum*; *Ledsham* (Ch, WRY), *Ledsam*, *Ledsome*, *Ledson*, *Leadsom*; *Micklem*, *Miklem* from Mickleham (Sr); *Mitcham* (Sr), *Mitchem*, *Mitchum*; *Tatham* (La), *Tatam*, *Tatem*, *Tatum*; *Totham* (Ess), *Tottem*.

-garth becomes *-gate*: *Applegarth* (NRY, ERY, Cu), *Applegath*, *Applegate*.

-house is frequently weakened to *-as*, *-es*, *-is*, *-us* or *-ers*: Backhouse 'bake-house', Baccas, Bacchus, Bachus, Backus; Barkhouse 'tannery', Barkas, Barkis; Bellhouse, Bellas; Broadhouse, Broadis; Brookhouse, Brockis, Brokus; Byas(s) 'house in the bend'; Caras(s), Carras, Caress, Caris(s), Carus 'marsh-house'; Childerhouse, Childers 'children's house'; Churchouse, Churchers, Churches, Churchus; Coultas(s), Coultous, Coultish, Cowtas 'colt-house'; Duckhouse, Duckers; Duffus, Duffes 'dove-house'; Haggas, Haggis, Haggish 'wood-cutter's hut'; Hillhouse, Hillas, Hillers, Hillis, Hellass; Kirkhouse, Kirkus; Malthouse, Malthus, Maltus, Maltas; Moorhouse, Morress; Newhouse, Newis(s); Nunhouse, Nunniss; Stannas 'stone-house'; Windus, Windows, Winders, Windes 'winding-house'; Woodhouse, Wodehouse, Woodus, Wooders, Woodisse.

-thwaite becomes *-waite* and *-white*, with various corruptions: Applewhaite, Applewhite, Ablewhite, from Applethwaite (Cu, We); Branthwaite (Cu), Branwhite; Crossthwaite, Crosswaite, Crostwight, from Crosthwaite (Cu, We, NRY) or Crostwight, Crostwick (Nf); Hebblethwaite (WRY), Hebblewaite, Hebblewhite, Hepplewhite, Ebblewhite; Hustwayte, Hustwitt, from Husthwaite (NRY); Satterthwaite (La), Satterfitt, Satterford,

Setterfield; Smithwaite, Smithwhite, Smorthwaite, Smorfit, Smurthwaite, Smurfit, Smallthwaite, from Smaithwaite (Cu), *Smerthwayte* 1530, *Smethwayte* 1552, or from some small clearing (ON *smár*, OE *smæl*) or 'smooth clearing' (OE *smēðe*) in Cumb or Yorks; Whitewhite, from *Whitthuait* (Cu) 'white clearing'.

wīc frequently loses its *w* and assumes various phonetic spellings: Bastick, Bassick, from Bastwick (Nf); Fullick, Follick, from Fulwick's Copse in Lurgashall (Sx); Pressick, Prissick, from Prestwick (Bk, Nb, Sr) or Prissick Fm in Marton (NRY); Sheppick 'sheep-farm', as at Shapwick (Do, So); Swannick (Db, Ha), though this may also be a nickname 'swan-neck'; Bloxwich (St), Bloxidge, Bloxsidge, Blocksidge; Bromwich (St, Wa), Bromage, Brommage, Bromige; Colledge, Collidge, from Collwich (St); Dullage, from Dulwich (Sr); Dunnage, Dunage, from Dunwich (Sf); Greenidge, Greenish, from Greenwich (K); Hardwich, Hardwidge, a variant of Hardwick 'herd-farm'; Harrich, Harridge, from Harwich (Ess); Horwich (La), Horridge;[1] Norridge, from Norwich (Nf); Prestwich (La), Prestage, Prestedge, Prestidge, Prestige; Woolwich, Woolich, from Woolwich (K), with Woollage, Woledge, Wolledge, though the latter may also be from Wollage Green and Woolwich Wood in Womenswold (K) or variants of *Worledge*, from OE *weorþlīc* 'worthy, noble, distinguished'.

Local surnames of varied origin

One result of these and other variations in spelling, combined with the changes in the forms of the place-names themselves, is that a modern surname may be derived from more than one place. Certainty of origin depends on the discovery of early forms of the surname and this involves family history and even then it is often impossible to reach a definite decision unless the pedigree of the name can be carried back to the fourteenth century or even earlier. The obvious derivation of *Cambridge*, for example, is from the University city, but Richard and Alan *de Cambrige* who were living in Staffordshire in 1182 and 1227, respectively, must have owed their name to Cambridge in Gloucestershire, for at this period the better-known Cambridge was known as *Cantebrigge* or *Cauntebrigge*. This later became *Caumbrigge* and *Cambrigge*, but no such spelling has been noted before 1348 and it did not become common until the last quarter of the fourteenth century. To prove that a surname Cambridge originated in Cambridgeshire, it is necessary to show that the family name developed from *Cantebrigge* (or an earlier *Grantebricge*) to *Cambrigge* alongside the development of the place-name.

---

[1] This may be from Hawridge (Bk) or one of the places in Devon named Horridge, all with a second element -*ridge*.

Fifield (O, W) and Fyfield (Berks, Ess, Gl, Ha, W) mean 'five hides', the origin, too, of Fifehead (Do), Fivehead and the curious Fitzhead (So), from one or other of which come the surnames Fifehead, Fifett, Fifoot and Fifield. *Sheffield* and *Leeds* may, at times, derive, not from Yorkshire but from Sheffield Park in Sussex or Leeds in Kent. Many surnames derive from villages or hamlets, or even from single farmsteads which took their name from some familiar topographical feature which might repeat itself elsewhere. Thus *Bedwell*, *Bidwell* and *Bidewell* 'spring or stream in a shallow valley' may come from Bedwell in Essex and Herts, Bedlar's Green (Ess), Bidwell (Nth, Beds, D, So), Biddles Fm (Bk), or from some place of the same name no longer on the map. *Barrington* may come from Cambridgeshire or Somerset, *Sorby* or *Sowerby* is a common place-name in Cumberland, Westmorland, Lancashire and Yorkshire, whilst *Tuddenham* may derive from any one of three places in Norfolk and Suffolk. *Kimberley* is found in three counties, *Addington* in four, and *Allington* in no less than nine.

The difficulty of identifying accurately the source of a modern surname is increased when we find that surnames apparently deriving from well-known places may also have some other, non-local, origin. *Worthing* is often, probably most frequently, from the Sussex place of that name, but early material proves conclusively the existence of a personal-name *Worthing* which had become a surname in the thirteenth century. So, too, *Buxton* or *Buckstone* is found early and often without any sign of a preposition and is clearly not always derived from Buxton in Derbyshire or Norfolk. One origin is certainly a personal-name, either OE **Bucstān* or, possibly, **Burgstān*. At times the alternative origin may be occupational, or a nickname: *Buskin*, from Buskin (D) or *buck-skin*, the skin of a buck, used particularly of breeches made of buckskin and, as a surname, for a worker in buckskin or leather; *Warboys*, from Warboys (Hu) or AFr *wardebois* 'guard wood', a nickname for a forester; *Saxby*, from Saxby (Lei, L) or from a nickname 'draw sword', corresponding to the French *Sacquépée*. *Chew* or *Chue* may be from Chew (So) or from OE *cēo*, a name applied to the smaller chattering birds, especially the jackdaw. The history of *Arundel* is complicated, but there is clear evidence that it derives both from Arundel (Sx) and from OFr *arondel* 'swallow'.

Surnames from lost or unidentified places

Some of the deserted villages of England can now be located on the ground and some have disappeared beneath the sea. Numerous other places have now disappeared from the map, not always villages, often farmsteads, sometimes merely physical features near which some family lived and from which they took their name. All trace of habitation may be gone, site and name may have been forgotten, but some of these places have left a memorial in modern surnames, some well known, others rare, and some still surviving in the district in which they originated. For some we can fix the parish where both place-name and surname were found, whilst for the site of others we can only speculate, assuming they came from the district where we meet them. *Bartindale* is from a depopulated place in Hunmanby (ERY), last mentioned in 1600. A lost place in Elmley Lovett (Wo), first recorded as *Inerdeshell* in 1275 and last as *Insoll* in 1642, is still commemorated by the surnames *Insall, Inseal, Insole, Insoll, Insull* and *Hinsull*, whilst in Lancashire, the lost name of the district south of the Roch, in Bury, *Lumhalghs* in 1324 and *Lomax* in 1592, has given us the modern surnames *Lomax, Lomas, Loomas, Loomis, Lummis* and *Lummus*. The Essex *Marriage*, found in that county in 1377 as *Marhach'* derives from a lost place in Finchingfield or Aythorpe Roding, from OE *(ge)mǣre* and *hæcc* 'boundary gate'. Marriage Farm in Wye (K) has the same meaning and this, like Marridge in Ugborough (D), 'meadow-ridge', gave rise to a surname in the thirteenth century.

Lists of names are weary reading, but are inevitable in a book such as this, and one more is justified by the difficulty of discovering the origin of these lost names. The list is not complete. The occasional date gives the latest known reference to the place.

From unidentified places:

Bedser (in or near Bexhill), Bettesworth (Sx), Chattey (Sx), Hollenrake, Hollinrake, Hollindrake, Hollingrake (probably near Wakefield), Pilbeam (Sx), Rawnsley (WRY), Robertshaw, Robinshaw, Robshaw (WRY), Sandeford, Sandiford, Sandifer, Sandyfirth (perhaps near Wakefield), Sidebottom, Sidebotham (Ch), Staniforth (probably near Sheffield), Winterscale, Wintersgill (Y).

From lost places:

Bagridge (in Woodlands, Do), Cruttenden (in Headcorn, K), Eckersley, Eccersley (in Leigh, La), Greethurst (in Yardley, Wo), Heberden, Hibberdine (1795; in Madehurst, Sx), Hubberstey (in Cockerham, La), Shillibeer,

47

Shillabear, Shellabear (1587; in Meavy, D), Smithwick (1608; in Lewes, Sx), Timberlake, Timblick (seventeenth century; in Bayton, Wo), Wadlow (seventeenth century; in Toddington, Beds), Westbroom, Wesbroom (in Woolpit, Sf), Wickenden (1542; in Cowden, K), Wicklow (a hundred meeting-place, Sf).

Surnames from minor and insignificant places:

Bonwick (Bonwick's Place in Ifield, Sx), Claridge (Clearhedge Wood in Waldron, Sx),[1] Cowstick (Cowstock's Wood in Danefield, Sx), Crittall, Crittle (Crit Hall in Benenden, K), Crittenden (in Brenchley, K), Enticknap (Enticknaps Copse in Dunsfold, Sr), Hawkley (Hawkley Fm in Pen sax, Wo), Henty (Antye Fm in Wivelsfield, Sx), Huffington (Ufton Court in Tunstall or Uffington Fm in Goodnestone, K), Huckstepp, Hucstep (Hucksteep Wood in Mountfield, Sx), Lindop, Lindup (Lindop Wood in Edensor, Db), Luxford (Luxford Fm in Crowborough, Sx), Maleham, Malham, Mallam (Malham Fm in Wisborough Green, Sx), Markwick, Markquick (Markwicks in Wadhurst, Sx), Mitchenall, Mitchener, Mitchiner (Michen Hall in Godalming, Sr),[2] Posford (Potsford Barn in Letheringham, Sf), Postlethwaite, Posselwhite, Posnett (a thirteenth-century manor; a field-name in 1840; in Millom, Cu), Prestney (Prestney's Fm in Great Horkesley, Ess), Prestoe, Pristo (from a lost *Prestall* in Deane (La), now Presto Lane), Swaffer (Robert *Swoffer* 1518, John *Swaffer* 1523, Robert *Swafford* 1549 CantW; from Swatfield Bridge in Willesborough (K), *Swatford* 1254 *Ass*), Thistlethwaite, Thistlewood (Thistlewood in Castle Sowerby (Cu), Twysden (Twysden or Twyssenden in Goodhurst, K), Wannaker[3] (Great, Little Wanaker, a field in Little Tey (Ess), *Wallakerbrydge* 1568 PNEss 623), Widdicks (White Dyke in Hailsham, Sx), Wigzell (Wigsell in Salehurst, Sx), Wreghitt (Wregetts in Wheldrake, ERY).

A very large proportion, perhaps the majority, of local surnames are descriptive of the place where a man lived, near a wood, by a hill, in a valley or on the heath. His place of residence could be described by any physical feature or by any object in the landscape, large or small, which could be easily distinguished. Some of these became actual place-names, usually of small, insignificant spots not important enough to find their way on to the map. Others remained merely as an attribute to distinguish a particular man and his family.

[1] Robert *de Claurugge* 1327 SRSx; *Clavregge* 1288, *Claregge* 1429 'cloverridge' (PNSx 406).

[2] Henry *de Michenhale* 1347 PNSr 309, Thomas *Mychinall*, John *Mychiner* 1583 Musters (Sr).

[3] Nicholas *de Walacre* 1276 *For*.

Originally, all such names began with a preposition: Adam *Ithelane* 1227 AssBeds (Lane), Ralph *in þe Hurne* 1279 RH (O) (Hern, Hearne, Hurne, Harn), Thomas *Beyendeyebeck* 1298 AssL 'on the other side of the beck', Simon *ate Hegge* 1327 SRSx (Hedge), Sarra *Bithebrok* 1327 SRSo (Brook), William *Undertheclif* 1327 SRDb, William *Onlehulle* 1332 SRSr (Hill), Geoffrey *uppe the Hurst* 1332 SRSx 'up the wooded hill' (Hirst, Hurst), John *Offyewode*, William *othe Wode* 1374 AssL (Wood). In most instances the preposition ultimately disappeared, but it has survived in a number of surnames: *Attlee, A'Court, Bywater, Overy* 'beyond the stream', *Underdown* 'at the foot of the down', *Uphill* 'up on the hill'.

In the earliest documents we find French or Latin forms: Basilia *de la Burne* 1219 FFEss (Bourne) 'stream', Henry *del Egge* 1221 AssWo, Henry *sub Egge* 1290 ShefA (Edge) 'dweller near or below some prominent edge, ridge or steep hill', Walter *en la Fenne* 1340 SRWo (Fenn). Many of these names are translations by the scribe of the corresponding English name, e.g. William *de la Nye* (1280 AssSo) is identical with William *Attenye* (1276 ib.), and the preposition usually disappears, but survives in a few compounds with English elements: *Dash, Dashfield, Dashwood; Delbridge, Delafield* and *Delahooke* (OE *hōc* 'bend' or 'hill-spur'), and also in *Surtees* which varies between 'dweller by the Tees' (Ralph *sur teyse* 1243 AssDu) and 'dweller at a place called Surtees' (Nicholas *de Surteys* 1315 Riev).

Much the most common of the prepositions used in forming these surnames is OE *æt*. This was followed by the dative of the article and the noun with its appropriate gender: *æt þǣm* (masc. or neut. sing.) became ME *at then, atten*; *æt þǣre* (fem. sing.) became ME *at ther(e), atter*. But by the thirteenth and fourteenth centuries, when these surnames begin to become common, the old inflected forms of the definite article gradually ceased to be used and masculine and feminine forms are used indiscriminately. The most common forms found are *atten, atter* and the uninflected *atte*. In colloquial speech, *atten ashe* and *atter ashe* came to be pronounced *atte nash, atte rash* and, with the loss of the preposition, gave us pairs of names like *Nash* and *Rash*, whilst *atte ashe* became not only *Ash* but also, occasionally, *Tash*, from *atash, a tash*.

Names like *Dale, Marsh, Park, Pond* and *Torr* are self-explanatory, but many of these surnames derive from uncommon place-name elements, many of them obsolete, and require explanation. A complete list, however, would become something like a dictionary of place-name elements. The index to Löfvenberg's *Middle English Local Surnames*, which deals with four counties only, fills 15 pages. Hence selection is essential and we shall concentrate on names with varied forms and those most needing interpretation, arranging them under the prepositions with which they were compounded. Early examples of all are known, but space does not permit this evidence.

at: A'Barrow, Barrow, Berrow 'grove' or 'hill'; A'Bear, Abear, Bear, Beer (OE *bǣr* 'swine-pasture'); Aborn, Aburn, Bourne, Boorn, Burn 'stream'; A'Brook, Brooke, Bruck; A'Deane, Adeane, Atherden, Dean, Dene, Dane 'valley'; Agate, Gate; Alder(s), Nalder, Nolder, Nolda, Older 'alders'; Aldritt, Eldrett, Naldrett, Neldrett (OE **alrett, *elrett* 'alder-grove'); Angle, Nangle (OFr *angle* 'nook or outlying spot'); Ash, Aysh, Dash, Daish, Nash, Naysh, Rash, Tash, Esh, Tesh; Asp, Apps, Happs, Hespe (OE *æspe, æpse* 'aspen'); Atherley, Atlay, Atley, Attlee, Alee, Lea, Lee, Leigh, Lay, Ley, Lye (OE *lēah,* 'wood, glade'); Atty, Tye 'common'; Athill, Athell, Attrill, Hill Rill, Rull; Athoke, Hook, Huck 'bend'; Atmeare, Atmer, Attmere, Mear, Meers 'pool'; Amoor, Atmore, Moor More; Atread, Attread, Attreed, Attride, Attryde, Read, Ride (OE **rīed, *rȳd* 'clearing'); Attack, Attock, Oak, Noake, Nock, Noke, Roake, Rock, Rook; Atteridge, Arridge, Ridge; Atterwill, Attewell, Attiwell, Attwell, Attwool, Twell(s), Wells, Will, Wooll, Woll 'spring, stream'; Attree, Attrie, Attrey, Atyeo, Eye, Nie, Nye, Nay, Ney, Raye, Rea, Ree, Rey, Rye, Yea, Yeo (OE *ēa* 'stream', *īeg, ēg* 'island, firm land in a fen');[1] Attru, Tree, Trew, True, Trow 'tree'.

Bache, Batch (OE *bæce* 'stream, valley'); Bench, Binks 'terrace, river-bank'; Bent 'grassy plain, heath'; Birchett, Burchett (OE **byrcett* 'birch-grove'); Bow (OE *boga* 'bow, arch, vault'; here 'an arched bridge'); Bye, Buy (OE *byge* 'bend of a river'); Clough, Cleugh, Cluff, Clow, Clew, Clue (OE *clōh* 'ravine or steep-sided valley'); Dane, Danes (OE *denu,* SE ME *dane* 'valley'); Denn (OE *denn* 'woodland-, swine-pasture'); Eaves, Eves, Reeves (OE *efes* 'border or edge' of a wood or hill); Ellen(s), Hellen (OE *ellen* 'alder'); Elm, Elmes, Nelmes; Etchells, Neachell (OE **ecels* 'piece of land added to an estate'); Gore (OE *gār* 'a triangular piece of land'); Gravatt, Gravett, Grevatt, Grevett (OE **grāfet, *grǣfet* 'a little grove'); Greaves, Greeves, Greve (OE *grǣfe* 'thicket, grove').

Hale(s), Hallowes, Hallas (OE *healh* 'nook, remote valley'); Ham, Hamme (OE *hamm* 'flat, low-lying land by a stream'); Haslam, Haslum, Hasleham (OE *hæsel*), Heslam (ON *hesli*) 'hazels'; Hatch 'gate'; Hay, Hayes, Hey, Heyes (OE *(ge)hæg* 'enclosure', 'forest fenced off for hunting') ; Haisell, Heazel, Hasell, Hazel (OE *hæsel*), Hessel (ON *hesli*) 'hazel'); Haslett, Haslitt, Hazlett, Hazlitt, Heaslet, Hezlett (OE **hæslett* 'hazel-copse'); Heal, Heales, Hele (a west-country form of *Hale*); Heald, Held, Hield (OE *hi(e)lde* 'slope'); Heck (a northern form of *Hatch*); Hern,

---

[1] The forms are confused. *īeg* should give *Nay, Ray, Rye*, etc., and *ēa* should become *Rea, Ree*. v. P. H. Reaney, *Dictionary of British Surnames* s.nn. *Yea* and *Yeo* are Devon and Somerset developments of *ēa*.

Hearn, Hurn (OE *hyrne* 'nook or corner of land or in a bend'); Hoad, Hoath (a Kent and Sussex form of Heath); Holles, Hollies, Hollen(s), Holling(s), Hollins, Holly (OE *holegn, holen*, ME *holi(e), holin* 'holly holm-oak'; Holme(s) (ON *holmr* 'flat land in a fen', 'land partly surrounded by water'); Holt 'wood'; Home(s) (variants of Holme and Hollen); Howe(s), Hoe, Hoo, Hough, Hoof, Huff (OE *hōh* 'projecting ridge of land, spur of a hill').

Knell, Knill (OE **cnyll* 'knoll'); Latch, Letch, Leach, Leche (OE **læcc, *lecc* 'stream'); Law, Lowe (OE *hlāw* 'hill, tumulus'); Leate, Leet (OE *(ge)lǣt* 'conduit, watercourse'); Leese (OE *lǣs* 'pasture'); Linch, Lince, Link (OE *hlinc* 'hill'); Lind, Lynd (OE *lind* 'lime-tree'); Lade, Loades (OE *(ge)lād* 'path, road, watercourse'); Lund, Lunt, Lound, Lount (ON *lundr* 'grove'); Lythe, Lyde (OE *hliþ*, ON *hlið* 'slope').

Mark (OE *mearc* 'boundary'); Marr (ON *marr* 'pool or marsh'); New (OE *ēow, īw* 'yew-tree'); Nind 'at the end of the village'; Nineham, Ninham, Ninnim (OE **innām* 'a piece of enclosed land'); Noar, Noah (OE *ōra* 'shore, bank, steep slope'); Oade, Noad, Nodes (OE *ād* 'pile, heap, funeral pile'); Orchard, Norchard; Over, Ower(s) (OE *ofer* 'bank, steep slope'); Parrack, Parrick, Parrock (OE *pearroc* 'paddock, enclosure'); Patt (OE **pætte* 'marsh'); Readett, Reditt, Riddett (OE **hrēodet* 'reed-bed'); Reading, Redding, Ridding (OE **rydding* 'clearing'); Rowntree 'rowan-tree'.

Sallows, Sallis (OE *sealh* 'sallow, willow'); Scales, Scholes (ON *skáli* 'hut, shed'); Seach, Sitch, Sykes (OE *sīc* 'small stream', 'gully, dip or hollow'); Seath (OE *sēað* 'pit, pool'); Shaw, Shafe, Shave, Shay (OE *sceaga* 'wood'); Slack (ON *slakki* 'shallow valley'); Slade (OE *slæd* 'valley'); Slape (OE **slæp* 'miry place, marsh'); Snead, Snea, Snoad (OE *snæd, snād* 'clearing, piece of woodland'); Soal, Sole (OE *sol* 'mud, wallowing-place for animals, pool'); Sparre (OE *spearr* 'enclosure'); Stumbles (OE **stumbel* 'tree-stump'); Twitchen, Twitching (OE *twicen* 'place where two roads meet'); Wald, Waud, Weald, Weild, Weld, Wolde, Would (OE *weald* 'forest, woodland'); Waylatt, Waylett (OE *weg-(ge)lǣte* 'cross-roads'); Woodgate, Woodgett, Woodjetts, Woodyatt 'gate to the wood'; Wray, Wroe (ON *vrá* 'nook, corner, remote or isolated place').

bove 'above', earlier *above(n)*: Bowater; Bowbrick 'above the brook'; Bowdon; Bowton, Bufton 'above the village'.

by, be 'by, near': Bidlake 'by the stream'; Bidmead 'by the meadow'; Byard, Byart (ME *bi yerd* 'by the enclosure'); Byatt, Byott, Bygate 'by the gate'; Bycroft; Bygrave(s), Bygreaves, Bygrove 'grove'; Bythesea 'by the sea, lake or pool'; Bytheseashore (pronounced *bitherseyshore*, with stress as in *Battersea*); Bytheway, Bythway, Byway, Bidaway; Bywater(s); Bywood.

ofer 'over, beyond': Overbeck 'beck, stream'; Overy 'stream, low-lying land'.

under: Underdown, Underhill, Undrell, Underwater 'south of the stream', Underwood.

Similar surnames are also formed from compound place-names, though many of these are actually used as place-names. Others remain unidentified, but may still exist, e.g. *Blackledge, Blacklidge* 'by the dark stream'; *Cladish* (Edward *Cladyche* 1494, John *Claydiche* 1499 CantW); *Claggett* (from *Claygate*); *Fairbanks*; *Fairhurst, Fairest* 'fair wooded-hill'; *Windebank, Windibank* 'windy hill'. Still others are common compounds, frequently noted both as place-names and as surnames, in counties where no trace of their survival can be found on the map: Whiteley, Whitla; Wheatcroft; Sheep-wash, Shipwash 'place for washing sheep'; Greenhill, Grinnell; Holyoak, Hollyoake, Hollyhock 'holy oak, gospel oak'.

SOME ELLIPTICAL FORMATIONS

In 1279 Ralph *de Bestuna* was living at the place now known as The Beesons in Sutton (C), 'the place to the east of the hamlet'. Similar names have been noted in Hampshire in 1248 (*Besteton, Biesteton*) and in Hertfordshire in 1286 (*Byeston*), and now survive as *Beeston*. The full form of the name was *bī ēastan tūne*; the *-an* was early weakened to *-e* and the preposition was usually dropped, giving *Esteton*, soon assimilated to *Eston*, which was the normal form of an original *ēast-tūn* 'east village'. This type of name was very common in Sussex at the beginning of the fourteenth century, almost invariably with the medial *e*, in parishes where there is no place-name ending in *-ton*. Surnames like *de Southeton* are found in 35 parishes and those of *de Westeton* in 22, whilst *Estetoune* and *Northetun* are similarly frequent. In one instance, we have a clue to the real origin of these surnames, for in 1327 Ralph *Biwestetoun* was assessed in the parish where, in 1296, we find William *de Weste-tun*. They clearly lived 'to the west of the hamlet' which had come to be called *bī westan tūne* '(place) to the west of the hamlet' and, with the loss of the preposition, *Westetun*, which would inevitably be assimilated to the common *Weston*. Thus, in Sussex, the surnames *Easton, Weston, Norton* and *Sutton*, whilst often deriving from places of that name, very commonly denote a man who lived to the north or south of the village or at a place originally named '(place) to the east or west of the village'.[1] Such names are found also in other counties and with other elements. *Eastwood* may derive from

---

[1] *Aston*, usually from a place of that name ('east farm'; occasionally 'ash farm'), is found in Surrey as *Aston(e)*, clearly from an original *Atte Stone* 'dweller by the stone': Thomas *A stone*, John *a stone* 1569, John *Astone* 1583 Musters (with others). In Surrey, OE *ēast* became ME *est*.

residence near the east wood, to the east of the wood, or at a place named Eastwood, whilst *Northway* and *Westaway* mean 'dweller to the north or the west of the road'. William *de Estbrok* lived at Eastbrook Fm in Dagenham in 1256, whilst William *Bestebroke* in 1296 and Alan *bi Estebrouk* in 1327 lived to the east of a brook in Sussex. Their surnames survive as *Eastbrook*, *Eastabrook*, *Easterbrook* and *Esterbrook*.

In Sussex we find another type of these names: John *de Sutingthun* 1296, Richard *de Sotinton* 1327, both in Bexhill, and William *de Sotiton* 1332, in Beddingham, who is probably to be identified with William *de Sutton*, assessed in the same parish in 1327. If this identification is correct, *Southeton*, etc., may also go back to an earlier *Southinton* and be parallel to a series of names particularly common in Worcestershire, where there are places named Sodington, Leigh Sinton and Sindon's Mill in Suckley. In Gloucestershire we have Siddington, and in Selbourne (Ha), Southington. Similar place-names were formed from *east*, *west* and *north* and survive in Ashington (So), Eastington (D, Do, Gl, Wo) and Norrington (Herts, W, Wo). As surnames, *Astington*, *Norrington*, *Sinton*, *Uppington* and *Westington* are all similar formations, from *ēast in tūne*, etc., '(place) east, etc., in the village'. Sindon's Mill was the place in Suckley 'south in the *tun*' as opposed to that 'north in the tun', now Norton Fm. All may similarly have become Easton, Sutton and Weston and all may, at times, be descriptive of the man rather than of the place, for in 1275, in Worcestershire, we find both Richard *Uppinton* and Adam *de Uppinton*. In view of these developments, it seems possible that the surname of John and William *Douninthetoun(e)* (1327 SRWo, 1375 AssL) may sometimes survive as *Dunton*.

A similar Scandinavian formation (sometimes partly anglicised) has also contributed to our surnames. The most familiar of these names is *Sotheby*, found also as *Suddaby*, *Sutherby* and *Suttaby*. Others are *Easterby*, originally purely Scandinavian, Peter *Austibi* 1204 P (Y), Robert *Oustinby*, William *Estyby*, Hugh *Estinby* 1297 SRY, *Nordaby*, Ralph *Northiby* (1256–84 CNat) and *Westaby*, *Westoby*, from ON *suðr í bý*, *austr í bý*, etc., '(the man who lived) south, east, north or west in the village'. *Dunnaby* is a hybrid, with OE *dūne* 'down'.

A few surnames indicate vaguely the quarter from which a man had come, *North*, *South*, *East* or *West*, earlier Agnes *Bynorth*, William *de la Sothe*, Ralph *del Est*, John *in le west*; Robert *bi*

Westen de Copford may actually have lived to the west of Copford. Sometimes the name takes the form of 'to the eastward', Hugh *Enesteward*, Robert *a Westeward*. The latter still survives as *Westward*, but the name of John *Anorthward* (1275 RH, Berks) seems to have been absorbed by *Northwood* and *Eastward* by Eastwood. A proof of this is provided by the modern form of Southward Downs in Aldbourne (W), earlier *Southwode*. The rare *Southward* has been further corrupted by confusion with *Southworth*. Southwood Fm in Walton-on-Thames is *Suthwude* in 1235, *Sutheworthe* in 1337. Both *Downward* and *Upward* still exist.

TOPONYMICS

This method of indicating the place of origin has been reinforced by the use of descriptive adjectives, William *le Northerne* 'the man from the north', now *Northern* and *Northen*, Geoffrey *le Westerne*, now *Western, Westren, Westron*. For *Southern*, we have a variety of modern forms, *Sothern, Southorn, Southan, Southon*, and *Suthern*, all from OE *sūðern* 'southern'. The surname, as one would expect, is found chiefly in the north and in Yorkshire and Derbyshire appears in the ME forms *le Sotherun* 1297, *le Sutheren* 1307, forms which must derive from ON *suðrænn*, an early literary example of which is found in the northern *Cursor Mundi* (a1300) in *sotherin englis*. This Scandinavian form has given the modern surnames *Sotheran, Sotheron, Southerin, Sudran, Sudron* and *Sutherin*.

Some of these toponymics have a French origin: *Estridge*, Peter *Estreis* 1148 Winton (Ha), from OFr *estreis* 'easterner', *Westrich, Westray*, Richard *le Westrais* 1206 AssL, *Surridge, Surrage*, Geoffrey *le Surreys* 1219 AssY. *Norreys* is from AFr *noreis* 'northerner' and may also have become *Norridge*. Here, too, may belong *Norris*, but this undoubtedly has other origins. It may be from a personal-name, *Noreis* de Blida, probably an original byname from *noreis*, but it is frequently from OFr *norrice* 'nurse', and may be a weakening of 'north house', Adam *de Northus, de Norhuse* 1206 Cur (Ess).

Other toponymics denote nationality: *English, Inglis, Scott, Irish, Welsh, Walsh* and *Wallis*, with *Gales* (*le Galeys, le Waleis*, central and northern forms of Fr *waleis* 'Welshman, Celt'). *Sayce* and *Seys* are from Welsh *sais* 'Saxon, Englishman'. Sometimes it is the county of origin which is specified: *Cornish, Cornes, Cornwallis*; *Devenish, Devonish*; *Kentish, Kintish, Cantes*; occasionally, the town: *Lunniss*, earlier *Londoneys* 'the Londoner'. *Wildash* and *Wildish* also belong here, deriving from OE **wealdisc* 'belonging to the Weald'. The inhabitants of the Weald were called Wealdish men and the surname was not uncommon in Kent in the forms *Weldisse* (1292) and le *Wealdessh* (1316).

THE MEANING OF LOCAL SURNAMES

So far, the local surnames discussed have been purely topographical. *Church*, *Cross* and *Street* must indicate the place at or near which the man lived. But the interpretation of other names is not always so simple. *Appleton* may well mean 'dweller near the orchard', but it might also denote a man who worked there. Men certainly did not owe their names to the fact that they lived in a *Kitchen*, *Pantry* or *Wardrobe*. Such names, topographical in appearance, preceded by *atte* or *de la*, must have reference to the place where the man worked and, in meaning, are really occupational surnames. Conclusive proof is provided by the name of Gilbert *del Bed* (1302 Cl). He certainly did not live in his bed but held the office of yeoman of the bedchamber, as did Lambert yoman of the Bedde in 1540.

With some names, both interpretations are possible. John *le Bruggere*, called also John *de Ponte*, lived in 1294 at Bridge End in Ockham (Sr). The Latin variant proves that he was also called *atte Brugge* and took his name from his residence near the bridge. In Essex, in 1332, we find another alternative: William *Breggeman* is identical with William *atte Bregge*. Ralph *le Punter* (1236 Cl), whose name is a parallel to *Bruggere*, from OFr *pont*, is described as 'custos pontis de Stanes'. Thus, *Bridge*, *Bridger* and *Bridgeman*, with *Pont*, *Ponter* and *Punter*, are identical in meaning, and each may denote either a dweller near a bridge or a keeper of the bridge, often, no doubt, one who collected the tolls there.

Richard Beselin *ate Bote*, a customary tenant of the Abbot of Battle, had to 'ferry the Bishop and his carriages and all the men in his service and all avers coming from Busshopestone Manor'. He thus owed his attribute to the services due from his holding. The surname occurs elsewhere in Sussex in 1332, William *atte Bote*, now *Boatte*, and this, with *Boater*, *Boatman* and *Bottman*, must be interpreted as 'boatman' or 'ferryman'. A similar explanation has been plausibly suggested for *Shipp*, John *atte Shype* of Quatford (1327 SRSa), 'possibly the boatman whose ferry formed the link with

Erdington, which, to this day, is in the parish of Quatford, though on the other side of the Severn'. *Mill* and *Millward* were interchangeable: John *atte Mylle* otherwise called *Mylleward* 1427 AD iv (Sx), whilst William *in the Wode* (1333 *SR* So) was a woodward for he was named William *Wodeward* in 1327 (SRSo).

Furlong and *Forlong* are from OE *furhlang*, literally 'a furrow long', which came to mean the length of a field and a division of an unenclosed field. The term was commonly used of the strips into which the open fields were divided, each allotted to a different villager, whose furlongs were scattered in various parts of the field. The land he cultivated was never a compact area such as we should describe as a field. Hence, John *de Forhlangh* (1250) and John *atte Forlange* (1327) could not owe their surnames to residence by their furlong. They lived in the village. In the fourteenth century *furlong* was used to translate the Latin *stadium* 'the course for foot-races' as in Wyclif's 'thei that rennen in the ferlong for the pris' and Chaucer's 'Yif a man renneth in the stadie or in the forlong for the corone'. Hence the real meaning of *Furlong* and *Furlonger* is 'the runner in a footrace' or, more probably, 'the winner of the prize of the crown in the race' and the two Johns above owed their name to their well-known exploits in the 'forlong'.

In the larger houses of the nobility, the household offices would necessarily employ a number of men performing various, often menial, duties. These would frequently be named from the section of the household to which they were attached, but might also be described by reference to their particular duties. Alan *de la Spense*, for example, worked at the buttery, hence his name (ME *spense*, OFr *despense* 'larder'). He is described in 1317 (AssK) as 'Alan de la Spense sometarius Domini Roberti de Shirlaunde'. He was a sumpter or pack-horse driver who carried the provisions to the buttery and was in the service of Sir Robert de Shirlaunde. He is also called Alanus *sometarius*, Alanus *serviens* and Alanus *homo Domini Roberti*. He clearly had no fixed surname and his descendants, if living today, might have been known by any of the names *Spence* or *Spens*, *Sumpter* or *Sunter*, *Servant*, *Sarvent* or *Sergeant*, or *Masterman*.

The purely topographical surnames ending in *-man* and *-er* are fully dealt with elsewhere.[1] Here we may add (with variants) some surnames, local in form, but really names of office or occupation.

[1] *v.* pp. 55, 200–203.

Culverhouse and *Duffus* must denote the keeper of the dovecot, whilst names like *Backhouse* or *Bacchus*, *Barkhouse* and *Barkis* should be regarded as descriptive of the baker and the tanner, of the place where he worked rather than where he lived. *Wardrobe*, *Wardrop* and *Whatrup*, like *Wardroper*, *Wardropper* and *Waredraper* are names of a household official, the man in charge of the robes, wearing-apparel, etc. *Panter* and the fearsome-looking *Panther* was the household officer who supplied the bread and had charge of the pantry. Robert *atte Panetrye*, assessed in the Sussex subsidy for 1332, is more likely to have been a worker in the pantry than the actual panter himself. Similarly we can explain *Buttery* or *Buttrey*, originally a place for storing liquor but early used of a room where provisions were laid up, whilst *Kitchen*, *Kitchin* or *Kitching*, with *Kitchener*,[1] *Kitchiner* and *Kitchingman*, *Kitcheman* and *Kitchman* denoted originally workers in the kitchen.

Sometimes the occupational nature of the surname is self-evident: *Boosey*, from OE *bōsig* 'ox- or cow-stall', hence 'cowman'; *Shippen*, OE *scypen* 'cattle-shed', hence 'cattle-man, cowman'; *Wick* and *Wicker* may denote either a dweller or a worker at the dairy-farm. *Hall*, *Haller* and *Hallman* are not likely to refer to the owner of the hall. He would be the lord of the manor and would have some more distinctive surname than *atte Halle* 'dweller at the hall'. These surnames must rather refer to one employed at the hall. OE *būr* 'cottage, chamber' might have given rise to a surname 'dweller at the cottage', but this would scarcely be distinctive, among all the cottagers of the village. It is much more likely to mean 'chamber-servant'. *Bower*, *Bowerman* and *Bowrah*, with their variants, are to be compared with such extinct surnames as *Bourwyman*, *Bourswain* and *Bourgrom*.

SIGN-NAMES

Previous writers have been of the opinion that many surnames derive from sign-names, but what evidence they have produced has been almost entirely from the sixteenth or seventeenth centuries, a period when the great majority of people already had established family names and the creation of a large number of new surnames is most unlikely. Many of these sign-names, too, are never found as surnames. Names of houses such as the Rose, the Harrow and the Plow were admittedly common in Elizabethan and Stuart London, but

---

[1] This may also be local, from Kitchenour (Sx).

how old such names are is unknown. To prove they have given rise to surnames, we need unequivocal examples from the thirteenth and fourteenth centuries and very few can be produced, whilst some of those previously adduced are now known to be of topographical origin. We should expect to find evidence in the towns, especially in London, but little is forthcoming. In the 1319 London Subsidy Roll, 950 persons, about half of those assessed, have local surnames, but of these only 11 can be regarded as sign-names (from six different signs): *Baskett, Cock, Ram, Rose, Swan* and *Vine*. Occasional examples have been noted elsewhere, but the total number is small. John *atte Belle* of 1332 (SRLo) probably lived at the sign of the Bell. *Cock* in London may be a sign-name, but in the country both *Cock* and *Hatt* were undoubtedly used of a hill or hillock. *Key* is usually from *quay*, from residence near or employment at a quay or wharf. *Harp* was used of a harp-shaped contrivance for sifting and cleansing salt and is found as a place-name in Essex and Somerset. *Eagle*, when not a nickname, appears as *de Aquila* or *del Egle*, from Laigle (Orne).

Occasional forms preceded by *atte* show that *Oliphant* 'elephant' (1318), *Pie* or *Pye* (1347), *Raven* (1344) and *Roebuck* (1313) were sometimes taken from signs. The London Brewers' records for 1423–6 give us the names of some London inns: *atte Katerine Whele, atte Cok & Sterre, atte Sarasynes hede*. These have never become surnames; here, like the simple names, they are used only as the address of a brewer, not as a surname, e.g. Petrus Andrew, atte Belle yn Holbourne; Nicholas Merton, atte Herte yn seynt John strete. Most Londoners had by this time acquired fixed surnames, but it is possible that such inn-names as the following were already old and may have become surnames: *atte hertishorn, atte Shippe, atte Mone, atte Crane, atte Gerland, the Rammeshed, atte Cristophore, atte panyer*. No example of *atte* with *Bull, Hart, Peacock*,[1] or any of the other suggested sign-names, has been noted as a surname.

[1] Cf., however, Simon petefyn, *atte pohenne* yn Bisshoppes gate stret 1424 *London English*, 183.

Chapter Four

SURNAMES FROM FRENCH AND CONTINENTAL PLACES

THAT many of our aristocratic surnames preserve the names of places in France has long been known and a craze for claiming a Norman origin has produced a crop of the wildest guesses. A mere superficial resemblance in spelling has derived *Barwise* from Barvaux and *Pudsey* from Puisey, despite the existence of places of these names in Westmorland and Yorkshire, whilst Baring-Gould's derivation of *Bisset*, really a nickname 'dark', from Bissey rivals in absurdity his explanation of *Longfellow* as 'a mutilated name from Longueville' and of *Longshanks* as 'a barbarous alteration of Longchamps'.[1] As a Devonshire man, he should have known that *Vowles* is a Devon pronunciation of *Fowle* and not from Veules, Fauvel or Vauville. *Twopenny* has no connexion with Tupigny. It is a nickname, whatever its real meaning may be.

PROBLEMS OF IDENTIFICATION

The identification of these French place-names is not seldom a difficult problem. Many of them are found frequently in widely

[1] An etymology still repeated, unfortunately, by a well-known historian.

59

separated parts of France, even in areas from which we know that immigrants came across the Channel, and the acclimatisation of these foreign names has provided some curious and interesting corruptions. The earliest examples are found in Domesday Book and some of these became the surnames of powerful aristocratic families, some of which still survive, though very many have died out in the course of centuries. These it is sometimes possible to locate exactly by a close study of family history and feudal relationships, but the lack of documentary evidence between 1086 and the middle of the twelfth century is such that for many families we are often left groping in the dark. Whatever other information we may have, if we are to reach a sound identification, we must see to it that the early forms of the surname correspond with those of the place to which we attribute its origin.

Among the surnames which have more than one place of origin are *Furnival*, less commonly *Furnifall*, from Fournival (Oise, Orne) and Furneaux from Fourneaux (Calvados, La Manche), which may also have become *Furnell*, *Fournel* or *Funnell* and so confused with surnames originating from one of the French places named Fournal or Fournel, and also with *Furnace* and *Furnish* from Furness (La). One Norman family took its name from Canteleu in Seine-Inférieure, another from Canteloup in Calvados; their surnames survive as *Cantelo*, *Cantellow* and *Cantlow*. Whilst Ferrers, earls of Derby, and Ferrers of Bere Ferrers and Newton Ferrers in Devon owe their names to two different places named Ferrières, one in Eure, the other in La Manche, both the Mortimers of Attleborough and those of Wigmore came from the same place, Mortemer-sur-Eaulne in Seine-Inférieure, though there is no reason to believe they were related by blood. *Claremont*, *Clermont* and *Clermunt* derive from Clermont, a common French place-name, that in Calvados occurring as *Clarus Mons* in 1198.

Even more complicated is the history of the Mandevilles and the Balliols. The Mandevilles, earls of Essex, came from Manneville (Seine-Inférieure), the Mandevilles of Earl's Stoke and Devon, from Magneville (La Manche), and the under-tenants of Montfort and the counts of Meulan, from Manneville-sur-Risle (Eure). The modern surname, which is found also as *Manville*, *Manvell* and *Manwell*, may derive from any of these places or from Manneville (Calvados). The origin of the Balliols is still more varied. First J. H. Round showed that the long-accepted origin of the Balliols of Barnard Castle, including the founder of Balliol College, Oxford, and a king of Scotland, from Bailleul-Neuville near Rouen was untenable. They were not Normans but came from Bailleul-en-Vimeu in Picardy. Then L. C. Loyd identified two other distinct families of Balliol, both from Normandy, one coming from Bailleul-sur-Eaulne (now Bailleul-Neuville) in Seine-Inférieure, the other from Bailleul-en-Gouffern in Orne.

That *Havill* and *Hovell* have two distinct origins is proved by the variant forms of the surname. Ralph *de Halsvilla*, a Domesday tenant-in-chief, must have come from Hauville (Eure) which is recorded as *Alsvilla* in 1050 and *Hasvilla* in the eleventh century, whilst Ralph *de Alta Villa* or *de Havill* (1198) and Henry *de Hautvill* (1242) must owe their surname to Hauteville-la-Guichard (La Manche), earlier *Hautteville*.

Where a place-name is particularly common, genealogy and history can sometimes determine from which a particular family came. Of the 58 places in France named Villiers, Loyd has given good reasons for identifying Villiers-le-Sec (Calvados) as the one from which one twelfth-century family came. Similarly, in spite of the frequency of places named Aubigny (17), Beaumont (46), Ferrières (22) and Neuville (58), the original home of certain families of *Daubeney, Beaumont, Ferrers* and *Neville* can be definitely located.

In all these instances this is only possible because they were holders of land, but many of those who left France for England were of a lower social class, men-at-arms, workmen, traders and merchants, of whose family history no record is known. In thirteenth-century London we find men who could not have been members of the aristocratic families whose names they bore: William de Furnival, tailor; John de Maundeville, brewer; Thomas de Neville, woolmonger; Thomas Seyncler, haymonger. There are no baronial families to account for the surnames of Henry de Arras, vintner; Thomas de Boloyne, merchant; or John de Paris, cook. They owed their surnames to the towns where they were born or where they had lived before migrating, and numerous others must similarly have been named from the smaller French places they had left.

SURNAMES FROM PLACE OF RESIDENCE

In France, as in England, many minor places were named from some neighbouring topographical feature, often from trees or woods.

From these places surnames might arise, but such a name as *Dubois* is clearly parallel to the English *Attwood*, denoting the actual place of residence. So, too, with the Channel Islands *Duquemin*, a Norman form of the French *Duchemin* 'one whose house was out on the country road' as opposed to the dweller in the village. But the form of the surname may indicate that it was derived from the place without any thought of its meaning. Roger *de Coisnieres* or *de Coyners* (now *Conyers*), for example, who was living in Yorkshire at the end of the twelfth century, clearly came either from Coignières (Seine-et-Oise) or from Cogners (Sarthe) and not from residence near a quince-tree. But Thomas *del Freisne* (1206) and William *a la Freyne* (1279) lived near an ash-tree (OFr *fraisne*) and the surnames *Frain*, *Frayne*, *Freyne*, *Frean* and *Freen*, like the corresponding English *Ash*, have lost their preposition, as have *Fay* and *Fey*, from OFr *fay* 'beech'.

Franey and *Freney* may have arisen either from a French village or from residence near an ash-wood (OFr *fraisnaie*). Ralph *de Caisned*, a Sussex under-tenant in Domesday Book, came from Le Quesney (Seine-Inférieure). Places of the same name are found also in Calvados and La Manche, whilst Chenay, Chenoy and Chesnoy are common French place-names. All mean 'oak-grove' (OFr *chesnai*, MedLat *casnetum*), whence the modern *Chainey*, *Cheyney*, *Cheyne*, *Chene*, with other variants including *Cheeney*, *Chesney* and *Chestney*.

Nor must we overlook the possibility that some of these French local surnames may have arisen in England. *Cowdray* may come from Coudrai (Seine-Inférieure) or from Coudray (Eure), but it is a common Sussex surname where it may well denote a man who lived near the hazel-copse which gave name to Cowdray in Easebourne or to Cowdry Farm in Birdham. In each case the surname is on record earlier than the place-name, whilst Cowdray has ousted the original English name of the place, *la Sengle*, which probably means 'a thicket of brushwood'. An English origin is also likely for *Dellew* 'by the water', *Dubois* 'by the wood' and *Dupont* 'by the bridge'. With the last we may compare *Pont* and its derivative *Ponter* which is certainly an English formation. Such names as *Dubarry*, *du Boulay*, *Dufresnoy*, *Duhamel* and *Dupuy*, of which no medieval examples have been noted in England, are late names brought from France by Huguenots or later immigrants.

Effects of English pronunciation and popular etymology

This preposition is retained occasionally as in *de Courcy, D'Abernon* and *Davers*, from Auvers (La Manche) or Auvers-le-Hamon (Sarthe). At times, forms both with and without the preposition survive: *Olley* and *Dolley*, from Ouilly, *Devereux* and *Everex*, from Evreux. In some names, an initial *D* was mistakenly regarded as the preposition and consequently dropped, so that we have both *Deville* and *Evill* from Déville, the former being also wrongly divided as *de Ville*, and, in the unaccented form *Devill*, confused with the nickname *le Devil*. Similarly, *Damary*, from *Daumeray*, is found as *de Amory*, which, with the loss of the preposition, is liable to confusion with the personal-name *Amery*.

To the ordinary Englishman, many of these French surnames were meaningless and difficult to pronounce and suffered more than their fair share of phonetic change and popular etymology. Beaufour becomes *Boffey* and *Buffey*, Bohun now appears as *Boon, Bone* and *Bown*, and Craon as *Crowne*. The element *-ville* is often anglicised as *-field*: *Blomefield* from Blonville, *Glandfield* by the side of *Glanville*, *Somervell* and *Somerfield* from Sémerville, and *Stutfield* from Etoutteville. *Grenville*, now often *Grenfell*, was pronounced *Greenfield* in Shakespeare's time, and has now, no doubt, often become indistinguishable from the English *Greenfield* 'dweller by the green field'. *Tuffield* and *Tuffill* now exist side by side with the original *Turville*.

Lison and Soissons are well disguised in the modern *Licence* and *Sessions*. Some of the identifications which early forms prove must be correct may appear at first sight as absurd and impossible as Lower's *Diamond* from *Dumont* or *Dinan* and Ewen's *Pheysey* from *Vessey*. To the phonetician, there is no difficulty in accepting Tourlaville as the source of the modern surname *Tollafield* and *Fancourt* or *Fancutt* from Fallencurt (Seine-Inférieure), whilst the early forms make it clear that Thouberville has given us *Turberville, Turberfield, Turbefield* and *Turbyfield*, which, with the change of *t* to *d*, not unknown in place-names and surnames, gives us the *Durbeyfield* of Hardy's Tess. *Scardifield* and *Scarterfield*, earlier *Scardevyle*, are from Ecardenville (Eure), whilst the development of *Baskerville* from Boscherville to *Baskwell* may be seen from the surviving forms: *Baskerfield, Baskeyfield, Baskwell*, with an intrusive *t* in *Basketfield* and an assimilation of *sk* to *st* in *Basterfield*.

In addition, we have a change of initial *B* to *P*, not common, but found elsewhere, in *Paskerful, Pasterfield* and *Pesterfield.* Less obvious, but still intelligible, is the development of *Sirdifield, Sirdyfield, Cedervall, Cederwell* and *Surrell* from Sourdeval (Calvados, La Manche), from which Baring-Gould gives also a modern *Sordwell.*

Tihel de Herion, the Domesday lord of Helion Bumpstead in Essex, still distinguished by his name, came from Helléan in Brittany. The family also held land in Haverhill, not far distant, on the other side of the Essex boundary. The family name is found in both areas between 1086 and 1570 in the forms *Helion, Elyon, Heline, Helon* and *Hellynge.* The attribute of Helion Bumpstead is recorded as *Elyns* in 1544, *Heleyns* in 1554 and *Hellyn* in 1570, and is still locally pronounced *Helen's.* The surname has persisted and, though not frequent, is still found scattered in northern Essex and southern Suffolk as *Elion, Elin* and *Hillen,* whilst *Helin* is found in London. The same family also held land in Devonshire where it has left its name in Upton Hellions. Here the attribute occurs as *Hyliun* in 1270, *Hylon* in 1385 and *Helling* in 1557. In the neighbouring county of Somerset the surnames *Hellings, Hellins* and *Hilling,* all rare, can still be found. Whether the bearers of these surnames ultimately trace their descent from Tihel the Breton, it is impossible to say, but the persistence to this day of these surnames within a limited area in or near which the family was long of no mean importance is, at any rate, suggestive and may be significant.

MULTIPLE ORIGINS

It must not be forgotten that some surnames of the kind we have been discussing may have other origins. The baronial family of Crèvecour, whose surname is now found as *Crawcour, Craker* and *Croaker,* etc., came from Crèvecœur in Calvados. There are places of the same name in the departments of Oise and Nord, whilst the surname may also be a nickname 'break heart', 'heart-breaker', for which we have an English parallel in the name of Richard *Brekehert* in Somerset in 1327. That *Membry* may be a form of *Mowbray* is proved by the name of John *Mowbray,* a freeman of Leicester in 1714, whose surname is spelled also *Memory* and *Membry,* which is also a variant of *Membury,* from a Devonshire place of that name. Without other evidence, it is impossible to decide whether the modern *Brewis* or *Bruce* goes back to the family of Briouze, lords of the rape of Bramber from 1086, or to that of a king of Scotland or to a worker at the brew-house. It is at least a salutary warning to those anxious to claim a Norman descent.

TOPONYMICS

In preparation for his invasion of England, William the Conqueror enlisted volunteers from Brittany and Maine, Flanders and Aquitaine. Some of these received their reward in land and their names are recorded in Domesday Book, some of them described merely from the district from which they had come, 16 Bretons, 10 Flemings, a Burgundian, a man from Maine and two from each of the provinces of Anjou, Lorraine and Poitou. To the archers and mercenaries who fought at Hastings were added, after the Conquest, a steadily increasing number of attendants in noble households, teachers and skilled workmen, traders and merchants. Seldom do we find mention of their names until records become more frequent in the thirteenth century and then we find many of them described simply as natives of the province or district from which they came. Burgundians, Picards and Loherings were numerous and with the extension of English dominion in France under the Plantagenets and the increase in the wine-trade with Bordeaux numerous immigrants came over from Anjou, Poitou and Gascony and have given us many surnames which still survive.

Bret and *Bretton* are particularly common, toponymics from OFr *Bret* (nom.) and *Breton* (acc.), alternating at times with a topographical name from OFr *Bretagne* 'Brittany', now *Brit(t)ain*, *Brittan*, *Britten* and *Brittney*. Normans, too, were numerous, but it is often difficult to decide whether *Norman* is from a personal-name, OE *Norðmann* 'a man from the north', a Scandinavian, especially a Norwegian, or from OFr *Normand* 'a Norman'. A clear instance is Nicholas *le Normand* (1221), which survives as *Normand*. From the Norman Pays de Caux, we have *Caw*, *Cawes* and *Cawse* (1166),[1] with the toponymic *le Cauceis* (c1140), now *Causey* or *Cawsey*, and from the Cotentin, *Constantine*, *Cossentine*, *Consterdine* and *Considine* (Geoffrey *de Costentin* 1153), with *Constance* and *Custance* (William *de Costenciis* c1150), from Coutances (La Manche), its cathedral city.

Less frequent are *Artois*, *Artis(s)*, *Artist* and *Artus*, from Artois

[1] The date is the earliest noted for the surname, excluding the occasional form from DB and Latin forms.

(1327); *Champain* (1195), with the toponymics *Champney(s)*, *Champness* and *Champniss* (*le Champeneis* 1219), 'the man from Champaign'; *Mansel(l)*, *Mancell*, *Maunsell* (*le Mansel* 1171), a native of Maine or its capital le Mans; *Main(e)*, *Mayne*, from the province of Maine (*de Meine* 1205) or from Mayenne (*de Meduana* 1212); and Vallis (*de Valeyse* 1275) from Valois.

Anjou, Lorraine, Picardy and Poitou, with Burgundy and Gascony are the provinces from which immigrants to England were particularly numerous. Lorraine and Poitou occasionally provide topographical surnames, *Lorrain(e)*, *Lorain(e)* (1333) and *Peto*, *Peyto* (1222). More common are toponymics: *Angwin* 'the Angevin' (1150), *Loring* or *Loaring*, from OFr *le Lohereng* 'the man from Lorraine' (1158), *Picard* (*le Pycard* 1276). Earlier examples are from OFr *Pohier* 'a Picard' (1127), now *Poor(e)* or *Power*; both modern forms have other origins, OFr *povre*, *poure* 'poor', just as *Picard* may also derive from a personal-name *Pichard*. OFr *Poitevin* 'man from Poitou' normally becomes *Poidevin*, but has undergone a variety of corruptions: *Podevin*, *Patvine*, *Potvin*, *Potwin*, *Portwine*, *Putwain*, *Puddifin*, *Puddifant* and *Puttifent*.

Whilst *Gower* is often from a French personal-name *Gohier*, from OG *Godeher* 'good army', and occasionally from Gower (Glamorgan), it also occurs as *Guwer* or *le Goher* (1230), from OFr *Gohier* 'an inhabitant of the Goelle', the country north of Paris, anciently *Gohiere*.

Gascoigne may be either a local surname, *de Gascoin* (1243), from Gascogne 'Gascony' or a toponymic *le Gascoyn* (1266) 'the Gascon'. It has many modern variants from AFr *Gascoun* 'Gascon' and the adjective *Gascuinz* 'of Gascony', including *Gaskain*, *Gasken*, *Gaskin* and *Gasking*. Bordeaux occasionally survives as *Bordeaux* (1297), but usually appears as *Bourdas*, *Bourdice*, *Bourdis*, *Burdas(s)*, *Burdess*, *Burdis*, *Burdus*, *Burders* and *Birdis*.

From the Duchy of Burgundy come *Burgoin(e)*, *Burgoyne*, *Burgon*, *Burgin*, *Bourgein* and *Bourgoin* (1086). The toponymic had several forms, John *Burgelun* (c1190), now found as *Burglin*, *Burlin*, *Burling* and *Burlong*, and Ralph *Burguignon* (1168), which now survives in the rare *Borgonon*. More than one form could be used of the same man: Nicholas *Burgelun* (1215 Bart) is also called *Burguine* in 1212 (now found as *Burgwin*). His wife, on her seal, used the form Felicia *Burgunung*. Similarly, John *le Borgiloun* (1310 LLB B) is alternatively named *de Burgoyne* (1319 SRLo).

66

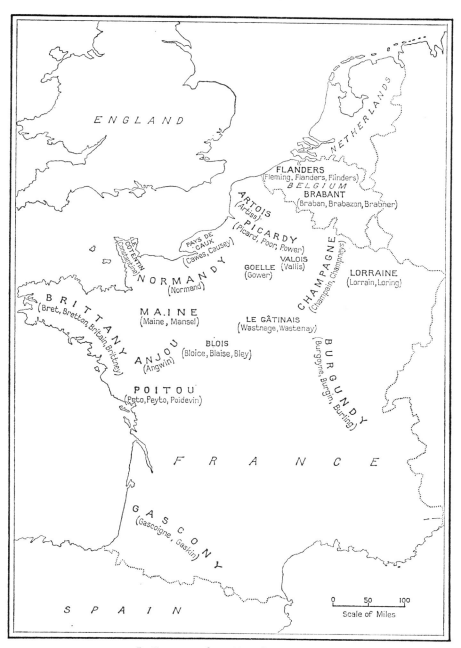

ENGLAND

NETHERLANDS

FLANDERS
(Fleming, Flanders, Flinders)
BELGIUM
BRABANT
(Braban, Brabazon, Brabner)

ARTOIS
(Artis)

PICARDY
(Picard, Poor, Power)

PAYS DE
CAUX
(Cawes, Causey)

VALOIS
(Vallis)

GOELLE
(Gower)

CHAMPAGNE
(Champain, Champneys)

LORRAINE
(Lorrain, Loring)

LE COTENTIN
(Constantine)

NORMANDY
(Normand)

MAINE
(Maine, Mansel)

LE GÂTINAIS
(Wastnage, Wastenay)

BRITTANY
(Bret, Bretton, Britain, Brittney)

BLOIS
(Bloice, Blaise, Bley)

ANJOU
(Angwin)

BURGUNDY
(Burgoyne, Burgin, Burling)

POITOU
(Peto, Peyto, Poidevin)

FRANCE

GASCONY
(Gascoigne, Gaskin)

SPAIN

0   50   100
Scale of Miles

I. *Surnames from French Provinces*

67

Theobald, count of Blois, nephew of Henry I, is called 'eorle Tedbalde *de Blais*' in 1116 (ASC) and the same form is used in 1135 for King Stephen. Elsewhere the surname, which might denote an inhabitant of the county or city of Blois, appears in the forms *de Bleys*, *le Bleys*, *de Bloy* and *le Bloy* which account for the modern surnames *Blaise*, *Blay*, *Bley*, *Blois*, *Bloice* and *Bloyce*. Later, the surname came to be pronounced *Blowes* and *Bloss*: John *Bloys* or *Blowes* (1497), Prudence *Blois*, *Bloyse* or *Blosse* (1634).

The district south of Paris and east of Orleans now known as le Gâtinais (Seine-et-Marne), formerly *Gastinois*, *Wastinensis*, has given us English surnames, both local and toponymic, with the Norman initial *W* for the central French *G*: *Wastnage*, *Was(t)nidge*, *Wastenay*, *Westnage*, *Westnedge*, *Westnidge* and *Westney* (1165). Occasionally we have a toponymic from the name of a village or town: *Druce*, *Drewes* (*le Droeis* 1225), from Dreux (Eure-et-Loire) and *Goy* (*de Goi* 1148, *le Guiez* 1166; Simon *de Guiz*, *le Goiz* 1212 Cur), from Gouy (Pas-de-Calais), an old fief, though there are other places of the name.

SURNAMES FROM PLACES IN FRANCE

No full account can yet be given of the place of origin beyond the seas of the countless men who appear in medieval England with surnames undoubtedly foreign. What has been done so far, selective and incomplete as it is, has already proved of value to genealogist, historian and philologist alike. L. C. Loyd, in the *Origins of some Anglo-Norman Families* (1951), confining himself to the feudal families of Normandy, has established the origin of some 315 families spread over the five departments of Normandy, with the addition of 16 from Brittany, the Somme and the Pas-de-Calais. He is concerned with families, not merely with local surnames, showing, e.g. the origin of *Bacon* (from OG *Bacco*) from Le Molay (Calvados), *Basset* (a nickname 'short') from Montreuil-au-Houlme (Orne), *Giffard* (OG *Gifard* or a nickname from OFr *giffard* 'chubby-cheeked') from Longueville-sur-Scie (Seine-Inférieure) and *Martel* (a nickname from OFr *martel* 'hammer') from Bacqueville-en-Caux (Seine-Inférieure).

In his *Old English Bynames* (1938) Tengvik deals with the topographical surnames of the tenants-in-chief and under-tenants of Domesday Book, whether surviving or obsolete. He is at pains to equate the forms of the surname with those of the place from which

68

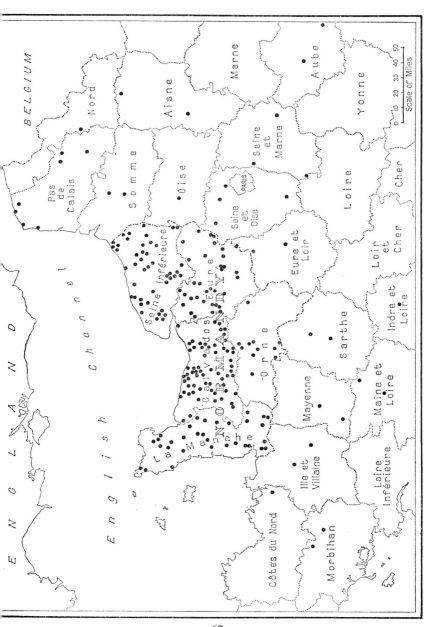

II. *The distribution of French place-names surviving as modern surnames*

he derives it and is careful to point out the many surnames which may have more than one place of origin.

The lists below have been compiled on a different principle. They (and the map) include only such surnames originating from places in France as are known to survive today. Names with more than one place of origin, even if mentioned in the text above, are not included, nor are the numerous names now obsolete, though many of these are of interest and importance and are still to be found on the map.[1] The surname is first found in Domesday Book unless a date is given; this is the earliest known reference to the surname.

With such differences of approach and the problems of multiple origin, statistics are of little real value, but it is quite clear that the great majority of these surnames came from Normandy itself.

Places in	*Loyd*	*Tengvik*	*Reaney*
La Manche	45	27	35
Calvados	93	50	68
Orne	15	4	12
Eure	48	34	34
Seine-Inférieure	92	26	45
	---	---	---
Normandy	293	141	194
From 22 other departments	15	42	49
	---	---	---
Total	308	183	243

Aisne: Soissons (*Sessions* 1181), Verly (*Varley, Verley, Virley*).
Aube: Clairvaux (*Clarvis* 1208), Troyes (*Troy* 1200).
Calvados: Abenon (*D'Abernon*), Airelle (*Dayral, Dayrell, Dar(r)ell* 1166), Anisy (*Danc(e)y, Dansey, Dansie, Dauncey*), Bayeux (*Bayeux, Bew(e)s* 1148), Beaufour (*Beaufoy, Boffee, Boff(e)y, Buffey*), Beaumais-sur-Dive (*Beam(e)s, Beamish, Beamiss* 1108), Bernières-sur-Mer (*Berners*), Blonville-sur-Mer (*Blom(e)field, Bloomfield, Blumfield* 1207), Boutemont (*Beautement, Butement, Bootman* 1172), Burcy (*Bursey, Bersey*), Caen (*Cain, Cane, Kane, Cam(m)*), Cahagnes (*Cain(e)s, Kaines, Keynes*), Cairon (*Car(r)on, Cairon, Charon*), Canteloup (*Cantel(l)o, Cantellow, Cantlow* 1130), Colombières-sur-Seulles (*Colombier*), Corbon (*Corben*), Courcy (*Decourcy, de Courcy, Coursey*), Courseulles-sur-Mer (*Coussell, Cusselle*), Crèvecœur (*Crawcour, Craker, Croaker, Croker, Crocker, Cre(e)gor* 1158), Cully-le-Patry (*Cully, Kewley*), Dives-sur-Mer (*Dives*), Donville (*Domvil(l)e, Dumville, Dunville, Dunfield* 1274), Escoville (*Scovell, Scovil* 1194), Falaise (*Fallas, Fallis*), Fontenay-le-Marmion (*Fontenoy* 1253), Glanville (*Glanvill, (de) Glanville, Glan(d)field*), Graye (*Gray, Grey*), Hérouville

---

[1] E.g. Belcumber Hall (Essex) commemorates a family from Bellencombre (Seine-Inférieure) and Saham Toney (Nf) one from Tosny (Eure). *v.* P. H. Reaney, *Origin of English Place-names*, pp. 60–6.

70

(*Harvell*), Hottot-en-Auge (*Hottot*), Isigny (*Disney* 1150), La Cressonière (*Cresner, Kas(s)ner* 1099), Lassy ((*de*) *Lac(e)y, Lassy*), Le Marais (*Mar(r)is, Mares*), Lison (*Lison, Licence, Lysons* 1195), Les Loges (*Loach*), Louvigny (*Lovney* 1242), Marigni (*Marnie, (de) Marney* 1166), Monceaux (*Mouncey, Mounsey, Mounsie, Monsey, Muncey, Munsey, Munsie, Munchay, Mungay*), Montpinçon (*Mompesson, Mumberson, Mumbeson* Hy II), Moutiers-Hubert (*Musters, Mustre*), Notre-Dame-de-Courson (*Curzon, Curson*), Noyers (*Nowers*), Ouilly-le-Basset (*Doyley, D'Oyley, Dol(l)ey, Dul(e)y, Dail(l)ey, Dayley, Olley, Ollie*), Percy-en-Auge (*Percy, Persey, Purcey*), La Pommeraye (*Pom(e)roy, Pomery, Pummery*), Port-en-Bessin (*Port*), Presles (*Prayer* 1161), Reinville (*Rainville, Renfield* 1166), Reviers (*Redvers, Reveres, Rivers*), La Rivière (*Rivers*), Rots (*Ros, Ross(e)*), Saint-Christophe-L'Anfernet (*Christopher* 1166), Saint-Clair l' Évêque (*Sinclair, Sinkler*), Sainte-Foy-de-Montgommery (*Montgomerie, Montgomery, Montgomrey*), Saint-Paul-de-Vernay (*Vernay, Vern(e)y, Varney* 1221), Savenay (*Savigny*), Secqueville-en-Bessin (*Satchwell, Setchfield*), Tessel-Bretteville (*Taycell, Tessel*), Thaon (*Tahan, Tahum*), Tilly-sur-Seulles (*Till(e)y, Tillie*), Tournai (*Tournay, Turney*), Tracy-Bocage (*Trac(e)y* 1130), Les Trois Minettes (*Tremlett, Trimlett* 1130), Vassy (*Vassie* 1203), Venoix (*Venes(s), Venis(e), Venus* 1130), Vienne (*Vian* 1084), Villiers-le-Sec (*Villar(s), Villers, Villiers, Villis* 1130), Villy-Bocage (*Villy* 1154).

Côtes-de-Nord: Dinan (*Dinan* 1155).

Drôme: Valence (*Vallance, Vallans, Valance* 1158).

Eure: Baudemont (*Balment* 1159), Beaumont-le-Roger (*Beaumont, Beaument, Beumant, Beauman, Beaman, Beamand, Beament, Beamont, Bemand, Bemment, Belmont*), Bec-Hellouin (*Bec, Beck(e)*), Bernay (*Berney, Burney, Burnie*), Boscherville (*Baskerville, Baskerfield, Baskeyfield, Basketfield, Basterfield, Baskwell, Paskerful, Pasterfield, Pesterfield* 1127), Bus-St-Rémy (*Boy(e)s, Boice, Boyce*), Caioullet (*Callaway, Calloway, Cal(l)way, Kellaway, Kelleway, Kelway* 1165), Candos (*Chandos*), Castellion (*Castellan, Castling*), Cormeilles (*Cormell*), Écardenville (*Scardifield, Scarterfield* 1235), Evreux (*Everest, Everiss, Everist, Everex, Everix, Dever(e)aux, Devereu(x), Deveroux, Deverose*), Épaignes (*Spain*), Ferrières-Saint-Hilaire (*Ferrers, Ferries, Ferris*), Gamaches (*Gam(m)age, Gammidge, Cam(m)idge* 1158), Gouville (*Wyvill(e)*), Harcourt (*Harcourt* 1055), Hauville (*Havill, Havell, Hovell, Hovil*), Ivry-la-Bataille (*Ivery, Ivory*), Livet-en-Ouche (*Livett, Livitt* 1135), Lyons-la-Forêt (*Lyons*), Manneville-sur-Risle (*Mandeville, Manvell, Manville, Manwell*), Minières (*Miners, Minors* 1130), Montfort-sur-Risle (*Montford, Montfort, Mountford, Mountfort, Mumford, Mundford, Munford*), Noyers (*Nowers* 1199), Pacy-sur-Eure (*Pac(e)y* 1158), Romilly (*Romilly* 1198,) Sacquenville (*Sackville, Sackwild*), Saint-Quentin-des-Isles (*St Quentin, St Quintin* 1135), Saint-Jean-de-Thenney (*Taney, Tawney* 1195), Thouberville (*Turberville, Turberfield, Turbefield, Turbyfield* 1115), Turville-la-campagne (*Turvill(e), Tuffield, Tuffill* 1131), Venables (*Venables* c1170), Vernon (*Vernon, Vernum, Varnon*).

Eure-et-Loir: Chartres (*Chartres, Charters, Chatters* 1179), Dreux (*Drew(e)s, Druce, Droy*).

71

Gironde: Bordeaux (*Bordeaux, Bourdas, Burders*, etc.).

Ille-et-Villaine: Espinay (*Spain*), Saint-Aubin-d'Aubigné (*Dauben(e)y, Daubney, D'Aubney, Dabney, Dobney*).

Indre-et-Loire: Tours (*Tours, Towers* 1150).

Maine-et-Loire: Angers (*Angers, Aungiers* 1207), Daumeray (*Damary, D'Amery, Dammery, Damri, Amori, Amory*), Saint-Laud (*Sandler, Sendler* 1148).

La Manche: Arcy (*D'Arcy, Darc(e)y*), Auvers (*Davers*), Beauchamps (*Beauchamp, Beachamp, Beacham, Beachem, Beecham*), Bohon (*Boon(e), Bone, Bown(e)*), Brix (*Bruce*), Cambernon (*Champernowne* 1172), Carteret (*Carteret, Chartrey* 1166), Coutances (*Constance, Custance* 1150), Ferrières (*Ferrers, Ferries, Ferris*), Gréville (*Greville* 1158), Hauteville-la-Guichard (*Havill, Havell, Hovell, Hovil* 1198), La Haye-du-Puits (*Haye* 1123), Lestre (*Lester*), Macey (*Mac(e)y, Mass(e)y, Massie*), Magneville (*Mandeville, Manvell, Manville, Manwell*), Marcy (*Mass(e)y, Massie*), Martinvast (*Matterface* 1166), Montaigu (*Montagu(e), Montacute*), Montbrai (*Mowbray, Mowbury, Moubray, Mumbray, Momerie, Mummery, Membry, Memory, Mulb(e)ry*), Montjoie (*Mountjoy, Mungay* 1219), Mortagne (*Morten*), Moyon (*Moon(e)*), Orglandes (*Oglander* 1144), Remilly (*Romilly* 1190), Saint-Clair-sur-Elle (*Sinclair(e), Sinclar, St Clair*), Saint-Hilaire-du-Harcouët (*Santler* 1219), Saint-Lô (*Sandler, Sendler*), Saint-Martin d'Aubigny (*Daubeney*, etc.), Sourdeval (*Sirdifield, Syrdifield, Cedervall, Cederwell, Surrell*), Vains (*Vaines, Vein* 1221), Valognes (*Valin(s), Vallin(s), Vallings*), Vauville (*Wavell, We(a)vill, Wevell*), Ver (*Vear(e), Vere*), Verdun (*Verden, Verdin, Verdon, Verduin, Varden, Vardon*), Vessey (*Vessey*).

Mayenne: Craon (*Crowne(s)*), Hercy (*Hercy, Hersee, Hers(h)ey*), Laval (*Laval(l), Lavell* 1130), Orange (*Orange*).

Morbihan: Helléan (*Elion, Elin, Hel(l)in, Hellin(s), Helling(s), Hellon, Hillen, Hilling(s)*), Rohan (*Rohan* 1190).

Nord: Douai (*Dowey, Douie*), Graveron-Sémerville (*Somervaile, Somervell, Som(m)erville, Summerville, Som(m)erfield, Summerfield*).

Oise: Beauvais (*Be(a)ves, Beavis, Be(e)vis, Beviss, Bovis*).

Orne: L'Aigle (*Eagle*), Alençon (*Allison, Dallinson, Dallison*), Aunou-le-Faucon (*Daunay, Dauney, Dawnay, Dawney, Dando, Daddow*), Bailleul-en-Gouffern (*Baillieu, Baillieul, Bal(l)iol*), Boucé (*Buss(e)y*), Briouze (*Brewis, Brewse, Browse, Bruce*), Chaumont (*Chaumont* 1200), Hautrive (*Hawtree, Hawtrey, Hatry, Daltr(e)y, Daultrey, Dealtry, Daught(e)ry, Daughtrey, Doughtery* 1155), Lacelle (*Lascelle(s)* 1150), Lucé (*Luc(e)y* 1135), Sai (*Say(e)*), Tournay-sur-Dive (*Tournay, Turney*).

Pas-de-Calais: Arras (*Arras, Aries, Aris(s), Darras* 1187), Béthune (*Bethune, Beat(t)on, Beeton, Betton* Hy II), Boulogne (*Bulleyn, Bullen, Bullin, Bullon, Bullan(t), Bullent, Boullen, Boullin* 1121), Le Boutimont (*Bootyman, Beautyman* 1208), Calais (*Callis*), Cuinchy (*Quincey, Quinsee, Quinsey, De Quincey* 1153), Gouy (*Goy, Goe* 1148), Marck (*Mark(e)*), Wissant (*Whisson, Wisson*), Cahu (a lost place near Boulogne), (*Keyho(e), Kehoe, Kew* 1195).

Saône-et-Loire: Cluny (*Clun(e)y, Clunie*).

Sarthe: Ballon (*Ballon, Bal(l)aam* 1176), Le Mans (*Mance, Manse* 1202).
Seine-et-Marne: Angerville (*Dangerfield* 1205), Gondouville (*Gonville* 1159), Lésigny (*Lesnie, Lisney* 1275), Provins (*Province, Provins* 12th).
Seine-et-Oise: Aincurt (*d'Eyncourt, Danecourt*), Chaussy (*Chasey* 1180), Étampes (*Stamp(s)* 1191), Montmorency (*de Montmorency* 1177), Pontoise (*Pontis, Puntis* 1190).
Seine-Inférieure:[1] Aumale (*Damerell, Damiral, Dammarell, Damrel(l)*), Bailleul-Neville (*Bal(l)iol* 1166), Bolbec (*Bulbeck, Bulbick*), Beuzeville-la-Giffard (*Bosvil(l)e, Boswall, Boswell* 1130), Bouville (*Bovill(e), Bovell*), Bouelles (*Bowell, Buell*), Cailly (*Cayley, Caley, Calley, Callie, Kaley, Kayley*), Canteleu (*Cantello(w), Cantlow* 1135), Canville-les-Deux-Églises (*Canwell, Canfield, Camwell, Cam(p)field* 1148), Clanville-en-Caux (*Clavell*), Colleville (*Colvill(e), Covell, Covil(l)*), Cressy (*Crecy, Cressee, Cress(e)y* 1171), Criel-sur-Mer (*Croyle, Kerrell, Kriel*), Dénestanville (*Dunsterville* 1130), Déville (*Devill(e), De Ville, de Ville, Devall, Deaval, Deaville, Davall, Davolls, Divall, Divell, Evill* 1107), Dieppe (*Dieppe* 1224), Émalleville (*Melvill(e), Malvin* 1161), Etocquigny (*Scotney* 1143), Etoutteville-sur-Mer (*Stutfield* 1106), Eu (*Doe*), Fallencourt (*Fancourt, Fancutt* 1166), Floques (*Flock, Fluck*), Freulleville (*Frillwell* 1107), Gerponville (*Jarville, Charville* (1258),[2] Gournai-en-Bray (*Gournay, Gorny, Gurney*), Grainville-la-Teinturière (*Grenville, Grenfell, Greenville, Greenfield, Granville, Gran(d)field* 1161), Longueville-sur-Scie (*Longueville, Longville, Longfield, Longwell* 1185), Louvetot (*Lout(t)it, Louttet* 1161), Manneville (*Mandeville, Manville, Manvell, Manwell*), Mesniers (*Manners* 1106), Monchaux (*Mouncey, Mounsey, Muncey, Munsey, Munchay, Mungay* 1130), Mortemer-sur-Eaulne (*Mortimer, Mortimore, Mut(t)imer*), Neufmarché (*Newmarch* Hy II), Néville (*Nevill(e), Nevile, Newill*), Normanville (*Normanville* 1106), Pavilly (*Pavel(e)y Pawley* 1172), Pierrepont (*Pier(re)point, Pierpont, Pearpoint, Pairpont, Spearpoint*), Rames (*Raimes, Reames*), Les Roches (*Roach, Roch(e)*), Roumare (*Romer* 1190), Saint-Léger-aux-Bois (*Salingar, Salinger, Seliger, Sel(l)inger*), Sommery (*Sum(e)ray, Sumrie*), Vatierville (*Waterfield* 1137), La Varenne (*Warren, Warran(d), Warrant*), Wanchy-Capval (*Wansey*).
Somme: Bailleul (*Bal(l)iol*), Dumart-en-Ponthieu (*Dummett, Dommett* 1150), Picquigny (*Pin(c)kney*).

OTHER CONTINENTAL SOURCES

From other countries on the Continent we have the toponymics *Al(l)mand, Almond, Allamand* and *Alliment* from OFr *alemaund* 'German', *Tyas, Tyes* (OFr *tieis* 'German'), *Den(n)es, Denness* (OFr

---

[1] Now *Seine-Maritime*.

[2] John, Laurence (*de*) *Jarpe(n)ville, Charpenevill* 1258, 1285, 1296 PN Ess 128, John *de Cherville* 1302 Petre, William *Jerpeville* 1327 SR (Ess), Gerard *de Charpeuile* 14th Petre, John *Gardeuill'* 1376 Ass Ess, John *Charfowle, -foule* 1467, 1483, John *Jardevelde* 1473, John *Charvell, Charvolle* 1522, 1537 Petre. This is the origin of Gerpins in Rainham (Ess) and may also be that of the rare surnames *Charpin, Sharpin, Sharvell* and *Sharvill*.

73

daneis) and *Dence, Dench* (OE *denisc* 'Danish') 'the Dane'. *Fleming, Fleeming, Fleeman, Flamank* and *Flament*, with five other variants, from AN *fleming*, OFr *flamanc*, and *Brabant, Braban, Brabon* and *Brabham* (Flemish *Brabant*), with *Brabazon* and *Brobson* (AFr *brabançon* 'a native of Brabant', remind us of the early medieval intercourse between England and Flanders, so common that in the fourteenth century an English form of the name developed by the addition of *-er* to the name of the Duchy, *Braba(y)ner*, which survives as *Brabiner, Brabner* and *Brebner*. Less commonly, these surnames were local in form: *de Brabayn, de Flandria*, the latter still in use as *Flanders* or *Flinders*.

We still have modern surnames from the towns of Antwerp (*Danvers, Danvis*), Bruges (*Bridges*), Ghent (*Gaunt, Gant*), Liège (*Luke, Luckes*), Louvain (*Loven*), and Ypres (*Dipper, Diaper*), and from the German Cologne (*Cullen, Cullin, Cullon*), and Lübeck (*Lubbock*). From Italy, we have the common *Lombard, Florence* and *Pleasance* or *Pleasants* from Piacenza, and *Romaine* and *Roman(s)*, all of which may also derive from personal-names. *Rome* and *Room(e)* may denote either natives of Rome or, more often, men who had made the pilgrimage to Rome, which is certainly the meaning of *Romer, Roomer* and *Rummer*. *Spain* usually denoted a Spanish merchant, whilst those from Portugal, known as *Portingales*, have given us the modern *Portugal, Portergill, Puttergill, Pettengell, Pettengill, Pettingale, Pettingall, Pettingell* and *Pettingill*.

Chapter Five

SURNAMES OF RELATIONSHIP

PATRONYMICS

AMONG the Anglo-Saxons and the Scandinavians, to whom hereditary surnames were unknown, it was often found convenient to identify a man by describing him as son of his father, e.g. Sired *Ælfredessuna* (987) 'son of Alfred' (OE *Ælfrǣd*), Yric *Haroldes sunu* (952) 'son of Harold' (ON *Haraldr*). Such names were not family names; they died with the man. A similar, natural method of description is found by the thousand in medieval documents in the Latin form, Willelmus *filius Roberti*. These, too, were descriptive and not family names.

From the Norman Conquest onwards, we find a different type in which the name of the father or of some ancestor is added as an attribute to the christian name: William *Leuric* (1086), from OE *Lēofrīc*, now *Leverich* or *Loveridge*; Richard *Fareman* (1086), from ON *Farmann*, now *Farman*; William *Bertram* (1086), from OFr *Bertran(t)*, from OG *Bertran(d)*, modern *Bertrand, Bertram, Bartram, Batterham*, etc. Some names of this type quickly became real family names, many of them still surviving as real patronymics, perpetuating the name of some early ancestor regarded as the father of the family, though, of course, the family is older than the surname.

METRONYMICS

In some instances, the parent named is the mother. Pre-Conquest examples are rare: Wulfric *Wulfrune sune* (997 ASWills), Eadric *Wynflæde sunu* (c1015 ASCh). They become more numerous after 1086 and are of every type: Godric *filius Brihtiue*, Æluric *Leueday* c1095 Bury (OE *Beorhtgifu*, *Lēofdæg*), now *Brightiff* or *Beriff* and *Loveday*, Robert *Gunnilt* Hy 2 DC (ON *Gunnhildr*), modern *Gunnell*, Henricus *filius Cecilie* c1180 Bury, William *Mariot* 1185 Templars.

Many of these metronymics are not easily recognised at first sight. Christian names are often recorded in the documents in forms still found, whereas surnames reflect the medieval vernacular pronunciation. *Agnes*, still found occasionally as a surname, *Agnes(s)*, was pronounced *Anneis*, *Annes* or *Annass* (cf. Fr *Anés*) and survives as *Annas*, *Anness* and *Annis(s)*. OFr *Cateline* was the form used for *Catharine*, hence the surnames *Catlin* and *Catling*. The Latin *Laetitia* 'joy', OFr *Lece*, is now found as both *Lettice*, *Letts*, *Letson* and *Letsome* and also as *Leece*, *Leeson* and *Leason*. Some of the names have a deceptive topographical appearance: *Baseley*, *Bazley*, by the side of *Bassill* and *Bazell*, from OFr *Basile* 'royal, regal', ultimately of Greek origin; *Sealey*, *Seeley*, *Ceeley*, from OE *sǣlig* 'happy, blessed', used as a woman's name, *Sely* filia Nicholai 1221 AssWo; *Sibley*, *Sebley*, from the Greek *Sibyl*; *Sisley*, *Sicely*, from *Cecilia* 'blind', the martyred patron saint of musicians, with pet-names *Ciss* and *Cissot*, surviving in *Sissons* and *Sisterson*.

Matilda, now known only as a christian name, unless it is the source of the very rare *Mattleson*, is from OG *Mahthildis* 'might-battle', found in ME as *Mathildis*, *Mahald*, *Mahaut*, *Mald*, *Maut*, *Maud* and *Molde*. Queen Matilda, wife of William I, is called both *Mahald* and *Mold* and the name was once one of the two most popular women's names and is still found as a surname in *Maude*, *Mahood*, *Mawhood*, *Mald*, *Malt*, *Mault*, *Mold Mould(s)*, *Moult*, *Mowles*, *Mowll*, *Mowat*, *Maudson*, *Maulson*, *Mawson*, *Mawsom*, *Molson* and *Moulson*. From its pet-names, we have also *Till(e)*, *Tills*, *Tilson* *Tillett*, *Tillott* and *Tillotson*.

Alice, the rival of *Matilda* in popularity, from OG *Adelhaidis* 'noble kind, sort', OFr *Aalis*, *Aliz*, occasionally preserves the old form *Alais* by the side of *Alis*, *Allies*, *Alliss*, *Allish* and *Hallis*. It was very common in the pet-form *Alison*, whence the modern *Al(l)ison*, *Alleeson* and *Hallison*.

76

Mabel is a shortening of *Amable*, from Latin *amabilis* 'lovable', which became *Anabel* and *Aneball* which was finally corrupted to *Hannibal* and *Honneybell*. As a surname it is found as *Mable, Mabl(e)y, Mabb(s), Mabson, Mabbett, Mabbitt, Mabbott, Mabbutt, An(n)able, Annible, Hannibal, Honeyball, Honneybell, Honniball, Hunnable, Hunneyball, Hunneybell, Hunnibal* and *Hunnibell*.

Some of these metronymics derive from personal-names which were always rare or have been long disused. *Parnall, Parnell, Parnwell* and *Purnell* are survivals of the once popular *Peronel*, from *Petronilla*, which has also given us *Penn* and *Pennell(s)*.

Neither OFr *Hersent*, OG *Herisin* (f) 'army-truth', nor OFr *Maissent*, OG *Mathasuent(a)* or *Magisind*, *Megisend*, were common names, but the former survives in the modern *Harsant, Harsent, Hersant, Hassent, Arson* and *Assen* and the latter as *Messant, Meazon* and *Mezen*. Occasionally we have a pet-name from the final element of a compound, modern *Line(s)* and *Lyne(s)* from *Lina*, a pet-form of such names as *Avelina* and *Emelina*, themselves surviving as *Aveline, Aveling, Emlyn, Emblin(g), Emblen* and *Emblem*.

The frequency of metronymics cannot be doubted. Our list is far from complete. Only three of the eight most common medieval women's names have been included. The remaining five include *Isabel, Juliana* and *Joan*, all productive of surnames, to which we might add *Pleasance, Precious* and *Prudence*, with such native names as *Alflatt* (OE *Ælfflæd*), *Audrey* (OE *Æðelðrýð*, Etheldreda) and *Ravenhill* (ON *Hrafnhildr*).

It was Bardsley who first drew attention to the numerous surnames which perpetuated the name of an ancestress. His views were subjected to much criticism by defenders of medieval virtue who regarded all such surnames as evidence of illegitimacy and were shocked by the picture of the moral degradation of medieval England which this implied. Whilst admitting that some of these names must be those of bastards, Bardsley himself (and others) have obviously been troubled by doubts. 'Even when the name is unquestionably feminine . . . illegitimacy is anything but an established fact.'[1] Ewen rightly criticises the statement of the *Complete Peerage* that Gervasius Caterine was 'presumably a bastard as being named after his mother', but his own views are too dogmatic and unproven: 'These names are no indication of base birth, as often erroneously

[1] C. W. Bardsley, *English Surnames* (London, 1875), p. 80.

supposed,'[1] whilst Weekley shirks any final conclusion: 'Even if illegitimacy were the only reason, that would not concern the philologist.'[2]

Among the various explanations offered are the adoption of children by women, posthumous birth and families 'where the mother was notoriously, and in an emphatic sense, the better half, in a family where the husband was content to sit in the chimney nook, and let the bustling Margery, or Siss, or Emmot take, whether in or out of doors, the lead in all that concerned the domestic relationship'.[3] The family of the medieval villager who neither ploughed nor harrowed nor reaped would have starved, and Geoffrey *Liggebiyefyre* (1301 SRY) and Henry *Lenealday* (1336 FrY) must have been men of this type. To these suggestions Weekley adds the children of a widow; in the case of second marriages, the distinguishing of the two families by their mother's names; the adoption of orphans by female relatives; and the suggestion that 'in a village which counted two Johns or Williams, and few villages did not, the children of one might assume, or rather would be given by the public voice, the mother's name'.[4]

Some of these suggestions are possible. Widows were numerous and it would be natural for the villagers to refer to the posthumous child as 'the widow's son' or to call him after his mother. Or, since, as we shall shortly see, an orphan might acquire the surname *Uncle* or *Neame* from his guardian, so when the natural guardian, the mother, still lived and took the place of the father in managing the family holding until her son came of age, this long and close association might well be perpetuated by giving the son his mother's name as a surname. William *Aumfrey* de Paston who held land granted him by Alice, daughter of *Aumfrey* de Paston, widow of Richard de Paston (13th CNat), may well have been a son of the widow Aumfrey. John *Organ* of Treworian took his surname from his mother *Organa*, wife of Ives de Treworian (1325 AD v). We have also to take into account the fluidity of surnames in the thirteenth and fourteenth centuries when an apprentice could assume the surname of his master and a daughter her father's surname or christian name, whilst a wife could assume her husband's christian name as her

[1] C. L. Ewen, *A History of Surnames of the British Isles* (London, 1931), p. 230; *A Guide to the Origin of British Surnames* (London, 1938), p. 138.
[2] E. Weekley, *Romance of Names* (London, 1922), p. 93.
[3] Bardsley, op. cit., p. 80.
[4] Weekley, op. cit., p. 92.

surname or retain her first husband's surname whilst a widow or after her second marriage. The use of surnames was regulated by no definite rules and the mother's name might have been acquired for many reasons.

But we cannot reject illegitimacy as a common cause. *Bastard*, rather surprisingly, has survived as a surname, and assize rolls, in particular, are full of prosecutions for rape and accusations of murder of concubines. Many a villein had to pay *leyrwite*, a fine for the incontinence of his daughter.[1] It was a common custom, too, that the heir to the family tenement should not marry until he entered on his inheritance. The other sons married only if they acquired land or some means of livelihood elsewhere. When marriage was long postponed there was, at least, a possibility of illegitimate births.

Medieval opinion on the subject differed from ours. Law and custom were in conflict. The common law excluded bastards from inheriting land and refused to allow that children born out of wedlock became legitimate on the subsequent marriage of their parents. The customs of many manors, however, were more lenient and allowed children born out of wedlock to inherit land under certain circumstances. The Church, too, was more merciful than the law. At the nuptial mass in the church, after the *Sanctus*, the couple knelt in prayer and a pall, the care-cloth, was stretched over them. According to Robert Grosseteste, Bishop of Lincoln 1235–53, it was already a custom before his time that any children born to the couple before marriage were placed beneath the care-cloth and were thenceforth regarded as legitimate.

In Miles Coverdale's translation of about 1541 of Bullinger's *The Christian State of Matrimonye*, we read:

After the hand fasting & makyng of the contracte, the church goyng and weddyng shulde not be deffered to long, lest the wicked sowe hys vngracious sede in the mene season . . . For in some places ther is such a maner, wel worthy to be rebuked, that at the hand fastynge there is made a great feast & superfluous bancket, & even the same night are the two hand fasted persones brought and layed together, yea certayne wekes afore they go to the church.

Homans has produced evidence that this sixteenth-century custom, which still survived in the Isle of Portland as late as the last century, existed in England in the thirteenth century. At Park (Herts) in 1271

[1] On medieval immorality 'an inseparable part of village life, both in England and abroad, right down the ages', *v.* H. S. Bennett, *Life on the English Manor* (Cambridge, 1938), pp. 245–8.

79

and at Wakefield in 1286, it was the custom to regard the elder son as the heir even if born before his parents' marriage, provided they had previously plighted their troth. It was the troth plight which was regarded as the important ceremony. The marriage might not take place until after a year or more, often after a child had been born. In this interval the father might die and one or both parents might decide not to proceed with the wedding; the child would then remain illegitimate and might well take its mother's name without censure or stigma for the custom accorded with the sentiment of the country-side.[1]

OTHER RELATIONSHIPS

At times, other relationships are expressed: Ioseph *frater* Beniamin 'brother' (1149 Holme), Robertus *nepos* Huberti 'nephew of Hubert', Robertus *nepos comitisse* 'nephew of the countess' Hy 2 DC, Gerardus *nepos episcopi* 'the bishop's nephew' c1162 ib. English formations are also found: Alwinus *Childebroder* 1066 Winton, William *Gamelstepson* 1296 Misc (Y), John *Lucebrother* 1327 SRSo, Henry *Prestesneve* 'nephew of the priest' 1327 SRSf, Robertus *Johannis Cousain* 'John's cousin' 1332 SRSx, John *Geppedoghtersone* 'grandson' 1336 Pat (Y), William *Nicolneve* 1374 AssL, John *Vicercosyn* 1379 PTY.[2]

The only names of this type to survive are certain compounds of -*magh* which will be discussed later.[3] We still have, however, some surnames which must be relics of this method of name-formation. The relationship is expressed, but the name of the actual relative does not appear. Some of these surnames have more than one origin. *Fadder* and *Fathers*, *Mothers* and *Brothers* may all derive from a well-established personal-name, ODa *Fathir*, *Mothir* and *Brothir*. But all are used also as nicknames: Robert *le Fader* 1201 AssSo, Alicia *le Moder'* 1279 RH (C), William *le Brother* ib. (O). The rare *Cyster* must be for 'sister', cf. Agnes *Vikercister*, Alice *Prestsyster servant* 1381 PTY. OE *fæder* was used of one who exercised protecting care like that of a father and the ME nickname may have had a similar meaning or may have been applied to one of outstanding character regarded as the 'father' of the village. *Mother*, too, may have com-

---

[1] *v.* the full discussion of 'Trothplight and Wedding' in G. C. Homans, *English Villagers of the Thirteenth Century* (Cambridge, Mass., 1942), pp. 160–76.

[2] For other examples of these and similar names in this chapter, *v.* P. H. Reaney, *A Dictionary of British Surnames* (London, 1958), pp. xv, xliv.

[3] *v.* pp. 203–4.

memorated the motherly qualities of the woman to whom the whole village turned in time of trouble or distress. *Brother* may have denoted a member of the brotherhood of some guild. *Daughter* is ill-documented, the sole example noted, late and corrupt in form, being Katheryn *Doctor* 1570 ChwWo, but it is, no doubt, the origin of the modern surnames *Daughters, Dauter, Darter, Dafter(s)* and *Daftor(s)*. From *son* we have the modern *Son, Soane(s), Soan(s)* and *Sone(s)*, John *Sune* 1203 P (Wa), Roger *le Son* 1327 SRSf, a name which may have been used to distinguish the son and heir from the father in whose house he had lived so many years that by the time he entered on his heritage it had become so commonly accepted that it ultimately became the family name. Or it may have been given to the son who worked the family holding which had been made over to him by his father on condition that he should continue to live in the house and be provided with food and shelter. *Daughter* might similarly have been used of a sole heiress who would ultimately inherit her father's land.

Among the less common names of this type are *Odam(s)* and *Odhams*, from OE *āðum*, ME *odame* 'brother-in-law, son-in-law', Nicholas *Odam*, John *Odames* 1327 SRSt, with *Gender(s)* and *Ginder(s)* of which examples are few and poor, Peter *Gindur* 1332 SRSr, John *Gendor* 1482 KentW. It is probably identical with the French *Gendre, Legendre*, which Dauzat regards as a surname of relationship which became a family name when a son-in-law inherited the house of a father-in-law.

Cousen(s), Cousin(s), Cosin and *Cuzen* are liable to confusion with *Cousans, Cussen, Cusson(s)* and *Cossins*. ME *cosin, cusin* was used not only of an actual cousin but also vaguely of any kinsman. It is occasionally found with *-ss-*, but such forms have usually a different origin. *Cussons* may be a local surname from Coutance (Peter *de Cusaunce* 1305 FFEss) or a metronymic from *Custance* (Constance), with pet-forms *Cust* and *Cuss*, one origin of both *Cusson* and *Cussen* (Robert *Custson* 1332 SRCu, Richard *Cusson* 1379 PTY 'son of *Cust*') which may also be 'son of *Cutt* (Cuthbert)', Henry *Cuttesone* 1329 ColchCt.

OE *ēam*, ME *eme* 'uncle' survives as *Eames, Heams* and *Hemes* and also as *Neam(e)*, from a mis-division of *min eme* 'mine uncle', a common form of address. From OFr *oncle*, too, we have *Uncle(s)* and *Ungles*. Radulfus *avunculus* is identical with Radulfus *Heam* (c1200 ELPN). *Uncle* is common as *(le) Uncle* from the twelfth century, but, especially in East Anglia, is also a patronymic from ON *Úlfketel* which became *Ulfkell*, *Ulkell*, *Unkell* and finally *Uncle*.

This group of names is particularly interesting as we can get a glimpse of the way in which such terms of relationship might have become family names. Throughout Kent in the thirteenth century it was the custom to entrust the heir of a man who had held land in gavelkind, if a minor on his father's death, to the guardianship of his mother, but if the mother were dead the wardship passed in some places to the mother's brother, the heir's *uncle* or *eme*, a custom which may have applied to holdings of countrymen, bond as well as free, in various parts of England.[1] Such a guardian, working the land and drawing the profits until the heir came of age might well have been referred to by the villagers as 'the eme' or 'the uncle', a term which, by long use, might ultimately have become the family name.

The nepotism of medieval popes and bishops was notorious and this partiality for nephews was not confined to ecclesiastics, to judge from the frequency of such surnames as Walterus *nepos Odonis* and the modern *Neave(s)*, *Neeve(s)* and *Neve(s)*, from OE *nefa*, *Nephew*, from OFr *neveu*, and *Neese* and *Neech*, from OFr *nies*, nominative of *neveu*. The frequency of these names is also due, in part, to the fact that OE *nefa* could be used of a stepson and, like the Latin *nepos*, of a grandson, whilst in ME it came to mean a prodigal or parasite, a 'neverthryfte or wastowre', a characteristic not surprising in view of the pampering to which many of these nephews were accustomed. At times, the frequency of these surnames of relationship may well have been due to distinctive attributes found necessary to distinguish members of the same family, especially when both christian name and surname were shared by all, e.g. John Darcy 'le fitz', John Darcy 'le frere',[2] John Darcy 'le cosyn', John Darcy 'le unkle', John Darcy 'le neveu', and John Darcy 'le piere' or the elder (1329–46 Fine, 1332–41 Cl).

SURNAMES OF WOMEN

Women's names are much less common in medieval documents than those of men and when they do occur they frequently consist of the christian name alone or of a description giving the name of the father or husband. At times, the christian name itself is omitted, the

[1] *v.* Homans, op. cit., pp. 191–2.

[2] This suggests that *Frear*, *Freer*, *Frier* and *Fryer* may sometimes mean 'brother'. They were certainly also derogatory nicknames from *friar*.

relationship alone being stated. All the types found for names of men occur also for those of women: Marieta *filia Aluric* 1148 Winton 'daughter of Ælfric', Alicia *filia Iuonis pastoris* 1185 Templars (Ess) 'daughter of Ivo the shepherd', Leflet *Ecregelesdocter* 1066 Winton, Margery *le Revedouctur* 1335 AD i (Wo), Emma *Nicoldoghter*, Alice *Gefdoghter* 1379 PTY, Joan *Jakdoghter*, Emma *Watdoughter* 1381 PTY,[1] Baldgiua *soror* (sister) *Osuuardi* c1095 Bury (Sf), Cecilia *soror capellani* 1327 SRSa, *Vxor Rogeri* 'wife of Roger' 1185 Templars (Lo), Elfleda *uxor Askilli* 1168 Holme (Nf), Matilda *uxor Roberti Selueni* c1140 ib., Joan *Tomwyf*, Alice *Lawranswyf*, Matilda *Diconwyf*, Margaret *Gudsonwyf*, Alice *Smythwyf* 1379 PTY, with longer descriptions, Agnes *Williamwyf Smyth* 'wife of William Smyth', Elena *Jonwyf Gibson* 1381 PTY.

The common form for a widow's name was 'Alicia que fuit uxor Knitt' (1231 Newark) 'Alice who was the wife of Knight' or 'Agnes quondam (formerly) uxor Warini Hereward' 13th CNat (Nth), but very frequently they are described simply as *vidua* or *relicta*, Edith *Vidua* 1185 Templars (Wa), Emma *Relicta Johannis* 'John's widow' 1296 SRSx, Johanna *relicta Edwardi Jakes* 1327 SRSo. A hint that about 1300 it was the surname by which the man was chiefly known is given by the very frequent omission in the Sussex Subsidy Rolls of the husband's christian name: Muriel *Relicta le Halgh*, Matilla *Relicta Hysmongere*, Isabella *Relicta Heryngmongere*, Alice Relicta *le Wyse* (1296). The woman's christian name was also often omitted: *Relicta Johannis Palmer, Relicta Preest, Relicta le Carter, Relicta Albyn, Relicta ate Stone, Relicta atte Lane* (1296). Matilda *relicta Candel* (1332 SRSx) is identical with Matilda *Candeles* (1327 ib.) and was, presumably, the widow of Ralph *Candel* (1296 ib.). Here, *Candeles* must be an elliptic genitive 'widow of Candel', a type of surname often found for widows, one origin of such names as Edwards and Riches, which will be discussed at greater length below. The Latin forms above are those of the clerk; they were never used by the widow's friends and relatives who used the common English word, Alice *Wedue*, Agnes *le Wydu*, which now survives as *Widdowes, Widders* and *Widdas*.[2]

---

[1] This type was actually used as a man's surname: Richard *Wryghtdoghter*, Robert *ffelisdoghter* and Cecilia his wife 1379 PTY. They must have owed their surnames to their mothers, daughters respectively of a man named Wright and of a mother named Felis or Felicia.

[2] ME *widewe* was also used of a widower: Peter *le Wydoue* 1297 SRY, John *le Wydewe* 1327 SRSf.

At Sevenhampton (W) in 1287 Reginald *Damemalde* held one yardland formerly of *Maud*, his mother. As her heir, he had taken his mother's name as his surname, '(son of) Dame (or the Lady) Maud'. A slightly earlier example of this type, which now seems to have disappeared completely, is found in the 1275 Subsidy Roll for Worcs, Robert *Dam perronele* (Parnell), with five others in that for 1327, including Walter *Damealis* and Robert *Dame Aldith*. About 20 examples occur in the 1327 roll for Somerset, only one actually the surname of a woman, Alicia *Damablie* (i.e. Dame Mabley or Mable); others are Robert *Dame Isabel*, Richard *dame Anne* and Adam *Damemagot*. It is an interesting formation which throws some light on the position of women in the fourteenth century. As with Reginald above, all these surnames must have been assumed by heirs of ladies who held land in their own right.

Many women, particularly in the fourteenth century, had surnames which they may have owed to their fathers or their husbands: Joan *Austin*, Isabella *Daye* (1327 SRSo), Agnes *Underwode* (1299 FFHu). Some were named from their occupation: Sarah *la Bredmongstere* 1311 LLB D, Alicia *Bredsellestere* 1317 AssK, sellers of bread, Alice *Matresmaker* 1381 PTY, whilst occasionally we have a nickname: Cecilia *la Fairewif* 1254 Oseney (O), identical with Cecilia *de Gloucestria* 1225 ib.

But women could acquire and vary their surnames in a bewildering fashion. They might take the name of their father: Emma Griffin, daughter of Ralph Griffin 1290 CNat; and this they might retain when married or widowed: Cecilia de Sanford, a widow, was the daughter of Henry de Sandford 13th AD v, but her sister's seal bore the legend S. ALIS. FILIA. HENDRICI. Maud, wife of Hugh, son of Huhelina, the fisherman and daughter of John Smith (*faber*) used her father's name on her seal: Matilda le Faber 14th AD vi. Emma Godȝer, wife of Robert Pacy (both villeins), was the daughter of Walter Godȝer 1290 CNat (Lei).

A wife might take the surname of her husband and retain it after his death: Christiana la Summonere, wife of Matthew le Sumener 1230 Pat (K); Agnes le Bele, widow of John le Bel 1213 Cur (Beds); Matilda de Doddebroc, wife (and widow) of Robert de Dodebroc 13th AD v. But the surname of husband and wife could differ: Matillis But, wife of William le Tipper 1214 Cur (Wa). Emma, wife of Reginald de Lavynton used a seal with the legend: S. EMME. DE. LITLECOTE. 14th AD v (W).

Some women took the christian name of their father or husband as their surname. The widow of Rickeman le Chaumberleng (1292 SRLo) was Agnes Rikemannes (1329 Husting). Isabella Estmar (1319 SRLo) took as her surname the christian name of her husband Estmer le Bouler (1298 LoCt), from OE *Eastmǣr*, which was the surname used by their daughter Katharine Estmare, widow of John de Aulton, in her will of 1351 (Husting). Amiel de Honesden late chandler is also called Amiel le Chaundeller. Of his two daughters, one, Johanna Amyel assumed her father's christian name as her surname, the other, Cristina la Chaundeller, was named from his occupation (1349 Husting).

The difficulties of identification which might arise from this haphazard use of surnames is well illustrated by the following example. Juliana, daughter of Thomas *Cross*, calls herself Juliana *Box* in her will of 1328 (Husting). She had been married to Henry *Box* who died in 1298 and became the second wife of John *de Luda* who was living in 1309 (LLB C), so that she retained her first husband's surname after her second marriage, but her daughter, Constance *de Luda*, took the surname of her father.

Only a large collection of examples can give a real impression of the variations in women's surnames before it became normal for a wife to abandon her maiden name and to assume that of her husband. The material is often insufficient to make the whole story complete. Writing of the entries in the fourteenth-century court book of Chertsey Abbey in Surrey, Elsie Toms points out as a remarkable fact that

When heiresses marry, they so often keep their maiden names, while their husbands change theirs to their wives' names . . . In one entry, a woman takes her husband's name, but when her father dies and she inherits his property, they both change to the father's name. Hugh atte Clauwe of Thorpe appears quite often as Hugh le Kach or Keach, because of his marriage to Alice le Keach; and when John atte Hethe of Cobham marries Lucy atte Grene, the remark is added 'He is now called atte Grene.'[1]

'To use the words of modern Irish countrymen,' remarks Homans, 'the family felt they ought to keep the name on the land.'

[1] Elsie Toms, *Court Book of Chertsey Abbey*, p. xxxviii, cited by G. C. Homans, *English Villagers of the Thirteenth Century*, p. 187.

JOHNSON, ROBINSON AND WILSON: DISTRIBUTION AND ORIGIN

Surnames such as *Adamson* or *Addison* and *Wilkinson* are commonly regarded as characteristically northern names and their frequency is generally attributed to Scandinavian influence. This, like so many generalisations on surnames, is based on superficial and insufficient evidence. The subject has not yet been thoroughly investigated. It will be a long task, requiring the collection and examination of thousands of surnames from every county over a period of some 300 years. The material already collected makes it quite clear that names of this type are not only widely distributed[1] but also late in becoming hereditary family names, whilst the great majority of those in use today are compounded with post-Conquest personal-names brought over from France.

The earliest known English example is Hering *Hussan sunu* (603 ASC), and one or two others are found in the eighth and ninth centuries at a time when Scandinavian influence was impossible. They become more numerous towards the end of the Anglo-Saxon period, and have been fully discussed in his *Old English Bynames* by Tengvik who, impressed by the local distribution of the type, rejects the general assumption of Scandinavian importation although he agrees with Ewen that the growing frequency of the suffix in the north during the ME period 'should certainly be attributed to Scandinavian influence'. Tengvik finds only 6 examples in Yorkshire (all from Scandinavian personal-names) and 1 in Durham, whereas Devon has 43, Hampshire 14, Somerset 12 and Kent 11, and Scandinavian influence in these four southern counties is negligible or non-existent. Of the personal-names with which -*sunu* is compounded, 111 are Old English, 24 Scandinavian, 12 Old German or Old French and 5 Celtic.[2] Especially during the last century of the Anglo-Saxon period, names of this type are found in the Latin form Æðnoðus *filius Godrici* (1060), a type common in Domesday Book and the Bury Documents, both of which Tengvik includes, thus accounting for the increase in OG and OFr personal-names in his totals: OE 94, ON 57, OG or OFr 86, Celtic 10.[3]

[1] Ewen discussing the growth in the use of the desinence 'son' in the North, cites 17 examples. Of these, only 5 are from north of the Humber, 2 are from Herts, 1 from Essex and 2 from Sussex. The remaining 7 are from the Midlands, Cheshire (1), Salop (2), Warwicks (1), Lincs (1), Cambs (1), Norfolk (1). *History of Surnames*, p. 172.

[2] G. Tengvik, *Old English Bynames* (Uppsala, 1938), pp. 147-8.

[3] Ibid., pp. 206-7.

This Latin formula is the normal method of indicating the relationship of father and son throughout the twelfth and thirteenth centuries, even in the north. Occasionally in early twelfth-century Yorkshire we have names like Gamel *Grimessune* and Ulf *Fornessuna*, the fathers, *Grim* and *Forne*, being both mentioned in Domesday Book, but the common form is Johannes *filius Grimkelli*, Robertus *filius Suartebrand*, whether the father's name is of English, Scandinavian or French origin, a type of name commonly translated (without the authority of the documents) as *FitzRalf*, *FitzWilliam*, etc., by historians and antiquaries who, at times, coin such hybrids as *FitzAilwin* and *FitzHarding*. It is only towards the end of the thirteenth century that names in -*son* begin to appear again, and they are rare: Adam *Saresone* 1286 LLB D, Geoffrey *Huwesson* 1290 CNat (Nth), William *Paskessone* 1293 FFC, Ralf *Maldesone* 1327 SRSx.

In the fourteenth century, names like Philippus *filius Walteri* are still common, but those like William *Collesson* (1300 CNat, Nth) gradually become more numerous. They are always a small proportion of the whole and are found in the north, the midlands and the south alike. The Subsidy Rolls give a general impression of their numbers and distribution:

		-son	-filius-			-son	-filius-
Cumb	1332	106	909	Cambs	1327	18	138
Lancs	1332	32	644	Suffolk	1327	7	163
Yorks	1297	2	525	Surrey	1332	9	4
	1301	4	1648	Kent	1334	3	12
	1327	12	534	Sussex	1296	0	23
Salop	1327	30	597		1327	4	5
Worcs	1275	0	259		1332	13	5
	1327	14	8	Somerset	1327	27	27
Warwicks	1332	27	121				

It is hardly conceivable that surnames like the Domesday *Godricsone* ceased to be used for a couple of centuries and were then suddenly revived. Radulfus *filius Godrici* may be a translation of *Godricsone*, but it may be merely a description, a device of some clerk or official to identify the man by reference to his closest relative, for a man could be called both Willelmus *filius Hermanni* and Willelmus *Hermannus* (1130–49 Holme), whilst there are a few examples of the equation of a simple christian name as a surname with a compound of -*sunu*: Aluuinus *Dode*, Aluuinus *Dodesune* (1066 DB). Surnames in -*son* must have continued in use, but they were not yet hereditary. They could be based on the father's surname: Robert

Ballardsone 1332 SRLa; William *Broun* and John *Brunnison* lived in the same Cambridgeshire parish, as did Henry *Law* and Richard and William *Lawisson* (1327 SRC); Hugh *Moserghson* was presumably the son of Thomas *de Mosergh* (1332 SRCu), whilst in 1379 PTY we find John *Payg'* and John *Paygson*, Adam *Warde* and John *Wardson'*, Richard *Parlebene* and Robert *Parlebeneson*, John *Knaresburg* and John and Richard *Knaresburghson*.

Towards the end of the fourteenth century, we find 35 examples of the *filius*-type and double that number of compounds of -*son* in a single Lincolnshire document (1374–5 AssL) and although that county has been described as the most Scandinavianised county in England, neither here nor in Yorkshire do we find a solitary example of -*son* compounded with an English or Scandinavian name. All are from French personal-names, both those of men (William *Dobson*, Robert *Jopson*) and of women (William *Cisseson* (now *Sisson*), Robert *Ibboteson*), with an occasional nickname, John *Brounaleynson*, with which we may compare John *Fayraliceson* (1327 SRY). Some of these names are not easy to interpret. Whether William *Smythesson de Beseby* was already surnamed *Smithson* or was the son of the smith of Beseby is not clear, and similar difficulties arise with John *Anabbleson o the Barn* and William *Ladyson de Screveby*. That surnames were not yet fixed is proved by five triple compounds like Walterus *filius Willelmi filii Rogeri*.

This last example appears to be a translation of a type of name common in Yorkshire in 1379–81 (PTY). John *Symson Rayner*, William *Tomson Wilkynson*. The first must mean 'John, son of Sym Rayner'; the second might be 'William, son of Tom Wilkynson' or 'William, son of Tom, son of Wilkyn'. Names in -*son* were beginning to become family names: William *Jonson* was presumably the father of Benedict *Willeson Jonson* and William *Willeson Johanson* and Robert *Hudson* of William *Robynson Hudson*. But John *Wrightson* was the son of Roger *Wright* whose wife was Elena *Wrightwife*. Even among the minor Yorkshire gentry surnames were only just becoming hereditary. John *Dyson* de Langeside owed his surname to his mother *Dionysia* de Langeside (1369), whilst a Thomas *Richardson* was the son of *Richard* de Schagh (1409). Joseph Hunter, the historian of Hallamshire, in his *Memoirs of the Wilsons of Bromhead*[1] demolishes the earlier pedigrees by proving errors of heralds and forging of documents. The family descended ultimately from

[1] *Yorks. Arch. Jnl.*, vol. 5 (1879), pp. 63–125.

William, father of John de Hunshelf or de Waldershelf (b. c1320), but owed its surname not to this William but to William (1369–87), father of John Wilson de Bromhead, who is called John son of William son of John de Waldershelf in 1398. 'This' (1380), he concludes, 'was the age at which that class of surnames which end in *-son* began to be assumed', a conclusion confirmed by the editor of the *Freeman or York*[1] who notes that it was not until after the reign of Henry IV that we find the son invariably taking his father's name; one of the last, if not the last instance to the contrary occurs in 1431 when we find 'Robertus de Lynby, filius Thomae Johnson'.

Our material, therefore, lends no support to the theory that surnames in *-son* are chiefly northern and of Scandinavian origin. They are found both before the Scandinavian settlement and later in the south, in areas unaffected by Scandinavian influence. Compounds with OE personal-names are more numerous than those with names of Scandinavian origin and after the Conquest the great majority are formed from names of French origin brought to this country by the Normans, from full names like *Davidson* and *Robertson*, from diminutives like *Robinson* and *Tillotson*, but chiefly from the pet-names common among the peasantry, *Dawson*, *Dixon*, *Mabson* and *Megson*. Occasionally compounds with OE personal-names survive, *Cuthbertson*, *Edmondson* or *Emonson*, *Edwardson* and *Wadeson*; compounds with Scandinavian names are equally rare, *Grimson*, *Gunson* and *Ormson*. Modern surnames of this type from French personal-names are ten times as numerous as those of English and Scandinavian origin combined. Curiously enough, French has no formation of this kind. It is a Teutonic type, common to England and Germany as well as Scandinavia.

It was not until the 1370s that names of this type began to become common and then chiefly in the north where surnames became hereditary later than in the south. Here, by about 1330, many, even of the peasants, had already acquired fixed family names, a fact proved by the numerous surnames derived from OE personal-names no longer in use, names used after the Conquest only by native Englishmen, a peasantry subject to Norman overlords. Some of these southern surnames were compounds of *-son* and still survive: William *Jonessone*, Richard *Pereson*, William *Hobbeson* (1327 SRSo), John *Dyesone*, Richard *Gibbesone* (1327 SRWo). In Somerset, Sussex and Worcestershire, where only one man in a hundred was without a

[1] P. xvi.

surname of some kind, there was little scope for the development of new surnames, but the position was very different in Yorkshire where one man in six and in Lancashire where one man in four had no surname. Here, the increasing tendency to use terms of relationship to particularise both men and women without surnames resulted in numerous names like *Nicholson* and *Watson*, a natural description of the son. For a time the surname varied with each generation. The son of John *Richardson* would be named William *Johnson* and his son would be Robin *Williamson* or *Wilson* until, some 50 years or so later than in the south, the son of John Wilson came to be called Robert Wilson.

It should be noted that many of these surnames contain the mother's name: *Alletson* (Allot, a pet-name of Alice), *Casson* (Cass, a short form of Cassandra), *Goodison* (OE *Gōdgyð*), *Ibbotson*, *Ibberson* (Ibbot, a diminutive of Ibb, from Isabella), *Mabson* (Mabel).

Others are taken from the father's occupation, the earliest noted being Ulfwin *Teperesune* (c1095 Bury) 'son of the tapper of casks', the beer-seller or taverner. Neither this nor William *le Harpersone* or Adam *le Skynnerson* (1332 SRLa) have survived, but we still have Cookson, Cuckson and Cuxon, Herdson, Hindson, Serjeantson, Sarginson, Sargeson and Surgison, Shepherdson, Sheppardson, Shepperson and Shipperdson, Smithson and Smisson, Taylorson, Wrightson, Rightson and Wrixon, along with Parsonson, Parsison and Parsizon. *Clarkson* is one origin of *Clarson*.[1] Margaret *Clarsome* was the wife of Francis *Clarsom* (1588). Both are called *Clarkson* in 1608. The once common *Revesson* is now *Reeson*, from OE (*ge*)*rēfa* 'reeve'; *Grieveson*, *Greavison* and *Greeson* are northern names with a similar meaning, 'son of the grieve or farm-bailiff' (ONorthumb *grǣfa*); also northern, but of Scandinavian origin, are *Graveson*, *Grayson*, *Grason*, *Graveston* and *Grayston*, 'son of the *greyve* or steward' (ON *greifi*).[2]

FITZALAN, FITZWILLIAM, ETC.

Surnames like Fitzalan and Fitzwilliam have acquired an aristocratic flavour, but are not necessarily a sign of noble birth, for we find *Cookson* 'son of the cook' in the form Gilbert *le Fiz Kew* (1279 AssNb). Modern survivals are compounded with French personal-names common in medieval baronial families though they were also

---

[1] Also 'son of Clara' and 'son of Clarice'.
[2] Also from a personal-name, ON *Greifi* 'count, earl'.

used of others of a less exalted state. Early examples are not easy to find, for they were generally Latinised as Robertus *filius Radulfi*, a form almost regularly translated by historians and others as Robert *fitz Ralph*, so that it is difficult to discover exactly at what period this particular type became a fixed surname. It is an Anglo-Norman formation which developed in England and has no parallel in France.

A few examples have been noted in the reign of Henry II. Very rarely we find *fil*, but the usual forms are *filz, fiz, fitz* and occasionally *fuiz*, from OFr *fils*, AN *fis*, pronounced *fits* 'son': Gervasius *fil Radulfi* 12th DC, Willelmus *le Fiz Simon* Hy 2 ib. (Fitzsimon), Rauf *le fuiz William* 1299 Whitby (Fitzwilliam), Roberd *filz Payn* 1305 SRLa (FitzPayn), Robert *le fuitz Wautier* 1329 Misc (Ess), Johan *fitz Waulter* 1350 AssEss (Fitzwalter, Fitzwater). Charles II used *Fitzroy* 'the king's son' as a surname for his illegitimate sons. Whether all the modern Fitzroys can claim descent from these royal bastards is doubtful. The name is first found in Essex in 1245 and in Sussex in 1296 in a Subsidy Roll (where king's sons are not likely to be found) in the form Henry *fis le Rey*, and is still found in Sussex as *Fillary* and *Fillery*. It may be a translation of *Kingson* 'son of the king' who had played the part in some pageant or play.

Some of these names have undergone curious corruptions. Oke-ford Fitzpaine (Do) occurs as Occeford *Fyppyn* in 1513 (LP), whilst *Fitzwilliam* is *Fewyllyam* in 1464 (Cl). *Fitz Hugh* survives also as *Fithie* or *Fithye*: Edward *Fythewe* or *Fitzhugh* 1492, 1477 GildY. *Fidgeon* and *Fidgen* are colloquial pronunciations of both *Vivian* and *Fitzjohn* and *Fennel* of *Fitz Neal*, whilst *Feehally* is a Liverpool version of the Irish *Feeharry* from *FitzHarry*, a pronunciation found in Surrey in the sixteenth century.[1]

A few surnames consisting solely of a personal-name in the genitive have been noted near the end of the twelfth century, e.g. Edricus *Keteles* (1188), Robert *Howeles* (1210), Stephen *Paynes* (1230). These survive as *Kettless, Howells* and *Paynes* and can only be elliptic genitives, 'Ketill's, Houel's or Payne's (son)'. Proof of this inter-pretation is provided by the surname of Robert *Dobes* who is twice

[1] John *Fyherre* 1572, *Fiharrye* 1596, Peter *Feeharrye* 1583 MustersSr.

so called in 1305, but appears in 1281 as Robert de Rokesle junior. He was the son of Robert de Rokesle senior who must often have been called by his pet-name *Dob* which his son adopted as his surname in the genitive form *Dobes* (now *Dobbs*) 'son of Dob', i.e. of Robert. Simon *Robes* (1319 SRLo) was perhaps identical with Simon de Bureford called *Robechon* late apprentice of John de Bureford (1311 LLB D). If so, his father's name was *Robechon*, a double diminutive of *Rob* (Robert), and his surname *Robes* means 'son of Rob(echon)' and now survives as *Robbs*.

This type of surname steadily increased in numbers in the fourteenth century, but its interpretation becomes complicated. Johanna *le Smythes* and Editha *le Priores* (1327 SRSo) could not have been the *son* of the smith or of the prior. Malyna *la Roperes* (1311 ColchCt), described as a servant, must have been either the servant of the roper or of a man called Roper. Similarly, Alice *le Parsones* and Margery *le Vikers* were servants respectively of the parson and the vicar, but it is doubtful whether shepherds and cobblers would have servants (Avice *la Schepherdes*, Nota *la Souteres* 1311, 1312 ColchCt).

These two women appear with numerous others who were regularly fined at court after court for selling ale at too high a price. They were usually described as 'the wife of John Carpenter', etc., but a certain number are mentioned by name, which almost invariably ends in *-es* (Joan la *Warneres*, Alice *Sayheres*). It is a reasonable assumption that they were widows (or wives) of men named *Warner* and *Sayher*. Margery *la Mazones* was the wife of Walter *le Mazoun* (1311 ColchCt) and, as we have already seen, Matilda *Candeles* was the widow of Ralph *Candel*. Agnes *Rickemannes* was probably the widow of *Rickeman* le Chaumberleng (1329 Husting, 1292 SRLo). In the Subsidy Rolls, it is not uncommon to find pairs of names like John *Serle* and Isabella *Serles*, David *Dobel* and Alice *Dobeles* (1327 SRSo), both assessed in the same parish and probably husband and wife. This will account for some of the rarer surnames such as *Carters* (Margerie *le Carteres* c1275 StThomas), *Fowls* (Agnes *Foweles* 1275 SRWo) and *Barrons* (Alice *le Barouns* 1332 SRWa).

For men, we find numerous similar names, both with and without the article: Adam *le Prestes* 1332 SRWa, which might mean either 'the priest's (son)', as in William *le Prestesson* 1293 FFEss, or 'the priest's (servant)', as in William *Prestesman* 1283 SRSf (now *Priest-*

man or *Pressman*). Similarly, *Parsons* and *Vickers* may commemorate either parentage or service: Eudo *homo persone* 1210 Cur, Henry *le Personesman* 1327 SRDb, John *le Personesone* 1312 AssSt, either of which might be represented by Roger *le Persones* 1323 AssSt, the latter surviving as *Parsonson*, *Parsison* and *Parsizon*; Gillebertus *filius vicarii* c1248 Bec, Roger *le Vikers* 1332 SRWa (*Vicars*, *Vickers*), the modern *Vickerman* and *Vicarage*, *Vickridge* and *Vickress* (Richard *le Vickeries*) 1327 SRSa, from ME *vikerie*, from Lat *vicarius* 'vicar'. Thomas *le Denes* 1332 SRWa (*Deanes*) is paralleled by Thomas *filius Decani* 1210 Cur, Willelmus *filius Dene* 1301 SRY and Henry *le Deneson* 1295, now *Denson* or *Densum* 'son of the dean'.

Whether these sons of parsons and priests were born in or out of wedlock is a matter of some interest and one on which little direct information is to be found. As Archbishop of Canterbury, Lanfranc found so many married priests that he did not dare decree their separation. In 1102, his successor Anselm forbade clerical marriage with the result that Henry I received large sums of money from priests for licence to live as before.[1] Even so distinguished an ecclesiastic as Henry of Huntingdon had doubts as to the wisdom of this policy:

About Michaelmas of this same year Archbishop Anselm held a Council in London, wherein he forbade wives to the English priesthood, heretofore not forbidden; which seemed to some a matter of great purity, but to others a perilous thing, lest the clergy, in striving after a purity too great for human strength, should fall into horrible impurity, to the extreme dishonour of the Christian name.

In the twelfth century we find bishops with wives and mistresses, whilst among the parish clergy marriage and illicit unions were common and it was not until the end of the thirteenth century that the custom of open marriage among clergy in holy orders was stamped out. There was a tendency for benefices to pass from father to son as a hereditary possession, especially where the parson was a member of a family of land-holders.[2] Sons of such priests had surnames (often varying) formed like others of the same class, well illustrated in the

[1] A. L. Poole, *From Domesday Book to Magna Carta* (Oxford, 1951), p. 183.
[2] *v.* P. H. Reaney, 'Celibacy and Clerical Marriage' (*Essex Review*, vol. XLVII (1938), pp. 82–5; A. R. Wagner, *English Genealogy* (Oxford, 1960), pp. 158–61; W. A. C. Sandford, 'Medieval Clerical Celibacy in England' (*The Genealogists Magazine*, vol. XII (1957), pp. 371–5, 401–3), and H. G. Richardson, 'The Parish Clergy of the 13th and 14th Centuries' (*Trans., R. Hist. Soc.*, 3rd Ser., vol. VI (1912), pp. 89–128).

pedigree of the sons of Stigand the priest (living in 1127) as revealed in the Holme Cartulary:

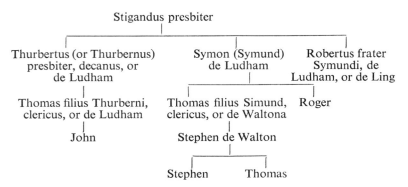

Stigandus presbiter

Thurbertus (or Thurbernus) presbiter, decanus, or de Ludham	Symon (Symund) de Ludham	Robertus frater Symundi, de Ludham, or de Ling
Thomas filius Thurberni, clericus, or de Ludham	Thomas filius Simund, clericus, or de Waltona	Roger
John	Stephen de Walton	

Stephen   Thomas

Gilbert Perdriz ('Partridge'), parson of Shoebury (Ess) in 1254 (*Ass*) had land in Dunton, Downham and Little Burstead. His daughter Willelma is named in 1262 as one of the possible heirs of her brother Paul fitz Gilbert who is also called Paul Perdriz.[1]

Stigand's sons had surnames from their office or their lands; Paul inherited his father's nickname. It is hardly likely that men of this class would be regularly called simply 'son of the clerk, the priest or the deacon'. Such vague descriptions would be more appropriate to the son of the poor village parson, often only in minor orders, frequently ignorant and ill-equipped, poorly paid and himself of peasant stock. Compelled by his poverty to cultivate his glebe, working in the common fields side by side with the villagers, fined and admonished like them in the manor courts, forbidden by his superiors to marry, only too often he fell from grace and shared the village vices. In 1295 the *Statuta Sinodalia* of the Bishopric of Winchester forbade the clergy to keep concubines. At the Hereford visitation of 1397, more than 60 rectors, vicars and chaplains were denounced as fornicators and adulterers and as keeping women from their husbands.[2] There can be little doubt that such surnames as *Presteson, Personesson*, etc., were bestowed by the villagers on the offspring of these weaker brethren.

Occupational surnames are not uncommon, as Osbert *le Smythes*, Hillarius *le Clerkes* (1327 SRSo), Gilbert *le Potteres* and Nicholas

---

[1] R. E. G. Kirk, *Feet of Fines for Essex* (Colchester, 1899–1910), vol. I, pp. 140, 196, 250.

[2] H. S. Bennet, op. cit., pp. 332–5.

94

le Cokes (1327 SRWo), but whether the reference is to a son or a servant we do not know. Both are possible, for we have the modern *Smithson* and *Smisson*, along with *Smidman* 'the smith's assistant' and *Cookes, Cookson, Cuxon* and *Cookman*. This final -*s* could be added to any surname (Hugh *Rabuckes* 1301 SRY), including local surnames: John *Byltons* (1327 SRC), Thomas *Bromes* (1327 SRSo), William *Chynnokes* 1359 Putnam (So), John *Pastons* (1327 SRWo). In some instances, like *Rhodes, Stocks* and *Stubbs*, this -*s* is a sign of the plural, but that is impossible where the source is an actual place-name: *Fullicks*, from *Fullewyke, Hunwicks, Hunnex, Honex*, from *Honeywick, Soames, Somes*, from Soham (C, Nf, Sf), and *Whitticase*, a variant of (Thomas) *Whitakers* (1616 GreenwichPR).

Most of these surnames, however, are based on personal-names and very many survive. We have OE names in *Edwards* and *Edmonds*, Scandinavian in *Siggers* and *Tubbs*, full French names in *Richards* and *Roberts*, diminutives in *Hutchings* and *Philpotts*, and numerous pet-forms as *Gibbs, Hicks* and *Hitches, Jeffs* and *Jeeves, Watts* and *Wills*.

Parsons and *Vickers* often derive from an original formation with a preposition: Ralph *del Persones* (1323), William *atte Persones* (1327), Henry *Attevickers* (1327), '(servant) at the parson's or the vicar's (house)'. We have the full form in 'Thomas *ate Presteshous*' (1327 SRC) which may well be the origin of the modern *Preshous*. *Cannons* and *Deanes* also belong here: Roger *del Kanonhous* 1301 SRY, Walter *ate Cannones* 1332 SRSr, Thomas *del Denes* 1297 MinAcctCo. In *Monks* or *Munks, Frears* and *Nunns*, we clearly have reference to workers at a monastery, a friary or a nunnery: Henry *de Monkes*, William *del Munkes* (1332); William *del Freres* (1327); Robert *del Nunnes, othe Nonnes* (1297), John *atte Nunnes* (1325). The master may be anonymous, William *atte Maystres* 1327 (*Masters, Marsters*), or may be identified by his occupation or by his name: Margaret *ate Budeles* 1332 SRSr (*Buddles*, 'servant at the beadle's'), Alice *at Someres* 1327 SRSx (*Somers*, 'servant at the sumpter's'); Richard *ad Saunders*, John *ate Henry'* 1327 SRC, William *del Dauks*, Diot' *del Daykyns*, John *del Piers*, John *del Symmes* 1379 PTY, Thomas *at Adamys* 1525 SRSx (now *Saunders, Heneries, Dawkes, Dakyns, Pierce* or *Piers, Simms* and *Adams*).

The modern *Stephens* or *Stevens* is found as Richard *Steuenes* 1332 SRWa, Alice *Stephenes* 1279 RH (Hu) and Sibilla *ate Stevenes* 1332 SRSr, so that it might mean either 'son of Stephen', 'servant of Stephen', 'wife (or widow) of Stephen' or 'servant at Stephen's house', and, in the absence of biographical information, the only certainty is provided by the medieval *ate*.

GEFFEN, HUDDEN, ETC.

In the Warwickshire Subsidy Roll for 1332, there are some 72 surnames ending in *-en*, with a smaller number in that for Worcestershire in 1327, whilst Ewen noted a few examples in that for Gloucestershire (1327). They are usually names of men, occasionally of women, and are found side by side with the more numerous common type *Hobbs* and *Watts*. The suffix is added to pet-forms of French personal-names common among the peasants, usually masculine (*Jacken*, *Kitten*, *Nicken*), occasionally feminine (*Maggen* (Madge), *Molden* (Maud), *Magoten*). The type survives in *Dawn* (Daw or David), *Edden*, *Geffen*, *Giffen*, *Hawken*, *Hobben*, *Hudden*, *Judden*, *Sellen*,[1] *Thommen* and *Tibbins* and has contributed to *Gibben*, *Hicken*, *Hitchen* and *Hullin*. The suffix *-en* is liable to confusion with *-in*, *-on* and *-un* which may become *-en*. Modern *Perren* and *Phippen* are diminutives of *Perre* (Peter) and *Phipp* (Philip). *Watten* may have been absorbed by *Watton*, *Jannen* by *Jannings* or *Jennings* and *Tommen* by *Tummon*.

It seems clear that in this suffix we have a genitive singular, *Geffen*, *Dawn*, etc., parallel to *Jeffs*, *Dawes*, etc., but the form is difficult. Our knowledge of the written language of the twelfth and thirteenth centuries in this area is scanty. Of the spoken language we know nothing. Presumably these pet-names of French origin were adopted at a time when the Old English system of declensions was breaking up and the inflexions were in a state of flux. They would be used most commonly in the nominative and when a possessive was required the common form of genitive in *-es* was normally used. It may be that in the West Midlands, when genitives of these pet-names were first required, the genitive singular in *-en* was still in use in the spoken language and persisted, side by side with that in *-es*, just as strong and weak plurals interchange in the Devonshire place-names *Hayes* and *Hayne*.

[1] From *Sell* or *Sill*, a short form of *Silvester*, surviving also as *Selvester*, or of *Silvein*, now *Sauvain* or *Selwyn*.

Chapter Six

SURNAMES FROM NATIVE PERSONAL-NAMES

S URNAMES formed by adding to the christian name that of the father or mother are numerous and early. A few are found before the Conquest and they steadily become more frequent from 1066 onwards: Aluuinus *Cubold* 1066 (OE *Cūðbeald*), Lemmer *Brihtmer* c1095 (OE *Beorhtmǣr*), Goduinus *Alfit* 1066 (OE *Ælfgȳð*, f), Æluric *Leueday* c1095 (OE *Lēofdæg*, f), Alfstanus *Clac* c975 (ODa *Klak*), Osgot *Sveyn* 1045 (ON *Sveinn*). Although, at this date, these were not hereditary surnames, they anticipate the modern *Cobbold*, *Brightmore*, *Loveday*, *Clack* and *Swayne*.

The general opinion is that such surnames are due to the dropping of *filius*. Tengvik has noted five instances which seem to support this view: Osbern *Hauoc*, Osbern *filius Hauoc*; Rainaldus *Croc*, Rainaldus *filius Croc*; in which two of the personal-names (*Hauoc* and *Dudde*) are Old English, two (*Baderon* and *Clamahoc*) Breton, and so introduced by Normans, and one (*Croc*) Scandinavian, though the christian name *Rainaldus* suggests a possible Norman origin.

It is difficult to believe in this 'dropping of *filius*' theory. A name of the type *Johannes filius Willelmi* was never used in everyday life by either Englishmen, Frenchmen or Scandinavians. It is Latin and a

97

documentary form. Where the font-name is French, it might possibly be a translation of Fitzwilliam, though such names are unknown in France and rare in English sources. If the font-name is English, *filius Dudde* might be a translation of *Duddesunu*, but it is unlikely that one-sixth of the Suffolk peasants of c1095 bore such names. There seems no alternative to regarding these forms as scribal descriptions. Walter Dudde was known to be the son of Dudda and he was so described in writing, in the clerk's Latin, *filius Dudde*. But in ordinary conversation, when his full name was needed, he was called Walter Dudde.

The origin of surnames of this type cannot, at present, be definitely decided. The majority of such names are not, as Smith states, from personal-names of Scandinavian origin. There are numerous examples from English and French personal-names and a smaller number from Celtic. Scandinavian influence may be partly responsible, especially in the Danelaw. The type does not become common in England until after the Conquest and we may be concerned with a French custom introduced by the Normans. Similar names are found in northern France in the tenth century and in the south and south-west in the previous century. The fact that similar formations from Old English personal-names are common in the south of England in the late thirteenth and the fourteenth centuries, and in eleventh-century Suffolk, suggests an independent formation in English. The frequency of the type may be due to all three influences, combined with its simplicity for everyday use and the analogy of similar simple attributes in the form of nicknames and occupation-names. It is noteworthy that such surnames from very common christian names like William and John are late formations.

OLD ENGLISH PERSONAL-NAMES

As hereditary surnames are not found in England before the Conquest, our chief interest is in those personal-names which continued in use after 1066 and gave rise to numerous patronymics and metronymics. Many of these are well-evidenced in OE sources and provide no difficulties apart from changes in form and pronunciation. For others, we have no direct evidence; they are not on record in OE; some can be paralleled in place-names, whilst for our knowledge of others we are dependent entirely on the forms of surnames and personal-names found only in ME documents and the correct interpretation of these is impossible without some knowledge of our pre-Conquest nomenclature. We are not concerned with the whole history of OE names; in fact, that cannot yet be written, for we know very little of the names in use in the first phase of the Anglo-Saxon conquest, whilst the material for their final decline and supersession by the new names brought over from France still awaits collection and treatment. A further difficulty is that the names recorded in OE are almost entirely those of the upper classes, whilst after the Conquest the old names lingered on only among the peasants.

OE personal-names are of two types: compound names formed from two distinct elements, as *Ælfrǣd* 'elf-counsel', *Sǣbeorht* 'sea-bright', *Wulfwīg* 'wolf-war', and simple names like *Bēda* and *Dudda* which are themselves of two types, *Gōda* and *Tunna*, short forms of such compounds as *Gōdwine* and *Tūnrǣd*, whilst others are from adjectives, *Brēme* 'famous', *Swēta* 'sweet', or names of animals, *Hengest* 'stallion', *Eofor* 'boar'.[1]

Originally, OE compound names had a meaning, *Ēadmund* 'prosperity-protector', *Sigerīc* 'victory-powerful', but the Anglo-Saxon system of indicating relationship by giving a child a name beginning with one or other element of his father's name, or by combining one element from the father's name with one from the mother's, soon resulted in meaningless compounds, e.g. *Hereswīþ* 'army-mighty' was the name given in the seventh century to their daughter by *Hererīc* 'army-ruler', nephew of King Edwin of Northumbria, and his wife *Breguswīþ* 'ruler-mighty'. According to his biographer, St Wulfstan, Bishop of Worcester 1062–95, who was born c1012, was given a name compounded of the first theme of his mother's name, *Wulfgifu* 'wolf-gift', and the second theme of his father's, *Æðelstān* 'noble-stone'. Their son's name, *Wulfstān* 'wolf-stone', had no more meaning as a name than had the names of his parents. Their sole concern was to give their son a name which would indicate his parentage. They were no more concerned with the meaning of the name than were those who called their children *Friðuwulf* 'peace-wolf' or *Wīgfrīþ* 'war-peace'. Hence, though it is customary, it is misleading to give the literal meaning of the name unless it is made quite clear that such names had become stereotyped and were given without any thought of the meaning.

[1] Except for *Tūnrǣd*, *Hengest* and *Eofor*, these survive as surnames: *Alfred, Alured; Seabridge, Seabright; Woolway, Beed, Dodd, Good, Tunn, Bream* and *Sweet.*

One other type of personal-name, that ending in *-ing*, is of importance, e.g. *Billing, Hearding, Lutting*. The suffix was originally used to indicate parentage, *Ida* (*wæs*) *Eopping*, Ida was the son of Eoppa, but it was purely descriptive and was not used as a surname. It was common in the plural in early place-names, as in Godmanham (ERY), recorded as *Godmundingaham* in 730, 'the village of Godmund's people', and also independently as a name. Most of these were probably original patronymics which had become a kind of byname, later used as an independent name. The son of a man called both *Dēorwulf* and *Dēora* was Wulfstan *Dēoring*, a patronymic which might well be associated with the adjective *dēor* 'brave, bold'. It was then regarded as a parallel to OE *dēorling* 'darling', *flīeming* 'fugitive', etc., and used as an independent name. A number of such names survive as surnames, *Dearing* (OE *Dēoring*), *Darling* (OE *Dēorling*), *Harding* (OE *Hearding*), etc., with others from unrecorded personal-names. In ME the suffix appears to have been used widely with a more general meaning and is found in a considerable number of obsolete surnames which still await collection and treatment.

Unrecorded personal-names in surnames

As with place-names, surnames are producing evidence of personal-names unrecorded in OE. For example, the existence of the OE **Pæcc, *Pæcci* or **Pæcca* postulated to explain a series of place-names including Patching, Paxford, Patchill and Packsfield in counties as far apart as Devon, Sussex and Essex, is confirmed when we find a woman named *Pacchild* living in Essex in 1166. In an Essex document of 1198, too, we find the sole evidence for OE **Hæfer* as a personal-name, long accepted as that contained in Havering-atte-Bower (Ess), Haveringland (Nf), Haversham and Hearndon Wood (Bk).

The modern surnames *Wackrill* and *Wakerel* derive from an OE **Wæcerhild* (f), 'watchful-war', first recorded c1130 in London as *Wakerilda*, in 1185 in Kent as *Wekerild*, in Middlesex in 1211, in Sussex in 1229, and, as a surname, thrice in Suffolk in 1188. Similarly, OE **Rædwīg* 'counsel-warrior', now *Redway*, is on record as a personal-name in Lincolnshire in 1165 and 1169 and in Worcestershire in 1185, in which county it had become a surname by 1221, Gilebertus *Redwy*. OE **Rimhild* (f) 'border-war', now *Rimell*, is found in Somerset, Hampshire, Norfolk and Shropshire as a personal-name between

1201 and 1209 and as a surname in Shropshire in 1219, Richard *Rimild* (SaG), in Worcestershire in 1327 and in Warwickshire in 1332. Numerous other examples could be cited, including previously unknown compounds, additional examples of personal-names recorded only once or twice in OE and the reappearance of OE names last recorded 200 to 300 years before the Conquest, including the famous name *Beowulf* which is found as *Beulfus* 1086 DB (Do), *Bowulfus* de Rugeberge 1196 P (D), and, as a surname, William *Bewolf* 1296 SRSx, William *Bewoulf* 1297 MinAcctCo.[1]

The post-conquest survival and decline of OE personal-names

Our knowledge of OE personal-names is both limited and abundant. We are dependent on the surviving literature and on the lists of witnesses to charters which are not only rare for the period before 750 but are very unevenly distributed over the country, most of them relating to Wessex and southern Mercia. In addition, we know little of the names common among the lower classes. Many names in use during the period of the migration disappeared within a few generations. Apart from this, up to about 900 there was little change in the character of the names used. From the tenth century there is a marked difference. Uncompounded names became rare, the compound names in use tended to become stereotyped and by the end of the century we find a distinct preference for a limited number of some 12 stems, particularly names in *Ælf-*, *Æðel-*, *Ead-*, *God-*, *Lēof-*, *Sige-* and *Wulf-*, all of which are well represented among modern surnames. But in an eleventh-century list of peasant names at Hatfield (Herts) we find short names for both men and women, *Dudda*, *Brada* and *Wine* (m), *Tate*, *Dudde*, *Lulle* and *Dunne* (f), side by side with the common *Ælfstān*, *Wulflāf* and *Wulfsige* and such names as the unique *Dryhtlāf*, with *Tilewine* and *Cēolmund*, once common but rarely found after the ninth century, and the feminine *Hereðrÿð*, of which the only other example is from the seventh century. There is no parallel to these Hatfield short names elsewhere. Among the 200 or so Suffolk freemen named in DB, we find only compound names, with a marked preference for stems in *Lēof-*, *God-* and *Wulf-*, the

---

[1] *v.* further, Olof von Feilitzen, 'Some unrecorded Old and Middle English Personal Names' (*Namn och Bygd*, vol. 33 (1945), pp. 69–98); P. H. Reaney, 'Notes on the Survival of Old English Personal Names in Middle English' (*Studier i modern språkvetenskap*, vol. XVIII (1953), pp. 84–112).

same name occurring more than once in the same village, so that the clerk was driven to differentiate by writing *et alter Godwine* 'and another Godwine'. Except for these peasant names DB records only the names of the upper, land-holding classes, thus giving an incomplete and one-sided picture, but among these names are 82 not recorded before the Conquest, of which 35 are found only in Norfolk, Suffolk and Essex. There is clear evidence, too, of the persistence of the ancient system of indicating family relationship by variation and repetition: *Beorht*wine was the son of *Beorht*mund and brother of *Beorht*nōð; Wulf*weard* was succeeded by his son Ēad*weard*.[1]

After the Conquest the new names brought over from the Continent by the Normans revolutionised the personal nomenclature of the country. It became fashionable for Englishmen to give their children French names, and by 1200 this practice was being followed by the peasants. At Winchester in 1066, one in twelve of the burgesses bore a French name, but these may have been French merchants and traders who had settled in the city. By 1115, however, we have clear evidence that men of English name and race had begun to give French names to their children: Willelmus filius Estmer (OE *Eastmǣr*), Radulfus filius Burewold (OE *Burhweald*), Robertus frater Goda. In 1148 all the children named bore French names whether their fathers had English, Scandinavian or French names. At King's Lynn in 1166 the process was less advanced. Of 17 fathers with Scandinavian names and 18 with English names, only half followed the new fashion.

There is reason to believe that Old English names survived longer in the provinces than in the capital where the fashion set by Normans would be followed more quickly. Old English names in London were often those of immigrants from the provinces. The old names were superseded by names introduced by the Normans, and many of those with French names in the first two or three decades of the twelfth century must have been Normans by birth. Those with English names at the same time were as a rule of English descent, as, probably, were those with English names later in the century. But it does not follow that a French name necessarily denotes French descent. As early as c1100 it was quite common for English people to give French names to their children, whilst there are only a few examples of sons or daughters of parents with French names being given English

---

[1] *v.* Olof von Feilitzen, *The Pre-Conquest Personal Names of Domesday Book* (Uppsala, 1937), pp. 31–2.

names. The earliest instances are found among the upper classes, both the clergy and patrician families. Some Englishmen with French names must have been born c1090 or earlier. After 1100 it became a fashion for English families to give French names to their children. Some families were more conservative than others and continued to use the old names. Some gave French names to one or more of their children and English names to another or others. Thus, in a very few generations the Old English christian names were altogether disused in London, apart from a few special names, Alfred, Edmund, Edward and Godwin. Edmund is frequent in London between 1250 and 1350, but Edward occurs only occasionally. Edward I does not seem to have been popular in London and the few Edwards were probably named after the saint, Edward the Confessor. It is unlikely, therefore, that the popularity of Edmund was due to Edmund, son of Henry III. Some, at least, of the London Edmunds came from East Anglia: Edmund de Suffolk 1309, Edmund de Bery 1346 (Bury St Edmunds), and others from places in Norfolk. These Edmunds were, no doubt, named after St Edmund, the martyr-king of East Anglia and founder of the monastery of St Edmundsbury, to whom a London church is dedicated.[1] In the three London Subsidy Rolls for 1292, 1319 and 1332, out of a total of 4,297 persons assessed only 36 bore English christian names, sharing 15 names among them. There are 42 English patronymics borne by 62 persons.

Even among the peasants, this fashion for adopting French names began early. Evidence is scanty and difficult to find, but already by about 1100 we find Suffolk peasants with French names. These Bury peasants must have been of native birth; their names were overwhelmingly English or Scandinavian, but some 34 out of over 600 bore such names as Robert (7), Ralph (3), Fulcher (2), Baldwin, Warin, Durand, Hugo, Hubert, Richard, Walter and William, but the persistence with which they clung to old habits and old names is proved by the large number of English and Scandinavian names still borne by the peasants on the Bishop of Ely's manors in Norfolk, Suffolk and Cambridgeshire in the survey of 1277 (*Ely*).

Occasional pedigrees put forward to support or resist a claim that a man was a villein shed some light on the names used by peasants in the twelfth century.[2] In all, there are eight of these which go back

---

[1] *v.* E. Ekwall, *Early London Personal Names* (Lund, 1947), pp. 87–100.
[2] H. M. Cam, *Liberties and Communities in Medieval England* (Cambridge, 1944), pp. 124–35.

three or four generations from 1206. It is impossible to go into details here. They have been fully discussed elsewhere.[1] The clearest way to show their real value is to reproduce the most important pedigrees with essential comments and then to summarise the whole. They come from Essex and Hertfordshire (1205), Suffolk (1206, 1214), Norfolk, Sussex, Bedfordshire and Cambridgeshire (1206).

The latest, from Suffolk, goes back four generations from 1214, giving the descent from Sirich (c1094), through his direct descendants Sired, Eillive and Salerna to Maud (1214). Here we have the repetition of the first theme in the names of father and son, *Sigerīc* and *Sigerǣd*, whose daughter Æðelgifu had a daughter and a granddaughter with French names. This repetition occurs also in other pedigrees, e.g. in Hertfordshire, Segar c1175 (OE *Sǣgār*) had a brother Seiet (OE *Sǣgēat*) and an uncle Seman (OE *Sǣmann*).

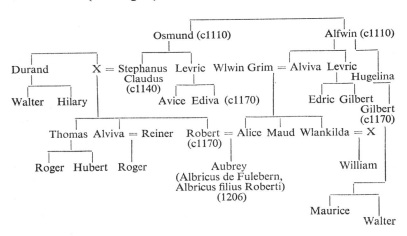

The most interesting name here is the otherwise unknown **Wlanchild* (f), *Wlankilda* filia Wlwini Grim, identical with (Willelmus filius) *Wlankilde*, which is found also as a surname in the neighbouring county of Suffolk, Warin *Wlankild* 1277 *Ely*. The second theme is *-hild*, common in women's names, the first is OE *wlanc* 'proud', found as a personal-name **Wlanc* in Longslow (Sa), thus confirming the existence of this name postulated by Ekwall. Two other compounds are found in late OE, *Wlancheard*, a moneyer in the reign of Ethelbert, and *Wlancþegn*, a moneyer *temp.* Cnut (Searle). The

---

[1] P. H. Reaney, 'Pedigrees of Villeins and Freemen' (*Notes & Queries*, vol. 197 (1952), pp. 222–5).

mutated *Wlenca* is found in Linchmere (Sx) and possibly in Lancing (Sx). *Wlencing* occurs in the AS Chronicle as one of the sons of Ælle and the founder of the South Saxon kingdom.

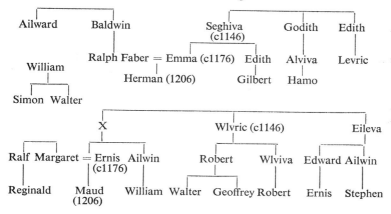

All the OE names in these eight pedigrees except *Osbert*, **Wlanchild* and **Wealdwine* are well known and well documented. All the men's names survive as modern surnames,[1] but of the women's names, only *Æðelgifu* (Ayliffe) and *Wulfgifu* (Wolvey). The number of persons bearing the name is given in brackets:

Old English: *masculine*: Ælfwine, Æðelweard, Æðelwine (2), Alwin, Ēadrīc, Ēadweard (3), Godwine (4), Lēofgēat, Lēofrīc (3), Ōsbeorht (2), Ōsmund, Sǣgār, Sǣgēat, Sǣmann, Sigerǣd, Sigerīc, **Wealdwine, Wulfrīc. 18 names, 27 persons.

feminine: Ælfgifu (3), Æðelgifu, Ēadgifu, Ēadgyð (2), Ealdgifu (2), Ealdgyð, Godgyð, Sǣgifu, **Wlanchild, Wulfgifu. 10 names, 14 persons.

Scandinavian: *masculine*: Anketillus, Broðor.[2] 2 names, 2 persons.

French: *masculine*: Adam (3), Aubrey (2), Alexander, Baldwin, Brian, Durand, Ernis (OFr *Erneis*) (2), Geoffrey (3), Gilbert (3), Hamo (2), Henry (3), Herman, Hilary, Hubert, Hugh, John (4), Jordan, Maurice, Michael, Peter, Ralph (5), Reynold, Reiner, Richard, Robert (5), Roger (3), Simon (2), Stephen (2), Thomas (2), Walter (4), Werric (OG *Werric*, OFr *Guerri*), William (7). 32 names, 68 persons.

---

[1] Alven, Alwin; Allward, Aylward; Alven, Alwin, Aylwin; Edrich; Edward, Ewart; Godwin, Goodwin; Levet; Leverage, Loveridge; Osmond, Sagar, Sait, Seaman, Sired, Search, Walwin, Woolrich.

[2] Modern Anketell, Ankill, Antell and Brothers.

feminine: Alicia or Aleis (4), Avice, Cristiana, Emma (2), Hawis (OG *Hadewidis*, OFr *Haueis*), Hugelina, Lecia, Margaret, Maud (Matilda, Matillis) (3), Salerna. 10 names, 16 persons.

Thus, from these twelfth-century peasant pedigrees from seven counties from Bedfordshire south to Sussex, it would appear that OE personal-names were being replaced by names of French origin, but some families were more conservative than others. The variety of personal-names used, both English and French, is noteworthy. On the whole, OE women's names show a stronger tendency to persist than those of men. The general picture is clearly revealed by this summary:

Generation	1st	2nd	3rd	4th	5th	Total
OE	15	19	6	1	0	41
Fr	5	26	41	8	1	81

When we turn to the early fourteenth-century Subsidy Rolls we find an overwhelming preponderance of French personal-names, English names seldom reaching 2 per cent and this only when two or three names were particularly popular. In Somerset, for example, where, in 1327, 124 persons shared 15 OE personal-names, 50 of these were named Edith, 41 Edward and 12 Edmund. In Worcestershire in 1275, 22 OE names were shared by 160 persons, including Osbert 49, Alfred 26, Edith 39 and Aldith 15. In Cambridgeshire, in 1327, Edmund accounted for 31 of the 54 persons who bore among them 19 OE personal-names, whilst in Suffolk the popularity of Edmund was even greater, 115 out of 207 being named after the martyr-king whose name survives in the title of the Bishop of St Edmundsbury and Ipswich and in Bury St Edmunds. Of the rest, who shared 15 different names, 59 answered to Seman. In six other counties, Lancashire, Yorkshire, Shropshire, Warwickshire, Surrey and Sussex, out of a total of 31,255 persons assessed, only 133 bore English christian names, sharing 48 different names among them. It would be interesting, and possibly instructive, to know the reason for this local partiality for certain names, especially as we shall find similar variations in the distribution of French personal-names. In these same rolls, we find, too, that surnames from English personal-names were only a small proportion of the whole, reaching 3·5 per cent in Worcestershire and Cambridgeshire, and 5·5 in Suffolk. The great majority of these are from personal-names no longer in use, thus confirming the decline of the native names and suggesting that these surnames had already become established family names.

The following table throws some light on the gradual disappearance of native names and emphasises the variation among different classes and in different places:

Source	Date	Total Names	OE	Personal-names Scandinavian	French
Winchester[1]	1066	243	173	6	20
	1115	274	85	18[2]	167
	1148	855	147	79[2]	596
Bury St Edmunds[3]	c1095	823	696	75	34
King's Lynn[4]	1166	214	81	50	83
Newark[5]	c1175	365	64	43	167

SURNAMES FROM OLD ENGLISH PERSONAL-NAMES

A complete list of all the modern surnames derived from OE personal-names would require a miniature dictionary, with others for surnames of Scandinavian and French origin. For this we cannot find space nor is it really necessary for in my *Dictionary of British Surnames* (pp. xxi–xxvi) will be found a list of OE personal-names surviving in modern surnames: monothematic 77, derivatives in *-ing* 42, dithematic 275, a total of 394, to which should be added *Hunting* (Hunting), **Spyrling* (Sperling) and *Ōsmund* (Osmond), with others for which evidence has since been discovered and which will be discussed below and a number of modern surnames which look as if they belong here but are as yet undocumented. In addition, there are, of course, large numbers of similar surnames now apparently obsolete, though some of them remained in use for centuries.

Dithematic names

Of the dithematic names, the most common to survive are those compounded with *Ælf-*, *Æðel-*, *Beorht-* (once much more frequent), *Ēad-*, *God-*, *Lēof-*, *Sǣ-* and *Wulf-*. Many of these cannot be recognised without some knowledge of the changes they underwent in ME. *Beorht-*, e.g. often became *Briht-*: *Beorhtgifu* (f), Berriff and Brightiff;

[1] Liber Winton (Burgesses).
[2] Probably Norman.
[3] Peasants. *Feudal Book of Abbot Baldwin* (Bury). The large number of names is due to the inclusion of those of both father and son in, e.g. *Lefstan Ulfuini filius*.
[4] Pipe Roll (Burgesses).
[5] Survey (Thoroton Soc., Rec. Ser., XVI, 1955). Townsmen.

Beorhtsige, Brixey; *Beorhtmann*, Brightman. *Ēad-* may become *Ed-* or *Ad-*, *Ēadgār*, Edgar, *Ēadmǣr*, Admer, and, with assimilation of consonants, *Ēadrǣd*, Errett, *Ēadstān*, Aston or Easton. In ME, *Lēof-* is often found as *Lev-*, *Liv-* or *Lov-* and gives a variety of modern forms: *Lēofgōd*, Lovegood, *Lēofrīc*, Leverich, Leverick, Loveridge; *Lēofwine*, Levin, Lewin, Livens, Lowin; *Lēofsige*, Lewsey, Livsey, Lovecy; *Lēofweard*, Livard, Luard. The modern form of *Wulf-* is usually *Woll-* or *Wooll-*, occasionally *Wolv-*, with various developments: *Wulfgēat*, Woolvett, Woolfit, Woollatt, Wollett, Woffitt, Ullyatt, Ulliott, Ullett; *Wulfrīc*, Woolrich, Wooldridge, Wolridge, Wolveridge, Woolwright; *Wulfsige*, Woolsey, Wolsey, Woosey; *Wulfweard*, Woolward, Woollard, Wolfarth.

In DB the OE themes *Ælf-*, *Æðel-*, *Eald-* and *Ealh-* were frequently reduced to *Æl-*, *Al-* or *El-*, whilst *Æðel-*, among other forms, appears as *Athel-*, *Adel-*, *Ade-*, *Ægel-*, *Ail-*, *Eil-*, *Al-* and *El-*. Unless, therefore, we have clear and unimpeachable forms, it is impossible to establish a definite etymology. Both *Aylmer* and *Elmer* are from OE *Æðelmǣr*, DB *Ailmer*, *Elmer* and *Aylward* from OE *Æðelweard*, but *Ailwardus grossus* and *Ailward judex* occur also as *Alfward* and *Ælward* (c1116 ELPN), forms which would normally be derived from OE *Ælfweard*, DB *Æluuard*, now *Allward*, *Elward*. At times, the ultimate etymology is made clear by alternative forms: *Alnodus* or *Ailnoð ingeniator* 1177 P, William *Aylnoth*, *Alnoth* 13th Lewes, undoubtedly from OE *Æðelnoð*, although some forms, taken alone, might point to OE *Ælfnoð*, **Ealdnoð* or **Ealhnoð*. As late as 1542 (*Petre*) the surname appears as William *Aylenouth*. Its modern forms are *Allnatt*, *Allnutt*, *Alner*, *Elnaugh* and *Elnough*. Similar problems arise with such names as *Aldred* and *Eldred*, *Aldrich*, *Aldridge*, *Eldredge* and *Oldridge*, *Alflatt* and *Elfleet*.[1]

Occasionally the fuller form survives: *Athelstan*, *Addlestone*, *Ethelston*, *Edleston* (OE *Æðelstān*). The DB *Aethericus* is for OE *Æðelrīc* and is now *Athridge*, *Atteridge*, *Attridge*, *Etheredge*, *Ethridge* and *Etridge* (Jacobus *Atteriche* 1276 RH (Berks), Richard *Etheriche* 1334 SRK).

Of the less common names, some with an unexpected development, we may note: *Brummer* (OE **Brūnmǣr* 'brown-famous', first noted in DB); *Burrage*, *Burridge* (OE *Burgrīc* 'fortress-powerful'); *Culf* (OE *Cūðwulf* 'famous-wolf', found as both *Cudulf* and *Cuulf* in

---

[1] For forms and discussion and for similar names, *v.* P. H. Reaney, *A Dictionary of British Surnames* (London, 1961).

DB); *Denbow, Dembow* (OE **Denebeald*); *Earwicker, Erricker* (OE *Eoforwacer* 'boar-watchman'); *Alsey, Elsey, Elsie* (OE *Ælfsige* 'elf-victory'); *Goodlake, Goodluck, Gullick, Cutlack* (OE *Gūðlāc* 'battle-play'); *Outright, Utteridge* (Johannes filius *Vghtrith* 1332 SRLa, Robert *Outright* 1327 SRSo; OE **Ūhtrīc* 'dawn-powerful'); *Redwin* (OE *Rǣdwine* 'counsel-friend'); *Siffleet* (OE *Sigeflǣd* (f) 'victory-beauty'); *Stanhill, Stonnill* (OE **Stānhild* (f) 'stone-war'). *Saywell*, which has been taken for a phrase-name, is a late development of *Sewell*: John *Saywell* or *Sewell* 1526 LP.

Some OE names have been influenced by Anglo-Norman pro-nunciation, e.g. *Alger, Aljer, Auger*, from OE *Ealhhere* 'temple-army', which became *Alcher, Aucher* and *Auger*. OE *Ælfhēah* 'elf-high' has become *Elfick, Elphick, Elvidge* and *Elvish* and, from a common Norman form, *Alphege*.

In the Parish Register of Staplehurst (K) we find three women named *Godleve* (1545–6), two named *Godlif* (1549) and one *Goodly* jaket (1554), a christian name identical with the OE **Godleofu* (f) 'good- or god-dear' which has given us the modern surnames of *Goodliff* and the less common *Godlove*. It is found as *Godelief* in Kent in 1197 and long survived in the county, *Godeleve* Gretys 1334 SRK, *Godlefe* 1508, and in the form *Goodlief* was the name of the wife of the Host of Chaucer's pilgrims.[1] It is probably also the origin of the christian name *Godly* which Bardsley records four times between 1579 and 1632 and found so objectionable.[2] The Staplehurst examples show that *Goodly* was the colloquial pronunciation of *Godleve* which could also become *Godly*. A similar development turned *good-wife* into *goody* and *huswife* into *hussey* (cf. Goody or Goodwyff Wilkes 1559 NED), both of which are found as surnames, Nota *Godwyf* 1311 ColchCt, *Husewyf* 1317 AssK, Rose *Husewif* 1192 P, now *Goodey* and *Hussey*. Both *Godley* and *Goodley* are usually local, but may well derive also from this sixteenth-century pronunciation which can be paralleled in other names. OE *Godgifu* (f) 'god- or good-gift' survives as *Goodeve* and *Goodiff* and probably also as *Goodey*. OE *Æðelðrȳð* 'noble-strength' is still common as the christian name and surname *Audrey* (whence *tawdrey*, from the showy but cheap necklaces sold at St Audrey's fair); OE **Bealdgȳð* (f) 'bold-combat' is now *Baldey*, OE *Wulfgifu* (f) 'wolf-gift' is one origin of *Wolvey* and *Wulffrīð* (f)

---

[1] As a surname, John *Godlyewe* 1334 SRK.

[2] C. W. Bardsley, *Curiosities of Puritan Nomenclature* (London, 1888), pp. 152–3.

'wolf-peace', Emelia *Woolfrey* 1664 HTSf, now survives as *Wolfryd*, *Woolfrey* and *Woolfries*.

Of the previously unrecorded names, we may note *Bucstān and *Pīkstān. The former is now *Buckstone* or *Buxton*, both of which may be local in origin, from Buxton (Db, Nf), but the distribution and frequency of the surname, regularly in the singular and without sign of a preposition suggest derivation from a personal-name. *Bucstān is a combination of OE *Bucca* and the common theme *-stān*. Or we may have an OE *Burgstān, with early loss of *r* as in *Burgheard*, now *Burchard*, *Burkett*, *Buchard*, *Burkard*, *Butchart* and *Buckett*. For *Pickstone* and *Pixton* no topographical origin seems possible. The name has been noted in some six counties, always without qualification, and is a compound of OE *Pīca, found in Picton (Ch, NRY) and Pickworth (L, R). It is the simplex from which was formed the recorded diminutive *Piichel*, found in Picklescott (Sa).

Monothematic names

It is a simple—and a dangerous—solution of the problem to assume that such names as *Cock* and *Hudd* are survivals of OE personal-names. The former appears as a personal-name in the twelfth and thirteenth centuries, but the surname is also clearly both local and a nickname, whilst *Hudd* is not from OE *Hudda* but from a pet-form of Hugh or Richard. What we need is clear evidence of the post-Conquest survival of the OE personal-name. OE *Botta*, for example, survives in *Botte* Buny 1222 and from this come both *Bott*, *Botson* and also *Botting* (OE *Botting 'son of *Botta*'). Similarly, OE **Butt(a)*, unrecorded but found in such place-names as Butsash (Ha) and Butley (Ch, Sf), was certainly in use in the eleventh and twelfth centuries (c1090–1170). It survives in *Butson* and formerly in (Richard) *Buttyng* 'son of *Butt*' (1327 SRSo) and is one source of *Butt* or *Butts* which is also clearly a nickname from ME *butt* 'thicker end, stump', probably used of a thickset person, and local from *atte Buttys*, from ME *butt* 'a mark for shooting', archery butts.

OE *Budda* 'beetle' is not recorded in independent use after the Conquest, and *Budd* is undoubtedly, at times, a nickname, Walter *le Bud* 1249 AssW. But *Budding* survives, and we have surnames like *Budecok* and *Budekin*, both regularly formed diminutives of a personal-name, so that *Budda* may also be the origin of *Budd* and of *Buddy* 'servant of *Budd*'.

110

Among the personal-names in use after the Conquest, we may note *Ceadda* (Chadd), *Creoda* (Creed), *Dodda* (Dodd) and *Pymma* (Pimm). Some colour-names also belong here occasionally, *Brown* (OE *Brūn*) and *White* (OE *Hwīta*), as do *Bishop, Knight* and *King*, all found as personal-names both before and after the Conquest. Of the previously unrecorded names, we may note *Bly* (OE **Blīða* 'gentle, merry'), *Glew* (OE **Glēaw* 'wise, prudent'), *Green* (OE **Grēne*), *Huck* (OE **Ucca*, a pet-form of *Ūhtrǣd*) with *Hug* (**Ugga*, a variant of **Ucca*: *Uctredus* pater Henrici et *Ugge* avus suus 1212 Cur).

Derivatives in -ing

Derivatives in *-ing* include some well-known names: *Browning* (OE *Brūning*, a derivative of *Brūn*, not uncommon from 1086 to the fourteenth century); *Downing* (OE *Dūning* 'son of *Dūn*') and *Dunning* (OE *Dunning* 'son of *Dunn*' or 'the dark, swarthy one'); *Golding, Manning* and *Whiting* (OE *Hwīting* 'son of *Hwīta*' or 'the fair one'). OE *Lēofing, Lȳfing* 'son of *Lēofa*' 'beloved' is now *Levings, Lewing, Liveing, Loving* and *Lowing*. From names not recorded before DB, we have *Fowling* (OE **Fugeling* 'son of *Fugol*' 'fowl', used as a personal-name), *Ravening* (OE **Hrǣfning* 'son of *Hrǣfn*' 'raven') and *Utting* ('son of *Utta*'). *Lucking* is from OE **Lēofecing* 'son of *Lēofeca*', a diminutive of *Lēofa* and *Lovering* from OE **Lēofhering*, **Lēofring* 'son of *Lēofhere*' 'beloved-army'.

Three names of mythological interest

Modern surnames preserve the names of Anglo-Saxon kings, earls, bishops and saints. But these were common personal-names. Some parents may have named their children in honour of some famous king or revered bishop or saint, but no proof is forthcoming. There are, however, three names of heroes whose mythological exploits were the subject of heroic legend and poems widely known and long remembered, 'the vain songs of ancestral heathendom', often passed on by oral tradition, though written versions may have been known to Alfred the Great. Our knowledge of all this comes from casual references which make it clear that some, at least, of these stories and certainly the names of their heroes had not been completely forgotten by Englishmen in the years following the Conquest.[1]

[1] *v.* R. M. Wilson, *The Lost Literature of Medieval England* (London, 1952), pp. 1–26.

The modern surnames which suggest a memory of these tales of the dim past are *Unwin*, *Wade* and *Wayland*. All three are susceptible of more than one interpretation and all persisted as English personal-names until the beginning of the fourteenth century. In DB we find *Hunuuinus* in Cambridgeshire and in 1166 in Norfolk, *Hunwine* de Batha, called also *Vnwine*. This is OE *Hūnwine*, found as a surname *Hunwyn(e)* in Cambridgeshire, Suffolk, Essex and Norfolk (1275–1308), now *Hunwin*. In these later examples, the *H* may be inorganic. Forms without the *H* are much more common and some may be from OE *unwine* 'unfriend, enemy', e.g. Walter *þonwyne* 1275 SRWo, clearly a nickname. As a personal-name OE *Unwine* (now *Unwin*) is found in Huntingdonshire, Worcestershire, Essex and Lancashire in 1188, 1221, 1272 and 1332, and as a surname from 1195, Rannulf *Vnwine* (Nf). In the numerous later examples it is impossible to decide between the personal-name and the nickname, but it is quite clear that the name was in use until 1332.

The story of *Unwen* 'son born beyond hope', with those of Hengest and Horsa, was current so long after the Norman Conquest that it was possible for these heroes to be classed with Waltheof.[1] References to the great Gothic hero, Unwine, are rare. He is probably identical with the Hunuil said to have been the son of Ostrogotha and in *Widsith* appears only as the son of Eastgota which suggests he was known as the hero of some story but no other mention of him is to be found before the fourteenth century. In the *Fasciculus Morum*, written perhaps before 1340, he appears 'in Elfland, where now, so they say, remain those strenuous warriors Unewyn and Wade'. He is mentioned in the alliterative *Morte Arthure*, and possibly appears with Attila in the shorter fifteenth century Latin version of the romance of *Waldef*:

At that time [i.e. after Arthur] there reigned in Norfolk a certain king called Attalus. In Suffolk ruled Unwyn, king of Thetford, who fought in single combat against Attalus. But the two were reconciled without the intervention of a mediator.

'Nowhere have we any hint of the deeds by which Unwine won his fame, unless perhaps the last reference preserves a dim remembrance of a single combat between Attila the Hun and Unwine the Gothic champion, both now shrunk to petty East Anglian kings. Yet for his name and fame to have lasted so long he must have been an important figure in Anglo-Saxon legend.'[2]

[1] R. W. Chambers, *Widsith* (Cambridge, 1912), p. 254.
[2] R. M. Wilson, op. cit., p. 9.

Wade is sometimes of local origin, Ordmar *de la Wade* 1188 P
(Nf), 'dweller by the ford' (OE *(ge)wæd*). As a personal-name, OE
Wada, from *wadan* 'to go' or OG *Wado*, occurs thrice in DB (He, Do,
So), and in Shropshire, Leicestershire, Suffolk, Bedfordshire and
Cornwall from 1176 to 1297. As a surname it is found in Essex,
Bedfordshire, Suffolk, Cheshire and Sussex from 1166. The persistence of the personal-name may be due, in part, to the tale of Wade,
originally a sea-giant, dreaded and honoured by the coast tribes of
the North Sea and the Baltic. 'In England the memory of Wade lived
longer than that of any of the old heroes of song, Weland only
excepted.'[1] The only reference to him in OE occurs in *Widsith*, 'Wada
ruled the Hælsings', and the first story concerning him appears in
the *De nugis curialium*, where he is connected with legends of Offa of
Mercia.

'A certain Gado, the son of a king of the Vandals, from love of adventure
left his home as a boy and wandered through the world redressing wrongs.
At last he comes to the court of King Offa who has just married the
daughter of the Roman emperor. On their return home the Roman guests
urge an attack on Offa, but the Romans are deterred by fear of his friend
Gado. But when Gado has been called off to the Indies the Romans send
a mighty army and refuse all Offa's terms of peace. In the meantime Gado,
having completed his task, is returning home when his ship, against his
will, carries him to Colchester. He greets Offa and, accompanied by a
hundred chosen knights, goes to the headquarters of the Romans in an
attempt to make peace but is repulsed. Thereupon he arrays the English
forces, placing Offa with the main body in the market-place of the town,
Offa's nephew Suanus with 500 men at one gate, and himself with 100 men
at the other. The Romans avoid Gado and concentrate their attacks on
Suanus who, at the third assault, appeals for help. Gado refuses, but as
Suanus prepares for the next attack commands him to fall back. The
enemy rush in and are met by Offa in the market-place, whilst their retreat
is cut off by Gado. A great slaughter of the Romans follows until quarter is
offered to the survivors, who return to Rome with their dead. It is improbable that much of the original Wade remains in this very much
romanticized story, though the boat which brings him to England against
his will is obviously the magic boat of which we hear later.'[2]

Among several medieval references to the tale, Chaucer, in the
Merchant's Tale (E 1424), has a reference to Wade's boat, the point
of which is not clear, whilst in *Troilus and Criseyde* (iii, 614) Pandarus
tells a tale of Wade:

'He song; she pleyde; he tolde tale of Wade.'

[1] *v.* R. W. Chambers, op. cit., pp. 95–100.
[2] R. M. Wilson, op. cit., pp. 16–17.

By the Tudor period, the old stories seem to have been forgotten but Speght, in his *Works of Chaucer* (1598), gives us the name of Wade's boat, Guingelot, a detail to be found nowhere else.

'Tales of this hero had flourished in England for almost a thousand years, yet the only one of them which has survived in any detail is that given by Map. And this Latin version probably has little in common with the vernacular stories of the hero which must have been common throughout the Middle Ages.'[1]

The modern *Wayland* or *Weyland* is sometimes of local origin, from Wayland (Nf), but is undoubtedly, probably more commonly, from the OG personal-name *Weland*, found as *Welland* (or *Welandus*) in the Devon DB, and as a personal-name from 1199 to 1318: *Weland* 1199 ClR (L, Sf), *Weilandus* 1185 Templars (So), *Welund* son of William the smith of Studley Royal (late 13th PN WRY vii, p. 73, n. 1), *Weyland* le Fevre 1318 Pat (Sf).[2] As a surname it occurs as John *Weland* 1194 CurR (Sf), William *Weiland* 1199 Cur (Ess), Osbert *Weland* 1219 AssY, John *Weylond* 1250 Fees (Sf).

'The two Germanic heroes who remained longest of all in popular legend were undoubtedly Weland and Wada. The first of them long remained famous as one of the greatest of smiths, and, although only allusions to his fame survive from England, his story appears in the Old Norse *Vǫlundarviða* and *Ðiðrekssaga*. The first tells how Weland and his two brothers wed three swan maidens. After seven years Weland's wife leaves him, whereupon he forges seven hundred golden rings one of which, having been stolen by King Nithhad's men, is given to the king's daughter Beaduhild. Weland himself is then captured, taken to the king's palace, hamstrung, and compelled to work in his smithy. After some time he succeeds in enticing there Nithhad's two sons, murders them, and makes jewels and goblets out of their eyes, teeth and skulls. Beaduhild then breaks her ring and brings it to Weland to repair. He violates her, regains his ring and with its aid is enabled to fly away, on his way alighting on the wall of the palace where he proclaims his vengeance.'[3]

In OE literature there is a reference to Weland's fame as a smith in *Beowulf* and to the sword Miming 'the work of Weland' in *Waldere*. In his translation of Boethius, when he comes to the Latin 'Ubi nunc fidelis ossa Fabricii manent', King Alfred perhaps misinterprets the name of the Roman hero and translates, 'Where are now the bones of Weland, or who knows where they be?'[4] The name occurs also in two

[1] R. M. Wilson, op. cit., p. 19.
[2] He had been assaulted by his master William Weyland of Byng and others.
[3] R. M. Wilson, op. cit., pp. 13–14.
[4] Ibid., p. 15.

Anglo-Saxon place-names, *Welandes stocc* (Bk) 903 BCS 603, and in *Welandes smiððan* 955 BCS 908, now Wayland Smith's Cave (Berks).

His fame lived on after the Conquest. Geoffrey of Monmouth refers to cups carved by Guillandus, whilst the hero of *King Horn* receives from Rimenhild a sword made by Weland and the equal of Miming. His fame lasted long in country districts, especially in Berkshire, as is shown by the occasional references of local antiquaries to the story and from its use in Scott's *Kenilworth*. 'Nevertheless the Middle English references show little knowledge of the actual story of Weland. In all probability it had already been forgotten by the time of the Conquest, and his name and fame as a smith were all that survived.'[1] We cannot prove conclusively that these names were actually given in memory of these three mythological heroes, but the cumulative evidence, scattered as it is, suggests that they may have been.

Some additional surnames from OE personal-names

In view of the abundance of material, both printed and in manuscript, which still awaits detailed examination, it is inevitable that from time to time we should find solutions of problems which had previously defeated us. Some few are dealt with below, though the evidence is not always so full and complete as we should like.

Alfille: *Alfilda* 1201 Cur (Sx), John *Alfild* 1309 EAS xxiii, Thomas *Alfyld* 1327 *SR* (Ess). OE *Ælfhild* (f) 'elf-war'.

Bartrick: *Brihtricus* 1066 DB (Sf), *Brictric* 1202 FF (Nf), 1206 Cur (K), Simon *Brightrich* 1317 AssK, John *Brihtric* 1333 ColchCt. OE *Beorhtrīc* 'bright-ruler'.

Brightling: John *Britlyng* 1381 AssC. OE *Beorhtling*; cf. Brightlingsea (PNEss 330).

Deniff, Denniff: William *Deneue* 1327 SRC. OE **Denegifu* (f), unrecorded, but found in Dennington (Sf), DB *Dingifetune*.

Edbro: John *Edboroue* 1479 SxAS 45, Thomas *Edborowh*, William *Edborowe* 1525 SRSx. OE *Ēadburh* (f) 'prosperity-fortress'.

Edgett: Robert *Ejote* 1409, John *Egeott* 1490, John *Egiott* 1534, Richard *Egett* 1541 *Petre* (Ess). OE **Ecggēat* 'weapon-Gēat'.

Elsegod, Elsgood: Margaret, Danyell *Elsegood* 1504 SIA xii, 1524 SRSf. Probably OE **Ealhgod* 'temple-god or -good'.

Elvey, Elvy, Elphee: *Elviva* 1325 Norw Deeds, Thomas *Elveve* 1488, John *Elvew* 1518 CantW. These late forms point clearly to OE *Ælfgifu* (f) 'elf-gift'. Earlier forms point equally clearly to OE *Ælfwīg* 'elf-war'. v. DBS, *s.n. Allvey*.

[1] R. M. Wilson, op. cit., p. 16.

Frewen, Frewin, Frewing, Frowen, Fruen, Fruin: *Freowinus, Freuuinus* 1066 DB (Sf, Ess), *Frewinus* c1150 Gilb (L), 1175 P (Ha), 1185 P (Nth), Richard, Henry *Frewine* 1221 *ElyA*, 1230 P (Ha), John *Froweyn* 1394 LLB H, Edward *Frewinge* 1665 HTO. OE *Frēowine* 'free-friend'. Occasionally we have forms with *Fra-, Frawin* 1192 P (Wa), William *Frawin* 1221 AssWa, from OE *Frēawine* 'ruler-friend', which may appear also as *Frewinus* (PNDB 253).

Frewer: Ærnaldus frater *Freware* 1180 P (Do), Edmunde *Frewer* 1568 SRSf. OE **Frēowaru* (f) 'free-shelter'.

Goldrich: *Goldric* 1086 DB (Ess), *Golricus* de Skegeness' 1218 AssL, Robert *Goldwright* 1500 *ERO*. OE **Goldrīc* 'gold-ruler'.

Hattrick: Claricia *Hatheric* 1275 SRWo, Alice *Haterich* 1332 ib. OE *Heaðurīc* 'war-ruler'.

Kindred: Roger *Kenrede* 1423 *Brabourne*, Wylliam *Kenered* 1524 SRSf. OE *Cēnrǣd* or *Cynerǣd*.

Linney: *Linniue* 1185 Templars (Herts), Alice *Linyeve*, William *Linyive*, Geoffrey *Lyneue* 1279 RH (C), Richard *Lyneve* 1327 SRSf. OE **Lindgifu, *Lindgeofu* (f) 'shield-gift'.

Onyett: Reginald *Honyet*, William *Honiet* 1275 SRWo, Peter *Onyet* 1279 RH (O), John *Oniet* 1327 SRSa, Peter *Honyot* 1327 SRWo. OE **Hūngēat* ' young bear-Gēat'.

Stidolph: John *Stithulf*, Richard *Stidolf* 1313 *Ass* (K). OE *Stīðwulf* 'hard-wolf'.

Wennell: Gilbert, Jacob *Wenyld* 1327 SRSf. OE **Wynhild* (f) 'joy-war'.

Wilfred: *Wilfrei* miles 1055 FeuDu, Robert *Wilfrith* 1275 SRWo. OE *Wilfrīð* 'will-peace'.

Wilmer: William *Wylemer* 1296 SRSx, Simon *Wilmer* 1296 Wak, 1327 SRC. OE **Wilmǣr* 'will-famous'.

Wimmer(s): Johannes *filius Winemeri* 1187 P (K), Richard, Roger *Winemer* 1279 RH (C), John *Wynmer* 1301 SRY. OE **Winemǣr* 'friend-famous'.

Winney, Winny: *Wengeua(m) uidua(m)* 1205 FF (Sf), Emma *Wyneue*, William *Wynyeue* 1327 SRSf, Thomas *Wynnyff* 1479 SIA xii, John *Wenef*, John *Wyny* 1524 SRSf. OE **Wyngeofu* (f) 'joy-gift'. The personal-names *Wenitha, Wennida* 1202 FFK are from OE **Wyngȳð* (f) 'joy-battle'.

Woolfield: Probably a popular etymology from OE *Wulfhild* (f) 'wolf-war', recorded four times in the tenth and eleventh centuries. Though rare, it must have survived the Conquest.

SCANDINAVIAN PERSONAL-NAMES

The Scandinavian Conquest and Settlement

Some 200 years before the Norman Conquest, in 865 A.D., a great Danish army, under a unified command, landed in East Anglia intent on conquest and settlement. In 866 they moved into Northumbria, captured York and ravaged Mercia and East Anglia where in 869 they defeated and killed Edmund, king and future saint. Almost the whole of Eastern England was now in Danish hands.

For nine years the Danish force had acted as a single military unit. In 874 it was divided into two armies, never to be reunited. In 875 Halfdan marched into Yorkshire, which he subdued, and in 876 he divided up the land, which the Danes ploughed and tilled, and the former pirates began to settle down as peaceful agriculturists. The second army, under Guthrum, invaded Wessex, but in 878 was forced to withdraw to Mercia, which was divided into two parts, one Danish, the other English. The ravaging of the south continued until 886 when Alfred the Great made peace with Guthrum and a common boundary was fixed between their territories, from the mouth of the Thames to the Lea, along this river to Bedford, and thence along the Ouse to Watling Street. East of this was the territory later to be called the Danelaw, where the Danes were supreme, speaking their own language, preserving their native customs and maintaining their own legal institutions.

There were three separate Scandinavian dominions, Northumbria (Yorkshire), East Anglia and Scandinavian Mercia. The most intensive settlement was in Yorkshire, where, until about 950, York was ruled by Scandinavian kings (some of them Norwegian Vikings from Dublin) and in Lincolnshire. East Anglia and Scandinavian Mercia were gradually subjugated by Edward, son of Alfred the Great. The southernmost counties of this area offered comparatively weak resistance and seem rapidly to have been re-anglicised, particularly the Danish regions of Buckinghamshire and the counties of Bedfordshire, Hertfordshire and Essex and southern Suffolk.

About 902, Norwegian Vikings from Ireland settled in Cheshire. They had become partly Hibernicised, used Irish personal-names and had adopted Irish words which they used in their place-names. They formed their patronymics in the Irish fashion, *Thorfinn mac Thore,* and formed their place-names in the Celtic way, with the defining element last, e.g. Aspatria 'Patrick's Ash', Kirkandrews and Kirkoswald 'the church of St Andrew and of St Oswald'. But they did not abandon their native language or their personal-names. Gradually these settlements were extended along the coastal areas north of the Mersey to Westmorland and Cumberland and east beyond the Pennines until, in 919, York was captured by Ragnall mac Bicloch, the first of a series of Irish Viking kings of York which lasted for 35 years.

Early in the eleventh century the Danes reconquered England, which came under the rule of Cnut and his sons (1016–42).

SCANDINAVIAN PERSONAL-NAMES

Our chief concern here is with those Scandinavian personal-names which still survive as modern surnames. This necessarily involves a brief general discussion of the Scandinavian methods of name-giving, but a full history cannot yet be written. The long wars and the isolation of the Danelaw have deprived us of early records, with the result that, apart from a few scattered mentions of isolated names, it is not until the compilation of Domesday Book that we have the first large collection of Scandinavian personal-names and place-names, a list which includes some 427 names of individuals and some 543 names of villages ending in -*by*. Very many of these contain a personal-name as first element, some of them ancient and rarely or never recorded in independent use. These villages were well-establish-ed in 1066 and may have been named at any time between 876 and 1066, many of them, no doubt, in the earlier half of this period. In the reign of Cnut a considerable number of immigrants from Scan-dinavia seem to have settled in England, some employed in the royal household and bodyguard, some acquiring land beyond the bounds of Danish England, and Scandinavian names are found in the southern and south-western counties.

These almost without exception were names of the military, land-owning classes. For the names of peasants we have to turn to post-Conquest documents. In a list of some 700 peasants on the manors of the Abbot of Bury St Edmunds c. 1095, about 8½ per cent are of certain Scandinavian origin, including *Lute* and *Challi*, not found elsewhere in an English text,[1] a proportion much less than in the Castleacre cartulary where, of the names of men of native ancestry in the twelfth-century charters, about 40 per cent are of Scandinavian origin.[2] Scandinavian names were still common as late as 1277 (*Ely*) among the peasants on the Norfolk and Suffolk manors of the Bishop of Ely.

In a similar study of the twelfth-century names recorded in the Norfolk *Holme Cartulary*, J. R. West notes 58 Scandinavian names

[1] D. C. Douglas, *Feudal Documents from the Abbey of Bury St Edmunds* (London, 1932), pp. cxvii–cxxi.
[2] Ibid., p. cxxi, n. 4.

in a total of 139 (41·7 per cent),[1] but he presses the evidence too far when he states that 'that percentage indicates that the population of Norfolk in pre-conquest days was almost equally divided into those of Anglo-Saxon and Scandinavian descent'.[2] The 'traditional names of the district' were borne by only one-quarter of those named, the remaining 75 per cent having names of French and continental origin, and we have no means of judging how many of these were post-Conquest immigrants. At this time, too, the name was no indication of nationality. Inter-marriage between Danes and English must here, as elsewhere, have led to the use in the same family of both Danish and English names, whilst there is clear evidence that by the twelfth century Scandinavians were already beginning to give their children the new names brought over from France.

The fullest and most illuminating of these studies is that of Sir Frank Stenton on the personal-names of the Danelaw.[3] He emphasises the value of twelfth-century charters and stresses the need for a full collection and critical examination of the Scandinavian names found in them, as, until this has been done, any conclusions must be merely tentative. Most of his material comes from the Lincolnshire Danelaw where Scandinavian settlement and influence was most intense. Here he finds that Scandinavian names outnumber the English. Of 507 names representing the personal nomenclature of the age before the Conquest, 266 (52–53 per cent) are of Scandinavian origin, comprising 119 distinct name forms. These include both names not particularly characteristic of the Danelaw, such as *Thorald* (now *Thorold*), *Swain* and *Thurstan* (ON *Þorsteinn*), and such common northern names as *Gamel* (ON *Gamall* 'old'), now *Gammell* or *Gamble*, *Grim* (ON *Grímr*), surviving as *Grime* or *Grimes* and *Tóli*, now *Tooley*, with characteristic names of comparative rarity such as *Airic* (ON *Eiríkr*), modern *Herrick*, and ON *Oddr*, now *Odd*.

Among the numerous compounds, all common also in Northern England, we may note ON *Farðegn*, ODa *Farthin*, now *Farthing*, and ON *Kolbrandr* (modern *Colbran*), but more significant than these are diminutives such as *Inga* and *Sigga* (Siggs), well-attested abbreviations of *Ingiríðr* (Ingrey) and *Sigríðr* (Syrett), *Hasti* from *Ásketill*, one origin of *Hastie*, ON *Steinki*, a short form of some name compounded with *Stein-*, with some half-dozen examples of *Anke*, from ON

[1] J. R. West, *St Benet of Holme 1020–1210* (Norfolk Rec. Soc., II, III, 1932), pp. 258–60.
[2] Ibid., p. 260.
[3] F. M. Stenton, *Danelaw Charters* (London, 1920), pp. cxi–cxviii.

Anki, a diminutive of *Arn-*, found also as *Hanke* and surviving as *Hanke* and *Hanks*. To these we may add the unrecorded *Samke, possibly a diminutive of ON *Sandúlfr, or from *Sanni*, a pet-form of ON *Sandi*. It is found as a surname in Suffolk, William *samke* 1221 *ElyA*, Wymark *Sanke* 1283 SRSf, and survives as *Sank*. A further example of this vitality is *Touillda* (f) 1066 DB, found in Essex and later in Suffolk and Norfolk and surviving as *Tovell* and *Tofield*, a rare surname from a rare Scandinavian personal-name of an unusual type, ON *Tófa-Hildr* (f), 'Hildr the daughter of Tófi'. One origin of *Goodhugh* and *Goodhue* is a rare ON compound **Guð(h)ugi*, recorded in the Essex DB as *Got hugo* and in Suffolk c1095 as *Godhuge*, with which we may compare **Ill(h)ugi*, found in Cambridgeshire and Norfolk in the twelfth century.

'If the Scandinavian like the English names were destined to become virtually extinct within three generations of the year 1200, this was not due to the inferiority of the northern stems. It happened because the peasantry as a whole had come to adopt the personal-names in use among the military class. Unlike most systems of nomenclature, above all unlike the English nomenclature of this region, the Scandinavian names of the Danelaw were to disappear before they had passed through any protracted phase of obsolescence.'[1]

SCANDINAVIAN METHODS OF NAME-GIVING

Like the Anglo-Saxons, the Scandinavians had both simple names and compounds: *Biǫrn* 'bear', one source of *Barne*, *Arnbiǫrn* 'eagle-bear', now *Arborn*; *Finnr* 'the Finn' and *Dólgfinnr*, surviving as *Finn* and *Dolphin*; *Geiri* 'spear', now *Garey*; *Arngeirr* 'eagle-spear'. Some of these ancient names are found only in place-names; others remained in use and survive as modern surnames, e.g. *Ingialdr* 'Ing's tribute', Ingoldisthorpe (Nf), Ingoldmells and Ingoldsby (L), and in the surnames *Ingall*, *Ingold* and *Ingle*.

The surnames *Gooderham*, *Goodram* and *Goodrum* appear in a variety of forms and some may be from ON *Guðrún* (f) or OE *Gōdrūn* (f). The surname is found in Lincolnshire, Norfolk and Suffolk and the personal-names *Gudram*, *Guðram* and *Guderam*, recorded in Lincolnshire from 1200 to 1214, with *Guderam* Gleve and John *Guderam* in Suffolk in 1283 (SR), suggest a man's name of Scandinavian origin. This is probably ON *Guðþorm*, found as *Guþrum* in the Thorney *Liber Vitae*, which survives in the York

[1] Stenton, op. cit., p. cxviii.

120

street-name *Goodramgate* 'Guthrum's Street'. We should expect the name of the leader of the Danish host and first Danish king of East Anglia to have been in common use.

Some ancient compounds, such as *Bertor, Brunketel* and *Ougrim*, are recorded only as personal-names in or after 1066 and appear to have left no modern survivals. But it is the frequent post-Conquest record of numerous personal-names found also in place-names combined with later formations such as *Rumfari* 'one who has made the pilgrimage to Rome' and the new diminutives discussed above which reveal the real strength and vitality of this Scandinavian nomenclature.

Bynames

The Scandinavians, unlike the Anglo-Saxons and the continental Germans, had a habit of using the same personal-name in different generations and branches of the same family. It was a common practice, too, for a man to name his son after some notable chief or a particular friend. 'The departure of the Scandinavian peoples from common Germanic custom is at this point so marked,' notes Sir Frank Stenton, 'that it requires some special explanation. In the opinion of most scholars, it is connected with the late survival in the north of the belief that the soul of an individual was represented or symbolised by his name, and that the bestowal of a name was a means of calling up the spirit of the man who had borne it into the spirit of the child to whom it was given.'[1]

The result of this custom was that in time there were so many men bearing the same name that it was found necessary to distinguish them by a nickname or byname descriptive of some physical characteristic, some habit or a reference to some particular incident. Many of these bynames were innocuous, some complimentary, others derogatory, characteristic of the gross humour and acute realism of the Vikings.

That these bynames soon came to be regarded as the man's real name is proved by the history of the place-name Scarborough. From the *Kormakssaga* we learn that two brothers Thorgils and Kormak went harrying in Ireland, Wales, England and Scotland. 'They were the first men to set up the stronghold which is called Scarborough.' From two poems which Kormak addresses to his brother, we know

[1] *Trans. R. Hist. Soc.* (4th Ser.), XXIV (1942), p. 17.

that Thorgils was nicknamed *Skarði* 'the hare-lip', hence the Scandinavian form of the name, *Skarðaborg*, named not from his personal-name but from his nickname. Thorgils died in 967; the brothers' expedition to England took place immediately after their return from one to Russia in 966, so that Scarborough must have been founded late in 966 or in 967.

By the end of the ninth century many of these bynames had come to be used as real personal-names; some of them lie concealed in English place-names, some were still in use in the twelfth century and are still found as surnames. *Blanda* 'the man who mixes his drinks' is the first element of Blansby (NRY); it was still used in Yorkshire in 1219 (Ass), Thomas *filius Bland*' and may survive in the modern surname *Bland*, though this is usually local, from Bland (WRY). *Bróklauss* 'the man without breeches', recorded in Lincs as a personal-name in DB and as a surname in the reign of Richard I (now *Brockless, Brockliss*), is the personal-name in Brocklesby (L). The modern *Cory* may be from ON *Kori*, as in Corby (L, Nth), or from *Kári* 'curly-haired', *Cari* DB, *Kare* Hy 2 Gilb, as in Careby (L), Carthorpe (NRY) and Corton (Sf), DB *Karetun*. ON *Skúli*, from the root of *skyla* 'to protect', found in Scoulton (Nf), Sculcoates (ERY) and Sculthorpe (Nf), is recorded as *Scula* (Nf) and *Escul(e)* (Nf, L, Y) 1066 DB, Lefstan *Scule filius* c1095 Bury (Sf), *Scul* c1155 DC (L), and, as a surname (now *Scowle*) in Robert *Scule* c1165 Bury (Sf), William *Scowle* 1274 RH (L), Richard *Scoule* 1297 SRY.

To these may be added: ON *Gípr* 'drunkard' (now *Gipp*), found both as a personal-name and a surname in twelfth-century Lincolnshire, *Káti* 'cheerful' (*Cates*), *Klak* 'clod' (*Clack*), *Kouse, Kause* 'tomcat' (*Couse*), *Lax*, a nickname from the salmon, the only example being Lax de Ludham 1141-9 Holme (Nf) (*Lax*), *Ormr* 'serpent' (*Orme*), *Orri* 'black cock', Roger *Orre* 1202 AssL (*Orr*), *Skarfr* 'cormorant' (*Scarfe*), *Skjótr* 'swift' (*Skeat, Sceats*), *Skeggi* 'beard' (*Skegg*), *Slengr* 'idler' (*Sling*), *Stori* 'strong' (*Storey*) and *Tryggr* 'true, faithful' (*Trigg*). The following, found only in place-names, are worthy of note: *Kisi* 'cat', *Loðinn* 'hairy', *Lútr* 'the bent', *Skammbein* 'short leg', *Skamlauss* 'shameless', *Skrauti* 'the magnificent', *Skúma* 'squinter', *Slóði* 'clumsy' and *Snípr* 'miser'.

Some late compounds

ON *Ketill* 'a round pot' or 'cauldron', an apt name for a round-headed man, became a common byname. In Iceland *Ketill* was fre-

122

quently used as a personal-name before 900 A.D. It became very popular in the Danelaw where it had given rise to 10 place-names before 1066: Kedleston (Db), Ketsby and Kettleby (L), Ab Kettleby and Eye Kettleby (Lei), Kettlestone (Nf), Kettlethorpe (L, ERY), Kexmoor (WRY) and Keystone (Hu); and to others later: Kettleshulme (Ch), Keskadale (Cu). It survives still as the surnames *Kettle*, *Kettless* and *Kittle*. But it was also used in the ninth century to form new compound names, some of which became widely popular and survive in numerous place-names and surnames: *Ketilbiǫrn* (Kettlebaston (Sf); *Kettleburn*); *Úlfketel*, *Úlfkell* (Oakerthorpe (Db); one source of *Uncle* and *Ungless*); *Þorketill*, *Þorkell* (Thirkleby (NRY), Thirtleby (ERY), Thurcaston (Lei), Thruxton (Ha, He), and in a variety of surnames, *Thurkettle*, *Thirkittle*, *Thurkell*, *Thurtell*, *Thorkell*, *Thirkhill*, *Thurtle*). *Ásketill* (Asselby (ERY); *Ashkettle*, *Axtell*, *Axcell*) is one of a number of compounds of *Ás-*, some of them ancient. Like *Þorketill* it was widely popular and common in Normandy, with a variety of forms which will be discussed later.

Danes and Norwegians

The north-west was settled mainly by Norwegian Vikings from Ireland. The common use of the terms 'Danelaw' and 'Danish England' assumes that the eastern and midland counties were conquered by Danes, an assumption amply confirmed by history, place-names and surnames. There can be little doubt that the Danish armies were a composite host, mainly Danes, but with an admixture of Norwegians and Swedes. In DB we find some men definitely stated to be Danes: Anunt dacus (ODa *Anund*, now *Annand*), Oinus dacus (ODa *Øthin*, Anglo-Scand *Oðin*, now *Othen*), Fin danus (ODa *Fin*, now *Finn*).

In the North Riding of Yorkshire the mixture of races is well illustrated by such names as Danby, Normanby and Ingleby, each of which occurs three times. These denote villages of Danes, Norwegians and Angles, and can have been given only by Scandinavians in districts where these races were in a minority. Irby (Ch, NRY) was similarly a village of Irishmen, Norwegian Vikings from Ireland, whilst Irton (NRY) is 'the farm or village of the Irish', both indicating that the Irishmen were outnumbered in the district, at Irby by other Scandinavians, at Irton by Anglians. So, too, Denaby (WRY) and Denby (Db, WRY) denote Danish settlements in a preponderatingly

English region, whilst Normanton, found four times in Nottingham-shire, thrice in Derbyshire and in Lincolnshire, and also in Rutland and the West Riding, is an English name given to a place inhabited by Norwegians in a district where Anglians were more numerous.

When we try to distinguish Danish and Norwegian personal-names in England, we are handicapped by the fact that Norse names are recorded in greater numbers than those of Denmark and Sweden. Many names found only in Norse sources may also have been used in Eastern Scandinavia. When a name is known to have been used in both Norway and Denmark, it can safely be regarded as of Danish origin if it is found in England only in the Danelaw. At times phon-etic criteria enable us to be definite. The surnames *Bond* and *Bondy* are from ON *Bóndi*, found in DB as *Bondi* (Ha, W, Do, Gl) and as *Bonde* (K). The Danish form of this name, ODa *Bundi*, is more common in DB, occurring as *Bundi* or *Bunde* (Wa, Y, Nf, Sf) and surviving as *Bound(s)*, *Boundy*, *Bundey* and *Bundy*. The modern sur-name *Ingrey* may derive from either ON *Ingiríðr* or Da *Ingrith*, OSw *Ingridh* (f). In DB it is found as *Ingrede* (Y), where the absence of the medial vowel is a criterion of East Scandinavian origin. It occurs later as *Ingreda* 1101–16 Holme (Nf), *Ingrith'* 1221 AssWa, Rogerus filius *Ingred* Ed I SRSf and as a surname, Thomas *Ingrid* 1279 RH (Hu), Reginald *Ingreth*, Nicholas *Hingreye* 1283 SRSf. The Norse form, not found in DB, was used also in the eastern counties: *Ingerithe, Ingeride* Hy 2, 1163 DC (L), *Ingerid* 1221 AssWa, Alexander *Ingerith'* 1221 *ElyA* (Sf).

Of the Danish personal-names which have given modern surnames, we may note: *Áki* (Oakey, Okey), *Aggi* (Agg), *Algot* (Allgood, Augood), *Alli* (Alley, Ally) *Auti* (Autie, Awty, Alty), *Brothir* (Brother, Brothers), *Elaf* (Ayloffe), *Fathir* (Fadder, Fathers), *Klak* (Clack), *Knútr* (Knott), *Mothir* (Mothers), *Segrim* (Seagrim), *Skeggi* 'beard' (Skegg), *Tóki* (Tooke, Toke, Tookey, Tuckey), *Tóli* (Tooley), *Tópi* (Toop) and *Vigot* (Wiggett).

Anglo-Scandinavian names

Some Scandinavian names were assimilated to an English form: ODa *Halfdan* 'half-Dane' (Haldane) became Anglo-Scand *Healfdene* (Alden); ON *sæfogl* 'sea-bird', especially the cormorant, not re-corded as a personal-name in Scandinavia but common in England after the Conquest, became Anglo-Scand **Sæfugol*, now *Saffell*,

Safhill; ON *Valþiófr* was anglicised as *Wælþēof* and survives in a variety of forms including *Walthew*, *Waldo*, *Waddy*, *Waddilove* and *Wadlow*. ON *Stigandr* (Stigand, Stiggants, Stiggins) was anglicised as *Stiand* (Styan, Styance, Styants). ON *Sprakkaleggr* 'man with the creaking legs' was adopted as **Spracaling*, modern *Sprackling*, *Spratling*, *Spradling*, *Spracklen*, *Sprackland*, *Spranklin* and *Sprankling*.

A few new compounds were formed, hybrids, of which we still have *Kilvert*, from ON **Ketilfrøðr*, anglicised as **Cytelferð* which became **Cylferð*; *Ketteridge*, *Kitteridge*, from **Cytelrīc*, a compound of ON *Ketill* and the common OE second theme *-rīc*; and **Þórgifu* (f), a compound of *Þórr* and OE *g(i)efu* 'gift', now *Turriff*.

Norman names

The Normans took with them to Normandy their characteristic Scandinavian names such as ON *Hrólfr*, ODa, OSw *Rolf*, sometimes Latinised as *Rollo*, the name of the first Duke of Normandy. This was common in England after the Conquest where it is sometimes Anglo-Scandinavian for it is found as the name of a Lincolnshire peasant in 1142, but it was more often of Norman origin, having become OFr *Roul*. It is the source of numerous modern surnames, including *Rolfe*, *Rolls*, *Roffe* and *Rowe*. The modern *Randolph* is ON *Rannulfr* 'shield-wolf', brought to England by the Normans as *Randulf* and often confused with the equally common OG *Rannulf* 'raven-wolf'.

In Normandy, as in England, the Normans adopted the native language of their conquered subjects, but whereas in England they brought over a flood of new personal-names which ultimately swamped those of native origin, in Normandy they quickly adopted the personal-names in use in France. The Conqueror himself was *William*, son of *Robert*, and his sons were named *Robert*, *Richard*, *William* and *Henry*, compounds of continental Germanic origin of a type with which the Normans were familiar. At the same time they retained a number of their native names, chiefly compounds of *Ás-*, *-ketel* and *Thór-*, and these, too, they brought to England but modified by a French pronunciation with the result that in post-Conquest England it is often impossible to decide definitely whether a man with a name of Scandinavian origin is English or Norman by birth.

Compounds of ON *Ás-* and the cognate OE *Ōs-* 'divinity, god' are numerous in England but the determination of their ultimate origin

K   125

is rendered difficult as, already before the Conquest, the English substituted their native *Ōs-* for the Scandinavian form, the name of *Ásketill*, leader of the Danish army from Repton to Cambridge in 874, appearing in the Anglo-Saxon Chronicle in the anglicised form *Ōscytel*. The native origin of *Ōsmǣr* (Osmer) and *Ōswine* (Oswin) is proved by their early occurrence, as is *Ōsmund* (Osmond), the name of an eighth-century king of Sussex, but *Osbern* and *Osgod* are not found in England before the eleventh century and are either anglicisations of ON *Ásbiǫrn* and *Ásgautr* or importations from Normandy. Despite the seventh and eighth century examples of OE *Ōsloc*, *Haslock* and *Hasluck* are from the ON *Áslákr*.

The whole problem is further complicated by the use in France of the OG cognates *Ans-* and *Ōs-*. In Normandy ON *Ásbiǫrn* and *Ásmundr* generally appear in the Saxon forms *Ōsbern* and *Ōsmund*, whilst the corresponding Frankish (OLG) forms *Ansger* and *Ansgot* are found for ON *Ásgeirr* and *Ásgautr* (anglicised as *Ōsgar* and *Ōsgod*). This *Ans-* later became *An-*. All the varieties appear in post-Conquest England with the result that we cannot be certain whether *Osgood* and *Hosegood* are from the late OE *Ōsgod*, from ON *Ásgautr* or from this Scandinavian name which was also common in Normandy. *Angood* is certainly from the Frankish *Ansgot*, *Angot*.

The post-Conquest clerks, who were largely of French birth or training, showed a marked tendency to give personal-names the continental spelling and pronunciation with which they were familiar, often giving a man's name in more than one form, but modern survivals prove that many of these varied forms were in actual use. ON *Ásketill*, for instance, preserves its Scandinavian form in *Ashkettle*, *Askell*, *Astell* and *Haskell* and the Frankish form in *Anketell*, *Ankettle*, *Anquetel*, *Ankill* and *Antell*. In Northern France it occurs also as *Anquetin* and *Asketin*, the latter giving us the modern surnames *Askins*, *Astin*, *Ashken*, *Haskins* and *Hastin*. Most of our *Osberns* and *Osberts* probably owe their name to the Saxon form common in Normandy.

Of the late compounds of *Thor-* a number were common in Normandy, where the initial *Th-* was pronounced *T-*, a pronunciation which often survives: ON *Þóraldr*, ODa, OSw *Thorald*, 'Thor-ruler' (*Thorold*, *Turrall*, *Torode*); ON *Þorfrøðr*, OSw *Thorfrith* (Turfery, Turfrey, Tuffery, Tollfree); ON *Þorgils*, ODa, OSw *Thorgisl* (Turgoose, Sturge, Sturgess); ON *Þorsteinn*, ODa *Thorsten*, common in England where it was anglicised as *Þurstān*, and in Normandy as

Turstinus, Turstenus which became Fr *Toustin, Toustain* (Thurstan, Tustin, Tusting, Tutin, Tuting); ON *Þorfinnr* (Turpin). In ON *Þorgeirr*, ODa, OSw *Thorger* 'Thor-spear' (Thurgar) and ON *Þorgautr*, ODa, OSw *Thorgot* 'Thor-Gēat' (Thurgood, Thorgood, Thurgate), the Norman pronunciation has not survived, although it is evident in early forms. In *Thorgood,* etc., the preservation of *Th-* may be due to the influence of *Thorogood* with which the name was confused. ON *Þorir*, ODa *Thorir, Thori*, is not found in Norway. *Tory*, by the side of *Thory*, is due to Anglo-Norman pronunciation in England. *Þorbert, Þurbert*, frequent in Normandy, is a hybrid compounded of ON *Þor-* and OG *-bert* (Turbard, Turbett, Torbett, Tarbert, Tarbath, Tarbutt).

In *A Dictionary of British Surnames* (pp. xxv–xxvi) is given a list of some 148 different Scandinavian personal-names which still survive in a variety of forms as modern surnames. Unfortunately a few names were omitted and others have since been identified. To this list should be added:

ON *Anki* (Hanks), ODa, OSw *Anund* (Annand), ON *Arnbiǫrn*, ODa, OSw *Arnbiorn* (Arborn, Arbon), ON *Asti* (Hastie), ON *Blanda* (Bland), ON *Bróklauss* (Brockless, Brockliss), ON *Flóki* (Flook) ON *Gípr* (Gipp), ON *Grípr*, ODa *Grip* (Gripp), ON *Guðrún* (f), ON *Guðþorm*, OSw *Guthormber* (Gooderham, Goodram, Goodrum), ON *Hildibrandr* (Hildebrand, Hilderbrand), ODa *Hildiger* (Hilger), ON *Kári, Kori* (Cory), ON *Káti*, ODa *Kati*, OSw *Kate* (Cates, Kates), ODa *Killi, Kille* (Kill), ODa *Klak* (Clack), ON *Krókr* (Crook), ON *Mundi* (Munday, Mundy), ON *Ǫgmundr*, OSw *Aghmund* (Ammon, Ammonds, Amon, Amond), ON *Orri* (Orr), ON *Auðun*, ODa *Øthin,* OSw *Ødhin*, Anglo-Scand *Ōðin* (Othen), ON *Skarfr* (Scarf, Skarf), ODa *Skeggi* (Skegg), ON *Skjótr* (Skeat, Skeates, Skett, Skeet, Sceats), ON *Skúl, Skúli* (Scowle), ON **Slengr* (Sling), ON *Tryggr* (Trigg), ODa *Wraghi* (Wragg).

With these 29 names we have a total of 177 Scandinavian personal-names surviving as surnames, compared with 420 OE names, a not unimpressive total, especially as it does not give a full picture. Many Scandinavian surnames of this type are undoubtedly obsolete and more will certainly be discovered. Their full importance can be realised only by the frequency with which many of them were used and by the many varied forms they have assumed.

Chapter Seven

NEW NAMES FROM FRANCE

DEVELOPMENT OF PERSONAL-NAMES IN FRANCE

AFTER the Roman conquest of Gaul, the native Celtic nomenclature gradually gave place to the Latin system which itself was submerged even more completely by Christianity and the barbarian invasions. The christians in the fifth century made a clean sweep of the Latin system of praenomen, nomen and cognomen (e.g. Marcus Tullius Cicero), recognising only a single name, that given at baptism either at birth or on conversion. The Frankish invaders, though compelled to abandon their native language, retained their ancient personal-names, which were used as baptismal names, and maintained the Teutonic system of one man, one name. The native population followed their example, but more generally in northern and central France than in the Midi where the Latin influence was more powerful.

In the North and Centre in the fifth century less than one-quarter of the names used were Germanic, in the sixth century one-half, whilst in the ninth they were almost universal.

For a long period the Church allowed complete freedom in the choice of baptismal names. In a list of men's names in use from 752 to 900, we find *Bernard, Herbert, Raymond* and *Richard,* all Germanic. The only exceptions are one Biblical name *Isaac* and two Latin names *Honoré* and *Loup.* In the twelfth century Germanic

128

names still predominate, but exceptions are more common, *Samson,*
Arthur (both probably from the *chansons de geste*), and three names
of saints, *Barthélemy, Josse* and *Mathieu.* Women, more liable to
changes of fashion, used mostly Graeco-Latin or Biblical names
(chiefly of saints): *Agnès, Béatrix, Constance, Denise, Elisabeth,*
Isabelle, Marguerite and *Marie.* The cult of the saints which began
in the ninth century had become common by the beginning of the
twelfth.[1]

CONTINENTAL GERMANIC PERSONAL-NAMES IN ENGLAND

It was this northern French system of nomenclature which the
Normans adopted and brought with them to England in the years
following the Conquest, the variety of names being steadily increased
as new immigrants came in from Flanders and northern France and,
later, under the Plantagenets, from farther south. The Conqueror
himself was accompanied by volunteers from various parts of western Europe, including Flemings and Bretons, and we find record of
names common on the Continent which never became acclimatised in
England, e.g. *Alfonsus,* frequent in Spain and Portugal, *Conrad,*
more common in Germany, *Enisant,* a Breton name, *Lanfranc,* a
Lombard name brought to England by the Archbishop of Canterbury, a native of Pavia, and the German *Winterhard,* found in DB and
twelfth-century Lincolnshire.

Most common of these Germanic names from Normandy were the
dozen or so personal-names which have remained in general use until
today, all of them having given rise to numerous surnames: *William*
(OG *Willihelm*), *Robert* (OG *Hrodebert*), *Richard* (OG *Richard*),
Ralph (OG *Radulf*), *Roger* (OG *Hrodger*), *Walter* (OG *Walter*),
Henry (OG *Heinric, Henric*), *Hugh* (OG *Hugo*), *Geoffrey* (OG *Gal-*
frid) and *Gilbert* (OG *Gisilbert*).

Biblical and saints' names were less common in the years immediately following the Conquest, but steadily became more popular
and more numerous. In DB we find examples of the Biblical *John,*
Matthew, Peter, Stephen and *Thomas,* and of the saints *Andrew,*
Eustace, Martin and *Nicholas.*

The gradual decline in the use of native personal-names and their
supersession by the new names from the Continent have been
treated above.[2] But what these new names were and how long they

[1] A. Dauzat, *Les noms de famille de France* (Paris, 1945), pp. 31–4.
[2] *v.* pp. 102–6.

were fashionable, these are problems which have never been satisfactorily discussed. Whilst the general trend is well known, the details are not. Definite statements on the relative frequency of various names are often made, but the basis on which these estimates are founded is either not given or they are made on insufficient evidence. The material available is enormous and no attempt has yet been made to collect and sift it. Forssner has produced a valuable monograph on the medieval names,[1] including a number which did not survive as surnames, but there are many omissions and he deals only with names of Germanic origin, thus excluding Biblical and saints' names. The *Oxford Dictionary of Christian Names* is selective, omitting numerous personal-names which survive as surnames.

As to their numbers, Weekley states categorically that 'The Middle Ages had a comparatively small stock of Christian names and relied almost entirely on fewer than two dozen for each sex.'[2] Miss Withycombe is more definite:

> In the late 12th century and early 13th century there were probably more christian names in use than at any subsequent period until the 20th century . . . But as the 13th century advanced, the stock of names shrank rapidly, and of those still in use a comparatively small number were borne by an increasingly large proportion of the population. The five names *Henry, John, Richard, Robert, William* together accounted for 38 per cent of recorded men's names in the 12th century, for 57 per cent in the 13th century, and for 64 per cent in the 14th century.[3]

This is substantially correct, but it seriously underrates the variety and number of christian names in use.

Here we make no pretence of completeness, but years of working on lists of medieval names have made it abundantly clear not only that the variety of christian names in use in the surname period[4] was extensive but also that there were fashions in names in different parts of the country and even within a particular county. The material given below is based on a detailed examination of the personal-names used in four twelfth-century documents and ten Subsidy Rolls, supplemented by two smaller unpublished collections of names from deeds of the thirteenth and fourteenth centuries in the Essex Record

[1] T. Forssner, *Continental-Germanic Personal-Names in England in Old and Middle English Times* (Uppsala, 1916).

[2] *Jack and Jill*, p. 15.

[3] E. G. Withycombe, *The Oxford Dictionary of English Christian Names* (Oxford, 2nd edn, 1950), pp. xxvii–xxviii.

[4] Christian names of the fifteenth century and later are not considered here.

Office relating to Aveley. The number of persons whose names are recorded varies from 339 at Aveley to over 11,000 in Somerset and Suffolk.

In the twelfth-century Holme Cartulary (809 persons) we find 115 different personal-names of post-Conquest origin and in the Lincolnshire Danelaw Charters of the same period (4,440 persons) 188. Of the 256 names in the Holme Cartulary and the Records of the Templars (1185), only 75 christian names are common to both. In the Subsidy Rolls the number of different names of this type varies from 91 in Lancashire and 97 in Shropshire to 158 in Cambridgeshire, 176 in Sussex, 182 in Kent and 227 in Yorkshire. In all, these lists include 333 men's names and 177 women's, a total of 510.

At Aveley in the thirteenth century, 306 persons shared 57 French names, whilst in the fourteenth century 63 French names were used by 549 individuals. Of these, William had declined from 20 to 18 per cent, whilst John had increased from 20 to 34 per cent; Robert, too, had lost ground, from 9 to 6 per cent, as had Geoffrey from 5 to 2 per cent, but Thomas had increased from 4 to 9 per cent. Of the rest, the only noteworthy feature is the late appearance of *Joce*, one instance of the rare *Fabian* (1250) and one each of *Asculf* (a Breton name), *Acius* (OG *Azo*, OFr *Ace*, surviving as *Ace* and *Aze*) and *Ingilram* (now *Ingram*).

In most of these documents *William* is the most popular name, in the twelfth century varying from 10 per cent at Holme to 15 per cent in the Danelaw charters and remaining supreme until the end of the thirteenth century, when he gives place to *John* in the Subsidy Rolls for Somerset, Suffok and Cambridgeshire (1327), Warwickshire (1332) and Kent (1334). In the twelfth century *John* varied from 2 to 7 per cent. By the end of the thirteenth century he accounted for 12 per cent in Worcestershire (1275), level with William, and 14 per cent in Sussex (1296) as compared with William's 15 per cent; in Somerset (1327), William was still 15 per cent, but John had risen to 20 per cent, whilst in Kent (1334) William had declined to 11 per cent and John had increased to 22 per cent.

The fourteenth-century Subsidy Rolls provide some curious facts which need explanation. It looks as if a number of personal-names common in the immediate post-Conquest period had become unfashionable or rare, whilst a few are surprisingly common in one county. For example, OFr *Arnaut*, OG *Arnald*, which has given us the surnames *Arnold, Arnall* and *Arnott*, with *Eustace*, OFr *Goscelin*,

Joscelin, from OG *Gautselin*, *Gozelin* (now *Jocelyn*, *Josling*, *Goslin*, *Gosling*, etc.), and OFr *Rainer*, OG *Raginhari* (now *Rayner*, *Reyner*), all recorded in DB, are never found as many as 10 times in any one county. *Ambrose*, *Ernest* and *Howard* do not appear in any roll. On the other hand, OFr *Hamo*, *Hamon*, *Hamond*, from OG *Haimo* (modern *Haymes*, *Hamon*, *Hammond*, *Hammans*) is found in Kent in 1334 as the name of 127 different men, its nearest rival being Sussex with 19. *Denis*, too, is particularly common in Kent, whilst *Thomas* increases in numbers from 45 in 1185 (Templars) to hundreds in the fourteenth century, being especially fashionable in Suffolk (642), Yorkshire (775) and Kent (934) where it comes third (9 per cent), followed by *Richard* (6 per cent). At the other extreme we have in Yorkshire (1301), 31 names not found in any other of these documents, with 13 more in Kent and 16 in Worcestershire.

In the 1296 Subsidy for Sussex, 32 men were named *Martin* as compared with 17 in Kent and Yorkshire, 18 in Suffolk and 19 in Cambridgeshire and Somerset. As a surname, it occurs 20 times in 1296, 23 in 1327 and 28 in 1332, a total of 71. Its nearest rivals were *Daniel* (38) and *Waryn* (36). Why was the name so popular in Sussex?

NAMES OF WOMEN

Of the 178 different women's names found in the above sources—and many others appear elsewhere—the most popular were Alice, Maud or Matilda, Agnes,[1] Margery and Margaret, Isabel, Juliana, Joan, Christiana and Emma. Of these, only *Alice*, *Matilda* and *Emma* are of Germanic origin; *Isabel* is a Provençal form of the Hebrew *Elizabeth*, *Joan* and *Juliana* feminine forms of the Hebrew *John* and the Latin *Julianus*, *Christiana* a Latin formation, *Christiana* 'Christian', *Margaret* from Lat *margarita* 'a pearl', ultimately of Greek origin; *Margery* was a French popular form of *Marguérite*. All these have given us surnames, most easily recognised. *Emma* is now *Emm* or *Emms*; *Margaret* survives only as *Margetts*, whilst *Margery* occurs also as *Margary*. As *Joan* shared the same spellings and pronunciation as *John*, it is impossible to decide when such surnames as *Janes*, *Joanes* and *Jeanes* are from the woman's name.

Names of OG origin include: OFr *Albree*, *Aubree*, OG *Alb(e)rada* 'elf-counsel' (f) (Aubrey); OFr *Heloïs*, OG *Heilwidis* 'hale- or sound-wide' (f) (Elwes); *Ingilsind(is)* 'Angle-journey' (f) (Inglesant); OFr

[1] For these and other women's names, especially *Agnes, Alice and Maud, v.* p. 76 above.

NEW NAMES FROM FRANCE

Iseut, Isaut, *Ishild 'ice-battle' (f), (Issard, Issott, Issolt, Izat, etc.);
OFr *Milesenda, Milessent,* OG *Amalasuintha* 'work-strong' (f)
(Millicent); *Aurildis, Orieldis* 'fire-strife' (f) (Oriel); OFr *Richeut,*
OG *Richild, Richeldis* 'powerful-battle' (f) (Richell, Rickell); OFr
Rohese, Roese, OG *Hrodohaidis* 'fame-kind' (f) (Rose, Royce, Royse).

To the saints' names already noted we may add: *Agatha* from Gk
ἀγαθός 'good', adopted in the OFr vernacular form *Agace,* now
Agass, Aggis, Aggus; Constance, preserved also in the vernacular
Custance; Ellen, the earlier English form of *Helen,* of Greek origin
'the bright one', surving both as *Ellen, Elleyne, Ellin* and *Hellen,*
Hellin; the Greek *Euphemia* 'auspicious speech', recorded as *Euphem-*
ma 1200–11 BuryS and *Effeme* 1283 SRSf (*Effemy, Effeney*); *Lucia,*
feminine of Lat *Lucius* (*Luce, Lucia*); *Sabina* (Lat) 'a Sabine woman';
the masculine *Sabinus* was also a saint's name; either may be the
origin of *Sabben, Sabin, Sabine.* Biblical names were not commonly
used by women, but we have *Eva* and *Eve,* the Hebrew *Sara(h)*
'princess' in *Sara* and *Sarra* and the Hebrew *Shushannah* 'lily'
surviving as *Susan, Sussams* and *Sussands.*

From the Classics come *Claris* (Lat *Claricia,* probably from *claritia*
'brightness'), *Florence* (Lat *Florentia* 'blooming'), *Marrable* (*Mirabell*
from Lat *mirabilis* 'wonderful'), *Pretious* (Lat *Preciosa* 'of great
value') and *Prudence* (Lat *Prudentia*). *Galiena,* not uncommon in the
thirteenth century, is the feminine of *Galienus* used in the same period
(*Galiena* 1210 Cur (Sf), 1219 AssY, *Galienus* 1212 Cur (Nf, Y)). This
is the medieval Latin form of *Galenus* (Galen the physician) which
survived as *Galen* (Turstinus *Galien* 1190 P (Y), John *Galen* 1358
Shef) and, with *Galienus* and *Galiena,* has contributed to the modern
Galleon and *Galliene.*

Men's names used for women

Today when the same name is used for both men and women we
make some distinction, e.g. *Denis* and *Denise, Leslie* and *Lesley,* at
times using a Latin form, *Philippa* and *Roberta,* but in medieval
England, whilst the women's names are given a Latin form, there was
no difference in pronunciation. Early examples are *Paulina* (1169) and
Eustachia (1214). In the thirteenth and fourteenth centuries they are
fairly common: *Colletta* and *Nicholaa* (from *Nicholas*), *Andrea,*
Jurdana, Dyonisia, Laurencia, Gervasia, Florentia, Philippa, Wyotta,
all easy to recognise and all found as surnames, though it is usually

impossible to prove these are not derived solely from the men's names.

One clear example of a metronymic is William *Anastasie* 1222 FFBk, from *Anastasia*, a fourth-century martyr, but the masculine *Anastasius* is found earlier, in 1188, and must be partly responsible for the surnames *Ansteys*, *Anstice*, *Anstis* and *Anstiss*. *Clement* and *Clements* must derive from the masculine *Clemens* 'mild, merciful' but, whilst the latter might have become *Clemence*, this, with *Climance*, probably represents the feminine *Clementia* 'mildness', still used as *Clemence* and *Clemency*. Less common are *Jakemina*, a deminutive of *Jacomus (James), now *Jackaman*, *Mazelina* found occasionally by the side of *Mazelinus* (OG *Mazelin*, OFr *Masselin*), now *Maslen*, *Maslin* and *Mazlen*, and *Marina* (1230 P (Nt), 1275 SRWo) with *Marinus* 1192 P (Lo), Lat *marinus* 'of the sea', both names of saints (modern *Marrin*).

The Spanish and Provençal *Sancha* or *Sanchia*, feminine of *Sancho*, from Lat *sanctus* 'holy', first appears in England on the marriage of Richard, Earl of Cornwall, to Sanchia daughter of the Count of Provence. The name has never been common (*Scientia* 1327 SRSf), but has given rise to the rare surname *Science*. *Gemma* (1219 AssY), *Jemma* (1283 FFEss) and *Jimma*, wife of Robert Elysent (1256 AssCh), were women, but *Gemme* brother of Gilbert (1251 AssLa) and *Gemme* Campion, whose wife *Magge* is mentioned (1306 Wak), were men. This must be the vernacular pronunciation of *James* (Jim), used of men and women alike.

Pet-names and diminutives

Many of the short, pet-forms used for women's names still survive as surnames and some of them have produced a variety of diminutives. *Cass* is a short form of *Cassandra*, the Trojan prophetess doomed to foretell the truth but never to be believed, curiously enough a common medieval name. *Minns* and *Mynn* are from *Minna*, a pet-name of some woman's name, perhaps from *Ismenia* (*Immine*), the source of *Emeney*.

Some of the common names have produced not only pet-forms but also a variety of diminutives in -*et*, -*ot*, -*on*, -*in* and double diminutives in -*elin*, often ringing the changes on both vowels and consonants. From *Margaret* we have *Maggs* and *Meggs* (*Megge* 1249 Misc (Y), James *Megge* 1528 FFEss), with *Meggett* and *Meggitt*,

134

variants of the common *Magota*, and *Mogg* (*Mogota* 1313 Wak) and from *Margery*, *Madge*; *Katherine* has given us *Caton*, *Cattel* and *Catlin* and *Custance*, the popular form of *Constance*, *Cust* and *Cuss*. To these we may add *Dye*, *Dyett* and *Dyott* from *Dionisia*, *Emms*, *Emmett* and *Emmott* from *Emma*, *Evetts* and *Evitt* from *Eve* and *Geeves* and *Jeeves* from *Geva* (Genevieve).

The colloquial pronunciation of *Juliana* was *Gillian* or *Jelian* and this survives as *Gillian*, *Gillions*, *Jillions*, *Gellion*, *Jellings* and *Jillings*, with the pet-forms *Gill*, *Gell and Jell* and a diminutive which survives as *Gillett*, *Gellett*, *Jillett* and *Jellett*, though this latter may also be from *Gillota*, a diminutive of *Gilia*, the feminine of *Giles*, often *Egidia*. The short form of both *Julian* and *Juliana* was *Jull* or *Jowe*, surviving as *Jull*, *Joll*; the diminutive of this was common as *Juetta* (f), whence the surnames *Jowett*, *Jewitt*, *Juett* and *Jewiss*. Equally varied are the derivatives of *Mary* and *Isabel*. Although *Mary* was never a common medieval christian name, its pet-forms were *Marriott*, *Marritt*; *Marion*, *Malyon*; *Mallett*, *Mallott*, *Malin*; *Moll* and *Mollett*. From *Isabel* we have *Ibbs*, *Ibbott*; *Libby*; *Tibbs*, *Tibbins*, *Tibbott* (*Tibota* 1279 RH); *Bibbs*, *Bibby* and *Bibel* (from *Bib-el*); *Bellett*, *Bellott* (from (Isa)*bel*).

From *Elizabeth* we have the surnames *Beth*, *Bett* and *Libby*. The modern *Betty* is now used as a distinct christian name, whilst *Bessie* and *Betsey*, with *Eliza* and *Lizzie* were once common. This use of more than one pet-name for the same person is well-illustrated by a novelist's observation:

'The Fairy Queen jostled past, and *Paulina* observed that she wore a new fur tippet and muff.
'"Hullo, *Polly*, have you found anything yet?" . ..
'The Demon King sauntered by.
'"Well, *Polly*? Pa's just coming" . . .
'But on the top step *Paulina* collapsed and began to cry . . . then a voice whispered "*Lina*", and she started; for only one person called her *Lina*.'[1]

Here, too, we should note certain diminutives of OG origin. OFr *Ameline*, *Emmeline*, a hypocoristic formation of OG names in *Adal-*, now survive as *Emblem*, *Emblen*, *Emblin*, *Embling*, *Emeline*, *Emlyn* and *Amblin* and have given us also *Amelot* and *Amlot* from OFr *Amelot*, *Emelot*. OFr *Aceline* is a feminine form of *Acelin*, from OG *Azilin*, a double diminutive of *Azo* (now *Ace*). This is more common than the woman's name which may have contributed to

---

[1] Eleanor Smith, *Ballerina*, pp. 10, 23.

Aslin(g), *Ashlin(g)* and *Astling*. OFr *Aveline*, OG *Avelina* (f), a double diminutive of OG *Avo* is now *Aveline* and *Aveling*. The *Egelina* (f) found in *Eglin*, *Eaglen* and *Eagling* is probably a Norman form of OG **Agilina*.

Though not a complete list, these names give some indication of the fullness and variety of women's names in medieval England and of the debt our surnames owe to them. To these we may add one or two rare names now obsolete: *Antigonia* 1219 Cur (Beds), *Argentina* 1196 P (Cu), *Assyria* Huband 13th AD ii (Wa), *Camilla* 1208 Cur (Ess), 1334 SRK, *Celestria* 1275 SRWo, *Diana* 1204 StP (Lo), *Imagantia* 1219 Cur (Sf), *Italia* 1214 Cur (Sx), *Lavinia* 1334 SRK, *Nigasia* 1203 Cur (Mx), *Prisca* 1327 SRSf, *Pupelina* 12th DC (L), *Pupelota*[1] 1296 SRSx, *Salerna* 1334 SRK.

NAMES OF MEN

Personal-names usually appear in the documents in a Latin form, *Egidius* for *Giles*, *Paganus* for *Payn*, *Vitalis* for *Viel*. The man registered as *Reginaldus* was called *Reynold* by his friends as is proved by occasional examples of *Renalt*, but more particularly by the modern surnames *Reynolds*, *Reynell*, *Renaud*, etc. (from OFr *Reinald*, *Reynaud*, OG *Raginald* 'counsel-might'). The modern christian name *Reginald* is a late resuscitation of the scribal Latin form. *Peter*, *Petre*, as a surname, though found in 1195, Ralph *Peter*, is rare, from the learned form of the christian name *Petrus*. The frequency of *Peters* is due to its late adoption by the Welsh. The popular form was *Per*, *Peres*, *Piers*, as in *Piers* Plowman and *Perkin* Warbeck, and this appears in 16 different spellings in such surnames as *Pierce*, *Pearce*, *Perris*, *Perse*, etc., and in the diminutives *Parkin*, *Parrott*, *Perrott*, *Porrett*, *Perrell*, *Perrin*, *Pirrett* and *Pirard*.

This Latinising tendency at times leads to difficulty. The modern *Jacobs* is certainly Jewish, but Agnes *Jacobes* is found in 1240, Walter *Jacob* and the christian name *Jacob* c1250 and William *Jacobson* in 1332, and these can hardly be Jewish. The name is found before the Conquest as that of an ecclesiastic, but how common it was after the Conquest it is impossible to say as *Jacobus* was used for both *Jacob* and *James*. The latter was not common, but there is clear evidence of its existence in England: *Jam'* de Sancto Hylario 1173-6; *Jamos* (*Jacobus*) de Vabadun 1221; *James* or *Jacobus* de

[1] *v*. p. 228.

Audithleg' 1255, *Jemes* or *Jacobus* Rossel 1297, 1304 Wenlok, whilst the surname is found as Walter *James* 1187 and Thomas *Jemes* 1279. In late Latin *Jacōbus* became *Jacŏbus* and *Jacŏmus*. From the former came French *Jacques*, English *Jacob* and Welsh *Iago*, from the latter, Spanish *Jayme*, OFr *James*, *Gemmes*, AFr *Jam* and English *James*. We have already noted the pronunciations *Jemme* and *Jimme* (now *Gem*). Such surnames as *Jacques*, *Jaquin*, *Jaquest* and *Jacquiss* are either late introductions from France or a refashioning of *Jakes*, etc., after the French. Camden notes such a tendency in the sixteenth century 'which some Frenchified English, to their disgrace, have too much affected'. *Jacquest* and *Jacquiss* are certainly English forms, whilst *Jakeways* preserves the dissyllabic pronunciation of *Jacques* found in Shakespeare.

This brings us to the problem of *Jack*. The ODCN, following E. W. B. Nicholson (1892), derives *Jack*, the common pet-name of *John*, from *Jankin*, a diminutive of *Jan*, *Jehan* (John). According to this theory, *Jankin* became *Jackin* and was then shortened to *Jack*, a process completed by the beginning of the fourteenth century. Both *Jack* and *Jake* are certainly found for *John* towards the end of the thirteenth century: *John* or *Jacke* le Warner 1275, *John* or *Jakke* de Bondec 1279, *Jake* or *John* de Couentre 1292. *Jankin* was a four-teenth-century diminutive of *John*: *John* nicknamed *Janekin* de Bocking Ed 3; *Janekyn* Hastang (1319) was the son of *Jone* Hastang and was called 'young John' or 'John junior' to distinguish him from his father was who still living. But we have record of Petrus filius *Jake* in 1195 and Normannus filius *Jacce* in 1218 and it is difficult to believe that these can come from *Jankin*. In France, *Jacques* (James) was so common a name that it became the normal term for a *peasant*, just as in England, *Jack* became a synonym for *man* or *boy*. It would be strange if so popular a French name did not appear in England. Though rare, undoubted examples of *Jacques* are found: *Jacobus* or *Jakes* Amadur, *Jakes* or *James* Flinthard 1292. The surname dimi-nutives *Jackett*, *Jacklin*, *Jakins* correspond to the French *Jaquet*, *Jacquelin*, *Jacquin*, from *Jacques*, whilst *Jakes*, *Jeeks*, *Jex* show the same vowel-development as *James*, *Jeames*, *Jem*.

Names of Germanic origin

In England Germanic names were usually adopted in their French form. OG *Drogo*, the name of a son of Charlemagne, probably of

Frankish origin (OSax (gi)drog 'ghost, phantom') became OFr *Dreus, Drues* (nom.) and *Dru, Driu, Dreu* (acc.). From the latter we have the surnames *Drew* and *Dru*, with two diminutives, *Drewell* and *Drewett* or *Druitt*. The nominative form does not appear to have been used in England for *Drewes* and *Druce* are invariably local in origin. But with some names, both forms were used and still survive, e.g. OG *Odo, Otto* 'riches', OFr *Odes, Otes* (nom.), *Odon, Otton* (acc.), is now *Oades, Oates, Oaten, Otten* and *Otton*, along with the compounds OG *Authard, Othard, Odard* 'riches-hard' (Odart), OG *Odger, Ogger* 'wealth-spear', OFr *Ogier* (Odgers, Oger), OFr *Otuel* (Ottewell), OG *Otwich*, OFr *Otoïs* (Ottoway, Otway) and the diminutive *Odelin* (Odlin, Odling).

Some names show little variation in form: *Barnard, Bernard* (OG *Bernard* 'bear-brave', OFr *Bernart*); *Baynard* (OG *Beinhard*), found in DB as *Baignard* and *Bangiard*, survives also as *Banyard* and *Bunyard*, due, no doubt, to the Englishman's difficulty in pronouncing the French *n* mouillé; *Gumbel* (OG *Gunbald* 'battle-bold', OFr *Gombaut*); *Gundrey* (OG *Gundric* 'battle-ruler', OFr *Gondri*); *Gunter* (OG *Gunter* 'battle-army', OFr *Gontier*); *Harger* (OG *Hariger, Harger* 'army-spear'); *Harmer, Hermer* (OG *Her(e)mar* 'army-famous'); *Herbert, Harbard* (OG *Hariberct, Her(e)bert* 'army-bright', OFr *Herbert*); *Mauger, Mager, Mayger, Major* (OG *Madalgar, Malger* 'council-spear', OFr *Maugier*); *Mayne* (OG *Maino, Meino* 'strength'); *Maynard* (OG *Maganhard, Meginhard* 'strength-strong', OFr *Mainard, Meinard*); *Mayner* (OG *Maginhari* 'army-might'); *Rabbetts, Rabbitts* (OG *Radbodo, Rabbodo* 'counsel-messenger'); *Rumbold, Rumble* (OG *Rumbold*); *Wareing, Warin, Wearing* (OG *Warin*, AFr *Warin*, OFr *Guarin*); *Wishart, Wiskar, Wesker, Whiscard, Whisker, Wysard, Vizard* (ONFr *Wisc(h)ard*, OFr *Guisc(h)ard*, compounded of ON *vizkr* 'wise' and OG *hardu* 'bold', apparently a purely Norman name).

So numerous are these continental-Germanic personal-names that we can do little here but select. We should note that the popular *Walter* was pronounced *Wauter*, found as a christian name, *Waterus*, as early as 1135 and was still in use in the fifteenth century (*Water* Dey 1479), whence the modern surnames *Water(s), Watters* and *Watterson*, with *Watkin* and *Watts* from the pet-name *Watte* (1292). *Baldwin* (OG *Baldwin* 'bold-friend') was a popular name both in Flanders and in post-Conquest England, whilst *Lambert* (OG *Landberct, Lambert* 'land-bright', OFr *Lambert*), often, with *Lamb-*

kin, clearly the name of Flemish immigrants, was probably introduced from Flanders where St Lambert of Maestricht was highly
venerated. The diminutive *Lambin* still survives as *Lampen, Lampin,
Lamping* and *Lamming*. OG *Engel-, Ingelramnus* 'Angle-raven', OFr
Enguerran, Engerann, now usually *Ingram* and occasionally *Engerran*,
was also used by Flemings, though some of the name came from
Champagne and also Normandy, including Ingelram Count of
Ponthieu, brother-in-law of the Conqueror. *Archibald*, too, was often
a Flemish name (OG *Ercanbald* 'previous-bold', found in DB, OFr
Archamboult). Its modern forms are varied, including *Archambault,
Archbold* and *Archbutt*. In sixteenth-century Kent it had assumed the
form of *Archepoll*, now represented by *Ashbolt, Ashpool* and *Ashpole*.

Among the less common names are: *Bence* (OG *Benzo*); *Beringer,
Bellenger, Bellhanger, Benninger, Benger* (OG *Beringar* 'bear-spear',
OFr *Berengier*); *Claringbold, Claringbull, Clarabut, Clarenbone* and
Cladingbowl are from OG *Clarembald*, a hybrid from Lat *clarus*
'famous' and OG *-bald* 'bold', OFr *Clarembald, Clarebald, Clarem-
baut; Eckhard, Eckert, Eckett* (OG *Eckhard* 'edge-hard'); *Frederick*
(OG *Frideric* 'peace-rule'), not a common medieval name in England
though it occurs in DB. The name became common under the
Hanoverians, and the modern surname is probably often of German
origin. Occasional examples of the colloquial form *Frari* are found
from 1198, and this still survives as *Frarey*; *Grimmond* (OG *Grimund*,
OFr *Grimond*); *Grimward, Grimwade, Grimwood* (OG *Grimward*
'helmet-guard'); OG *Grimbald* 'helmet-bold' was more common and
is now *Grumball, Grumble, Grimble* and *Gribble*; *Maffre* (OG *Mathe-
frid* 'power-peace', OFr *Mafreiz*); *Savary, Savory, Savoury* (OG
Sabaricus, Savaricus, OFr *Savari*); *Tancred* (OG *Tancrad* 'thought-
counsel'); *Tankard* (OG *Tancard* 'thought-hard'), the earliest example
being *Tankardus* the Fleming (1175).

Falk, Falkous, Faulkes, Fawke, Fawkes, Fawcus and *Fakes* are
varied developments of OG *Falco* 'falcon', OFr *Fauque, Fauques*
(nom.). The accusative *Faucon* may sometimes be the origin of *Falcon*, though this is usually from the name of the bird. More common
was OG *Fulco, Folco* 'people', OFr *Fulco, Fouques*, a name which
was hereditary with the Counts of Anjou. Henry II's chamberlain of
Anjou was named *Fulc*. The personal-name is found in DB, but did
not become common in England until Anjou came under English
rule. It seems to have been chiefly used by men of some position,
though not entirely, for we have Fulco portarius, a porter (1149

NthCh) and Fulco faber 'the smith' (12th DC). It occurs as a surname in the twelfth century, but with the loss of Anjou the christian name seems to have fallen out of favour. It is rare in the fourteenth-century Subsidy Rolls, though it continued to be used by certain families. The modern surname is found in at least 28 different forms, including *Folk* and *Fulk*, *Foulkes*, *Foakes*, *Fooks*, *Fowke*, *Voak* and *Volkes*.

Fulk is really a short form of such compounds as OG *Fulcard* 'people-brave' (*Folkard*, *Folkerts*, *Foucard*) and the common OG *Fulcher* 'people-army', OFr *Foucher*, *Fouquier*, which as a surname, has now 19 different forms, including *Fulcher*, *Fulger*, *Fulker*, *Fucher*, *Fudger*, *Futcher*, *Folger*, *Folker*, *Foker*, *Foulcher*, *Foulger*, *Foucar*, *Foulagar*, *Volker*, *Fullagar*. It had a pet-form *Fuche*, now *Fuche*, *Fudge*, *Fuge* and *Fuidge*.

OG *Theudobald* 'people-bold', OFr *Theobald*, *Teobaud*, *Thibaut*, *Tibaut*, a common name both on the Continent and in England, is proved by its modern forms to be of French origin: *Tibald*, *Tidball*, *Tibballs*, *Tibbles*, *Tebbett*, *Tebbutt*. The spelling *Theobald* is a learned form, regularly pronounced *Tibbald* in the sixteenth and seventeenth centuries. A similarly common name is OG *Theudoric*, OFr *Thierri*, *Terri*, now *Terry*, *Tarry* and *Torrey*. Many of the early ME bearers of this name were Flemish or German merchants, frequently described as *Teutonicus*, *Alemannus* or *Flandrensis*.

Biblical names

Much the most common Biblical name was *Adam*, particularly popular in Yorks and Lancs. *Elias*, the Greek form of the Hebrew *Elijah*, was *Elis* in ME. *Elias* is now found occasionally as a surname, but is usually *Ellis*, with such variants as *Ellice*, *Elles*, *Heelis* and *Helis*. *Absalom*, from Hebrew *Abshálóm* 'father of peace' was commonly *Apselon* or *Aspelon* in ME and has given not only modern *Absolom* and *Absolon* but also *Aspenlon*, *Asplen*, *Asplin*, *Aspland* and *Ashplant*. Common, too, was *Solomon*, often in the form *Salamon* (OFr *Salomon*, of Hebrew origin, meaning 'peace'). It was not confined to Jews, being found as the name of a cleric, a chaplain and a canon, and survives also as *Salman*, *Salmon*, *Salmond*, *Sammon* and *Sammonds*. Also popular, though much less so than *Adam*, were *Abel*, *Abraham*, *Daniel*, surviving also as *Dannell*, *Dennell* and *Denial*, *David*, with its French popular form *Davy* and *Joseph* (*Jessopp*, *Jessupp*).

140

Isaac, Samuel and *Saul* were rare, but had sufficient vitality to produce surnames. They were not confined to Jews and, like *Abraham* and *Absalom*, are found both as christian names and surnames at a time when the Jews had been expelled from England. Rare, too, were *Jude* and *Gabriel*. *Noah* (now *Noyse, Noise* and *Noe*) was not particularly popular and its common use as a surname is probably due to the medieval drama as is *Moyse, Moyses, Moyce* and *Moyes*, from OFr *Moise*, Hebrew *Moses*. This also occurs as a Jewish name, *Mossus* cum naso (1183), but Ailmer *filius Mosse* or Almer *Moss* (1153–68) was probably English. *Jeremiah*, found in its Greek form *Jeremias* in 1189, was popularly pronounced *Jeremy* as in the modern surname. *Job* now survives also as *Jobe, Jope, Jopp, Jubb, Jupe* and *Jupp*. Though it had other origins, its popularity as a christian name is proved by the diminutives *Jobbins, Joblin, Jobling, Joplin* and *Jopling*. The learned Greek form *Tobias* of the Hebrew *Tobiah* 'Jehovah is good', survives also in the popular form *Toby*. It was a rare name, but is found as that of *Tobias*, the first prior of Thoby Priory in Essex (1142–50) and as the name of a Suffolk priest in 1286, *Tobias* de Chatesham (AD ii, iii). The modern *Maccoby* may be of Jewish origin, from *Maccabaeus*, but it occurs at Norwich in 1289 as a sole name (NorwLt). *Gamaliel* is found in Yorkshire in 1196 (P) and the Biblical *Ananias* in Essex (1205 Cur) and was still in use in Devon in 1654, *Ananias* Colle (HartlandPR).

The Hebrew *Shimeon* 'hearkening' appears in the English version of the Old Testament as *Simeon*, occasionally *Shimeon*, but in the New Testament as *Simon* (except in one instance). The forms were kept distinct, as separate names, in the Middle Ages, *Simon* being much more common both as a christian name and as a surname. By the side of *Simeon, Simeons* and *Simion*, we have five different forms from *Simon*, including *Simon, Simons* and *Symon*. Here the Hebrew *Shimeon* may have been influenced by the Greek Σίμων, from σιμός 'snub-nosed'. But the problem is complicated by the fact that after the Conquest, in England, *Simund* was a common AFr form of *Simon*. Wycliffe uses *Symound* for Simon Peter; Simon de Montfort is called *Simond* by Robert of Gloucester, Adam *Cimond* (1292 SRLo) is identical with Adam *Simon* (1292 LLB A) and Adam son of *Simon* (1290 Pat), whilst Prompt Parv (c1440) gives *Symounde* as the English form of Simon. Thus the surnames *Simond, Simmonds* and *Symonds* and others of the 14 different varieties, including *Simmons, Simmance, Simmence* and *Semmens* may all derive from the Biblical name *Simon* or *Simund*. But there are other complications which make a definite etymology of any one surname difficult or impossible. *Simund danus* (1066 DB, Wa) was a Dane as was *Simon* or *Simundus* (ib., Wo), who is elsewhere called '*Simund quidam, genere Danus*'. This is ON *Sigmundr*, ODa *Sigmund* 'victory-protector', already confused with *Simon*. Some examples of *Simund* may be Anglo-Scandinavian; others may have been brought over from Normandy where we also have to reckon with OG *Sigmund*. The popularity of *Simon* (or *Simond*), however, is proved by its pet-forms *Simms* and *Symes* and its diminutives *Simcock* and *Simkin*, its diminutive *Simonett*, *Simnett*, the once common *Simon-el*, a surname from 1200 to 1561, well known as that of Lambert Simnel, and the undocumented modern surname *Simblet* which would appear to be from a double diminutive *Sim-el-et*.

Names of saints

The most common of the saints' names were those still in use today and easily recognised: *Andrew*, *Bartholomew*, *Clement*, *Denis*, *Gregory*, *Laurence*, *Lucas* and *Luke*, *Martin*, *Nicholas*, *Peter* (discussed above), *Stephen* and *Thomas*. The name of the founder of the Benedictine order, a popular name, occasionally appears in its Latin form *Benedictus* 'blessed', but from the twelfth century even as a christian name is usually *Beneit*, the colloquial French form, which as a surname survives as *Bennett*. The surnames *Benedict* and *Bennedik* appear to have no connexion with the christian name. They are found only as surnames, *Benedicite* (from 1221), from Lat *benedicite* 'bless (you)', a nickname, no doubt, from a favourite expression. The common *Samson*, *Sampson*, *Sansom*, *Sanson*, found as *Sanson* in DB, is not from the Biblical *Samson* of Gaza. Both christian name and surname are common in England in districts where Bretons were numerous and derive from OFr *Sanson*, *Samson*, probably of Celtic origin, for it was the name of a Welsh bishop (fl. 550) who crossed over to Brittany and founded the abbey of Dol where he was buried and venerated as a saint. *Brice*, too, popular both in England and France, is probably of Celtic origin. It was the name of St Britius, successor of St Martin as Bishop of Tours.

The Lat *Augustinus*, from *augustus* 'venerable' was common in its Latin form as a christian name, but *Augustin* as a surname is a rare and learned form. The modern surname is *Austin* or *Austen*, from OFr *Aoustin*, the vernacular form, found as a christian name in 1224 and as a surname in 1275. *Vitalis* (OFr *Vitel*, *Viel*), from Lat *vitalis* 'pertaining to life, vital', was the name of some ten saints. It is found in DB and the twelfth and thirteenth centuries both in its learned Latin form and in the northern French form *Viel*, and survives in the surnames *Vial*, *Viel* and *Vital* and also as *Vidal*, but the absence of early forms of this suggests that it was a later immigrant from Languedoc. Somewhat similar in meaning is *Vivian*, Lat *Vivianus*, from *vivus* 'living', a name not uncommon in England in the twelfth century. Its modern forms provide an interesting lesson in phonetic development including as they do, *Videan*, *Vidgeon*, *Fiddian*, *Fidgen*, *Phethean* and *Phythian*.

The less common saints' names include: *Adrian* (Lat *Hadrianus* 'of the Adriatic'), in England probably due to its assumption by Nicholas Brakespear, the only English pope (d. 1159); *Ambrose*, of Greek origin, 'divine, immortal'; *Antony*, an Egyptian ascetic; *Bastin*, a pet-form of *Sebastian* 'man of Sebastia', a city in Pontus, a Roman legionary martyred under Diocletian; *Boniface*, a third-century saint martyred at Tarsus, and the name of a number of popes; *Crispin*, *Crippen*, the patron saint of shoemakers, martyred at Soissons c285 (also a nickname from Lat *crispinus* 'curly'); *Damyon*, a Cilician martyr (303) whose relics were supposed to have been discovered at Milan by St Ambrose; *Fabian*, a third century pope and martyr; *Ledger*, *Leger* (OG *Leodegar* 'people-spear', OFr *Legier*), a seventh-century bishop; *Leonard*, *Lennard* (OG *Leonhard* 'lion-bold'), hermit and patron saint of captives, a name much less common than one would expect in view of the number of churches dedicated to him; *Mark*, curiously rare as a christian name, the surname being often local in origin; *Pollitt*, the popular form of the Greek *Hippolytus* 'letting horses loose' (*Ipolitus* 1207–14 Cur, Ess, Y, K) to whom the church of Ippollits (Herts) is dedicated (called *Polytes* in 1412); *Silvester*, *Siviter*, from Lat *Silvester* 'dweller in the forest', the name of three popes, apparently first used in England by clerics; *Urban*, Lat *urbanus* 'of the city', an occasional christian name from 1197; *Valentine*, a derivative of Lat *valens* 'strong, healthy' and *Vincent*, Lat *vincens* 'conquering', both third-century martyrs.

St George, the patron saint of England, was a Roman military tribune martyred at Nicomedia in 303. His cult was brought to England by returning crusaders, but the name was curiously rare. It is found as *Georgius* in Yorkshire in 1185 (of Greek origin, 'farmer');

143

the surname has not been noted before 1348, Agnes *Jeorge* (FFEss). It was not until after the Hanoverian succession in the eighteenth century that the name became popular.

In England, *Patrick* (OIr *Patraicc*) was chiefly northern, its earliest examples being Latinised as *Patricius* 'patrician', found also in Lincolnshire, where it is probably to be identified with the French *Patrice*, *Patris*, *Paris*, still surviving in the surnames *Paris* and *Parris*.

St Pancras, best known to most people as the name of a railway station, came of a family of wealth and position, Roman by his up-bringing, though not by birth. His parents were heathen and his father before his death entrusted Pancras to his brother Dionysius, adjuring him by all the gods to take care of the child. Dionysius moved with his nephew to Rome, took a house on the Caelian Hill, and both were baptised by the Bishop of Rome. A few days later Dionysius died during the persecution of Diocletian (303). The young Pancras, aged fourteen, was denounced and executed with the sword. Of the eight churches dedicated to him, all but one are in the south-eastern counties, three in Sussex,[1] where we find our only references to the surname, Richard *Pancras* 1296 SRSx, John *Pancrace* 1525 SRSx. Bardsley gives the christian name *Pancrace* Grout in 1532 and the surname Robert *Panckridge* in 1698 in London, a name which still survives, though rare. The etymology is confirmed by his note that in 1630 *Pancradge* church was the common pronunciation. There was also a St Pancras of Taormina (first century) to whom seven churches in the west of England are dedicated.

The Hebrew *Mattathiah* 'gift of Jehovah' was Latinised as both *Matthaeus* and *Mathaeus* which in France became respectively *Mathieu* and *Mahieu*, very popular names in England, which have given us the surnames *Matthews* and *Mayhew*, *Mayho* and *Mayo*. *Maurice* (Lat *Mauritius* 'Moorish, dark, swarthy', from *Maurus* 'a Moor') is the learned form, *Morice* c1175 Newark, *Moriz* 1185 Templars, the common, popular one, whence the surnames *Morrice* and *Morris*. *Paul* (Lat *paulus* 'small') is not common as a christian name. Its frequency is disguised under such forms as *Poll* (1209), *Powel* (c1260), *Pole* (1275) or *Poul*. The attribute of Wickham St Paul's (Ess) appears as *Pol(l)* 1285, *Poel* 1327, *Poulis* 1343, *Powel* 1358, *Poles* and *Poole* 1607. Pole Hill in Chingford is a relic of the

---

[1] *v.* F. Arnold-Forster, *Studies in Church Dedications* (London, 1899), vol. I, pp. 169–70, 489–91.

manor of Chingford *Pauls*, all of which help to explain the modern surnames *Paul*, *Pawle*, *Pole(s)*, *Poll*, *Poole*, *Powell* and *Powles*.

Michael, of Hebrew origin, 'Who is like the Lord?', is the learned form in which the christian name is almost invariably found. The popular pronunciation was from the French *Michel* which survives as the surname *Mitchell*. The OFr popular form in the north was *Mihiel*, as in the place-name Saint-Mihiel. This is found late as a christian name in England (*Mihil* 1549), but is probably much older and is still found in the surnames *Mihell*, *Myhill*, *Miall* and *Miell*. Butler, in *Hudibras*, rhymes *St Michael's* with *trials*. In ME *Michaelmas* is found both as *Mielmasse* and *Mighelmasse* and the *Cursor Mundi* has a form *seynt Myghhell*, surviving in *Miggles*, *Mighall*, *Mighell* and *Mighill*. In Orkney *St Michael's* is pronounced *St Mitchell's*. St. Michael's, Cornhill, was *Saint Mihills* in 1626. Miles's Lane (London) was *Seint Micheleslane* in 1303 and *Saynte Mighelles Lane* in 1548. *Michel* is found as a christian name in 1297 Wenlok (*Michel le wafrer*) and in 1327, but examples are rare. In 1198 *Michael* de Middelton' held a quarter of a carucate in Middleton (W) by service of keeping the king's wolf-hounds. About 1219 William *Michel* received $3\frac{1}{2}d$. per day for keeping two wolf-hounds, and in 1236 Richard *Michel* held a cotset in Middleton for a similar service. The relationship between these men is not stated, but it appears a reasonable assumption that they were of the same family and that *Michael* de Middelton had two sons who derived their surname *Michel* from their father's christian name. The clerk gave the christian name its usual learned form, the surname in the form in common use.

Names of Classical origin

Many of the saints' names were of Greek or Latin origin. Apart from these the number surviving as surnames is small, much the most popular being the Greek *Alexander* 'helper of men', still found in its learned form. In the Middle Ages its vogue was, no doubt, due to the French romance of Alexander and the name appears in England in its French form *Alisandre*, from which, as early as 1248, was formed the pet-name *Sandre*, whence the modern surnames *Sandars*, *Sanders* and *Saunders*. In 1327 it occurs as a surname *Elysandre*, a form underlying the Scottish surnames *Elesender*, *Elshener* and *Elshender*. The name of the first Christian emperor, *Constantinus*, a derivative of Lat *constans* 'steadfast', OFr *Constantin*, *Costantin*, was early adopted

as a christian name. It occurs in DB and has given the modern surnames *Constantine* and *Cossentine*, but the real medieval pronunciation is represented by *Costins* and *Costain*, with its pet-form *Coste*,
recorded in 1175 and still a surname. From the full name we also
have *Consterdine* and *Considine*. The Lat *Horatius* was introduced
into England from Italy in the sixteenth century in the form *Horatio*
but it is found as *Oratius* presbiter in Essex in 1193 (P) and, though
rare, has become the surname *Orriss* or *Orys*, appearing as Richard
Oras (1312 FF) and Richard *Orys* (1516 ib.), both from Essex, and
as Henry *Orris* (1674 HTSf).

Dauzat is of opinion that Fr *Payen* which still had its original
meaning 'peasant' in OFr was, like *Paysan*, a nickname given in a
town to an immigrant peasant, adding that *païen* was already applied
as a surname to children whose baptism had been delayed. This
suggests he had in mind the old meaning of *paganus* 'heathen', but it
was a curious practice to name a newly baptised child either 'peasant'
or 'heathen'. The whole history and meaning of *pagan*, formerly
misunderstood, has been made clear by Weekley.[1] It comes from the
Lat *paganus* 'peasant' (from *pagus* 'a village'), which in late Latin
took the sense of *heathen*. The *Oxford Dictionary* has now withdrawn
the traditional derivation:

'The explanation of Lat *paganus* in the sense non-Christian, heathen, as
arising out of that of villager, rustic, has been shown to be chronologically
and historically untenable, for this use of the word goes back to Tertullian
(c202), when paganism was still the public and dominant religion . . . The
explanation is now found in the Latin use of *paganus* = non-militant,
civilian, opposed to *miles*, soldier, one of the army. The Christians called
themselves *milites*, enrolled soldiers of Christ, members of His militant
Church, and applied to non-Christians the term applied by soldiers to all
who were not enrolled in the army.'

In England there is no shred of evidence for the use of the word
as a nickname, not a solitary example with the definite article.
Paganus[2] was introduced from Normandy where it had already become a personal-name, no doubt, without any thought of its possible
meaning. It is found in DB as *Pagen*, was very popular in the
twelfth and thirteenth centuries, often as *Pain* or *Payne* and is not
uncommon in the fourteenth-century Subsidy Rolls. As a surname it
is now usually *Pain* or *Payne*, but appears also as *Pagan*, *Payen* and

[1] E. Weekley, *Words Ancient and Modern* (London, 1946), pp. 73–5.
[2] It was also used as a woman's name: *Pagana* mother of Robert de Gravele
13th AD ii (Sf).

Pane. In 1086 (DB) Radulfus *filius Pagani* is also called Radulfus *Paganus* and *Paganel*, that is, as son of Paganus he had adopted his father's christian name as his surname, *Paganel* 'little Payne' distinguishing him from his father. This diminutive and also *Painot* (1176) still survive as the surnames *Paynell, Pannell, Pennell* and *Panet, Pannett.*

Classical names formerly found in medieval England further illustrate the variety of names in use: *Achilles* 1199, 1228 FFHu, William *Achilles* 1202 Fees (Sa), 1263 AssSt, possibly surviving as *Achille* and *Achilles*; *Aeneas*: *Eneas* filius Hugonis Hy 2 Seals (Y), *Eneas* 1263 AssLa, 1381 AssWa; *Aristotile* 1196 P (Hu); *Cesar* clericus 1185 Templars (Y); *Ciprianus* 1182–1211 BuryS (C); *Charlemayn* 1230 P (Wo), John *Charlemayne* 1353 Putman (W); *Eusebius* Ailbrit 1279 RH (Hu); *Hector* 1190 P (Sf), John *Hector* 1568 SRSf (now *Hector*); *Ygnatius* filius Athelwaldi 1207 Cur (Nf), common in Spain as *Inigo*; *Juvenalis* 1203 Cur (Nth), William *Juvenal* 1222 Cur (Nth), probably the origin of the rare *Juvenile*; *Nicodemus*, found as a surname, William, Agnes *Nichodemus*, 1310 ColchCt; *Lucianus* de Scille 1212 Cur (Db); Hugo *Pirramus* 1206 Cur (Lei); *Virgil* 12th DC (R), *Virgilius* 1237 StP (Ess), 1332 SRSx, 1334 SRK, *Virgil* Chapman 1296 SRSx, Reginald *Virgil* 1201 P (Ha), Isabella *Virgile* 1296 SRSx.

THE BRETON ELEMENT

The large Breton contingent which fought at Hastings was rewarded with lands in England. At their head was Earl Alan of Richmond, a cadet of the ducal house, with a fee of the first importance in Lincolnshire, East Anglia and neighbouring counties. In the south-west Judhael of Totnes had a fief which in the twelfth century owed service of 70 knights. In thirteenth century Suffolk was a 'Breton soke'. There is, in fact, hardly a county in which this Breton element is not found, and in some counties its influence was deep and permanent ... The Breton colony founded by Earl Alan of Richmond can still be traced, late in the twelfth century, by personal-names which give a highly individual character to records relating to the country round Boston, itself a town of Breton creation, and Louth. In these districts, as also in the North Riding of Yorkshire, Breton settlers of the eleventh and twelfth centuries preserved their ancient personal-nomenclature with a conservatism resembling that of the Anglo-Scandinavian peasants among whom they lived. It was something more than the establishment of a few score knights and sergeants in military tenancies. It must have had the character of a genuine migration, though a migration on a small scale.[1]

The strength of this Breton influence is not fully revealed by the Breton personal-names on record. Already at the time of DB, many Bretons bore names of Germanic origin common throughout Normandy and northern France. Geoffrey de Wirce, who came from La Guerche near Rennes, held a fee which included the whole of the Isle of Axholme; Oger the Breton was lord of Bourne in Lincolnshire and Maino Brito head of an estate at Wolverton (Bk). In 1086 we find men named Willelmus, Waldin and Radulfus with the attribute *Brito* 'the Breton'. *Herveus*, origin of the modern *Harvey*, a common name among the tenants of Count Alan, appears also as *Herueu, Herui, Hervicus* and *Herevi*, sometimes from OG *Herewig, Herewicus* 'army-war', but also from OBret *Aeruiu, Hærviu* 'battle-worthy', a clear survival of which is the surname of Richard *Herfu* (1327 SRSx). In Brittany the English name Alfred enjoyed peculiar favour. It is found there in the ninth century with 17 examples in a single cartulary between 1100 and 1150. Judhael of Totnes, the son of an Alfred, was succeeded by another Alfred. Alfred of Lincoln was not an Englishman but a Breton, his heir was Alan. Joel of Lincoln (d. 1051) must have been a Breton settled in England under the Confessor.[2]

In twelfth-century Lincolnshire, Alan was as common a name as Simon and more popular than Henry and Adam. Other common Breton names were Brian, Conan, Jarnegon, Justin (with its pet-form Just), Mengi, Samson and Tengi, all surviving as modern surnames. The christian name of Judhael de Totnes is still found as a surname in Devonshire as Jewell, and elsewhere as Jekyll and Joel. In Essex, Helion Bumpstead, and in Devon, Upton Helions, owe their attributes to Tihel de Herion, their Domesday lord who came from Helléan in Morbihan. His christian name, that of a Cambridgeshire reeve of the Bishop of Ely in 1086 (*Thiellus, Tehel*), was borne by a Bumpstead peasant, Tihel the fisherman, in the reign of Henry II and survived in Essex until the thirteenth century and is found as a surname at Barking in 1206 (Roger *Tihell*), whilst his surname, though rare, still lives on in Essex and Suffolk, in Devon and Somerset. Wiggens Green in Helion Bumpstead owes its name to the family

[1] F. M. Stenton, *The First Century of English Feudalism* (Oxford, 1932), pp. 24–6.
[2] J. H. Round, *Feudal England* (London, 1895), pp. 327–9.

of John *Wygayn* whose eponymous ancestor may well have been an actual follower of Tihel the Breton. Bretts in Aveley owes its name to John *le Bret* 'the Breton'. In Aveley is a field, Bumpstead Mead, the last relic of a Bumpsted Hall named from Gilbert de Bumsted ad Turrim who seems to have been accompanied to Aveley by Bumpstead men of Breton descent whose names are found in the district in the thirteenth century (*Wygan, Hervey, Alan, Bryce*).

Hervey de Ispania, probably a Breton from Espinay (Ille-et-Villaine), was a considerable tenant of the Honour of Richmond in 1086 and has left his name in Willingale Spain, Spains Hall in Finchingfield and Spaynes Hall in Great Yeldham where later we find under-tenants with Breton names, *Mingy* and *Jikel*, the latter surviving in Jeckyll's Farm in Finchingfield.

Breton personal-names still in use as surnames include: *Allain, Allan, Allen, Alleyne* (OBret *Alan*, OFr *Alain*, the name of a Welsh and Breton saint); *Brian*,[1] *Bryant, Brice, Conan* (OBret *Conan*, the name of Breton chiefs, kings and a saint); *Jekyll, Jeckell, Jickles, Jiggle, Jockel* (OBret *Iudicael*, name of a Breton king, which became *Iedecael*, modern *Gicquel, Jezequel*); *Jernegan, Jerningham* (OBret *Iarnuuocon, Iarnogon* 'iron-famous'); *Joel, Jewell, Joule, Jowle, Juell* (OBret *Iudhael*, from *Iud-* 'lord, chief' and *haël* 'generous'); *Josse*,[2] *Joyce, Joysey, Jowsey* (OBret *Jodoc*, the name of a saint, son of Judicael, who had a hermitage at the modern Josse-sur-Mer); *Jukes, Jewkes* (from *Jukel*, from *Judicael*); *Mingay, Mingey* (Bret *Menguy* 'stone dog', from *men* 'stone' and *ki* 'dog'); *Sampson* (*v.* above, p. 142); *Tingay, Tingey, Tengue, Tanguy, Tangye* (*Tanguy, Tanneguy*, a common name in Brittany, from St Tanguy, one of the entourage of St Pol of Leon; Bret *tān* 'fire' and *ki* 'dog'); *Wigan, Wigand, Wigens, Wiggans, Wiggin* (OBret *Uuicon, Guegon*, from *guen* 'white' and *con* 'high'), *Wymark, Waymark* (OBret *Wiuhomarch* 'worthy to have a horse').

Pet-names

Already in OE we find pet-names in use: *Tuma* for *Tumwine* in the seventh century and *Ælle* for *Ælfwine* in the tenth, and such forms as *Wine* and *Wulfa* for *Winefriŏ* and *Wulfwine*. Names of this type continued to be formed and a number still survive in surnames, some

---

[1] In the north, from ON *Brján*, OIr *Brian*.

[2] *Josse* and *Gosse* derive also from *OG Gozzo*, OFr *Joce, Gosse*.

otherwise unrecorded. But most of the pet-names in modern surnames are of post-Conquest formation and some are difficult to identify. Examples are found in the twelfth century; they become more numerous in the middle of the thirteenth and in the fourteenth are common. They are found among all classes and are derived from Old English, Scandinavian and French personal-names alike: *Cutt* (1279) from OE *Cūðbeorht*, is found as a surname at Newark in 1175 (Walter *Cut*) and *Cudd* in 1358. *Ugga* (1212) is from OE *Ūhtrǣd*; *Asti* (1203) is a pet-form of ON *Ásketill* (now *Hastie*); *Lamb* (1161) is for *Lambert*, *Gibb* (1179) for *Gilbert*, *Lina* (1181) for *Adelina* or *Emelina* (now *Lines*), whilst the Breton *Sanson*, *Samson* has given *Sanne* (1260) and *Samme* (1275), both still preserved in *Sanne* and *Sans*, *Sam* and *Sammes*.

Not all pet-names are so easy to identify. The modern *Hudd*, found as a personal-name as early as 1177, is clearly for *Hugh*. In 1212 the father of *Hugo filius Johannes* is later referred to as Johannes pater ipsius *Hudde*, whilst *Hugo* Sturdy is identical with *Hudde* Sturdi (1219, 1230). But it appears to have been used also as a pet-name of *Richard*. Bardsley's *Ricardus* de Knapton and Cristina *Hud*wyf is not absolutely conclusive, but his *Ricardus* dictus *Hudde* de Walkden (1346) leaves no doubt. *Hull*, too, was used for *Hugh*: *Hulle* le Bule (1201), probably from the diminutives *Hulin*, *Hulot*. John *Hulle*sone Rudd held a tenement formerly *Hugh* Rudde's. John was the son of *Hulle* or *Hugh* Rudde. *Pell*, frequent as a personal-name from 1274, is a pet-form of *Peter*, with a diminutive *Pelly*, also a modern surname. *Pelle* de Hoveden (1296) was a *Peter* and *Pelly* Wyth (1278) is identical with *Peter* son of John. This pet-name was still in use in Suffolk in 1764. *Hann* is at times a pet-name for *John*, from *Jehan*, but was certainly used also for *Henry*, *Hanne* or *Henry* de Leverpol (1323); Richard *Hanne*sone (1379) is identical with Ricardus filius *Henrici* (1365). Camden gives *Hann* as a pet-name of *Randolph*.

Some of these names followed normal phonetic laws of assimilation: *Ibb* for *Isabel* or *Ilbert*; *Judd*, from *Jurd* (Jordan); *Phipp* from *Philip*; *Tebb*, *Tibb* and *Tipp*, from *Tedbald* or *Tidbald*, the popular pronunciation of *Theobald*. *Bett* was sometimes a woman's name, *Betta* Caperun (1247), from *Beatrice* or *Elizabeth*, but it was also used for men: *Bettinus* Beaumond and *Bette* his brother (1289), *Bette* the bocher (Piers Plowman). This was a pet-name for *Bettin*, earlier *Bertin*, undoubtedly used for both *Bertram* and *Bertelmew* (Bartholo-

150

mew). *Ebb* is not only for *Isabel*, with a diminutive *Ebbitt*, but also from the masculine *Herbert* which has given both *Hebb* and *Ebb*. In the manuscript, the christian name of *Ebbi* le Estreis (1218 AssL) is an interlineation for the cancelled *Herebertus*.

In others, the name begins by anticipating the following medial consonant: *Dand* (1246) for *Andrew*, *Bibby* (1240) for Isabel. Some pet-names are formed from the second syllable of the full name. *Pott* (1115) from *Philipot*, itself a diminutive of *Philip*; *Coll* (1247) from *Nichol* (the diminutive *Colin* occurs in 1191); *Belle* from *Isabel*; *Sander* (1248) from *Alexander*. Voiced and voiceless consonants were used indiscriminately: *Dicke, Digge*; *Hikke, Higge*; *Gepp, Gebb* (Geoffey); *Judd, Jutte*. Vowels were unrounded, *Rob, Rab, Nobb, Nabb, Dobb, Dabb*, all from *Robert*; or rounded, *Malle, Molle* (Mary); *Magge, Mogge* (Margaret), whilst the changes were rung on the consonants, *Rick, Hick* and *Dick*, from *Richard*. The numerous surnames from pet-names include *Addey* and *Addis* (Adam), *Bate, Batt* and *Batty* (Bartholomew), *Clem* (Clement), *Daw* and *Dow* (David), *Gregg* and *Grigg* (Gregory) and *Law, Low* (Lawrence). With such varieties of the same name, it is not surprising that we cannot always identify the original of those that are rare or that confusion should arise. In 1400 Drew Barentyn appealed to the Council to correct his christian name to *Drew* in the list of freemen of the City where it had been entered as *Andrew*, an indication that *Drew* was regarded as a pet-name of Andrew for which there appears to be no other evidence.

Diminutives[1]

The most common diminutive suffixes are *-et, -ot, -un, -on, -in* and *-el*, with double diminutives in *-el-in, -el-ot, -in-ot*. These may be added to the full name and many are both masculine and feminine: *Ablott* from *Abel-ot, Luckett* (Luke), *Garnett, Warnett* (OG *Guarin, Warin*), *Rawlin* (OFr *Raoul*, OG *Radulf*), *Pagnell* (OFr *Pagenel*); to a short form of an OG name: *Gaudin* (OFr *Gaudin*, from OG *Wald-*), *Jobin* (Job), *Amiel* (Amy); or to a pet-name: *Linnett* (Lina), *Batten* (Bartholomew), *Dodgin* (Dodge, i.e. Roger), *Hewell* (Hugh).

OG *Avo* (Aves) has diminutives *Avel* and *Aveline*. We should, therefore, expect that *Avina* (1221), now *Avins*, was another diminutive, but as one *Avina* (1221 AssGl) was also called *Avicia*, the name was used as a hypocoristic of *Avicia* (Avis). Similarly, *Amiot* was used

---

[1] The diminutive suffixes *-cock* and *-kin* are discussed below, pp. 209–17.

as a pet-form of *Amis* or *Ames* for *Amiot* de Wudestoch' (1191 P) is identical with *Amisius* de Wodestoke (1250 Eyns). OFr *Bodin*, OG *Baudin*, common as *Bodin* or *Boydin*, was used as a pet-name for *Baldwin*: *Baldewyn* de Huntindon 1283 Husting, *Boydin* de Huntingdone 1293 LLB C. The diminutive is frequently used side by side with the full name: *Adam* de Bidyk is also called *Adinet* (a diminutive of *Adam*), now *Adnett*; *Robinus* or *Robertus* de Leie (1212 Cur).

Double diminutives include:

-el-in: *Hamlin* (OG *Haimo*), *Hewlins* (*Hugh*), *Hubling* (from *Hubb*, a short form of *Hubald* or *Hubert*), *Sablin* (Sabin), *Wakelin* (OG *Walho* or *Walico*, OFr *Walchelin*), *Wastling* (OG *Wazo*, *Wazelin*).

-el-ot: *Barlett* (OG *Berard*), *Bartlett* (from *Bertelmew*, *Bartholomew*), *Giblett* (from *Gibb*, *Gilbert*), *Roblett* (*Rob*), *Walklate*, *Walklett* (OG *Walho*, *Walico*).

-en-el: *Avenel* (OG *Avo*), *Parnell* (from *Per* 'Peter', *Peronel*, Lat *Petronilla*).

-in-ot, *-in-et*: *Dabinett* (*Dab* from Robert), *Picknett* (*Pik-en-et*, *Pik-en-ot*, from OFr *Pic*, originally a nickname), *Rabnott* (*Rab* from *Robert*), *Simnett* (*Simon*).

SURNAMES FROM POST-CONQUEST PERSONAL-NAMES

Numerous surnames from the new personal-names introduced by the Normans have been discussed already. No complete list has yet been made. In any case, it would be too long to be included here. In the *Dictionary of British Surnames* surnames from some 339 of these personal-names are included, but this seriously underestimates their number for it includes only distinct name-forms and takes no account of pet-names or diminutives nor, of course, of the many surnames of this class now obsolete. The full impact of these French names on our nomenclature can be realised only by considering the whole of these as well as the many varieties assumed by the modern surnames. The popularity of *Hugh* is clearly shown by its 14 variants in modern surnames and by its numerous diminutives of which some 90 different forms survive, and the list is certainly not complete. No modern representative, for instance, has been found of *Hudelin*, already a surname in 1208 and 1247. The following lists of the varied developments of a few of the most common surnames will give some indication of what we owe to these new-comers from the Continent.[1]

---

[1] For the various forms of *Peter*, *v.* p. 136, of *Agnes, Maud, Mabel, Mary* and *Isabel*, pp. 76–7, 135.

OFr *Gislebert, Gil(l)ebert, Guilbert*, from OG *Gisilbert* 'pledge- or hostage-bright'; pet-name *Gibbe*, with diminutives *Gibun, Gibelin, Gibelun, Gibelot*:

Gilbert, Gil(l)bard, Gilb(e)art, Gilburt, Guilbert, FitzGilbert, Gilbertson.

Gibb, Gibb(e)s, Gibson, Gibbeson, Gipson, Gypson, Gibben(s), Gibbin(s), Gibbings, Gibbon(s), Giblet, Giblin, Gibling.

OFr *Hue* from OG *Hugo* 'heart, mind'; pet-names *Hudd, Hull*; diminutives *Huel, Huet*; *Huget, -in, -un*; *Hugelin*; *Hudel, Huchon*:

Hugh(es), Hugo, Ugo, Hue, Huws, Hew,[1] Hew(e)s, How(s), Howe(s),[2] FitzHugh, Fitzhugues, Hughson, Hewson, Hooson, Hoosun, Huson.

Hudd, Hudden, Huddle, Hudson, Hutson, Hudman, Hudsmith; Hull(e)s,[3] Hulson.

Hewet(t), Hewat, Hewit(t), Howat(t), Howett, Howitt, Huet(t), Huitt, Huot; Hewetson, Hewitson, Hewison, Huetson, Huison, Huitson.

Hugget(t), Huggin(s), Hugon, Huggon(s), Huggonson, Huglin.

Hewlett, Hewlitt, Howlett, Hulatt, Huleatt, Hul(l)ett, Hullot, Hewlins, Hewlings, Howlin, Howling(s), Huelin, Hulance, Hulin, Hullin(s).

Hutchin(s),[4] Hutchings, Hutchence, Hutchens, Hutcheon, Hutchons, Hotchen, Hotchin, Houchen, Houchin, Howchin; Hutchinson, Hutcherson, Hutchingson, Hutchison.

Laurence, from Lat *Laurentius* '(man) of Laurentum'; pet-names *Lawe, Lowe, Lar*, diminutives *Lariot, Larkin*:

Laurence, Laurance, Laurens, Lawrance, Lawrence, Larrance, Lorence, Lorenz, Lowrance, Lawrenson.

Lawr(e)y, Lawrie, Lorie, Lorrie, Lory, Lowrey, Lowrie(s), Low(e)ry, Loury, Lowri(e)son, Lorriman, Loryman, Lorrison.

Law,[5] Law(e)s, Low, Low(e)s, Lawson, Lowson.

Larrett, Larkin(s), Larking, Larkinson, Lorkin(g).

Nicholas, from Lat *Nicolaus*, from Gk Νικόλαος 'victory-people'. Popularly *Nicol*,[6] with pet-forms *Nick* and *Coll*, with diminutives from each:

Nicholas(s), Nicolas, Nicklas(s), Nickless, Nickolay, Nicolai, Nicolay.

Niccols, Nichol, Nichol(e)s, Nicholds, Nicholls, Nicol(e), Nicoll(e), Nickal(ls), Nickell, Nickells, Nickels, Nickle, Nickol(ls), Nickolds, Nickols, Nicolls, Nicholson, Nickelson, Nicolson, Nickerson, Nickinson, Nickisson, McNichol, McNicol, McNickle.

Nicholetts, Nicklen, Nicklin.

Nick(e)s, Nix, Nickson, Nix(s)on.

---

[1] Also from ME *hewe* 'domestic, servant'.

[2] Also local, from OE *hōh* 'spur of a hill' or ON *haugr* 'mound, hill'.

[3] Also from Hull (Ch) or, occasionally, OE *hyll* 'hill'.

[4] From OFr *Huchon*, a double diminutive of *Hue*, common in Picardy, corresponding to OFr *Hueçon, Huesson*.

[5] More often from OE *hlāw* 'hill'.

[6] *Nicholas Godman* (1295) is also called both *Nicol* (1293) and *Colle* (1286, 1294 Wenlok).

Coll(s), Colle, Coull, Coule(s), Cowle(s).

Collard, Collet(t), Collete, Colin, Collin(s), Collen(s), Collyns, Collinson, Collis(s)on, Collerson, Colcock, Colkin.

Philip, from Gk Φίλιππος 'horse-lover', was commonly *Phelip* in ME and often contracted to *Philp* or *Phelp*, with pet-forms *Phill, Phip* and diminutives *Phillin, Phippin*, etc. From the diminutive *Philip-ot* was formed *Pot* which itself had a diminutive *Potel* and a lost double diminutive *Potelin*:

Philip(s), Philipse, Philipp(s), Philliphs, Phillipps, Phillips(e), Phelips, Phelops, Philp(s), Phillp(s), Phelp(s), Phalp, Philip(p)son, Phillipson.

Fill(s), Filson, Philson; Phillins, Phillot(t); Phil(l)cox, Philcott.

Phipps, Phippard, Phippin.

Philpin, Philbin, Philben; Philippot, Philpot(s), Philpott(s), Phillpot(s), Phillpott(s), Pilpot.

Pot, Pott(s); Pottell, Pottle; Potkin(s).

OG *Ric(h)ard* 'powerful-brave' became OFr *Richard*, AFr *Ricard*, both of which have survived in England with numerous pet-forms and derivatives. One of the four most popular names among the barons, it quickly spread to the peasants who shortened it to *Rich* and *Rick*, from which they coined *Hich, Hick* and *Dick*, each with its own diminutives:

Richard, Richard(e)s, Ritchard, Richardson, Richarson.

Rich,[1] Riche(s), Ritch.

Hitch(es), Hytch; Hitchen(s), Hitcheon, Hitchon, Hitchin(s), Hitching(s); Hitchcock, Hitchcox, Hitchcoe, Hitchcott, Hiscoke, Hiscock(s), Hiscox, Hiscott, Hiscutt, Hiskett, Hedg(e)cock, Hedgecoe; Hichisson, Hitchman, Hitchmough.

Ricard(s), Ricarde, Riccard, Rickard, Rickard(e)s, Rickeard, Rickerd, Rickert, Ricket(s), Rickett(s).

Rick(s), Rix, Rickson, Rix(s)on, Rixom.

Dick(e), Dicks, Dix, Dickson, Dix(s)on; Digg(es); Deek(e)s, Deex, Deakes; Dickels, Diggle(s); Dicken(s), Dickin(s), Dickings, Dickons, Dykins, Dekin, Dekiss; Diggen(s), Diggin(e)s, Digings, Dig(g)an, Diggon; Dicketts; Dickenson, Dickinson, Dickerson, Dickeson, Dickison, Dickason.

Hick, Hick(e)s, Hickish, Hix; Hickin, Hicklin(g); Hickmott, Hickmet, Hickmer, Hickmore; Hickman; Hick(e)son, Hix(s)on; Higgs, Higson, Higman; Higgett, Higgitt, Higgott, Higgins, Higgens, Higgon(s), Higginson.

In 1379 we have *Higdon* de Slynesby (PTY), whilst in 1432 *Richard* Hogge is also called *Higdon* Hogg (EwenG), a christian name found also in 1313, *Richard* son of *Hykedon* (ChambAcctCh) and in *Hickedun* 1221 AssWo. In 1301 we have *Richedon* Makedance (SRY), in 1317 Richard *Rickedoun* (AssK) and in 1557 William *Rigden* (ArchC 34). The latter must be a contraction of *Ricard-un*, a diminutive of *Ricard*, whilst *Hikedun* must be a variant of this. Both *Higdon* and *Rigden* still survive. Some similar names are derived from other compounds of OG *Ric-*: *Richell, Rickell(s)*, from OFr *Richeut*, OG *Richild(is)* (f); *Richold*, from OG *Richold* (m) or

[1] Also a nickname, 'the rich', or 'dweller by the stream' (OE *ric).

154

OG *Richoldis* (f), both found as personal-names in England; *Rickward, Rickwood, Rickcord, Record(s)*, from OFr *Ricoart*, OG *Ricward* 'powerful-guardian'.

OFr *Robert*, from OG *Rodbert* 'fame-bright'. Pet-names, *Robb, Rabb, Dobb, Dabb, Hobb, Nobb, Nabb*; diminutives, *Robet, Robot, Robin; Robelin, Robelot; Robeçun, Robechun*. *Bobin* or *Babin* is found only in the compounds: *Dunbabin, Dunbobbin, Dunbebin, Dunbavin, Dunbavand, Dunbevand, Donbavand* 'dun (dark) Bobin or Babin':

Robert(s), Robart(s), Robearts, Robards, Robberds, Robers, Robertson, Roberson.

Robb(s), Robe, Rob(e)son; Rob(b)ins, Robyns, Robbings, Rob(b)ens, Robinson, Robison; Hor(r)abin, Horobin ('grey Robin'); Ropkins; Roblett; Roblin; Robjant, Robjohn(s).[1]

Rabb, Rabbatts, Rabbet(t)s, Rabbits, Rabbitt(s); Rablan, Rablen, Rablin; Rabjohn(s).[1]

Dobb(s), Dobbe, Dobson, Dopson; Dobbin(s), Dobbyn, Dobbing(s), Dobing, Dob(b)inson, Dobbison.

Dabbs, Dabson; Dabinett.

Hob(b), Hobb(e)s, Hobbis(s), Hobson, Hopson; Hobbins; Hoblin, Hoblyn, Hobling; Hobgen, Hupgens;[2] Hopkin(s), Hopkyns, Hopking, Hobkinson, Hopkinson.

Nobbs, Nobes, Nop(p)s; Noblet(t).

Nabb(s), Napp.

OFr *Roger*, OG *Rodger* 'fame-spear' had few diminutives, *Roget, Rogerun*, but the pet-forms *Dodge* and *Hodge* were common:

Roger(s), Rogger, Rodger(s), Rogerson, Roginson, Rodgman, Roggeman; Roget(t).

Dodge; Dodgen, Dodgeon, Dodgin, Dudgeon; Dodgson, Dodgshon, Dodgshun, Dodson, Dudson.

Hodge, Hodges(s), Hodgson, Hodgshon; Hodgens, Hodgin(s), Hodgeon, Hodson;[3] Hodgett(s); Hodgkin(s), Hodgkiess, Hodgkis(s), Hadgkiss, Hodgskin(s), Hochkins, Hotchkin, Hotchkis(s), Hodgkinson, Hodgkison.

Thomas, an Aramaic name, 'twin', with pet-name *Tom* and diminutives in -*in*, -*et* and -*el-in*:

Thomas, Tomas; Thomazin, Thomasset, Thom(p)sett, Tom(p)sett, Thomasson, Thomerson.

Thom(s), Tom, Tom(e)s, Tombs, Toomb(e)s, Thom(p)son, Tom(p)son, Tomsen; Thomline, Tomalin, Tomlin(s), Tomline, Tomblin, Tombling(s), Thomlinson, Tomlinson, Tombleson, and in North Lancs, Townson, Tolson, Toulson, Towlson; Tamlin, Tamlyn, Tamblin(g), Tamblyn, Tamplin; Tomkin(s), Tomkies, Tomkys, Tompkin(s), Tom(p)kinson.

[1] A double diminutive of *Rob* from the Picard *Robichon, Robuchon*, OFr *Robeçon*; cf. *Hutchings* above.

[2] William *Hobjohn, Hopjohn* 1524 SRSx, perhaps 'rustic, boorish John'.

[3] In Lancashire, *Hogeson* is common before 1582 and *Hodson* and *Hodgeon* are clearly the same name.

William, from OG *Willihelm* 'will-helmet', which in NE France and Flanders became *Willelm*, in Central France *Guillaume*. Both have given surnames, the former being more common. Pet-form *Will*, with diminutives in *-et, -ot, -in*.

From *Willelm*:

Williams, Willyams, Willems, Welliam, Williamson, Fitzwilliam(s); from *Willemin*: Wellemin, Wellerman, Wel(l)man, Willmin, Wil(l)man, Willament, Williman, Williment, Willimont, Willment; from *Willemot*: Willmot(t), Willmett, Willmotts, Wilmot(t), Wilmutt.

Will, Will(e)s, Willis, Wyllys, Wil(l)son, Willeson, Willison, Wylson.

Willet(s), Willats, Willett(s), Willitt(s), Willott; Wilcock(e), Wilcocks, Willcock(s), Wil(l)cox, Wilcockson, Wilcox(s)on; Wilkin(s), Wilkens, Wilkings, Wilkinson, Wilkerson.

From *Guillaume*:

Gillam, Gil(l)ham, Gilliam, Gillum; from *Guillemin*: Gil(l)man, Guillerman, Gel(l)man.

Chapter Eight

SURNAMES OF OFFICE

High officers of state

Steward had various meanings, 'an officer of the royal household (a995) and 'an official who controls the domestic affairs of a household' (c1000). After the Conquest it was used as the English equivalent of OFr *seneschal*, of 'the steward of a manor' (1303) and of 'the manager of an estate' (c1386). The Lord High Steward of Scotland was the first officer of the Scottish king in early times; he had control of the royal household, great administrative powers, and the privilege of leading the army into battle. The office, described as *senescellatus Scotiae* in a charter of 1158, fell in to the Crown upon the accession of Robert the Steward as Robert II, whence the name of the royal house of Stuart. Both in Scotland and in England the surname derives from the lesser offices. In Scotland the term was used of a magistrate originally appointed by the king to administer crown lands forming a stewartry, but there, as in England, every bishop, earl and manor had a steward who was often a man of birth and position, who had to ride hard, hold courts and supervise the bailiffs and the reeves. The surname is no proof of royal descent as James VI emphasised when he said that all Stewarts were not 'sib' to the King. *Seneschal*, found also as *Senchell* and in the Norman forms *Senescall*, *Senecal* and *Sensickle*, was an official in the household of a sovereign or great noble to whom the administration of

M   157

justice and the entire control of domestic arrangements were entrusted, but was later used in a wider sense, 'steward', 'major-domo'.

High officers of state in the Norman royal household were often named from their office. This frequently became hereditary and the title persisted as a surname, but it was usually abandoned on the conferment of an earldom, e.g. William Marshall, Earl of Pembroke. In this instance, the memory of the office is still preserved in the office of the Earl Marshal, whilst the highest rank in the army, that of Field-Marshal, recalls its former military duties. But OFr *mareschal*, like similar terms used of high office, had a variety of meanings, 'one who tends horses, especially one who treats their diseases', used of a shoeingsmith, a farrier and a horse-doctor. The surname is very common as *Marshall* and in the Norman forms *Marskell* and *Mascall* and is often equated with *Smith* and *Faber*.

Other surnames of the same type include: *Butler* (OFr *bouteillier*) 'servant in charge of the wine-cellar', usually the head servant, but in some early examples an officer of high rank nominally connected with the supply and importation of wine; *Chamberlain* 'officer charged with the management of the private chambers of a sovereign or nobleman', Thomas *Chaumberleng'* serviens Regis (1196); *Chambers*, local in form, from *de la Chambre*, was originally official with the same meaning. To pay *in cameram* was to pay into the exchequer of which the *camerarius* was in charge. The surname also applies to those employed there, Nicholas *atte Chambre* dictus *Clerk*. It was later used of a chamber-attendant, 'chamberman, chambermaid'.

Hugh *le Despencer* (d. 1265) was justiciary of England. His son is called Hugh *þe Spenser*, the form which survives (OFr *despensier*, AFr *espenser*) 'dispenser (of provisions)', a butler or steward. Side by side with this, we have *Spence*, *Spens* (*del Spens*), from ME *spense*, OFr *despense* 'larder', one who worked at or was in charge of the buttery, e.g. Alan *de la Spense*.[1] David *le Lardener* (c1170) was the officer who superintended the pannage of hogs in the forest (AFr *lardiner*), now *Lardner*. This was an extension of the duties implied by his alternative name *Larderer*, a derivative of OFr *lardier*, originally 'a tub to keep bacon in', later, 'a room in which to keep bacon and meat', hence 'officer in charge of the larder'. *Napier*, *Napper* 'naperer, one who has charge of the napery or table-linen', not noted in NED before 1880, was already a surname in 1148. *Wardroper*,

[1] *v.* p. 56.

Waredraper, with *Wardrobe*, *Wardrop* and *Whatrup* (from *de la warderobe*) was the 'officer of a royal household in charge of the robes, wearing-apparel, etc.'. *Chancellor* goes back ultimately to Lat *cancelli* 'lattice, enclosure, balustrade, railings'. The chancel of a church was so called because fenced off with a latticed screen and the chancellor was originally an officer who stood near the screen before the judgement-seat, hence 'usher of a law-court', 'custodian of records' and later 'secretary'.

Officers of the law

Judge is less common than *Justice*, originally an abstract noun, but as early as 1172 used of judicial officers and sometimes of lesser officials. William *Justyce* (1253 Lewes) was a constable. The original English terms *Deemer* (OE *dēmere*), one who pronounces the verdict, and its feminine form *Dempster*, chiefly northern, still survive. *Lawyer* is occasionally found as a surname in ME. *Lawman* (ODa, OSw *Lag(h)man*, ON *Lǫgmaðr*) is found as a personal-name in DB in Yorkshire and Essex, and was still in use in Yorkshire in 1219 and in Lancashire in 1246, where it certainly became a patronymic. But it was also used as a common noun. Alwold and Brictric *Lageman* (DB) were 'lawmen' of Lincoln (Anglo-Scand *laȝman* 'one whose duty it was to declare the law'). The advocate is represented by *Muter* or *Mutter* (OE *mōtere* 'public speaker'), used of a lawyer who argues cases in a court of justice, less common in ME than *Playtur* or *Pleidur* (from OFr *plaitier* 'to plead' and *plaideor* 'pleader'). The latter has completely disappeared, but was in common use from 1170. The former has been absorbed by *Plater* 'a maker of plate-armour', from which it became indistinguishable in pronunciation. The *Crier* (OFr *criere*, *crieur* 'crier') was an officer of the court of justice who made public pronouncements, preserved order, etc. The *Sizer* was a member of the assize (ME *sysour*), a sworn recognitor. Nor must we omit *Spickernell*, *Spicknell*, from ME *spigurnel* 'a sealer of writs', an office of importance.

Of the lesser officials we may note *Catcher* or *Ketcher* (ME *cachere* 'one who chases or drives', 'a huntsman', NED), but probably also used in the same sense as the more common diminutive *cacherel* which was frequent both as a name of office and as a surname in Norfolk in 1275. The *cacherels* were the bailiffs of the hundred and had an unpleasant reputation for extortion and oppression. The

159

Suffolk *Catchpole, Catchpoll, Catchpoule*, lit. 'chase-fowl', was originally 'a collector of poultry in default of money', a tax-gatherer, and later a petty officer of justice, especially a warrant officer who arrests for debt.

Jailer was used of the man in charge of such gaols as Newgate, Nottingham and Colchester, and, as a surname, survives chiefly in the Norman spelling and pronunciation (ONFr *gaiolere*), *Gailer, Galer, Gayler*; occasionally it is from OFr *jaioleur*, now *Jailler*. The hangman has left no surnominal survivors, John *Hangeman* 1327 SRSf.

Manorial officials

The *Bailiff* or *Bailey*, with *Bayliss* (OFr *bailif* (acc.), *baillis* (nom.), later *bailli*) or sergeant, whatever his title, was a free man of importance as the mouthpiece of the lord by whom he was appointed. At Droxford he received £6 per annum as compared with the ploughman's 8*s*. and the shepherd's 4*s*. He lived in the manor-house at the lord's expense and was the general supervisor of agricultural policy. It was his duty to see that the services due were not evaded or ill-performed and to direct and determine the men's work.[1] Originally meaning 'carrier', later 'manager, administrator', the term was also used of the public administrator of a district, the chief officer of a hundred or of an officer of justice under a sheriff, a warrant officer, pursuivant and a catchpoll.

Beadle or constable, messor or hayward—it is impossible to separate their duties for the terms were interchangeable. He was either chosen by the lord or elected by the homage, one of the lesser men of the village. He had to make all summonses ordered by the hallmote, levy distresses, take pledges, make attachments and collect fines. In fact, he acted as the village policeman.[2] The surname survives in various forms. *Beadel* and *Beedle* may be from either OFr *bedel* or OE *bydel*. The latter has also given *Biddell, Biddle, Buddell* and *Buddles*. Other possible meanings are 'messenger of justice, under-bailiff, tipstaff', 'apparitor', 'mace-bearer', 'crier or usher of a law-court', 'town-crier'. The alternative *Sargeant* (OFr *sergent, serjant*) was a very common surname, probably in general 'servant',

---

[1] *v.* H. S. Bennett, *Life on the English Manor* (Cambridge, 1938), pp. 162–6.
[2] *v. ibid.*, pp. 178–82, and G. C. Homans, *English Villagers in the Thirteenth Century* (Cambridge, Mass., 1942), pp. 290–1.

latinised as *serviens*. It was commonly used of the king's sergeants, tenants by military service under the rank of a knight and of officers of justice, e.g. William Roculf bailiff of Worcester (1320 Pat) and John de Halteby constable of Ipswich (1315 Pat). *Constable* (OFr *cunestable*, from Lat *comes stabuli* 'count of the stable') may also denote 'the chief officer of the household or court', 'governor of a royal fortress', 'military officer' and 'parish constable'.

Of all the manorial officers, the two most important were the hayward and the reeve. The original duties of the former seem to have been to protect the fences round the Lammas lands when enclosed for hay (Coulton), hence his name, OE *heȝe-weard* 'guardian of the fence or hedge'. This *heȝe* was a dead hedge easily erected and removed, forming an enclosure (OE *(ge)hæg*) from which, to judge from the early and regular variation between *heiward* and *haiward*, and from his more general duties of preventing cattle from breaking through into the enclosed fields and growing crops, the hayward seems also to have been called *(ge)hægweard* 'enclosure-protector'; cf. (from *Piers Plowman*): 'Canstow . . . have an horne and be haywarde, and liggen oute a nyghtes, And kepe my corn in my croft fro pykers and þeeues?' It was his duty to see that breaches in the hedges were repaired and straying cattle impounded, to serve under certain conditions as an officer of the hallmote, to levy distresses, make attachments and collect fines. *Hayward* is a very common surname; its Latin equivalent *Messer* (OFr *messier, messer* 'harvester', from Low Lat *messarius* 'hayward'), frequent in the Middle Ages, is now rare.[1]

The *Reeve* was 'only a little less important as one of the management of a manor than he was as the chief officer of a village'. He was of servile origin, usually elected by the villeins for a year at Michaelmas, though his term of office was frequently extended. Men paid fines to escape the onerous duties involved. Though a villein, he was a man of substance, holding a yardland, strictly accountable to the lord for all that concerned the manorial economy. As reeve, he was quit of all or a large part of the services due and was often paid a stipend with such perquisites as a horse in the lord's stable or a special piece of land as reeve. He ate at the lord's table in the manor house from Lammas to Michaelmas (i.e. during harvest) and was responsible (with the bailiff or sergeant) for the management of the lord's demesne farm, especially for overseeing work-services owed by

[1] *v.* Homans, op. cit., pp. 66–7, 293.

villeins. He had to see 'that the keepers of all kinds of beasts do not go to fairs, or markets, or wrestling-matches, or taverns, whereby the beasts may go astray without guard or do harm to the lord or another, but they must ask leave and put keepers in their places that no harm may happen'. Some collected the lord's rents, took over tenements which had escheated to the lord, distrained men to do homage and fealty, had power of giving permission to villeins' daughters to marry outside the manor and had custody of the rolls of the hallmote. More often than not it was the reeve and not the bailiff who accounted every year for the income and outgo of the manor-rents, profits of courts, sales of corn and stock and all expenditure.[1] In Northumbria the term used was ONorthumb *grǣfa*, originally 'governor of a province', later 'overseer, manager, head-workman on a farm, farm-bailiff', surviving as *Grieve(s)*. In Yorkshire we have ME *greyve*, from ON *greifi* 'steward', 'a person in charge of property', the origin of the modern *Grave(s)*.

Although not, strictly speaking, surnames of office, manorial tenants often held their land on condition of performing particular duties. In the Durham *Boldon Buke* of 1183 it is frequently the work required which names the tenement, not that of the tenant, e.g. *Quidam carbonarius* 'charcoal-burner' (now *Collier*) holds one toft, a croft and four acres and finds the coal for making the iron-work of the ploughs. Similarly, the smith and the miller held their land in return for specific services. The *Miller* was commonly one of the most considerable men of the village. The lord had a monopoly of the village mill and the villeins were compelled to take their corn to his mill to be ground. The revenue of the mill came from the multure, that share of the flour which the miller kept in payment for his services. The mill was usually let to farm to the miller, the village capitalist, who was always suspected of adding to his gains by sharp practice, by using false measures and other frauds. He was forbidden to water or change corn sent to him or to give worse for better. He was not to keep hogs or more than three hens and a cock; 'gluttonous geese' especially were forbidden.[2] The miller was also known as *Milner* and *Millward*, *Millard* and *Mellard* and, less commonly, by the French terms *Mulliner*, *Mullender* and *Mullinger* (OFr *molinier*).

The frequency of *Smith*, our most common surname, is due

---

[1] *v.* Homans, op. cit., pp. 298–300, and Bennett, op. cit., pp. 169–78.
[2] Ibid., p. 285; Bennett, op. cit., p. 135.

chiefly to the blacksmith who was ubiquitous. We find him on every manor and in the towns where the smiths congregated in such streets as Smythen Street in Exeter, but partly to workers in other metals who could also be called simply *smith*. OE *smiþþe*, too, has contributed to the name, Robert *atte Smyth* 1332 SRSx, 'worker at the smithy'. The surname is even more common than would appear for it survives also in the Lat *Faber* and the French *Feaver* (OFr *fevere*) and *Ferrar* and *Farrer* (OFr *ferreor* 'worker in iron') which has also become *Farrow*. In the manor, the smith was of less substance than the miller. He might be a free-holder or a villein and he held his land in return for his work. At Aldingbourne in Sussex, for example, the smith's widow held four acres of land and in return rendered 100 horse-shoes a year to the lord's chamber, 50 with eight holes and 50 with six, without nails, for which she received 25*d.* She had to shoe the steward's hackney at all his comings if needed and for this she had 1*d.* for the four shoes. She also had to shoe the sergeant's horse and the carter's horse all the year at 1*d.* for the four shoes. In addition, she was to make of the lord's iron and mend and sharpen the irons of two ploughs all the year and to charge nothing, to mend the irons of the other two ploughs when needed and for this the lord was to pay. She had her coals of the lord's wood at the three terms and her dinner while the lord stayed on the manor. The lord was to plough all her land till sowing was done.[1]

Just as the peasant was not allowed to grind his corn where he wished, so he was forbidden to bake his bread at home or anywhere save in a special oven constructed for the purpose and belonging to the lord. Many peasants had no means of baking at home. The lord's oven was generally rented to an individual or to the peasants as a body. The village oven or bakehouse was a communal convenience.[2] Hence we have not only the common surnames *Baker* and *Baxter* but also *Ovens*, John *Attenouene* 1276 AssSo, from OE *ofen* 'oven', *Backhouse*, *Bacchus*, *Backus*, Robert *atte bachus* 1289 NorwDeeds, 'worker at the bakehouse', with the French *Bullinger*, *Pullinger* and *Pillinger* (OFr *boulengier* 'baker'), *Furner* and *Fournier* (OFr *furnier*), and *Pester*, *Pistor* (AFr *pestour*, *pistour*, Lat *pistor*).

Like the *Smith*, the baker is found in towns, too, congregating in such streets as Baxter Street in Bury St Edmunds. In fourteenth-century London there were two types, one the substantial tradesman, using his own capital, who had to choose between brown bread and

---

[1] Homans, op. cit., p. 286.　　[2] Bennett, op. cit., p. 135.

white and was not allowed to sell bread in his own house but might have it hawked about by regratresses or sell it from a hutch in the market on Wednesdays and Saturdays. He had to deal with the breadwomen at thirteen to the dozen and to stamp all his bread with a seal.[1] The other class was that of bakers who worked upon material supplied by their customers. Sometimes both methods were combined. The 'public baker' was a widespread institution in medieval London.

These bakers, like the miller, were full of tricks. In 1327 John Brid, baker, was accused of 'falsehood, malice and deceit' in that he had skilfully and artfully caused a certain hole to be made upon a table of his called a moulding-board pertaining to his bakehouse after the manner of a mouse-trap, there being a certain wicket warily provided for the closing and opening such hole. And when his neighbours and others who were wont to bake their bread at his oven came with their dough, such dough having been placed on the aforesaid table, the said John had one of his household sitting in secret beneath the table who carefully opened the hole and bit by bit craftily withdraw some of the dough, falsely, wickedly and maliciously.

With this discovery, a raid was made on the public bakehouses of the City and no less than nine others were found provided with fraudulent tables, beneath which in many cases lay an accusing litter of dough. The sentence passed by the civic jury on these malefactors was a fine specimen of medieval justice. All the bakers with dishonest moulding-boards were to stand till vespers in the pillory; and those under whose tables dough was found were to have a quantity of dough suspended from their necks.[2]

Such surnames as *Shepherd*, *Swinerd* or *Swinnard* 'swine-herd' and *Nothard* or *Nutter* (ON *naut* 'beast, ox', neat-herd) may be something more than mere occupational-names. They may refer to a specific office or service undertaken for the benefit of the community. More often than not, perhaps, each family designated one of its members to be shepherd for its own sheep. Many custumals stipulate that no tenement need send its shepherd to reap and carry the lord's corn: he could not be spared from his job of keeping the sheep on the fallows and out of the corn. It was also common for the men of a

---

[1] This gave name to *cocket-bread* (AFr *cokette* 'a seal'), a leavened bread or loaf slightly inferior in quality to the wastell or finest bread. It also appears to have been called *cockin-bread*. From this Henry *Cockin* (1207) and John *Coket* (1221) took their surnames, now *Cockin*, *Cockett*, as did Ralph *Cocunbred* (1209).

[2] G. Unwin, *Finance and Trade under Edward III* (Manchester, 1918), pp. 25–6.

village to choose village neatherds, village shepherds and village swineherds, to keep the stock of all the village and the neighbours assessed themselves for the wages of the common herdsmen;[1] cf. *Tunnard* (OE **tūn-hierde*) 'guardian of the village or town animals'.

Among the lesser officers of the manor, we may note *Granger* 'one in charge of a grange or outlying farm', farm-bailiff; *Parker* 'keeper of the park', usually a deer-park; *Warrener* or *Warner,* the officer employed to watch over game in a park or preserve, and the *Pinder,* responsible for impounding stray beasts on the manor.

Social classes

'Till long after the Conquest earldom meant an office and barony meant a tenure, while neither had its modern sense of a title of honour.'[2] There is no evidence that any of these earls or barons ever accepted either term as a surname—they had their own, to which they clung. *Baron,* especially when applied to peasants, was a nickname, proud or haughty or bold as a baron. The term was anciently applied to freemen of the cities of London and York who were homagers of the king and also to the freemen of the Cinque Ports who had the feudal service of bearing the canopy over the head of the sovereign on the day of coronation. Gervase *le Cordewaner* or *camerarius* was also called Gervase *Baronn,* no doubt because he was alderman of Aldgate Ward 1250–6 (ELPN). Eleventh-century names such as Leofric *Eorl,* Harold *Eorl* denoted rank. OE *Eorl* was used as a personal-name, but only one doubtful example of this has been noted after the Conquest, Stephanus *filius Erli* c1250 Rams (Nf). The surname was regularly a nickname, *le Erl* (Earl).

It is to the tenants of the Normans, not to their barons and knights, that we owe the surnames which denote status. They are not strictly surnames of office, but on the manor such terms as cotter and franklin were as distinctive as those of hayward and reeve. Why a man should be called simply *Free* (OE *frēo*), *Fry* (OE *frīg* 'free') or *Villain* (AFr *villein* 'serf, bondman, servile tenant') is not clear. All were either freemen or villeins and both were so numerous that these terms do not seem sufficiently specific as surnames to distinguish one man from another. Thuresson has found some 28 different surnames —most of them obsolete—which were used to describe various kinds

[1] Homans, op. cit., p. 63.
[2] A. R. Wagner, *English Genealogy* (Oxford, 1960), p. 89.

of manorial tenants. We are not concerned here with the history of the English social classes. On that Sir Anthony Wagner has thrown a flood of light.[1] The problem is full of difficulties for the meaning of the terms commonly used varied from time to time. Our purpose is much more limited both in scope and in time—to discuss only those classes which have given us surnames and this will not take us beyond the end of the fourteenth century.

In the village there were usually two social classes, the more substantial *husbonds*, bonds who had houses (late OE *hūsbonda* 'householder' (now *Husband*), from OE *hūs* 'house' and ON *bondi* 'husbandman, peasant, churl', now *Bond*), in contrast with the villagers of the poorer sort who were called *cotters* because their dwelling-places were only cots or cottages. In the thirteenth century a *husbond* was not simply a married man, but a man of a certain class, a substantial farmer, holding from 10 to 40 acres, one of the middle class of villagers.[2] In the country in the Middle Ages a man could keep himself alive by taking work as a farm labourer, but he could not keep a wife or found a family unless he held land. No land, no marriage—that was a rule.[3]

The household, rather than the family, was the actual working unit. The person who held the tenement, the holder, the husbond, was the head of the household and directed the husbandry of the tenement.[4] He was held responsible for the good behaviour of the members of his household. If they did evil, he was bound to produce them in court and even answer for the damages they had done.[5]

Many even of the more substantial of the husbandmen were not able to support on their tenement a full draught of oxen apiece. In groups of two or more they would become partners or marrows and pool their oxen to form common teams which then ploughed the lands of all the partners[6] (now *Marrow*, from ME *marwe* 'companion, mate').

At the lower end of the scale were those with dependent cottages on the messuage who might be married and keep house for themselves. They were called undersettles or coterells, lesser cotters, who had to share the works owed to the lord. The cotters had a cottage

---

[1] A. R. Wagner, *English Genealogy* (Oxford, 1960), pp. 84–177.
[2] Homans, op. cit., p. 72.
[3] Ibid., p. 137.
[4] Both *Holder* and *Household* survive as surnames.
[5] Homans, op. cit., p. 209.
[6] Ibid., p. 81.

and some 5 acres of land, a small tenement and a household with fewer work services. These classes have given us the surnames *Coterell, Cotter* and *Cotman*.[1] The predecessor of the DB *cottarius*, the eleventh-century *kotsetla*,[2] seems to have bequeathed the modern surname *Cotsell* of which no early examples have been noted. *Workman* recalls the *werkmen*, villeins who did customary works in contrast to *molmen* who paid rent. On some manors they had to labour three or four days a week for the lord. *Thrall* or *Thrale* is from OE *þræl*, from ON *þræll* 'a villein, serf, bondman'.

'The delineation of classes must often be in a measure arbitrary and subjective. Still in England a threefold grouping, into franklins or yeomen, husbandmen, and cotters or cottagers, seems over some centuries to correspond, if only roughly, with a felt reality.'[3] This coupling of franklins and yeomen illustrates one difficulty. Both terms have become surnames, *Franklin* 'a freeman' is common from 1195. *Yeoman*, originally 'young man', later 'a servant or attendant in a noble house, ranking between a sergeant and a groom or between a squire and a page' is much rarer, first noted in 1296 in Sussex and in the fourteenth century in Shropshire, Lancashire, London and Staffordshire (one example in each). 'The sixteenth century was in some respects the great age of the yeoman'[4] and it is doubtful whether the surname ever had reference to the status or class of yeomen. It was used in 1375 of a foot-soldier and in 1387 of a freeholder under the rank of a gentleman.

The franklins formed a small class of freemen, but not all freemen were franklins. At Ramsey in 1184–9, four hides of land made a knight's fee, but many knights held less than a full fee, though none less than one and a half hides. The franklins held half a hide, some more, some less, and they ought and were accustomed to aid the knight to do service. Elsewhere in the thirteenth century they held tenements smaller than those of the feudal gentry, the lords of the manors, and larger than those of the middle class of villagers. They did not owe military service nor were they sergeants. They paid rent (often not heavy) and were freeholders in spite of being husbandmen and villagers. They were quit of all (or most) labour services, did suit at the courts of the hundred and the shire and attended the king's justices in eyre when sitting in the neighbourhood. At the lord's

[1] Homans, op. cit., pp. 210–11, 244.
[2] *v.* F. M. Stenton, *Anglo-Saxon England* (Oxford, 1947), pp. 466–7.
[3] Wagner, op. cit., p. 126. For Franklins and Yeomen, *v.* pp. 125–30.
[4] Ibid., p. 128.

harvest and bedrepes they had to find a man to reap, at the lord's food, and to be present, with a rod in hand, for three days to see that the reapers worked well and fruitfully. During the harvest they fed at the lord's table. Later, members of this class throve and gained much power and wealth[1] as can be seen from Chaucer's description of the franklin who had been knight of the shire and sheriff.

'Was no-wher such a worthy vavassour,' he concludes, recalling an earlier term. *Vavasour* is not a common surname, but was frequent in the twelfth and thirteenth centuries. It derives from OFr *vavassour*, Lat *vassus vassorum* 'vassal of vassals' and was used of a feudal tenant ranking immediately below a baron. The status of the vavassor varied with time and place. In England at the time of Domesday the vavassors were men of very moderate estate. By the twelfth century the whole of military society was divided into two great classes, barons and vavassors. The surname also survives rarely as *Vawser* and as *Vassar* (OFr *vasseor* 'vassal').

Names of office as nicknames

When we meet such twelfth-century names as Talebotus *prior* 1121 Bury and Daniel *abbas* 1148–53 ib., we know that these were official titles for they can be identified as Prior of Bury St Edmunds and Abbot of St Benet of Holme. Similarly, Johannes *monachus* (1146–9 Holme) and Yvo *decanus* (1186–1210 ib.), two of the innumerable names of witnesses to charters, refer undoubtedly to a monk and a dean. But in the following centuries such surnames as *Abbott*, *Prior* and *Dean* are much too frequent to be taken literally. They are clearly names of the working classes who could never have held such high office and must be regarded as nicknames given because of some fancied resemblance in appearance or character to the official commemorated. This is made particularly clear in the case of *Minchin* and *Nunn*. The former, from OE *mynecen* 'nun' is not common but all the examples noted are names of men. Hence it must be a nickname, 'meek and demure as a nun', unless, as often, it was given in derision to one of a most un-nunlike character. The earliest example of *Nunn* refers to a twelfth-century nun. Later, when the christian name is that of a woman, this may be a surname of office or a nickname 'demure'. Applied to a man (as most commonly), it is a nickname. Monks and friars, too, like those above, were bound by vows of

[1] Homans, op. cit., pp. 248–50.

celibacy and so could not found families and pass on a family name. *Fryer*, *Friar* or *Frear* might also mean 'brother'. *Monk* is also found in the French forms *Moon* and *Munn* (AFr *moun* 'monk') and *Moyne* (OFr *moine*). Geoffrey le Moine was constable of Newcastle in 1219, hardly a post for a monk.

That these names were often nicknames is proved also by their form: John le prest le chaucer c1250 Clerkenwell; John called Prest, bureller 1333 SRLo; William Priour, cossun 'horsemonger' 1283 LLB B; from the Norwich Deeds: Richard Priur, lindraper (1300), Adam le Frere, merchant (1303); Roger le Mounke, baker (1318).

The common *Clarke* owes its frequency in the first place to the numerous clerics who never took higher orders but had the privilege of benefit of clergy. The earliest examples are of this type: Richerius *clericus* 1086 DB, Willelm *ðe Clerec* c1100 OEByn. The original meaning of the term was 'a man in a religious order, cleric, clergyman'. As all writing and secretarial work in the Middle Ages was done by the clergy, the term came to mean 'scholar, secretary, recorder or penman'.

In the thirteenth and fourteenth centuries many merchants and tradesmen were called clerks, professional men whose chief business was to draw up deeds, etc. The clerk was not necessarily a professional scrivener but a man who could read and write and the surname is often a nickname.[1] John Clerk of the Vintry (1276 LLB A) is called John le clerc coroner in 1292 SRLo, John de Vintry, coroner 1303 LLB C, and John Clerk of the Vintry 1317 Husting. He was alderman of Vintry 1300–9. John de Northalle, a skinner by trade, was also called a clerk, i.e. literate. He was sheriff of London 1336–7 and an alderman. He, too, was also called John le Clerk and in his will (1349), John de Northall called Clerk. William called le Clerk, butcher (1336 Husting), was tenant of a shop at the Shambles of St Nicholas and Warden of the Butchers. His real name was *atte Noke* (1328), son of Richard atte Noke. Of other London clerks, one was a fishmonger, one a potter and one a ceynturer 'a maker of waist-belts or girdles' (now *Century*).

In thirteenth-century Norwich clerks were exempt from tithings. But there were many clerks in the city, e.g. the clerks of the Bailiffs, who can hardly have been in ecclesiastical orders at all. They were married,[2] held civic offices, and lived and traded as citizens. All

[1] PopLond, pp. xxxi–xxxii.
[2] Hence *Clarkson*, a common surname from 1306.

such were bound by the law of frankpledge. One of the bailiffs was Galfridus clericus or Kempe (1293). John le Clerc de Rugham was a barber (1313), whilst Laurentius clericus and his wife were accused of breach of the assize of ale.[1]

Cardinal and *Pope* can never have been used as surnames of office in medieval England. They are either nicknames, the former for one like (or unlike) a cardinal or with a partiality for dressing in red, the latter for one of an austere, ascetic appearance, or they were pageant-names. In the Middle Ages every opportunity was seized to brighten the life of the common folk by the production, in the provinces and in London alike, of elaborate pageants and municipal shows of welcome at the state entries of royal and illustrious visitors, at coronations and royal marriages, the earliest being that at the wedding of Henry III to Eleanor of Provence in 1236. The triumphant return of Edward I after his defeat of William Wallace at Falkirk in 1298 is described in Stowe's 'Survey of London' from which we may quote one much later:

One other show in the year 1377, made by the citizens for disport of the young prince, Richard, son to the Black Prince, in the feast of Christmas, in this manner: On the Sunday before Candlemas, in the night, one hundred and thirty citizens, disguised, and well horsed, in a mummery, with sound of trumpets, sackbuts, cornets, shalmes, and other minstrels, and innumerable torch lights of wax, rode from Newgate, through Cheape, over the bridge, through Southwarke, and so to Kennington, beside Lambhith, where the young prince remained with his mother, and the Duke of Lancaster his uncle . . . In the first rank did ride forty-eight in the likeness and habit of esquires, two and two together, clothed in red coats and gowns of say or sandal, with comely visors on their faces; after them came riding forty-eight knights in the same livery of colour and stuff; then followed one richly arrayed like an emperor; and after him some distance, one stately attired like a pope, whom followed twenty-four cardinals, and after them eight or ten with black visors, not amiable, as if they had been legates from some foreign prince.

Here we have plausible origins for six surnames, *Squire, Knight, Emperor*[2] or *Cayzer, Pope, Cardinal* and *Leggatt*, and we should doubtless find others did we but know the names of the minstrels.

[1] NorwLt, p. lxvii. Note, too, *Nutter* (OE *nōtere* 'scribe, writer') and *Scrivener*, a derivative of *Scriven* (OFr *escrivain* 'writer, copier of MSS, clerk').

[2] A medieval surname, now obsolete. *Lempriere* survives in the Channel Islands.

The church, too, and other festivities have contributed their share. The ceremony of the 'Boy Bishop' was widely popular in the twelfth and thirteenth centuries, occurring first at York in 1221 and at St Paul's in 1235. During his year of office the boy bishop was a person of considerable importance and acquired as many remunerative privileges as the modern Beauty Queen. There can be little doubt that he frequently retained the name of his office, and to this many of our Bishops owe their surname.

In addition there was the *Abbot*, more usually the *Lord* of Misrule who has contributed to both surnames and the various *Kings*. *Rex Fabae* 'King of the Bean' occurs in 1334. Every village had its May-day King and at the feast of the Epiphany one of the company was always elected king, whilst *Rex* or *Roy* was not seldom a distinction among the minstrels. In 1306 five *Roys* are mentioned by name, whilst one of the minstrels of Edward II was William de Morlee 'roy de North'.[1]

The medieval drama

The characters in the Coventry Play include Adam and Eva, Caym and Abelle, Abraham, Isaac, Moyses, Gabryell, Joseph and Nycodemus, all of whom, with the exception of Cain and Nicodemus have given us modern surnames which are certainly, at times, patronymics. Caiaphas is prominent in the trial scenes with Pilate and is found as a surname from 1200 to 1529, William *Caifas* 1200 Cur (C), Adam *Caiphas* 1279 RH (C), John *Caiaphas* 1529 CantW. Pounce Pilat of the York Plays had already given rise to a surname which was fairly common in the twelfth and fourteenth centuries and still survives as *Pilatt*, *Pillatt* and *Pilot*. His praenomen, Lat *Pontius*, Fr *Pons*, Burgundian *Point*, was the name of a saint of Asia Minor whose cult was widely spread, but the surname may also be due to the drama (modern *Points*, *Poyntz*, *Punch*, the last from ONFr *Ponche*).

The boastful ranting of the braggart Herod must have made him a favourite with the audience, but it is difficult to decide how far his name was used as a surname. He is variously called *Herode* and *ser herowde*, whilst *Magnus Herodes* was the title of the fifth of the Wakefield Plays. This might well have given the modern surname *Herod* from such early examples as William *Herode* 1279 AssNb and Peter *Herodes* 1297 SRY, but Seman *Herodes* is identical with Seman

[1] E. K. Chambers, *The Medieval Stage* (Oxford, 1925), vol. ii, p. 238.

Erode or *Harrold* (1297 SIA x, 190–1) and this might be from one of the ME forms of *heraud*, *herault*, *herode*, *haraude* 'herald' (now *Herald*, *Heraud*, *Herod*). The problem is complicated, too, by the fact that the modern *Harold*, *Harrod*, etc., may derive from either ODa *Harald*, OG *Hairold*, *Herold* or OE *Hereweald*. In DB, King Harald's name occurs (among other forms) as *Herold*, *Herouldus* and *Herolt*. The evidence is too conflicting for certainty. Dauzat derives the rare French *Herode* from the Biblical name which Michaëlsson considers a suitable nickname from the name of the King of the Jews who slaughtered the Innocents and is often mentioned in the *chansons de geste*.

Lazarus has not been noted as a medieval christian name, but it is that of a character (*Lazar*) in the York Plays. The modern *Lazar*. is descriptive, from *le Lazur* (1280), ME *lazare* 'leper'. The Coventry characters include Veritas, Misericordia, Justicia and Pax which may well be one source of the abstract surnames *Verity*, *Mercy*, *Justice* and *Peace*.

The medieval minstrelsy

The precursor of the medieval drama was the medieval minstrelsy. In 1086 Berdic *ioculator regis* held three vills and five carucates of land in Gloucestershire (DB).

During the reign of the Angevin and Plantagenet kings the minstrels were ubiquitous. They wandered at their will from castle to castle, and in time from borough to borough, sure of their ready welcome alike in the village tavern, the guidhall, and the baron's keep. They sang and jested in the market-places, stopping cunningly at a critical moment in the performance to gather their harvest of small coins from the bystanders. In the great castles, while lords and ladies supped or sat around the fire, it was theirs to while away many a long bookless evening with courtly *geste* or witty sally. At wedding or betrothal, baptism or knight-dubbing, treaty or tournament, their presence was indispensable. The greater festivals saw them literally in their hundreds, and rich was their reward in money and in jewels, in costly garments, and in broad acres. They were licensed vagabonds, with free right of entry into the presence-chambers of the land.[1]

They wore coats of many colours, with their instruments on their backs, had shaven faces, close-clipped hair and flat shoes. At the knighting of Prince Edward in 1306 the minstrels were paid from five marks to twelve pence each. But they were given to dicing, had

[1] E. K. Chambers, *The Mediaeval Stage* (Oxford, 1925), vol. i, p. 44.

a hard life on the road and were likely to die like a dog in the ditch, under the ban of the church and with the prospect of eternal damnation before their souls.[1]

The normal medieval Latin term for minstrel in the widest sense was *ioculator* (OFr *jouglere, jougelour*). The Earl of Hereford granted a tenement to his jester, *Folebarba* 'meus joculator et homo meus' (1141–3 HeCh). As a term for minstrels of the lighter type this had to compete with the English *gleeman* and with *minstrel*. Its common use is for the lower type of minstrel or buffoon and in particular, in the exact sense of the modern *juggler*, for a conjurer or *tregetour*[2] (OFr *tre(s)geteo(u)r*, ultimately from Lat **tra(ns)iactare*, 'one who works magic or plays tricks by sleight of hand; a conjurer or juggler').

Minstrell as a surname is rare, in fact the only early example is instructive. Hugo *Harper* de Wolpet, *tregettour*, alias dictus Hugo *Mynstrall* de Bildeston, *jogelour* (1483 EwenG 90). Here we have four distinct terms applied to the same man, all of which survive as surnames, a clear indication of the difficulty of applying precise interpretations to these names. The varied terms applied to minstrels include menestrel, trouvère, ribaud, bordeor, jougler, chanteur, lecheor and pantonnier and sometimes harlot, japer, gabber and jangler.[3] They were habitually distinguished by the name of the musical instrument they played. The singer often became a mere story-teller, *gestour, disour* and *segger*, all classed as minstrels. At the knighting of Prince Edward in 1306, they included Janin *le Citoler*, Johan *le Croudere*, Henri *le Gigour*, Guillaume *le Harpour*, Janin *le Lutour*, Paulus *Menestrallus*, with le menestrel ove les cloches (the minstrel with the bells), Janin *Lorganistre*,[4] Gillotus *le Sautreour*, Martinet *le Taborour*, Wauter *le Trounpour*, Robert *le Vilour*, and Perle in the Eghe. In 1339, at Durham, we meet Thomas *Fole* 'the fool', probably identical with Thomas *Fatuus* (1337).[5]

Most of these are still in use as surnames: *Crowther, Crowder* (from ME *crouthe, croude* 'fiddle', a fiddler), *Harper* (OE *hearpere*), *Harpur* (AFr *harpour*), *Luter* (OFr *leuteor* 'lute-player'); *Salter* is sometimes identical with *Sauter* or *Sawter*, metonymic for *Sautreour* 'a player on the psaltery', a stringed instrument like a harp (OFr *saltere*). William *le Saltere* is also called *le Salterer* (1279 AssNb),

[1] E. K. Chambers, *The Mediaeval Stage* (Oxford, 1925), vol. ii, 48.
[2] Ibid., ii, 231.　　　　[3] Ibid., ii, 233.
[4] Obsolete, but *Organer* may mean either 'a maker of organs' or 'musician, a player of the organ'.
[5] Ibid., ii, 234–8.

N　　　　　　　　　173

i.e. *Psalterer*. William *le Sautreour* was minstrel to the Lady Margaret, Queen of England (1304 LLB C). *Taberer*, *Tabborah*, with the metonymic *Taber*, are from ME *tabere* 'to play on the drum', a drummer; *Taberner* is a similar derivative of ME *tabourne* or OFr *tabourner* in the same sense. *Trumper* (OFr *trompeor* 'trumpeter'); *Vieler*, *Viola* (AFr *violour* 'player on the viol', fiddler). *Foll* (OFr *fol*) may denote either 'fool' or 'foolish, silly'.

Of the various names for minstrel, there still survive: *Arlott*,[1] *Boarder*, *Border*, often 'a maker of boards or tables', but also from AFr *bourd(e)our* 'jester, joker, buffoon'; *Chanter* (OFr *chanteor* 'enchanter, magician' but also 'singer, chorister'); *Gaber*, *Gabor*, with *Gabb*, William *le Gabber* 1230 P, Gerard *le Gabur* 1275 RH (Sf), from OFr *gab* 'mockery, deceit'; *Juggler* 'juggler'; *Letcher* (also 'lecher'); *Tredgett*, *Trudgett*, metonymic for *Tregetor* 'juggler, mountebank'; *Jester* (ME *gester* 'a mimic, buffoon, merry-andrew', 'a professional reciter of romances'); *Sayer* (besides other meanings, sometimes a derivative of OE *secgan* 'to say', 'a professional reciter').

Some of these names of musicians may at times be nicknames given to men who had other surnames, who did not make their living by their music, but were affectionately remembered by the friends and neighbours they entertained. John *le Luter* (1319 SRLo) is identical with John *de Acon*, called *Le Lieutour* (1332 AD). He was assessed at 40*s.* and was clearly a man of wealth, probably a merchant, perhaps a vinter (he was associated with a wine-broker), certainly not a professional lute-player. Robert *le Pipere* (1319 SRLo, now *Piper*) is probably identical with Robert le Pipere, dyer (1310 LLB D). Adam *le Horner* (1297 SRY) is also called *le Harpour*, 'a blower of the horn', whilst *Hornblower* may be due to the use of the horn as part of his daily work. In the Middle Ages workmen were called to work by the ringing of bells or by a horn. In 1320, at Carnarvon, William de la Grene was paid 1*d.* per week 'for blowing the horn' to summon the builders to work, whilst Langland's hayward used a horn to give warning of a raid by thieves.

Then we have the mimes. Henry I had his *mimus regis*, by name Raherus, who made large sums by his *suavitas iocularis*, founded St Bartholomew's Hospital and became its first prior.[2] The performance of the mimes made up in versatility for what they lacked in decorum.

---

[1] *v.* p. 5 above.

[2] Chambers op. cit., i. 48. His name is preserved in the surname *Rayer* (OG *Radheri*, *Rather* 'counsel-army').

There were the tombeors, tombestres, or tumblers, acrobats and contortionists. The crowd of dancers was variously designated sautours, sailyours and hoppesteres. A second group includes the jugglers or tregetours, practitioners of sleight of hand.[1] Of these, we still have as surnames: *Tumber* (OFr *tombeor* 'tumbler, dancer'); *Sailer, Saylor, Seyler* (OFr *sailleor* 'dancer'); *Hopper* (a derivative of OE *hoppian* 'to hop, leap, dance'). The *hoppesteres* and the *tombestres* were women.

[1] Chambers op. cit., i, 71.

Chapter Nine

SURNAMES OF OCCUPATION

I N spite of the large numbers which have become obsolete, surnames of occupation are more numerous than would at first appear and their classification is often difficult. We have already seen
that many local surnames really denote a man's occupation,[1] e.g.
Castle, John *del Castel* (1307 Wak), may mean 'dweller by a castle',
but is more likely to be equivalent to *Castleman*, one employed at a
castle. In fact, we find also Richard *Castell* alias *Casteler* (1554 NQ
198, 4) where the lost alternative makes it clear we have here a
parallel to *Kitchen* and *Kitchener*. *Tabor* 'drum' is used for 'drummer',
Pepper was a dealer in pepper, a pepperer or *Spicer*, for which we still
have also the metonymic *Spice*. This frequent use of metonymy
gives a satisfactory explanation of such names as *Meale*, *Orledge* or
Orlich (OFr *orloge* 'clock'), *Purse*, etc.[2] The numerous compounds of
-man, *-smith*, *-wright*, *-maker* and *-monger* will be discussed in the
following chapter.[3]

Some pastoral occupations

The limitations imposed on the previous chapter dictated the omission of the non-official occupations. Chief of these is *Herd* 'herdsman', with its numerous compounds, many now obsolete, others
obscured in form: *Calvert*, *Calvard* 'calf-herd', *Coltard*, *Coulthart*

[1] *v.* pp. 55–7. [2] *v.* pp. 19, 245–6, 274. [3] *v.* pp. 197–200, 204–9.

'colt-herd', *Coward* 'cow-herd', *Ewart*, at times for 'ewe-herd', *Gathard* (William *Gotehird, the Gatherde* 1285, 1287 AssCh), 'goat-herd', *Geldart* 'tender of the 'geld' (sterile or barren) cattle', *Gossard Gozzett* 'goose-herd', *Hoggard* 'keeper of the hogs', both pigs and sheep, *Lambert*, sometimes 'lamb-herd', *Nothard, Nutter* 'keeper of the beasts or oxen' (ON *naut*), *Oxnard* 'oxen-herd', *Stothard, Stothart, Stuttard* 'keeper of horses or bullocks' or 'oxherd' (OE *stott* 'an inferior kind of horse', in ME also 'steer, bullock'), *Swinnard* 'swine-herd', *Weatherhead* 'keeper of the wethers, sheep or rams'.

Here, too, we should include *Barker* (OFr *berchier, berkier*) 'shepherd', *Looker, Luker* 'shepherd', *Bover* (OFr *bovier, buvier*) 'oxherd', Daniel *le bouier* 1191 P, *Vatcher, Vacha* (OFr *vachier*) 'cow-herd'.

Forestry and hunting

Most of the terms used are common and need no explanation: *Forester* (*v.* p. 18), *Varder* 'verderer', a judicial officer of a royal forest, *Woodward*; *Hunt, Hunter, Huntman*, with the French *Venner* (OFr *veneor*), *Falconer, Fowler*, with the French *Osler* (OFr *oiseleor* 'bird-catcher, fowler'). *Berner* is at times from OFr *bernier* 'keeper of the hounds'.

THE TOWNSMEN: ARTISANS AND DEALERS

In the towns the number of occupational-names is bewildering. Fransson and Thuresson in their two books devote nearly 500 pages to the subject and they deal only with a dozen counties. Very many of these names no longer survive. My own collection includes some 285 obsolete occupational-names. Some were long and clumsy, unsuitable for permanent use as surnames, such as *Baiounsfeuere* 'maker of crossbow arrows', *Haryngbredere* 'roaster of herrings', *Payndemeynere* 'maker or seller of white bread', *Tothedrawer* 'tooth-drawer', and these have simply disappeared, whilst others have been replaced by shorter, synonymous terms, often metonymic.

One reason for the number of these names is that at a time when surnames had not yet become fixed a man might be distinguished now by his father's name, now by his place of birth or residence, or by his occupation and this could vary without being incorrect, e.g.

John le clerc, coroner (1292 SRLo) is identical with John de Vintry, Coroner (1303 LLB C) and John called Clerk (1286 LLB A). His real name was *de Vintry* (probably inherited); *Clerk* and *Coroner* denote different aspects of the post he held. In London, dishers were makers of wooden measures for wine and ale who had to have each a mark of his own placed on the bottom of each measure, samples of the marks to be submitted to the Chamberlain. They could be named either from the objects they made (John *le Disshere* 1304 LLB C) or from their use of the lathe (John *le Turnour* 1347 LLB F). Both *Disher* and *Turner* still survive. Similarly, William *le Pinour* (1292 SRLo), 'a maker of combs' (OFr *peigneor*, *pignor*) was also called *le Horner* (1295 LLB A) from the material he used (*Pinner*, *Horner*).

French and English terms

In the earliest documents, occupational-names usually appear in a Latin form. As a rule this is purely scribal, but the Lat *Faber* 'smith', *Pistor* 'baker' and *Sutor* 'shoe-maker' still survive.

Fransson estimates that one-third of the occupational-names were of French origin. Until well in the thirteenth century, at least, French was the language of all educated people, whilst the lower classes spoke English. It was natural for French-speakers to use French terms, and many occupational-names were certainly introduced into England after the Conquest. Clerks of French origin undoubtedly translated many English occupational-names into French, whilst the lower, English-speaking, classes, already partial to French personal-names, may well have adopted some of the French occupational-names. Many of these are now obsolete; some became part of the ME vocabulary and are still in use; others, though rare, still survive.

One result of this was that the same man could appear at one time with an English, at another with a synonymous French name. That of Humfrey *le Syur*, *le Sawyere*, *le Sayhare* (1270 AssSo) appears in both French and English forms which have given the modern *Sewer*, *Sawyer* and *Sayer*, all meaning 'sawyer' (OFr *seieor*, *scieur*, *saieur* 'sawyer', ME *saghier*, from *saghe*, *sawe* 'to saw'). *Glover* (OE *glōf* 'glove') is paralleled by *Gaunter*, *Ganter* (OFr *gantier* 'maker or seller of gloves'), *Nayler* (OE *nægel* 'nail') by *Clower*, *Cluer*, *Clore* (OFr *clou* 'nail'; 'maker of nails'),[1] *Needler*, *Nelder*, *Nadler* by the

---

[1] Stephen *le Cloer* (1292 SRLo) is probably identical with Stephen *le Nayler* (1319 SRLo).

rare *Aguilar* (OFr *aigullier*, *agullier* 'maker of needles'), *Netter* by *Retter* (OFr *retier* 'net-maker'), *Roper*, *Raper* (OE *rāp* 'rope') by *Corder* (OFr *cordier* 'rope-maker'), *Sadler* (OE *sadol* 'saddle') by *Seller* (OFr *selier*, *seller* 'saddler') and *Baster* (OFr *bastier* 'sadler), *Wheelwright* by *Rower*, *Royer* (OFr *roier*, *rouwier* 'wheelwright'), and *Wright* (OE *wyrhta* 'carpenter') by *Carpenter* (AFr *carpenter*).

The real English term for a butcher was *flesh-hewer*, once a fairly common surname which may partly be the origin of the rarer *Flesher*, but has been confused with and absorbed by *Fletcher* (OFr *flechier* 'a maker of arrows'). Fletcher Gate in Nottingham was formerly *Flesshewergate* 'the street of the butchers'. The normal term today is the French *Butcher* but we also have the very rare *Maskery* and *Massacrier* from OFr *macegref* and *macecrier* 'butcher'.

Of the less common French names which survive we may note: *Avner* (OFr *avenier* 'oat-merchant'), *Century* (John *le Ceinturer* 1275; OFr *ceinturier* 'maker of waist-belts'), *Gabler* (OFr *gabelier* 'tax-collector'), *Gellner*, *Gellender* (Richard *gelinier* 1214 P (C); OFr *gelinier* 'poulterer'), *Hamper* (OFr *hanapier* 'maker of goblets'), *Habbeshaw* (OFr *haubergier* 'maker of hauberks or coats of mail'), *Harbisher* (OFr *herbergeor* 'lodging-house keeper').

Some English terms are now similarly rare: *Bloomer* ('a maker of blooms' (OE *blōma*) or ingots of iron, iron-worker), *Bookbinder* (Willelmus *ligator librorum*, *le Bocbynder* 1273, 1311 Oseney), *Booker* (either OE *bōcere* 'writer of books, scribe' or from ME *bouken* 'to steep in lye, bleach', a bleacher), *Clouter* (a derivative of OE *clūt* 'a patch', patcher, cobbler), *Felters* 'a maker of felt', *Hafter* 'a maker of hafts or handles for tools', *Halter* 'maker or seller of halters' (in 1301 Henry *le Haltrehere* was owed 62*s*. by the Commonalty of London for halters for horses), *Honer* 'a sharpener of tools, grinder', *Kitter* 'a maker of wooden tubs, milking-pails, etc.', *Stringer* 'maker of strings for bows'; cf. Ralph *le Bowestrengere* 1319 SRLo, *Sucker* (from OE *sūcan* 'to suck'; probably a 'blood-letter' which was also a surname), *Whittier*, *Whittear*, *Whitehair* ('white-leather dresser', one who taws skins into whitleather).

The specialisation of medieval industry

Quite apart from these linguistic doublets, many occupational-names occur in various forms without any apparent difference in meaning. We still have *Flaxman*, *Flexman* and *Flexer* 'dresser or seller of flax' (OE *fleax*), but *Flaxbeter*, clearly a flax-dresser, *Flex-monger*, equally clearly a dealer, and *Flexhewer*, a reaper, are obsolete, as are *Lynman* (OE *līn* 'flax'), synonymous with *Flaxman*, *Lyndraper*, once common, and *Lyner* and *Lynger* (OFr *linier*, *lingier* 'maker or seller of linen cloth). *Linter*, though always rare, still survives (OFr **linetier* 'flax-dresser'). Similarly, we have *Sacker* 'a maker of sacks or coarse cloth, sackcloth' (OE *sacc*), *Secker* (ON *sekkr* 'sack') and *Sacher* (OFr *sachier* 'maker of sacks') but *Sakman* and *Sacwebbe* (the actual weaver) have gone. So, too, *Poghwebbe* 'a weaver of bags' (OE *pohha*) is obsolete, but the more general term *Pougher* survives. *Purser* or *Pusser* was a maker of purses (OE *purs*), but the corresponding French term (OFr *boursier*), now lost, was used as a synonym; Robert *le Pursere* (1319 SRLo) was identical with Robert Neel, *burser* (1338 LoPleas) and Robert Neel, *pouchemaker* (1344 ib.) and was an associate of William de Borham, *pouchmaker*, a surname now lost, though *Poucher* and the metonymic *Pouch* survive. *Pouch*, therefore, was used not only of a pouch or bag but also of a purse.

In the Middle Ages walls of 'wattle and daub' were extremely common. Wattling consisted of a row of upright stakes the spaces between which were more or less filled by interweaving small branches, hazel rods, osiers, reeds, etc. On one side, or more usually on both sides of this foundation earth or clay was daubed and thrust well into the interstices, the surfaces being smoothed and usually treated with plaster or at least a coat of whitewash. Closely allied to daubing was pargetting or rough-casting, in which mortar or a coarse form of plaster was used instead of clay or loam. All these operations had their occupational-terms which have become surnames, but the workmen were not always limited to one operation. At Corfe in 1285 Stephen the Dauber pargetted the long chamber and it is not always possible to decide whether the daubers were really daubing or whitewashing.[1] Hence the modern surnames *Watler*, *Whattler*, *Dauber*, *Dober*, *Plaster*, metonymic for *Plasterer*, *Pargeter*, *Pargiter*, *Whiter* 'whitewasher' and also *Clayre* or *Clare*. The clayer was engaged in plastering with mud in wattle and daub work, called *torching* in 1278, *plastering* in 1368 and *claying* in 1486.[2] Robert Pany is described both as a *mason* and as a *plasterer* (1319 SRLo).

Very often an artisan did not make only the article denoted by his surname. The girdler, for example, made not only girdles but also

---

[1] Building, pp. 188, 190, 191.   [2] Ibid., p. 189.

small articles of metal work; Geoffrey de Bradelee is called both *girdler* (1303 LLB C) and *bokelarius* 'buckle-maker' (1312 LLB D); the pinner made wire articles in addition to pins. The metal-worker might be named from the general term *founder* or *potter*, from the metal used, *Brasier*, 'a worker in brass', *Latner* (OFr *laton* 'brass'), *Peutherer* 'a maker of pewter vessels', or from the articles made, *Panner* 'a caster of pans' (formerly also *Pannegetter*, OE *panne* 'pan' and *gēotere* 'founder'), *Lorimer* 'a maker of spurs'.

Fransson has noted the great specialisation of trades in ME and the many names of trades found within a group. 'Whatever group of trade-names one looks up in this book, one will find persons who have surnames of occupation that comprise such a small part of a common trade that it is surprising that they could live by this.'[1] Some of these, as he suggests, may have been side-lines, e.g. *Bledere* and *Blodleter*, *Vershewere* 'one who carves verse inscriptions on stone'. Specialisation seems to have been greatest within the cloth industry, where he finds 165 names. The weavers are particularly common, but also the dyers of cloth, which group alone comprises 25 surnames. There are 18 different surnames denoting makers or sellers of hats, caps, hoods, etc. The metal industry provides 108 names, whilst the makers and dealers in provisions supply 107 surnames.

Among the less common surnames which have survived, we may note *Alefounder*, John *Alefondere* 1381 FFEss, still to be found in Essex and Suffolk, the inspector of ale, appointed by the Court Leet. He examined it as it was poured out (Lat *fundere* 'to pour out') and he had his perquisites, at Cockerham (La) in 1483, either a gallon of ale or else a taste of each vessel. *Bracegirdle*, William *Brigerdler* 1281 LLB B, John *Brachgyrdyl* or *Brecchegirdle* 1540 Bardsley, Roger *Brachegirdle* or *Brasgirdell* 1556 ib., John *Bretchgirdle* 1561 Pat (Wa), now metonymic, originally 'maker of breech-girdles', ME *brigerdel*, OE *brēcgyrdil*.[2] *Brader* (from OE *bredʒan* 'to braid, plait') 'a maker of cords'; *Brayer* 'a maker or seller of pestles' (OFr *breie, broie*); *Fainer* (OFr *fenier* 'haymonger'); *Threader* (from OE *þrǣd* 'thread') 'one employed to keep the shuttles threaded in weaving'; *Thrower* (from OE *þrāwan* 'to throw'), probably 'thread-thrower', one who converts raw silk into silk thread; *sylkthrowster* was a London occupational-term in 1423 (Thuresson).

Setter was a common occupational-term and surname in thirteenth and fourteenth-century London. Ekwall notes[1] that in 1317 Alexander *le Settere* received £10 in part payment of £40 due for an embroidered choir cope bought of him, and undertook well and befittingly to complete it 'of the same breadth around as a certain cord'. This must mean that Alexander le Settere made embroidered copes himself, that he was an embroiderer. *Settere* must be a derivative of ME *setten* 'to set', 'to put (an ornament, fitting, piece of furniture, etc.) in a place allotted or adapted to receive it; to fit, fix', also 'to fix (a stone or gem) in a surface of metal as an ornament; formerly also on a garment'. This was also a building term 'to set or lay stone or brick'. 'The layers, setters, or wallers, who placed in position the stones worked by the (free) mason.' All three names survive, *Layer*, *Setter*, *Waller*.

The Spicers

One of the most interesting features of the study of names is that one is always liable to make fascinating discoveries in the most unexpected places. In his delightful book on *Greek Byways*, T. R. Glover has an illuminating chapter on *Diet and History* in which he writes that

'In medieval England cattle were poor beasts, ill bred and ill fed. There was not enough meadow to raise hay to keep them alive through the winter, herds were slain in November, the meat salted down and men lived on preserved meat. Those who fancied their food insisted on meat dishes being very heavily seasoned and spiced. The beasts that were spared—and they were few—barely survived on straw and tree-loppings, exposed, if sheep, to scab and rot, if cattle to the murrain. Whatever country people could stand, this was no diet to promote the health of the towns, least of all when towns were so full of every kind of filth and smell . . . Throughout the Middle Ages, then, the supreme necessity of diet, if it is to be palatable, is spice . . . pepper, ginger, anything to get the stuff down!'[2]

Spices of all kinds were mixed with drinks. In Piers Plowman, Beton the Brewstere greets Glutton with:

> 'I have good ale, gossib', quoth she,
> 'Glutton, wilt thou assaye?'
> 'Hast thou aught in thy purse,' quoth he,
> 'Any hote spices?'
> 'I have pepir, and peonies,' quoth she,
> 'And a pound of garleck,
> And a farthing-worth of fenel-seed
> For fastyng dayes.'

[1] SRLo, pp. 357–8.
[2] T. R. Glover, *Greek Byways* (Cambridge, 1932), pp. 45–7.

All these Glutton could not resist and instead of going to Mass he went into the tavern and, having supped 'a galon and a gille', got gloriously drunk.

All this has left its impress on our surnames, all those surviving, except two, being metonymic. The *Spicer* was also the medieval apothecary or druggist. *Sauser* 'maker or seller of sauces' was common but, like *Saucemaker*, has disappeared. *Garlick* and *Mustard* or *Mustart* have absorbed *Garleker* and *Garlekmongere*, *Mustarder* and *Mustardman*. The French *Ayler* (OFr *aillier* 'garlic-seller') survives, Luke *le Ayler* 'peverer' 1287 LLB B. The trade-name *pepperer* seems never to have become a surname but both the English *Pepper* and the French *Peever* (OFr *peyvre* 'pepper') still survive, but not *Peverer* (OFr *pevrier* 'pepperer'). *Peppercorn* 'undoubtedly the sobriquet of a spicer or pepperer' was once fairly common and Bardsley's comment is supported by 'Ricardus *pepercorne, spysar*', but it is probably also due in some instances to the peppercorn rent by which land was often held just as *Gilliver* might also refer to a rent of a clove of gilly-flower. It is from OFr *girofle*, *gilofre* 'clove', used for sauces, hence probably a grower of gillyflower or a sauce-maker. *Leak* or *Leek* is often local, but the modern *Leaker* and the obsolete *Lekman* suggest it may be metonymic for a seller of leeks. *Ginger* and *Fennell*, a plant cultivated for use in sauces, are always metonymic.

Cakes and ale

The baker, whom we have already discussed, was sometimes named from the kind of bread he made, *Whitebread* or *Whitbread*,[1] a seller of the white, i.e. the best bread, made of wheat, *Blamphin*, *Plampin* (OFr *blanc pain* 'white bread'). The preliminary operations are represented by *Bolter*[2] (OFr *buleteor* 'a sifter of meal'), *Boutflour* 'sift flour', a nickname for the miller, and *Dower* 'a maker of dough' (OE *dāh*). *Cake* or *Cakes* is from ME *cake*, a comparatively small, flattened sort of bread, originally round or oval, usually baked hard on both sides by being turned in the process, metonymic for a cake-maker (*Cakyer* and *Cakaman* are obsolete), as is *Cakebread* for a maker of *cakebrede*, of the finer and more dainty quality of cake. *Flann*, *Flawn* and *Flanner* (OFr *flaonnier*) represent the maker of flawns, a kind of custard or pancake. *Wafer* is metonymic for *waferer* (AFr *wafrer*), a maker or seller of wafers or thin cakes. The

---

[1] Also for 'white beard'.   [2] Also 'a maker of bolts'.

waferers seem to have been chiefly concerned with the provision of the eucharistic bread but also sold sweet, spiced cakes, the 'wafers piping hot' which Absolon the clerk gave to Alison. *Wastell*, too, is metonymic for the common *wasteler* or *wastelmonger*, a maker or seller of *wastels*, a north-eastern French form of *gastel*, modFr *gâteau*, 'a cake or bread made of the finest flour', whilst the *Wigger* made wedge-shaped cakes or buns (ME *wygge*).

Drink gave rise to an abundance of surnames, surviving and obsolete, occupational and nicknames, usually, like *Taverner* and *Vinter* or *Vintiner* 'wine-merchant' frequent and of obvious meaning. Besides the common *Brewer* and *Brewster*, we have *Brasseur*, *Bracer* and *Brasher* from OFr *braceor*, *brasseur* 'brewer', *Malster* the feminine form of *Malter*, both used only of men, and *Maltman*, with *Malthouse*, *Malthus*, *Maltus* and *Maltas*, originally *atte Malthuse* 'worker at the malt-house'. *Maltmaker*, *Maltmelnere* 'miller' and *Maltmetere* 'measurer' are obsolete. *Meader*, *Medur* (Alexander *le Meder*, *Medarius* 1180 Oseney, from OE *meodu* 'mead', Lat *medarius* 'a maker or seller of mead') has superseded *Medemaker*. *Tapper* (OE *tæppere* 'tapper of casks') was a beer-seller or tavern-keeper, whilst *Tapster* was used only of women who sold ale. The *Tipler*, too, was a seller of ale or tapster (ME *tipeler*), not a boozer.

Weavers, fullers and dyers

The weaver is represented by a variety of names: *Webb* (OE *webba* (m) or *webbe* (f) 'weaver'), *Webber* a derivative of this, *Webster*, feminine in form but usually used of men, *Weaver*, a derivative of OE *wefan* 'to weave' and *Tisser* (OFr *tisseur* 'weaver').

The raw cloth had to be *fulled*, i.e. scoured and thickened by beating it in water, a process known as *walking* because originally done by men trampling upon it in a trough. Hence *Walker* by the side of *Fuller* and *Tucker* from OE *tūcian*, originally 'to torment', later 'to tuck'. These surnames seem to be characteristic of different parts of England. In general, in ME *Fuller* is southern and eastern; *Walker* belongs to the west and the north; *Tucker* is south-western. *Fuller* (also *Voller*) is from both OE *fullere* and OFr *fouleor*, the French form being found all over England, often a translation of *walker* or *tucker*. The feminine *fullestre* survives in the rare *Folster* (Emma *Fullestr'* 1327 SRSx). *Fulloon*, *Fullen* is from OFr *fulun* 'fuller'. *Wolbeter* was also an occasional ME surname.

The teaseler drew up from the body of the cloth all the loose fibres with *teasels*, the dried heads of the 'fuller's thistle' and has left his name as *Tazelaar* or *Tesler* 'one who teasels cloth'.

Dyer (OE *dēagere* 'dyer') is also found in the feminine form *Dyster*, used both of men and women, and *Dexter*, a Suffolk form noted also in Leicestershire and Warwickshire. In the north we have the Scand *Lister, Litster, Lidster, Ledster* and *Lester*, from ME *lit(t)e*, ON *lita* 'to dye'. The once common *Teynturer* (OFr *teinturier* 'dyer') has completely disappeared.

The most common dye used appears to have been woad (OE *wād*), a blue dyestuff obtained from the plant, in great demand in the Middle Ages, from which we have *Wader, Wademan* and *Wodeman*. This is more common today but rarer in ME than the French *Waider, Weider* (OFr *wesdier, waisdier* 'dyer with or seller of woad'). The ME spelling *Wodeman* is indistinguishable from *wodeman* 'wood-man'. That ME *wōdman* from OE *wādmann* existed is proved by the modern *Wadman* and *Wader*. Similarly, ME *Wodere* is indistinguishable from *wodere* 'woodman'. ME *wōdere* 'woad-merchant' certainly existed for Robert *le Woder* de Merthone is identical with Robert de Merthone, *wayder* (1276 LLB B). OE *wādere* became ME *wōdere* and should give a modern *Woader* or *Woder*. The latter may well have been confused with and absorbed by the more common and more readily understood *Wodere*, now *Wooder*. *Cork* is metonymic for *Corker*, a derivative of ME *cork* 'a purple or red dyestuff', one who sells purple dye; or synonymous with *Corklittster*, a dyer of cloth with 'cork'. *Madder* or *Mader* is metonymic for *maderer* 'a dyer with or seller of madder' or *maderman* or *madermonger*.

The goldsmith

In addition to these many specialised terms and the application to a single man of two or more synonymous occupational-names, we find also the opposite tendency, the use of a single general term both for the merchant or capitalist and for the small craftsman who actually did the work. Many of the early mayors and sheriffs of London had been at one time or another goldsmiths as well as vintners. They minted the king's money, acted as his exchangers and undertook the repair of the crown jewels or negotiated for a new supply, generally with the technical and financial assistance of Italian experts. In this sense, Gregory de Rokesley, Mayor of London 1275–81, was a goldsmith. But he was also a vintner or wine-merchant and he dealt largely in wool. Here we are concerned with the goldsmith's trade as a distinct profession. First and foremost the goldsmith was a highly skilled craftsman. He did not necessarily own the precious metals in which he worked. We find him going to the Guildhall to acknowledge the receipt of articles of plate entrusted to him by royal or noble personages for his manipulation. But more often he was a dealer as well as a worker in the precious metals. The first charter of the craft (1327) authorises the goldsmith to buy gold and silver plate, but only in the row of shops called Goldsmiths' Row in Cheapside where their work may be overlooked, and not in back streets where stolen goods might be received. Other sources show us that the goldsmith's profession embraced men of every degree of wealth, from the merchant of aldermanic status to the poor craftsman.[1]

Apart from *Goldsmith* itself, the only surviving surname of the craft is *Finer* (OFr *fineur* 'refiner of gold, silver, etc.'), but there are medieval examples of *Goldbeter*, with the synonymous French *Orbatour*, *Goldehoper* 'maker of gold rings' and *Orgraver* 'gold engraver'. *Silver* is sometimes metonymic for a silversmith, *Silverhewer* or *Sylverour*. From their activities as moneyers, we have *Conyer* (from OFr *coynier* 'to stamp money, to mint'), *Minter* (OE *myntere* 'moneyer'); *Money* may be metonymic for *Monemaker* (1381 PTY) or for *Monier*, John *monier* c1198 Bart, Gilbertus *le muneur* or *monetarius* 1230 P (Y), from OFr *monier*, *monnoyeur* 'moneyer'.

OFr *orfevre* 'goldsmith' was a common medieval name. It usually appears as *Orfevre*, *Orfeuere* and *Orfeure* and is now probably represented by *Orfeur* and *Offer*. But occasional early forms, William *le Orfere* 1265 Pat, Nicholas de Norhamptone *orfrer*, William atte more *orfrer* 1292 SRLo, with Henry *le Oriffere* 1269 AssSo, suggest another likely origin also. Both the Londoners can be identified with goldsmiths and it is possible that *orfrer* meant 'a maker of orphrey or gold embroidery', from ME, OFr *orfreis*, from MedLat *aufrisium*, a modification of Lat *auriphrygium*. The modFr for a maker of orphrey is *orfroisier* which probably accounts for *Officer* (Adam *le Orfreyser* 1302 MKS). In the thirteenth century we have Alicia *aurifrigeria* which might well be for *orfrer*.[2]

---

[1] G. Unwin, *Finance and Trade under Edward III* (Manchester, 1918), pp. 26–7.
[2] *v*. SRLo, p. 357.

Cordwainers

The term *cordwainer* was applied in the thirteenth century to men of widely different social status. Early in the Middle Ages Cordova acquired a wide reputation for the leather which its craftsmen prepared from goats' skins and the manufacture, which afterwards spread to Barcelona, Northern Spain and Provence, supplied one of the main articles of commerce at the Champagne fairs. The merchants who dealt in it were called cordwainers. Gervase the cordwainer, who was the king's Chamberlain of London in 1227, and sheriff 10 years later, derived his name from the cargoes of Spanish leather which he brought to London.[1]

At the end of the thirteenth century the leading cordwainers or skinners of London gave Spanish merchants 'shipping orders' and received credit of from £30 to £75. Lesser merchants took small parcels worth £5 to £10. But by far the commonest transaction was for small groups of lesser merchants and shop-keepers to combine to buy a cargo. Most of the cordwainers of the fourteenth century were small craftsmen and shop-keepers. The gild rules forbade a member to have two shops, but this could be got round by setting up a man of straw like Richard 'the Sewer'. In 1281 he was provided with a stock worth £11. 13s. by a leather-merchant and a cordwainer. He covenanted to remain in their service for three years and to render yearly accounts. He was to be provided with all necessaries and a yearly stipend of one mark.[2]

Richard *le Cordewaner* who was threatened in his house in Wood St whilst cutting leather (1299 LoCt) was clearly a shoemaker. *Cordwainer* was common in ME and appears in 1474 as *cordener* (NED). The surname, therefore, survives as *Cordner* or *Codner*, but is usually metonymic, from OFr *cordoan* 'Cordovan leather': *Corden, Cordon, Cordwent, Corwin*. AFr *corviser*, OFr *corveisier*, fairly common from 1135 to the fourteenth century, is apparently obsolete. The shoemaker also appears as *Sewer* (OFr *suor*), the Lat *Sutor* and as *Souter, Sowter, Sueter, Suter, Sewter* and *Suiter* (OE *sūtere*). *Cobbler* is extinct (Emma *le Cobelere* 1289 NorwLt), but is of interest as in London cordwainers had to use new leather in making shoes, whilst the cobblers were restricted to the use of old leather in mending them. Other footwear is represented by *Clog* for *Clogmaker*

---

[1] Unwin, op. cit., p. 29.   [2] Ibid., pp. 30–1.

(1387), *Patten* and *Pattin* for *Patener* or *Patynmaker*. *Pattens* were a kind of clog made of wood or iron, often used by ecclesiastics, probably to protect the feet from the chill of the bare pavement of the church. *Hoser* or *Hosier* may be a derivative of OE *hosa* 'hose', a dealer or maker of stockings and socks, not recorded in NED before 1403, but the earliest forms (*Husier* 1180) point to an OFr **hosier*, from OFr *heuse, hose* 'boot', hence 'a shoemaker'. The term is sometimes used as a synonym of *Chaucer* (OFr *chaucier*), a maker of *chausses* (OFr *chauces* 'clothing for the legs, pantaloons, hose'). In 1484 these were 'chauces of yron or legge harneys', but ME *chawce* was a general term for anything worn on the feet, boots, shoes, etc. As Baldewyn *le Chaucer* lived in Cordwanerstret and other London taxpayers of the same name lived in Cordwainer Ward, the early chaucer was probably a worker in leather, a maker of leather breeches, boots, etc.

The most common of the general terms for workers in leather was *Skinner* (ON *skinnari*), but there was also an English *Shinner* (from OE *scinn* 'skin'). *Leather* and *Leatherman* denote a dealer or a worker in leather (cf. the lost *Lethercarver*). *Fell* and *Feller* may sometimes be synonymous with the lost *Felmonger*, whilst the rare *Pelter* or *Pilter* (OFr *peletier*) was a fellmonger, furrier or dresser of fells, and *Currier* a leather-dresser (OFr *conreeur* 'currier'). Some of the more particularised occupations have already been dealt with, but we may add *Pilcher*, from OE *pylece* 'a pilch', a maker or seller of pilches (an outer garment made of skin dressed with hair).

The potters

The potters of fourteenth-century London were not makers of earthenware but workers in copper and brass, and bell-founders. The early potters, like the early cordwainers, were importers of foreign goods, mostly kitchen-utensils, known as *dinanderie*, brass-work of Dinant near Namur, of European reputation. These *marchands batteurs*, as they were called, brought large quantities of their wares to England and took back English wool and tin.

Two wealthy London merchants, Walter and Richard the Potter, each an alderman, both made their wills in 1280. They lived in Cheapside and had much property in London, a shop in Bury St Edmunds and land at Boston and Winchester. Richard's nephew, Walter the Potter junior, and Henry, Walter's brother, and Alan, another nephew, were extensively engaged in the same business.

Walter the Potter junior and Henry his brother gave Aubrey le Pecherous a shipping order for £34 worth of dinanderie.

But a home industry was growing up. In October 1288 John the Potter contracted with the Abbot and convent of Ramsey to make them a new lavatory 'of good and durable metal, 30 ft long and 2½ ft high, with 16 copper keys of subtle design and richly guilt, and fillets through the centre' for £30 and a gown, one-third to be paid in advance to enable him to get materials. John was to ride down to Huntingdonshire with his two journeymen, the abbot to find food for horses and men whilst they stayed. Master and men were each to have two loaves of bread and two gallons of beer, a dish of meat or a dish of fish every day; one of the master's loaves was to be 'monks' bread' and both his gallons to be drawn from the convent cask, whilst his men were to be content with the bread and beer given out in the hall to the servants of the abbey.[1]

Richard of Wymbush, a working potter, cast a bell for Holy Trinity Priory, Aldgate, and in 1312 contracted to supply another as nearly as possible in tune with the first. The second bell, though not so large as the first, was to weigh over a ton. Richard was to have six months to complete the task and the Priory was to lend him the first bell to work by.[2]

The bell-founder is now represented by *Billiter* (OE *belle* and *gēotere* 'bell-founder') and by *Sainter, Santer, Senter,* and *Center* (OFr *saintier* 'bell-founder'). The demand for bells could hardly have been large enough to enable a craftsman to specialise entirely in that branch; a bell-maker would always have been primarily a founder and according as the main portion of his trade lay in casting buckles and other fittings for belts (whence *Buckler* and *Belt,* for the lost *beleter*), or pots, or bells, he would be known as a girdler (now *Girdler, Gurdler* and *Gurtler*), a potter or a bell-founder. Most of the known London bell-founders used the title 'potter'. Ekwall has noted that Edmund *Seintier* (1168 ELPN) is called a moneyer. Most moneyers were goldsmiths, but occasionally other metal-workers had a die in the mint (one was a *Spurrier*) and a bell-founder may have acted as a moneyer. Several bells were cast for Westminster Abbey by Edward Fitz Odo, the famous goldsmith of Henry III. William *Founder* (now obsolete as a surname) cast both bells and cannon. His trade stamp, bearing his name and a tree, appears on a number of bells and hints at his real surname—clearly *Woodward*.

[1] Unwin, op. cit., p. 31.   [2] Ibid., p. 33.

In two successive entries in 1385 he is called William *the founder* and William *Wodeward* and in 1417 cannon were supplied by William *Wodeward, founder*.

At Exeter about 1285 Bishop Peter de Quivil assured the proper care of the bells of the cathedral by granting a small property in Paignton to Robert *le Bellyetere* as a retaining fee, Robert and his heirs being bound to make or repair, when necessary, the bells, organ and clock of the cathedral, the chapter paying all expenses, including the food and drink of the workmen, and these obligations were duly fulfilled for at least three generations. In 1454 a Norwich bell-founder was called Richard *Brasier*[1] (now *Brasier, Brazier, Braisher*, 'a worker in brass'). An earlier term was *Brasgetere* 'brass-founder'.

The maker of earthenware pots was a *Crocker* or *Croker* (from OE *crocc*). The *marchands batteurs* and makers of *dinanderie* are now represented by the surname *Bater* (OFr *bateor* 'one who beats'), a coppersmith or dealer in beaten copper or brass ware. Stephen *le Coperbeter* (1286 LLB A) is identical with Stephen *le Batur* (1292 ib.).

Our treatment of these names has necessarily been selective, but enough examples have been given to illustrate how specialised they were and to prove that a mere dictionary etymology is insufficient to show how many of them were really used. Others will be discussed in the next chapter. This we will end with one or two names of interest.

OE *hēawere* 'hewer' is not a common term in surnames but survives, usually well-disguised, in *Furzer* 'furse-cutter' and *Fusier*: Gratia *Furshewer* 1560, Joanna *Firsheer, Furshewre* 1590, 1594, Ann *Forschouer, Furzier* 1672, 1786, Elizabeth *Fuzier* 1765 HartlandPR (D); *Stonehewer, Stonier, Stanyer* 'stone-cutter' and *Woodier, Woodyear, Woodger* 'wood-cutter'.

Armer, Larmer is metonymic for *armourer* 'a maker of armour', also 'linen-armerer', a tailor who made gambesons, tunics worn under the habergeon (William *Gambeson* 1297 MinAcctCo (R), now *Gamson* or *Gameson*). Henry *Horpol*, armourer, was Warden of the Tailors in 1328. He was paid for 100 aketones, stuffed jackets or jerkins worn under the mail, and 100 bacinettes or basnets, a small steel (or brazen) head-piece. He was thus both an armourer and a linen-armourer;[2] cf. Richard *le Aketonmaker* 1328 MESO and the undocumented *Bassnett*. OFr *heaumier* 'maker of helmets' is now

---

[1] *v.* L. F. Salzman, *English Industries in the Middle Ages* (Oxford, 1923), pp. 145–54.
[2] PopLond, p. 144.

Homer. Limmer and *Lumner* are from OFr *enlumineor, illumineor* 'an illuminator of manuscripts', Ralph *le Liminur*, Robert *le Luminur* 1230 Oseney, Reginald *le Eluminur* 1257 ib., *le Ylluminor* 1265 FF (O).

Plumer and *Plummer* are often difficult to keep apart. *Plumer* and *Plomer* are from OFr *plumier* 'a dealer in plumes or feathers'. John de Cestrehunte, *fethermongere* (1280 LLB A) is called *plumer* in 1281. *Plummer, Plimmer* and *Plummber* sometimes occur as *Plumer*, but Osbertus *le plumer* or *Plumbarius* (1221–2 Cur) was certainly a plumber. The earliest examples, e.g. Godric *Plumberre* (1102–7 Rams), seem to be a direct formation from OFr *plomb* 'lead', later assimilated to OFr *plummier* 'plumber', Ernaldus *le plummer* 1225 LeicBR.

Chapter Ten

SOME COMMON COMPOUNDS

Man, Mann derive, no doubt, at times from OE *Mann* 'man', a personal-name still in use, though not common, in the twelfth century. The usual source is OE *mann* 'man', but the exact meaning is not always clear. It probably often means 'servant' as in many of the compounds below. Sometimes it may correspond to a phrase like *homo Bainardi* 'the man of Bainard', one who owed him feudal service. At times we may have reference to a lower rank in the social scale, *nativus* 'bondman'. In 1279 Ralph de Ginges granted to Simon de Duntona Peter *Man* son of Robert *Man* his *nativus* with all his family and all his chattels for 40*s.* sterling. These bondmen seem to have acquired a surname descriptive of their status.

Surviving compounds of -*man* are exceedingly numerous and many others have become obsolete. The meaning varies and for some of the surnames there is more than one explanation. *Waterman* may be the 'servant of Walter' (Adam *Walterman* 1260 AssY), or it may mean 'waterman, water-carrier' synonymous with *Waterlader* (1197), a carter of water for sale (William *le Waterman* 1249 Oseney), or *Waterberere* (1381), a carrier of water from a spring or conduit for domestic use, a term surviving in Waterbeer St in Exeter. *Readman, Reedman, Redman* may denote a cutter of reeds or a thatcher, or it

192

may be a nickname 'red man', or derive from Redmain in Cumberland. *Woodman* is usually from OE *Wudumann*, but may also be occupational, *le Wodeman*.

From personal-names

A number of OE personal-names in *-mann* still survive as surnames: Ashman (*Æscmann*), Blackman, Blakeman (*Blæcmann*), Broman, Brooman (*Brūnmann*), Dearman, Dorman, Durman (*Dēormann*), Dodman, Dudman (*Dudemann*), Goldman (*Goldmann*), Kinman, Kynman (*Cynemann*), Sweatman, Sweetman, Swetman (*Swētmann*), Whatman, Wheatman, Watman (*Hwætmann*), Winman (*Winemann*). Some of these personal-names are not actually on record in OE: Elfman (**Ælfmann*), Gladman (**Glædmann*), Hardman (**Heardmann*), Howman, Hughman, Human, Uman (**Hygemann*), Lilleyman, Lilliman, Lillyman, Litman, Lyteman, Lutman, Lulman (**Lȳtelmann*), Strangman, Strongman (**Strangmann*), Whiteman, Whitman, Wittman (**Hwītmann*), Wightman, Weightman (**Wihtmann*). Sometimes the suffix is from *-mund*: Eastman, Eastment, Astman, Esmond (*Ēastmund*), Warman (*Wærmund*; also 'chapman', from OE *waru* 'articles of merchandise, goods for sale'), Osman (OE *Ōsmund* or ON *Ásmundr*), Chillman, Chilman (**Cildmann* or *Cēolmund*). Godman, Goodman, Goudman, Gutman may be from OE *Godman*, OG *God(e)man*, ON *Guðmundr* or OE *Gūðmund*; or a nickname 'good man', as is proved by Henry *le Godman* 1275 RH (C).

ON personal-names have given Farman (*Farmann*), Lawman (ON *Lǫgmaðr*, ODa *Lag(h)man*, Thurman, Thorman (ODa *Þormund*) and Westman (*Vestmaðr* 'man from the west', especially Ireland).

Godsman, Goodsman, Goodisman are from OG *Godesman*, Coleman, Colman, Coulman from OG *Col(e)man* in the south and OIr *Colmán* in the north.

Occasionally *-man* is a corruption of *-min* in OFr personal-names: Gillman, Guillerman, Gelman, Wellerman, Wellman, Wilman, Williman (OFr *Guillemin*, AFr *Willemin*, diminutives of *Guillaume, Willelm*), Jackaman (*Jakemin*, a diminutive of *Jacqueme* 'James'). Bateman, Baitman, Batman are from *Bateman* 'servant of Bartholomew', used early and often as a christian name.

Names of servants

In the fourteenth century we find numerous surnames of servants so long and elaborate that they must be regarded as descriptions rather than names. They are found only in legal documents and are intended as a means of identification. Such names as the following can never have been in common use: *Nicholas Rogeresseriaunt le Norreys* 1297 Coram (C), i.e. Nicholas the sergeant of Roger le Norreys; *Ricardus*

193

Willames baillif Pickerell (ib. Wa), Richard the bailiff of William Pickerell. For practical purposes the names would be shortened and the men referred to as Nicholas *Rogeres sergeant* or Nicholas *the sergeant* or even Nicholas *Rogeres*, etc. We still have surnames like *Harryman* and *Matthewman* and we know that one meaning of *Parsons* and *Vicars* was 'the servant of the parson or of the vicar'. A clear case of simplification by dropping the master's surname is: Robert *Alcockesknave*, the servant of *Alcock* le Marscal (1350 Putnam, La), with which we may compare: William *Collecnape* 1191 P (L) 'servant of *Colle*', a pet form of Nicholas; William *Man Norry* 1297 SRY; Felicia *Williamserjaunt* 1310 AssSt; John *Watknave* 1325 Wak (Y).

Most common of the suffixes employed are *-servant* and *-man*, with a number of examples of *-sergeant* and *-knave* and a few more definite terms. *Serjant* is sometimes a doublet of *-servant*; Saerus *Thomasservant* Clench, servant of Thomas Clench, parson of Birdbrook (Essex), is also called *Thomasserjaunt de Clench* (1319 Pat). But other sergeants may have been officers of justice. *Knave* is at times equated with *-man*: *Villanus Rauvesman Bagot* is identical with *Villanus Raulynesknave Bagod* (1312 LLB D) and may well mean 'the villein of Ralph Bagot'. In other instances it may mean 'valet'. Among more specific occupations we have: William *Peresshephird le Coliere* (1334 Pat, Herts), the shepherd of Peter le Coliere; John *Elysessometer de Middilton* (1288 Pat, Sf), the pack-horse driver of Elys de Middilton; Robert *Heryngkartere* (1332 SRLo), a carter of herrings; Thomas *Botonerescartere* 1380 AssWa, Thomas the carter of a man named *Butner* 'a maker of buttons'; John *Thelavediescartere Engayne* (1327 Pat, Ess), 'carter of the Lady Engayne', wife of John Engayne, lord of White Notley; Robert *Williamesheyward de Maundevill* (1322 Pat, W), 'hayward of William de Maundevill'; William *Robertspage Chysell* (1400 Pat, Nth), 'page of Robert Chysell'.

These surnames of the servants cannot be regarded as established family names but those of the masters were most probably hereditary surnames; some are known to have been well established before this period. The majority of the masters belonged to the upper or middle classes. Some are expressly stated to be nobles or gentry or clergy and to have had a chamberlain, an usher, a warrener, a bailiff or steward or a chaplain and were clearly men of rank or wealth or both. Some appear to be tradespeople or yeoman farmers. Sir Simon

Ward was a Sheriff of York and one of the leaders at the Battle of Boroughbridge in 1322. Three of his servants are mentioned: William *Simundeschamberleyn Ward*, Robert *Simundescok Ward* and Gilbert *Simundesusher Ward* (1318 Pat, Y). The case of John Hastang is interesting. His surname, well established from the twelfth century, is from a Norman personal-name *Hastenc*, ultimately from ON *Hásteinn*, and survives as *Hastain* or *Hasting*. He had a pantler and a private chaplain, Henry *Jonespaneter Hastang* and Richard *Jonesprest Hastang*. He was living in 1319 (AssSt) and had a son John, who had his own servant, Henry *Janekynesmon Hastang*. To distinguish him from his father of the same name, the son is called by the diminutive *Janekyn* 'John junior'.

Some half-dozen of these surnames point to the maintenance of private chaplains and one to that of a hermit: Stephen *Hamondesheremyt of Hesseye* (1348 Pat, Y). These, with John *Johanesprest* (1332 EwenG, Bk), give the clue to the meaning of certain compounds of *-prest*: Richard *Hoggeprest* 1327 SRSx, Lucia *Hogeprest* 1332 ib.; as both are assessed in the same parish, Lucia was probably the wife of Richard who had died between 1327 and 1332; Adam *Jakeprest* 1332 SRSx; Robert *Grymeprest* 1285 AssLa, John *Grymprest* 1524 SRSf. These are probably simplified forms of such names as John *Thomasprest Dorward*, using the christian name of their employer, though the meaning might be 'priest of a man surnamed *Hogge*', etc., for *Hodge*, *Jakes* and *Grime* were all established family names before 1300. Thomas *Pilcheprest* 1301 SRY and John *Saltprest* must certainly be from *Pilch*, metonymic for *Pilcher*, 'a maker or seller of pilches', outer garments made of skin dressed with hair, and *Salt*, from Salt (St), Nicholas *de Salt* 1199 AssSt.

The only surviving compounds of *-priest* are *Hollinpriest* and *Allpress*. The former, of which no early examples have been found, Weekley suggests may denote 'a pious hermit among the hollies. It is found in Cheshire, where *Hollin-* names, such as *Hollingshead*, are numerous.' But such a formation would be rare or unique and *Hollin* may well be a surname. *Hollen* and *Hollins* are variants of *Hollies* 'dweller by the holly or holm-oak'. At first sight, Robert *Morprest* 1286 Pinchbeck (Sf) and Richard *Mosoprest* (*sic*) 1275 SRWo, suggest support for Weekley's interpretation, but both *Moor* and *Moss* are common surnames, the latter being either 'dweller by the moss' or a form of *Moses*.

That some of these surnames were nicknames is clearly proved by the names of Wulfstanus *cognomento uuilde preost* (1040–2 Lambeth MS 1212, f.330) and Robert *Wildprest* (13th Guisb), William *le Wyseprest* (1298 AssSt) and *Allpress*, found without a christian name as *Aldeprest* (1194 P, Co) and as a surname, as Thomas *Alprest* (1279 RH, C), 'the old priest'. With these we may compare the surviving *Oldman* and *Oldreive* and such lost names as Richard *Aldegrom* 1198 P (K), Ædwinus *Wildegrom, Willegrom* 1182–4 P (St), Robert *le Wyldreve* 1296 SRSx and William *Wildecnave* 1327 SRWo. As *Godecnave* (1220) 'good boy or servant' occurs as *Goddeknawe* in the thirteenth century and has become confused with *Goodenough, Goodnow* and *Goodner*, so *Wildecnave* may have contributed to *Wilner*. To this class, in spite of its topographical appearance, belongs William *Wodeprest* 1200 Cur (W), Adam *le Wodeprest* 1207 FFBk, 'the mad priest'. Similarly, *Woodsmith* and *Woodmason* may also be from OE *wōd*, ME *wod(e), wood* 'frenzied, wild', which became confused in spelling and pronunciation with *wood*; cf. Shakespeare's pun 'And here am I, and *wood* within this wood'. The ME Adam *le Wode* 1221 AssWo has contributed to the frequency of *Wood*, from *atte Wode*.

Compounds of *-man* 'servant' with personal-names, some in their pet-form, are common and many more have become obsolete. Early examples are in the form *Rotbert' homo bainardi* 1086 InqEl (Sf), *Gold homo abbatis de Ely* 1086 ICC (Sf), *Ærnulf' homo Willelmi* 1170 P (Ha), where the relationship was probably feudal, 'Arnulf who owed feudal service to William' and was his *man*. Personal-names are found in: *Butman* (OE Butt), *Falkman* (OFr Fauque, OG Falco), *Folkman* (OG Folco), *Gassman* (OFr Gace, OG Wazzo), *Lukeman, Luckman, Markman, Pakeman, Packman, Paxman* (OFr Pasques, Paque), *Payman* (OE Pæga), *Tookman* (Anglo-Scand Tōka) and *Tumman, Tummon* (Tom), and pet-forms in *Addyman* (Adam), *Dowman* (David), *Fugeman* (OFr Fuche, from OFr Fulcher), *Hickman, Higman, Hitchman* (Richard), *Hobman* (Robert), *Hodgman, Rodgman, Roggeman* (Roger), *Hudman* (Hugh and Richard), *Jackman, Lammiman* (Lambin, from Lambert), *Lorriman* (Laurence), *Pateman* (Patrick), *Potman* (Pot, from Philipot) and *Sandeman* (Alexander; cf. Thomas *Alysaundresman* 1297 Coram (Bk), John *Saundirman* 1379 PTY).

The curious *Mortleman, Mortelman*, which, according to Weekley 'suggests a dramatic personification of the uncertainty of human life', probably belongs here. Examples are rare and late: Thomas *Mortiman* 1588 RothwellPR (Y), Francis *Mortlemens* 1638 HorringerPR (Sf), George *Mortelman* 1674 HTSf. Much earlier in Yorkshire we find William *Martinman* (1301 SRY). In names containing

196

three liquids, *r—n—n*, loss or interchange is common and *Martinman* might have become *Martiman* or *Martilman*. Rounding of *a* to *o* is found in such names as *Warboys* and *Worboys*, *Warlock* and *Worlock*. Though not strictly parallel, a similar change might have taken place in *Martilman* which could have been regarded as a dialectal pronunciation of *mortal-man* and re-spelled accordingly.

From surnames, we have: *Grubman*, *Pennyman*, *Pannaman* and *Snowman*. In other instances, the status or occupation of the master is expressed: *Ditterman* (*Diter* 'public crier, summoner'), *Ladyman*, *Leachman*, *Leechman* (*Leech* 'physician'), *Maidman*, *Maidment*, *Maitment* ('maidens'), *Masterman*, *Monkman*, *Needlaman*, *Needleman* (*Needler*, *Nadler* 'maker of needles'), *Priestman*, *Smidman*, Henry *Smythman* 1379 PTY ('the smith's assistant'), *Surgerman* (OFr *surgier* 'surgeon') and *Tuckerman* (*Tucker* 'fuller'). Confirmation of this interpretation is found in Lincolnshire in 1374 when John de Barnby, *chaumberleyn*, and William *Chaumberleynman* were both accused of killing William de Cantelupo (AssL).

Names of occupation and office

Occasionally surnames in -*man* have reference to office or status: *Alderman*, *Shirman* 'sheriff, bailiff or steward'; *Smallman*, a tenant who was coupled with thanes and drengs in an order which suggests he was inferior to both; *Spackman*, *Speakman* 'advocate, spokesman'; *Sturman* 'steersman' and probably also 'captain, master of a ship'. The first recorded bearer of the name, Edricus *Stirman*, was the commander in 1066 of the sea and land forces of the Bishop of Worcester in the service of Edward the Confessor; *Tiddiman*, *Tidiman* 'the chief man of a tithing, a headborough'.

More often the surnames denote actual occupations in town and country alike, workers on the land and tenders of cattle, makers and sellers of manufactured articles. The specialisation in medieval trades resulted in numerous occupational names long obsolete, as *Burelman* 'a maker or seller of *burel*', a coarse woollen cloth of a reddish-brown colour; *Fetherman*, *Hardwareman*, *Smereman* 'a dealer in fats, lard or butter'; *Semylman* 'a maker or seller of *semels*', cakes of fine wheaten flour; *Timberman*.

Many of the surviving surnames are common descriptive terms: *Ackerman* 'farmer', *Boatman*, *Bowman*, *Chapman*, *Chipman* 'merchant, trader', *Flodman* (OE *flotmann* 'sailor'), *Plowman*, *Totman* 'look-out man', *Trotman*, identical with *Trotter* 'messenger', *Waithman* (ON *veiðimann* 'hunter'), *Watchman*. *Wakeman* recalls the title of the chief magistrate of Ripon, replaced by *mayor* in 1604. He was the head of the body of *wakemen* whose duty was to blow a cow's horn every night at nine o'clock. If between that time and sunrise any burglary took place, it was made good at the public charge. *Walkman* is a variant of this; cf. 'Angels ben called walkmen and wardeyns for they warne men of perylles that may fall' (1398 NED).

Many of the names specify the article made, the material used, or the commodity sold: *Barleyman, Cheeseman, Clayman* 'one who prepares clay for use in brick-making', equated in ME with *Dauber*; *Cowlman* 'a maker of cowls' for monks; *Elliman, Ellerman, Elman, Ulman* (OE *æle*, OFr *uille* 'oil'); *Ferriman, Flaxman, Flexman, Glassman, Grassman*, earlier *Graysman, Gresman* (OFr *graisse, gresse* 'grease'); *Harringman* 'seller of herrings', *Leapman* (OE *lēap* 'basket'), *Maltman, Millman* (Roger *le meleman* 1275 SRWo, a dealer in meal), *Pyman* 'a maker or seller of pies' (cf. Peter *Piebakere* 1320 LLB E, Adam *le Piemaker* 1332 SRLo); *Pearlman* (cf. Simon *le Perler* 1291 LLB A, from OFr *perle* 'pearl', a seller of pearls or, perhaps, a maker of glass pearls or paternosters); *Pearman, Cherryman*, a grower or seller of pears or cherries; *Pikeman*, either 'a pikeman' or 'a fishmonger'; three Londoners named *Pikeman* in 1292 were certainly 'sellers of pike' or 'fishmongers'; *Saltman* (John *Saltman* 1327 SRSf, a dealer in salt).

Sedgman, which might refer to a cutter of sedge, appears to be equivalent to *seggethakker*; this we should take to be a man who roofed buildings with sedge but it had a wider application, synonymous with *Dauber*; in 1428 a *seggeman* named Brown was paid 7*s.* for thatching walls at King's Hall, Cambridge. *Schoolman* (Philip *Scoleman* 1309 SRBeds) is to be associated with the medieval *schoolman* 'a subtle, sophistical reasoner', a follower of the scholastic theologian John Duns Scotus who had died in 1308, whose surname survives as *Dunce* or *Duns*. This cannot be the modern *dunce* which is not recorded before 1527; like Hugh *de Duns* (c1150), his family probably came originally from Duns in Berwickshire.

Whilst the interpretation of many of these surnames is obvious, others preserve ME terms now rare or obsolete. Of the first class, we may note *Shearman, Sharman, Sherman* 'a shearer of woollen cloth', *Shipman, Smythyman, Smitherman* 'worker at the smithy', *Spearman, Stoneman, Stringman*, equivalent to *Stringer*, 'a maker of strings for bows', *Taberman*, like *Taberer, Tabborah* and *Tabor*, 'a drummer', *Tolman* 'a collector of tolls', *Tubman* 'a maker of tubs', a cooper,

Wainman, Wenman, Whenman 'wagoner', *Woodman, Wolman* 'dealer in wool' and *Yeatman, Yetman* 'gate-keeper'. *Slayman* (Henry *Slayman* 1279 RH, C) preserves ME *sleye* 'a weaver's reed or shuttle'; *Spellman* 'a professional story-teller', like *Speller*, is from OE *spell* 'discourse, homily, story', and is sometimes confused with *Spillman* (OE **spilemann* 'jester, juggler'), used also as a personal-name. *Tillman* and *Tileman* have been confused and may derive from either OE **tilmann* 'husbandman, farmer' or *tile-man* 'maker of tiles'. *Trussman* means 'baggage-man, porter' (OFr *trousse* 'bundle, package', which survives as *Truss*).

    Kissman and *Cushman* are not well evidenced: Simon *Cusheman* 1514 LP (K). They are two of several rare surnames of which *Kisser* and *Kissa* are most frequently recorded: William *Kisere* 1224–46 Bart, Richard *le Kisser(e)* 1288 LLB A, 1300 LoCt, Hugh *le Kysser* 1292 SRLo, *le Cussere* 1294 LLB A, *le Kissere, le Kischere* 1307 Husting, Benjamin, Edward *Kishere* 1738, 1750 Bardsley. The simple *Kiss, Cuss, Cusse* and *Cush* occur as Thomas, William *Kisse* 1327 SRSf, William *Kysse* 1328 FFSf, Lawrence *Kyshe* 1573 Bardsley. This was explained by Riley as 'a maker of "cushes" or armour for the thighs'. But A. H. Thomas suggested that the kissers were leather-dressers or dealers. In support of this, Ekwall notes that John Tilli in 1292 was alternatively described as 'kisser' and 'cordwainer' and that Edmund Haringeie, leather-merchant (1386), was a brother of Ralph atte Brom, *kissere* (1349). The names would appear to derive from OFr *cuisse* 'thigh' and Riley's explanation is supported by Godefroy's OFr *cuissel, quissel* 'partie de l'armure qui protège les cuisses' and by Cotgrave's OFr *cuissaux* 'cuisses, armour for the thighs'. It may be that this was protective armour of leather and that *Kissman, Cushman* and *Kisser* denoted makers of this, whilst *Kiss, Cuss* and *Cush* are metonymics from *cuisse*, with the same meaning.

    In the country, compounds of *-man* were in common use as names for the men in charge of animals and the meaning is generally obvious: *Bestman* 'beasts', *Bullman, Cappleman* (ME *capel, capul* 'nag'; also 'dweller near or worker at the chapel'); *Coltman; Foreman, Forman, Fourman* (OE *fōr* 'pig'; 'swineherd'); *Goatman, Henchman, Hensman, Hinckesman* (OE *hengest* 'stallion'); *Herdman, Heardman, Hurdman; Kidman, Oxman; Palfreyman, Palfreeman, Palfreman, Palferman, Palframan, Palphreyman, Polfreman, Parfrement* (palfrey); *Runcieman, Runciman, Runchman* (rounceys); *Steadman, Stedman, Steedman, Stedmond* (OE *stēda* 'stud-horse, stallion'; also 'farmworker', from OE *stede*); *Tupman* (ME *tup* 'ram'). Farmyard birds are represented by *Gooseman* and *Henman* and the bee-keeper by *Beeman*.

In other instances, it is the place of work which is specified and these can be regarded either as occupation-names or as names of servants: *Bowerman*, *Grangeman* (John *Greyngeman* 1381 PTY), *Hallman*, *Houseman*, *Kitchingman*, *Kitcheman*, *Kitchman* (kitchen), *Parkman*, *Templeman* 'worker at the Temple' or 'servant of the Templars'.

Surnames from place of residence

Names like *Heathman*, *Hedgeman* and *Moorman* are clearly toponymics, indicating the place at or near which the man lived. They run parallel with names in *atte* and *-er*, but are less common and more widely distributed, though their chief home is in Sussex, Kent and Essex. All three types frequently survive: *Crouch*, *Croucher*, *Crouchman* 'dweller by the cross'; *Hatch*, *Hatcher*, *Hatchman* 'gate'; *Wald*, *Walder*, *Waldman* 'forest-dweller'. That there was no difference in meaning is proved by the variation of form in the name of the same man. John *atte Vanne* (1330 ColchCt) is identical with John *Vanneman* (1336 ib.) and was probably of the same family as John *Vanner* or *Fanner* (1373, 1377 ib.), 'dweller in the marsh', now *Fann*, *Vann*, *Fanner*, *Vanner* or *Vannah*. John *atte Cleve* (1361 ColchCt) is called John *Clever* in 1365, 'dweller on the cliff', now *Cleeve*, *Cleever*. In the Sussex Subsidy Rolls, in particular, the forms are interchangeable. John *atte Gore* is assessed in North Stoke in 1296, Stephen *Gorman* in 1327, and William and John *Gorman* in 1332, 'dweller by the triangular piece of land' (*Gore*, *Gorman*). Hugo *atte Broke* is assessed in all three years in Coombes, in 1327 and 1332 as Hugo *le Broker*.

The earliest examples noted are *Hacheman* 1196, *Dunman* 1199, *Punter* 1214, *Crucher* 1220 and *Marshman* 1233 (*Marshman*, *Mashman*). Examples of both types are most common in the fourteenth century, especially in the Subsidy Rolls, an indication that these were country names, found chiefly among the smaller farmers and agricultural workers. Toponymics in *-er* are particularly common in Sussex and Kent and are found also in the neighbouring counties of Surrey and Hampshire and sporadically elsewhere. Where they survive, modern forms in *-er* or *atte* are added. The most common names are:

Beechman, Beech, Beecher 'beech-tree'; *Brookman, Brook, Brooker, Brucker; Crossman, Cross; Delleman, Dell, Deller; Downman, Dunman, Down, Downer; Denman, Dean, Deaner; Flashman, Flash, Flasher* (ME *flasshe* 'pool or marshy spot'); *Flatman, Flatt* (ON *flatr* 'level ground'); *Furseman, Forsman, Furse, Furzer; Heaseman, Hayesman, Easman, Hayes, Hease, Heyes* (OE *hǽs* 'brushwood'); *Hedgman, Hedge, Hedger; Knapman, Knapp, Knapper* (OE *cnæpp* 'hillock'); *Knowlman, Knoll, Knowler, Knowlder* (OE *cnoll* 'top of the hill'); *Lakeman, Lake, Laker* (OE *lacu* 'stream'); *Marman* ('mere'); *Pitman, Pettman, Putman, Pitt, Pett, Putt, Pitter, Putter* (OE *pytt* 'hollow'); *Rothman* ('clearing'); *Rushman, Rush, Rusher, Risher* ('rushes'); *Sloman, Slowman, Sluman, Slough, Slowe* (OE *slōh* 'slough, miry place').

Downman may also be a late corruption of *Downham*: Robert *Downnam* or *Doneman* or *Downeman* 1579 Oxon. Similarly, *Debenham* (Sf) or *Debnam* has become *Deadman* or *Dedman* (Francis *Debnam* or *Deadman* 1684 HTSf), *Hadenham* (Bk) is found as *Hadman* (John *Hadenham, Hadman* 1524 SRSf) and *Tudman* is a colloquial pronunciation of *Tuddenham*, Nf, Sf (Thomas *Tudman*, William *Tudman* (1524 SRSf). *Swetman* is sometimes for Swettenham (Ch), Edmund and Jone *Swetnam, Swetman* 1649, 1652 StourtonPR (W), and *Putman* for *Putnam* from Puttenham (Herts, Sr), Edward *Putman* or *Putnam* 1621 Oxon. A similar development accounts for *Wusteman, Woosman* and *Worsman* from the Lancashire *Wolstenholme*. *Twyman* is said to be a late development of *Twynham* or *Twynam*, from Twineham (Ha, Sx), whilst Weekley derives *Tottman* from Tottenham (Mx). For this we have an early example in Robert *Toteman* 1202 P (Ess), which is clearly from OE *tōt-mann* 'look-out man, watchman'. It is not safe to assume this development of *-nham* to *-man*. Only unequivocal examples can prove it. *Godliman* preserves the old local pronunciation of Godalming (Sr). *Stalman* is from Stalmine (La).

In a few surviving surnames we find *-man* added to a place-name: *Chesterman, Honickman*, from Honeywick (Sx), found as a surname as *Hunwick, Hunnex, Honex* and *Honick*, and *Penkethman, Penkeyman*, from Penketh (La). The obvious meaning of these names, as Weekley suggests, is 'the man from Chester, or from Honeywick or from Penketh'. Fransson, who gives seven other examples, takes a similar view. It is true that *-er* is added to a place-name. We still have *Borlindor* 'man from Barline' in Peasmarsh (Sx), *Bylander*, from

Byland (NRY), *Crassweller*, *Cressweller*, 'man from Cresswell',
Ramseyer from Ramsey, *Rippiner* from Ripon (John *Rypponer* 1575
FrY), *Rylander*, *Wheeliker* from Wheelock (Ch) and *Risbridger* and
Rusbridger which in one instance undoubtedly means 'the man from
Ridgebridge' in Surrey, whilst in Sussex it was probably from Rice
Bridge in Bolney.[1] The obsolete *Rumbridger* (John, Clement *Rum-
bryger* 1525 SRSx) is found in the same parish where in 1327 lived
John *de Rumbrugg*' (1327 SRSx). It is an interesting name, 'dweller
at Rumbridge', a lost place in Wittering, now beneath the sea, last
mentioned in 1398, which is to be identified with the *þri beorgas* 'the
three barrows' of an Anglo-Saxon charter. In ME this would become
at thrum bergen, which by a common misdivision of words and a
confusion of *berg* and *bregge* became *at the rumbrugge*. The place
was then called *Rumbridge* and a man who lived there, *Rumbridger*.
Nicholas *Kolhoker* (1296 SRSx) must have lived by Colhook Common near Petworth, whilst the Shropshire *Breadner* may similarly
derive from Bredon in Worcestershire, in which county there was
living in 1275 a man named William *le Tybtoner* (1275 SRWo), 'the
man from Tipton' in Staffordshire (*Tibintone* DB). *Crumpler*, too,
probably belongs here and may well mean 'the man from Cromwell'
(Nt). The place-name, pronounced *Crummell*, is found as *Crumbwell*
and *Crumwell*. *Crumbweller* could well become *Crumbler*, *Crumpler*,
whilst *Crumweller* could come to be pronounced *Crumler* and later
Crumpler.

In spite of these parallels, the surnames in which *-man* has been
added to a place-name have a different origin. They occur chiefly in
Yorkshire and Cumberland, where toponymics in *-er* are very rarely
found. In the earliest documents in which these names occur, we
frequently find pairs of names such as Richard *de Halton* and Richard
Haltounman, Adam *de Multon* and John *Multonman*, John *de Scaffoll*
(probably from Scawfell) and Adam *Scaffolman*, Thomas *de Scoreby*
and Adam *Scorebyman*. Most of the place-names can be identified
and it is in these areas where we find numerous names like John
Talbotman (1327 SRY) and John *Alaynman*. In all, *-man* must here
mean servant, 'servant of a man surnamed Penketh or Halton or
Scoreby', especially as we find *-son* similarly added to a surname:
Thomas *de Mosergh*, Hugh *Moserghson* (1332 SRCu), John *Payg*,
John *Paygson* (1379 PTY). George *Bredyman* (1561 Pat, Ha) probably owed his surname to an ancestor who had been servant of a

[1] *Rushbridge* and *Ruzbridge* also survive.

man from Long Bredy (Do). Lost examples include: Adam *Crassedalman* (1332 SRCu) from Crossdale (Cu), Peter *Crayman* (1369 LLB G) from Cray (K); John *Caldwellman*, Richard *Rowleyman* (1381 PTY), William *Leytoneman* (1386 AD i, W), Roger *Tankerlayman* (1387 FrY), John *Barnestoneman* (1439 FrY).

Nicknames

Oldman, Newman, Nyman and *Youngman* are clearly nicknames for the old, the new and the young servant. Physical characteristics gave rise to names such as *Bradman* 'broad', *Fairman, Langman* and *Longman* 'tall', and mental or moral qualities to *Hardiman* 'bold', *Holyman, Merriman, Merriment, Muddeman, Muddiman* 'brave, courageous', *Prettyman* 'cunning' or, perhaps 'servant of *Pretty*', *Proudman, Skillman* 'trustworthy', *Snellman* (John *Snelman* 14th AD i, Ess) 'active, bold', *Starkman* 'firm, unyielding', *Stolerman* 'sturdy, courageous', *Trueman, Truman, Trewman, Troman, Trowman* 'faithful, trusty' and *Wildman*. *Gentleman* means 'a man of gentle birth', whilst *Sleeman, Sliman, Slyman* may denote either 'a cunning, sagacious man', 'a dweller by the grassy slope' or 'a maker of slays'.

COMPOUNDS OF -*maugh*

Maw, Mawe and *Mowe*, though they have more than one origin,[1] may also be identical with *Maufe* and *Muff*: William *Mawe* 1275 RH (Nf), William *Mogge, Mugh* Ed I NottBR, Robert *Mouth, le Mogh* 1336–7 ib., William *Magh'* 1381 PTY, from ME *maugh*, used vaguely of a relative by marriage, in the north of a brother-in-law; cf. 'Mow, husbondys syster, or wyfys systyr or systyr in law' (Prompt-Parv). As the compounds are common in the north, the source may be ON *mágr* 'brother-, father- or son-in-law, OE *māga* 'relative, son', OE *māge* 'female relative' or OE *magu* 'child, son, servant'. The common interpretation is 'brother-in-law', but as there has been considerable confusion between the four forms in ME, 'relative of, son, descendant of' is as near as one can get. The first element is usually a personal-name, often a pet-form, but sometimes a surname. These compounds were not uncommon in Yorkshire, Lancashire and Cumberland, and are found occasionally as far south as Essex. The

[1] OE *Mawa*, a nickname from the sea-mew (OE *mǣw*), or 'dweller by the meadow' (OE *mawe*).

normal development of -*maugh* would be to -*maw*, -*mow* or -*mauf*. The final *f* interchanged with *th*, which at times became *t*, and we have a variety of more or less phonetic spellings, including -*moor* and -*more* for -*maw*.

The most common and best evidenced of these surnames is that which survives in the forms *Watmough*, *Watmore*, *Watmuff*, *Whatmaugh*, *Whatmoor*, *Whatmore* and *Whatmuff*, 'the relative of *Wat*', a pet-form of *Walter*. The earliest example is Robert *Waltersmaghe* (1305), the ultimate original of the modern *Wadsmouth* and *Wasmuth*, with which we may compare Hugo *Watmouth* (1599). Other surviving examples are *Dymott* (Adam *Dyemoghe* 1332 SRLa), from a pet-form of *Dionysia*, *Hickmott*, *Hickmet*, *Hickmore*, *Hickmer* and *Hitchmough*, from *Hick* and *Hitch* respectively, both pet-forms of *Richard*, and *Mattimoe*, William *Matheumogh* 1327 SRDb, Ann *Mathemore* 1619 GreenwichPR, from *Matthew*. *Willmott* is usually a diminutive of *Willelm* (cf. Fr *Guillemot*), but the modern *Willmouth*, *Wilmoth* suggest that this might also be from -*magh*, perhaps actually from (John) *Wilkemoghe* 1332 SRLa.

Most of the compounds are based on an uninflected genitive. Where the genitive in -*es* is employed, this combines with -*mouth* and assumes the form of -*smith*: *Goodesmith*, John *Godesmagh* 1351 FrY, Margaret *Godsmyth* 1525 SRSx, 'relative of (OE) *Gode*'; *Hudsmith*, Thomas *Huddemogh* 1332 SRLa, William *Hudmagh* 1379 PTY, Thomas *Huddesmawth* 1464 FeuDu, Cuthbert *Hodgemaght*, *Hodgemaughthe* 1545–6 NorwW (Nf), Ralph *Hudsmyth* 1582 PrGR (La), 'relative of *Hudd*' a pet-form of *Hugh* or of *Richard*; *Taylorsmith*, John *Tailliourmoghe* 1379 PTY, 'the tailor's relative'.

Examples of which no modern trace has been found include: Galfridus *Cokesmahc* 1183 Boldon, Richard *Pittesmug*, *Putesmug(e)* 1240 *ERO* (Ess), Thomas *Putesmoge* 1270 ib., William *le Barnemawe* 1276 RH (Y), William *Julianemough* 1316 Wak (Y), John *Gibbemogh* 1324 LaCt, William *Penymawe* 1327 SRSa, Adam *Duncanmaugh*, Thomas *Nicholmagh*, William *Raynaldmagh* 1332 SRCu, William *Robertmoghe*, Henry *le Portermogh*' 1332 SRLa, John *Elysmagh*, Richard *Gepmouth* 1379 PTY, Richard *Letmore* 1662 PrGR (La) and, possibly, John *Buckmote* and Wyllyam *Buckmott* 1525 SRSx.

COMPOUNDS OF -*smith*

The smith was a worker in metal and many of the numerous compounds of -*smith* are descriptive either of the metal used or of the article made. *Coppersmith, Goldsmith* and *Silversmith* are self-explanatory. *Leasmith, Leesmith* and *Leysmith,* John, William *Leysmith* 1319 *SR* (Ess), are from ONFr *aley, alay* 'a mixture of metals', ME *lay* 'a kind of pewter'. *Leadsmith,* Jacob *le Ledsmyth* 1329 MESO (Nf), does not seem to have survived. *Blacksmith,* the existence of which was vouched for by Lower, *Brownsmith, Greensmith* and *Whitesmith* denote workers in iron, copper and brass, and tin, from the colour of the metals used. *Greysmith* is probably 'a worker in lead', though it might possibly mean 'the grey, the old smith' on the analogy of such names as Agnes *Greyadam* 1297 MinAcctCo. Randolph *Redesmyth* 1396 NottBR was a worker in red metal, a goldsmith.

Arsmith, Ralph *le Orsmyth* 1292 *Ass* (La), means 'coppersmith', from OE *ārsmiŏ. Harrowsmith* and *Harrismith* are probably corruptions of *Arrowsmith,* a maker of arrow-heads which, it was ordered in 1401, 'shall be well boiled or braised, and hardened at the points with steel'. *Naysmith, Naismith, Naesmith, Nasmyth* and *Neasmith* denote a cutler, a maker of knives (Roger *Knifsmith* 1246–89 Bart), whilst *Shoesmith* or *Shoosmith* was 'a shoeing-smith', a maker of iron horse-shoes. *Locksmith* and *Spearsmith* are self-explanatory. *Wildsmith,* which Weekley explains as 'the smith in the wild, rather a Forest Lovers sort of figure' has a much more prosaic explanation. It is found also as *Wilesmith, Weldsmith* and *Whilesmith* and occurs in Essex in 1319 and 1327 as *(le) Welsmyth* which is from OE **hwēolsmiŏ* 'wheel-smith', a maker of wheels, especially the iron parts, whilst the *Wheelwright* was concerned with the parts made of wood.

Among lost names of this type, we may note: *Ankersmyth* 'anchor', *Bladsmyth* 'blades of knifes or swords', *Bokelsmyth* 'buckles', *Boltsmith* 'bolts or arrows', *Comsyth* 'combs' (Alicia *Comsmyth* 1590 RothwellPR), *Hildsmith* 'sword-hilts' (William *Hyldsmyth* 1275 RH, C) and *Balismith,* noted only in north Worcestershire, with a characteristic Anglian form, probably 'a smith who used a pair of bellows'.

For a number of these compounds of *-smith* we have, at present, no early forms and can only speculate as to their meaning. Weekley explains *Shawsmith* and *Brooksmith* as 'the smith who lived near the wood or the brook'. The former may be a corruption of *Shearsmith* and the latter of Broxmead (Sx). This was *Broksmegl* in 1296 and gave rise to the surnames of William *de Broksmegl* (1296 SRSx) and Ralph *de Broxmele* (1332 SRSx). The form of the surname would normally develop like the place-name which had become *Brocksmede* by 1556 and *Brooksmead* by 1689 which, as a surname, might well be corrupted to *Brooksmith*. In *Fordsmith, Muirsmith, Northsmith, Woodsmith, Caldersmith* and *Crowlesmith*, the first element has every appearance of a place-name but all occur as well-established surnames. Is the meaning 'the smith who lived by the ford, to the north, at Crowle', etc., or have we here undocumented examples of compounds of *-magh* such as *Goodesmith* and *Hudsmith*? In some instances, the first element is undoubtedly a personal-name or a surname. Is *Joysmith* to be interpreted 'Joy the smith' (*Joy* occurs as a man's name) or 'the smith who worked for Joy'? The former appears to be supported by *Clarksmith*, the latter by William *Joyneve* (1395 AssL), 'nephew of *Joy*', and John *Joymeyde* (1275 RH, K) and Geoffrey *Joyemaiden* (1279 RH, C), 'Joy's maidservant', where the surnames must already have been hereditary, deriving from the mother's name. Similar problems arise with *Daysmith, Drakesmith, Marksmith, Martinsmith,*[1] *Owensmith, Okeysmith, Orrinsmith*[2] and *Whitlamsmith*. In all, if the development to *-smith* is late, the source may be *-maugh*. For (John) *Watersmyth* (1333), Fransson suggests 'a smith who uses a hammer driven by water', which appears to be somewhat far-fetched. It might be 'smith of *Walter*' or, possibly, 'Walter the smith'.

COMPOUNDS OF *-wright*

The *Wright* was a carpenter or joiner, a worker in wood, though other materials are sometimes specified. In Kent the surname took the form of *Wraight*, whilst the common ME *writh* found in Norfolk appears today as *Wraith* and *Wreath*. Some names in *-wright* go back to OE personal-names in *-rīc* which in ME underwent various irregular developments, occurring as *-rich, -richt, -riht* and *-right*, which is often confused with *-wright*: *rick*, too, is a common development. *Oughtright* (OE *Ūhtrīc) has been influenced by the spelling of *outright*. OE personal-names have given modern *Allright, Allwright, Oldwright* (Æðelrīc), *Goodrich, Goodwright* (Godrīc), *Search, Searight, Seawright* (Sǣrīc), *Whitteridge, Whitewright* (Wihtrīc), and *Woolrich, Woolwright* (Wulfrīc). *Cuffwright* is probably from OE *Cūðrīc*. OE *Bealdrīc*, which survives as *Baldridge*, appears at Greenwich in 1633 as *Boldright* and survives occasionally as *Boldwright*,

---

[1] This might well be 'Martin's maugh'.

[2] This may contain the surname *Orren, Orrin*, from a woman's name *Oreyna* (1317 AssK).

whilst the curious *Horsewright*, noted in Suffolk (John *Horsewright*, Robert *Horsewreath* 1524 SRSf), is probably from OE *Ōsrīc*. The surname is not well evidenced but may be the modern *Ostridge*, *Ostrick*, though this is certainly sometimes for *ostricer* 'a keeper of goshawks, hawker, falconer'. For the Suffolk *Horsewright*, we may compare the modern *Orsborn* for *Osborn* and *Horsegood* for *Osgood* and the place-name Horse Godly, earlier *Osgodleye* (PN WRY iii, 58).

This confusion of *-rich*, *-ridge* and *-rick* with *-wright* also affected compounds of *-wriht*, some of which developed irregularly: *Bowrick* (Robert *Bowwright* 1332 SRCu), *Deathridge*, *Detheridge* (John *le Dethewright'*, *le Dedewrighte* 1299, 1327) 'a maker of tinder' (OE *dȳð*). *Cartwright*, *Kortwright* is found also as *Cartrick*, *Cartridge* and probably *Cardrick*. *Cartridge* is rare. Guppy gives it as peculiar to Worcestershire, where it may be the descendant of (John) *le Cartwereste* (1275 SRWo). In Brighton it may represent the ME *Karkeridge* which derives from a lost swine-pasture of Little Chart in Cranbrook (K),[1] first mentioned as *cadaca hrygc* in an original Anglo-Saxon charter of 843 (BCS 442). *Wrixon* is identical with *Wrightson* 'the wright's son'.

Most of the surviving compounds of *-wright* denote the article made and are self-explanatory: *Arkwright*, *Artrick*, *Hartwright*, *Hattrick*; *Boatwright*, *Boatright*; *Ploughwright*, *Plowright*; *Shipwright*; *Sievwright*, *Sivewright*, *Seivwright*, *Severwright*; *Tellwright* 'tilemaker, brick-maker'; *Wainwright*, *Wainewright*, *Wainwrigt*, *Wenwright*, *Winwright* 'wagon-maker'; *Wheelwright*. *Limrick*, Hugo *le Limwryte* 1279 RH (Bk), denotes a maker of lime, a limeburner. *Chalkwright* has disappeared. *Cheesewright*, *Cheesright*, *Cheswright* and *Chesswright* 'a maker of cheese', became *Cherrett*, *Cherritt* in Suffolk: Nicholas and Jane *Cheswright*, *Cherritt* 1655, 1660 DenhamPR.

Lost compounds include: *Basketwricte* 1229 Pat (L), *Bordwreghte* 1332 SRSx (OE *bord* 'board, table'), *brandwirchte* 1115 Winton (OE *brand* 'sword'), *le Briggwricht* 1230 P (Lo), (Hugh) *le dublerwrith* 14th YDeeds I, a maker of wooden dishes (OFr *doublier* 'dish', surviving as *Doubler*), (John) *Fanwryghte*, *Vanwrighte* 1379 AssEss (OE *fann* 'a winnowing basket'), *le Glasewrith'* 1301 SRY 'glass', (Richard) *le Hayrewritte*, *le Heyrere* 1284, 1292 MESO (OE *hǣrewyrhta* 'a maker of cloth made of hair'), *le Kystewrycthe* 1332 MESO (ME *kyste* 'chest, coffer'), *le Kittewritt'* 1275 Wak (ME *kitte* 'a wooden vessel made of hooped staves', tubs or milking-pails), *le Lattewrichte* 1268 MESO (OE *lætt* 'lath'), *Nawrith'*

1301 SRY (OE *nafu, nafa* 'nave' of a wheel), *le Orewrycthe* 1332 MESO (OE *ār* 'oar'), (Roger) *Sleywricte* 1230 Cur (Wo) 'a maker of slays', a weaver's reed or shuttle), *le Tunewrith* 1246 AssLa (OE *tunne* 'a tun'), *le Wycchewrichte* 1256 FF (So) (OE *hwicce* 'chest, coffer').

Two nicknames survive: *Micklewright* 'the big wright' and *Woodwright*, probably 'the mad wright'.

COMPOUNDS OF -*maker* AND -*monger*

Both these suffixes were common in ME surnames, but few survive today. The names of makers were more numerous than those of dealers, Fransson and Thuresson together giving 99 compounds of -*maker* and 40 of -*monger*, and their lists are by no means complete. One reason for the disappearance of so many of these names is, no doubt, their length, but many of them are synonymous with other forms of the same or a similar meaning and the tendency was to preserve the shorter names, many of them metonymic. We have, e.g. in ME, Richard *le flexmongere* 1294, Crispin *Flaxbeter* 1219, Robert *Flexhewer* 1367, Richard *le Flexere* 1316 and William *Flexman* 1279, but of these only *Flaxman* or *Flexman* and *Flexer* are still in use. Some of these surnames survive only as the name of the thing made or sold: *Matresmaker* (1381) has given place to *Matters* (Alexander *Matras* 1379 PTY) and *Pesemongere* (c1198) 'seller of peas' to *Pease*. Such survivals are noted below.

The only modern examples of compounds of -*maker* are: *Bowmaker* (John *le Boumaker* 1281 LeicBR), a rare name; *Dightmaker* for which no evidence has been found; *Millmaker*, Adam *le Melemakere* 1274 Wak (Y), 'maker of meal, miller'; *Reepmaker*, identical in meaning with *Ripper*, Adam *le Ripiere* 1279 RH (O), a maker of baskets, from OE (*h*)*rip* 'basket', which survives as *Reep*; *Shoemaker*; *Slaymaker, Slamaker* 'maker of slays or weaver's shuttles'; the last two are found also as *Shoemark* and *Slaymark*. With *Lackmaker* we may compare *Lackner*, both unevidenced, and the obsolete *Lakensnither*, Arnald *Lakensnyder* 1380 FrY. This Fransson takes to be of Dutch origin, MDu *lakensnidere* 'a seller of cloths and sheets'. But he admits the possibility of a derivation from OE *lacen* 'sheet' and *snīðan* 'to cut'. The fact that *Snider, Snyder* is found in Sussex, John *Snyther* 1332 SRSx, clearly a derivative of OE *snīðan* in the sense 'cutter, tailor', seems to confirm the English origin. *Lackner* is thus 'a maker of sheets' and *Lackman* (with *Lack*), with a similar meaning, is from ME *lake* 'fine linen'.

Among lost compounds of *-maker* are: Henry *Barkemaker* 1662 *HTEss* 'tanner' (*Barker*), Hugh *le Flekmaker* 1319 Cl (Y), 'maker of *flekes* or wattled hurdles' (cf. *Flekeman* 1292, *Flekewynder* 1327), Hugo le *Gerthmakere* 1289 NorwLt, ME *gerth* 'girdle', Hugo *Lastemaker* 1395 NottBR 'maker of lasts', wooden moulds of the foot used by shoemakers (*Last, Laster*, Thomas *le Lastur* 1275 AssSo), John *Mururmaker* 1378 AssWa 'mirror-maker', Thomas *Schetilmaker* 1361 ColchCt, 'maker of *shuttles*' for weavers (*Shitler, Shutler, Shettle, Shuttle*), John *le Tanckardmaker* 1298 LoCt (*Tankard*), Thomas *Tassemaker* 1349 FrNorw, from OFr *tasse* 'cup' (*Tass*), John *Weymaker* 1386 LLB H 'whey'.

It is impossible to deal adequately with the obsolete compounds given by Fransson and Thuresson. They include common terms like *Candelmaker* (cf. *Candler*), *Clokkemaker*, *Dofkotemaker*, *Harpemaker*, *Medemaker* 'mead', *Piemakere* and *Saucemaker*, along with rarer terms such as *Aketonmaker* (ME *aketon* 'stuffed jacket or jerkin'), *Brigendermaker* (ME *brigander* 'body-armour for foot-soldiers'), *Pundermaker* (ME *punder* 'auncel', a kind of balance) and *Tauelmaker* (OE *tæfel* 'die, game with dice or tables', a maker of dice or of boards on which games of chance were played).

Only two compounds of *-monger* appear to have survived, one fairly common, the other very rare. *Ironmonger, Iremonger* (OE *īren* 'iron') and *Icemonger, Isemonger* (OE *īsen* 'iron'), with *Strumanger* and *Struminger*, rare names, Thomas *le Strumonger* 1285 Oseney (O), Thomas *Straumonger* 1346 MKS, 'dealer in straw' (OE *strēaw* and *mangere*). Lower vouches for the survival a century ago of *Fellmonger* 'dealer in skins' and *Woodmonger*.

Obsolete examples include *Cornmonger* (frequent), Alexander *Shepmongere* 1227 AssBeds 'sheep', Margaret *le Buttermonggere* 1306 LoCt, and Emma *le Sclopmongere* 1317 Oseney (O), 'a seller of slops, outer garments, tunics, etc.' (*Sloper*). Others, noted by Fransson or Thuresson, are: *Alemonger, Bakmonger* 'seller of pastries, pies, etc.' OE (*ge*)*bæc* 'bakemeats', *Clothmongere, Horsemongere, Lusmanger* (ME *lus* 'pike'), *Madermanger, Waxmongere*.

THE SUFFIX *-cock*

Surnames in *-cock*, which are not uncommon and were once much more numerous, have given rise to much speculation. Ewen lists no less than 16 possible origins, but his discussion is marred by assumptions and his failure to realise that the confusion between *-coc* and *-cot* is often due to the difficulty of distinguishing between *c* and *t* in medieval script. It is inconceivable that *Hwituc* should become *Wytcok* 'to give it an intelligible sound to the modern ear'. The name survives as *Whittock* or *Whittuck*. The suffix in *Laycock* is -*ock*, not *cock*. This surname derives from Lacock (W) or Laycock (WRY), both diminutives of OE *lacu*, **lacuc*, 'little stream'. There is no evidence that *cokke* 'a short pipe or waterspout' was ever used for a conduit. Residence near this gave rise to the surnames *Conduit* or *Cunditt*. Richard *atte Cocke* of London (1323) may have lived at the sign of the Cock, but OE *cocc* meant 'haycock, heap', and *atte Cokke* must often mean 'dweller by the hillock'. Weekley's suggestion that David *atte Kokes* referred to a boat called a 'cog' or 'cock' is unlikely. The formation is parallel to that of *atte Persones* and denotes a man who lived at the house of one named *Kok* and was his servant, now *Cocks* or *Cox*. -*coc* may also be for 'cook'; Aluuinus *hamelecoc* (1086 ICC) is identical with Aluuinus *cocus bedellus* (1086 DB). He was nicknamed 'the maimed, mutilated, scarred' (OE **hamol*, **hamel*), was a cook (*cocus*) and a King's beadle.

Glasscock is a corruption of *Glascott*, Walter *de Glascote* 1332 SRSt, from *Glascote* (Wa). There is at present no evidence for *Glascocke* earlier than 1667. *Elicoc*, a diminutive of *Elie* (Elias or Ellis), survives not only as *Ellicock* and *Elcock* but also as *Ellacott*, *Ellicott* and *Hellcat*: *Elecocc* (son of Elias) 1246 AssLa, Ralph *Hellecoc* 1202 AssL, William *Elicot*, *Ellacot* 1573, 1606 Hartland PR(D), Anna *Hellicate* 1673 Bardsley (Du). The two suffixes are confused in other names, but which is original can usually be decided by attention to the medieval spellings. *Heathcock*, Walter *Hathecok* 1274 RH (Ess), is a nickname from the heathcock, the black grouse. *Heathcote*, Godfrey *de Hetcota* 1166 P (Db), denotes a man who came from Heathcote (Db, Wa). *Jeffcock*, Geoffrey *Geffecoke* 1327 SRWo, is a derivative of *Jeff*, a pet-form of Geoffrey. The modern surname is more common as *Jeffcoat*, *Jeffcote*, *Jephcott*, etc., but the correctness of this etymology is proved not only by the early -*coke* but also by the fact that the surname does not appear as *Jeffcott* before 1616.

Some of these compounds, like *Heathcock*, are nicknames from birds: *Peacock*, *Woodcock* and *Grewcock*, *Grocock*, *Growcock*, *Growcott*, *Groucutt*, a compound of ME *grew* 'crane' and *co(c)k*, similar to that of *Peacock*. All the medieval forms end in -*co(c)k*, Margeria *Groucok* 1275 SRWo. *Moorcock*, too, may be a nickname from the moorcock, but as we find a personal-name *Morecok* Chep-

210

man 1327 SRSo, the surname may also be a patronymic. *Hedgecock*, John *Hechecok* 1327 SRC, is probably identical with *Hitchcock*. John *Wedercok* 1196–1237 Colch (Ess) probably owed his nickname to some instability of character which reminded his acquaintances of the fluctuations of a weathercock.

In most of these surnames, -*cock* is compounded with a personal-name, usually of a man, occasionally of a woman, in its pet-form. The majority of these personal-names are of French origin, intro-duced into England after the Conquest: Roger *Hogecok* 1260 AssC (Roger), John *Halcok* 1270 ArchC v (Harry), William *Thomecok* 1327 *SR* (Ess), Richard *Belecok* 1275 SRWo (*Bele* or *Bell*, from Isabel). Of OE origin are: Simon *Budecok* 1275 RH (Nf), from OE *Budda*, surviving as *Budd*; Henry *Godecoke* 1327 SRC, from OE *Goda*; Amicus *Odecok* 1275 RH (Nf), from OE *Odda* or ON *Oddr* (now *Odd*). OE *Lufa* has given *Luuecok*, *Leucok* Schayfe 1246 AssLa, now *Lowcock*, *Locock*, *Luckcock*, *Luckcuck*, *Luckock*, *Lucock* and *Lewcock*.

In these compounds, -*cock* must have been regarded as a kind of affectionate or diminutive suffix for very many of them are recorded as personal-names and the fact that we occasionally find names like Geoffrey *Geffecoke* (1327 SRWo) and Hugo *Hullecok*, where *Hulle* is a pet-name for *Hugh*, suggests that -*cock*, like -*kin*, was sometimes used to distinguish the son from the father. The earliest examples of -*cock* are two from the twelfth century, both surnames: Robert *Fretecoc* 1176 P (Beds), 'eat, devour the cock' (ME *frete*) and John *Pilecoc* 1199 P (G1), 'pluck the cock' (ME *pile*). The first noted as a personal-name is *Peacock* in 1086, but this is probably an original nickname. Then comes *Alecoc* in 1204, a pet-form of some name in *Al-* (now *Alcock*). They begin to appear more often about 1250 and gradually increase in frequency until the middle of the fourteenth century. They were clearly names in common use among the lower classes, among those who were too poor for assessment in the early Subsidy Rolls where personal-names of this kind are rare but sur-names more frequent, though not common, presumably those of men who had begun to rise in the social scale.

The personal-names from which the following modern surnames derive have been found in independent use: *Adcock*, *Atcock*, *Hadcock* (*Adecok* 1246, from *Adam*), *Badcock*, *Battcock* (*Bat*, a pet-form of Bartholomew, or OE *Bada*), *Beacock* (*Be*, from *Beton* or *Beatrice*), *Hancock*, *Handcock* (*Hannecok* le Nunne (1297 Wak) is also called *Henricus* 1297 SRY),

Heacock, Hickox, (Hēa-coc, from OE *Hēah), Hitchcock, Hitchcox, Hiscock, Hiscox, Hitchcott, Hiscott, Hiscutt, Hiskett (Hitch,* from *Richard), Litcook (Litecock* 1246, from *Lit,* a short form of *Litman* or *Litwin),*[1] *Maycock, Meacock, Mycock (May,* from *Mayhew,* i.e. *Matthew), Silcock, Silcox (Sill,* from *Silvein* or *Silvester), Wilcock, Willcox (Will,* from *William).* Other compounds of *-cock* with pet-forms of common christian names must have existed, e.g. *Philcox* (Philip), *Sandercock* (Alexander), *Simcock* (Simon), *Tilcock* (Matilda).

The squeamishness which insists on spelling *Rowbottom* as *Robathan* and pronouncing it *Roebotham* and in pronouncing *Bottom* as *Bot-tom* and *Sidebottom* as *Siddybottarm,* also says *Coburn* for *Cockburn, Cofield* for *Cockfield, Coeshot* for *Cockshott, Glasscoe* for *Glasscock,* and *Sandercoe* for *Sandercock,* and has succeeded in concealing all connexion with *-cock* in *Alcoe, Badcoe, Bayco, Hedgecoe, Hitchcoe* and *Simco,* as in *Coeshall* for *Coxall* or *Coggeshall,* from Coggeshall (Ess).

This may give one clue to the etymology of *Jellicoe* which occurs in 1553 (Pat) in Derbyshire as John Dawson alias John *Jelicoke,* in the Chester Wills as James *Jelicoe* in 1648 and John *Jolycoe* in 1667, and in Thomas Rugg's *Diurnal* as 'one *Jellico*' a Quaker of Chester (1660). *Jolliffe* and *Jolly* are both from ME *jolif, joly* 'joyous, mirthsome, sprightly, spirited' which occurs in a number of nicknames, as Roger *Jolifboye* 1308 PNEss 326, Robert *Goleboye* 1317 AssK. The change of *o* to *e* is found in *Jessop* from *Josep* or *Joseph* in 1379 (John *Jesop*), but is not well evidenced before the sixteenth century. It is parallel to the colloquial *jest* for *just* and *jedge* for *judge* which is found in the variation between *Justice* and *Jestice,* and, surprisingly, between *Hodge* and *Hedge* (1610 LewishamPR). For *Jelley* our earliest forms are Thomas *Jely* 1472 Cl (Ess), Robert *Jely* 1524 SRSf and this is probably identical with *Jolley* as is *Jelliff* with *Jolliffe.* John *Ielyffe* (1569 MustersSr) is almost certainly identical with John *Ioolyf* (1574 ib.).[2] Hence *Jelliman* and *Jelleyman* are also probably late developments of *Jollyman,* Richard *Jolyman* 1379 PTY and *Jellicoe* may well derive from *Jolif-cock* 'the joyous, sprightly boy'.

No other nickname in *-cock* survives, but a few obsolete examples have been noted: William *Newecok*' 1317 AssK, William *Petykok* 1430 FeuDu, Robert *Wytcok* 1275 RH (W) and William *le Yongecok* 1324 EwenG (Wo). Here, as with Richard the *grangecok* 1313 EwenG

[1] Or, possibly, 'little cook'.
[2] But *Jelley* (and *Jellis*) may also be from *Giles;* cf. Gilly Gate in Pontefract, named from the church of St Giles (PN WRY ii, 76).

212

(Nth), the meaning is probably 'boy' or 'servant', for *cock* was used as a nickname for one who strutted like a cock and became a common term for a pert boy, being used of scullions, apprentices and servants.[1] The boy in *Gammer Gurton's Needle* is always so called:

'My Gammer is so out of course, and frantyke all at ones,
That *Cocke*, our boy, and I poor wench, have felt it in our bones.'

William le Keu *Williamesservaunt* Hod (1336 Pat) is also called William *Williamescok* Hood, whilst Richard *le Personescok* of Long Stanton (1312 Pat) was the servant of Peter, parson of the church of St Michael, Long Stanton. Occasional examples occur in which *-cock* is compounded with a surname: Robert *Bunchekok* 1327 SRSf, 'servant of a man named Bunch', the hunch-back; Simon *Payncok* 1327 SRC. The only modern survival seems to be *Johncock* 'John's servant' as in John *Jonescok* Herun (1302 Pat), 'John, servant of John Herun'.

<h2 style="text-align:center">THE SUFFIX -kin</h2>

Not all modern names in *-kin* originally contained this suffix. *Buskin* is a simplified pronunciation of *buck-skin*,[2] Roger *Buckeskyn* 1281 FFEss, Walter *Buskyn* 1281 Cl, used of a maker of breeches made from the skin of a buck or for a worker in buckskin or leather. Richard de Gravele called *Bokskyn* was an apprentice of Walter Polyt *fuyster* 'maker of saddle-trees' (1311 LLB D). *Donkin* is a variant of *Duncan* and *Gaskin* of *Gascoigne*, whilst *Paskin* (*Pasken* de Stafford, Ralph *Pasken* 13th StThomas) is from the OW personal-name *Paskent*, MW *Pascen*, from Lat *Pascentius*. *Dickin* and *Hickin* are from *Dicoun* and *Hicun* or *Hicin*, diminutives of pet-forms of *Richard*. Occasionally an original *-kin* appears in a disguised form in modern surnames, *Bulgin*, Walter *Bulekin* 1200 P (Sx), is a nickname 'little bull', whilst *Watking* is for *Watkin*, a late development found also in *Hopking*, *Hosking* and *Larking*. In others, *n* has been lost in *-kins*: *Hipkiss*, *Hodgkiss*, *Simkiss*, *Tomkiss*, *Watkeys*, *Watkiss*, *Jenckes*, *Jenks*.

The diminutive suffix *-kin*, of Teutonic origin, is found early in German and Dutch, but there is no trace of it in Old English. The Oxford Dictionary, relying on the literary evidence and Nicholson's

---

[1] Cf. *Cok* mon garcon, a groom of John de Langeford (1293–7 Wenlok).
[2] Also local, from Buskin (D).

Pedigree of Jack (which does not account for the facts),[1] notes that the suffix had only a limited use in English. 'It appears to occur first in some familiar forms of personal (chiefly male) names, which were either adoptions or imitations of diminutive forms current in Flanders and Holland, where such forms appear already in the tenth century.' The earliest examples cited are *Janekin, Malekin, Watekin* and *Wilekin* 'found as early as 1250, and evidently then in familiar use'.

In the light of the surname material, this needs some modification. *Walterkin* is found in Oxfordshire in 1200 and *Wilechin* in Northumberland in 1166 and must have been a well-established name as it occurs as a surname in Hampshire in 1180. Some half-dozen other personal-names of this type have been noted in the twelfth century, with others in the early years of the thirteenth. They increase in numbers after about 1250 and are most common in the second half of the fourteenth century, apparently going out of fashion about 1400. They were thus most common during the period when surnames were in process of formation and of the 100 surnames of this type noted more than 60 survive.

A Flemish origin can confidently be ascribed to some of these names. *Derekin* del Acre 1197 P (Nf) is mentioned in association with *alter Flandrensis* 'another Fleming', and the surname survives as *Derkin, Darkin* and *Darking*,[2] William *Derkyn* c1250 Gilb (L), Richard *Darking* 1525 SRSx. *Lambkin* and *Lampking* are diminutives of a pet-form of *Lambert*, a name found in Flanders; cf. *Lambekyn* Flandrensis 1178 P (Nb), *Lamkynus* de Braban (of Brabant) 1379 PTY. *Lambert* de Colon' (of Cologne) 1199 Cur (Ha) is alternatively named *Lambekinus*. With *Gilkin* we may compare *Gilkinus* de Braban 1296 FrY. *Godkin* appears to be purely continental in origin: *Godekin* de Kyureld, a merchant of Alemain (1275 RH), *Godkin* de Reulle of Estlond, an Easterling, 1338 Misc (L), William *Godkynsman* of the Rye 1327 Pat. *Sessekin* 1195 P (Ess) does not look English, whilst *Hardekin* (1175 P, Nf), the source of *Harkin* and *Harkiss*, John *Hardekyn* 1327 *SR* (Ess), is probably the same name as *Heardcyn*, a moneyer of Edward the Confessor, and probably a continental.

It is curious, however, that some of our earliest forms have the French *-quin*: *Wilechin*, son of a moneyer of Newcastle-upon-Tyne, 1166 P (Nb), Richard *Willechin* 1184 P (Ha), William *Potechin* 1166

---

[1] *v.* P. H. Reaney, *Dictionary of British Surnames*, p. 179, *s.n.* Jack.
[2] This might be from the local pronunciation of Dorking.

P (Nf). The latter is compounded with *Pot*, a pet-name for *Philpot*, a diminutive of *Philip*, a common name introduced into England from France. *William* also came from France and was for centuries one of the two most popular christian names in England. These names, *Wilkin* and *Potkin*, with, possibly others, may have been introduced into England from north-eastern France, where *Willeme* was the normal form of the French *Guillaume*. From Flanders the suffix *-kin* spread into France, where it survives in such names as *Gosquin*, *Hanequin* and *Willequin*.

It is noteworthy that the great majority of English surnames in *-kin* are compounded with pet-forms of common names of French or Biblical origin: *Adkin*, *Atkin*, from *Adekin* 1191 P (Nf), from *Adam*; *Alkin*, *Aukin*, (*Alkin* the Yonge 1296 AssCh), probably from *Alan* or *Alexander*; *Batkin*, a diminutive of *Bate* (Bartholomew), *Batekyn* 1274 RH (Ess); *Ruskin*, *Roskin*, a diminutive of OFr *Rosce*, OG *Rozzo*, *Rosekin* 1220 FFEss. Other common surnames of this type are *Dawkins* and *Daykin* (David), *Hodgkin* (Roger), *Hopkin* (Robert), *Jenkins* (John), *Makin*, *Meakin* (from *Mayhew*, Matthew), *Parkin*, *Perkins* (*Per*, Peter), *Silkin* (Silvein or Silvester), *Simkin* (Simon), *Tomkin*, *Tamkin*, *Tonkins* (Thomas) and *Malkin*, *Maulkin* (*Mald*, Matilda). *Benskin*, *Binskin* is not evidenced early: William *Benskyn* or *Benchekyn* 1508 CantW, Jamys *Bynskyn* 1525 SRSx. It is probably a diminutive of OG *Benzo*, occurring as *Bence* 1175 P(Y), *Benze* 1178 P (Nb), found already as a surname in 1066 DB, Osmund *Benz*, and surviving as *Bence*.

Occasionally *-kin* is compounded with a personal-name of English origin: *Dodkin* (OE Dodda), *Lovekin*, *Lufkin* (Lufa), *Luuekin* 1221 AssSa, *Hoskin*, from *Osekin* 1274 RH (Lo), a diminutive of *Os-*, a short form of such names as *Ōsgōd*, *Ōsbeorn*, etc., and the obsolete William *Budekin* 1279 RH (C), from OE *Budda* and Adam *Swetekynes* 1323 AssSt (OE *Swēta*). The only evidence found to support the general opinion that *Hawkin* is for *Halkin*, a diminutive of *Harry* is *Halkin* 1315 PN Db 102. *Havekin* (1248–1365) is the normal form, for *Havek-in*, a diminutive of OE *Hafoc*, and not a name in *-kin*.

It would appear, therefore, that *-kin* was adopted in English from Flemish and used freely as a diminutive suffix added to the pet-forms of those common names of French origin which were particularly used by the lower classes. It is noteworthy how often we find the same names compounded with *-cock*. In our documents they form a very small proportion of the whole, usually about one-half of 1 per cent.

Compounds which can be proved to be of purely Flemish origin are rare and are confined to names which were in common use. Most of the Flemings either went back home, taking their names with them, or, when they were not called simply *Fleming, Flanders, Brabant* or *Brabason*, were given English occupational-names or nicknames. The fourteenth-century Dutchmen of Colchester left no permanent influence on the surnames of the district.

Neither christian names nor surnames in *-kin* are common in the Subsidy Rolls. Nor are they frequent in the towns. From the abundant material used by Ekwall in his studies of London names for the period 1086–1350, only three christian names and three surnames of this type have been noted: *Hankin* de Arras 1292 SRLo (now *Hankin, Hanking*), *Bankyn* de Brounlexk 1319 SRLo, a merchant of Florence and *Notekyn* de Lincolne (ib.), whose name might be one origin of *Nutkins*; two of the surnames still survive, John *Oskyn* 1292 SRLo and John *Maikyn* 1319 SRLo (*Hoskin, Makin*); the third, John *Cotekyn* (ib.), may, like the modern *Coste* and *Costins*, be a hypocoristic of *Constantine*. Among the 2,700 names in the Norwich Deeds of 1285–1341 there are only four surnames of this type, including *Malkin* and *Lamekyn*, with the obsolete Robert *Thornekyn*[1] (1334) and Thomas *Ridekyn* (1336). In these documents, however, we have only the names of the upper classes, officials and owners of property. It was clearly not among these but among the artisans of the towns and the labourers of the countryside that names in *-kin* and *-cock* were popular. There is some evidence, however, that the diminutive meaning of these names was realised and that they were used at times as pet-names or to distinguish father from son. William de Ros is called also *Wilekin* 1200–1 Cur (K), and Symond Skynner, *Symkyn*, 1466 AD v (Lo), whilst we have seen that *Janekyn* was used to distinguish the younger John Hastang from his father of the same name.

Instances of the suffix added to common nouns in the fourteenth century are rare and this will account for the complete lack of nicknames, for later formations could have no influence on surnames. William *Boykin* 1255 FFEss, a surname found also in Cambridgeshire and Suffolk, may be a diminutive of *boy*, whilst the modern *Webkin* and the obsolete Richard *Revekyn* 1327 *SR* (Ess) look like 'little weaver' and 'little reeve', names of similar meaning to Thomas *Litelsmyth* 1327 SRSo, William *Lytelgrom* 1212–23 Bart. The only nickname to survive is *Bodkin*, a name which has been regarded as a

[1] Probably an error for *Thomekyn*.

diminutive of *Baldwin*, a derivation proved impossible not only by the early forms, *Baudechoun* or *Baudewin* (*le*) Chaucer 1292 SRLo, 1293 LLB A, always with *au*, never with *o*, and with a suffix which cannot be -*kin*, but also by the preservation of the *ch*: William *Bawchyn* 1551 NorwDep, George *Bachin* 1677 FrYar, modern *Balchin*. Another suggestion, equally impossible, is ME, OFr *baudekin*, medLat *baldakinus*, from *Baldacco*, the Italian form of Bagdad, 'a rich embroidered stuff originally made with warp of gold and thread and woof of silk'. The early forms of the surname are Robert, William *Bodekin* 1279 RH (O,C), Peter *Bodekyn* 1297 MinAcctCo, 1331 AssSt, and Nicholas *Boydekyn* 1327 SRSx, forms identical with those of *bodkin* 'a short pointed weapon, a dagger, poniard', on record from 1386 (NED). The surname must be occupational, a maker or seller of these weapons, or it might be a nickname for one notorious for its use.

Chapter Eleven

NICKNAMES

ENGLISH, unlike French, has no distinctive terms to distinguish between *sobriquets* and *surnoms*, a drawback which has its advantages. *Nickname*, from *eke-name* 'an additional name', is an elastic term which is used here for a name or description which is added to or substituted for the proper name of a person. It does not include pet-names or diminutives of personal-names and is applicable equally to those descriptions which refer only to a particular person and to those which have become family names. Most of our earliest examples were personal and died with the man: Edricus *Cecus* 'the blind' (1066 DB), the nickname of Edricus de Laxefelde, Robert *Nagod* 'no good', 'good for nothing' (Hy I ELPN), with numerous other examples in the following two or three centuries.

But already in 1086 in DB we find nicknames which had become family names, e.g. Robert *Gernon* or *Grenon* 'moustache', a facial adornment unusual among the Normans—all those on the Bayeux tapestry are clean-shaven. We cannot be certain whether Robert was the first of the name, but his descendants inherited it as a family name and held some of their possessions for nearly 300 years where it developed into *Garnon*, *Garnett*, *Garnish* and *Garland*,[1] all of which

[1] v. P. H. Reaney, 'Gernon, Garland and Garnish' (*Trans. Essex Arch. Soc.*, vol. XVII (1926)), pp. 172–8.

survive today[1] in addition to *Grennan* and, more commonly *Garnham*. Four Essex farms, Garnons in Wormingford and three named Garlands were actually held in 1086 by Robert Gernon. Wlfwin *Grant* or *Grand* (c1125) of London had a son William called *grandis* or *legrant* (c1150, 1160) who inherited his father's name and was probably father of Thomas *Grandus* (c1200). The nickname is OFr *grand*, *grant* 'great', 'tall' (now *Grand*, *Grant*, *Legrant*), but here evidently means 'the elder, senior' to distinguish him from Wulwinus *juvenis* 'the young, younger' (c1130),[2] thus illustrating the difficulties of interpretation.

DIFFICULTIES OF INTERPRETATION

Nicknames arise spontaneously from some fortuitous chance. Those which are particularly apt persist and the unfortunate recipient, no matter how strong his objection, has no option but to endure it. They are not given deliberately as names but suddenly blossom forth in jest, derision or anger, and the circumstances, if known, are soon forgotten. Julian Franklyn, for example, in the enlightening introduction to his valuable *Dictionary of Nicknames*,[3] tells us that during the Second World War he was known to all ranks as 'Felix', 'but no amount of careful (and guarded) inquiry could reveal when, why or by whom the nickname was bestowed . . . The reason why the nickname "Felix" remained unaccounted for was simply because the man who originated it did not himself realise he had done so.'[4] One of my schoolmasters, Arthur Watson, was 'Joe Plug' when I entered the school and 'Joe Plug' when I left, but no one knew why. Other schoolmasters of my acquaintance were 'Wally' and 'Mike' to generations of schoolboys, names accepted without question or explanation. They had certainly no connexion either with their christian name or their surname, for their initials were J. T. and A. H. P.

Occasionally it is possible to trace the origin of the form of the nickname, even though its original meaning is obscure. The chemistry master in my first school rejoiced in the name of 'Bublum Squeaks', a corruption of 'Bubble and Squeak' which had no culinary association. He was excitable, no disciplinarian, with a voice which rose

---

[1] But *Garnett*, *Garnish* and *Garland*, as surnames, have also other origins.
[2] ELPN, pp. 152–3.
[3] This deals only with modern nicknames, not with those which gave rise to family names.
[4] Ibid., p. xiv.

higher and higher to a shrill squeak as he vainly tried to make himself heard above the uproar in the laboratory. Another, 'Kip', was originally called 'Skipper'—why, nobody knew. This soon became 'Kipper', was shortened to 'Kip', and when, years later, his son entered the school, he immediately had to answer to 'Little Kip'. *Bong* owed his nickname to a peculiar pronunciation in his common cry, 'Don't *bong* the door!'

At times, the point of the nickname, in part, at least, is clear. My headmaster was known as 'Old Bogey', a name of affection in spite of its appearance. He was a strict disciplinarian, but invariably just, and when he did punish, the culprit knew he was getting no more than he deserved. The nickname applied to his appearance; he had a good head of shaggy grey hair with a face buried in a shaggy grey, untidy beard from behind which he gazed benevolently over his flock or glared at the individual as circumstances demanded. 'Tubby' is usually an accurate description, but 'Tiny' is often used of a hefty giant in the first eleven.

Nicknames often go by contraries, e.g. Moyses *Euelegrom* (c1214 *WAM* 5165) is identical with Moyses *Godegrom* (c1244 ib., 5247). From time to time, too, the novelist reveals his observation of life and throws light on the development of nicknames, e.g.

'The young priest, one of the three chaplains of Dean Peyramole, lived up to his name of Pomian or Appleman, for he had apple-round red cheeks and waggishly smiling eyes.'[1]

With this we may compare the surviving *Sweetapple*, the medieval Richard *Swetchicke* 1315 HPD (Ess), Nicholas *Swetemouth* 1327 SRY, William *Swetmylke* 1288 Ipm (Db) and the contrasting John *Sourhappell* 1381 PTY and Ralph *Surmylk* 1290 NorwLt.

As examples of euphemism, we may note:

'She was called Piguno, but what that nickname meant nobody knew. If it were meant to refer to the dove-like nature of this crone, it would be sheer euphemism, like that of the ancients when they called an especially treacherous body of water the "benevolent sea" in order not to anger it by a characterization of its real nature. Piguno was no dove; rather a crow, hardened by wind and weather, a many-wrinkled crone, a demon of curiosity, and a dangerous know-all. Her real name was Maria Samaran.'[2]

'He was known to the rest as Curly because of his premature baldness. His hairless head was an unlined dome rising incongruously from a brow already considerably wrinkled.'[3]

[1] Franz Werfel, *The Song of Bernadette*, c.3.
[2] Ibid., c. 6.
[3] E. Burgess, *Divided we fall*, p. 54.

Offensive nicknames may be really tokens of friendship or affection. 'Many nicknames that sound to the polite ear offensive, even cruel, are not so intended and the person who answers to them does not feel himself either insulted or hurt.'[1] This, too, must apply to many medieval nicknames but proof is never forthcoming.

Previous writers have given examples of modern nicknames used in place of or to supplement surnames, especially where the same surname was particularly common.[2] The following is new. It is from a novel, but the novelist obviously knew his characters and their idiosyncracies:

'Yet old Bacca Chops was not always talking gamecocks. He had much lore at his fingers' ends and taught me a great deal about other things too. One evening when I knew him better I commented on his own nickname, to his amusement [Jacob Tranter, or Bacca Chops, as everyone called him from his habit of chewing plug tobacco].[3]

'"We all have nicknames here," he said. "I'd tell you your brother's but like as not he'd lie in wait and wring my neck for it—so I shan't."

'I tried to persuade him to take the risk but he turned the question. "Nay, I daredn't, my lass," he said, "but let me tell you a tale about Black Country nicknames as a whole, and I don't suppose there's any county in the land that can match this one for its names . . . Well, there was a gentleman came to Wedgebury one day and got off the hossbuss and asked a street-corner lounger if he could direct him to the house of Mr Foster. "Ay, no doubt I can," said the man. "But thee mun tell me fust which Foster it is thee want'st. Is it Gentleman Foster, or Jonah Foster, or Billy Gunner Foster, or Old Shake Tupty Foster, or Joel Tenney Foster, or Ode Wag Foster, or Tom Jonder Foster, or Ode Mouldyhead Foster, or Ode Boggan Foster?" The stranger was mystified. "Well, what does he do for a living?" asked the Wedgebury man. "He's a screwmaker," answered the other. "Oh," said the lounger, "well thee want'st Ode Foxy Jack Foster. That's who thee want'st." And so he did, when it came to it! What do you think of that!

'I was bemused by the wealth of names and could think of nothing much to say to the schoolmaster for a while. Then I asked, "Why Mouldyhead Foster?"

'"Well, it seems that the man's hair was growing grey in patches," said Jacob Tranter. "You know, like mine!" And he lifted his brown Derby hat so that I might see. Then he fumbled in his jacket-pocket. "I've got something here to do with this," he said, taking out a leather pocket-book from which protruded an envelope, addressed and franked. "Look at this," he said. "This actually came through the post to an old friend of my father's

[1] Julian Franklyn, *Dictionary of Nicknames* (London, 1962), p. xvii.
[2] S. Baring-Gould, *Family Names and their Story* (London, 1910), p. 298; C. L. Ewen, *A History of Surnames of the British Isles* (London, 1931), p. 330.
[3] Henry Treece, *The Rebels* (London, 1953), p. 167.

many years ago. That'll show you what nicknames we had in this district, years gone by."

'I took the yellowing envelope and read the faint black superscription. It ran:

> To Mr Wilkes, Darlaston, near Wednesbury.
> Not My Lord Wilkes,
> Not Gentleman John Wilkes,
> Not Soft Water Jack Wilkes,
> Nor They Wilkes,
> Nor Brick End Wilkes,
> Nor Whackey Wilkes,
> Nor Dowker Wilkes,
> Nor Dragon Wilkes,
> Nor Hockey Wilkes,
> Nor Bullet Wilkes,
> Nor Darkey Wilkes,
> Nor Fagler Wilkes,
> Nor Tizzie Wilkes,
> Nor Dunty Wilkes,
> Nor Gallimore Wilkes,
> But Bacca Box Wilkes!
> *That's the man!!'*[1]

In the few instances where the document gives an explanation of the nickname, this is not always what we should expect. Wlfricus *Niger* (Black) got his nickname because on one occasion he went unrecognised among his foes with his face smeared with charcoal (c1080 OEByn). The name of Lefwinus *Prat* (ib.) is similarly glossed (*id est*) *Astutus* 'because, when captured by the enemy, he often escaped by cunning'. Ordericus Vitalis gives the name of Edricus Streona (1006–16 ib.) as 'Edricus cognomento *Streone*, id est acquisitor', i.e. 'acquirer, miser', and notes that Ralph *Basset* was raised by Henry II from an ignoble stock and from the very dust, *de ignobili stirpe et de pulvere*. The usual meaning is 'of low stature', 'small', perhaps 'a dwarf'.

Nor must we forget that nicknames may have more than one meaning and may belong to two or more classes of surnames. *Milk* may be a nickname for one whose drink was milk, effeminate, spiritless, for one with milk-white hair or for a seller of milk. *Poor* and *Power* may both derive from either OFr *Pohier* 'a Picard' or OFr *povre*, *poure* 'poor'. Both terms appear in ME as *poer* and *poure*, and if the name is not well-evidenced certainty is impossible. But occasionally the evidence is clear; Richard *le Poier, le Pouer* 1297 MinAcctCo was

[1] Treece, op. cit., pp. 171–2.

clearly a Picard; Roger *Pauper, le Poer, le Povr'* 1211–12 Cur equally certainly was 'Poor'. Traditionally, William Malet, founder of Eye Priory, owed his surname to his warlike prowess in beating down his foes in battle *ut malleo* 'as if with a mallet', the iron mace of the Middle Ages. When William Malet was banished in 1109, his son Hugh took the name of *Fichet* which was retained by his son Hugh, although his eldest son reverted to *Malet*. This undoubtedly implies that Hugh regarded both surnames as nicknames with very similar meanings, both suited to a knight expert in the use of lance and mace. But some early forms of the name are *Malait*, a nickname, 'accursed', whilst the three tenants-in-chief of DB who are invariably called *Malet* probably brought with them a Norman patronymic, a diminutive of *Malo*, the popular form of the name of St Maclovius, a sixth-century Welsh monk who worked in Brittany, which survives in Saint-Malo and in the church of Saint-Maclou in Rouen. In England, the chief source of the name is probably *Mal-et*, a diminutive of *Mall* (Mary), on record from 1199.

EARLY COLLOQUIALISMS AND SLANG

Whilst sifting and sorting my very large collection of nicknames, I have frequently been impressed by their fundamental similarity to the essentials of slang, a subject much too vast for discussion here, and quite unnecessary, as the work has already been done by that master of the subject, Eric Partridge. Those who wish to get a sound idea of the background behind both slang and nicknames should read his two chapters on 'Slang Characteristics' and 'The Essence of Slang', with his 'Sketch towards the History of English Slang'. In the following brief quotation, we might very well substitute 'nicknames' for 'slang', remembering, of course, that the recorded history of slang begins roughly after surnames were established:

'We may note a very different characteristic of slang: that of the difficulty in assigning a correct etymology to so many of its units, for Slang, usually indirect, depends upon metaphor and allusion (often very far-fetched) and irresponsible mutilation. The metaphors and allusions are generally connected with some temporary phase, some ephemeral vogue, some unimportant incident; if the origin is not nailed down at the time, it is rarely recoverable.'[1]

[1] Eric Partridge, *Slang Today and Yesterday* (2nd edn, London, 1935), p. 31; *v.* also pp. 10–44.

The slang of the Roman legionaries of the late Empire laid the foundations for modern French. Examples are well known, the most common, perhaps, being *testa*, originally a brick, later a pot, then a slang term for the head, now the standard French *tête*. From this was formed a derogatory nickname *testard*, probably 'big head', which now survives as *Tester*. In English an analogous sense-development gave us the slang *nut* and *block*, whilst in Chaucer we find Arcite swearing 'by my pan', glossed by Baugh as 'skull', but more probably slang for 'head'. OE *panne* was 'a metal or earthenware dish or vessel', and the sense-development here is exactly parallel to that of *testa*. This may be one origin of the modern surnames *Pan* and *Pans*, recorded from 1176, though they may also be metonymic for *Panner* 'a maker or caster of pans'.

Penny-father, a slang term for a miser, first recorded by NED in 1549, has a much longer history. It was the nickname of Godwinus *penifeder* in Winchester in 1066 and survives as *Pennyfather*, *Pennefather*, *Pennyfeather*, *Penfare* and *Pannifer*. In the sixteenth century *Palliards* was a fashionable slang term for 'those whose fathers were beggars born'. It derives from OFr *paillart*, *paillard* 'a low or dissolute person', from OFr *paille* 'chaff, straw', plus the pejorative suffix *-ard*, 'one who sleeps on the straw' in barns and out-houses. It is first recorded by NED in 1484, but was a surname in 1103 (OEByn), Ælgares *Paiardes* (gen.), and, though rare, survives as *Paillard*.

Not only do nicknames, at times, carry back the history of a word for 300 or 400 years; from time to time they provide us with forms of importance for the etymology of the word. Lack of context may prevent us from discovering the real meaning, but the form itself may throw doubt on etymologies previously proposed. If the nickname of John *Pifle* 1344 FFSf means what it appears to mean, the suggestion that *piffle* is a blend of *piddling* and *trifling* would appear to need reconsideration. Boselinus *Curmegen* was living in the reign of Henry I (Rams). His surname looks suspiciously like *curmudgeon* 'an avaricious, churlish fellow, miser, niggard' (1577 NED). Skeat derived it from *corne-mudgin* 'a corn-dealer' which the Oxford Dictionary dismisses as a nonce-word and gives the derivation as unknown. Partridge in *Origins* also states the origin is obscure, but suggests a possible association with the Scottish *curmurring* 'a low rumbling or murmuring'. The nickname solves no problems, but, if it really is an early example, carries the word back over 400 years.

No satisfactory etymology of *gibberish* has been put forward. First recorded in NED c1554, it occurs as a nickname 200 years earlier: Gilbert *Gibriche* 1332 SRCu and then as William *Gyberyssh*, *Gybrysh*, *Gybrych*, Robert *Geberyche* 1525 SRSx, Clement *Gibberishe* 1549 StaplehurstPR (K). The possibilities are too varied and uncertain to be discussed here, and the problem is complicated by the occurrence of a field-name is Gosford (O), *Giberis* 1225, *Gyberichs* 1359 PNO 268, *Gyberiche* 1359 Frides.

Humble-jumble is recorded once in NED in 1550 as 'humble iomble or hotch potch', described as a riming formation on *jumble*. A similar riming formation is found as a nickname 350 years earlier, William *Humbelcumbel* 1204 P (Nt/Db), in which the first element would appear to be from MD *humpelen*, LG *humpel* 'a small heap, hump', whilst the second is from *cumble*, *comble*, OFr *combler* 'to load, oppress' (1388 NED), found as a noun in 1694 in the sense 'heap'. Earlier, we have *cumber*, both noun and verb, 'overthrow, overwhelm, destruction' (1303), more common as *encumber*. Du Cange has *combri* 'impediments', from LowLat *cumbrus* 'a heap', from Lat *cumulus*, whilst Chaucer has '*combre-world*, that may of nothyng serve', an encumbrance to the world (by living too long), Troilus 4, 279. In the same poem (2, 1037) he has 'Ne *jompre* ek no discordant thyng yfeare', i.e. don't confuse the different terms of medicine and love. This is clearly a variant of *jumble* 'to mix together confusedly', well evidenced in the old name of High St, Shrewsbury: *Gumbellestolestrete* 1288, *Gumbelestolstre* 1300, *Gumbelstrelstret* 1343, *Gombelstolstrete* 1394,[1] 'the street of the jumble-stalls', where goods of all kinds were heaped and mixed together, reminiscent of the modern *jumble-sale*. Both *jumper* and *jumble* are probably frequentative forms of *jump* 'to make to jump, shake about, confuse'. Hence we have not only a duplication of sound but also of meaning, *humbel-cumbel* 'heap-heap', *humble-jumble* 'heap-heaped confusion'.

Before the sixteenth century there are no English writings on slang and the earliest were vocabularies of thieves' slang, an unlikely source for the nicknames that were common to all classes. But slang there always was, and a careful study of the language of Chaucer provides examples of colloquialisms and slang which enable us to see something, at least, of the mentality of his characters, their language and thoughts, their likes and dislikes, the tales they

[1] *Trans. Shropshire Arch. and Nat. Hist. Soc.*, 3rd Ser., VI (1906), pp. 384–6, and VII (1907), pp. 321–3.

loved to tell and those they delighted to hear. His characters were representative of their age and the more we understand them, the better we are able to realise the conditions under which they lived, the way they thought and talked, the essentials of the medieval life so productive of nicknames. For nicknames are of the earth, earthy; they developed on the farm and in the market-place, among farm-labourers, artisans and tradesmen no less than among hard-bitten knights and soldiers with their broad rumbustious humour. We shall not find definite explanations of nicknames but we shall see trends and possibilities, and we cannot fail to realise that we have discovered clues to the interpretation of some terms which, at first sight, seem hopelessly vague and indefinite and hints that others may have unsuspected shades of meaning.

This background is well summarised by Bardsley. After noting that there were nicknames as early as the times of Bede, he continues:

'With the incoming of the Normans, however, came a great change. The burlesque was part of their nature. A vein for the ludicrous was speedily acquired. It spread in every rank and grade of society. The Saxon himself was touched with the contagion, ere yet the southern blood was infused into his veins. Equally among the high and the low did such sobriquets as "le Bastard", "le Rouse", "le Beauclerk", "le Grisegonel" (Greycloke), "Plantagenet", "Sansterre", and "Cœur-de-lion" find favour. But it did not stay here; the more ridiculous and absurd characteristics became the butt of attack. In a day when buffoonery had become a profession, when every roughly-sketched drawing was a caricature, every story a record of licentious adventure, it could not be otherwise. The only wonderment is the tame acquiescence on the part of the stigmatized bearer.'[1]

Some of Chaucer's proverbial sayings have a remarkably modern look. Partridge notes that 'When . . . Chaucer wrote *There been mo sterres, god wot, than a paire*', he suggests the modern English *there's more than one pebble on the beach* or the American *there's more than one tin can in the alley*.[2] Still more modern are: They walwe as doon *two pigges in a poke*' (A 4278) and *mordre wol out* (B 4242), whilst 'But I woot best *where wryngeth me my sho*' (E 1553) differs little from *where the shoe pinches*; his '*I sette nat a strawe* by thy dremynges' (B 4280) reminds us of *I don't care a fig*; (She preyseth nat his pleyyng) *worth a bene* (E 1854) is now colloquial, a proverbial expression recorded by NED in 1297: 'Al nas *wurth a bene*.' The bean was regarded as typical of things of small value and this accounts

[1] C. W. Bardsley, *English Surnames* (London, 1875), p. 424.
[2] *Slang*, p. 43.

for one meaning of *Bean*.[1] The modern *Straw*, attested by Thomas *Straw* 1367 ColchCt and the historical Jack *Straw*, may also have a similar meaning,[2] though it must also have been applied to a dealer in straw (cf. *Strumanger*).

It is not always easy to distinguish colloquialism from slang, especially as our knowledge of the everyday language of ME is limited. But when, after his night with the miller's daughter, Aleyn wakes his friend with the call, 'John, thou *swynes-heed*, awake', his friendly, affectionate term of address was clearly slang and suggests that such names as *Swinstead*[3] (John *Swynesheved* 1288 NorwLt) and *Lambshead* were not always derogatory. When Oswald the Reve described his heart as *mowled* 'grown mouldy' he was using metaphor, but when he applied the same term to his hair, it was slang: 'Myn herte is also mowled as myne heris' (A 3870).[4] Clear examples of Chaucer's slang are: 'an old wydwe, a ribibe', a kind of fiddle (D 1377), 'an old rebekke' 'fiddle', applied to an old crone (D 1573) and 'olde stot' 'bullock', addressed contemptuously to an old woman (D 1630), a nickname still surviving as *Stott*.

Absolon, waiting at night outside her window for a kiss from the carpenter's wife, calls her by three different terms of endearment which must all be slang:

'What do ye, hony-comb, swete Alisoun,
My faire bryd, my sweete cynamome?' (A 3698–9)

And again, later:

'Lemman thy grace, and sweete bryd, thyn oore!'[5] (A 3726)

Modern slang still describes a girl as a 'bird', though not quite in Chaucer's sense. It is curious that this vague, indeterminate, generic term should be so common as a surname (*Bird*) and this sense 'darling, sweetheart' may have contributed to its frequency. The word was originally used especially of young birds and was applied to the young of animals in general. For 'generations of vipers', Wyclif has 'eddris and eddris *briddis*'. In ME it also meant 'child, young man,

[1] Also a nickname from ME *bēne* 'pleasant, genial, kindly', metonymic for a grower or seller of beans, a nickname from the 'king of the Bean' on Twelfth Night, and from a personal-name.
[2] Cf. also, 'Straw for thy Senek, and for thy proverbes!' (E 1567).
[3] Also local, from Swineshead (Beds, L).
[4] Cf. Ode Mouldyhead Foster, *supra* p. 221.
[5] I.e. favour.

maiden', also suggestive of modern slang, and, as a nickname, must have been used as a kind of affectionate diminutive.

As a parallel to this we may note the Hoost's 'murye wordes' to Chaucer:

> 'He in the waast is shape as well as I:
> This were a popet in an arm t'embrace
> For any woman, small and fair of face' (B 1890–2)

Popet, 'a small or dainty person', is a diminutive of OFr *poupee* 'a baby', 'puppet', where Cotgrave's 'baby' means 'doll', from VL **puppa* 'a doll', from Lat *pūpa*, originally 'a girl child', then 'a puppet or doll', applied later to any child (there was also a Lat *pūpus* 'a boy child'), then to the young of animals, hence the modern *puppy*. It was used as an early term of endearment, 'little one, darling', usually, but not always of girls. Where colloquialism ended and slang began is not clear, but it early became a nickname, modern *Poppett*, *Poppitt* (William *Pupet* 1191 P (Wa), Jordan *Popet* 1285 Wak), with a pejorative, William *Popard*, *Pupard* 1221 Cur (Herts), which may now survive as either *Poppett* or *Popper*. From this was formed a double diminutive *popelot*, 'a beloved young woman';

> 'In al this world, to seken up and doun,
> There nys no man so wys that koude thenche (imagine)
> So gay a popelote or swich a wenche' (A 3254)

a description of the carpenter's wife to which Chaucer later adds:

> 'She was a prymerole, a piggesnye' (A 3268)

'a primrose and a cuckoo flower', slang descriptions of a woman like 'peach' and 'daisy'. The modern surnames *Poplett*, *Puplett* are recorded as a surname, Tomas *Pupelot* 1214 P (C) and as a christian name, *Pupelota* 1296 SRSx, by the side of a similar diminutive, John *Popelyn* 1327 SRSf, though our earliest examples of this are *Popelina*, *Pupelin* (1214 Cur, L, Bk), a woman's name formed from the nickname, 'little dear, little darling'.

One other example and we must leave Chaucer for the moment. Cutting short the poet's own 'Tale of Sir Thopas', the host rudely dismisses it:

> 'Now swich a rym the devel I biteche![1]
> This may wel be rym dogerel' (B 2114–15)

[1] 'I consign to the devil.'

228

This is generally accepted as the earliest reference to *doggerel* and is probably slang. Its origin is unknown, but it may be a derivative of *dog*, in a pejorative sense as in *dog-Latin, dog-cheap*, though Weekley derives it from Lat *doga* 'a cask-stave'. The history of the word can now be carried back over 100 years from the nicknames of William *Doggerel* 1277 AssSo, Alice *Dogerel* 1321 EwenG (Beds), surviving in the rare *Doggrell*. This can hardly have reference to rime and the complete absence of context is a serious handicap. The form suggests that of *cockerell, duckerell, pickerell* 'little pike' and OFr *poutrel*, MedLat *pultrellus* 'colt', all diminutives and all surviving as modern surnames, *Cockerell, Dockerell, Duckrill, Pickerell, Putterill, Pottrill*, etc. To these we may add *mongrel*, probably 'a little mixture', 'a hybrid', and *dotterel*, a species of plover, 'a very foolish bird', used also of 'a silly person'; cf. 'Dottrell, fowle, idem quod Dotarde' (c1440 PromptParv), from ME *doten* 'to be foolish'. As a nickname this is found in Suffolk as early as 1182–1211, William *Doterel* (BuryS), in Staffordshire in 1292 and in Yorkshire in 1301, now *Dottrell*. It looks as if this was originally a derogatory diminutive 'little dotard', later applied to the bird which is easily caught. *Doggerel* may similarly have meant 'a little dog', used as a pejorative nickname, and then applied derisively to wretched poetry, irregular verse, its irregular rhythm suggesting the antics of a young dog. Though we have no surviving surname from *dog*, one formerly existed.[1]

THE CLASSIFICATION OF NICKNAMES

Before we attempt to classify nicknames, we must be sure what they mean, and that at once excludes large numbers and proves that many so-called nicknames have an entirely different signification.[2] Even when we have a quite simple meaning, we can never prove that the nickname does not mean the opposite of what it says[3] or that it is not used with some special, unexpected sense.[4] For the meaning, we must get back to the original medieval form; that of many modern names, apparently nicknames, is definitely misleading. *Weatherhead* has no connexion with *-head*; it was occupational, a man in charge of sheep, John *le Wetherhirde* 1297. *Mulberry* is local, a variant of *Mowbray*, Roger *de Mulbrai* c1130, Richard *Mulberye* 1381, from Montbrai (La Manche), as is *Rasberry* or *Raspberry*, from

---

[1] *v.* p. 262.
[2] Cf., e.g. *Rumbelow, Prettejohn*, p. 12.
[3] *v. Black*, p. 222.　　　　[4] *v. Basset*, p. 222.

Ratsbury (D), Marioth' *de Radespree* 1242. So, too, is *Grisenth-waite* which Bardsley, citing Anne *Griselwhite* from an old Norfolk register, regards as a compound of 'Grissell' and 'white'. Earlier, it was (Richard) *Grysethwayte* 1520 FrY, from Gristhwaite (NRY), with substitution of *-white* for *-thwaite*, as often. *Limmage*, Weekley explains as for *l'image*. We certainly have *Image*, not noted before 1563, which is metonymic for *Ymagour* (1305) 'a maker of images, carver, sculptor'. No example of *image* with the definite article has been found. *Limmage* is the local pronunciation of Lyminge (K). *Greengrass*, which Weekley associates with food for cattle, is from a lost place in Suffolk, Alice *de Grenegres* 1275. *Collar* is a form of *Collier* 'charcoal-burner' and *Whisker*, a variant of *Wishart*, from ONFr *Wischard*, OFr *Guischard*. The frequent explanation of *Wool-ward* as 'clothed in wool', 'to go *woolward*', to undergo the penance of wearing outer woollen garments without any linen under-dress, is most unlikely as a nickname. It is the normal development of OE *Wulfweard*, a personal-name still in use in the late thirteenth century. No example suggests a nickname. The illustrative material adduced consists entirely of instructions to undergo this penance or the man's own statement that he is doing so. Besides, the absence of a garment which could not in any case be seen is an unlikely source for a nick-name.

'*Medlicott* for "medley coat", i.e. motley seems to be certified by Peter *Miparty* (*Fine R.*), Fr *mi-parti* corresponding exactly to mot-ley.'[1] In spite of the French parallel, no one has yet produced an example of *Medlicott* as a nickname. It is undoubtedly local in origin, from Medlicott (Sa) and all early examples come from its county of origin: Lewelin *de Modlincot* 1255 RH (Sa), John *de Modlycot*' 1327 SRSa, William *Medlicott* 1641 SaAS (3rd Ser.), IV. Weekley made good use of the comparative method, a valuable aid, which must, however, be used with caution. There are undoubtedly numerous parallels between English and French surnames, but there are also many differences, and it is dangerous to draw comparative deductions without definite proof of the existence of the name in this country. We have not in England the endless series of diminutives of personal-names like *Arnaud, Naud, Naudot, Dot, Dottin*, etc., found in France, or surnames compounded with prefixed prepositions as the French *Degeorges, Derobert, Auclerc, Aufrere, Aupetit*.

Diamond, pronounced *Dimmond*, and the obsolete *Demon* look

[1] Weekley, *Surnames*, p. 148.

like nicknames. The former Bardsley explains as 'son of Dymond', but gives no evidence for such a personal-name. *Dimont* and *Dimond* he takes as local, from Dinant, noting that they are Devonshire names which have come directly across from Brittany. Weekley derives *Diamond* from OE *Dægmund*, but no medieval examples of this have been found. He also notes *Diamanda* (1349), an earlier example of which occurs in 1221 (Cur), one of the fanciful names given to women in the Middle Ages, but two examples of this rarity will not account for *Diamond* and its varieties. I have elsewhere explained *Dayman* as both a personal-name (1331) and an occupational-name 'herdsman' from 1224 and there can be little doubt that this is the origin of the whole series. In the Hartland Parish Register (Devon) for 1765 we find record of the burial of Joannah *Dyman*, Mr Wm *Dayman*'s wife. The surname is common, appearing with 29 different spellings of which *Dayman*, *Deyman* and *Demon* are most common, the two former from 1559 to the eighteenth century, the latter disappearing by 1569. An excrescent *t* or *d* is added in the seventeenth century and the name is found as *Dieman* 1609, *Deymant* 1627, *Dimon* 1671, *Daymand* 1685, *Diamond* 1738 and *Dyment* 1817. We also find the alternative John *Deyman* alias *Dymond* 1698 DKR 41 (D). The modern variants surviving are *Dayman*, *Deman*, *Demant*, *Diamond*, *Diamant*, *Diment*, *Dimond*, *Dimont*, *Dyment* and *Dymond*. These late examples are invaluable in illustrating the development of a name, but are useless for etymological purposes without early medieval forms.

Nor must we forget that a nickname may have more than one meaning and that an apparent nickname may belong to more than one class. *Bear* is usually a specifically Devonshire local name from OE *bær* 'pasture', especially a swine-pasture, but a common nickname origin is proved by the frequent *le Bere* (1159 P) and its Latinisation, Willelmus *Ursus* (1182 StCh), one with some characteristic of the bear (OE *bera*), 'savage', 'unapproachable', 'unsociable', one who lived in isolation. The Devon place-name is also found as *Beer*, which, as a surname, may also be from a personal-name, OE **Bera* or ON *Biórr*, or a nickname from OE *bēor* 'beer', a seller of beer, taverner or metonymic for a brewer (cf. John *le Berebruer* 1329 AD iv). We have also *Godbear*, *Godbeer* 'good beer' (also an oath-name) by the side of *Goodale* and *Goodall* 'brewers or sellers of good beer or ale', with the derogatory William *Sourale* (1301 SRY).

It is obvious, therefore, that any classification of nicknames must be broad and general, and comprehensive treatment of each surname is impossible if we are to avoid endless repetition and innumerable cross-references. Briefly, we shall deal with:

1. Physical and External Peculiarities (including nicknames from dress, accoutrements, etc.)
2. Mental and Moral Characteristics (excluding peculiarities of relationship, dealt with above)
3. Nicknames from animals, birds and fishes
4. Names from oaths, street-cries and phrase-names
5. Names of indecent and obscene connotation

Chapter Twelve

NICKNAMES FROM PHYSICAL AND EXTERNAL CHARACTERISTICS

Height and build

QUITE a number of nicknames are purely general, descriptive of height and build, and many are self-explanatory: *Bigg, Lang* or *Long, Tall, Greet* (great), *High, Much* or *Muckle,*[1] with the French *Grand, Grant* and the Scandinavian *Storr* (ON *stórr* 'big'), whilst the lack of size is indicated by *Little, Low, Short, Smale* or *Small, Murch* 'dwarf' and the French *Bass* or *Bassett, Curt, Court* and the diminutives *Curtin, Pettitt*. Obesity and its opposite were natural subjects for comment: *Fatt, Plump, Thick* and *Thynne*, the East Anglian *Craske* 'fat and lusty', *Gaunt, Lean, Meager*, all 'thin', *Lank* 'tall and thin', with the French *Grace, Grass* 'fat' and the metaphorical *Buss* (OFr *busse* 'cask') and *Barrell*, used in the sixteenth century of 'the ydell and *barrell bealies* of monkes' and still common as a children's nickname for 'fatties',[2] *Spire, Sprigg, Stick* and *Twigg* 'tall, thin,

---

[1] *Lardge* and *Large* are from OFr *large* 'generous'.
[2] I. and P. Opie, *The Lore and Language of Schoolchildren* (Oxford, 1960), give both *barrel* and *barrel-belly*, p. 168.

233

slender', with *Scatchard*, a derivative of ONFr *escache* 'a stilt'. *Scachard* is a pejorative, a nickname for a long-legged bird like the heron, later applied to a man. To these we may add: *Broad* or *Bradd*, *Straight*, *Round* 'rotund and plump' and *Bullett*, a diminutive of OFr *boule* 'round'. Physical defects are stigmatised in *Cromb*, *Crumb* (OE *crumb* 'bent, crooked, stooping'), *Crump* (OE *crump* 'bent'), *Crook* (ON *krókr* 'crooked'), *Wrong* (late OE *wrang*, also from ON, in the same sense) and *Yapp* (OE *gēap* 'bent').

Above the neck

There is scarcely a single part of the visible human anatomy which has not at some time given rise to a nickname, descriptive, derisory or complimentary. Hundreds of these have disappeared, but a surprisingly large number survive, the most common subjects of comment being the head, with its adornments of hair and beard—or their absence, legs, foot and neck. The proof that such vague terms as *Head, Hair, Hand, Mouth* and *Tooth* are undoubtedly, at times, nicknames is found in certain early prepositional forms. Hubertus *cum testa* 1130 P, Godefridus *cum capillo* c1200 Dublin, Henry *Mytehare* 1254 ELPN (*mid the here* 'with the hair'), Johannes *cum manu* c1200 Dublin, Michael *od la Buche* 1225 Pat (now *Bouch*, from OFr *bouche* 'mouth'), Hugo *cum dentibus* c1111 ELPN. All these must have reference to some physical peculiarity, a man with a big mouth or prominent teeth, well illustrated by that 'gracious piece of dialogue' aptly quoted from some comic paper by Weekley:

> 'Who was that bloke as I see yer with last night?'
> 'Wot? 'Im with the face?'
> 'No; the other one.'[1]

Descriptive compounds are numerous: *Broadhead, Greathead, Fairhead, Whitehead, Redhead, Roughhead, Rowed* and *Ruffhead*, with obsolete examples like *Milkheved* 'white', *Swarteheved* 'black' and *Potheved* 'like a pot'. In compounds, *-head* is often reduced to *-ett*: *Blackett* (Thomas *Blakehevede* 1301 SRY), *Perrett* (Robert *Perheved* 1273 RH) 'pear-shaped', *Smollett* (John *Smalheued* 1332 SRWa) 'small'. Sometimes the name is metaphorical: *Brasnett* (Roger *Brasenhed* 1434 FrNorw), *Brassett* (Richard *Brassehevede* 1301 SRY), 'hard as brass', with which we may compare 'brasse-head buls' (1613 NED) and *Bulled, Bulleid* (Robert *Buleheved* 1195 P), one noted for his bull-headed impetuosity, and *Dowsett* (usually

[1] *Surnames*, p. 126.

234

a diminutive of *doux* 'sweet'), probably one of the opposite temperament, 'pleasing, agreeable' (Thomas *Dowcehed* 1444 *ERO*, John *Dousett*, *Dowced* 1555, 1556 ib.), *Durrad* (Adam *Durheued* (1332 SRCu) 'hard head'. Compounds with the name of an animal or bird are not uncommon, but the real meaning is obscure: *Cockhead*, *Cockshed*, *Coxhead*, *Lambshead*, *Ramshead*, *Dockett* and *Duckett* 'duck', *Doggett* 'dog' and *Duffett* 'dove'.

Apart from *Hair* and *Hare*, both of which have other origins, we have the simple *Lock* (OE *locc* 'lock of hair'), probably for one with fine curls and the French derivatives of *hure*, *Hurran* or *Hurren* and *Hurrell*, probably denoting an abundance of hair, possibly 'shaggy-haired', as opposed to *Coppell*, *Cupples* 'short hair', from OFr *curt peil* (Walter *Curtpeil* 1200, John *Curpel* 1221, Robert *Coppayl* 1381). Otherwise, compounds usually refer to curls or colour: *Curl*, *Croll*, *Crisp*, *Cripps*, *Crispin* and *Crippen*; *Fairer*, *Fairfax* (cf. Alice *Witfax* 1289 Misc, 'white hair'); *Blacklock*, *Blakelock*, either 'black' or 'fair'; *Harlock*, *Horlock*, *Horlick* (OE *hār* 'grey'); *Sherlock* (OE *scīr* 'bright, shining') and *Silverlock*. *Lockless* denoted one with straight hair, without curls, whilst *Lovelock* was a nickname for a dandy, a wearer of pendant locks of hair falling over the ears and cut in a variety of fashions. They were common in the sixteenth century and apparently much earlier. Or it may have denoted a maker of these.

Lack of hair does not permit of a similar variety of epithets. ME *ballede* was used originally of rotundity or corpulence, later of baldness (c1386 NED). The seal of Madoc *le Balled* (14th AD iv) gives his name as Madocus *Calvus*. ME *ballard* was a pejorative for a bald-headed man. Where Wyclif has 'Stye up, ballard!', Coverdale translates, 'Come vp here thou balde heade'. The OE *calu* (*calewa*) 'bald' survives as *Callow*, whilst *Nott* is from OE *hnott* 'bald-headed, close-cropped'. By the side of these we have a number of French survivals, *Chaff*, *Chafe*, *Chave*, *Caff*, *Cave*, from OFr *chauf*, *cauf*, Lat *calvus* 'bald', the diminutives *Chaffin*, *Chauvin*, *Caffin* and *Cavell* (Roger *Calvel*, *Chauuel* 1190, 1195), and *Pelly*, *Le Pelley* (OFr *pele*, ModFr *pelé* 'bald').

Facial hair we have already met in *Garnon*, but it was the beard which provided an abundance of nicknames. *Beard* itself, and *Barbe* (Hugo *Alabarbe*) are both found as early as 1086, and the Scandinavian *Skegg* (ON *skegg* 'beard') in 1379. Compounds are descriptive of colour or shape, but few survive: *Fairbeard*, *Fairbard*, *Blackbird*,

235

a corruption of *black beard*, *Whitbread*, sometimes for white beard and *Goldbard* for golden beard. The 'Bearded Lady,' remarks Ewen, 'is represented by Alice Barbe Dor' (1246 Nth).[1] He did not realise that the lady was a member of a well-known Cambridgeshire family and had inherited the name 'golden beard', which may survive as *Barder*. Among the obsolete examples we may note William *Museberd* 1198 P, 'mouse', Thomas *Dustiberd* 1229 Pat (So), Peter *Seilberd* 1230 P, John *Spadeberd* 1246 AssLa (1598 NED), Roger *Thistilberd* 1260 AssC.

The face itself is commemorated in *Vidler* 'wolf-face' and the lost (Geoffrey) *Vis de Chat* (1185 P) 'cat's face'. The rest of the facial anatomy is little more productive of nicknames: *Durden* (William *Duredent* 1154) 'hard tooth', *Airrless*, *Arliss* and *Harliss* 'ear-less', *Penderel*, *Pendrell*, 'hang-ear' (Fr *pendre*, *oreille*). *Earthroll* and *Earthrowl*, of which Lower found two examples in London in 1852, still survive, though very rare. It must be OE *ēar* 'ear' and *þyrel* 'hole' and we can only agree with Lower: 'How "ear-hole" became a surname I do not venture even to guess.'

Reference to the eye is somewhat more frequent, to colour, in *Blackie*, *Brunyee* 'brown', Ralph *Greyeye* 13th CNat, *Goldney*, *Whitey*, *Fairey* and *Farey*; descriptive in *Bradie*, *Broady*, with occasional comparison with an animal, Ralph *Musege* (1180 P) 'mouse', Roger *Wulfesege* 1168 P, 'wolf's eye', one origin of *Woolsey*, or to a bird, *Goosey*, *Hawkey*, *Hawksey*. Of lost nicknames, we may note *Belymuð* 'with a mouth like a pair of bellows', *Chykenmouth*, *Butermuth*, *Blak in the mouthe* (probably with black teeth); *Nose* and all its compounds have disappeared, including *Langnase*, *Rynose* 'crooked', *Torcheneys*, *Kattisnese* and *Oxenose*. But *Wroot* (OE *wrōt* 'snout') is still with us, presumably because its meaning was forgotten.

Both *Neck* and *Halse* (OE *heals* 'neck') are rare, and most of their compounds have disappeared: *Longhals*, *Bulehals*, *Gaythals* 'goat', along with *Shortnekke*, *Blaknekke* and *Doggenecce*. Symon *Nekeles* 'neckless' was probably identical with Symon *Chortneke* 'short neck' (1275 RH). Gone, too, are Agnes *Neckepayne* (1297 MinAcctCo), Geoffrey *Neckebon* (1316 FFC) and Alan *Waghals* (1240 *Ass*Sf), 'wagneck'. But we still have *Swannick* (John *Swaneke* 1279 RH), parallel with Edgyue *Suanneshals* (1066) 'swan-neck', *Whittles* or *Whitehouse* (William *Whitehals* 1369 FrY), whilst (Robert) *Schorthals* 1189 P may still survive as *Shorthouse*.

[1] *Guide to the Origin of British Surnames* (London 1938), p. 101.

Colour-names

Colour-names refer as a rule to complexion or hair. *Blache* and *Blatch* are palatal forms of OE *blæc* 'black' which in ME occurs both as *blacke* and *blake* (now *Black, Blake*), the latter being then indistinguishable from ME *blake* from OE *blāc* 'bright, shining; pale, wan', both meanings being found also in the French *Blanck, Blank* (OFr *blanc* 'white, fair') and *Nares* (AFr *neir* 'black'). Fair hair or a blond complexion seem to have been thought particularly worthy of note: *Blunt, Blount* and the diminutive *Blondel, Blundell* (OFr *blund, blond* 'blond, fair, yellow-haired'). In Joce *Blonthefed* 1195 P (L), 'fair head', the reference is clearly to hair. We now prefer *Golden, Goolden* and *Goulden* (cf. Richard *Guldenheved* 1222 DBStP), but *yellow* was a common medieval description. Bardsley cites an early Thomas *Yalowehair* and notes not only Chaucer's reference, 'Her hair was yellow, and clear shining', but also a description of the hair of Henry VII's queen, 'her faire yellow hair hangyng down pleyne behynd her back'; cf. also Jordan *le Yelewe* (1234 Oseney), a surname which survived in Suffolk as late as 1674 (widow *Yellowe* 1674 HTSf). Other variants of this colour are *Faugh* (OE *fealu* 'of a pale brownish or reddish yellow colour'), *Favell* (OFr *fauvel* 'fallow-coloured, tawney'), used also as early as 1325 as a symbol of cunning, duplicity or hypocrisy, and *Flavell* (Thomas *Flavell* 1493 FrY).

Read, Reed and *Red* are all from OE *rēad* 'red'. *Rudd* is *ruddy* from the root of *rudduc* 'red-breast', *Rous* from OFr *rous* 'red', *Russell* from its diminutive, *Soar* and its diminutive *Sorrell* from OFr *sor* 'reddish-brown', with which we may include *Sanguine, Sangwin*, from OFr *sanguin* 'of a sanguine complexion'. *Gray* and *Grey*, like *Hoar* and *Hore* (OE *hār*), *Biss* and its diminutive *Bissett* (OFr *bis* 'brownish or dark grey'), refer to grey hair, as sometimes do *Grice* and *Griss* (OFr *gris* 'grey'), and certainly *Grisson, Grissom* (OFr *grison* 'grey'). Particularly common is *Brown*, from both OE *brūn* and OFr *brun*, whence the French diminutives *Brownett* and *Brunet*. *Dunn* is OE *dunn* 'dull brown, dark, swarthy', *Colley, Collie*, from OE **colig* 'coal-black', *Swart* from ON *svartr*, OE *sweart* 'swarthy', whilst *Snow* is metaphorical. Haylwardus *Snew* (c950 OEByn) is said to have been so called *propter albedinem* 'owing to his snow-white hair'. An interesting compound is *Nutbrown*, found also in the reverse order, *Brownnutt, Brownnutt* and *Brownhut*, 'brown as a nut', with which we may compare Roger *Perbrun* 1270 Misc (Nf), 'brown as a pear'.

Here, too, belong certain names which have also other meanings. *Farren, Farrant, Ferran, Ferrand* may be from OFr *Ferrant*, OG *Ferrand*, but were also nicknames from OFr *ferrant* 'iron-grey', used in England of the colour of a horse. *Moore, More* are variants of *More*, the vernacular form of OFr *Maure* 'a Moor' or 'swarthy as a Moor'. It occurs early as a nickname, William *le Mor* 1221 AssSa, and also as a diminutive, *Morrell* (OFr *morel* 'brown, dusky'). In France *brun* is said to have been applied to the hair, *maure* to the colour of the skin. Moisy noted that in Normandy *cheval morel* was used of a black horse. *Morris* also may be a nickname, Agnes *la Morise* 1275 SRWo, 'Moorish, dark as a Moor'. *Sarson* (sometimes 'son of Sara') must always have been a nickname in England. It is found as early as 1148 in Winchester, Stephanus *Sarazinus*, and undoubtedly as a nickname in 1201, Philip *le Saracin* (AssSo), Stephen called *Saracen* 1281 AssCh. It probably referred to a swarthy complexion, but may also have been a pageant-name. In France the surname belongs especially to the Midi (in the North they were called *Mores*), and Dauzat remarks that *Sarrazin* had preserved its ethnic meaning which *Maure* lost early in France, to become metaphoric.[1]

Descriptive nicknames compounded with a personal-name

Brownjohn, clearly a nickname, 'John with the brown hair or brown complexion', is one of a number of medieval surnames, a few of which survive: *Dunbabin* and *Dunbobin* 'dun (dark) Babin or Bobin', pet-names for Robin (cf. Robert called *Brounerobyn* 1311 ColchCt), *Horrabin, Horabin, Horobin* 'hoar (grey) Rabin or Robin', with the obsolete *Broun Edrith* (i.e. Edrich) 1255 RH (Sa), Adam *Brounadam* 1329 ColchCt, Agnes *Greyadam* 1297 MinAcctCo, John *Whithobbe* 1381 FFEss 'fair Robert'.

Similar compounds, with other descriptive epithets, usually attached to common christian names, were used, apparently, to distinguish one John or Will from the many others of the same name in the village. At first they were pure individual nicknames, but some ultimately became surnames: *Petinicol* 1279 RH, *Jolyrobin* 1332 SRCu, *Litelwatte* 1340 LoPleas, William *Litelmold* 1289 RamsCt, Richard *Godedick* 1301 SRY, Roger *Petywill* 1303 Misc, John

[1] *Les Noms de famille de France* (1945), p. 186.

Literolf 1332 SRSx, Richard *Longe Ion* 1340 AssC, John *Jolifion* 1377 FFC, Richard *Goderichard* 1383 AssWa, William *Faireellis* 1674 HTSf.

Littlejohn is probably the most common of the survivors and *Gaukroger* 'clumsy Roger' the most interesting. *Goodjohn, Gudgeon,* appears to be attested by the French *Bowgen, Budgen* (Robert *Bonjohan* 1297 MinAcctCo), but the earliest forms are clearly from the fish, 'greedy' (gudgeon) or 'big-headed', or one who will take any bait, 'credulous, gullible'. Although definite identifications are impossible in Subsidy Rolls, those for Sussex suggest that *Pidgen, Pidgeon, Pidgon* and *Pigeon* may also be for *Petit Johan* 'Little John': Relicta *Pygon* 1296, Relicta *Pijohan,* John *Petijohan,* John *Pyion,* John *Petiion* 1327.

Goodhugh, Goodhue, Goodhew, which may sometimes stand for 'good Hugh', is certainly also from ME *god* and *hewe* 'good servant', a parallel to *Goodhind,* but is▪probably, as a rule, from ON **Guð(h)ugi,* the opposite of *Ill(h)ugi,* the earliest examples being a personal-name. *Littlecole* would appear to be an English pet-form of *Petinicol* above, whilst Robert *Litteldick* (1640 LeiAS xxiii) looks like an ancestor of a modern *Littledyke,* but this evidence is insufficient to decide which is the original form. *Younghughes* and *Younghouse* are probably identical, 'Young Hugh'; cf. Thomas *Youngjohnson* 1374 Misc (Cu), no doubt 'son of Young John'.

Middle is a difficult name to explain. It is sometimes local but also occurs as a nickname, Richard *le Midel* 1279 RH. It is probably to be taken with John *Middeljohan* 1381 FFSf, Peter *Morejohn* 1425 ArchC 48, and *Littlejohn* above, either the middle one of three brothers all named John or one intermediate in size between a little John and a greater (*More*) John. *Hobgen, Hupgens* is a different type of compound, clearly a combination of *Hob* (Robert) and *John,* William *Hopjohn, Hobjohn* 1524 SRSx. I have previously explained it as perhaps 'rustic, boorish John', but the discovery of such surnames as *Jakharry* and *Watfilip* suggests doubts.

From neck to foot

Armstrong and *Strongitharm* are well-known English nicknames. From French we have also the obsolete Richard *Beaubraz* (1335 ERO), 'fine arm', the rare *Bradfer,* William *Braz de fer* (1205 P), 'iron-arm', now largely absorbed by *Bradford,* and *Fairbrass,*

Farbrace, Firebrace, John *Fierbrace* 1196, Rober *Ferbraz* 1221, John *Farbrace* 1533, from OFr *fer, fier* 'bold, fierce, proud' and *bras* 'arm'. *Shoulders* still survives, a nickname, possibly, for one with broad shoulders, as do *Rump* and *Tout,* ME *toute* 'buttocks, rump' (cf. Roger *Scarpetout* 1327 SRSx).

But it is the hands, legs and feet which have always attracted apt comment or derisive description and the hands less than the lower extremities. *Hand* itself is rare in compounds, *Goodhand, Whitehanp* and the hybrid *Bonnan,* Peter *Bonhand* 1327 *SR* (Ess), OFr *bon* 'good' and OE *hand,* with the obsolete *Clenehand, Lefthand* and *Littelhand. Main(s)* and *Mayne(s)* are both at times undoubted nicknames, Walter *Asmeins* 1223, 'the man with the hands', a plural form often found, though not always surviving: *Bellemain,* Nicholas *Belesmains* 1210, 'beautiful hands'; the opposite *Malemaynes* 'evil hands' long survived as a surname in Essex; *Fortman,* William *Fortesmains* 1219 'strong hands', found also as a hybrid, Thomas *Maynstrang* 1279 RH; *Quartermaine, Quarterman, Quatermaine* 'four hands', perhaps 'mail-fisted', with the obsolete Robert *Curtesmains* 1208 Misc, 'short hands' and Robert *Tortesmains* 1169 P, 'twisted hands'.

OE *bān* 'bone' is often used of the legs, both alone as *Baine(s)* or *Bones,* and in compounds such as *Langbain* and *Longbones, Smallbone(s)* and *Fairbain* and in *Cockbain* 'cock-legs' and *Rawbone* 'with legs like a roe'. The term most frequently used is OE *sceanca* 'shank, leg' which survives as *Shanks* 'the man with the legs', and in numerous compounds most of which are obsolete: *Crookshank(s), Cruickshank(s)* 'crooked leg', in early forms always singular, *Sheepshanks* 'with legs like a sheep', a type formerly common: *Doggeschanke, Pyshank* 'magpie-legs', *Philipschank* 'sparrow-legs', *Folesanke* 'with legs like a foal'. *Legg* is from ON *leggr* 'leg', of which the only compound seems to be *Whitelegg.* The French *jambe,* Rannulf *Jambe* 1221 AssWa, is now found only as a compound, though a diminutive of the Norman form *gamb* survives in *Gammon,* Margery *Gambun* 1209 P, 'little leg'. *Belgian, Belgion* and *Belgeonne* are corruptions of the AFr *bele jambe* 'fine leg' and *Fulljames* of *Foljambe,* from OFr *fol* 'foolish, silly' and *jambe,* probably in the sense 'useless, maimed leg', for OFr *fol* was used of something useless or of little value: *farine folle* 'milldust', *figue folle* 'a good-for-nothing fig'. Among the lost nicknames, we may note: *Baresanke, Barebayn, Barleg* 'bare', *Brunshanks, Greyschanke, Schortbayn, Longleg, Longschankes, Bridbayn* 'bird-leg', *Kitebein* 'kite-leg'.

The nickname origin of *Foot* is attested by Gregorius *cum pede* 1271 FrLei and Henricus *Pes* 1290 ShefA. As with leg, comparisons with birds and animals are frequent in both English and French forms: *Crowfoot, Duffett*, Richard *Dovefote* 1301, *Forfeitt* 'pig-foot' (OE *fōr* 'pig'), *Grayfoot* 'badger', with *Pedler* (AFr *pie-de-levre* 'hare-foot', 'speedy, nimble'), *Harfoot* 'hare-foot', and the obsolete *Pedeken* 'dog-foot', *Piedurs* 'bear-foot', *Pedebef* 'ox-foot', *Piggesfot, Lomesfot* 'lamb', *Oxefot*. Descriptive of the foot are: *Barefoot, Barfoot, Bearfoot*, Robert *barefot* c1160, Reginald *Berfot* 1203, 'bare' (OE *bær*), *Broadfoot, Fairfoot*, Adam *Fairefot* 1328 WhC, *Goldfoot*, Robert *Geldenefot, Gildenefot* 1188 P (OE *gylden* 'golden'), *Platfoot* 'flat', *Playfoot*, probably 'splay-foot', *Lightfoot*, one with a light, springy step, a speedy runner, messenger (cf. *Lyghtefot Nuncius*, a messenger in one of the Towneley Plays and John *Litefot*, cacher, 1274 RH); *Proudfoot*, with its curious corruption *Proundfoot*, one who walks with a haughty step. Gilbert Proudfoot was sheriff of London c1140 and, remarks Ekwall, 'it is interesting to find that the first known bearer of the name was a sheriff, thus a person who might be justified in walking with a proud step'. *Ruffett* is 'rough foot'; *Whitefoot* has its French parallel in *Blampey, Blampied*, Richard *Blancpie* 1198 P, from OFr *blanc, pied*. Note, too, William *Dustifot* 1221 AssWo, William *Sarfoot* 1297 SRY, 'sore', Annabel *Squatfot* 1339 Misc, 'short and thick', Richard *Wrongfot* 1260 AssC, 'twisted', and John *Hotfot* 1327 SR (Ess), probably another name for a messenger; cf. Chaucer's 'And Custance han they take anon, foot-hoot' (B 438), i.e. hastily, quickly, which may survive as *Footitt, Foottit*, Roger *Vothot, Fothot* 1291, 1295 ELPN.

All nicknames from OE *wamb* 'belly' have disappeared, e.g. *Cuwambe* 'cow', *Pesewombe* 'pease', i.e. small, *Wombestrang* 'strong belly'. But *Pauncefoot* does belong here. It is usually explained as 'paunch-face', from OFr *pance*, ONFr *panche* 'stomach' and OFr *volt* 'face'. But Harrison rightly noted that the second element is OFr *volt* 'vaulted, arched', hence 'the man with the arched and rounded belly', a much more attractive etymology than 'paunch-face'. The surname has also become *Paunceford* and *Ponsford*, both of which may also be local, from Ponsford (D).

Nicknames from physical defects

Some surnames denoting physical defects were probably purely descriptive: *Boss* is sometimes from ME *boce, bos*, OFr *boce* 'protuberance, swelling', 'a hunch or hump on the back', metonymic for a hunchback, *Bossey*, from OFr *bocu* 'hunch-backed', whilst *Bunch* is from OE *bunche* and *Bunney* from OFr *bugne*, 'a swelling',[1] in the same sense; *Blind*, *Deave(s)*, from OE *dēaf* 'deaf', *Domm*, *Domb* 'dumb' (cf. Alan *le Mute* 1274 RH), *Stamer* (OE **stamera* 'stammerer'), *Stutter(s)* 'stutterer'. *Born* is from OFr *borgne* 'one-eyed', 'squint-eyed'; cf. Simon *Monoculus* 1212, a parallel to the obsolete English (Stephen) *le Oneyede* 1293 AssSt, 'with one eye'.

Some complimentary nicknames

Blessed, *Blest*, *Blissett* and *Blissitt*, all derive from ME *iblescede*, past participle of OE *blētsian* 'to make sacred', in the sense 'happy, fortunate' (c1175 NED), Alicia *Iblessed* 1297 MinAcctCo, John *le Blessed* 1327 SRSt, John *le Blest* 1332 SRSx, whilst *Mignot*, *Minet*, *Mynott* are from OFr *mignot*, 'dainty, pleasing', Peter *Mignot*, *Minnot* 1191, 1201 P (K). Other simple names are: *Bell* and *Bew*, Robert *le Beu*, *le Bel* (OFr *bel*, *beu* 'beautiful, fair'), *Bone*, *Bunn* (OFr *bon* 'good'), *Fair*, *Fayer*, *Phair* 'fair, beautiful', *Good* and *Legood*, Gilbert *le Gode* 1212 Cur (OE *gōd* 'good'), but most complimentary nicknames are compounds of one or other of these terms, the nickname often surviving from both English and French sources, and some may have been courteous forms of address: *Bellamy*, 'fair friend', *Bonnamy*, 'good friend', *Goodfriend*, William *Godfrend* 1210 P 34 (W), *Goodfellow*, used also by Chaucer as slang for 'a disreputable fellow', 'a rascal',[2] *Bellham*, *Belhomme* 'fair man', *Fairman*. *Beldam*, *Beldham* is probably a derogatory nickname from AFr *bele-dame*, 'fine lady', Godfrey *Beledame* 1296 SRSx. ME *beldam* 'grandmother' is not recorded before c1440 and the sense 'aged woman, hag' not until the sixteenth century. *Bonham*, *Bonhomme*, 'good man' is paralleled by the English *Goodman*, Henry *le Godman* 1275 RH; the French *bon enfant*, corresponding to the English *Goodchild* (cf. also *Goodbairn* and *Fairchild*), survives as *Bonafont* and *Bonifant* and later became *Bullivant*, a development revealed by such names as Henry *Bolyvaunt* 1524 SRSf, William *Bonyvant* 1540 RochW, George *Bulliuant*, *Bulliphant* 1624–5 SolihullPR (Wa). This appears also to have become *Pillivant*, Judith *Pellefant* 1618 HartlandPR (D), Andrew *Pellevan* 1621 ib., Jane *Pellifant* 1629 ib.,

---

[1] *v.* also *Bunyan*, pp. 10–11.
[2] *Bonfellow* is a corruption of *Boutflour*.

Andrew *Pilliphant* 1633 ib., though it is possible that these Devonshire names may be local, from Pilliven in Witheridge. But *Sillifant* is also found in Devonshire, 'happy, blessed child', from OE *sǣlig*, which survives as *Ceeley, Cely, Sealey, Seeley, Selly, Silley, Silly, Zealey* and *Zelley*; cf. also *Sillibourne, Silabon, Silburn* 'happy bairn'.

Bonser, Bonsier is OFr *bon sire* 'good sir', no doubt, like the English *Goodsir* and *Sweetser, Switzer,* used as a term of address. *Beausire* and *Bowser* are from OFr *bel, beau* and *sire* 'fair sir' and are well attested: Roger *Beausire* 1202 Fees (He), Walter *Beausire,* Thomas *Belesire* 1301 SRY. In the sixteenth century the name appears to have been confused with *Belsher,* Alexander *Belsier, Belshyre* 1542 Oseney. This is a comparatively rare form of *Belcher,* surving also as *Bewsher, Beuscher, Bewshea, Belshaw, Bewshaw* and *Bowsher.* All the early examples of the surname have *ch,* Thomas *Belcher* 1219 AssY, Richard *Belechere* 1274 RH (Gl). Later, we have Margaret *Bewcher* 1530 SIA i, William *Bewshawe* 1539 FrY, Henry *Belsher* 1662 *HTEss. Belechere* must be a nickname from OFr *bel(e)* and *chiere,* originally 'pretty face', later 'pretty look', one of a pleasant, cheerful demeanour. In the York Plays it is used as a term of address, often derogatory. Herod, bidding the messenger approach, addresses him, 'And, bewcher! wele ye be', and when Annas orders a boy who had been bound to be brought in, the soldier announces, 'Lo, here is the belschere broght that ye bad bring.' For the form, we may compare *Goacher, Goatcher, Goucher,* Willelmus dictus *Godechere* 1343, 'one of good aspect, cheerful appearance', and, for the earlier meaning, *Goodfare,* 'one of good appearance, demeanour', from ME *feyr,* from OFr *aferir* 'to be proper, meet'.

Contrast with these the compounds of *mal* 'bad, evil': *Maliphant,* Geoffrey *Malenfant* 1205, 'naughty child', *Malzer,* William *Malesoveres* c1144 Riev, William *Malesour', Mala opera* 1219 AssY, 'evil deeds', *Manclark, Moakler, Mockler,* Roger *Malclerc* 1194, Walter *Mauclerc* 1207, John *Manclerk* 1428 NorwW, 'bad clerk'. Walter *Mauclerc* (1275 RH) was bishop of Carlisle and Pierre de Bretagne, similarly nicknamed, was unfrocked (Dauzat); cf. *Bunclark* 'good clerk'; *Mauduit, Mawditt, Mudditt,* Gunfridus *Maledoctus* 1084, William *Malduit* 1086, 'badly educated', *Mauleverer* 'poor harrier', *Marwood,* William *Malreward* 1169 P, Richard *Malregard* c1170 Riev, Walter *Marreguard, Marreward* Hy 2 Bart, OFr **malregard, *malreward* 'evil regard, evil eye', preserved in Goadby Marwood (Lei).

One origin of *Welcome, Wellicome* is 'well-kempt', 'well-combed', Ralph *Welikempt* 1275 SRWo, Lovekyn *Welikembd* 1285 *Ass* (Ess), referring to well-kept hair or a well-trimmed beard, later to one of elegant appearance. *Welfitt*, William *Welifed* 1195 P (D), 'the well-fed', would apply to a well-nourished body; cf. William *Welshapen* 1240 *Ass* (Sf).

NICKNAMES FROM COSTUME, ACCOUTREMENTS, WEAPONS, ETC.

The modern forms of *Greenhead* and *Whitehead* conceal the fact that originally the second element was sometimes *-hod* and that these nicknames were bestowed on men with a partiality for a green or a white hood. So, too, with *Fairhead, Blackett*, Ralph *Blachod* 1327 SRSf, *Colledd*, John *Colhod* ib., 'coal-black', *Horrod*, Richard *Horhod* 1293 AssSt, from OE *hār* 'grey' and Stephen *Greyhod* 1327 *SR* (Ess), whilst *Hoodlass, Hoodless* denoted one who wore no hood and John *Furhode* 1301 SRY preferred fur and Walter *Straythod* (ib.) a narrow hood. *Gildersleeve*, Roger *Gyldenesleve* 1275 RH (Nf), 'the man with the golden sleeve', appears to be the sole survivor of *sleeve*, though we formerly had William *Grenescleue* 1246 AssLa and Richard *Blacsleve* 1334 SRK and Geoffrey *Curtemanche* c1284 Lewes, 'short sleeve'. With *Broadbelt* we may compare *Broadribb* and *Brodribb*, and William *Brodgirdel* 1275 RH (Nt), all indicative of girth, and the obsolete William *Wytbelt* 1277 Wak and Henry *Fayrgirdel* 1301 FrLei.

Of the undoubted nicknames from dress all that remain are *Hussey*,[1] *Hosey*, on record from 1086 as *Hosed, Hosatus*, from OFr *hosed*, Lat *hosatus* 'booted' and *Shorthose*, surviving also as *Shorthouse, Shorters* and *Shortus*, a translation of the French *Curthose* 'short boot', contrasted with (Robert) *langhose* 1277 *Ely* (Sf). To this we may add Ernulf *Letherhose* 1199 P (O), William *Redschoz* 1332 SRSt, 'red shoes', Robert *Heighschoo* 1327 SRY 'high', William *Smalsho* 1378 PNEss 481, but the surviving *Smallshaw* is from a place of that name in the West Riding, William *Welschod* 1260 AssY, and certain compounds of *kirtle* and *skirts*: Adam *Sortkyrtell* 1256 AssNb 'short gown', Robert *Witkertel* 1316 Wak 'white', John *Grenekertil* 1351 AssEss, Henry *Sidskirte* 1332 SRLa 'narrow', John *Longskirts* 1662 HTEss.

[1] Also from ME *huswyf* 'mistress of a family', 'wife of a householder'.

Metonymic occupational-names from costume, animals, etc.

Such simple names as *Hood, Cape* and *Cope, Capp* and *Mantell* are too frequent and too vague in meaning to serve as nicknames. They are a few of a very large number of surnames like *Buckle, Meale, Pearl, Pouch* and *Rope* where the name of the article made or the commodity dealt in was used by metonymy for the maker or dealer. So, too, surnames from animals like *Colt* and *Goate* may not only be nicknames from some similarity to the animal in appearance or habit but may also denote the man in charge of these animals. In some instances we still have a series as *Colt, Coltard* 'colt-herd', *Colter* and *Coltman, Goate, Goatman*, just as we have *Cheese, Cheeseman*, and *Cheesewright* and once had *Cheeser*. Of the medieval *Garlek, Garleker* and *Garlekmonger*, only *Garlick* now remains. We have already seen that *Kitchener, Pantry, Buttery*, etc., in spite of their original local form, must be occupational-names and that *Hall, Haller* and *Hallman* denote a servant at the hall. These metonymic formations are exceedingly common and provide a reasonable interpretation of names difficult to explain as nicknames.

Conclusive proof requires a number of examples where the same man is named both literally and metonymically from his occupation. Specific examples are not common but there is enough evidence for reasonable certainty. In *Cofferer* 'maker of coffers' and *Coverur* 'one who covers or roofs buildings', the final -*er*, -*ur* would inevitably be slurred in pronunciation, giving the modern *Coffer* and *Cover*. In *Peever* and *Peffer* we have the same man, William *Peyforer, le Peyfrer, Peyfore* 1293, 1301, 1324 FFEss, named from both OFr *peyvre* 'pepper' and *peyvrier* 'pepperer', whilst AFr *wafre* 'wafer' and *wafrer* 'maker or seller of wafers' alternate in the name of Simon *le Wafre, le Wafrer* 1212 Fees (He), 1221–2 AssSa, AssWa (He). Once, at least, the simple *Hawk* is used by metonymy for 'hawker' or with reference to the holding of land by providing hawks for the lord. In 1130 (P), Ralph *Hauoc* owed the exchequer two 'Girfals', gerfalcons or hawks.

In the following instances, both the literal and the metonymic form of the name is used of the same man: William *Slinger, Slinge* c1248 Bec (Wa), Gilbert *le Palfreyman, le Palefray* 1264 Misc (Y); Matilda *le Welker* or *le Welke* 'seller of whelks' 1279 RH(C); Richard *le Sporiere, Sporon* 1281 LLB B; Hamo *Hode, Hodere* 1317 AssK; Thomas

Parment or *Parmenter* 1509 LP (Nth).[1] Ralf *Belancier* (sic), i.e. scale-maker, who, according to Stow, was sheriff of London in 1316, is called in the *French Chronicle of London* Rauf *la Balance*.[2] Henry *le Gaugeor*, collector of Customs in the port of London (1306 Fine), William *le Gaugeour*, gauger of wines in England, Ireland and Wales (1327 Fine) and Nicholas *Gauge*, of the office of the tronage of wools in Lynn (1330 Fine) owed their surnames to their occupation, now *Gager, Gaiger*, from AFr *gaugeour* 'gauger', 'exciseman', and *Gage, Gauge*, from ONFr *gauge* 'a fixed measure', metonymic for a measurer or tester.[3] *Troner* was the official in charge of the *tron* or weighing machine, called also *Poyser, Poyzer*. The metonymic *Trone* still survives, William *Trone* 1285 FFSf. With this evidence, there need be no hesitation in accepting as metonymic occupation-names *Horsnail, Horsnell* 'maker of horse-shoe nails', *Matters*, Alexander *Matras* 1379 PTY, identical in meaning with Alice *Matresmaker* 1381 ib., *Plumb* for plumber (now *Plummer*), *Plume* for *Plumer* 'dealer in feathers' and a host of others.

To return to costume. *Burnell*, except when occasionally a personal-name, is used only as a nickname for one with a brown skin or brown hair; cf. Chaucer's Daun Burnell the Asse (B 4502) and Daun Russell the fox (B 4524). But *Scarlett*, OFr *escarlate* 'scarlet' can hardly have been used as a nickname for a scarlet face is too ephemeral for permanent description. It must be metonymic for a dealer in 'scarlet', the name of a cloth already in 1182 (P), 'x ulnis de escarlato'. Other cloths, too, were named from their colour and when used as surnames must refer to makers or dealers: *Blanchet, Blanket*, a surname from 1275, from OFr *blankete*, ME *blankett* 'white or undyed woollen stuff used for clothing', first recorded in NED c1300, but in use in 1182 (P), 'ix ulnis de blanchet'. In 1363, a statute to restrict the dress of the peasantry ordered that all people not possessing 40 shillings' worth of goods and chattels were not to wear any manner of cloth but blanket and russet wool of twelvepence[4]— cheap and too common to serve as a nickname distinctive of dress. *Blewett* and *Bluett*, OFr *bleuet* 'bluish', a surname already in 1086,

---

[1] Of these, there survive *Sling, Slinger*; *Palfrey, Palfreyman*; *Welker*; *Spurrier* 'spur-maker', *Spurren* 'spur'; *Hodd, Hood, Hodder* 'maker of hoods'; *Parmenter, Parmiter*, 'tailor'.

[2] Weekley, *Surnames*, p. 166. Survives as *Ballance, Ballans*.

[3] In 1356 the Gauger of wine received a fee of 1*d*. per tun, half paid by the buyer, half by the seller (G. E. Unwin, *Finance and Trade under Edward III* (Manchester, 1918)), p. 283.

[4] C. W. Bardsley, *English Surnames* (London, 1875), p. 455.

was certainly the name of a cloth dyed blue,[1] but Dauzat notes that *bleu* in the Middle Ages was used of 'le teint blafard', dull, wan, lurid, and cites examples referring to the face and cheeks, a parallel to the English *Blaw*, *Blowe*, Randulphus *Bla* 1202 AssL, Richard *Blawe* 1260 AssC, from ME *bloo*, *blow(e)*, a midland and southern form of ON *blá* 'livid, leaden-coloured'.[2]

Here, too, belongs *Burnett*, OFr *burnete* 'dark brown', also 'a wool-dyed cloth of superior quality, originally of a dark-brown colour' (1284 NED), again much older: *caligas de burneto* 'hose of burnet' (1200 Oseney), *una roba de burnetta* (*cum bissis, cum cuniculis*), a dark-brown robe, apparently trimmed with doe-skin or rabbit-fur (1214 P). *Burrell* and *Borell* also derive from a coarse woollen cloth (OFr *burel* 'reddish-brown'), so common that, in 1172, 2,000 ells were bought at Winchester for the soldiers in Ireland and the coarser and cheaper Cornish burels were distributed to the poor by the royal almoner.[3] So common was this as a material for the dresses of the poorer classes that *borel-folk* came to be used as a regular term for the uneducated. The surname is clearly metonymic for *Bureller*, frequent in medieval London for dealers in *borel*. They seem to have been drapers, members of the capitalist or at least of the employer class, distinct from weavers with whom they had frequent disputes.[4] *Lambswool*, Adam *Lambeswulle* 1295 AssCh, would appear to be a costume-name, a distinctive dress, as is *Slaven*, *Slavin*, Roger *Sclavin* 1177 P (Sf), from ME *sclaveyn*, *slavyne*, OFr *esclavine* 'a pilgrim's mantle' (c1290 NED), from MedLat *sclavina*, apparently from *sclavus* 'slave' or *Sclavus* 'Slav', described by Cotgrave as a seaman's gown, sufficiently distinctive for notice and comment.

Surnames from equipment, weapons and armour

Numerous surnames refer to the weapons, defensive and offensive, with which man protected his body. These are not easy to classify. They may be metaphorical like *Fortescue*, *Foskew* 'strong shield', a doughty protector, or metonymic, *Sword*, *Soord*, for *Sworder* 'a maker of swords' and *Spear* for *Spearman*. In *Dagger*, the reference

---

[1] Cf. iiij pannis de *blueto* emptis pro clericis . . . iiij ulnis et dimidia *blueti* pro Pikardo 1290 Wenlok, p. 166.
[2] Dauzat explains the French *Bluet* as 'blue-eyed', from the cornflower (Fr *bluet*, *bleuet*).
[3] L. F. Salzman, *English Industries in the Middle Ages* (Oxford, 1923), p. 197.
[4] Ibid., p. 199.

may be to either a maker or seller, to one known regularly to carry a dagger, or to one proficient in its use. *Burdon, Bourdon,* OFr *bourdon* 'a pilgrim's staff' is a real nickname. Common terms must refer to makers or dealers. By the Assize of Arms of 1181 every adult man had to be provided with at least a knife and a staff or club, an ordinance which must have led to a great increase in their manufacture and sale, hence such names as *Club, Staff, Kidgell* 'cudgell', *Baston,* Ernald *Bastun* 1191 P (OE *bastun* 'stick'), *Hansard, Handsheart,* OFr *hansard* 'cutlass, poniard', *Trunchion, Trounson* 'truncheon, club'. From armour we have: *Armer, Armour, Larmer,* metonymic for armourer, *Gamson, Gameson,* William *Gambeson* 1297 MinAcctCo, a wadded doublet worn under the armour; *Habbeshaw,* William *le Haubergier* 1201, a maker of hauberks or coats of mail; *Habershon Habberjam, Habbijam,* a maker of habergeons, sleeveless jackets of mail or scale armour; *Harness,* Philip *Harneis* 1285, from OFr *harneis,* for a maker of harness or suits of mail (cf. William *le Hernesemaker* 1300 LoCt).

When we pass to the artillery, the reference is clearly occupational, to the man who worked the machine: *Quarrell,* OFr *quarel* 'a short, heavy, square-headed arrow or bolt for cross-bow or arbalest', an arbalester; *Mangnall,* OFr *mangonelle* 'a war-engine for throwing stones'; *Springall,* OFr *espringalle,* AFr *springalde* 'an engine of the nature of a bow or catapult used in medieval warfare for throwing heavy missiles'.

Two undoubted nicknames, both early and well documented, and both with other interpretations, are *Mallett*[1] and *Martell.* The latter is a nickname from OFr *martel* 'hammer', the *martel de fer,* the iron hammer or mace of medieval warfare. The first bearer of the name was Charles, son of Pépin d'Héristal 'qui martela les Sarrasins' at the battle of Poitiers in 732 and was thenceforth Charles *Martel.* In England, the name may later be occupational, 'smith'; cf. Geoffrey *Handhamer* 1296 SRSx,[2] John *Handax* 1327 SRY. These less martial implements were probably metonymic for workmen proficient in their use, as *Pigache,* Richard *Pigace* 1176 P, from Norman–Picard *pigache,* Fr *Pigasse,* 'pick-axe, hatchet', and the obsolete Roger *Bilhok* 1243 AssSo, Thomas *Brodax* 1214 P.

We may conclude with two rare surnames the exact significance of which is not clear: *Paffard,* Willelm *Pafard* 1100–30 OEByn, from

---

[1] For *Mallett, v.* pp. 135, 223 *supra.*
[2] NED has no example of *hand-hammer* between 1050 and 1606.

OFr *pafard* 'shield', a large oval or quadrangular buckler carried by arbalesters, and *Tarves, Tarvis*, Nicholas *Talewaz* 1199 FFEss, Robert *Talvace* 1296 Wak, Thomas *Taleuas* 1327 SRSf, William *Turphas, Turface* 1400, 1424 *Petre* (Ess), Robert *Talface* 1520 NorwCt, Margaret *Talves* 1524 SRSf, explained by Cotgrave as:

'*Talevas*, a large, massive, and old-fashioned targuet, having, in the bottome of it a pike, whereby, when need was, it was stuck into the ground.'

Nicknames from coins and numbers

Penney, Penning and *Halfpenny, Halpenny* are usually nicknames from the coin. Halfpenny Field in Elm (Cambs) was so called because the tenants had to contribute a half-penny for each acre to the repair of the neighbouring Needham Dyke. Some such custom or a similar rent may account for the nicknames. *Farthing*, sometimes from ON *Farðegn*, ODa *Farthin*, more often local, used of a measure of land, must occasionally have been a nickname. Both John *Ferthinge* and Margery *Halpenny* were tax-payers in Pershore in 1327 (SRWo). *Shilling* is always from the coin. There is no medieval evidence for a personal-name.

Besant is from ME *besant*, OFr *besan*, Lat *byzantius* (*nummus*), a gold coin first minted at Byzantium. The earliest reference to the coin is c1179 (Bart), 20 years earlier than that in NED (c1200), but the first bearer of the name, Lefwin *Besant*, was a London moneyer in 1168 (P). Why these coin-names were given, it is usually impossible to say. Thomas Beckett, archbishop of Canterbury, was born in London in 1118 and before entering the Church received a business training in the office of a relative Osbert *Huitdeniers*, a rich City magnate and justiciar of London in 1141, whose nickname 'eight-pence' must have been given in jest. Where there is no clue of any kind, speculation is of no value.

Ducat, William *Duket* 1314 FFSf, is from OFr *ducat*, It *ducato* 'a gold coin', late Lat *ducatus* 'duchy', so called because when first coined c1140 in the Duchy of Apulia, they bore the legend: 'sit tibi, Christe, datus, quem tu regis, iste *ducatus*', 'may this *ducatus* (a pun on *ducat* and *duchy*) which Thou dost rule be given to Thee, O Christ'. It also bore the effigy of a *duca* or duke. *Ducat* is a 'restored' spelling; it is spelled *duket* by Chaucer and *ducket* by Shakespeare, and the surname has been inextricably mixed with *Ducket* (of varied origin).

Nicknames of this type still survive: *Hallmark, Allmark, Almack, Awmack,* Robert *Alfmarck* 1279, Adam *Halfmark* 1296, Emma *Halmark* 1324, John *Awmack* 1722, 'half-a-mark'; *Dismore, Dimmer,* Robert *Dimars* 1220, Roger *Dismars* 1225, John *Dismore* 1576, OFr *dix mars* 'ten marks'; cf. also Alan *de duabus marcis* 1202, Batholomew *Dewmars* 1334, 'two marks', which may have been absorbed by *Dimmer*; *Sissmore, Sizmore,* Thomas *Sysmore* 1432 *Petre* (Ess), 'six marks'; *Seppings, Sippings,* Nycolas *Sevenpennys,* Hamond *Sepens* 1524 SRSf, Francis *Sipins,* George *Sepings* 1674 HTSf, 'seven-pence'; *Twopenny, Tuppenny, Tippeny,* Thomas *Twapens* 1260 AssY, Thomas *Twapenis* 1297 SRY, 'twopence'. *Moneypenny,* Richard *Monipenie* 1211, *Manypeny* 1229, 'many pennies', may be a nickname for a rich man or, ironically, for a poor one. To these we may add *Darree, Darry, Denre, Denry* and *Derry,* William *Darri, Derri* 1200 Cur, from OFr *darree, denree* 'penny-worth'; cf, Fr *Danré, Danrée* 'surnom probable de marchand' (Dauzat).

Obsolete coin-names include: William *Duzedeners* 1190 Eynsham, Thomas *Quatresoz* 1300 LLB C 'four sous', Alicia *fouerpenys* 1285 Pinchbeck (Sf), John *Fifmark* 1335 AD ii, John *Fivepeni* 1279 RH (O), Henry *Sixpons* 1381 AssWa, Andrew *Tenmarc,* Fulco *Twelpenes,* Geoffrey *Tventimarc* 1279 RH (C).

Certain modern surnames consist solely of a number, *Two, Twelve, Twelves, Eighteen* or *Eteen,* for none of which have we any early material. *Fower* (Ralph *Four* 1219 AssL) is from OFr *fouuer,* Lat *focarius,* 'keeper of the hearth' or a scavenger (Fowar or clensare, *mundator, purgator* PromptParv); *Six* is a variant of *Sicks,* for *Siggs* or *Sykes; Forty* is local, from places like Forty Green or Forty Hill. The existence of such names is attested by Matilda *Eleven* 1275 SRWo, Elizabeth *Thirteen* 1780 SfPR. A hint of their origin is given by the alternative names of William *Vintesisdeners* 1251 FrLei, called also William *Sixandtwenti* 1271 LeiBR; cf. also Simon *Sixanttwenti* 1253 FrLei. But no satisfactory explanation is forthcoming. Weekley's speculations are unsupported by evidence and unlikely. He cites Robert *Quinzanz* '15 years' and suggests that *Eighteen* may have represented the age of an ancestor, but that will not explain the Lancashire *Twoyearold* (William *Two yer old* 1311 Ronton) or Thomas *Twowynterold* 1327 *SR* (Ess), Adam *Fivewinterald* 1246 AssLa, Margaret *Tenwynter* 1476 SIA xii, or Laurence *Sixweeks* 1570 FrLei. Nor have we any parallel for the equation of *Twelve* with *Twelftree* or *Twelvetree(s).* The latter is probably local, from residence near a group of 12 trees, a place-name similar to Sevenoaks. No English names are known parallel with the French Robertus *Quatuor Boum* or Geffroi *as ij Moutons*, the man who owned four oxen or two sheep. Dauzat explains the French *Trois, Cinq, Dix* and *Dixneuf* as names given to foundlings from the day of the month on which they were found abandoned. We know nothing of the naming of foundlings in medieval England. More likely is his explanation of *Cinq-sols* 'two-pence-halfpenny', an old hereditary surname of the family of Cinq-sols de Marolles, a nickname from the real or supposed poverty of these nobles. We may get a glimpse of the truth from the fifteenth-century classification of nails according to their price per 100: Threpeny nayl, fourepenynayll, fyfepenynayll, sixpenynayle, x peny nayle.[1] All these surnames cannot refer to nailmakers but it is possible that some, at least, of the nicknames may be from the salesman's repeated shouting of the price of his wares.

Bardsley explains *Twentyman* as 'the twynterman', one who tended twinters, i.e. two-year-old beasts. But his examples are all late and all *Twentyman*. Lower, again without evidence, took the surname as a translation of *vintenarius*, a fourteenth-century name for the officer in command of 20 armed men. He may well have been on the right track, for at Vale Royal in 1278, Carnarvon in 1282 and Harlech in 1286, the labourers were organised on a semimilitary basis under *vintenarii* (foremen or gangers), though, judging from their numbers, their gangs must have been considerably more than the 20 implied by their title;[2] cf. also Robert *Tuelfmen* 1327 SRY, William *Twentipayr* 1315 Wak.

[1] L. F. Salzman, *Building in England* (Oxford, 1952), p. 315.
[2] Salzman, op. cit., p. 54.

Chapter Thirteen

NICKNAMES FROM MENTAL
AND MORAL CHARACTERISTICS

Nicknames denoting mental and moral characteristics, both complimentary and uncomplimentary, are numerous, formed not only from adjectives, *Doughty* and *Daft*, but also from nouns, *Fear*, ME *fere* 'comrade', ME *fere*, OFr *f(i)er* 'fierce', or the noun *fear*, Rogerus *Timor* 1200 Cur, *Sleeper*, abstract terms, *Counsell*, *Wisdom*, and compounds, *Goodlad*, *Truelove*. Many of them are self-explanatory and a list would be long and tedious. Others, as we have seen, are misleading, as the ME meaning of the word differs from that in use today,[1] whilst many preserve terms now rare or obsolete. Very many, too, have completely disappeared as surnames.

Complimentary

Of obvious meaning are *Noble*, *Sage*, *Gay*, *Perfect* and *Parfitt*, *Constant*, *Ready*, *Bold*, *Hardy*, *Meek*, *Valiant*, *Sharp*, *Smart*, *Steady* and *Stern*. But *Hastie* is from OFr *hastif*, *hasti* 'speedy, quick', *Sartin* from OFr *certeyn* 'self-assured, determined', *Fates*, *Laffeaty*, William

---

[1] For *Sadd, Moody, Simple.* v. pp. 4, 5.

Affaitied 1162, Henry *la Faitie* 1199, William *Fayt* 1359, from OFr *afaitié* 'affected, skilful, prudent'.

Quant is from ME *coint, quoint*, Lat *cognitus*, originally 'knowledgeable', 'skilful'; in French it came to mean 'neat, fine, trim', a sense used derogatively in the diminutive *Quantrell, Quintrell*, OFr *cointerel* 'a beau, a fop'; in English it meant 'famous', 'remarkable', 'curious, strange', 'cunning, crafty', later used to denote a whimsical and antique prettiness. Chaucer uses *queynte* in a variety of senses, all different from that of today, 'strange', 'curious', 'unfamiliar', 'ingenious', 'skilful', 'clever', 'crafty'. Similarly he uses *Coy* (OFr *coi*, earlier *quei*, Lat *quietus* 'quiet, still') for 'quiet', not in its modern sense of 'bashful', with reference to the smile of the Prioress, 'ful symple and coy', whilst the Host addresses 'Sire Clerke of Oxenford':

> 'Ye ryde as coy and stille as doth a mayde
> Were newe spoused, sittynge at the bord;
> This day ne herde I of youre tonge a worde' (E 2)

Ventre, Venture and *Vigar, Vigor* are from OFr abstract nouns, *aventure* 'chance, hazard' and *vigor* 'vigour, liveliness', *Venters, Ventrers, Ventris* and *Vigars, Viggers, Vigrass, Vigus*, from the corresponding adjectives *aventurous* 'the venturous' and *vigoro(u)s* 'hardy, lusty, strong'. Unsuspected meanings are found in *Root* (OE *rōt* 'glad, cheerful'), *Rank* (OE *ranc* 'strong, proud'), *Baud* (OFr *baud* 'gay, sprightly'), *Bream* (OE *brēme* 'vigorous, fierce', earlier 'famous, noble'), *Bragg* (ME *brag(ge)* 'brisk, lively, mettlesome'), *Bean* (ME *bēne* 'pleasant, genial, kindly'), *Crank, Cronk* (ME *cranke* 'lusty, vigorous', 'in high spirits'), *Crease* (OE *crēas* 'fine, elegant'), *Cruise, Cruse, Crews* (ME *crus(e)* 'bold, audacious'), *Fane, Fayne, Vane, Vayne* (OE *fægen*, ME *fein, fane* 'glad, well-disposed', proverbially opposed to 'fools': 'Fayne promys makyth folys fayne'), *Lythe, Lyde* (OE *līðe* 'mild, gentle', but now 'pliant, flexible, active'), *Toward* (ME *toward* 'compliant, docile').

From terms no longer in use (or rare) come: *Leal* (ME *lele*, OFr *leial* 'loyal, faithful'), with the abstract *Lawtey, Leuty, Lewtey* (OFr *leaute* 'loyalty'), *Dowsett, Dowcett* (AFr *doucet*, a diminutive of *doux* 'sweet to eye or ear, pleasing, aggreeable'), *Edmead, Edmed, Edmett, Edmott, Eadmeades*, Gervase *Eadmede*, Roger *Edemede* 1334 SRK, Joan *Edmed* 1485 CantW, Robert *Edmets* 1604 StaplehurstPR (K) (OE *ēadmēde* 'humble'), *Figgis* (AFr *fikeis*, OFr *ficheis* 'faithful'), *Frais, Frose* (OFr *freis* 'full of vigour, active', 'blooming, looking healthy or youthful'), *Galliard, Gaillard, Gaylard, Gaylord, Gallard*

S   253

(OFr *gaillard*, ME *gaillard*, *galiard* 'lively, brisk; gay, full of high spirits'), *Glew*, *Glue* (OE *glēaw* 'wise, prudent'), *Happe* (OE *gehæp* 'fit'), *Hendy* (ME *hendy* 'courteous, kind, gentle'), *Kedge*, *Ketch* (an East Anglian dialect word, 'brisk, lively'; '*Kygge* or ioly' Prompt-Parv), *Orpet* (OE *orped* 'stout' strenuous, valiant, bold'), *Prew*, *Prow*, *Prue* (ME *prew*, *prue*, OFr *prou*, *preu* 'valiant, doughty'), with *Prewett*, *Pruett*, a diminutive of this; *Prowse*, *Prouse*, *Prewse*, *Pruce* (ME, OFr *prous*, *prouz* 'valiant, doughty'), *Sturdee*, *Sturdy*, *Stordy* (OFr *estordet*, *estourdi* 'reckless, violent', in ME 'impetuously brave, fierce in combat'), *Tait*, *Teyte* (ON *teitr* 'cheerful, gay'), *Worledge*, *Wolledge*, *Woollage* (OE *weorþlīc* 'worthy, noble, distinguished').

Abstract nouns

Courage is sometimes local, from Cowridge End (Beds), but was also undoubtedly a nickname, John *Curage* 1249 AssW, from OFr *corage*, *curage*, used as an adjective, 'stout' of body. *Danger*, too, is an abstract name, from OFr *dangier* in one of its early senses, 'power, dominion' or 'hesitation, reluctance, coyness'; cf. Gerard *Daungerous* 1275 RH (L), used by Chaucer with the meanings 'power over a person', 'restraint', 'reluctance', 'distant manner', 'haughtiness', hence 'difficult to approach, distant, haughty, grudging'. OFr *purchas*, too, had a variety of meanings, 'eager pursuit', 'pillage' and was used as a name for messengers and couriers. Bardsley notes 'Purchase the Pursuivant' in the reign of Henry VI. But the general meaning of the verb was 'to acquire' and the noun is found in Chaucer in the senses 'acquisition, profit, gain from begging'. It was a common surname from 1190 and survives in a variety of forms including: *Purchase*, *Purches*, *Purchese*, *Purkess*, *Pirkiss*, *Porkess*, *Porcas*. In ME, OFr *deintié*, *dainté*, now *Dainty* and *Denty*, was both a noun 'pleasure, tit-bit' and an adjective 'fine, handsome, pleasant'. It is ultimately from Lat *dignitat-em*, OFr *deintiet*, and the modern surnames *Dainteth*, *Daintith* and *Dentith* (Agnes *Deynteth* 1379 NottBR) preserve the archaic ME *deinteth*.

Among abstract nouns of obvious meaning, we may note *Bliss*, *Chance*, sometimes, perhaps, for a gambler, like *Hazard*, *Hasard*, *Hassard*, from OFr *hasard*, ME *has(s)ard* 'a game at dice', metonymic for (John) *Hasardour* 1366 ColchCt, 'a dicer, gamester'; *Pride*, with *Orgill*, *Orgles* (OFr *orgeuil* 'pride'); *Reason*, *Raisin*, *Raison*, *Rayson* must, at times, be from ME *resoun*, *reisun*, OFr *reison* 'reason';

Henry *Raisun* 1221 *ElyA*, Walter *Reysun* 1251 AssY, Geoffrey *Resun* 1275 RH (Sf), Henry *Reson* 1279 RH (O). But it may also be either a nickname from OE *ræsn* 'a beam', 'one stout and solid as a beam' or metonymic for a maker of beams called *walplates* or *sideresons* or for a workman who placed them in position; cf. '4 beams called 'rasewepeces' [*sic*] 1286, 'le resin' of the porch of the Constable's hall at the Tower 1348, 'raysynnys' 1415.[1] Here, too, belong *Boast* 'vain talk', *Burr* 'a burr', used by Shakespeare of one who sticks like a burr, a person difficult to shake off, *Marvell* (cf. William *le Merveillus* 1186 P), *Plenty*, Simon *Plente* 1230 P (OFr *plente* 'abundance'), *Sollas*, Robert *Solace* 1269 AssNb (ME *solas*, OFr *solaz* 'comfort') which confirms *Comfort* as an abstract name (William *Cumfort* 1269 AssSo), from ME *cumfort*, OFr *cunfort* 'strengthening, encouragement, aid, succour, support', used of one who strengthens or supports, a source of strength. But this is also a late development in Surrey of *Comport*. Comforts Farm in Oxted owes its name to the family of Ambrose *Comporde* (t. Eliz), whilst Comfortsplace Farm in Godstone is *Comports Place* in 1559 and is to be associated with a family which appears as (*de*) *Cumpwrthe* 1204, *Compworthe* 1294 and *Comport* 1601 (PNSr 317, 334). Bardsley, too, notes Richard *Comport* alias *Comfort* of Chislehurst.

Less obvious are: *Manchip, Manship* (OE *gemǣnscipe* 'community, fellowship'), *Theedam, Theedom* (ME *þeodam*, *þeedom* 'thriving, prosperity'), *Worship* (OE *weorþscipe* 'worship, honour, dignity'). *Prudence* is an early woman's name and the surname is probably always a metronymic. *Marriage* does not belong here. It is always of local origin and a warning against relying on modern forms for etymologies of undocumented names. The present spelling dates only from the seventeenth century, Alice *Marriage* 1616 Bardsley (Wa), Robert *Marriage* 1663 ER 57 (Ess). In Essex and Suffolk it derives from a lost place in Finchingfield or Aythorpe Roding, OE (*ge*)*mǣre-hæcc* 'boundary-gate', found as a surname as William *Marhach*, *Mar(r)ach* 1377 AssEss, Widdow *Marrage*, Thomas *Marridge* 1662 HTEss, in Kent, Joan *Marach* 1413 CantW, from Marriage Farm (K), 'boundary-ridge', and in Devon, where it occurs as a surname as *atte Marigge* 1276, probably 'meadow-ridge' (PND 285). All would be pronounced *Marridge* which popular etymology, unconcerned with the real meaning, re-spelled as *Marriage*.

[1] Building, p. 203.

Uncomplimentary

Surnames descriptive of uncomplimentary or unpleasant mental and moral characteristics almost invariably require explanation. We still have *Dullard, Rough, Savage* and *Slack* 'lazy' (also local), but the unfortunate possessors of obviously derogatory names have usually succeeded in shedding them, whilst obsolete terms and French names unintelligible to their bearers have persisted, e.g. the French *Gulliver, Galliver, Gulliford* and *Galliford*, William *Gulafra* 1086, William *Galliford*, Thomas *Gollafer*, William *Gullifer* 1664 HTSo, from OFr *goulafre* 'glutton', a common name, and the rarer French *Saffer, Saffir*, Robert *le Saffere* 1275 SRWo, from OFr *saffre* 'glutton' still survive, but the English Simon *le Glutun* 1201 P (Nt) has completely disappeared, though, curiously enough, both *Greed* and *Greedy* persist, whilst *Best* 'the beast' owes its survival to a popular belief that the name was one to be proud of and *Doll* 'foolish' was not associated with folly.

Job, Jobe, Jope, Jopp, Jubb, Jupe, and *Jupp* form a complicated series of more than one origin. The variation between *Jop* and *Job* is similar to that in *Gepp* and *Gebb*. One source is undoubtedly the Hebrew *Job* 'hated, persecuted', found as a personal-name from 1185 to at least 1296 in the forms *Jop, Jubb* and *Job*, a frequent character in medieval plays. But we have also, without doubt, a nickname, Matthew *le Jop* (Edw III), from OFr *jobe* 'a fool', and also from ME *jubbe, jobbe*, a large vessel for liquor, holding four gallons, hence one who could carry that quantity, or occupational, a maker of *jubbes*, and also a maker of *jupes*, 'long woollen garments for men', from OFr, ME *jube, jupe*, in ME used also of a light surcoat worn over armour and a rough or padded garment worn under armour.[1]

So numerous are names of this class that we can only take them as they come: *Bask* (ME *baisk, bask*, ON *beiskr* 'bitter, acrid'); *Boggis, Boggers, Boggs* (ME *bogeys* 'inclined to bluster or bragg, puffed up, bold'); *Breare* (OE *brǣr* 'prickly thorn-bush', 'sharp as brere', Chaucer); *Buffard* (OFr *bouffard* 'often puffing, much blowing, swelling up, strutting out; also swelling with anger, Cotgrave); John *Bunglere* 1368 *ERO*; *Crust* (OFr *crouste* 'crust of bread', used of one hard as crust, obstinate, stubborn); *Chopin, Chopping* (OFr *chopine*, an old measure; '*Chopine* a chopine; or the Parisien halfe pint; almost

---

[1] For this, *v.* the article on *Jumper* in E. Weekley, *Words Ancient and Modern* (London, 1946), pp. 60–2.

as big as our whole one (Cotgrave); cf. Fr *chopiner* 'to tipple'; 'tippler'); *Craske* 'fat or lusty'; *Deuters* (from ME *duten*, OFr *duter* 'to hesitate'; 'timid or wavering in opinion, one who dilly-dallies'); *Droop* (ME *drup* 'dejected, sad or gloomy'); *Dwelly* (OE *dweollic* 'foolish, erring'); *Gauche* (OFr *gauche* 'left-handed, awkward'); *Geake, Jeeks, Jex* (ME *geke, gecke* 'fool, simpleton'); *Gedge* (ME *gegge*, a contemptuous term applied to both men and women); *Gerish* (ME *gerysshe* 'changeful, wild, wayward'); *Giddy, Geddie* (OE *gydig* 'possessed of an evil spirit', 'mad, insane'); *Gigg* (ME *gigge* 'a flighty, giddy girl', used as a nickname for a man); *Grill* (ME *grille* 'fierce, cruel'); *Harker* (a derivative of ME *herkien* 'to listen', an eavesdropper); *Jealous* (ME, OFr *gelos* 'wrathful, furious'); *Keech, Keetch* (ME *keech*, a lump of congealed fat; the fat of a slaughtered animal rolled up into a lump; used in the sixteenth century for a butcher; 'Did not goodwife Keech the Butcher's wife come in then?' (Henry IV); 'I wonder that such a Keech can with his very bulke Take up the Rayes o' th' beneficiall Sun, And keepe it from the Earth' (Henry VIII), where the reference is to Cardinal Wolsey, a butcher's son; *Langrish*, Robert *le Langerus* 1200 Cur; *Mallory*, Geoffrey *Maloret* 1086, Richard *Mallorei* 1155 (OFr *maloret* (maleuré, maloré) 'the unfortunate, the unlucky'); *Mussard* (OFr *musard* 'absent-minded, stupid'); *Pretty, Pritty* (OE *prættig* 'crafty, cunning'); *Ramage, Ramadge* (OFr *ramage* 'wild', used of a hawk 'living in the branches', MedLat **ramaticus*, from *ramus* 'branch'); *Samways* (OE *sāmwīs* 'dull, foolish'); *Sorrie* (OE *sārig* 'sorry, sad'); *Soures*, Gilbert *le Sour* 1279 RH (OE *sūr* 'sour'); *Stunt* (OE *stunt* 'foolish'); *Tardew, Tardif* (OFr *tardif*, Fr *tardieu* 'slow, sluggish'); *Treacher* (OFr *trecheor* 'deceiver, cheat'); *Wroth, Wroath* (OE *wrāð* 'angry, fierce').

Compounds of un-, -less and -thorough

Unwin, undoubtedly, at times, a nickname, Walter *þonwyne* 1275 SRWo, i.e. *the onwyne*, from OE *unwine* 'unfriend, enemy', and the curious looking *Onraet*, William *Unred* 1208–13 P 36 (Ch), John *Onrett* 1275 (OE *unrǣd* 'without counsel, evil counsel') are survivals of a common OE formation used also in ME nicknames. The latter was applied to King Ethelred, usually, and mistakenly called 'the Unready'. There is no early authority for the nickname which was a punning allusion to the meaning of his name, *Æðelrǣd* 'noble-counsel', *unrǣd* 'without counsel'. *Shortreed* 'short, limited counsel' also survives; cf. Chaucer's 'My wit is short', William *Thinnewyt* 1285 AssCh and Robert *Smalred* 1176 P (Y), '(of) little counsel'.

Obsolete examples noted are: Ædgarus *unniðing* 1170 P (Nb), 'not a rascal, an honest man'; Leuricus *Unsiker* 1188 BuryS (Sf), 'not free from guilt, danger or doubt, unsure'; William *Unskole* c1200 EChCh; probably OE **unscola* 'not a learner', 'ignorant'; Robert *le Uncuthemon* 1278 AssLa, Adam *Huncouthe* 1379 PTY, 'unknown, strange'; Hugo *Unscriven* 1219 AssY, 'unshriven'; John *Unnyredy* 1334 SRK, Thomas *Untroth* 1522 GildY.

Here, too, we may note certain compounds of OE *lēas* 'free from, void of, destitute of, without'. They are of all types but best treated together. Uncomplimentary nicknames are: *Careless*, *Carless*, *Carloss*, OE *carlēas* 'free from care', probably 'unconcerned, careless'; *Lawless* 'uncontrolled by the law, unbridled, licentious', often for 'lawless-man' or *Outlaw*; *Reckless*, *Reatchlous*, *Rickless* (OE *rēcelēas* 'careless, reckless'); *Thewless*, *Thewlis* (OE *þēawlēas* 'ill-mannered', 'destitute of morals or virtue, vicious'); *Wanlace*, *Wanlass*, *Wanless*, *Wandless*, John *Wanlesse* 1509 LP (ME *wanles* 'hopeless, luckless'); with the obsolete Thomas *Redeles* 1524 SRSf 'without counsel', Robert *Sorhgeles* 1246 AssLa 'sorrow-less', Robert *Wytelas* 1275 SRWo 'witless'.

Lovelace, *Loveless*, *Lowless*, with the variation between *Loveles* and *Lovelas*, must also be 'loveless, without love'. It is just possible that we may sometimes have 'love lass' from ME *las(se)*. cf. Alan *Luveswain* 1166. But the suggested 'love lace', a dandy, is unlikely. OE *laz*, ME *las* meant 'cord'. The sense 'lace' is not recorded in England before 1550 and the surname dates from before 1250. In 1630, in the GreenwichPR, it occurs as Anne *Loverlace*. *Goodless*, *Gudless*, appears to be attested by *Sotelass*, presumably 'sweet lass', as 'good lass', a parallel to the well-documented *Goodlad*, but the only evidence is William *Godlesse* 1525 SRSx, which might well be for 'god-less'. *Hoodless* and *Lockless* we have met earlier. To these we may add: Adam *Sporeles* 1219 AssY 'without spurs', William, John *Blodles* 1199 P, 1346 Pat, John *Peniles* 1332 SRCu, and three referring to the loss of a relative, William *Faderlas* 1198 Cur, 1382 Misc, Walter *le Moderles* 1275 SRWo and John *le Wyfles* 1327 SRSx.

Thorogood, *Thoroughgood* is complimentary and self-explanatory, though there is evidence of confusion with *Thurgood*. But *Goodenough*, *Goodnow*, *Goodner*, *Goodanew*, early and well-attested, is one of a group of names, politely derogatory, reminiscent of the school-

NICKNAMES FROM MORAL CHARACTERISTICS

master's 'Very Fair', either non-committal or damning with faint praise. In fact, our earliest example might well have come from a school report, Wimund *bonus satis* 1184 France (So). This surname has also absorbed *Godecnave* 'good boy or servant'. So, too, *Whitenow*, Thomas *Wytynowe* 1327 SRSo, 'white or fair enough' has absorbed *Whiteknave*. *Oldknow*, William *Aldinoch* 1203 P, is 'old enough', but for what? Obsolete are Robert *Welynogh* 1260 AssC (? a valetudinarian), William *Langynow* 1360 Misc (Do).

Toogood cannot, as Bardsley claims be a variant of *Thurgood* nor s it to be associated with *Duguid* which is Scottish, though it is found in Wiltshire in 1467 (Cl), John *Doogode*. It is a formation parallel to that of *Dolittle*, *Doolittle* and means 'do good'. *Toogood* is well-documented as *Togod* from 1200, *Tougod* 1297, *Togoud* 1332 and in the BishamPR (Berks) it appears as *Toogood* and *Twogood* 1763 and *Tugwood* 1761–70. *Twogood*, *Tugwood* and *Towgood* all survive. It means simply 'too good', an early English variant of 'unco guid' and this meaning appears to be confirmed by *Sargood*, presumably from OE *sār* 'sore' in its sense 'very' as in 'sore afraid'. We still have *Trapnell*, William *Tropisnel* 1183, from the French *trop isnel* 'too swift' and the French have *Trodoux* and *Troplong*. Other examples of this type of name are the obsolete Hamon *Toproud* 1287, Adam *Overprud* 1222, with which we may contrast Hugh *Proud of Noght* 1348 Misc (Y). But *Littleproud* is a hybrid, a compound of OE *lȳtel* and OFr *prut*, *prud* 'worth, value'. The wife of Henry *Lytilprud* (1301 NottBR) was Hawisie '*Crist a pes*' whose constant cry 'Christ have peace' suggests her husband deserved his nickname of 'Little worth'.

Here, too, we may include nicknames, both complimentary and otherwise, where dispositions are characterised by reference to the weather: *Fairweather*, *Fareweather*, ME *fair weder* 'weather not wet or stormy', one with a bright and sunny disposition, *Merryweather*, *Merrywether*, from *merry*, a common term for fair weather, a gay or blithe fellow, *Foulweather*, *Foweather* and *Fowweather*, ME *foul weder* 'wet and stormy', and *Rowedder* 'rough'. *Allweather* and *Many-weathers* blew neither hot nor cold, one whose temper was unpredictable. Now obsolete are: John *Coldwedre* 1327, Alexande *Ilwedyr* 1316, Alexander *Starkweder* 1327 SRSf 'rough'.

Uncomplimentary abstract names

Derogatory abstract names are much less numerous than those which are complimentary: *Atter* (OE *ātor*, ME *atter* 'poison, venom'); *Bismire* (OE *bīsmer*, *bīsmore*, originally 'shame, disgrace', later used of a shameless creature, a lewd person, a pander or bawd); *Gabb* (ME, OFr *gab* 'mockery, deceit'); *Gain, Gaines, Dingain, Engeham, Ingham*, William *Inganie* 1086, Vitalis *Engaine* 1130 (OFr *engaigne*, Lat *ingania* 'trickery, ingenuity'); *Travell* (OFr *travail* 'exertion, trouble, hardship'); *Wrench, Wrinch* (OE *wrenc*, ME *wrench* 'wile, trick, artifice').

Some obsolete nicknames

William *le Cruel* 1251 AssY; Jordan *le Cursede* 1284 Wak; Gille *Fraward* 1230 P (Y); Robert *le Glorius* 1219 Cur (O); Hedolin *le Restif* 1208 FFL; John *Ryghtwyse* 1327 SRSo; John *Rightwise* 'righteous' was High Master of St Paul's School 1522–32; Lecia *Wrangwyse* 1301 SRY, Thomas *Wrangwysh* 1457 FrY (from OE **wrangwīs*, the opposite of *rihtwīs*); John *Skamful* 1301 SRY; Walter *Petitcurteis* 1279 RH (O); Ailwin *Softe* 1195 P (Ess), John *Soft* 1524 SRSf; William *le Wilfulle* 1275 RH (C); Reginald *Gargoyl* 1348 LLB F; Geoffrey *Snob* 1274 RH (Ess); Ralph *Snivel* 1206 Cur (Nf); Thomas *le Spewere* 1247 AssBeds; Baldewin *tyrant* 1169 P (D); Henry *le Weper* 1237 Oseney; Alexander *Mirthe* 1279 RH (C); Gilbert *Rage* 1208 P (O); Hagena *Jugement* 1130 P (Nf); Adam *Testimonie* 1279 RH (O); John *Muchegod* 1275 SRWo; Ralph *Muchelorne* 1327 SRSx; Walter *Nosuch* 1275 RH (W); Petronilla *Notegood* 1375 FFSf; Geoffrey *Nutemuche* 1199 FrLei; Cybilia *Fayrwit* 1327 SRSo; Nicholas *Swetemouth* 1327 SRSf; Thomas *Moderlove* 1296 SRSx; Roger *Scortfrend* 1243 AssDu; William *Teredlad* 1301 SRY.

Chapter Fourteen

NICKNAMES FROM ANIMALS, BIRDS AND FISHES

S OME names of animals and birds are still used as more or less offensive descriptions of people, as goat, pig and goose; duck is often affectionate and in some parts of the country has become a common term of address. All are long-established surnames and may have been used at times with a similar meaning, but the interpretation of these nicknames often presents difficulties. They frequently appear in such forms as William *le gat* 1139, Richard *le Pyge* 1327 SRSa, Hugh *le Gos* 1227, clearly nicknames ascribing to the individual the possession of some quality characteristic of the animal or bird. But, like *Palfrey*,[1] they may be occupational, *Goate* metonymic for *Goater* and *Goatman* 'goat-herd', *Pigge* for the obsolete (Robert) *Pighurde* 1332 SRSx, and *Goose* for *Gooseman* or *Gossard* 'goose-herd'. Even when the nickname origin is certain, more than one meaning may be possible. *Hare* may denote either speed or timidity. Harald Harefoot, the son of Godwin, owed his nickname to his fleet-ness of foot 'for he was a good runner', but already in the fourteenth century the timidity of the hare could be contrasted with the boldness

---

[1] *v.* p. 245.

261

of the lion: 'liouns in halle, and hares in the feld' (c1325 NED). Many
of these nicknames, too, have other origins: *Goate* may be local,
Peter *atte Gote* 1327, 'dweller by the water-course or sluice'; *Lamb*,
sometimes a nickname, Roger *le Lamb* 1279, may be a personal-
name, *Lamb* dispensator 1161, a short form of *Lambert*, or a sign-
name, William *atte Lamme* 1320.

ANIMALS

Scarcely any farmyard animal has failed to provide a nickname, with
the conspicuous exception of the dog and the horse, though these,
too, were once nicknames: Rogerus *Canis* 1200 Cur, Roger *le Doge*
1296 SRSx, with the derivatives Syward *Dogheafd* (now *Doggett*)
1177–95 Seals, Matthew *Doggenecce* 1275 RH, Symon *Doggeschanke*
c1246 Calv, Lucas *Doggestayl* 1279 PN Wt 10. Late OE *docga* is
found, but the common term in OE was *hund* which survives in the
rare *Hound*. We still have, too, *Curr* (1180), the French *Kenn*, William
le Chien (*Chen*) 1183, Simon *le Ken* 1327 (AFr *ken, chen*, OFr *chien*)
and *Brack*, ME *braches* (plur.), OFr *braches*, plural of the diminutive
brachet, which survives as *Brachett* and *Brackett*. From this plural
was apparently deduced an English singular *brache* 'a hound which
hunts by scent'. Nicholas and John *Spanyel* 1327 SRSf were named
from the spaniel, literally 'a Spanish dog' (c1386 NED), now *Span-
yol*; *Tarrier* 'a hunting dog', a surname in 1193, is first recorded in
NED c1440; *Tike*, originally an opprobrious nickname now proudly
accepted by Yorkshire Tikes, was fairly common in the twelfth and
thirteenth centuries, Walter *Tike* 1141–9 Holme, in ME 'a mongrel',
from ON *tík* 'a bitch'; also obsolete are William *Grehound* 1327 *SR*
(Ess), Peter *le Welp* 1289 AssCh (OE *hwelp* 'puppy') and John *Whipet*
1478 ER 54, ultimately from ME *whippen* 'to whip', which came to
mean 'to move smartly', hence the name of this speedy dog.

In France *Cheval* is curiously rare as a surname; it is found occasionally in England, Rober *Cheval* 1208 ChR, where *Horse* has
completely disappeared, though it occurs sporadically from 1150 to
1545. It is probably metonymic for *Horseman*, Walter *Horseman*
c1248 Bec, or for such obsolete names as Aluuin *Horsthein* c1095
Bury, Adam *Horsdrivere* 1199 P, John *Horssecnawe* (i.e. horse-knave)
1292 Glapwell, Ranulf *Horsleche* 14th AD vi, 'horse-doctor', and
William *Horskeper* 1524 SRSf. Ricardus *cum equo* 'with the horse'
1327 *SR* (Hu), suggests that occasionally it denoted the possession of

a horse.[1] *Colt* and *Foale*, however, with the French *Pullen, Pulleyne* (OFr *poulain* 'colt') and *Putterill, Puttrell, Powdrill* (OFr *poutrel* 'colt') are common, with reference, probably, to one of a lively, frisky disposition.

Most of the farmyard animals which gave rise to nicknames are of English origin and need no interpretation: *Boar* (cf. *Wildbore, Wilber*); *Galt, Gault, Gaute* (ME *galte, gaute*, ON *goltr* 'boar'); *Bull* 'corpulent, strong, headstrong', *Bullock, Farr* (OE *fearr* 'bull'); *Calf, Kidd*:

> 'Therto she koude skippe and make game,
> As any kyde or calf folwynge his dame'
> (Chaucer A 3259)

Haver, John *le Haver* c1270 Petre (OE *hæfer* 'he-goat'); *Hogg* (OE *hogg* 'pig'), *Ram* 'strong', *Sheep* 'gentle' and, possibly, 'foolish', 'easily led astray'; *Stede, Steed* (OE *stēda* 'a stud-horse, stallion'); *Steer* (OE *stēor* 'young ox'), *Stirk* (OE *styrc* 'bullock'), *Stott* (ME *stot* 'stallion', 'bullock').

From Scandinavian come *Gait* (ON *geit* 'goat') and *Grice, Griss* (ON *gríss* 'pig'); cf. *Willgrass, Willgress*, Gilbert *Wildegris* Hy II 'wild pig', and from French: *Bellar(s), Bellers*, Hamo *Beler* c1166 DC (OFr *belier* 'ram'), *Boff, Leboff* (OFr *boef* 'bullock'), *Cheever, Chivers* (AFr *chivere, chevre* 'she-goat'), probably 'agile', *Mutton, Motton* (OFr *mouton* 'sheep'), *Purcell, Purssell* (OFr *pourcel* 'little pig'), *Torr* (OFr *tor* 'bull'), *Toril*, William *Torel* 1159 P, 'little bull', *Veal* (OFr *veel* 'calf').[2] To these we should add *Mule, Moule, Mowle* (OE *mūl*, ME *moul* 'mule', which would have become *mowl*, but was ousted in the thirteenth century by OFr *mule*) and *Fortnam, Fortnum* (OFr *fort anon* 'strong young ass').

Catt is not only a pet-form of *Catharine* but also a nickname, Robert *le Cat* 1167, Adam *le Chat* 1203, denoting some feline characteristic or habits, often, no doubt, from the wild cat, Richard *Wildecat* 1176 P. *Puscat* is an old name which, though rare, still survives in London, Robert *Pusekat* 1256 AssNb.

Another group of names comes from animals of the chase: *Buck*, which may be from OE *bucca* 'he-goat' or OE *bucc* 'a male deer', *Brock* (OFr *broque, brock* 'a young stag'), *Brockett* (ME *broket* 'a

---

[1] Nicholas *atte Horse* 1327 SRSx would normally be taken as a sign-name, but it might well mean 'dweller by the low-lying land where horses were kept', often *Horsea* or *Horseye*.
[2] Difficult to distinguish from AFr *viel* 'old' and *Viel*, i.e. *Vial*, from *Vitalis*.

stag in its second year with its first horns'), *Deer* (OE *dēor* 'wild animal', 'deer'), probably 'swift' (cf. *Wilder* 'wild animal'); *Rae* and *Ray*, northern forms of the midland and southern *Roe*, *Roo* (OE, ON *rā*, ME *rō* 'roe-deer'; cf. Chaucer's *the dredful ro*, i.e. 'timid, fearful'); *Roebuck*, *Roback* 'roe-buck', *Prickett* 'a buck in his second year', and *Stagg*, with *Hare* and *Leveret* (AFr *leveret* 'young hare'). With these we may include the obsolete Ranulphus *Polkat* 1327 Pinchbeck 'polecat', and *Rat*, once common. *Mowse* 'mouse' survives as do *Brock* 'badger', *Fox* and the northern *Todd*, with *Colfox* 'coal-fox', the brant fox, Chaucer's 'A col fox, full of sly iniquitee' (A 4405), its ears and tail tipped with black; *Cony* and *Conning* 'rabbit', with *Ferret*; *Squirrell*, *Scurell*, *Squirl* probably denote agility or thrift; *Tortice*, *Tortiss* is ME *tortuse* 'tortoise' 'slow' and Want (OE *want* 'mole').

As a surname, *Wolf* is very seldom without the article *le* in the thirteenth and fourteenth centuries and must be a nickname. It is often equated with the French *Love*, Robert *le Love* 1279 (AFr *louve* 'wolf') and at times alternates with the diminutives *Lovell*, *Lowell* and *Lovett* (AFr *lovel*, *louet* 'wolf-cub') which are common and widely distributed. *Low* (with various other meanings) is OFr *lou* and *Lew* from AFr *leu* 'wolf'.

Bear is undoubtedly, at times, a nickname. The animal was well known to the medieval population from bear baitings and the antics of the beast at fairs. The bear-ward or keeper of performing bears gave rise to the surnames Fulko *le Bereward* 1180 P, Edward *Bereward* 1356 LLB G, and has left his name in Bearward St in Northampton and formerly also in Nottingham and London. *Camell*, usually from Queen or West Camel (So), is occasionally a nickname (1200, 1332), perhaps in the sense 'a great, awkward hulking fellow' as used by Shakespeare, 'A Dray-man, a Porter, a very Camell.' *Leopard*, *Leppard* must be a nickname, but *Tigar* is OFr *Tigier*, OG *Thiodger* 'people-spear', found as a personal-name in DB and as a surname from 1305. *Whale* is another undoubted nickname, Hugh *le Whal'* 1249, from OE *hwæl*, ME *whal* 'whale', used of any large fish, including the walrus, grampus and the porpoise. The original sense was 'roller' and the name may refer to gait or to size and weight. *Lyon*, *Lyons* provides problems. It may be from *Lyon*, the popular pronunciation of *Leo* or *Leon*, *Lyon* son of *Lyon* 1293, or a nickname from the lion, William *le Leoun* 1290, or local, Azor *de Lions* 1159. As the early forms all end in -*s*, this must be from Lyons-la-Forêt

(Eure) and not from the better-known Lyons, earlier *Lugudunum*, French Lyon.

Chaucer thus describes the Miller's wife:

> 'Fair was this yonge wyf, and therwithal
> As any wezele hir body gent and smal' (A 3233)

a comparison one would not expect, but clearly physical, descriptive of her small and slender body. As a surname the English *weasel* has naturally not survived, William *Wesele* 1193 P, Matillis *Wesel'* 1206 AssL, but we still have two nicknames of French origin, with the same meaning, which, as the terms were not part of the general vocabulary, have persisted, both with a clear popular etymology: *Marter, Martyr*, Robert *Lamartre* 1130, William *le marter* 1275 (OFr *martre*, ME *martre, marter* 'weasel') and *Mustell, Mustill, Mustol, Muzzel, Muzzle*, Robert *Mustail* 1175–90, William *Mustol'* 1208 (OFr *musteile, mustoile* 'weasel'). Various meanings are possible, some, no doubt, due to the place of the weasel in folklore. In Suffolk the wife of a labourer had a child ill. She consulted a wise woman who advised her to put milk into a saucer and 'stand it out abroad' at night. Should a weasel drink of the milk, she was to give what it left as a medicine to the child. The Roman *mustelam habes* 'you have a weasel in your house' was applied to an unfortunate whom luck always seemed to pass by. In medieval days, 'the weasel which constantly changes its place' was taken for 'a type of the man, estranged from the word of God, who findeth no rest'. In the west of Ireland weasels are held to be spiteful and malignant, and old witches sometimes take this form. It is considered extremely unlucky to meet a weasel first thing in the morning; still, it would be hazardous to kill it, for it might be a witch and take revenge.[1]

Marmion, found also as *Marmin, Marmon, Marment* and *Marmont* (OFr *marmion* 'marmot', 'monkey'), 'one of those nicknames that the Normans loved to inexorably bestow on one another',[2] early became a family name, being borne by Roger Marmion (1115–18) and his descendants for six generations until the death of Philip Marmion, last of his line c1292. *Ape*, Toraldus *le Ape* 1231 Oseney, no longer survives.

---

[1] v. H. M. Doughty, *Chronicles of Theberton* (1910), p. 130.
[2] J. H. Round, *Feudal England* (London, 1895), pp. 191–4.

Nicknames from birds are at least as common as those from animals; they range from the familiar *Cock* and *Henn* to birds of prey like *Eagle* and *Kite*, songsters like the *Nightingale* and the *Lark*, the harsh-voiced *Crow* and *Rook*, the humble *Sparrow* and the gorgeous *Peacock*. The reason for the nickname is not always clear. *Coot*, originally the name of various swimming or diving birds, especially the Guillemot, was later restricted to the bald coot whose appearance and traditional stupidity gave rise to attributes like 'as bald (or as stupid) as a coot' and to Skelton's 'The mad coote, with a balde face to toot'. *Drake* may be from OE *draca* 'dragon', which, like OFr *dragon*, was used in ME of a battle-standard as well as of a serpent or a water-monster and must, at times, be metonymic for *drakere* 'standard-bearer' (surviving as *Drakers*). Sir Thomas Smith, in his *De Republica Anglicana*, speaking of his contemporary Sir Francis Drake, asserts that *Drake* was not his family name but an assumption from the name of a sort of serpent and adds that the Dunkirkers fitted out a fine ship called the Dog for the purpose of hunting and perhaps catching this *sea-serpent*. But the surname may also be from ME *drake* 'male of the duck' which is certainly found in *Sheldrake*, *Sheldrick*, *Shildrake*, *Shildrick* 'sheldrake', a bird of the duck tribe, remarkable for its bright and variegated colouring. *Nottage, Nottidge* derives from the nuthatch, a bird of a bold disposition and sprightly gestures, but it is difficult to see why the titmouse should give rise to a nickname. This is the usual explanation of *Tidmas, Tidmus, Titmass* and *Titmuss*, but no evidence is given. My earliest example is Edward *Titmouse* 1662 *HTEss* which may well be a popular etymology for an earlier *Titmarsh* which may come from Tidmarsh (Berks) or from Titchmarsh (Nth), *Titemerse* 1206, which was certainly the original home of William *Tytemers* 1279 RH (C).

Let us turn to Chaucer's catalogue of birds (not complete) in the *Parlement of Foules* (334–64):

Most of these birds have given us surnames: *Goshawke, Gosshawk*, Robert *Goshauek* 1332 SRWa, 'fierce and rapacious'; *Falcon, Faucon*; *gentyl* is not the attribute one would expect, but it is so called because in hawking it was carried perched on the fist; *Sparrowhawk, Sparhawk*, often from a personal-name, OE *Spearhafoc*; *hardy*, again, is not the obvious description; it must usually be regarded as a bird of prey, here the foe of the *Quayle*, itself a nickname, noted for its supposed amorous disposition and timidity; elsewhere it is the lark which suffers:

'What myghte or may the sely larke seye,
Whan that the sperhauk hath it in his foot?'

(*Troilus and Criseyde*, iii, 1191)

The merlioun or merlin, the smallest of the hawks, has not become a surname but we have the simple *Hawk*, often a personal-name, but also a nickname, 'savage, cruel', and sometimes metonymic for *Hawker*; *Haggard* (ME, OFr hagard 'wild, untamed', used of a hawk), *hagard hauke, faulcon, hagard* 'a hagard, a faulcon that foraged for herself long before she was taken'; *Buzzard, Buszard* (OFr *busart* ME *busard* 'buzzard', an inferior kind of hawk, useless for falconry, used also of a worthless, stupid, ignorant person); *Mushett, Muskett* (OFr *mouschet, mousquet* 'a muskett, the tassel of a sparhauke', 'a lytell hauke'); *Tarsell, Tassell* are probably ME *tercel* 'a male hawk', used by Chaucer both as an adjective and as a noun, later *tassell* (Shakespeare), a diminutive of *tiers* 'a third', 'so tearmed because he is, commonly, a third part less than the female' (Cotgrave).[1] In popular opinion, every third bird hatched was a male. ME *tierce* is used of the third of the canonical hours, the third of a pipe and the third card, in all instances originally an adjective, later a noun, and hence may be the source of *Terse*, Henry, Robert *Ters* 1221 *ElyA* (Hu), AssWa, used in the same sense as the diminutive *tercel*.

Lark and its fuller form *Laverack* (OE *lāwerce*) survives as a nickname for a songster and *Dove* for one gentle as a dove. *Swann* has various origins, from OE *Swan*, an anglicising of ON *Sveinn* (now *Swain*), OE *swān* 'herdsman, swineherd, peasant' and OE *swan, swon* 'swan', here called *jelous* because of the ferocity of the male during the breeding season. *Owles*, with the diminutive *Owlett*, is from OE *ūle* 'owl', ultimately derived from its hoot or screech, a wise old bird, a nocturnal bird, an ill-omened bird which warns of impending death. *Crane* 'the giant' because of its height, along with the French *Grew* (and *Grewcock*), *Heron* and *Stork*, all long-legged birds, provide apt nicknames for tall men with long legs.

The actual names of many of these birds, like Chaucer's 'crane with his trumpet-like sound' are ultimately echoic and hence suited to nicknames: *Crow, Craw*, with the cognate *Crake* (ME *crake* 'crow' or 'raven'), from its croak, *Coe* and *Coo* (ME *co, coo*, the midland form corresponding to the northern *ka*, ON *ká*, 'jack-daw', one

[1] (William) *Tassell*' 1206 Cur (Sx) must have a different origin.

267

source of *Kay. Chew* and *Chue* are from OE *cīo, cēo* (not found in ME), a bird of the crow family, a name applied to all the smaller chattering species, especially the jackdaw. The later form *chough* is probably the source of *Chuff*, aptly described by Chaucer as 'the thief'. So, too, 'the janglynge' (chattering) *Pie*, the 'skornynge' *Jay*, the chatterer with its querulous screech. But thrice Chaucer compares a woman to a magpie, giving us additional possible meanings for the nicknames *Pye* and its diminutive *Pyatt*. The miller's wife was 'proud, and peart as a pye' (A 3950), whilst both the merchant's wife and the wife of Bath were cheerful, 'jolif (or joli) as a pye' (B 1399, D 456).

No surname from 'the false lapwynge' has been noted; that from the peewit, too, is now lost, William *Piuet* 1209 P (Ess). OE *stær*, ME *stare* 'starling', may be the origin of *Stares* of which no early examples have been found, but ON *stari* 'starling' survives as *Starey* and *Starie*. The modern *Starr*, Leuenot *Sterre* 1066 DB, frequently found as *sterre*, is from OE *steorra*, ME *sterre* 'star', occasionally as a sign-name. *Starling* is, at times, a patronymic. 'The tame ruddok' (OE *ruddoc* 'robin-redbreast') is now *Ruddock, Ruddick* and *Rudduck*, with which we may compare Thomas *Cokerobyn* 1297 Wak, first recorded by NED 400 years later (c1699).

'Coward' is not the obvious epithet one would apply to the kite, a bird of prey we should rather describe as rapacious. Besides *Keat, Keet* and *Kite* (OE *cȳta*, ME *kete, kyte*) 'greedy glede', we also have *Glide, Gleed* (OE *glida*, ME *glede* 'kite').

The cock is here the clock that rouses the little villages, just as the Pilgrims' host was the rooster who wakened them all in the morning:

'A-morwe, whan that day bigan to sprynge,
Up roos oure Hoost, and was oure aller cok,
And gadred us togidre alle in a flok'   (A 822)

Apart from the difficulty of distinguishing *Cock* from *Cook*, cock had other meanings.[1] It became a common term for a pert boy who strutted like a cock and was used of scullions, apprentices and servants and, in ME, also of 'one who rouses slumberers, a watchman of the night' and was applied to ministers of religion. The evidence is scanty, no references being given between Chaucer (1386) and 1614, but the latter appears conclusive: 'No noyse to waken the Sybarites, unless the Cockes, the Ministers . . . Few will beleeve Christs Cocke, though he crowes to them that the day is broken.' Earlier examples of

[1] *v.* pp. 58, 210.

this use are *Cristescoc* 1148 Wint, Johannes *Cristescoc* 1185 Templars (L), 'servant of Christ'; cf. Walter *Godescoc* 1366 FFEss 'servant of God'.

In calling the *Sparrow* (OE *spearwe*, lit. 'flutterer') 'Venus sone', Chaucer is referring to the Classical tradition that the sparrow was sacred to Venus. Hence it was popularly regarded as especially amorous and serves to characterise the Somenour:

'As hoot he was and lecherous as a sparwe'   (A 626)

Shakespeare, too, takes the bird as symbolic of feathered lechery. Lucio, concerning the seemingly austere Angelo (in *Measure for Measure*), remarks, 'Sparrows must not build in his house-eaves, because they are lecherous.'[1] The French *Musson*, Roger *Muissun* 1166 P (Sa), Adam *Mussun* 1206 Cur (Gl), from AFr *muisson* 'sparrow', also survives. *Nightingale*, also *Nightingall* and *Nightingirl* (OE *nihtegale* 'nightsinger'), *Swallow* and *Turtle* are all modern surnames, the latter from OE *turtla*, ME *turtel* 'turtle-dove' (often, too, a variant of *Thurkell*), a bird said never to take a second mate. OFr *arondel* 'little swallow' survives as *Arundel* though this is more often from Arundel (Sx).

The earliest example of *Peacock*, also *Peecock, Pacock, Pocock*, and formerly *Paycocke*, the name of a family of Coggeshall wool-merchants, is a Domesday burgess of Colchester, probably a nickname used alone (300 years earlier than the first example (1374) in NED), but certainly also a personal-name, *Pecoc* de Briminton 1285 AssCh, used as a woman's name in Colchester in 1357, *Pecok*, sometime wife of John Arwesmith (ColchCt). But usually the surname is a nickname denoting vanity, one proud of his fine feathers. The miller of Trumpington

'As any pecock he was proud and gay'   (A 3926)

The name is a compound of *-cocc* with OE *pāwa, pēa*, whence the modern *Paw* and *Powe, Pea* and *Pee*, and ON *pá*, ME *pō*, modern *Poe*, all ultimately from Lat *pavo* and all used both as personal-names and nicknames. With the peacock we should naturally associate the popingay or parrot with its bright colours and its fondness for repetitive imitation of human speech, a natural source of nicknames. But Chaucer suggests other possibilities, 'ful of delicasye', from its

---

[1] Eric Partridge, *Shakespeare's Bawdy* (London, 1961), pp. 190–1.

lascivious reputation. After the successful conclusion of his business, the Merchant

> 'hoom he gooth, murie as a papejaye'   (B 1559)

and, curiously enough, it is coupled with the sparrowhawk, the thrush and the wood-pigeon as a bird of song:

> 'The briddes synge, it is no nay,
> The sparhauk and the papejay,
>   That joye it was to heere;
> The thrustelcok made eek his lay,
> The wodedowve upon the spray
>   She sang ful loude and cleere'   (B 1956)

And again,

>   'Januarie,
> That in the gardyn with his faire May
> Syngeth ful murier than the papejay'   (E 2320)

The surname was common and survives as *Papigay*, *Pebjoy*, *Pobgee*, *Pobjoy*, *Popejoy* and *Popjoy*, from OFr *papegai*, ME *papejay*, *popingay* 'parrot'. *Parrot*, too, is a nickname, William *le Perot* 1277, now *Parrott*, *Perrott*, etc., difficult to distinguish from the personalnames *Perret*, *Perrott*, diminutives of *Perre* (Peter), from which the parrot itself is named. Why the *Pheasant* is called 'skornere of the cok by nyghte', is not clear; it has been suggested that as the cock crows at dawn, so the pheasant crows at sunset before he goes to roost. *Drake* and *Stork*[1] we have already met, but Chaucer notes other characteristics; the drake kills young ducks, and stories are told that the stork had a habit of tearing its mate to pieces for infidelity.

'The waker goos' is a reference to the classical story of the sacred geese of Juno which warned the Romans of the Gallic attack on the citadel. But vigilance can hardly be the reason for the English nickname. The bird is noted for its shyness and extreme wariness which render approach particularly difficult, hence 'a wild goose chase', an unsuccessful undertaking, commemorated in the surnames *Wildgoose*, *Wildgust*, *Widgust* and *Willgoss*. In addition to the simple *Goose*, which must often mean 'silly', we have *Graygoss*, Richard *Graigos* 1249 AssW, Jonathan and Mary *Graggiss*, *Greygoose* 1771, 1779 DenhamPR (Sf), with the obsolete Widow *Greengoose* 1674 HTSf, William *Fassegos* 1187 P (Nth) and Richard *Patergos* 1327 SRSf. *Barnacle*, a surname of more than one origin, may sometimes

---

[1] *v.* also pp. 266, 267.

be a nickname from the barnacle goose which is also called in ME *clake, clayk, cleck* (c1455 NED), probably named from its call, *claik* 'the cry or call of a goose' (1549 NED), from ON *klaka* 'to chatter, twitter', whence *Clake, Cleak*, William *Cleike* 1176 P (Y). *Gannet*, John *Ganet* 1208 P (Glam), 1230 Cl (O) is from OE *ganot* 'the solan goose'.

'The cukkow ever unkynde' or unnatural lays its eggs in the nest of other birds and the young cuckoo ultimately kills its foster-mother. As a surname, this was common, Warin *Kuku* 1191 P, and, rather surprisingly, survives as *Cuckow*, which was probably used in the sense 'cuckold', less common as a surname, Uluric *Cucuold* c1095 Bury, Richard *Kukuel, Cucuel* 1194 P (Nb), 1197 P (D), from OFr *coucuol, cucault*, ME *cokewold* (now *Cockwell, Cockwill*), but a very common term in ME and later for a married man whose wife has been unfaithful, a fertile subject for story, jest and derision. The merlin scathingly addresses the cuckoo:

'Thou mortherere of the heysoge on the braunche
That broughte the forth, thow [rewthelees] glotoun!
Lyve thow soleyn, wormes corrupcioun!'   (*Parl. Foules* 612)

Heysoge is the hedge-sparrow, preserved in *Sugg* and as *Pinnock, Pinnick* (ME *pinnock* 'hedge-sparrow').

The cormorant has not given us a surname but its Norse equivalent *skarfr* survives as *Scarfe* 'ravenous'. *Raven*, 'wise' because in classical legend endowed with the gift of prophecy, is often from a personal-name, ON *Hrafn* or OE **Hræfen* (whence *Revan*), but also a nick-name from its colour or its cry, and occasionally from a sign-name. The name is found also as *Corb* (OFr *corb*) with the diminutives *Corbet* and *Corbin, Corf* (OFr *corf*) and *Corp* (ON *korpr*, OFr *corp* 'raven'). The *Crow* we have already met; its 'vois of care' is a reminder that it is a bird of ill omen. The throstle (OE *þros(t)el*), now found as *Throssell, Thrussell* and *Thrustle*, and the thrush (OE *þrysce*), now *Thrush, Thresh*, both singing birds, were supposed to live to a great age. The fieldfare, 'frosty' because a winter bird, once provided a surname, Ralph *Feldefare* 1284 Wak, of interest, though it has not survived, because the Oxford Dictionary has no example between c1000 and 1375.

Some additions

Of the 34 birds in Chaucer's catalogue, only four are not now found as surnames; the remaining 30 have suggested numerous parallels and there are more to add, commemorating colour, song and other characteristics, *Duck* and, occasionally, the unrecorded *Duckett* (OFr *ducquet*, a diminutive of *duc* 'leader, guide', one of the names of the owl, so called because thought to serve as a guide to certain birds), with *Digg* and *Digges* (ME *digge* 'duck'). Other farmyard birds are *Gander*, *Henn*, *Chick* and *Chicken*, the latter often used as a term of endearment. *Diver* and *Ducker* or *Duker* (ME *douker* 'a bather' or 'diving bird') were diving birds and may not belong here. *Heathcock* and *Moorcock* are certainly nicknames; *Partridge* may refer to a hunter or catcher of partridges. In *Rook*, the reference may be to colour or persistent hoarse croaking. *Butter* is from OFr *butor* 'bittern', noted for its 'boom' in the breeding season and called 'bull of the bog'. Down to the marsh ran the wife of Midas

> 'And as a bitore bombleth in the myre,
> She leyde hir mouth unto the water doun'   (D 972)

and unburdened her heart of the dreadful secret that her husband had two ass's ears.

Perkyn Revelour, the merry, lively apprentice of the Cook's Tale,

> 'Gaillard he was a goldfynch in the Shawe' (A 4367)

Goldfinch is one of a number of surnames from birds of the finch family, including *Goldspink*, *Finch* itself, with *Fink* and *Vink*, perhaps 'simpleton', *Spink* (ME *spink* 'finch', especially a chaffinch), *Pink* and *Pinch* (OE *pinca*, *pinc* 'chaffinch'), and *Pinchen*, *Pinching*, *Pinshon Pinson* and *Pinsent*, from OFr *pinson*, *pineon*, Norman-Picard *pinchon* 'finch', used as a symbol of gaiety, 'gai comme un pinson' (Dauzat); *Alpe* and *Alps*, an obsolete name for the *Bullfinch*, Richard *Bulvinch* 1275 SRWo, Richard *Bulfinch* 1296 SRSx. *Woodcock*, a bird popularly regarded as brainless, as a surname means 'fool, simpleton, dupe', whilst *Pidgeon*, *Pigeon* is 'one easy to pluck', and *Culver* (Thomas *Colvere* 1334 SRK), from OE *culfre* 'dove, pigeon' is confirmed by Walter *Cylfrebrid* 1221 AssWo. The woodpecker has given us a variety of names, probably due to its place in folklore: *Pike* and *Pick* are, at times, from OE *pic*, Lat *picus* 'woodpecker'; from OE *speoht, *speht, ME *speight*, we have *Speight*, *Spaight*, and from OFr *espech(e)*, *espek*, *Speake*, *Speck*, *Speek* and *Speke*.

Obsolete bird-names include OE *clodhamer* 'a field-fare', not in NED, but reappearing in the surnames of Robert and Elias *Clodhamer* c1260 *ERO*, John *Cledhamer* 1433 W'stow Wills; Richard *Curlu* 1269 Ipm (Nf), Mathew *Snype* 1293 Pinchbeck (Sf), Robert *Dunnebrid* 1183 P (Y),

Thomas *Dunfugell* 1291 AssCh (dun-coloured), Alfwinus *Pirfugel* c1250 Rams, Roger *Purfoghel* 1296 SRSx (OE *pūr* 'bittern').

INSECTS

With the exception of *Bee* 'busy, industrious' and *Papillon* 'butterfly', the symbol of lightness and grace, nicknames from insects are derogatory: *Drane* and *Dron* 'drone', lazy; *Breese, Breeze*, Robert *Brese* c1175 Newark (OE *brēosa* 'gadfly'); *Budd*, Walter *le Bud* 1249 AssW (OE *budda* 'beetle'), not recorded in independent use after the Conquest; Brihtmerus *Budde* c1025, 'fat, corpulent', so called *pro densitate* 'because of his thickness'; the nickname is attested by the French *escarbot*, John *Scarebot* 1212 Cur (Y), and *Wigg*, Ailmer *Wigga* c1130 ELPN (OE *wicga* 'beetle'); *Lobb* (OE *lobbe* 'spider'), *Midge, Migge*, Adam *Migge* 1296 Wak, and *Wasp*. *Stout* may sometimes be OE *stūt* 'gnat', which itself was once a nickname, Margaret *Gnatte* 1274 RH.

FISHES

Previous writers have shown a marked disinclination to admit the possibility of nicknames from fishes.

'We may quote,' says Bardsley, 'the famous chapter on "Snakes in Ireland": "There are no snakes in Ireland", and say there are no fishnames in England. They possessed no individuality so to speak; they led a dull and monotonous life.'[1]

With this Ewen is in strong agreement, whilst Weekley considers that such names are not numerous and probably at first occurred only in regions where fishing or fish-curing were important industries.[2] Attention has been paid chiefly to modern forms which have rightly been discounted, though often for the wrong reason. Ewen, e.g. dismisses *Bream* and *Brill* as names brought over by Dutchmen, but the former is an old name in England from OE *brēme* 'famous' or OE *Brēme*, whilst the latter is certainly local, from Brill (Bk). Bardsley dismisses *Chubb* as a variant of *Jubb* or *Job* on the strength of the alternatives William *Chubbs* or *Jubbs* (d. 1505) which throw no light on the ultimate origin. There is no confusion in ME,

[1] C. W. Bardsley, *Dictionary of English and Welsh Surnames* (Oxford, 1901), p. 31.
[2] E. Weekley, *The Romance of Names* (London, 1922), p. 226.

Richard *Chubbe* 1180, which must be from ME *chubbe* 'chub', used also of a 'lazy, spiritless fellow, a rustic, simpleton', whilst Bailey has '*Chub*, a Jolt-head, a great-headed, full-cheeked Fellow', a description reminiscent of that of the chevin, another name of the chub from OFr *chevesne*, Fr *chevin*; 'the cheuyn is a stately fish'; 'Chevins and Millers thumbs are a kind of jolt-headed Gudgeons' (now *Cheavin*, *Chevins*, *Chevis*). *Gudgeon*, Bardsley regards as an imitative form of *Goodson* or *Goodison*, which may be so in some instances, but he gives no evidence. 'Greedy gudgeon' suggests some character and the forms of the surnames *Gudgeon* and *Gudgin* are clearly identical with those of ME *gojon*, OFr *goujon*, which might also mean 'big-headed', or one who will take any bait, 'credulous, gullible'. *Gurnett*, too, Alexander *Gurnard* 1275, is clearly a nickname from ME *gurnard*, *gurnade*, a fish with a large spiny head and mailed cheeks, with a throat almost as big as the rest of its body, so called because of the grunting noise it makes.

Some of the fish-names are undoubtedly metonymic. Alexander *le pik* (1292 SRLo), now *Pike*, was a fishmonger and owner of a ship. William, Robert and Stephen *Pikeman* (ib.) were also fishmongers and all four owed their surnames to the fish they sold. Alexander was actually nicknamed 'the pike' (ME *pike*), just as Matilda *le Welker* 1279 RH (C), now *Welker*, 'seller of whelks', is also called *le Welke*. *Mullett*, too, may sometimes mean 'seller of mussels' (OFr *mulet*). *Pickerell*, *Pickrill* mean 'young pike'. *Herring* and *Harenc* (OE *hǣring*, OFr *hareng* 'herring') may be from the fishmonger's cry or metonymic for *le Heryngmonger* 1212 or *le Heringman* 1327, and *Mackrell*, too, from OFr *makerel* 'mackerel', early examples coming chiefly from Durham, Yorkshire and Lincolnshire. *Tench* 'a fat and sleek fish', *Trout* and *Sturgeon*, the royal fish, are all clearly fish-names, as is *Shad* (OE *sceadd*), the importance of which is shown from the existence of a 'shad season' in OE times. *Smelt* (OE *smelt* 'sardine') is found as a personal-name in OE and this is usually regarded as the source of the surname, but John *le Smelt* (1334 SRK) is an obvious nickname. *Crabbe* may be from OE *crabba* 'crab', either for one who walked like a crab or for a cross-grained, fractious individual or it may be from ME *crabbe* 'wild apple', used also of crabbed, ill-tempered persons.

Chapter Fifteen

OATH-NAMES, FAVOURITE EXPRESSIONS AND PHRASE-NAMES

MANY names of fish, vegetables, etc., as we have seen, were bestowed on sellers and dealers, often, no doubt, because of their habit of trying to attract buyers by calling out the name of their wares. At times they would add some complimentary description to which their customers would retort with some derisory epithet. A few of the former survive, but none, apparently, of the latter. *Goodcheap* and *Goodchap* are compounds of OE *gōd* 'good' and *cēap* 'barter'. ME *good cheap* was used of a state of the market good for the purchaser, when prices were low, and the nickname could be used both of one who gave a good bargain and of one who vociferously claimed he did. The French equivalent has disappeared, though it is still used as the name of a shop, Geoffrey *Bonmarche* 1300 LoCt; cf. also Thomas *Bargayn* 1297 SRY. *Goodale, Goodayle, Goodall* and *Goodhall* all denote a brewer or seller of good ale, though the customer might have a different opinion, William *Sourale* 1301 SRY. Similarly, John *Fresfissh* (1320 LLB E) and Alexander *Fresharing*, fishmonger (1277 LLB B), owed their names to their constant cry of 'fresh fish', 'fresh herrings', but Robert *Evelhering* (1327 SRSf) and Robert *Rotenheryng* (1297 SRY) were apparently stigmatised as sellers of stale and not so fresh fish, though such names, whilst derogatory occupation-names, were not necessarily apt descriptions of the product sold, for Rotten Herring Staith in Hull and *Rotten-herringland* in Welwick owe their names to the family of John *Rotenhering* (1348), a family of wealth and importance.

Among lost names of this type we may note: Ralph *Godbarlich* 1240 Ass (Sf) 'barley', Richard *Godfugel* 1189 P 'good fowl', John *Fresschebred* 1327 SRSf, Staingrim *Bonpain* 1166 P 'good bread', William *Godmel* 1266 CNat, Adam *Godwhete* 1327 SRSf, William *Swetmylke* 1288 Ipm, Thomas *Sourmylk* 1307 Wak, John *Swete bi ye bone* 1225 AssSo, presumably a butcher, and Reginald *Swetbone* 1377 LLB H, John *Megresauce* 1201 P, and Walter *Smalfis* 1249 Misc, though this was also a nickname, John *le Smalfisch* 1327 SRSo.

GREETINGS AND FAVOURITE EXPRESSIONS

From such names it is an easy step to nicknames from favourite expressions of which more survive. *Goodday* and *Goodenday* are both from a salutation on meeting or parting: 'Have a good day!', 'God give you a good day'; cf. Walter *Godemorwe* 1327 *SR* (Ess), 'good morrow', and the French *Bonger, Bonjour*, Alice *Bonjour* 1327 SRSx. The early forms make it clear that *Goodyear*, with its variants *Goodyer, Goodier* and *Goudier* are from ME *goodyeare, goodier, goodere, goodyeere*, an expletive here elliptic for 'as I hope to have a good year'. *Goodspeed*, too, is from a similar expression, 'God yow speede' (A 769), a wish for success for one setting out on an enter-prise, parallel to the French (Riche) *Boneaventure* 1267 FFEss, Thomas *Bonantur* 1376 LLB H, with which we may compare Robert *Gudechaunce* 1381 PTY and Chaucer's

'Freend, for thy warnyng God yeve thee good chaunce' (G 593)

Godbeer and *Godber* may be nicknames, 'good beer', but may also be forms of *Godbehear, Godbehere* and *Goodbehere*, John *Godbehere* 1456, Geoffrey *Godbeherinne* 1277, either 'May God be in this house' or 'May it be well in this house'; cf. Gilbert *Godbiemidus* 1219 AssL, 'May God be with us', and the French *Dugard, Dieu (te) garde* 'God guard (you)'; *Wardie*, Engelram *Wardedeu* 1220 Cur (Nth), appears to be a Norman version of this, 'Guard (us), God'; *Debney*, Robert *deulebeneie* 1162, 'God bless him', paralleled by the English Olive *Goadebles* 1269 Pat; cf. Robert *Godesblescynge* 1225 AssSo.

Drinkale, now also *Drinkall, Drinkald, Drinkhall, Drinkell, Drinkill* and *Drinkhill*, Thomas *Drinkhale* 1281, is a nickname from the customary courteous reply to a pledge in drinking, *drinc hail* 'drink good health or good luck'; cf. John *Heylheyl* 1281 LLB B and Walter *Allehaile* 1221 AssWo.

Obsolete nicknames from what were clearly the man's favourite expression, all of French origin, include: John *Jevousdy* 1301 SRY, 'I tell you', common to Chaucer's friar, Robert *Jedyben* 1286 FFSf, William *Wibien* 1212 Cur (L) 'oui bien', Robert *Taisezuus* 1177 P (Nf) 'keep quiet', William *Jurdemayn* 1279 RH (C) 'tomorrow', Ranulf *Tutbien* 1223 Pat (Nf), Hugh *Tutprest* 1249 AssW 'quite ready', Walter *Tutfayt* 1310 AD v (Nf) 'all done, quite done', perhaps surviving in *Tuffey*, Fulco *Prentut* 1155 FeuDu, 'take everything', or a nickname 'rapacious', John *Pernezgarde* 1270 AssSo 'take care!'. In Thomas *Tutlemund* 1219 AssY, the meaning is not clear, but the name survives in France as *Toulemonde*.

OATH-NAMES

The speech of Chaucer's pilgrims, which must be regarded as typical of his times, is interlarded with a considerable variety of oaths, from the mild 'by my trouthe' and the common 'God woot' to the drunken miller's 'By armes, and by blood and bones' (of Christ). Not uncommon are the French 'pardee', the man of law's 'depardieux', 'parfay' (with the English 'by my fey') and 'paraventure', but most include the name of the Deity: 'a Goddes name', 'God me save', 'by Goddes saule', 'for Goddes love', 'for Goddes sake' and 'Goddes mooder'.

When the Man of Lawe had ended his tale, the Host called on the parson:

> '"Sir Parisshe Prest," quod he, "for Goddes bones,
> Telle us a tale, as was thi forward yore.
> I se wel that ye lerned men in lore
> Can moche good, by Goddes dignite!"
> 'The Parson him answerde, "*Benedicite!*
> What eyleth the man, so synfully to swere?"
> Oure Host answerde, "O Jankin, be ye there?
> I smelle a Lollere in the wynd"'

and, when, with another oath, 'for Goddes digne passioun', he remarks that the parson will now preach to them, the Shipman interrupts,

> 'Nay, by my fader soule, that schal he nat' (B 1166–78)

277

To the Parson's mild rebuke, the Pardoner, much later, in his tale adds a much more emphatic denunciation, too long to quote in full, confirming the profanity of the contemporary Englishman and shewing that some, at least, regretted it and preached against it:

'Gret sweryng is a thyng abhominable . . .
But ydel sweryng is a cursednesse . . .
          I wol thee telle al plat,
That vengeance shal nat parten from his hous
That of his othes is to outrageous.
"By Goddes precious herte", and "By his nayles",
And "By the blood of Crist that is in Hayles" . . .
Now, for the love of Crist, that for us dyde,
Lete [leave] youre othes, bothe grete and smale'   (C 631–59)

It is not, therefore surprising that a man should receive as a nickname the oath to which he was particularly partial. Some of these still survive, usually in a disguised form, and numerous others have completely disappeared. *Godsafe, Godsave, Godsalve, Godseff* and *Godsiff* are all from ME *on* (*a*) *Godes half* 'in God's name, for God's sake', a surname common and widely distributed and already hereditary in London by 1216. *Mothersole* may be a popular pronunciation of Moddershall (St), but is also clearly an oath-name, Ralph *Modersoule* 1313 Cl (La), 'by my mother's soul', and has also absorbed the nickname Richard *Modisoul* 'brave, proud soul'; cf. *Godsal*, William *God saule* 1197 FF, 'good soul', 'an honest fellow'. *Mordue, Mordey*, William *Mortdew* 1551 NorwDep, though the evidence is late, is probably from French *mort-dieu*, corresponding to the later but common English oath *'sdeath*. Most of the survivors are of French origin: *Pardew, Pardey, Pardoe, Purdue*, Henry *Pardeu* 1332 SRWa, from *par Dieu*, probably shortened from *de par Dieu* (Lat *de parte Dei*) 'in God's name', common in Chaucer as *pardee*; *Purday, Purdey, Purdie, Purdue*, Gilbert *Purdeu* 1227 AssBeds, Fr *pour Dieu*; the modern *Purefoy* is misleading, a popular etymology, 'pure faith', which arose when *per, par* and *pur* came to be pronounced alike. Its real origin is seen in William *Parfei* 1195 FF, Robert *Parfoi* 1296 SRSx, Adam *Parmafey* 1327 SRSf, AFr *par fei*, OFr *par foi* 'by (my) faith'; (William) *Purefay* does not occur until 1412.

Obsolete names of this type include: Geoffrey *Godesgrace* 1220 Cur, William *Godthanke* 1275 RH (Nf), John *Bythegodom* 1296 SRSx, Richard *Godesname* 1298 LoCt, John *Godwot*, Walter *Goduspart* 1327 SRSo, Richard *Godeswones* 1378 AssWa (wounds), William *Godhelp* 14th AD iv (Sr), which survived to 1632 (GreenwichPR), Henry *Godsake* 1514 NorwW,

278

Steven *Godswyll* 1596 Musters (Sr), Robert *Mouthergod* 1258 FFSf, 'by the mother of God'; William *Halupetur* 1279 RH (Hu), 'Holy Peter', Richard *Holifader* 1327 SRSo, William *Haligod, Holygod* 1327 SRSf, SRSo, Richard *Holigost* 1354 Putnam (Sa); Simon *Helpusgod* 1296 SRSx; Roger *Paraventur* 1279 AssNb, Alan *Par le Roy* 1302 SRY, Richard *Parmoncorps* 1332 SRSx. We will end with Roger *Foulmoth* 1286 Wak, 'foul mouth', whose language must have been particularly atrocious to earn him this nickname.

PHRASE-NAMES

Origin and interpretation

So far as form goes, some of these oath-names should really be included with phrase-names, a term not entirely satisfactory, as there are two distinct types, the first consisting chiefly, but not entirely of oath-names, some of which belong to the second type, imperative-names, again an unsatisfactory term as the verb may merely be the verbal stem and there is no clear indication in English that it was an imperative. For proof of this we must turn to late Latin and early French where imperative and indicative had different forms. The earliest example is the fourth-century *labamanos* (for Lat *laua manus* 'wash the hands'), used of a receptacle for washing the hands. As Lebel puts it, one was thought to say to this receptacle 'wash my hands', as if it were personified. This type of formation steadily increased in numbers and survives in *garde-manger* 'larder, pantry, meat-safe', used in the Middle Ages of a cook, *gâte-sauce*, lit. 'spoil sauce', now 'scullion', 'pastry-cook's boy', 'bad cook', *pique-assiette* 'pick plate', 'a sponger'. In the tenth-century *Torna-vent* 'tourne, vent!', 'turn, wind!', used of a weather-cock, the noun is in the vocative.

The interpretation of these names is often difficult. They may be simple occupation-names, *Torne-miche* 'turn loaf', a baker, *Fille soie* 'spin silk'; or derogatory, *Gaste farine* 'spoil flour', a bad miller or a bad baker. But *Manjue pain*, 'mange pain', 'eat bread', Lebel suggests, is probably a nickname 'good for nothing'; eaters of bacon were regarded as hypocrites. In Franche-Comté, to eat wolf's liver was to learn secrets: *'Il sait tout, dit-on, il a mangé du foie de loup.'* Such proverbs and such ideas were part of the popular language of which we know nothing and many of these surnames remain unintelligible for a literal translation leaves us guessing at the meaning.[1]

[1] *v.* P. Lebel, *Les noms de personnes* (Paris, 1946), pp. 69, 88–90, 95–6; A. Dauzat, *Les noms de famille de France* (Paris, 1945), pp. 208–9.

Native or imported from France?

Whether these 'imperative-names' in English are indigenous or imported from France is a difficult problem. They occur early and often in the Romance languages and Jespersen is of opinion that such formations as *pick-pocket, make-peace, turn-coat, saw-bones* ('surgeon') and *catch-penny* seem to be modelled on the French formations. He notes *picke-purse* and *lett-game* 'spoil-sport' in Chaucer and *cutte-pors, pick-porse* and *picke-herneis* in Langland, with a rapid increase later 'so that in Shakespeare we find at least 25 of them'.[1]

As so often, surnames compel us to revise this view for imperative-names are found much earlier and are much more numerous than common nouns of similar formation. Of some 380 surnames of this type, 26 are first recorded in the eleventh century (10 in DB), 83 in the twelfth, 175 in the thirteenth and 85 in the fourteenth. Some occur frequently; others are later, whilst there is in addition a number of modern surnames which look as if they are of this type for which, at present, no early evidence has been found. Of those recorded in the eleventh century, 11 are purely English formations, 8 are French and 1 is a hybrid. Of the English formations, Ailric *Brenebrec* 'burn breeches', Ædric *Hopeheuene* 'hope for heaven', Uluric *Pichele Cruste* 'pick the crust', Ædric *Scaldehare* 'scald hare', Æilmer *Stachecoc* 'spit (roast) the cock', Godric *Stichehert* 'stick (kill) hart', Aluricus *Stikestac* 'stick (kill) stag' and Godlef *Crepunder Huitel* 'creep under cloak', a name for a coward, are all from a list of Suffolk peasant names (c1095 Bury) where French influence is unlikely; Wulfwine *Spillecorne* c1055 'destroy (waste) corn', Eylwyne *Stikehare* 1053 'kill hare' are early for French influence and have frequent parallels later, whilst Alriz *Wordepund* 1086 InqEl (OE **Weorðepund* 'worship (esteem) pound') is a purely English name for a miser. There is certainly evidence of French influence which later becomes more obvious in the appearance of French and English doublets but there seems no reason to doubt that some, at least, of these names are of English origin.

Formations and meanings

In English there are two distinct formations; (i) verb plus noun, John *Cloutpate* 1301 SRY, John *Wakedogge* 1377 AssEss, and (ii) verb

[1] O. Jespersen, *A Modern English Grammar* (Heidelberg, 1922), p. 223.

plus adverb or a prepositional phrase: *Gover*, Gilbert *Gofaire* 1240 Oseney, 'go fairly', either one who walks beautifully or, more probably, one who goes gently, uses gentle means; cf. Margerie *Gangefayre* 1451 Rad (C); *Doolittle*, Hugo *Dolitel* 1204 P (R), 'do little', a nickname for an idler; cf. the French John *Faypew* 1334 LLB E, 'fait peu' and contrast Martin *Dofayr* 1301 SRY; *Fallowell, Fallwell, Followwell*, John *Falleinthewelle* 1332 SRSt, found also in Cambridgeshire, Shropshire and Yorkshire.

Meanings vary. The name may simply be (i) occupational: *Copestake, Copestick, Capstack, Capstick*, Geoffrey *Coupstak* 1295 FrY, a hybrid from OFr *couper* 'to cut' and OE *staca* 'a stake', 'cut-stake', a woodcutter; *Fettiplace*, Thomas *Faiteplace* 1210 Oseney, AFr *fete place* 'make room', an usher; *Threadgold, Threadgill, Thridgould, Tredgold* 'thread gold', an embroiderer; (ii) derogatory: *Bailhache*, the name of a recent judge, *Baylehache marescallus* 1154 EngFeud (Sf), with the more English form *Ballachey* and the diminutive *Ballhatchet, Balhetchett*, John *Ballechett* 1620 GreenwichPR, OFr *baille hache* 'give axe', an executioner; *Boutflour, Boughtflower*, John *Bulteflour* 1303, ME *bulte* 'to sift', 'sift flour', a miller; *Catchpole, Catchpoll, Catchpoule*, Aluricus *Chacepol* 1086 DB, OFr *chacepol*, ONFr *cachepol* 'chase fowl', a collector of poultry in default of money, a tax-gatherer, a warrant officer who arrests for debt; (iii) a nickname, complimentary: *Makepeace* 'peace-maker', *Parlabean, Parlby*, Richard *Parlebien* 1200 P, Richard *Parlebeen* 1352 ERO, Robert *Parleby* 1607 LeiAS xxiii, OFr *parle bien* 'speak well'; (iv) uncomplimentary: *Butlin*, Robert *Butevilain* 1130 P, OFr *boute-vilain* 'hustle the churl'; *Hakluyt* 'hack little', a lazy woodcutter (from 1255, not Dutch); *Scattergood* 'scatter goods', a spendthrift or, possibly, a philanthropist.

To deal systematically with this mass of names, most of which are obsolete, poses many problems. Classification by formation would lead to constant repetition and innumerable cross-references, whilst grouping according to meaning is an almost impossible task for a single phrase-name may have more than one meaning. Some we can explain literally, but what the name actually meant to the man's contemporaries we do not know, whilst others are a complete mystery. Consequently, we shall eschew system and group and discuss names as seems most convenient.

Drinkwater has its parallel in the French *Boileau* and is to be compared with *Bevin, Bivins*, Godfrey *Beivin* c1160 CartAntiq, AFr *bei vin* 'drink wine', a suitable nickname for an Englishman whose favourite drink was wine and not the more usual ale. In France, where wine was the normal drink, Dauzat takes *Boivin* to be a nickname for a heavy drinker. But in medieval England, with its lack of sanitation, to drink water was dangerous and unnatural, too, for 'Ale for an Englysshe man is a naturall drynke'; it was drunk at all times, taking the place not only of tea, coffee, etc., but also of water, and it was cheap and plentiful. A thirteenth-century writer, describing the extreme poverty of the Franciscans when they first settled in London (1224) writes: 'I have seen the brothers drink ales so sour that some would have preferred to drink water.'[1] The nickname may have been bestowed on a man so poor that he could not afford to drink ale even when it was four gallons a penny. But it was also used ironically of a tavern-keeper, and, perhaps, of a tippler. Margery *Drynkewater* was the wife of Philip le Taverner (1324 LLB E), whilst Thomas *Drinkewater* (1328 Husting) was landlord of *Drinkewaterestaverne*.

Telfer, with its modern variants *Telford*, *Talfourd*, *Tolver* and *Tulliver*, was the nickname of William I's minstrel, described by Guy of Amiens in 1068 as 'Incisor-ferri mimus cognomine dictus':

> In the very van of William's army at Senlac strutted the minstrel Taillefer, and went to his death exercising the double arts of his hybrid profession, juggling with his sword, and chanting an heroic lay of Roncesvalles.[2]

It is first recorded as a surname a1103, Dunning *Taillifer*, in Devon, and dates from the tenth century in France as the nickname of the Duke of Angoulême, OFr *taille fer* 'cut iron', 'iron-cleaver', aptly suited to a warrior who could cleave clean through the iron armour of his foe. But the French regard it as occupational, ironic for a tailor, Lebel citing not only *Taille fer*, *tailleeur* from a 1292 Paris tax-roll but also *Taille boys*, *engraveres* from Lyon in 1388, engraver or wood-carver. This corresponds to *Tallboy*, *Talboys*, OFr *taille bosc* 'cut wood', 'woodcutter', and *Cutbush*, but the earliest English examples date from 1086 when we have two tenants-in-chief and two under-tenants of the name and they are unlikely to have been either woodcutters or wood-carvers. There must be some other explanation to which we have no clue, a clear warning against dogmatism.

[1] L. F. Salzman, *English Industries in the Middle Ages* (Oxford, 1923), p. 286.
[2] E. K. Chambers, *The Mediaeval Stage* (Oxford, 1925), vol. i, p. 43.

Some occupational-names

There are, however, undoubted examples of occupational-names and these not always derogatory, e.g. those in which *-loup* or *-love* 'wolf' is preceded by a verb: *Catchlove* 'chase wolf', *Cutliffe*, John *Cutloff* 1512 AD vi (Y), Francis *Cutlove* 1603 SRDb, *Pritlove*, *Pretlove*, Richard *Prykkelove* 1296, 'prick, kill', *Truslove*, *Truslow*, *Trussler* 'bind, carry off', *Bindloes*, *Bindloss*, *Bindless*, Alan *Byndlowes* 1301 'bind wolves', *Spendlove*, *Spendlow*, *Spenlow*, *Spindlowe*, found also in France, for which Weekley's explanation *espand-louve* 'disembowell' is probably correct, Richard *Hachewolf* 1297 MinAcctCo, 'hack, cut', Ranunph *Grindelove* 1256 AssNb, all 'wolf-hunter', 'wolf-trapper'.

Drawater, *Hackwood* and *Culpepper*, *Colepeper* 'gather pepper', a spicer, are certainly occupational, as, no doubt, is *Knatchbull*, William *Knecchebole* 1334 SRK, ME *knetch*, *knatch* 'to knock on the head', 'fell bull', a butcher. *Trusher*, William *Trussehare* (1206) 'carry off the hare' was probably a poacher as Edhiva *Cachehare* (1240) 'chase hare' may have been (one source of *Catcher*), but the reference here might have been to speed as in Bernard *Turnehare* (1224) 'turn hare' (one of several sources of *Turner*), one so speedy that he could outstrip and turn the hare though the latter might also be a nickname for a coward, one just brave enough to face and drive off a hare, the opposite of *Turnbull* which must refer to strength or bravery, a name acquired in some unrecorded exploit. Dauzat, however, explains the French *Tournebœuf* as 'drover'. *Warboys*, usually local, from Warboys (Hu), is occasionally occupational, Richard *Wardebois* 1207 P, John *Gardeboys* 1280 LLB A 'guard wood', a forester, from OFr *warder*, *garder* and *bois*. *Hornblow*, *Horniblow* and *Orneblow*, synonymous with *Hornblower*, are rare examples in which the object is placed before the verb; cf. Thomas *Blauhorn* 1303 Pat. *Rideout* is explained by Chaucer's description of the monk in the Shipman's Tale:

> 'an officer, out for to ryde,
> To seen hir graunges and hire bernes wyde'   (B 1255)

and by that of the monk in the Prologue:

> 'An outridere, that lovede venerie'   (A 166)

These monks were officers of a monastery whose duty it was to visit and supervise the outlying manors, but the term was not necessarily limited to ecclesiastics.

Some nicknames

Most of the nicknames of this type which have survived are complimentary: *Lovejoy*, Philip *Loveioy* 1596 Musters (Sr), *Winlove*, William *Wynloue* 1390 AssL, but *Turnpenny*, Ralf *Turnepeny* 1227 AssBk, *Winpenny*, *Wimpenny*, Richard *Winepeni* 1219 SaG, with John *Wynnegold* 1327 SRSf, John *Turnegold* 1329 LoPleas, Abraham *Cathermonie* 1193 Riev with Adam *Gaderpeynye* 1285 AssLa and John *Lovegold* 1466 LLB L were probably noted for their love of gain, their acquisitiveness or even miserliness.

Flambard, *Flambert* was undoubtedly derogatory. It was common, first borne by Rannulf Flambard, bishop of Durham (1099–1128), 'the agent of Rufus's worst oppressions'. He was a Norman clerk of humble family, chaplain of William I and keeper of the King's seal in 1086. Under Rufus he became justiciar and the chief agent of the king's will. Arrogant, ambitious and largely responsible for the extortions which characterise the reign of Rufus, he was described by Archbishop Anselm as 'non solum publicanus, sed etiam publicanorum princeps infamissimus',[1] not merely a tax-gatherer but the most infamous head of all the tax-gatherers. The name by which he is commonly known is a shortened form of the original, Randulf *Passflambard* 1128 ASC E, *Passeflambart* 12th LibEl, 'pass on the flaming torch', another example of the importance of background knowledge in interpreting these names.

Of the complimentary names, we may note *Standalone*, *Standerline*, 'a resolute, self-reliant man', *Standfast* 'steadfast, resolute', *Standwell*; cf. 'Beo stalewurðe & stond well' (a1225 NED) and John *Standepert* 1374 AssL, Henry *Standinnough* 1702 LewishamPR; *Startifant*, *Sturtivant*, John *Stirtavant* 1404 Pat, 'start forward', probably a nickname for a messenger, like *Startup* and *Golightly*, *Gallatly*, *Gelletly*, 'go lightly'; cf. also John *Startout* 1381 ArchC 4, Robert *Styrtover* 1320 Shef, to which we may add *Treadwell*, Seeman *Treddewel* c1248 Bec, Symon *Tredeven* 1275 SRWo, John *Tredebas* 1327 SRC and John *Stepesoft* 1260 Oseney. *Steptoe* is evidenced late, William *Steptoe* 1665 HTO, but is probably older; cf. *Step to* 'to address oneself vigorously to a task'; 'Step to it, man . . . Steppe to it agayne and take better holde' (1530 NED).

Somewhat similar to the above is a group of names compounded

---

[1] A. L. Poole, *From Domesday Book to Magna Carta* (Oxford, 1951), pp. 114, 171.

with OFr *passe-*: *Passavant, Passant,* 'passe avant' 'go on in front', like Startifant, 'a herald or messenger'; *Parsloe, Parslow, Parsley, Paslow, Pasley, Pashley, Pashler,* Radulfus *Passaqua* 1086 DB, Ralph *Passelewa* 1106 Bury, OFr *Passelewe* 'cross the water'; cf. Alan *Pasewater* 1439 NorwW, Richard *Passewelle* 1327 SRSo; *Passmore,* Richard *Passemer* 1199 P, OFr *passe mer* 'cross the sea', 'seafarer, sailor', a type of surname common in both England and France; cf. Richard *Passeboys* 'wood', Adam *Passebusck* 1297 SRY 'bush', Alfwin *Passeculuert* 1166 P, and the French *Passedouet* (canal), *Passefons* (fountain), *Passepont* (bridge), *Passerieu* (stream). These Dauzat plausibly suggests mean 'one who has to cross the bridge, stream or water, or pass the spring or fountain to reach his home'. *Perceval, Percival, Percifull, Purcifer* and *Passifull* is a similar compound, *perce val* 'pierce the valley'. Such names were common also in France: *Percebois* 'wood-borer', *perce-roche* 'rock-piercer', *perce-forêt* 'forest-piercer' which Harrison interprets as 'keen hunter'. It might also mean a poacher. William *Percevent* 1221 Cur 'pierce wind' was, no doubt, renowned for his speed, as was William *Scherewind* 1187 P (Cu), 'cut wind', from OE *sceran* 'to cut' (*Sherwin*) and Richard *Wyndswyft* 1301 SRY. Similarly, *Pearcey, Pearsey, Piercy* 'pierce hedge', from OFr *haie* 'hedge', which may have been used either of a hedge protecting a forest or enclosure or of a military work. Hence, either 'poacher' or 'warrior famous for forcing his way through fortifications'.

Shakespeare, Wagstaffe, etc.

Former controversies about such names need no longer detain us. The formation is clear and established, a verb followed by a noun, often the name of a weapon.[1] It is the meaning which is doubtful for a variety of different incidents may have given rise to the nickname and these we shall never know. In addition to *Shakespeare*, we still have *Shakelance, Shakeshaft, Shackshaft, Shakeshift* and *Shakesheff,* and by the side of these, *Wagstaffe, Waghorne* and Walter *Waggespere* 1227 AssLa. The earliest meanings of *shake* are 'to brandish, to agitate (some part of the body), to wag, flap, etc.', and of *wag* 'to

---

[1] For *Shakespeare*, v. C. W. Bardsley, *Dictionary of English and Welsh Surnames* (London, 1901), *s.n.*, E. Weekley, *Words Ancient and Modern* (London, 1946), pp. 204–8, and P. H. Reaney, *Dictionary of British Surnames* (London, 1961), *s.n.*

brandish (a weapon) defiantly', well illustrated by Weekley's quotations:

'Heo scæken on heore honden speren swithe strong' (Layamon)

'Schaftes thai gan schake' (Sir Tristram)

'Thei schulen schake lockis, as the whelpis of liouns' (Wyclif)

'Be not afrayde for the Kinge of the Assirians—he shal wagg
(A.V. lift up) his staff at thee' (Coverdale)

One obvious explanation is that some of these were common nicknames for a spearman or soldier, active and vigorous, who brandished his lance or spear and made it quiver in preparing his throw. *Waghorne* is a name for a trumpeter (or a huntsman) whose habit of wagging and flourishing his trumpet can be seen on many a television programme. The -*staff* names can hardly refer to soldiers. The reference here may be to one proficient at the quarter-staff or to the common practice in medieval England of carrying a staff which gave rise to such surnames as *Langstaff* or *Longstaff* or they may be nicknames for a bailiff, catchpoll, beadle or other officer of the law, whose tipped-staff, furnished with a silver top or iron spike, has given us the noun *Tipstaff* which survives as a surname, though no early examples have been found. Bardsley noted that in 1392 one Roger Andrew was publicly indicted for pretending to be an officer of the Marshalsea, which he did by bearing a 'wooden staff with horn at either end, called a *tipstaffe*'. Chaucer's lymytour (a friar with a licence to beg in a particular area) 'wente his wey . . . with scrippe and tipped staf', whilst

'His felawe hadde a staf tipped with horn'
(D 1736, 1740)

And, of course, some of these nicknames may have been given to men noted for their excessive use as offensive weapons.

Shackman, *Shacklady* and *Shakelady* have some other origin. *Shacklock*, *Shatlock* and *Shadlock*, Roger *Schakeloc* 1187, may be names for a gaoler either as a shaker (or rattler) of locks or from ME *schaklok* 'fetters', but the plural form of the name of Adam *Schakelokes* (1316) is a nickname for one with a habit of shaking back his long hair; cf. Geoffrey *Schakeheved* 13th Rams (Hu), John *Shakeleg* 1333 ColchCt, Alan *Waghals* 1240 *Ass* (Sf) 'neck', John *Wagheberd* 1297 MinAcctCo. *Waple*, Everard *Wagepole* 1169 P, Geoffrey *Waupol*, *Wagpoll* 1271 LeiBR, 'wag pole' is equivalent to *Wagstaffe*, but

Wagpoll suggests an alternative 'wag head'. Enigmatic are William *Schaktre* 1301 SRY and Richard *Schakerake* 1379 *Coram* (Ha). *Saxby*, usually from Saxby (Lei, L), is also (John) *Sacheespee* 1183 P, 'draw sword', a name for a trainer in swordmanship (cf. Fr *Sacquépée* and Richard *Dragheswerd* 1240 *Ass* (Sf), but was confused in the popular mind with the *shake-* names and became (John) *Shakespey*, now *Shakesby*. To these we may add *Breakspear, Brackspeare*, the surname of the only English Pope, 'break spear', which, as Bardsley remarks, 'would be cheerfully accepted as a nickname by the successful candidate in the tournament' or, of course, in actual battle; cf. Denis *Brekelaunce* 1308 RamsCt (Sf).

Medieval punishments

Some of these phrase-names obviously refer to the men who inflicted one or other of the cruel penalties imposed by medieval law: *Brend, Brent* and *Brind* are ME terms meaning 'burnt, branded'; *Brennan, Brennand, Burnand*, Reginald *Brennehand*' 12th, 'burn hand'; Matilda *Brendhand* 1295 Barnwell, 'burnt hand', now *Brennand*, had suffered this punishment; Henry *Brendcheke* 1279 AssNb; Gwydo *Cuthand* 1310 ColchCt, Ralph *Hackenose* Ed I Malmesbury; *Crakebone* 'crack bone', 'break bone'; cf. Langland's

'Quikliche cam a caccepol and craked a-two here legges,'

and the hybrid *Brisbane, Brisbourne*.

Obsolete names

Many obsolete names have already been used for comparative purposes; those that remain are too numerous to list in full nor will any such list ever be complete. Here we deal with some of the most common types, with some rarities, omitting those given by Weekley:[1] Richard *Bindedeuel* 1188 P, Roger *Byndecart* 1296 SRSx, Archil' *Brechecastell* 1166 P, John *Brekaldoun* 1327 SRSx, Walter *Brekebac* 1269 AssSo, Adam *Brekeleg* 1243 AssSo, Walter *Brekheved*, master of a ship, le Godeyer, of Lynn 1336 Misc, William *Brekewomb*' 1199 P; William *Brindboyf* 1301 SRY 'burn cow', Adam *Cachcapel* 1327 SRSa 'chase nag', William *Cacchemayde* 1339 Clerkenwell, William *Cachepeni* 1278 AD v, Richard *Chasegrey* 1327 SRSa 'badger', Thomas *Cuttegos* 1247 AssBeds, Alan *Cutteharing* 1206 AssL, Symon *Cuttepurs* 1275 Burton, Richard *Drawebac* 1327 SR (Ess), Walter *Dragestrawe* 1240 *Ass* (Sf), Henry *Drink al up* 1282 FFEss, William *Drinkepin* 1206 ChR, 'one who drinks a peg' (pegs were fixed on the inside of large drinking vessels), William *Etecroue* 1361 LLB G, Ralph *Ferebule*

[1] *Surnames*, pp. 270–7.

1169 P, William *Fretehoxe* 1379 *SR* (Ha) (ME *frete* 'eat, devour' ox), John *Gedirwit*, John *Gedirstanes* 1332 SRCu, Thomas *Grindebofe* 1332 SRLa, Ralph *Hackbon* 1277 Misc 'hack bone', a butcher, Goduuine *Hachelard* c1095, a seller of bacon, Hugo *Hakepetit* 1202 P, Geoffrey *Hakkeches'* 1227 AssBeds 'cheesemonger', Nicholas *Hopyndore* c1265 WhC, William *Hopperoket* 1271 HPD; Hugo Hoppeoverhumbr, *Uppeoverunnbr* 1220 Cur (Sx) probably lived 'up, beyond the Humber', a fairly common name of small streams, though not noted in Sussex; Richard *Huchese* 1200 Cur, Aluricus *Huchepain* 1177 P (C), John *Hucketrout* 1301 SRY, ME *hucke* 'to bargain', hawkers or sellers of cheese, bread and trout.

Hugo *Likkeberd* 1230 P (C) 'lick beard', Leofric *Liccedich* 1119 Rams (Hu) 'lick dish', William *Lykkedoust* 13th AD i (Ess), Geoffrey *Lickefinger* 1206 Cur (Nf), Ralph *Likkeloue* 1309 SRBeds, John *Makebeter* 1327 SRSo, Nicholas *Makebotere* 14th AD v (W), Richedon *Makedance* 1302 SRY, Robert *Makefayr* 1332 SRSr, Ralph *Makelitel* 1204 P (He), Simon *Makesac* 1327 SRC, Robert *Mangebien* 1185 P (Nf) 'eat well', Warin *Mangeharneis* 1228 *FF* (Ha) 'eat armour'; Simon *Pyckeble* 1327 SRSf 'corn', Baldwin *Pikechese* 1209 FFEss, William *Pykhare* 1221 *ElyA* (Nf), John *Pykehuskes* 1316 Wak, Adam *Pickpese* 1283 SRSf, Richard *Pilecat* 1166 P (Nf), ME *pile* 'pluck, rob', Roger *Pilecrowe* 1175 P (Nf), William *Pilegold* 1272 *Ass* (Ha), Gilbert *Pylewhey* 1327 SRSo; Richard *Pynnefowel* 1315 LLB E 'pen, shut up the fowls', Richard *Pynsweyn* 1327 SRSf; Philip *Pleywel* 1327 SRWo, Cristina *Prykefysh* 1332 SRSx, John *Prikehurt* 1208 P (Sf) 'hart', Nicholas *Prikpeny* 14th AD ii (Do); William *Quelhoxe* 1288 *Ct* (Ha), ME *quelle* 'kill'.

John *Rydefayre* 1381 PTY, Roger *Rokbot* 1285 CNat, Ædwinus *Scaldhot* 1187 P (Ess), Ædric *Scaldehare* c1095 Bury, Robert *Scaldecoc* 1222 Cur (Herts), Robert *Scaldeharing* 1209 P (C), nicknames for a cook; Richard *Escorcebæf* 1183 P (Y) 'skin ox', Fr *écorcher* 'to flay, tear; fleece', Peter *Escorcheberd* 1183 P (Sx), William *Scorchfrent* 1327 SRC, William *Escorcheueille* 1170 P (Nf); Adam *Singsmal* 1301 SRY, Agnes *Singalday* 1309 SRBeds, Edmund *Singgemasse* 1187 Clerkenwell; John *Skipop* 1292 SRLo 'skip up', Roger *Sparebutter* 1321 Wak, John *Sparwatre* 1327 SRY; Geoffrey *Sitadun* 1285 FFEss, Thomas *Sitequyt* 1358 ib., William *Slengbutre* 1230 P (K), 'sling butter', presumably a waster; William *Spillebred* 1297 MinAcctCo (Y), ME *spille* 'to destroy, waste', Roger *Spillebark* 1306 NorwDeeds i, derogatory for a tanner, Alexander *Spillecause* 1275 RH (L), William *Spillegod* 1201 AssL 'goods', Adam *Spilgold* 1332 SRCu, John *Spilhaver* 1301 SRY 'oats', Robert *Spilring* 1276 RH (Y), Richard *Spiltimbir* 1331 Wak (survived to 1598 in Essex), John *Spylwater* 1524 SRSf, Robert *Spillwode* 1308 Wak; William *Tirevache* 1172 P (Ha), perhaps 'tear cow', ME *tiren* 'to tear a prey', Simon *Tirhare* 1327 SRY, either 'tear' or 'tire hare', Alexander *Tyrelitle* 1183 P (Y); Osbert *Triphup* 1249 AssW, Walkelin *Trussevilain* 1204 P (Bk), Robert *Turnevileyn* 1240 FFEss; William *Wassepoke* 1184 P (Beds), 'wash bag', Robert *Wassepot* 1199 Cur, Roger *Waspail* 1130 P (W), 'wash pail', John *Washewhite* 1684 NorwDep, Emma *Wastecerueise* 1191 P (Ha), 'spoil ale', AFr *waster*, Fr *gâter*.

Miscellaneous

Henry *Pende-, Pundecrowe* 1293 AssSt 'pen crow' (OE *pynden* 'to pen'), one who attempted the impossible, an utter fool, like the Somerset yokels who built a wall round the field to prevent the cuckoo from flying away, Herueus *Milkegos* 1288 NorwLt and Malkyn *mylkedoke* 'milk duck' of the Coventry play. Reginald *Pendeleu* 1301 SRY may be a parallel, 'put the wolf in the pound', or it may be a nickname for a wolf-trapper. The following, though not all phrase-names, deserve record: Mucheman *Wetebede* 1235 Ch (C), John *Levetoday* 1279 RH (C), Thomas *Haldebytheheved* 1301 SRY; William *Gatorest* Hy III Gilb (L), Serle *Gotokirke* 1279 RH (C), William *Gawell* 1284 AssLa, 'go well', Adam *Gobigrounde* 1327 *SR* (Ess), Robert *Gobytheweye* 1327 SRSa, John *Go inthe Wynd* 1334 LLB E, John *Gobiside* 1379 PTY, Nicholas *Gabyfore* 1430 FeuDu, Hugh *Wendowai* 1332 SRCu; Adam *Hanggedogge* 1262 ForSt, Ædricc *Al for druncen* c1095 Bury, William *Aydrunken* 1279 AssNb, Robert *Ayredy* 1379 PTY, Walkinus *Alrebest* 1197 P (Berks), William *Partut* 1183 P (D), Henry *Bredandale* 1272 FFSt, Adam *Fayrarmful* 1246 AssLa (recorded as slang for 'a little short person' from the sixteenth century), William *Fayrandgode* 1301 SRY, Adam *Richeandgod* 1334 SRK, Ralph *Badinteheved* 1275 RH (Bk), William *Hipythesike* 1301 SRY, Adam *Potfulofale* 1302 SRY, Elias *Overandover* 1311 NottBR, John *Alswo* 1317 AssK, Henry *Altheworld* 1327 SRY, Robert *Natheles* 1330 AD ii (Ha), *Adam Yat godmade* 1379 PTY, Robert *Monelyght* 1442 RochW.

NAMES OF INDECENT OR OBSCENE CONNOTATION

Lovers and philanderers

'Les coureurs de femmes', as Dauzat neatly terms them, are commemorated in certain French surnames: *Lamoureux, Chéradame* (cher à dame), *Aimlafille*, whilst *Lami* he explains as 'lover'. In England we have *Lover* and *Lovelady*, the mere existence of which suggests the philanderer, as does the French *Amor, Amour*, Adam *Amour* 1327 SRSf and *Blandamore*, Richard *Playndeamours* 1284 AssLa, OFr *pleyn d'amour*, with its English equivalent *Fullalove, Fullerlove, Fulleylove*, Henry *ffulofloue* 1327 SRC. *Paramor, Parramore*, OFr *par amour* 'with love', 'lover, sweetheart', is a clear instance for the modern meaning was well established in Chaucer, where the Wife of Bath remarks:

> 'My fourthe housbonde was a revelour;
> This is to seyn, he hadde a paramour'   (D 453)

Finnemore, OFr *fin amour* 'fine, perfect love' can have no hidden meaning, but *Drew*, OFr *dru*, originally 'sturdy', later 'lover', and

Drewery, Drury, OFr *druerie* 'love, friendship', 'love-token', 'sweet-heart', are to be compared with the French *Ledru* 'lover' or 'homme à femmes' (Dauzat). *Leman, Lemon,* ME *leofman, lemman,* originally 'beloved man', came to mean 'lover, sweetheart' and was often used as a term of address without any sense of obloquy. In the Townley Plays it is applied to the Virgin, but already in Chaucer it had de-generated in sense, being used affectionately by one adulterer to another. There is no doubt of the meaning of *Copner,* OE *copenere* 'paramour' or of *Letcher,* Adam *le Lechur* 1249 AssW, ME *lech(o)ur,* OFr *leceor* 'lecher', a rare surname, probably often disguised as *Leger. Lickorish, Licrece* and *Liquorish,* Ralph *Lycorys* 1348 AssSt, is from ME *likerous* 'lecherous, wanton', a term used by Chaucer of the Miller's wife:

> 'And sikerly she hadde a likerous ye'   (A 3244)

and of the punishment for lechery:

> 'And likerous folk, after that the ben dede,
> Shul whirle aboute th'erthe alwey in peyne'
> > (Parlement of Foules, 79)

Language and ideas of Chaucer's contemporaries

However objectionable or immoral were the habits which gave rise to these names, no exception can be taken to their form. But there are numerous nicknames which are undoubtedly obscene. The great majority have long ceased to be used; some which survive are now well disguised, whilst many others which have often more than one innocent meaning must, at times, have been used with an indecent connotation of which abundant proof can be found in Chaucer and other medieval literature (as well as in the Elizabethan and Restora-tion dramatists). We have already seen that the talk of Chaucer's pilgrims was liberally interlarded with oaths. The language of the time was much less inhibited than that of today and much that we regard as indecent or obscene was to them normal and natural. In an age when sanitation was non-existent the normal functions of the body and its various parts were referred to openly and without shame by their ordinary everyday terms, no watering down from water-closet to W.C. and then to lavatory, and finally to toilet. Life was much more communal. They slept naked, whole families, with their guests, in a single room. In the Miller's Tale, one bedroom housed the miller and his wife, their baby and their grown-up daughter, and two clerks. There was little room for reticence here and one result was the nature of the tales they told and enjoyed. Their humour was broad, their jests and jokes hilarious, and often cruel. No tale was more appreciated than the elaborate devices resorted to by a wife to deceive her husband or some swain's successful or unfortunate adventures in pursuit of a seduction. The actual day-to-day talk of the populace was undoubtedly less restrained than that of the poets as is clearly proved by the nicknames bestowed on friends and enemies alike which prove, too, that this kind of language goes back at least to the twelfth and thirteenth centuries.

There can be no doubt that many a *Bullock* was once a *Ballock* (OE *bealluc* 'testicle'). The earliest examples are Lewinus *Balloc* and Alueredus *Caddebelloc*, 1066 Winton, in which both elements have the same meaning. The simple nickname was not uncommon and survives in the modern 'Ballocks in brackets: a term of reference to a bow-legged man, sometimes used in a quite inoffensive spirit' (Franklyn). Occasionally we have a compound, Robert *Blakeballoc* 1243 AssSo, Roger *Ruchballok* 1288 NorwLt and Roger *Gildyn-ballokes* 1316 Wak, a translation of the Latin Hunfridus *aurei testiculi* 1086 DB (Ess), which became the French hereditary surname of the family of Helye *Oriescuilz*, lord of the manor of Sandford Orcas (Do) in 1177, where the attribute still preserves the nickname in a disguised form. But already in the twelfth century there was confusion with *bullock*: Radulfus *Witebullock, Whiteballoc* 1196, 1197 P (Co), Laurence *Ballock, Bullok, Bollock* 1281 LLB B.

The normal OE name for the membrum virile was not uncommon as a surname in the twelfth and thirteenth centuries, Robert *Pintel* 1179 P (Sf), and in the compounds Hugo *Humpintel* 1187 P (? for *Huni-*), Alan *Coltepyntel*, John *Swetpintel* 1275 RH, William *Dogge-pintel* 1361 Ass (Lei), but none survive, nor do any of the numerous synonyms for the pudend found in Chaucer and Shakespeare, though *-tail*, used both of the male and the female organ, is not uncommon in compounds, sometimes with reference to coition. When the merchant had reproved his wife for borrowing money from the monk which he had had to pay, the point of her offer to repay him well and readily from day to day is clear:

'I am youre wyf; score it upon my taille'   (B 1606)

and is emphasised by the ending:

'Thus endeth now my tale, and God us sende
Taillynge ynough unto oure lyves ende'   (B 1622–3)

291

Hence such nicknames as Alicia *Pryketayle* 1275 SRWo, John *Wryngetayl* 1341 LLB C, John *Swalwetayl* 1365 ColchCt and Richard *Wagetail* 1187 P (St). The last suggests that *Waghorn, Wagstaffe, Waple* (earlier *Wagpole*) and even *Shakespeare* may sometimes belong here.[1]

Shakelady is clearly a nickname for a libertine, as is probably *Tiplady*, though, as the earliest example, Johanna *Tippelevedy* 1301 SRY, is a woman's name, the real meaning may be 'the lady of Tippe', a pet-form of *Theobald*, recorded in 1204. Other names of this type are evidenced only late and may or may not belong here. *Toplady*, John *Taplady* 1400 AD vi (Db), might be compared with Richard *Toppelord* 1168 P (D), whilst *Toplass, Toplis* and *Topliss* are even later, Robert *Topples* 1596 Shef. For these, Weekley refers to Scene 1 of Act I of *Othello*, but as Toplas Fm in Ashleyhay (Db) is called *William Toplis house* in 1629 and as there was a Thomas *Topleys* in the parish in 1619 (PN Db 521), these names may really be local in origin. *Gotobed* was used by Shakespeare of coition.

Goats and monkeys are Shakespeare's types of animal lustfulness:

'As prime as goats, as hot as monkeys'

and in often taking sparrows as symbolic of feathered lechery,[2] he is in tune with Chaucer:

'As hoot he was and lecherous as a sparwe'   (A 626)

To Shakespeare, too, the buck and the stag, with their horns, were symbolic of the cuckold[3] (cf. *Cockwell*), whilst Chaucer anticipates our 'mad as a March hare' in

'this Somonour wood were as an hare'   (D 1327)

an animal, regarded originally, owing to its excitability in rut, as a symbol of generative power, which came to be typical of incontinence.[4] Dauzat takes a similar view of the buck, the pig and the stag and there can be little doubt that in some instances this was the characteristic which gave rise to such names as *Buck, Goate, Hare, Pigg, Sparrow* and *Stagg*, and probably also to *Ram* and *Bellar*,

[1] It has been shown that ME *burdoun*, MFr *bourdon* (now *Burdon*), 'a pilgrim's staff', 'lance', also meant 'phallus'. *v. Notes & Queries*, vol. 204 (1959), pp. 435–6; 205 (1960), pp. 404–6.

[2] Eric Partridge, *Shakespeare's Bawdy* (London, 1961), pp. 122, 190–1.

[3] Ibid., pp. 81, 192.

[4] B. Rowland, 'Wood . . . as an hare' (*Notes & Queries*, vol. 208 (1963)), pp. 108–9.

William *Tup* 1227 Cl (Y) and, possibly, to *Tupper*, a sense not unknown in modern nicknames:

'Ramsey (or Mr Ramsey): is a nickname given to a lascivious person. From *ram*, a male sheep whose abilities are proverbial.[1]

Colt must also be included here for Chaucer's Reve and the Wife of Bath, despite her forty years, both had 'alwey a coltes tooth' (A 3888, D 602), the desires of youth, a tendency to wantonness.

Clear proof of this interpretation is provided by *Stallan, Stallen, Stallon* and *Stallion*, from OFr *estalon* 'a stallion', applied to a person, 'a begetter', 'a man of lascivious life'; cf. 'þe monke þat wol be stalun gode . . . He schal hab wiþute danger. xii. wiues euche ȝere' (c1305 NED). In Shakespeare's use of bull as 'a man regarded as an habitual copulator' and town bull for 'the most notable fornicator and womanizer in a village or township',[2] we have a survival of an ancient medieval custom to which both *Bull* and *Boar* must be indebted:

'Under the champion husbandry, just as the fields were village fields, so the cattle ran in a village herd. And in some parts of England the increase of the herds was provided for just as it is on the ranges today, by allowing bulls to run free with the cows. This gave Chaucer a chance in the *Parson's Tale* to develop a neat simile for lecherous priests. He wrote:
'"Swiche preestes been the sones of Helie, as sheweth in the Book of Kynges, that they weren the sones of Belial, that is, the devel. Belial is to seyn 'withouten juge'; and so faren they: him thynketh they been free, and han no juge, namoore than hath a free bole that taketh which cow that hym liketh in the town. So faren they by wommen. For right as a free bole is ynough for al a toun, so is a wikked preest corruption ynough for al a parisshe, or for al a contree."'

'Free bull' and 'free boar' are not limited to literature. They were technical legal terms. They were franchises; the right to keep a bull or boar was the privilege of the lord, or one of the lords, of many a village.[3]

Two examples remain of words which would now be avoided in polite speech. Weekley cites *Baysers* and *Brendhers* which he doubtfully associates with (horse?). The first is certainly a hybrid, OFr

[1] Julian Franklyn, *A Dictionary of Nicknames* (London, 1962), p. 89. *v.* also Partridge, op. cit., pp. 81, 176, 210.
[2] Partridge, op. cit., pp. 81, 207, 162.
[3] G. C. Homans, *English Villagers of the Thirteenth Century* (Cambridge, Mass., 1942), pp. 60–2.

baise 'kiss' and OE *ears* 'backside'. The latter is probably Cutte *Brendhers* 1279 RH (C), a compound of ME *brend* 'burn' and *ears*, with intrusive *h*, a name which must be due to some such tale as that of Chaucer's Miller or to some similar exploit;[1] cf. also Alestan' *braders* 1066 Winton. The second is a typical example of the same broad, rumbustious humour, but from a higher social class. About 1250 (Fees) Rolland *le Pettour* is recorded as holding land in Hemmingstone (Sf) by serjeanty of appearing before the King every year on Christmas Day to do a jump, a whistle and a fart (*unum saltum et unum siffletum et unum bumbulum*). In another record he is called Roland *le Fartere*, a habit regarded as perfectly natural and a source of considerable amusement to Chaucer's contemporaries, the Clerk of Oxenforde's delicacy being noted with naïve surprise:

> 'But sooth to seyn, he was somdeel squamous
> Of fartyng'[2]   (A 3337)

Pettour is from OFr *peter* 'to break wind' and, as the word was uncommon, the meaning was forgotten and it survives in the Ipswich surname *Petter*[3] and probably in *Pethard*, William *Petard* 1296 SRSx. Curiously enough, it survives in French as *Pétard*, *Peton* and *Petot*, and probably in *Pétain*, but Dauzat notes that one family of *Pétard* had licence to change its name to *Pérard*.

Obsolete nicknames

Godwin *clawecuncte* 1066 Winton, Simon *Sitbithecunte* 1167 P (Nf), Jocelin *Prinketail* 1210 Cur (Wo); John *Prikehard* 1213 Cur (Sf); cf. Chaucer's 'He priketh harde and depe as he were mad' (A 4231) where the meaning is obvious; Gunoka *Cunteles* 1219 AssY, John *Fillecunt* 1246 AssLa, Peter *Huniteil* 1268 ELPN, Thomas *Hunicod* 1275 RH (K), Nicholas *Streketayl* 1275 RH (L), Richard *Scittebagge* 1277 *Ely* (Sf); cf. *Schitebroch* (Weekley), for -*breech*, mill called *Scitepilche* 1279 PNO 181, a derogatory name for the miller, *Shitface*, strangely enough complimentary, and *Shitpot*, an aggressive nickname, expressive of dislike and contempt (Franklyn 96); for the term in place-names, cf. PNEss 117 and

---

[1] *v.* particularly A 3732–5, 3800–13.

[2] This was one of the accomplishments expected of the lower type of minstrel. *v.* Chambers, *Mediaeval Stage*, vol. I, p. 72, n. 6, and *Piers Plowman*, Passus XVI, 205–8.

[3] This may also be 'dweller in the hollow' (OE *pytt*), but not when the suffix is -*our*. Other examples of the surname are John *le Petour* 1299 LLB B, John *Pethour* 1519 NorwDep.

Ekwall, *Street-names of London, s.n.* Sherborne Lane, p. 155; John *Shepenkertel* 1327 *SR* (Ess), OE *scypen* 'cow-shed'; Agnes *Strokeher*, Roger *Strokehose* 1296 SRSx, Alexander *Haripok* 1299 FrY, Robert *Harilas* 1301 SRY, Robert *Clevecunt* 1302 SRY, Ernald *Pokestrong* 1309 Abbr (St), Peter *Strekelevedy* 1316 Wak, John *Strokelady* 1327 SRC, Roger *Louestycke* 1327 SRSa, Bele *Wydecunthe* 1328 Sibton (Nf).

Chapter Sixteen

THE
GROWTH OF FAMILY NAMES

TYPES OF NAMES USED

WE have already seen that originally a man had only a single name, OE *Godwine* or *Leofric*, ON *Brand* or *Gamel*, and, after the Conquest, *Robert*, *Adam* or *Peter*. Such simple names are found by the hundred in twelfth-century documents, but steadily decrease in numbers during the thirteenth and fourteenth centuries. But already before the Conquest we find names with an additional attribute, Ælfuuard *æt Dentune*, Cytel *Clacces sune*, Osferð *swadebeard*, i.e. 'spade-beard' (963–92 ASCh). These were not hereditary surnames; the name was used of only one man and it died with him.

After the Conquest such attributes are found in increasing numbers, especially such names as Radulfus *filius Osberti* and Ricardus *filius Edwini* (1185 Templars), a type long found, a description not a surname, identifying the man as 'the son of Osbert or of Edwin'. Any attribute could be used, provided it was definite and distinctive: Gaufridus *clericus*, Galfridus *clericus de Fordham* or Galfridus *de Fordham* (1147–68 Holme), Robertus *frater magistri Ade clericus* or Robertus *de Gernemut'* (1175–1210 ib.). There were, too, innumerable patronymics, local surnames, occupational-names and nicknames of

296

which abundant examples have been cited in earlier chapters. That the following are pure descriptions needs no proof: Agnes *filia Hugonis prepositi de Dodesthorp* 'daughter of Hugh, the reeve of Dogsthorpe' (c1290 CNat), Willelmus *filius Willelmi filii Johannis de Walton* (1276–90 ib.), Willelmus *filius Ricardi filii Roberti de Placea de Scotere* (1256–84 ib.). But some names make it clear that the man had more than one surname, e.g. Bartholomeus *tabernarius de Oxonia*, Bartholomew *Taverner de Oxonia*, Bartholomeus *Bysshoppe Tabernarius de Oxonia*, or *Bysshop de Oxonia* (1366–1402 Eynsham). The only certainty here is that he lived at Oxford which was not part of his surname.

HOW MUCH OF THE NAME IS REALLY A SURNAME?

In the *Inquisitio Comitatus Cantabrigie* and the *Inquisitio Eliensis* of 1086, we are given parallel lists of the jurors of certain hundreds. The attributes often vary, e.g. Ricardus *fareman* (ICC) appears as Ricardus *praefectus huius hundredi* in InqEl, 'reeve of the hundred', Baldeuuinus *cum barba* 'with the beard' is identical with Baldeuuinus *cocus* 'the cook' and Godwinus *nabesone* with Goduuine *de fulburne*. It is quite clear not only that these were not family names but that the local attributes were not part of the surname but indicated merely the village which the man represented, for Leofwin (InqEl) appears as Leofwin *de Bodischesham* (ICC), Robertus *Anglicus de Fordham* as Robertus *de Fordham*, Godlive (InqEl) is Godlid *de Stanton* (ICC). These men were not lords of manors but villeins, so that Stanhard *de Severlei* and Frawin *de Curtelinge* had no real surname; they simply represented the villages of Silverley and Kirtling.

These and other early local attributes may thus be purely descriptive, not part of the surname, a statement of the man's place of residence. In the towns we shall note that it was quite common for an immigrant to be named from the village or town he had left, e.g. Robert *de punfreit* (1292 SRLo) had left Pontefract (Y) for London, and such names frequently became family names.[1] But in the thirteenth-century *Carte Nativorum* the villeins of the Abbot of Peterborough frequently have added to their name that of the village where they lived and had acquired land, e.g. Richard Gryffyn *de Wytherinton*, Thomas Giuur *de Wytherington*, with others too numerous to cite. That these local attributes were not part of the

[1] *v.* pp. 346–51.

surname but merely indications that the man lived in Werrington is made clear by such successive names as Robertus filius Simonis ad crucem *de Wytherington* and Rogerus filius Galfridi Holyman *de eadem* 'of the same village', whilst Salamon *de Wytherington* is almost certainly to be identified with Salamon filius Willelmi filii Salamonis *de Wytherington* who apparently had no surname. Galfridus *filius Durandi* (*de Glinton*) was of the same family as Robert *Durant*.

The jurors of Wisbech Hundred in 1302 (FA) include Andrew Faber of Tyd, Nicholas Aufre of Neutone, John de Multone of Leveryngtone, John de Wyltone of Wisbech, William de Skyrebeke of Elm and William Wylmete of Welle, the final place-name in each instance indicating the village from which the juror came. In the fourteenth century, when surnames were becoming more general, the juror's village was not named except occasionally where the surname is common (e.g. *Smith, Chapman* or *Barker*). A late example comes from the Lincolnshire assizes of 1361 when William Martyn *de Scothorn*', Robert Benet *de eadem* and Walter Huck *de eadem* were summoned as jurors (AssL).

In the towns it was quite common for a man to be described by a composite name, any part of which might later become a fixed surname, e.g. in Norwich: William *de Devenschyre le Wayte* (1287 NorwLt), Walter *Plukkerose of London le Bursere* (1301 ib.), Robert *Pillecrowe of Aldeburgh wrighte* (1315 ib.). In London, we have *Alan de Sutton called Ballard, saddler* (1303 LoCt), John *Whitlok de Ewelle* (1309 LLB D), called also John *de Ewelle* (1319 SRLo), Simon *de Elyngham, fundour* (1312 LLB D) or Simon *le Founder* (1318 LLB E). John *de Grenewych*, an apprentice, son of Richard *de Bekynham*, had adopted the surname of his master, Peter *de Grenewych* (1312 LLB D). This was a common practice. Sometimes the new surname became the family name, at others it was discarded and changed again.[1]

An interesting and somewhat complicated example has been noted by Ekwall.[2] *John Frank*, son of John *de Aslyngfeld*, in his will of 1349 stipulated that he was to be buried in St Stephen Colman Street near *Alice* his mother, and disposed of goods acquired from *William de Stebeneth* his late brother. He made his former master *Richard Kysser* guardian of John his nephew, son of William de Stebeneth, and mentions a bequest from *Margaret Frank*, widow of *Simon Frank.*

[1] For other examples, *v.* pp. 338–42.   [2] Var, p. 39.

Here we have two brothers with different surnames, neither apparently that of their father. It might be suggested that they were half-brothers, but John had changed his surname as William de Stebeneth may have done. He might have been an apprentice of Andrew de Stebenhethe, smith or cutler (1298–1310). John Frank, on the other hand, cannot have taken his master's surname, unless Richard Kysser had the surname *Frank*, a name by which he is never known. The probability is that John Frank got his new surname owing to the connexion with the Franks indicated in his will. Simon Frank, whose will was enrolled in 1332, was probably a son of *John Frank*, a batour, whose will was enrolled in 1304. He, like Simon, was of the parish of St Stephen Coleman Street. Simon Frank had a daughter *Alice* and it is reasonable to suppose that she was John Frank's mother. If so, John Frank probably adopted his mother's surname. Or he may have been taken care of by his grandparents and acquired their name.

Thus far we have been concerned with the lesser folk, but there is abundant evidence of similar vacillation and variation in the surnames of the land-owners and baronial classes, at times even when they had inherited family names. G. J. Turner has noted an instance in which a single man is referred to by three different surnames in five documents between 1241 and 1248, once as Oliuerus *Clericus*, twice as Oliver *de Opton* and twice as Oliver *de Stilton*. His wife was a daughter of Alicia de Stilton and he had land in Stilton.[1]

Some of these names are purely descriptive: Robertus filius Jalf patris Muriellis uxoris Roberti filii Roberti (1219 AssL); Simon pater Sabine uxoris Nicholai de Radestan (1221 AssWo); Baldewinus filius Roberti filii Randulfi de Grimesbi (Hy 2 DC); some suggest varieties which may have been in actual use: Eudo filius Henrici de Broclosebi, Eudo filius Henrici de Auforde, Eudo de Auford (12th DC). Variation between the father's name and a place-name was common: Willelmus filius Hermanni, Willelmus Hermannus, Willelmus de Caletorp, Willelmus de Hobosse (1140–66 Holme). The names of clergy varied with a change of incumbency or office, or as they rose to higher orders.

Some of these surnames could never have become family names. Some contain the germ from which a hereditary surname might develop. William *le Syur called le Gos* of Tamenhorn (1293 AssSt)

---

[1] G. J. Turner, *A Calendar of the Feet of Fines for the county of Huntingdon* Cambridge Antiq. Soc., 8vo Pub., no. XXXVI, 1913), p. xviii.

had a brother Alan who was called Alan *Gos*, which suggests that this was the real family name. Tamenhorn was presumably their place of residence. Martin *le Marchaunt*, coroner of Wisbech Hundred in 1279 and 1286 is named Martin *de Leverington* in 1299. He was succeeded by his son called indifferently John *de Leverington*, John *son of Martin* and John *le Marchaunt* (Miller). Any one of these three varieties may have become the family name. Innumerable examples of this kind can be found in the twelfth to fourteenth centuries, a period during which hereditary surnames became more numerous.

In England there were no hereditary surnames before the Conquest. They were brought by the Normans from France, where the heredity of fiefs was sanctioned by the Capitulary of Kiersy-sur-Oise in 877. This led gradually to the adoption of hereditary surnames taken from the fiefs. A few are found in the ninth century and the practice gradually became more common, but at the time of the Conquest it was still a novelty but, to quote Freeman, 'a novelty which was fast taking root'. Hugo de Montgomeri was a tenant-in-chief in Staffordshire in 1086. Roger, Lord of Montgomery in Calvados, was made Earl of Shrewsbury by the Conqueror in 1074.[1] The surname derives from an old Norman fief and was borne by an ancestor of Roger in the tenth century.[2] But these surnames could and did vary. Ricardus *filius Gisleberti* was named not only from his father's christian name but also from his French castle of Bienfaite, Ricardus *de Benefacta*, from that he held in Kent, Ricardus *de Tonbrige* and, from his Suffolk lordship, Ricardus *de Clara*, which ultimately became the family name.

In 942 William Longsword, Duke of Normandy, made Hugh de Calvacamp Archbishop of Rouen. He handed over to his brother Ralph the domain of Tosni which formed part of the estates of the archbishopric and both fief and surname were passed on to his descendants. His great-grandson, Ralph de Tony, fought at Hastings and his lands and his name descended from son to son until the extinction of the male line in 1309 when the heir, Alice de Tony, succeeded, and the surname finally disappeared on her marriage

[1] A. R. Wagner, *English Genealogy* (Oxford, 1960), p. 70. For other Norman families, *v.* also pp. 51–70.
[2] A. Dauzat, *Les noms de famille de France* (Paris, 1945), p. 132.

before 1310 to Guy de Beauchamp, Earl of Warwick. Ralph's younger brother Robert, however, abandoned his own surname for that of *de Stafford* where most of his English lands were situated.[1]

One of the chief difficulties in deciding when an early surname became hereditary is the absence of documentation between Domesday Book (1086) and 1155 when continuous national records begin. The names of many of the DB land-holders reappear in the twelfth century with the same surname and in connexion with the same land. The presumption is that both family and surname had continued in the interval, but we lack conclusive proof. Tengvik[2] gives a list of hereditary bynames found in DB based on the mention of father and one or more sons, occasionally also of a grandson, or of two or three brothers all bearing the same surname, but this is not always conclusive. He includes, for instance, Robertus *Balistarius* and Hugo *Balistarius* his son. Robert held Worstead (Nf) in 1086 by serjeanty of performing the duties of *arbalistarius* and his son Odo *albalistarius* (c1140 Holme) inherited the land and the office and owed his surname (now *Arblaster* or *Ballister*) either to inheritance or to his office. But he is also called Odo *de Wrthesteda* (c1150 Crawford) and his son Richard and his grandson Robert were both called *de Worsted* (1166, 1210 Holme).

In all, Tengvik gives some 50 of these hereditary surnames of which 32 are taken from the fief, including names which must have persisted as family names such as Bohun (*Boon*), Brus (*Bruce*), Ferrers, Lacy, Mohun (*Moon*), Mortimer, de Oilgi (*Doyley*), Percy and Pomeroy. Six are patronymic, including Giffard, Paynell and Peverell, and among the 13 nicknames are Bassett, Gernon, Malet and Matravers. To these we must add *Gresley* which is not to be confused with later surnames from Greasley (Nt) and Gresley (Db). Early forms of *Gresley* are clearly from a nickname, OFr *greslet* 'marked as by hail', i.e. pitted or pock-marked. 'The descent of the Gresleys from a Domesday tenant-in-chief is uncommon in the highest degree. Drakelow, which their ancestor held in 1086, remained in the family down to the present century . . . The present baronet is twenty-eighth in descent from the Domesday tenant.'[3]

Two English families, Arden and Berkeley, owe their surnames to this period. The former Round referred to as 'a house enjoying a

---

[1] *v.* Wagner, op. cit., p. 65.
[2] OEByn, pp. 13–22.
[3] Wagner, op. cit., pp. 65–6.

distinction perhaps unique. For it had not only a clear descent from Ælfwine, sheriff of Warwickshire before the Conquest, but even held, of the great possessions of which Domesday shows us its ancestor as lord, some manors which had been his before the Normans landed, at the least as late as the days of Queen Elizabeth', whilst Dugdale notes that his son (Turchil *de Eardene* or *de Waruuic* DB) 'was one of the first here is *England*, that in Imitation of the Normans, assumed a Sirname; for so it appears that he did and wrote himself *Turchillus de Eardene*, in the Days of K. *Will. Rufus*'.[1] With the Berkeleys there is some doubt. Berkeley Castle in Gloucestershire has been theirs for eight centuries since Henry of Anjou (later King Henry II) gave it to their ancestor Robert, son of Harding, in 1153 or 1154. The identity of Harding is not certain, but he was certainly an Englishman and 'on any showing Mr. Robert Berkeley, now of Berkeley, is twenty-fourth in descent from Harding, whose father was probably a thane Eadnoth living before the Conquest'.[2] Among other extant families whose English origin may be assumed, though the proved or highly probable descent goes back only to the twelfth century are Lumley, Fitzwilliam and Assheton.[3]

An obvious method of identifying a man was by reference to his father, and descriptions like Herald *filius Radulfi* (DB) are common in the three centuries after 1086. As a surname, the father's name was added to the christian name as a byname and where both forms are used of the same man we have the beginning of a hereditary surname. Whether it continued as the family name can be decided only when we have sufficient documentary evidence:

Rogerius filius Corbet, Rogerus Corbet 1086 DB (Sa)
Radulfus filius Pagani, Radulfus Paganus ib. (So)
Radulfus filius Balduini, Radulfus Baldewinus Hy 2 DC (L)
Godebald filius Lurc, Godebald Lurc 1166 P (Nf)
Ailmerus filius Mosse 1153–68, Almer Mosse 1186–1210 Holme (Nf)
Robertus filius Akar', Robertus Akari 1199 CurR (Hu)
Andreas filius Amauri, Andreas Amauri 1200 Oriel (O)
Galfridus filius Angod, Galfridus Angod 1208, 1235 Fees (Bk)
Godwinus filius Elfare, Godwinus Elfare 1221 *ElyA* (Nf)
Paganus le Cachepol, father of William Payn 1285 *Ass* (Ess)
John Gerveis son of Gervase de Pelsedun 1299 AD vi (K)

[1] Wagner, op. cit., 47–8.　　[2] Ibid., pp. 48–9.　　[3] Ibid., p. 51.

William Morisse, Willelmus filius Mauritii 1300 *ERO*
John le fiz Michel 1292 SRLo, John Michel 1301 LoCt

Nicknames probably became hereditary early. They may at times be applicable to both father and son but are usually personal and particular. The following names were probably already hereditary:

Reginald Ridel son of Hugh Ridel 1156–80 Bury (Nth)
Ralph Belet son of William Belet 1176 P (Sr)
William Brese son of Roger Brese 1210 P (Nf)
William Shepescank, Gilbert his brother, John Sepesank' 1224 Cur (Nf)
John Caritas, Simon Caritas, brothers 1265 FrLeic
William Lefthand, Ralph Lefthand 1268 FrLeic
Peter Wedercok son of Simon Wedircok 1302 Miller (C)
John Melkesop, William Melkesop 1327 SRSo
John son of Peter Sokelyng and John Sokelyng junior 1329 FFK
John Jolife son of Peter Jolife 1332 NorwDeeds
William Godchep son of John Godchep 1374 AssL

Clear evidence of heredity:

A charter of 1153 of Agnes de Sibbeford, wife of Ralph Clement, is witnessed by Hugo Clement and William, son of Richard Clement, who is later called Willelmus Clemens, with a brother Robertus Clemens (1155 Templars)
Thomas Noel, founder of Ronton Priory, is so called in 1182–5. His father was Robert Noel (ib.), who is called Robertus Noelli filius (c1150 StCh)
Goce[1] Ketel, brother of Peter Ketel; Thomas Ketel son of Peter Ketel c1200, 1218–22 StP (Lo)
Nigel Brun father of Roger Brun; Roger Brun brother of William Brun 1219 AssY
Eda Elger, daughter of Walter Elger of Fornesete, Robert Elger her brother 1271 AD iv

When local surnames of address and occupational-names became family names, it is, at present, impossible to say. The former type is found from the twelfth century, but we seldom have any indication of a pedigree or when the name ceased to be descriptive and was used of all members of the family, or even whether there was more than one family living by the particular wood or hill. Nelmes in Hornchurch (Ess) was probably the home of Ernwin *de Ulmis* in the reign of John (PNEss 114). The surname occurs in the parish as *atte Elmes* in 1333, *atte Nelmes* in 1339 and *ate Thelmes* in 1356 and clearly became hereditary although it had changed, for Richard *de Ulmis* is called indifferently Richard *de Ulmis* (*de Havering*) and Richard *de Havering* (*de Ulmis*) and once Richard *de Havering* son of Reginald *de Ulmis*.

[1] Printed *Gote*. Probably an error for *Goce* or *Joce*. v. ELPN, p. 78.

It has been suggested that an occupational-name preceded by the article was a proof that the man followed the particular trade, whilst the absence of the article indicated a hereditary surname. But from the twelfth century forms of both kinds are found for the same man: Henry Taneur, le Tanur 1166–7 P; Robert (le) Cupere 1176–7 P; Richard (le) Turnur 12th DC. Where the surname is followed by a different trade-name, it was, probably, already inherited: Roger le Parcheminer, butcher 1294, John le Combister, fishman 1315 NorwDeeds; Peter le Barbier Pybaker 1319 SRLo; John Faber carnifex 1327 SRSf; John le sauser, felter, son of John le sauser 1331 FrY; John le Fysscher, pistor 1353 Putman. But not always, e.g. Johannes Byller, baxter, filius Henrici Holtebyman, milner 1427 FrY. This is confirmed by such pairs as the modern Archer, Larcher; Feaver, Lefeaver; Usher, Lusher, etc.

Whilst evidence for the heredity of surnames steadily increases from the twelfth century onwards, there is abundant proof that, even among the landed classes, surnames were far from stable in the thirteenth and fourteenth centuries. Richard de Glanville held Glanville in Calvados down to the loss of Normandy in 1205 (Loyd). But Bartholomew de Glamuill', joint sheriff of Norfolk and Suffolk 1170–5, was a descendant of Robert de Glanuill' the DB holder of Honing and an ancestor of William de Glaunville who held in 1210–12, yet he appears in the Holme cartulary as Bartholomeus (1127–34), Bartholomeus filius Hugonis (1134–40) and Bartholomeus de Glamuill' (1141). But the surname was undoubtedly hereditary, for in a charter of Bartolomeus de glamuilla of about 1150 he refers to his father William, whilst six of the witnesses include Hervey, Randulf his son, Roger, William, Osbert and Reginald, all called de Glanville (Crawford).

Ralph, son of Robert Puintel de Walsham, had two brothers, William de Criketot and Ralph Cangard (12th Holme). He is also called Ralph de Crichetot (1141–9 ib.), with a son Hubert de Criketot (1163–6 ib.).

Philip de Powyk (1147–54 Holme) was a brother of Geoffrey Ridel (1153–68 ib.), a son of Richard Basset, and is called Philip Basset in 1185 (RotDom).

Griffin de Tweyt (1153–68 Holme) had a son Osbern de Thurgerton

(1140–53) who married Cecilia, daughter of Roger de Curcun. Their son was Robert de Thweyt (1153–6) or de Curcun or Robert Curcun de Thweyt (1186–1210). His son was Robert the Clerk.[1]

From twelfth century Danelaw charters:

Ralph de Cheurolcurt, Ralph de Clachesbi
Johannes filius Herberti, John de Orrebi
Adam filius Remigii (de Hakethorn), Adam Wodecok
Reginald Lequite, Reginald de Courtenay

In the thirteenth and fourteenth centuries similar variations are found, and here we often have real alternative surnames:

Robert Hastif, Robert de Disun 1202–3 Cur (Wa)
Ricardus filius Walteri, Ricardus de Cliue 1221 AssWo
Milo de Verdun, Milo de Creyton 1222 AssSt [2]
Roger Waudin, Rogerus Anglicus 1243 Fees (Sa)
Ralph le Verrer, Ralph Vicar 1311 ColchCt
Jordan de Newintone, Jordanus Pistor 1317 AssK
Nicholas Patyner otherwise called Nicholas Neuman 1395 Cl (Co)

This variation of surnames is sometimes implied:

Hugo de Burgo le Mazun 1257 Oseney
Johannes Gyffard dictus le Boef 1297 MinAcctCo
John Bulichromp called le Binder 1300 LLB C
Adam de Sutton called 'Ballard', sadler 1303 LoCt
William Cros le Bole 1305 LoCt
Peter le Taverner called Holer 1311 LLB D
Walter de Braylesham called 'le Cok' 1341 LLB F
Roger de Haveryng alias atte Sele 1343 LoPleas
Ralph de Eyr called Proudfot of Havering 1393 HPD (Ess)

The following names of freemen of York are so entered on the roll:

Thomas le Walche, de Selby, girdeler (1329)
Alan Hare, de Acastre, carnifex (1332)
Rogerus filius Johannis de Burton, de Eton in le Clay, boucher (1343)
Johannes filius Roberti de Gaunt, de Duffeld, mercer (1356)

With the fifteenth century such names become less common, but variation of surname continued and is found sporadically until the seventeenth century or later:

Robert Curson alias Betele 1410 AD iv (Lo)
Nichol Wigh oþerwise callyd Nicholas Ketringham oþerwise callyd John
    Segrave oþerwise callyd Nicholl' Pecche 1418 LondEng

[1] For the surnames of the family of Stigand the priest, *v.* p. 94.
[2] He held land in Creighton.

John Morys alias Rede alias Sclattere 1474 Oseney

Roger Harflete otherwise called Roger Cheker son and one of the heirs of Christopher Harflete otherwise called Christopher Atcheker . . . Raymond Harflete also called R. Atcheker 1508 ArchC 40

John Alforthe alias Aworthe alias John Surgion alias John Holford of Pountfret 1532 LP (Y)

John Salcot alias Capon, bishop of Bangor 1534 LP

Xʳ Septvans alias Harflete 1575 ArchC 40

Richard Bishop alias Hewson of London 1671 EA(NS) iv

There is evidence, too, that the surname of the document is not always that used by the man himself:

Robert le Botiler of Hertford. *Seal*: Robertus filius Willelmi (1275 AD iv)

John Cundy of Suthewyc. *Seal*: John Lungecot (1288 AD vi)

Agnes daughter of Rogerus piscator of Coventre. *Seal*: Agnes filia Petronille (1299 AD v)

Thomas le Diakne of Ikelyntone. *Seal*: Thomas filius Ricardi de Fonte (1300 ib.)

Angerus called Humfrey of Lapworth. *Seal*: Aungerus de Bispwod (1319 ib.)

Katharine daughter of John le Jay, wife of Roger Prodhome. *Seal*: Katerina Franceis (14th ib.).

A short selection of non-hereditary surnames:

Galfridus del Bec filius Rogeri de Cauces Hy 2 DC (Db)

Reginald le Taylor, son of William de Tamworth 1262 FrLeic

John Kneyth' son of Eudo le Provost de Redeswelle 1285 *Ass* (Ess)

Adam Berenger de Enefeld filius Simonis de Benyton 1285 Bart

William de Horsted, son of Geoffrey le Chapman of Mergate 1287 NorwDeeds

Luke le Ayler 1287 LLB A; his son, Walter le Mazerer 1306 LLB B

Richard de Lincoln, son of Richard de Stalham 1288 NorwDeeds

Joceus le Gerdelere son of Gilbert Pollard 1314 *Petre* (Ess)

John de Refham son of William de Laxton 1334 NorwDeeds

Roger de Ellerton, mercer, son of Roger Alcok 1379 FrY

John de Moreton, son of William de Dalby 1391 ib.

TRANSFER OF SURNAMES

In London, in the thirteenth and fourteenth centuries, it was quite usual for the surname of an apprentice to be replaced, either temporarily or permanently, by that of his master which in many instances became the family name. Robert *Podifat* (1288 LLB D) was an apprentice of Roger *le Fuyster* (1312 LLB D), who is also called

Roger *Podifat* (1320 LLB E). Robert had therefore adopted his master's nickname as his surname.[1]

There is evidence of the same custom at York, Norwich and elsewhere, though less well documented:

Agnes de Scothowe servant of William de Scothowe le Especer 1289 NorwDeeds
William Payne serviens John Payne 1323 FrY
William Bowyere serviens Walteri Bowyere de Luda 1374 AssL
. . . Shortnekke serviens Johannis Shortnekke 1381 SRSf
Thomas Gauke, cocus, filius Roberti Nyd servientis Simonis Gauke (1424 FrY). Here, Thomas bore the surname of his father's master which had probably been assumed earlier by his father.
John Tegeantservant *alias* John Servaunt Tegeaunt *alias* John Tegeant of Westminster, servant 1509 LP [2]

LONDON SURNAMES

As with the nobility, hereditary surnames became fixed early among the patrician classes of London, the families which provided aldermen, sheriffs and mayors. Brichtmar de Haverhill (1147), sheriff in 1174–6, had a son William (sheriff 1190–1, alderman c1200) who had two sons Thomas (alderman 1205–6) and James, all called *de Haverhill*. *Basing* was a common London surname from about 1190 to 1269. *Viel* persisted certainly from 1229 to 1311. John *Vitalis* or *Viel* (1237) is also called John son of Vitalis and must have been the son of a man named Viel, perhaps Viel Parmentarius (1169). Richard Renger, a merchant, alderman, sheriff 1220–2 and mayor 1222–7 and 1238–9, is also called Ricardus *filius Reinger*. He had two sons Richard Reynger (alderman) and John Renger. Like many of the wealthy Londoners, the family acquired a landed estate and has left its name in two Essex farms, Ringer's Fm in Terling and Ringers in Shalford.[3] *Sperling* the alderman (c1130) was, no doubt, the ancestor of the family which can be followed for some 200 years, usually under this surname, occasionally as *filius Esperling* (1173) and *Alderman* (Hy 2).[4]

These early hereditary surnames were more common than would at first sight appear. Ekwall has noted that William *Joinier*, sheriff

---

[1] For a full discussion, *v.* pp. 338–42 below.
[2] For servants' names, *v.* pp. 193–7, 201–3, 212–13.
[3] ELPN, pp. 120, 133.
[4] Ibid., pp. 62–4.

1222–3, an alderman and mayor 1239–40, first appears as William *le juinnur* in 1204. But he was not a joiner. He was a merchant who imported wine and merchandise, silk cloths and other goods and exported wool. He sold the King a chasuble, an alb stole and baudekin cloth. He appears to have been a mercer and his surname must have been inherited. John Peucier 'leather-seller' and Godwin Ladubur 'renovator of old clothes' both occur in a list of moneyers of 1168. Neither surname can have any reference to their occupation and both must have been inherited.[1]

From the latter part of the thirteenth century onwards the abundant records provide much material for the study of surnames including those of the lower classes, but it is often complicated and difficult to handle. What is clear is that surnames were still not generally settled. A man could be named after his father or from his occupation, from his place of residence or from the place from which he had come to London, or from a nickname, or, at times, from his mother or some other relative. One man might have several surnames used indifferently or in combination and the testator not seldom uses as his name a surname different from that he had in his youth. The surnames of immigrants and the masters' surnames assumed by apprentices are discussed elsewhere.[2] Which of these surnames survived is largely a matter of choice or accident and cannot be settled without much detail and documentation. Examples are scattered throughout this book and here we may note a few late examples of unstable names:

Richard Eswy, brother of Thomas de Basinges 1275 Husting
John le Poter 1284 LLB A, John de Totenham potter 1302 LLB B
Gilbert Ladde 1305 LLB B, Gilbert de Seint Need called Ladde 1306 ib.
Richard de Foxton, son of Adam Mody 1314 Husting
William de Whetelee cordwainer 1353 LLB G, William Lovel called
    Whatelee, cordwainer 1380 Husting

Ekwall, whose knowledge of London surnames was unrivalled, was of opinion that 'in the early fourteenth century usage as regards surnames had not yet acquired the fixed character it had later, and we must conclude that the christian name was still the most important part of the name, that by which people were called in ordinary speech—I am here referring to middle-class London society. But the implication of this variation in surnames should not be overestimated. There can be no doubt that in the early fourteenth century surnames on the whole had acquired a fixed character.' It was the surnames of young people that were most liable to change. Many of the apprentices with new surnames were demonstrably newcomers to London. The surnames of adult people cannot be proved to have been so liable to change and where variation did take place it was most likely to develop in the case of immigrants.[1]

THE COMMON FOLK

For the moment we will remain in the town, this time Norwich, where we have an interesting example of the value of access to a number of different documents. John the Subdean appears usually as John *de Berstrete*, from the district so called. But he lived not in that district but in Tombland. In 1290 Hamo, son of Simon *atte Hollegate*, was living in this street leading out of Berstrete, but no one would suspect this Simon to be a brother of John until he found his son Hamo called in another deed 'Hamo, son of Simon *de Berstrete*' and nephew and heir of John *le Den*. The father of John and Simon was also called John *de Berstrete*, so that *de Berstrete* had, to some extent, become the family name. But in the first Roll we find mention of John *le Mercer*, Dean of Norwich, who must be John *de Berstrete*. In the deeds of this period there occurs several times in the neighbourhood of Holgate a 'John, son of Simon *le Mercer*' and, although it cannot be proved, yet, considering the occurrence of 'John', 'Simon', 'le Mercer' and 'Holgate', it seems most probable that this was the elder John de Berstrete, and that the Subdean was called 'le Mercer' from his grandfather. Yet it would plainly be incorrect to take 'Mercer' for a settled family name and call him 'John Mercer, Dean of Norwich'.[2]

Such detailed information is very seldom available to elucidate the surnames of the common folk of the countryside or the town. Their names usually occur in isolation with little, if any, information of their relatives. For their genealogies we need a long, continuous series of Court Rolls and those published provide only odd scraps of family history on which we have to theorise and speculate. We have a long list of the peasants on the Bury St Edmund's manors c1095. Of 660, more than half (359) had a single name only; 104 were described by their father's name (Goduine *Stanardi filius*, Ulfuine *Teperesune*); 163 had bynames of various kinds (Ordric

---

[1] Var, pp. 48–9.   [2] NorwLt, p. xcii.

Wihgar, Æiluuin *de Mor*, Godui *longus*, Uluric *Blodleter*)—a clear indication of the rise of surnames, but with no suggestion that they were hereditary. We know that up to 1206 hereditary surnames were unknown among the villeins.[1] Surnames were still in a state of flux in 1277 on the Ely manors of Norfolk and Suffolk (*Ely*). It is clear from the Subsidy Rolls that in the south at least a large proportion of the surnames must have become hereditary but we have no proof; there is no indication of relationship (except of widows).

The fourteenth-century *Carte Nativorum* contains numerous names of the villeins on the manors of the Abbot of Peterborough in the latter part of the thirteenth century. Every kind of surname is found, from a single name to descriptions like Robertus *filius Willelmi filii Audelin*, patronymics such as Robertus *Harold* and Galfridus *Huwesson*, local (John *atte Grene*), occupational (Osbernus *le Taylour*) and nicknames like Willelmus *dictus Louel*, Henricus *Puttok* and Radulphus *Greyeye*. Many of the surnames varied and it is quite clear that, in general, they were still unstable, but a number show signs of developing into family names, whilst some were already hereditary.

Robert *Hereward*, living somewhere about 1250, had two sons, Richard and Ascelin; the latter also had two sons, Warin and Matthew. All the men except Richard are at some time named *Hereward* which seems to have been their family name, but Warin is also called 'son of Ascelin Hereward de Glinton' and Warin de Glinton (a1290).[2] Ralph *Matefrey* is identical with Radulphus *filius Matefridi de Undele* (1274–95). It is the only surname given to any member of the family and appears to be the beginning of a family name. *Gere* also appears to be already a fixed surname, appearing in three successive generations from about 1275 to 1310,[3] whilst the nickname *Folesanke* 'with legs like a foal' occurs as the surname of father, son and grandson between 1227 and 1245.[4] Other evidence points in the same direction, showing that the country folk were gradually acquiring fixed surnames in the thirteenth century.

The absence of genealogical information in the Subsidy Rolls is a serious handicap, but Fransson has very plausibly suggested means by which this may to some extent be overcome.[5] He gives seven instances from 1296 onwards where two men with the same christian name and surname are styled *senior* and *junior*, plausibly suggesting

---

[1] See the villein pedigrees on pp. 104, 105.
[2] Cf. CNat, p. 107.   [3] Ibid., p. 8.
[4] Ibid., p. 78.   [5] MESO, pp. 36–8.

they were father and son. To these we may add: Henry Loe junior, William de Wymbeldon' junior 1275 SRWo, Willelmus Sutor (junior), John Gromet (antiquior) 1301 SRY, William Magge (junior), William Harneys (junior), John Norman (junior) 1327 SRSf and Robert Lucas senior, junior, John Willing senior, junior 1327 SRSo.

In the Subsidy Rolls, the repetition of local or occupational surnames in the same village cannot be regarded as a sign of heredity, but where we have two or more surnames from the same nickname in the same village, as Roger and William *le Rede* in Blythburgh, William and Adam *Prat* in Clopton and John, Alexander and Richard *Pesecod* in Reydon (1327 SRSf) this can hardly be regarded as a mere coincidence; they must refer to members of the same family. Similarly, two or more men with the same patronymics in the same village, especially if the surname is uncommon, were probably relatives; Thomas and Hamo *Sarle* (Little Stonham), Gilbert and James *Wenyld* (Yaxley), Roger and Thomas *Bence* (Bungay), Simon and Adam *Yongwyne* (Great Saxham), all in 1327 SRSf. In fact, an analysis of the Subsidy Rolls produces impressive evidence that in the early fourteenth century a considerable number of such names must have been already hereditary. In 1275 SRWo we find such evidence in 59 different parishes; in 1327 SRSf in 188 parishes and in 1327 SRSo in 137; in one parish in the last county there are 9 different surnames of this kind, shared by 28 persons, including Sparke (5), Martyn, Stevene and Gille (4 each), Harding (3), Edward, Sevare, Sharpe and Wylecok (2 each), surely no mere coincidence.

When material is available, a further test is to compare different documents of different periods relating to the same village. For Suffolk, where in 1095 we can find no hint of hereditary surnames among the Bury peasants, we have two surveys of the manors of the Bishop of Ely for 1221 and 1277 in which many peasants have no surname. In 15 parishes we find the same surname in 1221 and 1277 as in the subsidy of 1327, and these can safely be regarded as hereditary. Only two or three parallels are found, as a rule, in any one parish, but in Glemsford six names occur in both 1221 and 1277, two in 1277 and 1327, and one (*Curteis*) in all three years. In Rattlesden, seven surnames occur both in 1221 and 1327, *Haliday* twice in each year, *Barun* twice in 1221, *Hardheved* twice in 1327.

For the Bury manors we have a Subsidy of 1283 for Blackburn Hundred, unfortunately damaged, with the loss of many names, and

311

surveys of five hundreds c1188–90. These surveys are much less detailed than those of the Ely manors and contain many fewer names. In 27 parishes we find some of the surnames of 1327 also in one or both the earlier documents, cumulative evidence that the surnames were becoming hereditary throughout the county. In Stanton, Nicholas *Wluric* of 1283 probably owed his surname to *Wuluricus* filius fabri of 1188. *Cat* is found in all three documents, *Hubert* and *Kenne* in 1283 and 1327, *Cauel* and *Brunston* in 1188 and 1327. In Hopton, Honington and Troston six, in Walsham five and in Culford, Rickinghall and Ixworth Thorpe four surnames occur in both 1283 and 1327.

All this fits in with a noteworthy feature of the southern Subsidy Rolls—the large number of surnames formed from OE personal-names no longer in use in the county: Worcestershire (1275) 203, Somerset (1327) 208, Suffolk (1327) 441. The complete disappearance of these personal-names proves that the surnames must have become family names.

YORKSHIRE SURNAMES IN 1379

In the north, especially in Lancashire and Yorkshire, hereditary surnames became fixed later than in the south. In the fourteenth-century Subsidy Rolls the proportion of men with no surname is much greater than in the south and, on the whole, family names seem to have developed some 50 years later, though some of the smaller landed gentry had fixed names earlier. Five generations of the Sampsons occur with the same surname from before 1273,[1] whilst the Abrahams owed their surname to a certain Abraham whose grandson John Abraham was grandfather of William Abraham of Nawton who held the land in 1298.[2]

Among the Freemen of York some names were hereditary, e.g. Robertus le batour, carnifex 1311, Thomas le hosteler, mariner 1331, Henry de Beverley son of John de Beverle 1338; others were not, William Belle son of Andrew le taillour 1316, Thomas le parchemyner son of John le hatter 1334, John de Hoveden son of John de Worne, seller 1361.

In 1379 PTY there is distinct evidence that many occupational surnames were not yet hereditary. Twenty-two men named *Smyth*

---

[1] 1301 SRY, p. 119, n.   [2] Ibid., p. 50, n. 2.

are described as *smyth* or *faber*; 20 *Taylours* and 12 *Websters* followed these trades, 8 *Wrights* were either wrights or carpenters and 7 Walkers fullers or walkers; in all some 138 of these artisans had surnames such as John Littester, lister; John Sowter, sutor, etc. At the same time there is a clear indication that many trade-names were hereditary: John Taylour, smyth; Thomas Cartwryght, draper; Robert Ploghman, osteler; John Mylner, souter—in all 95 (neither total claims to be complete). To these we may add John Saunder, senior, junior; John Gobisid senior and William Gobisid; John de Corby senior, junior, all pointing to established family names.

This West Riding Poll-tax of 1379 (19,600 names) provides material quite unlike that found in the south and paralleled only by the East Riding Poll-tax of 1381. The *filius*-type of name is much less common than in 1327; that in *-son* much more frequent. What is especially noticeable is the frequency of names in *-wyf* and *-doghter* and those of servants in *-man*, *-servant*, *-woman* and *-mayden*, besides names indicating other relationships in *-brother*, *-cosyn*, *-syster* and *-stepson*:

Magota Williamwyf, Joan Jonkynwyf, Alice Gefraywyf
Joan Tomdoutter, Rosa Anotdoghter, Alice Wilkynsondoghter
    In two instances we have a man's surname: Robertus ffelisdoghter et Cecilia vxor ejus; Richard Wryght doghter
William Mathewman, Magota Mathewwoman; Joan Vikerservant; Joan Prestewoman; Alice Martynmayden; Robert Parsonbrother, Henry Parsoncosyn, Alice Prestsyster, John Robertstepson
    In these names, the suffix was often added to the surname and the master, etc., may be named separately: John Odson, Alice Odsonwyf; John de Wykelsworth, Joan Wykelsworthdoghter; Emma Hurle, Joan Hurlemayden
    Similarly names in *-son* were also based on the surname: John Payg, John Paygson; Richard Parlebene, Robert Parlebeneson; cf. William Saunderson, Alice Saunderdoghter; William Milnerson, Agnes Milnerwyf
    The wife of Robert *Wright* was Elena *Wrightwyf*; his son John *Wrightson*.

The sons of William Jonson are named William Willeson Johanson and Benedict Willeson Johnson; that of Robert Hudson was William Robynson Hudson. Wives were similarly named: Margareta Wilkynwyf Raulynson, Agnes Dycounwyfdouson. Occasionally we have proof of a hereditary surname: Adam Siluermouth was clearly the father of John Adamson Siluermouth and Robert Hyrd of John Robynson Hyrd; cf. Agnes Williamwyf Smyth (1381 PTY).

It is abundantly clear that in the north surnames became hereditary much later—about 50 years—than in the south. It was not until about 1370–80 that many of the land-holders named Wilson, Dyson, etc., acquired real family names and they were clearly ahead of the common folk.[1]

WHY DID SURNAMES BECOME HEREDITARY?

The rise of surnames, according to the accepted theory, was due to the Norman Conquest when the Old English personal-names were rapidly superseded by the new christian names introduced by the Normans. Of these, only a few were really popular and in the twelfth century this scarcity of christian names led to the increasing use of surnames to distinguish the numerous individuals of the same name.

This is an oversimplification. Bynames—both English and Scandinavian—are found in England before the Conquest. Some Normans had hereditary surnames before they came to England. Evidence is accumulating that the OE personal-names lived on longer than has been supposed, a fact confirmed by the large number of modern surnames to which they have given rise and which must have been in living use after the Conquest. The new French personal-names, too, were more varied than is commonly believed. A few, William, Robert, Richard and John, certainly became much more popular than the rest, but it was not from these that the earliest patronymic surnames were formed.

It is often assumed that men 'adopted' their surnames. Some certainly did, but the individual himself had no need for a label to distinguish him from his fellows. The development of the feudal system made it essential that the king should know exactly what service each knight owed. Payments to and by the exchequer required that debtors and creditors should be particularised. The lawyers saw to it that the parties to transfers of land or those concerned in criminal proceedings could be definitely identified. Monasteries drew up surveys and extents with details of tenants of all classes and their services. And later the net was thrown wider in the long lists of those assessed in the Subsidy Rolls. It was the official who required exact identification of the individual. His early efforts often consisted of long-winded descriptions attached to a personal-name. Any description which definitely identified the man was

[1] v. pp. 88–9.

satisfactory—his father's name, the name of his land or a nickname known to be his. The upper classes—mostly illiterate—were those with whom the officials were chiefly concerned and among them surnames first became numerous and hereditary. It is noteworthy that in London, with its organised government and elaborate records, surnames became fixed early among the patrician classes.[1]

WHEN DID SURNAMES BECOME HEREDITARY?

This question, often put to me, can be satisfactorily answered only in the most general terms—at any time in the 300 years following the Norman Conquest. In England, family names were first introduced by the Norman barons, mostly taken from their French fiefs, but also from the name of an ancestor or from a nickname. The practice became fashionable and gradually spread to the lords of smaller manors. The system was found useful by officials and lawyers who gradually extended it to men who held no land, naming them by reference to their father, by a nickname or from their place of residence, often varying the description, until in time the combined influence of fashion and convenience provided all men with a fixed surname.

Throughout this long period the process continued at different rates not only in different parts of the country but also among the different classes. From the twelfth century there is a steady increase in the growth of family names among the land-holders, at the same time with considerable variation of name. Up to 1200 the peasants had no fixed surnames, but there are signs of their development from about 1225 and they became steadily more common as the century advanced and were in fairly general use about 100 years later. The north was less advanced than the south and here many surnames, even among the landed gentry, did not become hereditary until about 1380, some not until after 1400.

For the towns, apart from London, our information is unsatisfactory. There were surnames of all kinds in Winchester in 1066, in King's Lynn in 1166 and in Newark about 1175 but little or no evidence of heredity. London, as always, was exceptional. Its abundant records prove that the patrician classes had fixed family

---

[1] P. H. Reaney, *Dictionary of British Surnames* (London, 1958), pp. xxxviii–ix. I see no reason yet for modifying this general statement.

names in the twelfth century, but that in the thirteenth and fourteenth centuries among the middle and lower classes there was considerable variation in the names used; a man might be known by more than one surname at different times or might have changed his name, having assumed or had imposed on him the surname of a former master or of some relative.

Here we come to the end of the 'origin' of English surnames. What follows is largely a matter of change and variation and the influx of new surnames from abroad. The modern form of many of our surnames is, however, due to the Parish Registers. In these, from late Elizabethan times, we find the solution of many problems. The parson was often dealing with illiterates; he had no previous spelling of the name to guide him; he merely wrote down what he heard—or thought he had heard. At a time when there was no recognised system of spelling, his phonetic efforts were apt to vary and these, combined with the genealogical material in the registers, prove clearly that Farrer, Farrah, Farrey and Farrow are but a single name, that Dayman and Diamond are identical, and that Fusier undoubtedly derives from *Fursehewer*. Other problems will undoubtedly be solved by a study of other registers, but the task will be long. The material used for this book is but a very small part of that available, and the full story of our names will not be known until the rest has been fully examined and sifted and for this we need much more time. The way to progress and success is co-operation. What we really need is an English Names Society to round off and supplement the work of the English Place-name Society.

WELSH SURNAMES

Although our subject is the origin of English surnames, we cannot altogether ignore those of Wales. Long before Wales came under English rule there was much coming and going across the border. Welsh personal-names are found in England in DB and steadily become more numerous. After the creation of the future Edward II as Prince of Wales in 1301 increasing numbers of Welshmen settled in the border counties.

None of these Welshmen had hereditary surnames. For a couple of centuries more they clung tenaciously to their ancient system by which a man's name gave his pedigree for several generations, a type of name still found as late as the sixteenth century (*ap* means 'son of'):

Morgan ap Llewelyn ap Jevan ap Jenkin 1454 AD (Monmouth)
David ap Ithell ap Hoell ap Gruffith LLoit 1500 ib. (Flint)
Jevaun ap Rees ap David ap Grono 1548 ib. (Denbigh)

As the Registrar-General in his Annual Report for 1853 puts it, 'Hereditary surnames were not in use even among the gentry of Wales until the time of Henry VIII, nor were they generally established until a much later period; indeed, at the present day they can scarcely be said to be adopted among the lower classes in the wilder districts, where, as the marriage registers show, the christian name of the father still frequently becomes the patronymic of the son.'

But Welsh surnames appear in the border counties from the twelfth century. When a Welshman settled in England he was treated by his new neighbours—at any rate so far as his name was concerned—as an Englishman. Most of their surnames were patronymics from ancient Welsh personal-names such as William *Hoel* 1183 P (W), William *Craddoc* 1205 P (Wo), John *Morgan* 1214 Cur (Berks), Roger *Lewelin* 1255 AssSa, Walter *Meyler* 1255 RH (Sa), Richard *Cadigan* 1273 RH (Wa), William *Madoc* 1274 RH (Sa). All these still survive and each personal-name is found earlier in England: *Morganus* filius *Hoel* 1166 P (Sa), OW *Morcant* and *Houel*, now Morgan and Howell, *Cradoc* (*Caradoch*') 1177 P (He), OW *Cara-dawc, Cradawc*, from Lat *Caratācos*, now Craddock, *Lewelinus* 1198 P (Sa), W *Llyelin*, now Llewellin, *Meilerus* 1160 P (Sa), W *Meilyr*, OW *Maglorīx*, now Maylor or Meyler, *Caducan* 1161 P (Wo), OW *Cadwugaun*, now Cadogan, *Madoch* 1066 DB (Gl), *Madoc* 1160 P (Sa), W *Madawc*, OW *Matōc*, now Maddocks or Mattocks. Exactly when these names became hereditary we cannot say, but their frequency and their persistence as surnames prove this must have been long before the Welsh abandoned their pedigree-names. They are English surnames, formed in England after the English manner.

The records of the border counties show, too, the development in England of other types of Welsh names. Some Welshmen had a nickname, not hereditary but peculiar to the individual: David ap Jorwerth *Vachann* (W *fychan*, mutation of *bychan* 'small, little'), now Vaughan; Gruffydd ap Jorwerth *Gogh* (W *coch* 'red'), now Gough, Gooch; Madog *LLoit* Bannour (W *llwyd* 'grey'), now Lloyd (all 1391 Chirk). These nicknames came to be used as the sole surname, and finally as family names: Cadogan *Vaghan* 1327 SRSa, David

Y   317

Gogh 1391 Chirk, Richard *Loyt* 1327 SRWo. Galfridus Lloyt son of Jevan Lloyt ap Tudor (1459 SaG) had adopted his father's nickname as his surname.

In 1327 in Shropshire (SRSa) about one man in five had a Welsh surname, including 10 nicknames, some 25 short pedigree-names (David ap Gwyn) with the same number of patronymics formed after the English fashion from Welsh names (Richard Owen). Later Shropshire documents give some idea of the gradual development of hereditary surnames. In the Extent of Chirk (1392–3) most of the surnames were of the longer pedigree type, Madog ap Jevan ap Jorwerth, 'Madoc son of Evan, son of Yorwerth'. In the Shropshire Guild Records in 1450 we still find names like Lodowicus ap Dauid de Salop, but Hugo Morys, son of Maurice ap Phelip had adopted his father's christian name as his surname, as had Geoffrey Jones, son of Jeuen ap Mapefflur (1459) and John Meredith, son of Meredith ap Llewellyn ap Madoc (1501).

John *Evans*, provost of Shrewsbury 1558, was admitted a burgess in 1505 as John *Jevans*. He was the son of John *ap Jeuan* of Llanvair Caereinion (Montgomery), carpenter. He was a corvisor by trade, later 'gentleman', and MP for Shrewsbury in 1547. Hugh *Edwardes* was the son of *Edward* ap John, mercer and burgess of Shrewsbury (1552) and founder of Shrewsbury Royal Grammar School. His descendants were called *Edwardes* for some 300 years.

Among the Chirbury ratepayers of 1604 were David ap William, Mawd Evans, John ap David, John ap Oliver, Thomas ap Hugh, William Hughes, Jewan ap Edward and Robert ap Edward, a list which shows the tenacity with which the Welsh clung to their *ap* or *ab* and illustrates the difficulty of discovering when these names finally lost their initial vowel. *Evans* and *Hughes* are typical 'Welsh' surnames, *ap Hugh* is now *Pugh* or *Pew* (John *Pewe* 1584 MustersSr) and *ap Edward* has become *Bedward* or *Beddard*. We still have *apSimon, Abadam, Badams, Badham* (Hoel *ab Adam* 'son of Adam' 1255 RH (Sa), John *Ab Adham* 1310 ParlWrits, Rychard *Badam* 1570 LedburyPR), and *Abethell* or *Bithell* 'son of Ithel', W Ithell, MW *Ithael*, which survives as *Ithell, Iddols* and *Idle*. Occasionally a trace of the initial vowel survives: *Upjohn* (Roger *ap John* 1638), *Uprichard*. But the rest now begin with B- or P-: *Bevan* 'son of Evan', *Brobyn, Probin* 'son of Robin', *Probert* 'son of Robert'. Some of these names preserve OW personal-names: *Bowen* 'son of Owen', *Preece* or *Price* 'son of Rhys', the most prolific being from OW

Enniaun, ultimately from Lat *Anniānus*, though the personal-name seems to have been associated with W *einion* 'anvil' for 'stability, fortitude' and doubtfully with *uniawn* 'upright, just'. This survives as *Ennion, Eynon, Inions, Anyan, Onians, Onions* and *Hennion* and, compounded with *ap* or *ab*, as *Pinnion, Beynon, Benian, Benyon* and *Binyon*. In 1455 in Worcestershire and in 1486 in Gloucestershire this acquired a pseudo-topographical form John and Alexander *Baynham* which still survives.

An interesting example of variation and the late development of a Welsh surname comes from Essex. Lewis Johan or Jon or John occurs frequently from 1414 to 1447. He was a Welshman who in 1424 secured testimonials from the Mayors of Tenby, Pembroke, Carmarthen and Cardigan and the Provosts of Newborough and Kidwelley to the effect that he 'was born a free man of free parents and of noble and gentlemanly stock'. He had already married, without the king's consent, the sister of Sir John de Vere and acquired lands in France and Essex. *Loys Johan* 'son and heir of *Loys Johan* (1447) by 1449 had become *Lewis Fitz Lowys* son and heir of *Lewis John*, knight. Occasionally we have *alias Lowis* (1462, 1484), otherwise from 1468 to 1514 the family name occurs only as Fitz Lowys or Fitz Lewes. The normal Welsh surname would have been *ap Lewis*, but neither this nor *John* satisfied a family of increasing wealth who had made good marriages and produced two knights one of whom was attainted (and later pardoned) for high treason. Hence the aristocratic French *Fitz Lewes*.[1]

We have already seen signs of the development of such common Welsh surnames as Evans, Edwards and Hughes. One clear example of heredity is John Edwards son of William Edwards (1536 Chirk), but this type of name was still being coined in the nineteenth century. In Merionethshire, for example, it was still not uncommon for a man to take his father's christian name as his surname, e.g. William Roberts son of Robert Williams. The three sons of Evan Thomas and Gwen Jones were known as Howal Thomas, Hugh Evans and Owen Jones, surnames derived (i) from the father's surname, (ii) from his christian name, (iii) from the mother's surname. The frequency of Jones, Williams, etc., brought a need for further distinction and a tendency developed to create double surnames by prefixing the name of a house, parish or the mother's surname, as Cynyddlan Jones,

---

[1] *v. Petre* (numerous deeds from A 831 to A 2070); *Feet of Fines for Essex*, vols. III, IV (*v.* Index *s.nn.* FitzLewes, John, Lewes).

Rhondda Williams, etc. In the following generation a hyphen was often introduced,[1] Nash-Williams, etc. As a Welshman wrote in 1932:

Most of our [Welsh] surnames are derived from a number of christian names and are borne by so many individuals and families in common that, generally speaking, Welsh surnames may well be said to have ceased to be distinctive as single surnames. It has been necessary, for at least two or three generations, when reference is made to a particular person bearing a common Welsh surname, to add either his personal-name, his calling, his place of abode, or some other distinguishing feature, to mark him down among his fellows. Sometimes two or more of these alternatives have to be added, and even a nickname occasionally becomes handy![2]

[1] C. L. Ewen, *A History of Surnames of the British Isles* (London, 1931), p. 208.
[2] T. E. Morris, 'Welsh Surnames in the Border Counties of Wales' (*Y Cymmrodor*, XLIII (1932)), pp. 93–4.

Chapter Seventeen
THE HOMES OF FAMILY NAMES

ONLY one serious attempt has been made to deal with the distribution of English family names, that of Guppy, which will be discussed later. As with other aspects of the history of surnames, the abundant material still awaits collection and analysis. The modern distribution of surnames is no safe guide. Families have migrated from county to county, surnames have changed and many modern surnames have more than one origin. Accuracy is impossible unless we can trace back the family surname to an unequivocal form which establishes its origin and for this we must delve deep into genealogy, ever on guard against equating impossible forms[1] and alive to the dangers of succumbing to the fascination of family pride in legendary origins.

The title of this chapter, too, is open to more than one interpretation. When a family has been settled in a particular place or district for two or three centuries, that must be regarded as the home of both family and surname even though the ultimate source of the surname can be proved to be elsewhere. The Tremletts have lived in Devonshire since the twelfth century. The first known member of the family

[1] L. G. Pine (*They came with the Conqueror* (London, 1954), p. 135) rightly accepts Round's derivation of the DB Adelolfus de Merc, from Marck (Pas-de-Calais), one origin of *Mark*, but, with no evidence beyond the mere assertion, explains this as the origin of *Marris* which is found in DB as *de Maresc* and *de Maris*, from some French place Le Marais (OFr *marais* 'marsh').

appears in Normandy in 1094 and the surname derives from the hamlet of Les Trois Minettes in Calvados. Both family and surname are Norman in origin, but both have had a longer life in Devonshire.

Robert de Benethal' (1221 AssSa) and Philip de Benedhal (1255 RH Sa) were members of a family which owed its name to Benthall in Shropshire where they held the manor until the extinction of the male line in 1720. One of them, John Benthall, who died c1590, married the daughter of an Essex clothier of Halstead and settled there where the farm known as *Brenthall* in 1620 came to be called *Bentall's* Barn Farm through the influence of the surname of Arthur Bentall (c1633), which had become the Essex spelling. This Essex branch was prolific and declined in status from gentleman to baker and agricultural labourer, among other occupations. Frank Bentall (1843–1923), who began life working in his father's shop in Maldon, in 1867 moved to Kingston-upon-Thames where he opened a small draper's shop which has now developed into a great general store still managed by a Bentall. In the second half of the eighteenth century another branch of the family moved to Devonshire where they prospered, revived the old spelling of the name in 1843, and one of them in 1934 repurchased their ancestral estate in Shropshire.[1] Here both family and surname originated at Benthall in Shropshire, their home for nearly 500 years, but as younger branches lived in Essex for 300 years, in Devonshire for 200 and in Surrey for a century, these counties, too, must be regarded as secondary homes of the surname.

Some surnames have not moved far from their original habitat. In and around Tonbridge and Tunbridge Wells, and at Bromley and Bexhill-on-Sea, live a number of families named Durtnall, Durtnell and Dartnall. The surname, also found occasionally as Darknell and Dutnall, has been noted from 1240 and derives from a lost place *Durkinghole* in Leigh. Slightly more common, but within a similarly restricted area in and near Tonbridge and Tunbridge Wells, and on and beyond the Sussex boundary, at Edenbridge and East Grinstead, we have Wickenden, recorded from 1200 and deriving from a lost place *Wigendene* in Cowden, last recorded in 1542 and now known as Polefields, long owned by the Wickenden family, where 'ould mother wickenden of powlfields' died in 1626. Prosperous landholders in Cowden in the sixteenth century, they became so numerous that they had to be distinguished by an additional attribute to their

[1] *v.* A. R. Wagner, *English Genealogy* (Oxford, 1960), pp. 188–90.

surname: Wickenden de Ludwells, Thomas Wykinden de Cowden Streate (1558), Thomas Wickenden de Bechinwoode (1571), Thomas Wickenden de la hole (1589). But they fell on evil days. Joan Wickenden, who died in 1741, after receiving relief from the parish nearly all her life at the rate of 4s. per month, was spared the ignominy of a pauper's burial by the surprising discovery that she was possessed of £250 on her death, a sum which was spent in 1742 in the ceiling and restoration of the parish church of Cowden.[1]

DISTRIBUTION OF FARMERS' SURNAMES IN 1890

In *The Homes of Family Names* (London, 1890) H. B. Guppy's aim was 'to ascertain the homes of familiar surnames and to ascertain the characteristic surnames of each county'. He takes as his basis the names of farmers, 'the most stay-at-home class of the country', extracting them from Kelly's Post Office Directories and ignoring those with a relative frequency of less than 7 per 10,000 in a county. The rest he arranges by a system of proportional numbers per 10,000 of the farmers in each county. The family names are classified on a geographical basis:

1. *General names*, occurring in from 30 to 40 counties.
2. *Common names*, occurring in from 20 to 29 counties.
3. *Regional names*, occurring in from 10 to 19 counties.
4. *District names*, occurring in from 4 to 9 counties.
5. *County names*, established in 2 or 3 counties.
6. *Peculiar names*, mostly confined to one county.

The surnames of each county are arranged under these six classes, with notes on the characteristic names. These notes are based mainly on the county historians and are not confined to names of farmers. For his etymological material he relies chiefly on Camden, supplemented by such works as were available before 1890.

What Guppy has produced is a valuable mass of material on the distribution of the names of the farmers of the country about 1890, but he gives us very little information on the real homes of family names. He relies entirely on the modern form of the names, and most of his illustrative material dates only from the Tudor period or later. The very names of his farmers, too, prove that they came from more than one class, Bond, Freeman, Franklin, Knight, Squire and Page, all well attested. Yeoman, itself, found already as a surname in

1296, had not its modern meaning. It referred, rather, to 'a servant or attendant in a noble house, ranking between a sergeant and a groom or between a squire and a page'. Surnames, too, prove that many of these farmers traced their origin back to an ancestor who had followed some quite different occupation, Baker, Carpenter, Chandler, Goldsmith, Mason, Potter, Smith, Taylor and Turner, to mention only a few. Nor were these farmers so static as Guppy implies. Many of them had strayed far from their original home, like the Kents of Cambridgeshire and Cornwall, the Worcestershire farmers named Essex, the Cumberlands of Nottinghamshire and the Darbys of Essex and Worcestershire. From Cumberland came the Blencowes of Oxfordshire and the Blenkirons of Yorkshire, from Lancashire the Cheethams of Nottinghamshire and the Inskips of Bedfordshire. Some of them, too, had an ultimate origin in France, Baskerville, Daubney, Glanville and Lacey, among others.

When we compare Guppy's lists of 1890 with medieval lists of names for the same counties, we find marked differences. To take only one class. In the 1327 Subsidy Roll for Cambridgeshire, 22 of Guppy's 29 Peculiar Names do not appear; in that for Suffolk 30 out of 56 are missing. For Sussex he gives 63 names; of these 28 are not found in the three Subsidy Rolls for 1296–1332; 19 are missing from that for 1525; 15 do not appear in any of the Rolls. But at least 1038 surnames of 1296–1332 were still in use in the county in 1525.

In Worcestershire, of 49 Peculiar Names, 32 are absent from both the Subsidy Rolls of 1275 and 1327. In his Introduction to the 1327 Roll (p. xiv), F. J. Eld makes some interesting notes on the migration of the population. He includes material from a list of names of 1240 in the Register of St Mary's Priory, Worcester, and cites three Worcestershire Directories for 1820, 1841 and 1892. In Stoke Prior in 1327, 35 persons were assessed; of these families 22 appear in the Roll of 1275, and 25 in that of 1240. In the Directories 58 names are given for Stoke Prior in 1892; of these no more than 15 can be traced in 1841; and only 8 reach back to 1820. Thus in the thirteenth century, at the end of 87 years, 29 per cent of the population are found to be new-comers, whilst in the nineteenth century, after a shorter interval of 72 years, no less than 86 per cent appear to be immigrants.

It is obvious, therefore, that much work needs to be done on this aspect of surname history. It will be a long task demanding patient industry and accuracy and cannot be satisfactorily concluded without the co-operation of philologists, genealogists and historians. The philologist must establish definite etymologies and make clear where he is doubtful and where he has failed. The genealogist must base his pedigrees on the records, rely on the philologist for the identification of doubtful forms of surnames and, where proof fails, avoid or give good reasons for his speculations. The historian must serve both and provide a sound background. All that is attempted here is to give such facts as are relevant from a considerable collection of surnames, to suggest trends and possibilities and to indicate the lines on which progress may be made.

Curiously enough, Guppy finds a pattern in his material, but some of his theories, based as they are on the modern distribution of the surnames, seem unlikely or impossible to one whose impressions are based on the medieval material. 'He can here follow the migration eastward of the Welsh, and the intermingling of the Scottish and English peoples.' The latter statement ignores the fact that the Cheviots did not originally form a national or linguistic barrier. The Kingdom of Strathclyde stretched south of the border, whilst Lowland Scots was an English dialect in which, making due allowance for the development of local characteristics, vocabulary and names were very similar to those of Northern England.

Guppy seems to have regarded the county where he finds a family most numerous as their original home from which they marched forth to conquer:

'HARRIS—HARRISON.—These names, considered together, are distributed over England and Wales. Each, however, has its own area of frequency, Harrison in the north and Harris in the south, whilst they wage a sharp contest for supremacy in the midlands . . . A line drawn across England through the cities of Lincoln and Chester will define the northern border of the area of Harris. This name is at present most numerous in Monmouthshire and South Wales, in the southern midland counties of Oxford, Northampton, Warwick, and Worcester, and in the west of England, especially in Cornwall and Devon. It is less frequent in the eastern portion of its area, that is to say, from Lincolnshire south to Kent . . . Harrison is most numerous in Westmoreland, Lancashire, Yorkshire, and Lincolnshire. Further south we find it invading in numbers the area of the Harrises and fighting for the supremacy in the midland shires, victorious in some, as in those of Derby and Stafford, waging an equal contest in others, as in the county of Notts, and completely outnumbered in the advance southward into the counties of Warwick and Worcester. Pushing on, however, in greatly diminished numbers, the Harrisons have established outposts on the borders of the English Channel.

'In this struggle between the Harrises and the Harrisons, it is evident that

325

the former have been worsted. The Harrises, in fact, have been entirely on the defence. Not only have they been unable to make any successful inroads into the northern territory of the Harrisons, but they have not prevented their foes from forcing a way through their ranks and reaching the south coast.'[1]

Unfortunately *Harris* and *Harrison* do not seem to be well evidenced, but Guppy gives similar explanations for such pairs as *Richards* and *Richardson*, etc. I suspect that the difference is largely geographical and chronological. Surnames like Thomas Hughes and John Philippes are very common in Somerset in 1327 and are found in smaller, but increasing numbers elsewhere south of Lincolnshire and Norfolk, but are rare in the north. At this time hereditary surnames were well established in the south, but were still in a state of flux in the north where the common habit of describing a man as son of his father resulted in the late formation of numerous surnames like Richardson, Wilson, etc. In the south there was not the same scope for such formations though some, like the Somerset John Gibbeson of 1327, may be the precursors of some modern names of this type which are found in the south from 1066 onwards.

The Welsh trek towards London, whilst something more than a myth, conceals the fact that it was a late migration and that many so-called Welsh surnames were established in England long before any Welshman had a hereditary surname. Of the invasion of the Joneses, Guppy writes:

'Having occupied the English counties on the Welsh border in great force, the Joneses have advanced on the metropolis from their home in North Wales, and after founding colonies *en route*, in Northamptonshire and Bucks, they have pushed on to the shores of Essex and Kent.'[2]

Jones is found as a surname in Huntingdonshire in 1279, in Staffordshire in 1309, frequently in 1327 in Worcestershire, four times in Suffolk, eight in Shropshire and eleven times in Somerset and in 1340 at Glinton (Nth). Other 'Welsh surnames' occur about the same time: Hughes (4), Richards (3), Walters (8) and Williams (2) in Somerset in 1327. Similarly, surnames from Welsh personal-names are found in England: Meredith 1191 (St), Craddock 1205 (Wo), Morgan 1214 (Berks) and Maddock 1274 (Sa), all surnames of Welshmen, formed on the English model in England at a time when Welshmen in Wales had no fixed surnames but patronymics like

[1] Pp. 37–8.   [2] P. 42.

David ap Phelip (1327 SRSa), a type which survived until the sixteenth century, e.g. John ap Madog ap Gryffyd ap Res (1538 Chirk). Welsh surnames like Jones and Edwards are not found before 1450 and are often much later.[1]

According to Guppy, *Jones* accounts for 1,500 per 10,000 surnames in North Wales, 650 in South Wales, 650 in Monmouthshire, 500 in Shropshire, 350 in Herefordshire, 138 in Worcestershire and 105 in Gloucestershire. Outside the border counties the proportion does not appear excessive except in Northamptonshire (55). *Williams* is less numerous: 700 in North Wales, 650 in South Wales, 700 in Monmouthshire, 272 in Herefordshire, 158 in Shropshire, 109 in Gloucestershire, 60 in Worcestershire, from 40 to 8 elsewhere except in Somerset (44) and Cornwall (182). An overflow of Welshmen into the border counties was natural and inevitable, but the great preponderance of these English surnames borne by Welshmen cannot date from before the reign of Henry VII. There were Joneses in Shropshire in 1327 and these were almost certainly Englishmen. These and other 'Welsh' surnames have certainly spread farther east; we must remember, however, that Jones and Williams were English surnames long before the Welsh claimed them, but, though they derive from the two most common christian names, or rather because of this, they were not commonly used as surnames. Had they been, English surnames would have been swamped by Jones and Williams a couple of centuries before the Welsh adopted them.

LEICESTERSHIRE PEASANT FAMILIES

'Coming back to the village one talks to a man whose surname appears on the Wigston poll tax assessment of 1377, the descendant of John Mold and wife. Over a decaying shop the name of Vann shows that a descendant of Thomas Vanne, a Wigston farmer in Henry VII's time, lives on, rather precariously perhaps in these difficult times; Pawleys were peasant proprietors in the village in the 1440's and a Pawley still does building jobs in the village. Dands were here in Henry VIII's reign, and their name is still called in the school register.'[2]

Thus, briefly, does Dr Hoskins summarise the continuity of life at Wigston Magna in Leicestershire. But he does more. He takes us back to the beginning of the thirteenth century when these peasants first acquired surnames and reveals the rise and fall of families, the

[1] v. p. 319.
[2] W. G. Hoskins, *The Midland Peasant* (London, 1957), p. xx.

persistence of some, the extinction or departure of others, and the arrival from time to time of newcomers. Fascinating as is the story he unfolds, we could wish he had given us a complete list of the peasant names of, say, the thirteenth century. The seven or eight earliest names are almost all patronymics. Was this a characteristic of the village? Were there no nicknames or local surnames? Was Smith the only occupation name used by these peasant farmers?

Surnames commemorating an ancestor became established in the second half of the thirteenth century. Robert son of Godwin was living about 1202–21. About 1250 the father's name, OE *Godwine*, became the surname of the family which lived in the village for seven generations until its property was disposed of by Joan Godwyne in 1351. Rannulf the clerk of Wikingeston, living c1200, also gave his name to his descendants, but the surname seems to appear first as that of his great-grandson, Adam Randolf, in 1309. The family lived in the same house and held the same land until the time of John Randull (1424). In 1436, his son, Richard Randolff alias Randull, migrated to Leicester. *Rannulf* is ON *Rannulfr* 'shield-wolf', a name brought to England by the Normans as *Randulf*. A Wigston peasant is scarcely likely to have been of Norman origin, though by 1200 his father may have given him a Norman name. The Rannulf of 1200, however, may have been of Scandinavian descent, whilst the surname may have become assimilated to the more common Norman form, now found as *Randoll* or *Randle*.

The Herricks certainly bore a Scandinavian name, ON *Eiríkr*. The eponymous ancestor of the family has escaped detection. We first find the name as a surname, Henry *Eyrig* c1250. The family remained in the village until the twentieth century, though some of them had left earlier. John Herrick moved to Leicester c1470 where one, a goldsmith, became mayor in 1552 and another MP for Leicester in 1588. Another John Herrick migrated to London c1470 where he became a skinner. Of their origin, Dr Hoskins writes:

'It seems likely that the Herricks could trace their ancestry back to one Erik, one of the original Danish settlers, perhaps of the last quarter of the ninth century in the same village; and they may well have occupied the same piece of land since that distant date.'

The family is older than the surname but this is pressing the evidence too far. Other similar surnames at Wigston and elsewhere suggest that the Eric who gave name to the family probably lived about the end of the twelfth century. He may well have been of

328

Danish descent, but not necessarily so; for by this time a christian name was no proof of nationality. At King's Lynn in 1166, where the early Scandinavian names of the district were still preserved, we find men with Scandinavian personal-names giving their sons both English and French names: Wulnoth son of Turchil, John son of Anand, whilst Englishmen used both English, Scandinavian and French names: Aluric son of Godric, Gamel son of Godric, Richard son of Godwine. At Wigston, too, intermarriage between men of English and Danish descent must have led to the use in the same family of names of both races. The name Herrick is of Danish origin, but actual proof of the ultimate nationality of the family is lacking. They could not have owed their surname to a ninth-century Eric for it is quite certain that the surname was not in use until well after the Conquest. There may have been an Eric in the village in the ninth century, but the Eric to whom they owed their surname could not have lived until some 300 years later.

In drawing national or historical deductions from surnames it is essential that there should be no doubt as to their real meaning. The Wigston family of Swan is found in the village from 1273 to 1462 and not until 1445 is there any variation in the spelling of the name (*Swanne*). Dr Hoskins derives the surname from ON *Sveinn* which would give a medieval *Swein* and modern *Swaine* or *Swayne*, just as ON *Steinn*, modern *Staines* or *Staynes*, is the source of the surname of Richard, Simon and Amice Steyn of Arnesby (1252) who probably descended from Robert son of Steyn of Littlethorpe. *Swan* is often an occupational name from OE *swān* 'herdsman, swineherd, peasant' (Thomas *le Swan* 1327 SRSf), or a nickname from OE *swan* 'swan'. The complete absence of the article in the Wigston surname suggests that its real origin may be a personal-name, OE *Swān*. This is an Anglicising of ON *Sveinn* and is a form which would not be used by men conscious of their Danish origin. The etymological possibilities are too varied for dogmatism, but point to an English rather than a Danish origin for the family.

That Dann 'may possibly indicate a Danish origin' is an impossible assumption.[1] In ME this would be *Dench* or *le Deneys*, modern *Dench* or *Dennis*. In Wigston, the family does not appear before 1525 and the surname alternates between *Danne* and *Dand*. These Dannes may have moved from Galby or Frisby, where they appear under the name

[1] A. R. Wagner, *English Genealogy* (Oxford, 1960), p. 130; W. G. Hoskins, *Essays in Leicestershire History* (Liverpool, 1950), pp. 36, 51; *The Midland Peasant*, pp. xx, 227.

of *Dand* in 1296 and 1381. This was, no doubt, the original form of the surname, from a pet-name of *Andrew*.

Another Wigston family, that of *Balle*, probably a nickname 'the bald', lived in the village for a century from about 1265. Richard Balle, who died about 1364, failing other heirs, bequeathed his property for life to his son William of Penne who is earlier called William Balle. The change of surname is probably due to the fact that he had moved to Penn in Staffordshire and after some years returned to Wigston where he was then known as William of Penne or William a Penne, a surname which then continued in his family, his grandson being known as William a Penne in 1424. By 1452 the preposition had been dropped, John Penne.

Occasionally we learn the reason for departure from the village. In 1431 four members of the family of Swanne mentioned above were charged with breaking the Earl of Oxford's close at Wigston and depasturing beasts there. After this they seem to have found life in the village unpleasant, for in 1445 we find all four at Coventry, all described as 'of Coventre', two of them as hosiers, one as an ostler and one as a labourer.

From the middle of the fifteenth century there is clear evidence of a change in the population of the village. Some of the old families remained, but others left and new ones came in. 'In general it was the wealthiest and the poorest who tended to leave. In all we cannot assume that more than ten families in Henry VIII's reign had come through from 1377 . . . In 1524–5, eight or ten families out of 70 had persisted since the fourteenth century; about six out of every seven had come in since 1377.'[1] There were fresh immigrants in the late sixteenth and early seventeenth centuries,[2] and after the enclosure of the open fields in 1766[3] the village changed completely; with the introduction of frame-knitting came swarms of new families with new surnames.

This study of Wigston families makes it quite clear that no satisfactory conclusions as to the homes of family names can be drawn from the distribution of modern surnames. We must go back to the beginning, note the establishment and development of the surnames of the place, watch the extinction and migration of families and keep an eye open for new-comers. What we need is more studies of the kind provided by Dr Hoskins for other villages in various parts of the country, of villages where the conditions of life differed from that of

---

[1] *The Midland Peasant*, p. 87.   [2] Ibid., p. 171.   [3] Ibid., p. 250.

the peasants of Wigston whose open fields were not enclosed until the end of the eighteenth century, of villages in Saxon England free from Scandinavian influence, and of others among the hills and in the forests, for comparison with those of the Midland Plain.

SURNAMES OF NORWICH IMMIGRANTS 1285–1350

More than once it has been stated categorically and it is still a common belief that a surname like *Hackford* is a proof that the family once held land there. This is certainly true in many instances, but proof is necessary, for it is quite clear that the majority of the local surnames found in medieval towns originated in these towns. When a man named John left his native village of Hackford in Norfolk and took up his abode in Norwich, his new neighbours referred to him as John *of Hakeford* (in documents, *de Hakeford*), the John who had come from Hackford. If his descendants were known by the same name and continued to live in Norwich, the real place of origin of the surname, the home of the family name, was Norwich, not Hackford, the place of his birth.

Some of these immigrants already had surnames which they retained. Between 1280 and 1290, a number of men are found in Norwich who had come from the Norfolk village of Irstead, all tanners, e.g. William de Irstede (1288). Some of these were father and son, but two of them had other surnames, one Gervase Kempe de Irstede,[1] and another, Nicholas Godwyne de Irstede (1288). Still another, Adam de Irstede, who died in 1288, was the head of a third family, and, as his daughter was called Beatrice de Irstede in 1290, the surname had already become hereditary. Adam may have been a brother of Gervase, but it is most improbable that the other two were related, as Nicholas Godwyne married Gervase Kempe's daughter.[2]

The printed records of Norwich, unlike those of London, throw little light on the variation and change of surnames, but the Rev. W. Hudson, who had a wide knowledge of the unprinted records of the city, gives it as his considered opinion that 'while family names were certainly in use, they were not by any means in use as a general practice. Consequently the same person will figure sometimes with a name of origin, sometimes with a name of occupation, sometimes with a

---

[1] Margaret Kempe (1375) may have been a descendant of his.
[2] *Norfolk Archaeology*, XII (1895), pp. 74–5.

nickname, and to a casual reader his identity will be altogether un-suspected.'[1]

Elsewhere he has discussed the distribution of the places which contributed to this migration from the country to the city.[2] He concludes that 'We shall certainly be within the mark in assuming that the city of Norwich, towards the close of the thirteenth century, had attracted within its sheltering walls natives of at least 400 Norfolk, and perhaps 60 Suffolk, towns, villages and manors.' This general impression is more or less correct, though it ignores other counties, and some of his identifications are doubtful or incorrect. Unfortunately, the actual places are not given and his method is impressionistic, based on a calculation of place-names or surnames in the index of persons in the Conveyance Rolls for 1285–98, first under B, then to the end of H, with an estimate for the whole alphabet. This he supplements by a similar count of names under B in the Leet Rolls, assuming a similar proportion for the rest of the alphabet.

To check this and to establish the actual facts, a collection has been made of all the local surnames in the Norwich Deeds for 1285–1341[3] and the Leet Rolls for 1288–1350.[4] Only actual local surnames are included, such names as John Howard de Surlingham being ignored, for whilst this must mean 'John Howard who came from Surling-ham', we have no proof that the place-name was here used as a surname. Care has been taken to see that the forms of the surname correspond with those of the place-name with which it is identified. Where a surname may derive from any one of two or more places of the same name, it is disregarded. A few places have eluded identification.

The Norwich Deeds include occasional names of clergy and knights; many of the surnames, however, are clearly names of tradesmen, artisans, etc., but not of the lowest class as they were concerned in buying and selling property, much of it, however, small. The Leet Rolls include some men of standing. Hugo de Bromholm, once Constable of the Leet of Conesford, is described as a 'citizen of Norwich', a title used very sparingly and distinctively in the Conveyance Rolls. His property was of considerable value and subject to

[1] W. Hudson, *Leet Jurisdiction in the City of Norwich during the XIIIth and XIVth centuries* (Selden Soc., vol. V, 1892), p. xcii.

[2] W. Hudson, 'Notes about Norwich before the close of the Thirteenth Century' (*Norfolk Archaeology*, vol. XII (1895), pp. 66–70).

[3] W. Rye, *A Short Calendar of the Deeds relating to Norwich, 1285–1306; A Calendar of Norwich Deeds* (Norfolk and Norwich Arch. Soc., 1903, 1915).

[4] *Selden Soc.*, vol. V. The late Rolls for 1364–91 are not included.

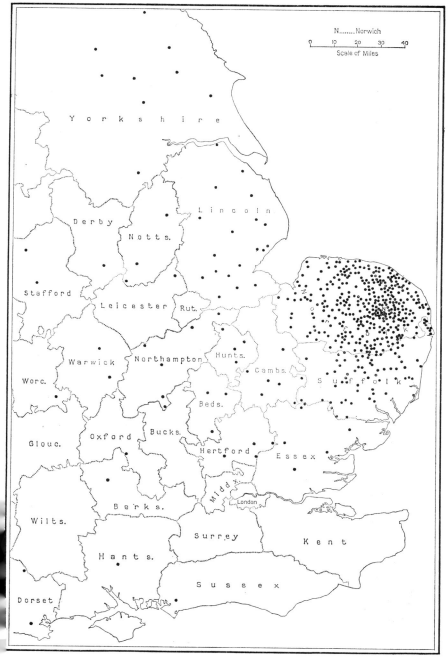

III. *Original homes of Norwich immigrants 1285–1350*

more than one law-suit after his death. 'Citizen' is mostly confined to 'merchants, lyndrapers and drapers who dealt in foreign goods and were men of the greatest substance'.

Most of the surnames in the Leet Rolls are those of jurors, tradesmen and artisans, e.g. flaxman, skinner, carpenter, fishmonger, bleacher, basket-maker, barber, fuller, carter. 'There is a marked absence of the names of those with whom the reader soon becomes familiar as the great holders of houses, lands, shops and stalls in all parts of the city.'[1] In particular, it is clear that many of the lower classes are included, breakers of the assize of ale, men fined because they were not in a tithing, or used false weights, committed nuisances or broke market regulations by selling warmed-up meat and pasties two or three days old, or by buying a drowned cow, cutting it up and selling the meat in small pieces. Accusations of theft, receiving stolen property, house-breaking, assault, etc., point also to the lower classes. Not all these men had local surnames, but the frequent addition of the occupation followed makes it quite clear that we are concerned largely with artisans and traders: Bartholomew de Tiveteshale le Especer 'spicer' (1290), Henry de Sithingg le Cuteler (1291), William de Sibeton le Cobelere (1296), Geoffrey de Wyketoft le messager (1306).

All identified local surnames are included on the map (p. 333). In the lists below, surnames known to survive are italicised. Modern variants are included in brackets. Many of these surnames are still found in Norwich and district, others elsewhere. Some of those apparently extinct survived for some centuries: Edmund Billingford 1557, Thomas Narford 1561, both in Norwich, and Richard Shipdam 1664, a freeman of Yarmouth.

It was clearly from the Norfolk countryside that Norwich drew most of its new-comers, from 351 places; 194 of their surnames still survive. The neighbouring county of Suffolk also made a considerable contribution, from 73 places, with 42 surnames surviving. Immigrants from other counties were few in number, coming from 77 different places. Of their surnames 57 survive.

Norfolk: Acle, Castle Acre, Alburgh (*Alborough*), *Alby*, Aldborough, Aldeby Alderford, Arminghall, *Antingham*, Ashmanhaugh, Ashwellthorpe olim Æscwelle (*Ashwell*), Aslacton, Attleborough, Attlebridge, Aylmerton, Aylsham, Bacton, *Bale*, *Banham*, Banningham, Barmingham, *Barney*, Barnham Broom (*Barnham*), *Barningham*, Barsham (*Barsam*, *Basham*),

---

[1] *Selden Soc.*, vol. V, pp. lxii–lxiii.

334

THE HOMES OF FAMILY NAMES

Bastwick (*Bastick*), Bawburgh, Bawdeswell, *Bayfield, Beckham, Bedingham, Beeston* (*Beeson*), *Beighton,* Belaugh, Bergh Apton, Bessingham, Besthorpe, Bickerston, Billingford, *Bilney,* Binham (*Bineham*), Bintree, *Bixley,* Bittering, *Blakeney,* Blickling, *Blofield* (*Blofeld*), *Bodham,* Bodney, Bowthorpe, *Boyland,* Bracon Ash (*Bracken*), Bradenham (*Bradnam, Bradnum*), *Bradfield, Bradwell, Brampton,* Brandiston (*Branston*), Brandon Parva (*Brandon, Branden, Brandom*), Breckles, Bressingham, Bridgham (*Brigham*), Briningham, *Brinton, Brisley,* Briston, Brockdish, *Broome* (*Broom*), Bromholm (*Bromham, Broomham*), Brumstead, Brundall (*Brundell, Brundle*), Buckenham, Bunwell, *Burlingham, Burnham, Burston,* Buxton, Caister (*Caistor*), Cantley (*Cantlay, Cantlie*), Carbrooke, *Carleton,* Caston, Catfield, *Catton, Cawston* (*Causton*), Claxton, Cley (*Clay*), Clipesby (*Clisby*), *Colgate* (*Colegate*), Colney, Coltishall, *Colton,* Colveston, Corpusty, Costessey (*Cossey*), Coston (*Corston*), Cranworth, Creake (*Creak, Creek*), Cringleford (*Cringlewood*), (Field) *Dalling, Denton,* Deopham, Dereham (*Derham*), Dersingham, Dickleburgh, Dilham, *Diss,* Ditchingham, Market Downham (*Dunham*), *Drayton, Dunston,* Earlham (*Erlam*), Earsham (*Esam*), *Easton, Eaton, Eccles,* Edgefield, Edingthorp, *Ellingham,* North Elmham, Erpingham, Fakenham, *Felmingham,* Felthorpe, *Feltwell, Filby* (*Filbee*), Flitcham, Flordon, Forncett, Foulden (*Fowden*), *Foulsham, Foxley, Framingham, Fransham* (*Frensham, Frenchum*), Frenze, Frettenham, Fritton, Fundenhall, Gasthorpe, *Gayton,* Gimingham, *Gissing,* Gooderstone (*Gotterson*), Gressenhall, Griston (*Grisson*), Guestwick, *Gunthorpe* (*Guntrip*), Gunton, *Hackford* (*Hackforth*), Haddiscoe, Hainford, *Hanworth,* Happisburgh, *Harling, Harpley,* Hautbois, Haveringland, Heckingham, *Heigham,* Helhoughton, Hellesdon (*Helsdon*), Hemblington, Hempnall (*Hemnell*), Hemsby (*Hinsbey*), Hempstead (*Hemsted*), Hethersett, Hevingham, *Heydon, Hickling,* Hindringham, *Hingham, Holkham,* Holverston (*Holverson*), Honing, Honingham, Horning, Horsford, Horstead (*Horsted*), Houghton, Hoveton, *Howe,* Hunworth, Illington, *Ingham,* Ingworth, Intwood, Irstead, Itteringham, *Kenningham,* Kerdiston, *Keswick* (near Norwich), *Ketteringham, Kimberley, Knapton,* Lakenham, Lamas (*Lammas*), Langhale, *Langley,* Larling, Lessingham, Letton (*Letten*), Limpenhoe (*Limpaney, Limpenny*),[1] *Lingwood,* Loddon, Lopham, Ludham, King's Lynn (*Lynn, Lenn*), Lyng (*Ling*), Markshall, Maslingford, *Marsham,* Martham, *Massingham,* Mattishall (*Matsell*), Mautby (*Mawbey, Mawby*), (Great) *Melton, Middleton, Mileham, Morley,* Morningthorpe, Morston, *Morton, Moulton,* Mulbarton, *Mundford* (*Munford, Mumford*), Mundham, Narford, Neatishead, Necton, *Needham, Newton,* Northwold, *Oulton, Palgrave,* Panxworth, *Paston, Pentney,* Pickenham, *Plumstead,* Poringland, Postwick, *Pulham, Quarles* (*Quarless*), Quidenham, *Rackheath,* Ranworth, *Raynham,* Redenhall (*Rednall*), Reedham, Reepham, Repps, Reymerston, Ringland, *Ringstead* (*Ringsted*), (Castle) *Rising,* Rockland, Rollesby, *Rougham, Rudham,* Runhall (*Runnals, Runnells*), *Runham, Rushall,* Ryburgh, Saham (Toney) (*Soames*), *Sall, Saxlingham,* Saxthorpe, Scarning, *Scottow* (*Scotto*),

[1] Weekley's derivation from Lympne (K) is impossible. This is a monosyllable, pronounced *Limm.* The *p* is a late intrusion.

335

Sculthorpe (*Sculthorp*), Sedgeford, Seething, *Sharrington*, *Shelfanger*, *Shelton*, Shipdam, Shotesham, Shouldham (*Shuldham*), Shropham, Sidestrand, Smallburgh, Snetterton, Snettisham (*Sneezum*), Snoring, *Sparham*, Spixworth, *Sporle*, Sprowston (*Sprowson*), *Stalham*, *Stanford*, Stanhoe (*Stanner*), Stanninghall, Starston, *Stibbard*, Stody (*Studdy*), *Stratton*, Strumpshaw, *Suffield*, Surlingham, Swaffham, Swafield (*Swaffield*), Swainsthorpe, Swannington, Swardeston, Tacolneston, Tasburgh, Taverham, *Thetford*, Thurning, Thursford, Thurton, Tibenham (*Tibbenham*), *Tilney*, Tivetshall (*Titshall*), *Tofts* (*Tufts*), *Tottington*, *Trimingham*, *Tunstall* (*Tunstill*), Tuttington, Tyby, Wacton, *Walcott* (*Walcot*), *Walpole*, (North) *Walsham*, *Walsingham*, *Walton*, Weasenham, Weeting, *Wells*, Wendling, *Weston*, *Whitlingham*, *Whitwell* (*Whittle*), Wickhampton, Wicklewood, Wiggenhall (*Wignall*, *Wignell*), *Wilby*, *Wilton*, Wimbotsham, *Winch*, *Winfarthing*, Witchingham, *Witton*, Wolterton (*Woolterton*, *Wooltorton*), Worstead, Wreningham, Wroxham, Wymondham (*Wyndham*), *Yarmouth*, Yaxham, *Yelverton*.

Suffolk: Badingham, Battisford (*Batsford*), Beccles (*Beckles*), Benhall (*Bennell*), Blundeston (*Blundstone*, *Blunstone*), Blythburgh, *Bradwell*, Braiseworth, Bramford (*Branford*), Brockford, *Brundish*, Bungay (*Bungey*), *Bures* (*Buers*, *Bewers*), *Bury*, Cavendish (*Candish*), Chelsworth, *Cockfield*, Coddenham, *Combs* (*Combes*, *Coombs*), *Corton*, Debach (*Debbage*), *Debenham* (*Debnam*), Dunwich (*Dunnage*), (South) Elmham, Elmswell, *Eye*, Finningham, Flixton (near Bungay), Friston (*Freestone*), Gapton, Gedding, *Gislingham*, Haverhill, *Hepworth*, Honington, Hoxne, Huntingfield, Ilketshall, Ipswich, Ixworth (*Ixer*), *Kenton*, Kersey (*Keresey*, *Kearsey Kiersey*, *Carsey*), Knettishall (*Kneeshaw*), *Linstead*, Lound (*Lund*), (Long) *Melford*, *Mendham*, Mendlesham, Mickfield, *Milden*, Mildenhall (*Mildinhall*), Nayland, Occold, *Orford*, *Parham*, Pettaugh (*Petto*), Rattlesden, *Redgrave*, Rickinghall (*Rignall*), Rothenhale, Sibton, *Sternfield*, Stuston, *Sudbury*, Syleham (*Sillem*), Thrandeston, *Thurston*, Westhorpe (*Westhorp*, *Westrope*, *Westrup*), Wissett, Witnesham, Woolpit, Worlingworth, *Wortham*.

Bedfordshire: *Bedford*, Limbury (*Limbrey*), Sandy (*Sanday*, *Sandey*).

Berkshire: Wantage.

Cambridgeshire: *Ashley*, *Cambridge*, (Castle) *Camps*, *Elsworth*, *Ely*, *Foxton*, Fulbourn.

Derbyshire: *Derby* (*Darby*).

Dorset: *Shaftesbury*, *Wareham*.

Essex: (Steeple) *Bumpstead* (*Bumstead*), *Colchester*, Mountnessing, Roding, *Sturmer*, *Totham*.

Hampshire: *Winchester*.

Hertfordshire: St Albans, Sawbridgeworth (*Sapsworth*), *Ware*, *Wormley*.

Huntingdonshire: Godmanchester, *Haddon* (*Hadden*), *Ramsey* (*Ramsay*), Raveley.

Leicestershire: *Sproxton.*

Lincolnshire: Aswardby, *Baston, Bennington, Catley, Dalby,* Folkingham, *Holbeach* (*Holbech(e)*), *Holland* (*Hoyland*), Kirkstead, *Leake* (*Leak, Leek*), *Lincoln, Lindsey* (*Lindsay*), *Louth,* Quadring, Sempringham, *Sleaford, Spalding, Waltham,* Wigtoft, *Wrangle.*

Northamptonshire: *Alderton,* Helpston, Heyford (*Hayford*), *Laxton,* Passenham (*Passingham*), *Welford.*

Nottinghamshire: (Sutton) *Bonnington* (*Bonington*), Darlton (*Darlington*), *Nottingham.*

Oxfordshire: *Oxford.*

Staffordshire: Newcastle-under-Lyme, *Stafford.*

Sussex: *Chichester.*

Warwickshire: *Coventry, Ladbrooke* (*Ladbroke*).

Worcestershire: Evesham.

Yorkshire: *Bedale, Doncaster, Driffield* (*Driffill*), Easingwold (*Easingwood*), *Malton,* Ripon (*Rippon*), Spaunton (*Spanton*), Upsall (*Upshall*), *York.*

MIGRATION FROM THE PROVINCES INTO LONDON 1147–1350

London records are more voluminous and more detailed than those of Norwich and this mass of material often enables us to identify definitely a man who was known by more than one name and sometimes, by piecing together information from various documents, to compile a family pedigree for two or three generations, with names of wives, sons and daughters, and, at times, of daughters' husbands and their relatives. Members of a single family might be known by different surnames; one man would retain his original surname, another would pass on a newly acquired surname to his descendants. We can often find an explanation for these variations of name; sometimes we can suggest a probable reason, though actual proof may be lacking, whilst, at others, we can merely prove that the name was changed. The variations include surnames of every type, but here we shall confine our attention to such as throw light on the places in the provinces from which men came to settle in London.

Most of our material will be taken from a series of valuable studies in which Professor Ekwall has accumulated a vast store of information on the surnames, families and population of medieval London.[1] Our purpose is much more limited than that of Ekwall. We are not concerned with the light thrown by these local surnames on the medieval dialect of London and the growth of Standard English nor with the number of immigrants from various places or the general problems of population.

This is important to us only as a proof that a single village could send more than one immigrant to London. The numerous Londoners named Lincoln, Norwich or York could not all belong to the same family. The surname *Kelsey* derives from either North or South Kelsey (Lincs). Hence came the family of Robert de Keleseye found in London from 1299 to 1375. Whether Robert was the first of the name in London, we cannot say. He may have been London born or a descendant of an earlier immigrant.

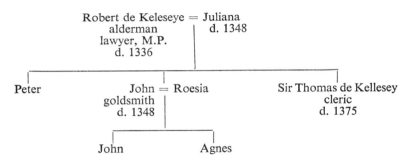

Changes of surname

Six other men with the same surname must have left Kelsey for London in the first quarter of the fourteenth century. They have no apparent connexion either with one another or with the family above. One was a maker of images and one a tapicer, whilst Stephen de Keleseye was indicted for assault in Westminster in 1320 and escaped from Newgate in 1325. Here, too, we have a clear case of the assumption by an apprentice of the surname of his master and father-in-law. Robert *Gumme de Keleseie*, late apprentice of Geoffrey de Brandone, mercer, (1322), clearly came from Kelsey. His real surname was

---

[1] E. Ekwall, *Variation in Surnames in Medieval London* (Lund, 1945) [Var]; *Early London Personal Names* (Lund, 1947) [ELPN]; *Two Early London Subsidy Rolls* (Lund, 1951) [SRLo]; *Studies on the Population of Medieval London* (Stockholm, 1956) [PopLond].

Gumme. His wife was Joan, daughter of Geoffrey de Brandone. He is called Robert *de Brandone*, late apprentice of Geoffrey de Brandone in 1322 and Robert *de Brandone*, mercer, in 1328.[1]

From Brancaster, Norfolk, came two family groups, both with property in London, descended from Alan de Brancestre (1284) and Thomas de Brancestre (1274). The relationship between these men is obscure, but they may well have been brothers.

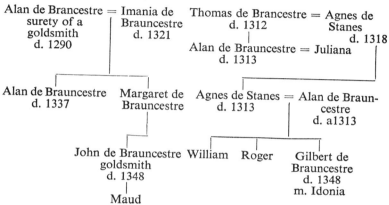

John de Brauncestre, son of Margaret and grandson of Alan, may have taken his mother's maiden name as his surname, or his father may have been an apprentice of his grandfather or of Thomas. In that case he would have taken his master's surname as his own. Alan de Brauncestre, husband of the younger Agnes de Stanes, cannot have been a member of the Brancaster family. He was probably a former apprentice and son-in-law of Thomas and adopted his surname and passed it on to his son. The elder Agnes de Stanes owed her surname to a previous marriage. She was stepmother of Alan, son of Thomas. A second Thomas de Brauncestre, junior, goldbeater, (d. 1309) was probably an apprentice of an early Brancaster whose surname he assumed.[2]

Examples of the adoption of a master's surname by an apprentice or servant are not uncommon. In 1221 William de Ely and Ralph de Ely were servants of William de Ely, merchant of London. In 1325 James de Kereseye was robbed at Basildon (Berks) by Adam de Kereseye, his servant, who died in Newgate jail. James came from Kersey in Suffolk and was probably a cloth-merchant.

[1] PopLond, pp. 173–5.   [2] Ibid., pp. 39–41.

Ralph son of Walter Fox de Malteby, co. Lincoln, late apprentice to Hugh de Gartone, mercer, in 1309–10 gave an undertaking to his master not to practise mercery in London, but Hugh withdrew his prohibition and Ralph was admitted in 1310. Ralph de Garton called Fox, who was a party to a transaction in 1310–11, is clearly the same man.

Elias de Salle, son of Walter Amy, late apprentice of John de Salle, chapeler 'hatter' or 'capper', was admitted in 1310–11. He must be identical with Elyas de Salle who in the same year was commissioned to supervise the sale of caps.[1]

John de Tyffeld, apothecary, (d. 1348) left his tenements in Bread Street to his wife Massilia, with remainder to Walter his son and John de Hurle his servant. Walter (d. 1356), also an apothecary, inherited his father's surname. The servant is John de Heurle called Tiffeld in 1350 and John de Tiffeld in 1355. He had assumed his master's surname.[2]

Geoffrey David de Helweton, taverner (1290), was executor of Robert le Eskot in 1295 when he is called Geoffrey de Helwethon. Later, he appears as Geoffrey de Helvetone, called Scot, taverner (1306) and Geoffrey Scot or le Scot, scrutiniser or broker of wine (1302–10). His real surname was David. He came from Helhoughton or Hellington (Norfolk) and must have been an apprentice of Robert le Scot, taverner (1281–90), whose name he assumed. In 1296 Geoffrey, with Juliana, widow of Robert, and John her son, was a debtor of a French wine-merchant.[3]

Many changes of surname cannot be proved to be due to the assumption of a master's surname. They may well be such, but other explanations may be possible. At times, too, the original surname ultimately survived. William Curteys de Bricklesworth (1330) is called *Curteys* in 1336 when sheriff and in 1339 when alderman but *de Brikelesworth* in 1336 when elected MP. His real surname was a nickname *Curtis*; he was a native of Brixworth (Nth) where his will was dated and he made bequests to the church there, where he desired to be buried. His surname seems to have varied throughout his life, but ended as *de Brikelesworth* which he used in his will and was the only name by which his son John was known.[4]

John de Stoppesle came from Stopsley (Beds). He was a tanner and had an apprentice called Symon de Stoppesle in 1311, Simon de

1 Var, p. 13.   2 Ibid., p. 13.
3 PopLond, pp. 156–7.   4 Ibid., p. 139.

Stoppeslee called Seman in 1340 and Simon Seman 1329–46. His real name was *Seman* (OE *Sǣmann*) which alternated with his master's surname. He may well have been born in London.[1]

Thomas de Blakeneye was warden of the drapers in 1328. His will was challenged in 1330 by Maurice Turgiz who stated that he was a brother and heir of Thomas whose real surname was thus *Turgis* (ON *Þorgils*, modern *Turgoose, Sturgess*). He may have come from Blakeney (Nf) or he may have been an apprentice of one of four earlier Blakeneys described as merchants and wool-mongers, one of whom was a citizen of Norwich who paid murage and contributed to a loan in London.[2]

Nicholas de Tryllowe (1339) is identical with Nicholas, son of Stephen Godynge de Trillawe, apprentice of John Matfrey, fishmonger (1311). Both he and his father clearly came from Thurlow (Sf), their real surname being *Godynge* (OE *Goding*).[3]

Luke de Grendone de Abyntone (1311) is also called simply *de Grandon* (1325), *le Chaucer* (1319) and *le Hosiere* (1326). He must have moved originally from Abington (Nth) to Grendon (Nth) whence he came to London, where he was described both as 'of Grendon' and from his occupation.[4]

Augustine de Bolhurste was assessed at 2*s.* in the Subsidy for 1319. He must have come from Bolnhurst (Beds) and set up as a lodging-house keeper in London for in all later references he is called Augustine *le Herberer* (modern *Harberer, Haberer*).[5]

The Cavendishes

A particularly interesting example is that of *Cavendish*. Eight men with this surname were living in London between 1298 and 1332. Geoffrey de Cavendysh, who seems to have died before 1299, was probably an actual migrant from Cavendish (Sf) to London. He had a house in St Lawrence Jewry and his son Geoffrey, a buckle-maker, was bequeathed tenements there by Walter Blondel in 1307. In 1324 John de Cavendisshe committed manslaughter and escaped. He is described both as 'son of Geoffrey de Cavedihs' and as 'brother of Geoffrey de Cavendisshe of London' so that he appears to be the son of the first Geoffrey. The brothers Geoffrey and John must have inherited their surname from their father.

[1] PopLond, p. 131.   [2] Ibid., p. 37.
[3] Ibid., p. 33.   [4] Ibid., pp. 143–4.
[5] SRLo, p. 304.

There is a third Geoffrey, son of Alice de Cavendihs, who was bequeathed houses in Broad Street by John de Cavendihs in 1303. This appears to be a different family. Of Henry de Kauendishe we know only that he was assessed at 8*d*. in the Subsidy for 1319. He may have been a not very successful recent immigrant from Cavendish. Roger and Walter de Cavendysch were legatees in 1311 of Geoffrey de Bradele who came from Great or Little Bradley (Sf). Their relationship is not stated. All these men owed their surname ultimately to migration from Cavendish, but some inherited the name and may have been born in London.[1]

But there were also other Cavendishes who owed their surname to the adoption by an apprentice of his master's surname. Thomas de Cavendisshe, son of William atte Watre de Ewelle, a former apprentice of Walter de Cavendisshe, mercer, was admitted a freeman of the City in 1312. He is frequently referred to in later sources as Thomas de Kavendish or Thomas Cavendisshe and regularly used this surname as his own, for his will is dated 1348 as that of Thomas de Cavendych, mercer or draper. He had come to London from Ewell in Surrey and left a bequest for a chantry in the church of St Mary of Ewell. His real surname would have been either *atte Watre* or *de Ewelle* and he adopted the surname of his former master, Walter de Cavendish, who is well evidenced in the records from 1304 to 1320.[2] These dates would suggest that he might be identical with the Walter above, the legatee of Geoffrey de Bradele, but the documents provide no proof.

The descendants of Thomas inherited his adopted surname, a matter of some interest as it is probable, though not conclusively proved, that he was the ancestor to whom Sir John Cavendish the chief justice who was murdered by a Suffolk mob in 1381 and the Dukes of Devonshire owe their surname.[3]

Social position of these immigrants

The men whose surnames we have discussed were of every rank and class, men of position and wealth, aldermen, sheriffs, mayors and wardens of crafts, substantial merchants, tradesmen and artisans, some of whom owned their own houses and shops, some technically paupers, exempt from taxation because the value of their movables

[1] PopLond, pp. 12–13.   [2] Var, p. 13.

[3] *v.* further, J. H. Round, 'The origin of the Cavendishes' in *Family Origins* (London, 1930), pp. 22–32, especially pp. 25–7 and 30–32.

342

was below a prescribed minimum, in 1319 half a mark (6s. 8d.). To decide how they got their name, whether they were original immigrants or were born in London, sons of earlier immigrants, whether they were apprentices who had assumed their masters' names, or whether they were landed gentry who brought with them to London an inherited surname derived from the land they owned, all this has compelled us to check our identifications by frequent references to family and other relationships. But, strictly speaking, this is irrelevant to our particular purpose, to ascertain the distribution of the places from which these immigrants came to London. Very rarely indeed can we say definitely that a particular man came from a particular place. We can seldom be sure that he was not a son of an earlier immigrant. What is to us incidental and supplementary material is part of a vast mass of information which throws light on various problems of the population of medieval London, problems fully discussed by Ekwall.[1]

Many men are mentioned only once, as Roger de Elveden, mirourer 'maker of mirrors' (1309 LLB D) and Hugh de Bonggey, armurer (1317 ib. E); these were probably new-comers. John de Kileworth, hosier, who came from Kenilworth, was taxed at only $13\frac{1}{2}d.$ in 1319, but by 1328 had become a warden of the hosiers and contributed largely to the City's loans of 1339 and later. He had evidently come to London and started business not long before 1319.[2]

Of men who already had hereditary surnames before they came to London, we may note Sir Robert de Cokesfeld (1281) who owned houses in London. He was a descendant of Adam de Cokefeld who held the manor of Cockfield (Sf) of the Abbot of Bury in the twelfth century. John de Charleton, mercer, assessed at five marks in the Subsidy of 1319, held the manor of Charlton in Otmoor (O) in 1325 (Pat). John de Pulteneye, merchant, alderman and three times mayor, who died in 1348, had a mansion, later called *Pultneysin*, in St Lawrence Pountney, a parish, with Laurence Pountney Lane, named from him. He was a grandson of Hugh de Pulteney of Poultney (Leics) where he is said to have been buried. He thus belonged to a landed family (modern *Poultney* or *Pountney*) and is an interesting example of a young man of this class who went into business in London.[3]

---

[1] v. *Two Early London Subsidy Rolls*, pp. 49–71; *Population of Medieval London*, pp. xxxix–xlviii.
[2] SRLo, p. 110.
[3] PopLond, pp. 197–8.

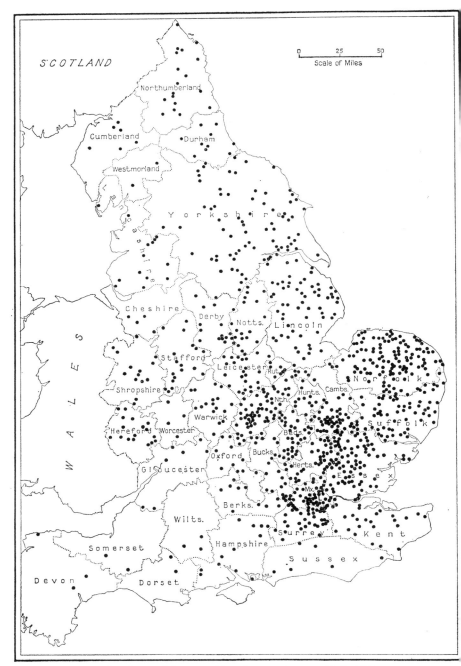

IV. *Original homes of London immigrants 1147–1350*

The original homes of London immigrants

Local surnames from English place-names are not numerous in early London sources. The earliest appears to be that of Brihtmer de Haverhell who is first mentioned in 1147. He came from Haverhill, just over the Essex boundary, in Suffolk, and, like his son William and his grandson Thomas, became sheriff. This surname survived, but others were not necessarily inherited. Herebertus de Oxon (of Oxford), cordewaner, living about 1205, had a son Gervase who is never called by his father's surname, but from his occupation, *le Cordewaner* (1238, 1250). He was sheriff in 1237–8 when he is called Gervasius *Camerarius*, and Gervase *Baronn* after he had become alderman of Aldgate, a nickname from his office, for sheriffs and aldermen were often called barons in early London records.

In the early thirteenth century, local surnames gradually became more numerous and by the end of the century were common and still increasing. Most of them, in the twelfth and thirteenth centuries, came from the counties round London, but in the fourteenth century there is a marked increase of such surnames from farther afield, particularly from the East Midlands. It is noteworthy that the south-western counties produced very few.

The accompanying map (p. 344) and the lists below include only the earliest example of the surname and only those which can be definitely identified. The general impression of the distribution can be safely accepted as approximately accurate. But neither lists nor map are complete, as it is frequently impossible to locate the origin of a surname, for often our only means of identification is the spelling of the place-name which may refer to more than one place. A man named Bentley may have come from Essex, Middlesex, Staffordshire or Derbyshire, a Nettlestead from Kent, Surrey or Suffolk, an Ormes-by from Norfolk, Lincolnshire or Yorkshire, all counties from which we know that immigrants came into London. Though likely, it is not safe to assume that a man came from the place nearest London. All such doubtful examples are, therefore, excluded, and, as a result, immigration from places in the Home Counties is certainly under-estimated.[1]

---

[1] Ekwall derives *de Boli(n)ton* from Bullington (L). The place-name forms, however, are identical with those of Bollington Hall in Ugley (Ess) where there was an early thirteenth-century family of the name which owned the manor. It was prolific and one of them, Richard (m. Alice), son of Robert de Bolyton of Uggele (1344 FFEss) is probably identical with Ekwall's Richard de Bolinton

345

The material, therefore, does not lend itself to accurate statistics, a fact emphasised also by Ekwall, whose figures are given for comparison. These, it should be remembered, include all the persons from a particular place; ours refer only to the number of places. For the general areas we have:

	Home Counties	East Midlands	West Midlands	Northern England	South and South-west	Total
Places:	234	449	107	113	57	960
Persons:	3,000	1,970	400	350	1,000	6,720

In drawing conclusions from these figures, account should be taken both of the size of the area and of its medieval population. London would be likely to attract greater numbers from the places nearer to it. The larger towns, too, made a considerable contribution. Men named Lincoln, e.g. numbered 55, Hereford 40, Bedford 34, Coventry 33, York 31. Of 29 immigrants from Cumberland, 20 were named Carlisle. Of 960 places marked on the map, 117 are in Norfolk, whilst 241 are scattered among 26 counties. The distribution of places in the chief areas, by centuries and counties is as follows:

	Home Counties						Northern Counties				
Century	Bk	Herts	Ess	Mx	Sr	K	Y	Du	Nb	Cu	We
12th		2	3	5	2	1	1				
13th	5	15	26	9	13	13	21	4	5	1	1
14th	18	22	42	14	28	16	55	6	13	5	1
Totals	23	39	71	28	43	30	77	10	18	6	2
Ekwall	175	450	850	500	400	400	215	37	30	29	9

	East Midlands								
Century	Beds	Nth	Lei	Nt	L	Hu	C	Nf	Sf
12th		1	1		3		2	3	5
13th	9	13	5	4	16	5	21	38	21
14th	24	48	18	13	47	8	23	76	38
Totals	33	62	24	17	66	13	46	117	64
Ekwall	150	225	76	67	265	48	220	500	320

In the lists below surviving surnames are italicised:

Bedfordshire: *13th: Bedford* (*Bedforth*), *Caddington*, Dunstable, Edworth, *Luton*, Pavenham, Roxhill, Sharnbrook (*Sherbrooke, Shambrook*), Silsoe: *14th:* Ampthill, Arlesey, Biggleswade, Bolnhurst, Chicksands,

---

(1300) who, with his wife Alice, was a legatee of Godfrey de Essex (PopLond 165). That William de Othelveso (1310) came from Oxhill (Wa), *Ochteselue, Otheselve* 13th, is unlikely. He almost certainly came from Audley End in Gestingthorpe (Ess), *Othelvesho* 1309 PNEss 430.

Elstow, Felmersham, *Flitton*, Goldington, *Harrold*, Hockliffe, Houghton Regis (*Houghton*), *Odell*, Pegsdon, Pertenhall, Podington, *Potton*, Sharpenhoe, *Shillington*, Stevington (*Steventon*), Stopsley, Sundon, Whipsnade, Wrestlingworth.

Berkshire: *12th: Windsor* (*Winsor, Winser, Wincer, Winzer*); *13th: Abingdon*, Hagbourne, Newbury; *14th: Bray*, Childrey, *Harwell, Reading*, Sindlesham, *Wallingford, Warfield.*

Buckinghamshire: *13th:* Beaconsfield, *Chalfont*, Colnbrook (*Colebrook, Colbrook*), Iver, *Marlow; 14th:* Amersham, *Aylesbury, Beekestone*, Biddlesden (*Bittleston*), Bledlow, *Brickhill* (*Brickell*), Buckingham, Chalvey, Cheddington, *Chesham*, Cippenham, Cublington, *Dagnall* (*Dagnell*), Hambleden (*Hambleton*), Lillingstone (*Lillingston*), *Slough*, Wavendon, *Wingrave* (*Wingrove*).

Cambridgeshire: *12th: Ely*, Sawston; *13th:* (Little) *Abington*, Babraham, Balsham (*Balsam, Balsom*), Bassingbourn, *Brinkley, Cambridge*, (Castle) *Camps, Caxton*, Dullingham, Duxford (*Doxford*), Fowlmere, Fulbourn, Ickleton, *Linton, Melbourn* (*Melborne*), Pampisford, *Quy, Shelford*, Swavesey (*Swasey, Swezey*), Thriplow (*Triplow*), *Trumpington; 14th: Barrington*, Bottisham, *Cottenham, Elsworth* (*Ellsworth*), Eltisley (*Elsley*), Harlton, *Harston*, Haslingfield, Hildersham, Hinxton (*Hingston*), Horseheath, Isleham, Knapwell, *Leverington*, Guilden Morden, *Over, Teversham*, Whaddon, *Whittlesey* (*Whittlesea, Whittlesee*), Whittlesford, *Wimpole* (*Wimple*), Wisbech (*Wisbach*), Witchford.

Cheshire: *13th: Wettenhall; 14th:* Blakenhall (*Blacknell*), *Bulkeley* (*Bulkley*), Tattenhall (*Tatnall, Tatnell*).

Cumberland: *13th:* Carlisle (*Carlile, Carlill, Carlyle*); *14th:* Cockermouth, *Dalston*, Greystoke (*Greystock, Grestock, Gristock*), Inglewood, Raughton.

Derbyshire: *12th: Derby* (*Darby*); *13th:* Ashbourne (*Ashburn*), Bakewell, *Shardlow* (*Shardelowe*), *Tissington; 14th:* Boyleston, Chaddesdon, *Coddington, Cowley* (*Colley*), Glapwell, Ilkeston, Ockbrook, Sandiacre, Sawley, Spondon, *Tideswell* (*Tiddswell, Tidsall*), Wadshelf.

Devonshire: *14th: Combe* (Martin), *Exeter* (*Hexter*), Woodbeer (in Plymtree).

Dorset: *14th: Blandford* (*Blanford*), *Shaftesbury* (*Shafsby*).

Durham: *13th: Biddick*, Coundon (*Condon*), *Durham, Stanley; 14th: Billingham, Eldon*, Hartlepool (*Harpole*), *Hunwick* (*Hunnick, Hunnex*), Staindrop (*Stainthorp*), *Stanhope.*

Essex: *12th: Bocking, Felsted* (*Felstead*), Hadstock; *13th:* Barking (*Barkin*), Billericay, Burstead (*Bustead, Busteed*), *Chignall* (*Chignell*), Chishall (*Chissell*), Cressing, Doddinghurst, *Dunmow* (*Dunmo*), *Dunton*, (Great) *Easton* (*Eyston*), Fingrith, Frowick, Hallingbury, *Harlow, Havering, Laver, Layer*, Mucking, Ongar, Parndon (*Parringdon, Parrington*), St Osyth, *Shenfield*, Theydon, Thunderley, Ugley, Writtle; *14th:* Audley End (in Gestingthorpe), Bardfield, *Berden*, Bollington Hall (in Ugley), Brentwood, *Broomfield*, (Steeple) *Bumpstead* (*Bumstead, Bumsted, Bunstead*), *Canfield*, Chelmsford, Clacton, *Clavering*, Codham, Corringham, Dedham (*Didham, Diddams, Diddems*), Elsenham, Emanuel Wood in

Chesterford (*Mannell*), Finchingfield, Hainault, *Halstead, Hedingham, Hockley* (*Hockly*), *Ilford, Leyton*, Mashbury, Matching, *Messing*, Navestock, Naylinghurst, Nunty's Fm (Pattiswick), Prittlewell, Roding, Roxwell, Great Sampford, Springfield, Stisted, *Stock*, Thremhall (*Tremmell*), *Tilbury*, Toppesfield, Ugley, *Warley, Yeldham*.

Gloucestershire: *14th: Bitton*, Bristol (*Bristow*), Charingworth, Gloucester (*Gloster*), Oddington, *Tewkesbury, Winchcombe*.

Hampshire: *12th: Basing, Winchester*; *13th:* Cadnam, Holybourne (*Halleybone, Hallybone, Hollobon*), Odiham, *Portsmouth* (*Portchmouth*); *14th: Clere, Ellingham*, Hamble, Itchel, *Ringwood*, Romsey (*Rumsey*).

Herefordshire: *12th:* Hereford (*Herford, Harford*); *13th:* Bromyard; *14th:* Bosbury, Breinton, *Byford, Ledbury*, Leinthall (*Lenthall, Lentell, Lentle*), Leominster, Marcle, Mintridge, Pedwardine, Pencombe, Shelwick, Shobdon, Snodhill, Stoke Lacy (*Stoke*), Weobley (*Webley*), *Wigmore*.

Hertfordshire: *12th:* Stortford, Watford; *13th: Barkway* (*Barkaway*), Braughing, Chelsing, Gaddesden (*Gadsden, Gadsdon*), *Hertford*, Hormead, Kelshall (*Kelsall*), *Munden, Pelham, Reed*, Sacombe, St Albans, Stevenage, Totteridge, *Ware*; *14th:* Aldenham, *Anstey*, Ashridge, Aye Woods, *Baldock*, Bengeo, Berkhamstead, Brickendon (*Brigden*), Broxbourne, Buntingford, Cheshunt (*Cheston, Chesson*), Croxley, Eastwick, Flaunden, *Gilston*, Hadham, Hoddesdon (*Hodson*), Hunsdon, Rickmansworth, Roxford, Sawbridgeworth (*Sapsworth, Sapsford, Sapsard, Sapsed, Sapsted, Sapstead*), Walkern.

Huntingdonshire: *13th: Huntingdon*, Ripton, St Ives, St Neots, Woodstone; *14th:* Alconbury, Bluntisham (*Blunsom, Blunsum*), Catworth, Godmanchester, (Great) *Gransden*, Leighton Bromswold (*Leighton*), *Stilton, Tilbrook*.

Kent: *12th:* Tonbridge (*Tunbridge*); *13th:* Borden, *Boughton, Brenchley, Bromley*, Lessness, Lewisham, Mereworth, *Romney* (*Rumney*), Ruxley, Sandwich, Shorne (*Shorn*), Sittingbourne, Wrotham (*Rootham*); *14th: Beckenham*, Benenden, *Canterbury*, Chilham, *Cobham*, Cobhambury, Copton, Greenwich (*Greenidge, Greenish*), Kemsing, *Lenham, Maidstone* (*Mayston*), Palstre, Selling, Stourmouth, Wiggenden, a lost place in Cowden (*Wickenden*), Yalding.

Lancashire: *13th:* Smethurst; *14th:* Chaigley, *Clitheroe* (*Clitherow, Cleatherow, Cluderay*), Dinckley (*Dunckley, Dunkley, Dunkerley*), *Furness* (*Furnace, Furniss, Furnish*), Henthorn (*Henthorne*), Knowsley, *Lancaster* (*Langcaster, Lankester, Loncaster, Longcaster*), Liverpool, *Manchester*, Martinscroft (E of Warrington), Pennington in Leigh (*Pinnington*), *Stanworth, Wigan*.

Leicestershire: *12th: Leicester* (*Leycestre, Lester, Lestor, Lessiter, Lisseter, Laister, Lasseter*); *13th: Bowden*, Garendon, Kimcote, Shangton, *Wartnaby*; *14th: Belgrave* (*Belgrove, Bellgrove*), Blaby, *Bosworth, Breedon* (*Breeden*), Garthorpe, Glen Parva (*Glenn*), *Loughborough*, Lutterworth, Mountsorrel, Mowsley (*Mousley*), Nailstone, *Peatling, Poultney* (*Pulteney, Pountney, Poutney*), Seagrave (*Seagrief, Seagrove, Segrave*), Sharnford, *Skeffington* (*Skevington, Skivington*), Thringstone, Wymeswold.

Lincolnshire: *12th: Boston*, Lincoln (*Linkin*), Whisby (*Wisbey, Wisby*);

13th: Barnoldby, Beck, Carlby, *Grantham (Graham),* Haconby, *Holbeach, Keal (Keel),* Lindsay, Louth, Spalding, Stainsby, Strubby, *Tattershall (Tattersall, Tattersill, Tattershaw, Tettersell, Tetsall),* Torksey, (West) *Torrington (Terrington),* Washingborough; *14th:* Ashridge, Atterby, *Bardney, Barkwith (Barkworth),* Beckfield, *Blyton, Bolingbroke (Bollingbroke),* Brackenborough *(Brackenboro, Brackenbury, Brackenberry), Cranwell, Crowle,* Dalderby, *Deeping, Elkington,* Elsham *(Elsom), Friskney (Freshney),* Gonerby, Gosberton, Grayingham, *Grimsby,* Haugham, Huttoft, *Kelsey,* Kirmond, Mablethorpe *(Maplethorpe, Mapplethorp), Maltby, Markby,* Messingham, *Mumby,* Navenby, Owersby, *Pinchbeck (Pinchback), Pointon (Poynton), Rasen, Sleaford, Stickney,* Swarby, Theddlethorpe, Thoresway, Threckingham, Tothby, Ulceby, Wainfleet, *Welby,* Wellingore, Whaplode, *Whitton, Willingham.*

Middlesex: *12th: Fulham (Fullam),* Isleworth, Lisson Grove, Paddington, Ruislip; *13th:* Chiswick *(Chissick, Chishick),* Edmonton, *Enfield (Endfield), Hackney, Harrow,* Hendon, Stanmore, Stepney, Tottenham; *14th: Barnet,* Bedfont, *Brentford,* Chelsea, Halliford, *Haringay,* Heston *(Hesten),* Islington, Laleham, *Mimms (Mims), Staines, Turnham* (Green), Uxbridge, Yeoveney.

Monmouthshire: *13th:* Monmouth.

Norfolk: *12th:* Larling, *Norwich (Norridge),* Snoring; *13th:* Castle Acre, Anmer, Aylsham, *Bayfield, Blakeney, Bodham,* Brancaster, Brockdish, Bromholm *(Bromham),* Cawston *(Causton, Cason),* Deopham, Dereham *(Derham),* Fincham, Foulsham, Gaywood, Harling, Helhoughton, *Ingham,* Ingoldisthorpe *(Inglethorpe),* Lamas *(Lammas),* Loddon, *Lynn (Lenn), Massingham,* Mundford *(Munford, Mumford),* Narford, Necton, Reepham, (Castle) *Rising,* Runhall *(Runnalls), Sall (Salle), Stalham,* Strumpshaw, *Trimingham,* Walsoken, Weasenham, Worstead, Wymondham *(Wyndham),* Yarmouth *(Yarmuth); 14th:* Attleborough, *Banham, Barney,* Bawdeswell, Blickling, Bradeston *(Bradstone),* Breckles, Bressingham, *Brisley, Burlingham,* Carbrooke, Catfield, Colkirk, Corpusty, Cressingham, Cringleford *(Cringlewood), Dalling,* Didlington, *Docking,* Edgefield, Egmere, Elsing, *Filby (Filbey, Philby),* Fundenhall, Garboldisham, Glandford *(Glanford),* Hackbeach, *Hackford, Hardingham,* Hellesdon *(Helsdon),* Hempnall *(Hemnell),* Hethersett, *Hickling,* Hilborough, Hilgay, Hindringham, *Hingham,* Honingham, *Horsford, Horsham, Ketteringham, Knapton, Marsham, Mileham (Milham),* Ormesby *(Ormsby), Paston,* Pickenham, Redenhall *(Rednall),* Riddlesworth, Rockland All Saints, Saxthorpe, Scarning, *Scottow (Scotto),* Sedgeford, *Shelfanger,* Shipdam, Shouldham *(Shuldham),* Shropham, Snettisham *(Sneezum),* Southery *(Suddery), Sparham, Sporle,* Stanhoe *(Stanner),* Stody *(Studdy),* Stradsett, Surlingham, Swardeston, *Thompson,* Thornham, Thorpland Hall in Fakenham, *Tilney,* Tichwell, *Walsingham,* Witchingham, Wreningham, Wroxham.

Northamptonshire: *12th: Northampton (Norrington); 13th:* Bozenham Mill in Hartwell, Brackley, *Braybrooke (Brabrook),* Dodford, Finedon *(Findon),* Oundle, Passenham *(Passingham),* Pattishall *(Pateshall, Passell), Rockingham,* Tiffield, *Titchmarsh, Upton, Walgrave (Walgrove, Waldegrave); 14th:* Astwick, Barby, *Blakesley (Blaksley, Blaxley), Bozeat,*

Brixworth, (Long) *Buckby* (*Bugbee, Bugby*), Bugbrooke, *Byfield, Catesby,* Cransley, *Daventry* (*Daintree, Daintr(e)y*), *Dingley,* Duston, Etton, Greatworth (*Greatwood*), *Grendon,* Guilsborough, Hackleton, *Harpole,* Helpston, Hulcote in Easton Neston, *Isham* (*Isom, Issom*), Kelmarsh, Kettering, Kislingbury, Lilbourne (*Lilburn*), Litchborough, *Lowick,* Lyveden in Aldwinkle, Maidford, *Maxey,* Northborough, Northolme House in Eye, *Old, Piddington,* Pitsford, Polebrook, Raunds (*Rands*), Scaldwell, Shutlanger, *Silverstone, Thornby, Wakefield* Lawn in Pottersbury, Wansford, Wappenham, *Weldon,* Wellingborough, Westhay in King's Cliffe.

Northumberland: *13th: Corbridge,* Hartington, *Morpeth,* Prendwick, Sweethope; *14th:* Bamburgh (*Bamborough, Bambrough*), Berwick, Broxfield, *Earle,* Glendale, Hawick, *Rothbury* (*Robery, Rowbery, Rowbury*), Settling Stones, *Swinburn, Tindale* (*Tindal(l), Tindell, Tindill, Tindle, Tyndale, Tyndall*), *Wark,* Weedslade, *Wooler* (*Wooller*).

Nottinghamshire: *13th: Blyth* (*Blythe, Blyde, Blye*), *Gotham, Nottingham,* Welbeck; *14th:* Bridgford (*Bridgeford*), Colwick (*Collick*), Cossall, Gringley on the Hill, Langar (*Langer*), Linby (*Limby*), *Markham,* Muskham, Oldcoates, *Selston, Sherwood, Willoughby,* Worksop.

Oxfordshire: *13th: Banbury* (*Banbery, Banberry*), *Burford* (*Burfoot*), Eynsham (*Ensom, Ensum*); *14th: Charlton,* Chipping Norton, Daddington, Epwell, *Headington, Thame, Witney.*

Rutland: *12th:* Luffenham (*Luffingham*); *13th:* Ketton; *14th:* Empingham, Glaston, *Oakham, Tinwell,* Whissendine.

Shropshire: *12th: Wenlock; 13th:* Bitterley, *Ludlow, Preen, Puleston,* Shrewsbury (*Shrosbree*), Whitchurch; *14th: Acton* Burnell, Idsall, *Kinnersley,* Knockin, *Pitchford* (*Pitchforth*), Pontesbury, Presthope, *Whittington.*

Somerset: *14th:* Crewkerne, *Taunton* (*Tanton*).

Staffordshire: *12th:* Tamworth; *13th:* Lichfield (*Litchfield*), *Stafford,* Wyrley; *14th: Audley* (*Audeley*), Bobbington, *Brinsford,* Butterton, Cauldon (*Caldon*), *Coven,* Enville (*Envill*), *Marchington, Oxley,* Penkridge, Kingswinford (*Swinford*), Tutbury, Uttoxeter, Wolverhampton.

Suffolk: *12th: Bury,* Dunwich (*Dunnage*), Haverhill, Ipswich, *Orford; 13th:* Beccles (*Beckles*), Brantham (*Braham*), *Bungay* (*Bungey*), *Cavendish* (*Candish*), *Clare, Cockfield,* Hessett, Kelsale (*Kelsall*), Lawshall, *Lidgate,* (Long) *Melford, Mendham,* Nedging, Rattlesden, Rickinghall (*Rignall, Rignell*), Rumburgh, Sibton, Stoke by Nayland (*Stoke*), *Thurlow* (*Thurloe, Trillo*), *Wetheringsett, Withersfield; 14th:* Aspall (*Aspel(l)*), *Bardwell* (*Beardwell*), *Bedingfield,* Blaxhall (*Blaxall, Blaxsell, Blaxill, Blacksell, Blacksill*), *Bradley, Byng,* Copdock, Little Cornard, *Cove, Debenham* (*Debnam, Deadman, Dedman*), *Dennington,* Eriswell (*Erswell*), *Glemham,* Gosbeck, Harkstead, Hobland Hall in Bradwell, Honington, Icklingham, *Kersey* (*Keresey, Kearsey*), Kettleburgh (*Kettleboro, Kettleborough, Chittleburgh*), *Kirkley* (*Kirtley, Kerley*), Knettishall, Knoddishall, Lavenham, Laxfield, Layham, *Nayland, Pakenham, Redgrave, Ringshall,* Saxham, Shadingfield, *Sudbury,* Swefling, Thelnetham, Whelnetham, Worlingworth, *Wortham.*

Surrey: *12th:* Camberwell, *Mortlake* (*Mortlock*); *13th:* Abinger,

Barnes, Battersea, Carshalton, Chobham, *Dorking (Dorkings, Darking),*
Ewell, *Guildford (Guilford, Gilford), Reigate,* Rotherhithe, Sanderstead,
Stockwell, Wandsworth; *14th: Banstead, Beddington,* Betchworth, *Bodley,*
Brookwood, *Burstow,* Caterham, Cheam *(Cheyham),* Chertsey, Chidding-
fold, Comforts Place in Godstone, *Croydon,* Dippenhall *(Dipnall),* Dunley
Hill in Effingham, *Eaton* (Farm in Cobham), Godalming *(Godliman),*
Godstone, *Kingston, Lambeth,* Leatherhead, Morden, Papercourt *(Pap-
worth),* Pipers Fm in Tandridge, Portley, Portnall in Egham, *Sheen,*
Tolworth *(Talwith),* Wiggie in Reigate *(Wigney).*

Sussex: *13th: Chichester, Lewes; 14th: Arundel,* Dencombe, Rudgewick,
Winchelsea.

Warwickshire: *12th: Warwick (Warrick, Wharrick); 13th:* Attleborough,
Coventry, Kenilworth *(Killingworth),* Mancetter, *Packwood; 14th:* Ashow,
Bordesley *(Bordsley), Broom* Hall in Lapworth, Chadshunt, Dassett,
Dunchurch, Fletchamstead, Idlicote, Itchington, Ullenhall.

Westmorland: *13th: Kendal (Kendall); 14th:* Warcop *(Warcup, Warkup).*
Wiltshire: *13th: Amesbury,* Teffont; *14th: Salisbury.*

Worcestershire: *13th:* Kidderminster *(Kittermaster); 14th:* Birlingham,
Feckenham, *Worcester (Worster, Wooster, Wostear).*

Yorkshire: *12th: Whitby; 13th: Beverley,* Doncaster *(Dancaster),* Drax,
Ellerker *(Elliker, Allaker, Alliker, Hellicar),* Fockerby, *Garton, Gisburn*
(Gisbourn, Gisborne, Gisbon), Knaresborough, Kneeton, Lead *(Leede),*
Malton, Middlesborough *(Middleburgh), Pontefract (Pomfret, Pomphrett,*
Pumfrett), Richmond, Scarborough (Scarbrough, Scarbrow), Stonegrave,
Thwing, Tickhill *(Tickel(l), Tickle), Wakefield, Wetherby (Weatherby,*
Wetherbee), York; 14th: Adlingfleet, Adwick, Ardsley, Arrathorne,
Barlby, *Bilham (Billham),* Bootham, Bridlington *(Burlington), Cave*
(Kave), Cayton, Cottingham, Driffield (Driffill), Dromonby, Faceby,
Firbeck, *Flaxton, Gilling, Grantley,* Guisborough, *Halifax (Hallifax),*
Hemingbrough, Hessle *(Hessel),* Holderness *(Holness),* Horbury *(Horberry),*
Hotham, Huggate *(Huggett),* Hunmanby, (Sand) *Hutton,* Kingston-upon-
Hull *(Kingston),* (South) *Kirkby (Kirby),* Knottingley, *Manfield,* Marking-
field, Maunby, Naburn, Nafferton, Ousefleet, Patrington, *Pickering,*
Pocklington, Poppleton, Ripon *(Rippon), Rossington,* Sandal Magna
(Sandall), Selby *(Selbey, Selbie),* Skipton, Swanland, *Thirsk (Trask),*
Toothill *(Tootal, Tootell, Tootill, Tootle, Tothill, Tottle, Tuthill, Tutill,*
Tuttle), Warter, Wauldby *(Walby),* Wawne *(Wawn),* Wentbridge, Wet-
wang, *Wharram (Wharam).*

HOMES OF SURNAMES REVEALED BY DIALECT OR VOCABULARY

In Middle English surnames often appear in a form which is clearly
dialectal and can be assigned to a particular area. *Royds* preserves a
West Riding (and Lancashire) pronunciation of *Rhodes,* found also
in *Hoyle* for *Hole, Oldroyd* and *Boothroyd. Nadler* is a medieval
Essex and London form of *Needler. Hele* and *Heale* are common in

Devon, less frequent in Somerset and noted occasionally in Hampshire, Wiltshire and Worcestershire. This corresponds to the more common *Hale*, found in counties as far apart as Shropshire, Lincolnshire and Sussex. The West Saxon *Weald*, found in Essex, Kent, Sussex, Hampshire and Oxfordshire, appears as *Wald* or *Wold* farther north, in Anglian counties. *Hoath* and *Hoad* are Kent and Sussex dialectal forms of *Heath* and *Lone* or *Loan* West Midland forms of *Lane*. These local surnames, referring to the place where the man lived, often remained common in their native districts and are a clue to the home of the family name. But care is always needed in drawing deductions, for in many of these, formed from common terms, the medieval dialect form has been replaced by the standard English one. The areas, too, are vague, whilst our knowledge of the essential characteristics of the Middle English dialects and their distribution is not so precise as we could wish.

Some topographical terms and formations are characteristic of particular areas. *Sole*, from *atte Sole* 'dweller by the pool', is common in Kent and found also in Surrey and Sussex. The south-east, too, is the home of place-names ending in -*ett* compounded with the name of a tree, *Aldritt*, *Eldrett*, *Naldrett* 'alder-grove', *Hazlett* 'hazel-copse', particularly common in Essex, Surrey and Sussex. *Etchells* and *Neachell* come chiefly from Staffordshire and Warwickshire. The home of *Bridger*, *Brooker*, etc., is the southern counties, especially Sussex and Kent, though examples are found elsewhere.

Some terms are confined to counties where there was a strong Scandinavian element. The Yorkshire *Storrs* is from ON *storð* 'a young plantation', *Scales* and *Scholes*, from ON *skáli*, ME *scale*, *scole* 'hut, shed', found as a place-name in Cumberland, Lancashire, Yorkshire and Norfolk. *Sotheby*, *Nordaby*, *Easterby* and *Westoby* are Scandinavian formations with which we may compare such Saxon surnames as *Astington*, *Sinton*, etc.[1] The Yorkshire *Grave(s)* is certainly Scandinavian, either from ON *greifi* 'steward' or from ON *Greifi*, a byname meaning 'count, earl'.

HOMES OF PATRONYMICS

Surnames from Scandinavian personal-names must usually have arisen in Scandinavian areas, though we must not forget that in the reign of Cnut many Scandinavians moved south. As a surname,

[1] *v.* p. 53.

Herrick comes chiefly from Leicestershire; *Copsey* (ON *Kupsi*, OSw *Kofse*) is found early in Durham, Yorkshire and Norfolk; ON *Valþiófr*, Anglicised as *Wælpēof*, with a variety of modern forms, including *Walthew*, *Waddy*, *Waddilove* and *Waddelow*, is distinctly northern, common in Durham, Northumberland and Yorkshire. Two rare surnames of Scandinavian origin, *Sank* and *Tovell*, with its variants *Tofield* and *Tuffield*, have been noted only in Suffolk. Scandinavian personal-names are found all over England in DB, but are naturally less common in the south and south-west. Some, however, found only in particular counties, are listed by von Feilitzen.[1] Of these 56 are found only in Yorkshire, 34 only in Lincolnshire, 6 only in Lincolnshire and Yorkshire, 41 only in the northwest, and 36 only in East Anglia. Some of these still survive as surnames: *Allgrim*, *Turpin* (Y), *Brockless*, *Fastolf* (L); *Dolphin*, *Duffin*, *Rankill*, *Seagrim* (NW); *Fathers*, *Fadder*, *Langbain* (East Anglia).

The problem of the distribution of OE and Scandinavian personal-names before the Conquest has not yet been tackled nor has any collection been made of those which continued in use after the Conquest. When this material has been assembled and sifted we shall be able to throw light on the homes of numerous family names derived from personal-names.

Of 83 OE personal-names in DB which are not recorded in pre-Conquest sources, 35 occur only in Norfolk, Suffolk or Essex.[2] In these counties, too, we find other names found only in late OE. The theme *Stān-* was popular. The late OE *Stānmǣr*, surviving as *Stammer(s)* and *Stānheard*, now *Stannard* or *Stonard*, and the unrecorded woman's name **Stānhild*, still found as *Stanhill*, *Stonhill* and *Stonnill*, are all East Anglian. *Kerrich* and *Kerridge* are Suffolk names, frequently found in that county from the thirteenth century, deriving from OE *Cynerīc* which occurs four times in the Suffolk Domesday. OE *Ælfhēah* continued in use after the Conquest in counties as far apart as Gloucester and Essex. The home of the family name, now usually *Elphick*, appears to be Kent where the personal-name is found as late as 1216, its popularity due, no doubt, to the veneration of St Alphege, Archbishop of Canterbury 984–1012, who was martyred by the Danes.

[1] O. von Feilitzen, *The Pre-Conquest Personal-Names of Domesday Book* (Uppsala, 1937), pp. 25–6.
[2] von Feilitzen, op. cit., pp. 13–14.

THE DISTRIBUTION OF SOME SURNAMES OF OCCUPATION

The Smith is ubiquitous. We find him on every manor and in the towns. The Shepherd and the Weatherhead, originally 'wether-herd', were countrymen, whilst the Spurrier, the Cutler and the Tanner worked in the towns. But some occupations were limited to a particular area. The *Reader* or *Reeder* thatched roofs with reeds and must have lived where the material he needed was plentiful. It is a fenland name, particularly common in Norfolk and found also in Cambridgeshire and Suffolk. *Scudder*, who appears to have been a dresser of white-leather, has been noted only in Norwich. Other surnames of tradesmen and artisans were certainly limited to particular areas, but no serious attempt has been made to tackle the problem, which is vast and complicated. One difficulty is that we are often unable to decide whether a man actually followed the occupation from which he was named or whether this was already an inherited family name. What we need is a full collection of surnames of occupation, localised and dated, care being taken to avoid including the same man twice. A series of distribution maps would be instructive and might well provide the economic historian with useful material.

Fransson and Thuresson have provided some material which is of use. The latter's material does not always agree with that from other sources. *Kitchingman* has been noted only in Yorkshire, but *Boatman*, which he finds only in Yorkshire, Surrey and Somerset, is found also in Norfolk and Suffolk, whilst *Ferriman* occurs in Berkshire as well as the north, and *Hafter* in Middlesex and Norfolk in addition to London and Sussex. Some of Fransson's conclusions are somewhat surprising, but must be accepted on the evidence he gives. The real difficulty in coming to any final decision is that his material is limited. He confines himself to 10 counties, Essex, Sussex, Hampshire, Somerset, Worcestershire, Staffordshire, Lancashire, Yorkshire, Lincolnshire and Norfolk. For these, his material is full and his results reliable, but we need a similarly full treatment of the other counties.

Milner and *Millward* 'keeper of a mill' are identical in meaning, but belong to different parts of England. *Milner* is characteristic of the north and the east, especially Cumberland, Lancashire, Yorkshire, Lincolnshire and Cambridgeshire. Its frequency in the Scandinavian counties suggests it may partly be due to ON *mylnari*. *Millward* is very common in the south and west, in Essex, Sussex, Hampshire, Somerset, Worcestershire and Staffordshire.

OE *īsenmangere* 'ironmonger', now *Icemonger* or *Isemonger*, is especially common in London, Kent and Sussex and is found in Essex and Hampshire; OE *īrenmangere*, now *Ironmonger*, is more widely distributed, in Lancashire, Yorkshire, Lincolnshire, Norfolk, Staffordshire and Buckinghamshire. In some of these counties, the surname is probably of Scandinavian origin, from ON *jarn, earn* 'iron'. *Iremonger* is the sole form noted in Somerset, is common in Worcestershire and has been noted also in Cambridgeshire, Essex, Oxfordshire and Herefordshire.

Fuller, Walker and *Tucker*, identical in meaning, are similarly found in different parts of the country. *Fuller* is southern and eastern, found especially in Norfolk and Essex. The French form *fouleour* is common everywhere and is now indistinguishable from *Fuller*. The common term in the west and north is *Walker*, corresponding in the south-west, especially in Somerset, to *Tucker*.

Wheeler is common in the south, especially in Essex, Sussex, Hampshire and Somerset, fairly common in Worcestershire, and found also in Staffordshire and Cambridgeshire. *Wheelwright* is more widely spread, found alongside *Wheeler* in Essex, Hampshire and Worcestershire. It is common in Yorkshire and Lincolnshire and occurs also in Derbyshire, Bedfordshire and East Anglia.

Whether words like *baxter, brewster*, etc., were originally feminine and later applied to men, or whether they were from the first used of both sexes, is a problem we need not consider. Such terms have given rise to numerous surnames, some of them very common, and they were more frequent in ME than they are today. It is the ME meaning which concerns us. The suffix was certainly feminine and still survives in surnames derived from occupations followed by women. *Simester* is from OE *sēamestre*, fem. of *sēamere* 'sewer, tailor', hence 'sempstress', but our two earliest examples, William and Peter *le Semestre*, were Lincolnshire men of 1275. Similarly, *Huxter* or *Huxster* is the feminine form of *Hucker* 'a retailer of small goods, pedlar, hawker', a common occupation of women, and, as a surname, usually that of a woman. But again our earliest example is a man, Walter *le Hokestere* of Essex (1285 *Ass*). *Souster* 'sempstress', from *sewestre*, feminine of *Sewer*, has been found only as the surname of women. *Brewster* is found much more frequently as the name of a man than of a woman, though we should have expected it to be commonly applied to a

355

woman in view of the innumerable women who were fined for charging too much for their ale. But they are usually referred to as wives of their husbands, with no mention of their own surname and often without even their christian name.

Fransson has examined fully the evidence for the counties with which he deals and has come to the conclusion that, so far as surnames are concerned, the difference between *Brewer* and *Brewster* is topographical.[1] *Brewer* is southern, *Brewster* midland and northern. Surnames in *-ester* are found throughout England, but are chiefly Anglian (100 examples in Norfolk alone), where they are commonly used of men, whereas in the Saxon counties they are comparatively rare and are used of women. Of 42 surnames in *-ester*, 16 are used only of women, 12 only of men, the remaining 14 being used of both men and women. Of the individuals bearing these surnames, 77 are women and 242 men.

The most common of these surnames are *Baxter*, *Lister*, *Webster* and *Brewster*, all occupations which might have been carried out by women, but all, as surnames, used most frequently of men. All, too, are Anglian surnames, found in Worcestershire, Warwickshire and Bedfordshire, and in the counties farther north. *Lister* 'dyer' is of Scandinavian origin, particularly common in Lancashire, Yorkshire, Lincolnshire and Norfolk. *Webster* is found also in Suffolk, where it is more common than *Webber* and less common than *Webb*, a Saxon name, from OE *webba* (masc.) or *webbe* (fem.), usually used of men. Fransson has only two examples of *Webber*, from Somerset (1340) and London (1378). Though rarer than *Webb*, it is found also in Essex in 1255 and in Suffolk in 1327. *Weaver*, a derivative of OE *wefan* 'to weave' is also rare in early sources, noted only in Sussex, Worcestershire and Cheshire.

Dyer is the southern surname corresponding to the Scandinavian *Lister* and the Anglian *Dyster* or *Dister*. *Dexter*, usually said to be limited to Suffolk, is found also in Leicestershire and Warwickshire. We have a similar series in *Thatcher* in the south, *Thacker* in the north, with *Theaker*, from ON *þekja* 'to cover', in Yorkshire and Lincolnshire, and occasionally in Norfolk and Bedfordshire. *Thaxter* has been noted only in Norfolk where it still survives.

---

[1] G. Fransson, *Middle English Surnames of Occupation, 1100–1350* (Lund, 1935), pp. 41–5.

Index of Subjects

London, 307–9; of London immigrants, 337–51; Welsh, 316–20; Yorkshire, 312–14; homes of, revealed by dialect, 351–2; patronymics, 352–3; occupational, 354–6; variation of, 298–9, 304–6, 308–9, 338–43; heredity, 300–3, 304, 307–8, 310–12, 314–16; transfer of, 306–7, 338–41; development of family names, 302–4; homes of family names, 321–3; migration of, 321–3, 324–6, 330; farmers' surnames in 1890, 323–7

toponymics, English, 54–5; in *-er* and *-man*, 200–1; French, 54, 65–8; continental, 73–4

women's names, 76–7; post-Conquest, 132–3; Saints' names, 133; Classical, 133; men's names used for, 133–4; pet-names, 134–5; diminutives, 135–6; obsolete, 136; surnames of, 82–5, 92

words antedated, 4, 224, 229, 249, 262, 268, 269, 271

-wright, compounds of, 206–8; obsolete names, 207–8

359

Index of Surnames

Obsolete surnames are not indexed. Where a letter (or letters) is enclosed in parentheses, forms both with and without that letter are found: e.g. Adkin(s) is for both Adkin and Adkins, Aud(e)ley for Audley and Audeley, Chum(b)ley for both Chumbley and Chumley, etc.

Alpe, Alps, 272
Alphege, 109
Alsey, 109
Alty, 124
Alured, 99
Alven, 105 n. 1
Alwin, 105 n. 1
Amblin, 135
Ambrose, 143
Am(e)lot, 135
Amery, 63
Ames, 152
Amesbury, 351
Amiel, 151
Amiot, 151
Amis, 152
Ammon(ds), 127
Amoor(e), 36, 50
Amori, Amory, 72
Amo(u)r, 289
Andrew, 142
Angers, 72
Angle, 50
Angood, 126
Angwin, 66
Anketell, Ankettle, 32, 105 n. 2, 126
Ankill, 32, 105 n. 2, 126
Ankin, 32
An(n)able, Annible, 77
Annand, 123, 127
Annas, Anness, Annis(s), 76
Anquetel, 126
Anstey, 348
Ansteys, Anstice, Anstis(s), 134
Antcliff, 28
Antell, 32, 105 n. 2, 126
Antin, 32
Antingham, 334
Antony, 143
Anyan, 319
Applegarth, Applegath, Applegate, 44
Appleton, 55
Applewhaite, Applewhite, 44
Apps, 50
ApSimon, 318
Aram, Arum, 42
Arblaster, 301
Arbon, 127
Arborn, 120, 127
Archambault, 139
Archbold, Archbutt, 139
Archibald, 139
Arden, 301, 302
Aries, Aris(s), 37, 72
Arkwright, 30, 207
Arliss, 236
Arlott, 5, 30, 174
Armer, 190, 248
Armour, 248
Armstrong, 239

Arnall, Arnold, 131
Arnott, 131
Arras, 37, 61, 72
Arridge, 50
Arrowsmith, 205
Arscott, 42
Arsmith, 205
Arson, 77
Artis(s), Artist, 65
Artois, 65
Artrick, 207
Artus, 65
Arundel, 46, 269, 351
Ash, 49, 50, 62
Ashbolt, 139
Ashbourne, Ashburn, 347
Ashken, 126
Ashkettle, 32, 123, 126
Ashley, 336
Ashlin(g), 136
Ashman, 193
Ashplant, 140
Ashpole, Ashpool, 139
Ashwell, 334
Askell, 126
Askin(s), 30, 32, 126
Aslin(g), 136
Asp, 50
Aspel(l), 350
Aspenlon, 140
Aspland, Asplen, Asplin, 140
Assen, 77
Assheton, 302
Astell, 126
Astin(s), 32, 126
Astington, 53, 352
Astling, 136
Astman, 193
Aston, 52 n., 108
Atcock, 211
Athell, 50
Athelstan, 108
Atherden, Atherley, 50
Athill, 36, 50
Athoke, 50
Athridge, 108
Atkin, 215
Atlay, Atley, 50
Atmeare, Atmer, 50
Atmore, 36, 50
Atread, 50
Attack, 50
Atter, 260
Atteridge, 50, 108
Atterwill, 50
Attewell, Attiwell, 50
Attlee, 49, 50
Attmere, 50
Attock, 50
Attread, Attreed, 50

363

Cheever, 263
Chene, 62
Cherrett, Cherritt, 207
Cherryman, 198
Chesham, 347
Chesney, 62
Chesson, 348
Ches(s)wright, 207
Chesterman, 201
Chestney, 62
Cheston, 348
Chevins, Chevis, 274
Chew, 46, 268
Cheyham, 351
Cheyne, Cheyney, 62
Chichester, 337, 351
Chick, 272
Chicken, 272
Chignall, Chignell, 347
Childerhouse, 44
Childers, 44
Chil(l)man, 193
Chipman, 197
Chishick, 349
Chissell, 347
Chissick, 349
Chiswick, 32, 349
Chittleburgh, 350
Chivers, 263
Cholmeley, Chomley, 26
Cholmondeley, 26
Chopin, Chopping, 256
Christopher, 58, 71
Chubb, 273
Chue, 46, 268
Chuff, 268
Chum(b)ley, 26
Church, 55
Churchers, Churches, 44
Churchouse, Churchus, 44
Circuitt, Cirket(t), 40
Clack, 97, 122, 124, 127
Cladingbowl, 139
Cladish, 52
Claggett, 52
Clake, 271
Clarabut, 139
Clare, 180, 350
Claremont, 60
Clarenbone, 139
Claridge, 48
Claringbold, Claringbull, 139
Claris, 133
Clarke, 24, 169
Clarksmith, 206
Clarkson, 90, 169 n. 2
Clarson, 90
Clarvis, 70
Clavell, 73
Clavering, 347

Claxton, 335
Clay, 335
Claygate, 52
Clayman, 198
Clayre, 180
Cleak, 271
Cleatherow, 348
Cleeve, 200
Cleever, 200
Clem, 151
Clemence, 134
Clement(s), 134, 142, 303
Clere, 348
Clermont, Clermunt, 60
Cleugh, 50
Clew, 50
Climance, 134
Clisby, 335
Clitheroe, Clitherow, 348
Clog, 187
Clore, 178
Clough, 50
Clouter, 179
Clow, 50
Clower, 178
Club, 248
Cluderay, 348
Clue, 50
Cluer, 178
Cluff, 50
Clun(e)y, Clunie, 72
Cobbold, 97
Cobham, 348
Cock, 58, 110, 210, 266, 268–9
Cockbain, 240
Cockburn, 212
Cockerell, 229
Cockerham, 26
Cockett, 164 n. 1
Cockfield, 36, 212, 336, 343, 350
Cockhead, 235
Cockin, 164 n. 1
Cockram, Cockran, 26
Cocks, 210
Cockshed, 235
Cockshott, 212
Cockwell, Cockwill, 271, 292
Coddington, 347
Codner, 187
Coe, 267
Coeshall, 212
Coffer, 245
Coggeshall, 212
Colbran, 119
Colchester, 336
Colcock, 154
Col(e)brook, 347
Col(e)gate, 335
Col(e)man, 193
Colepepper, 283

371

Cox, 210
Coxall, 212
Coxhead, 235
Coy, 253
Crabbe, 274
Crabtree, 4
Craddock, 317, 326
Crake, 267
Crakebone, 287
Craker, 64, 70
Crane, 58, 267
Crank, 253
Cranwell, 349
Crask(e), 43, 233, 257
Crassweller, 202
Crathern, Crathorne, 26
Craw, 267
Crawcour, 64, 70
Craythorne, 26
Creak, 335
Crease, 253
Crecy, 73
Creed, 111
Cre(e)gor, 70
Creek, 335
Cresner, 71
Cressee, Cress(e)y, 73
Cressweller, 202
Crews, 253
Crier, 159
Cringlewood, 335, 349
Crippen, 143, 235
Cripps, 28, 235
Crisp, 235
Crispin, 143, 235
Crittall, 48
Crittenden, 48
Crittle, 48
Croaker, 64, 70
Croasdell, 42
Crocker, 70, 190
Croker, 70, 190
Croll, 235
Cromb, 234
Cromwell, 202
Cronk, 253
Crook, 127, 234
Crookshank(s), 240
Cross, 55, 201
Crossdale, 42
Crossman, 201
Crossthwaite, Crosswaite, 44
Crostwight, 44
Crouch, 200
Croucher, 200
Crouchman, 200
Crow, 266, 267, 271
Crowder, 173
Crowfoot, 241
Crowle, 349

Crowlesmith, 206
Crowne(s), 63, 72
Crowther, 173
Croydon, 351
Croyle, 73
Croysdill, 42
Cruickshank(s), 10, 21, 240
Cruise, 253
Crumb, 234
Crump, 234
Crumpler, 202
Cruse, 253
Crust, 256
Cruttenden, 47
Cuckow, 271
Cuckson, 90
Cudd, 150
Cuffwright, 206
Culf, 108
Cullen, 37, 74
Cullin, Cullon, 74
Cully, 70
Culpepper, 283
Culver, 272
Culverhouse, 57
Cumberland, 324
Cunditt, 210
Cupples, 235
Curl, 235
Curr, 262
Currier, 188
Cursham, 29
Curson, 71
Curt, 233
Curtin, 233
Curtler, 27
Curzon, 29, 71
Cush, 199
Cushman, 199
Cuss(e), 81, 135, 199
Cusselle, 70
Cussen, Cusson(s), 81
Cust, 81, 135
Custance, 65, 72, 133, 135
Cutbush, 282
Cuthbertson, 89
Cutlack, 109
Cutler, 354
Cutliffe, 283
Cutt, 150
Cuxon, 90, 95
Cuzen, 81
Cyster, 80

Dabbs, 151, 155
d'Abernon, 63, 70
Dabinett, 152, 155
Dabney, 72
Dabson, 155
Daddow, 72

Daft, 252
Dafter(s), Daftor(s), 81
Dagger, 247
Dagnall, Dagnell, 347
Dail(l)ey, 71
Dainteth, Daintith, 254
Daintree, Daintr(e)y, 350
Dainty, 254
Daish, 50
Dakyns, 95
Dalby, 337
Dale, 49
Dalley, 1
Dalling, 335, 349
Dalli(n)son, 72
Dalston, 247
Daltr(e)y, 72
Damary, 63, 72
Damerell, 73
D'Amery, 72
Damiral, Dammarell, 73
Dammery, 72
Damrel(l), 73
Damri, 72
Damyon, 143
Dancaster, 351
Danc(e)y, 70
Dancock(s), 29
Dand, 151, 327, 330
Dando, 72
Dandrick, Dandridge, 29
Dandy, 29
Dane, 31, 50
Danecourt, 73
Danes, 50
Danger, 254
Dangerfield, 73
Daniel, 140
Dankin, 29
Danks, 29
Dann, 329
Dannatt, 29
Dannell, 140
Dannet(t), Dannit, 29
Dansey, Dansie, 70
Danvers, Danvis, 37, 74
Darby, 324, 336, 347
Darc(e)y, D'Arcy, 72
Darkin, 214
Darking, 214, 351
Darknell, 322
Darling, 100
Darlington, 337
Darras, 72
Darree, Darry, 250
Dar(r)ell, 70
Darter, 81
Dartnall, 322
Dash, 49, 50
Dashfield, 49

Dashwood, 49
Dauben(e)y, 61, 72
Dauber, 180, 198
D'Aubney, Daubney, 72, 324
Daughters, 81
Daught(e)ry, Daughtrey, 72
Daultrey, 72
Daunay, Dauney, 72
Dauncey, 70
Dauter, 81
Davall, 73
Daventry, 350
Davers, 63, 72
David, 140
Davidson, 89
Davolls, 73
Davy, 140
Daw, 151
Dawbarne, Dawborne, 21
Dawkes, 95
Dawkins, 215
Dawn, 96
Dawnay, Dawney, 72
Dawson, 89
Daykin, 215
Dayley, 71
Dayman, 231
Dayral, Dayrell, 70
Daysmith, 206
Deadman, 201, 350
Deakes, 154
Dealtry, 72
Dean, 50, 168, 201
Deaner, 201
Deanes, 93, 95
Dearing, 100
Dearman, 193
De Ath, De' Ath, D'Aeth, 11
Dearth, 11
Death, 11
Deathridge, 11, 207
Deaval, Deaville, 73
Deave(s), 242
Debbage, 336
Debenham, Debnam, 201, 336, 350
Debney, 276
de Courcy, Decourcy, 63, 70
Dedman, 201, 350
Deek(e)s, 27, 154
Deemer, 159
Deeping, 349
Deer, 264
Deeth, 11
Deether, 12
Deetman, 12
Deex, 27, 154
de Glanville, 70
Dekin, 154
Dekiss, 154
de Lacy, 71

374

Domb, Domm, 242
Dommett, 73
Domvil(l)e, 70
Donbavand, 155
Doncaster, 337, 351
Donkin, 213
Do(o)little, 1, 259, 281
Dopson, 155
Dorking(s), 351
Dorman, 193
Dottrell, 229
Doubler, 207
Doucett, 253
Doughtery, 72
Doughty, 252
Douie, 72
Dove, 267
Dow, 151
Dowcett, 253
Dower, 183
Dowey, 72
Dowman, 196
Down, 201
Downer, 201
Downham, 201, 335
Downing, 111
Downman, 201
Downward, 54
Dowsett, 234, 253
Doxford, 347
Doyley, D'Oyley, 71, 301
Drake, 266, 270
Drakers, 266
Drakesmith, 206
Drane, 273
Drawater, 283
Drayton, 335
Drew, 138, 151, 289
Drewell, 138
Drewery, 290
Drew(e)s, 68, 71, 138
Drewett, 138
Driffield, Driffill, 337, 351
Drinkald, Drinkale, 277
Drinkell, 277
Drink(h)all, Drink(h)ill, 277
Drinkwater, 281
Dron, 273
Droop, 257
Droy, 71
Dru, 138
Druce, 68, 71, 138
Druitt, 138
Drury, 290
Dubarry, 62
Dubois, 62
du Boulay, 62
Ducat, 249
Duck, 272
Ducker, 272

Duckers, 44
Ducket(t), 235, 249, 272
Duckhouse, 44
Duckrill, 229
Dudgeon, 155
Dudman, 193
Dudson, 155
Duffes, 44
Duffett, 235, 241
Duffin, 353
Duffus, 44, 57
Dufresnoy, 62
Dugard, 276
Duguid, 259
Duhamel, 62
Duker, 272
Dul(e)y, 71
Dullage, 45
Dullard, 256
Dummett, 73
Dumville, 70
Dunbabin, Dunbebin, 155, 238
Dunbavand, Dunbevand, 155
Dunbavin, 155
Dunbob(b)in, 155, 238
Dunce, 198
Dun(c)kley, 348
Dunfield, 70
Dunham, 335
Dunkerley, 348
Dunman, 201
Dunmo, Dunmow, 347
Dunn, 237
Dunnaby, 53
Dunnage, 45, 336, 350
Dunnicliff, 29
Dunning, 111
Duns, 198
Dunstall, 29
Dunsterville, 73
Dunston, 335
Dunton, 53, 347
Dunville, 70
Dupont, 62
Dupuy, 62
Duquemin, 62
Durden, 236
Durham, 347
Durman, 193
Durrad, 235
Durtnall, Durtnell, 322
Dutnall, 322
Dwelly, 257
Dye, 135
Dyer, 185, 356
Dyett, Dyott, 135
Dykins, 154
Dyment, Dymond, 231
Dymott, 204
Dysart, 29

375

389

Leet, 51
Lefanu, 35
Lefebure, Lefebvre, 35
Lefeaver, 35
Le Feuvre, 35
Le Fever, Lefever, 35
Leffingwell, 12
Lefroy, 35
Leger, 143, 290
Legg, 240
Leggatt, 170
Le Good, 35
Legood, 242
Legrant, 219
Le Hunte, 35
Leicester, 37, 348
Leigh, 50
Leighton, 348
Leman, 290
Lemay, 35
Lemon, 4, 290
Lempriere, 35, 170 n. 2
Lenfesty, 31
Lenham, 348
Lenn, 335, 349
Lennard, 143
Lentell, Lentle, 348
Lenthall, 348
Leonard, 143
Leopard, 264
La Patourel, 35
Le Pelley, 35, 235
Leppard, 264
Leppingwell, 12
Lesnie, 73
Less, 9
Lessiter, 348
Lester, Lestor, 72, 185, 348
Le Sueur, 35
Letch, 51
Letcher, 174, 290
Lethem, 15
Letsome, Letson, 76
Letten, 335
Lettice, 76
Letts, 76
Lettsome, 29
Leuty, 253
Leverage, 105 n. 1
Leveret, 264
Leverich, Leverick, 75, 108
Leverington, 347
Levet, 105 n. 1
Levick, 35
Levin, 108
Levings, 111
Lew, 264
Lewcock, 211
Lewes, 351
Lewin, 108

Lewing, 111
Lewsey, 108
Lewtey, 253
Ley, 50
Leycestre, 348
Leysmith, 205
Leyton, 348
Libby, 135
Licence, 63, 71
Lickorish, Licrece, 290
Lidgate, 350
Lidster, 185
Lightfoot, 241
Lilburn, 350
Lill(e)yman, Lilliman, 193
Lillingston, 347
Limbrey, Limbury, 336
Limby, 350
Limmage, 230
Limmer, 191
Limpaney, Limpenny, 335
Limrick, 207
Lince, 51
Linch, 51
Lincoln, 337, 338, 348
Lind, 51
Lindop, Lindup, 48
Lindsay, Lindsey, 337, 349
Line(s), 77, 150
Ling, 335
Lingwood, 335
Link, 51
Linkin, 348
Linnett, 151
Linney, 116
Linstead, 336
Linter, 180
Linton, 347
Lippingwell, 12
Liquorish, 290
Lisney, 73
Lison, 71
Lisseter, 348
Lister, 185, 356
Li(t)chfield, 350
Litcook, 212
Litman, 193
Litster, 185
Little, 233
Littlecole, 239
Littledyke, 239
Littlejohn, 239
Littleproud, 259
Littler, 42
Livard, 108
Liveing, 111
Livens, 108
Livett, Livitt, 71
Livsey, 108
Llewellin, 317

Momerie, 72
Mompesson, 71
Money, 186
Moneypenny, 250
Monier, 186
Monkman, 197
Monk(s), 95, 169
Monsey, 71
Montacute, 72
Montagu(e), 72
Montford, Montfort, 71
Montgomerie, Montgom(e)ry, 71, 300
Moody, 4
Moon(e), 58, 72, 169, 301
Moorcock, 210, 272
Moor(e), 18, 36, 50, 238
Moorhouse, 44
Moorman, 200
Mordey, Mordue, 278
More, 50, 238
Moresby, 16
Morgan, 317, 326
Morley, 335
Morpeth, 350
Morrell, 238
Morress, 44
Mor(r)ice, Morris, 16 n., 24, 28, 144, 238, 318
Morrisby, 15
Morrish, 28
Morsby, 16
Morse, 16 n.
Mort, 11
Mortelman, 196
Morten, 72
Mortiboy, xi
Mortimer, Mortimore, 60, 73, 301
Mortlake, Mortlock, 350
Mortleman, 196
Morton, 335
Mos(e)by, 16
Moss, 195
Mothers, 80, 124
Mothersole, 278
Motton, 263
Moubray, 72
Mould(s), 76
Moule, 263
Moulson, 76
Moult, 76
Moulton, 335
Mouncey, Mounsey, Mounsie, 71, 73
Mountford, Mountfort, 71
Mountjoy, 72
Mousley, 348
Mouth, 234
Mowat, 76
Mowbray, 64, 72, 229
Mowbury, 72

Mowe, 203
Mowle(s), 76, 263
Mowll, 76
Mowse, 264
Moyce, Moyes, 141
Moyne, 169
Moyse(s), 141, 171
Much, 233
Muckle, 233
Muddeman, Muddiman, 203
Mudditt, 243
Muff, 203
Muirsmith, 206
Mulb(er)ry, 72, 229
Mule, 263
Mullender, 162
Mullett, 274
Mullin(g)er, 162
Mumbe(r)son, 71
Mumbray, 72
Mumby, 349
Mumford, 71, 335, 349
Mummery, 72
Muncey, Munchay, 71, 73
Mund(a)y, 127
Munden, 348
Mun(d)ford, 71, 335, 349
Mungay, 71, 72, 73
Munks, 95
Munn, 169
Munsey, Munsie, 71, 73
Murch, 233
Muriel, 20
Murrell, 20
Mushett, Muskett, 267
Mussard, 257
Musson, 269
Mustard, Mustart, 19, 183
Mustel(l), 265
Musters, 71
Mustill, Mustol, 265
Mustre, 71
Mut(t)er, 159
Mut(t)imer, 72
Mutton, 263
Muzzel, Muzzle, 265
Mycock, 212
Myhill, 145
Mynn, 134
Mynott, 242

Nabb(s), 151, 155
Nadler, 178, 197, 351
Naesmith, Naismith, 205
Nalder, 50
Naldrett, 50, 352
Nangle, 50
Napier, 158
Napp, 155
Napper, 158

Nares, 237
Nash, 49, 50
Nasmyth, 205
Nay, 50
Nayland, 336, 350
Nayler, 178
Naysh, 50
Naysmith, 205
Neachell, 50, 352
Neame(s), 21, 78, 81
Neasmith, 205
Neave(s), 21, 82
Neck, 236
Neech, 82
Needham, 335
Needlaman, Needleman, 197
Needler, 178, 197, 351
Neese, 82
Neeve(s), 82
Nelder, 178
Neldrett, 50
Nelmes, 50
Nephew, 82
Netter, 179
Neve(s), 82
Nevil(l)e, 61, 73
New, 51
Newbury, 19
Newhouse, 44
Newill, 73
Newis(s), 44
Newman, 203
Newmarch, 73
Newton, 335
Ney, 50
Niccols, 153
Nichol, 153
Nicholas(s), 142, 153
Nicholds, 153
Nichol(e)s, 153
Nicholetts, 153
Nicholls, 153
Nicholson, 90, 153
Nickal(ls), Nickel(l)s, 153
Nickelson, Nickerson, 153
Nick(e)s, 153
Nickinson, Nickisson, 153
Nicklas(s), Nickless, 153
Nickle, 153
Nicklen, Nicklin, 153
Nickolay, 153
Nickol(d)s, Nickol(ls), 153
Nickson, 153
Nicolai, Nicolay, 153
Nicolas, 153
Nicol(e), Nicoll(e), 153
Nicolson, 153
Nie, 50
Nightingale, Nightingall, 19, 266, 269
Nightingirl, 269

Nikells, 153
Nind, 51
Nin(e)ham, 51
Ninnim, 51
Nix, 16, 153
Nixseaman, 16
Nix(s)on, 153
Noad, 51
Noah, 51, 141
Noake, 50
Noar, 51
Nobbs, Nobes, 151, 155
Noble, 21, 252
Noblet(t), 155
Nock, 50
Nodes, 51
Noe, 141
Noel, 303
Noise, 141
Noke, 50
Nolda, Nolder, 50
Nop(p)s, 155
Norchard, 51
Nordaby, 53, 352
Norman(d), 65
Normanville, 73
Norreys, 54
Norridge, 45, 54, 349
Norrington, 53, 349
Norris, 28, 54
Norrish, 28
North, 53
Northampton, 349
Northen, Northern, 54
Northsmith, 206
Northway, 53
Northwood, 54
Norton, 52
Norwich, 338, 349
Nothard, 164, 177
Nott, 235
Nottage, Nottidge, 266
Nottingham, 237, 350
Nowers, 71
Noyse, 141
Nunhouse, Nunniss, 44
Nunn(s), 95, 168
Nutbrown, 237
Nutkins, 216
Nutter, 164, 170 n. 1, 177
Nye, 50
Nyman, 203

Oade, 51, Oades, 138
Oak, 50
Oakey, 124
Oakham, 350
Oaten, Oates, 138
Odam(s), 81
Odart, 138

395

INDEX OF SURNAMES

Odd, 119, 211
Odell, 347
Odgers, 138
Odhams, 81
Odlin(g), 138
Offer, 186
Officer, 186
Ogbourne, 9
Oger, 138
Oglander, 72
Okey, 124
Okeysmith, 206
Old, 350
Older, 50
Oldham, 30
Oldknow, 259
Oldman, 196, 203
Oldreive, 196
Oldridge, 108
Oldroyd, 351
Oldwright, 206
Oliphant, 58
Olley, Ollie, 63, 71
Onians, Onions, 319
Onraet, 257
Onyett, 116
Orange, 72
Orchard, 51
Orfeur, 186
Orford, 336, 350
Organer, 173 n. 4
Orgill, Orgles, 254
Oriel, 133
Orlebar, 39
Orledge, Orlich, 176
Orme, 122
Ormsby, 349
Ormson, 89
Orneblow, 283
Orpet, 254
Orr, 122, 127
Orren, Orrin, 206 n. 2
Orrinsmith, 206
Orriss, Orys, 146
Orsborn, 207
Osbern, 126
Osbert, 126
Osgood, 30, 126, 207
Osler, 177
Osman, 193
Osmer, 126
Osmond, 105 n. 1, 107, 126
Ostrick, 207
Ostridge, 9, 207
Oswin, 126
Othen, 123, 127
Otten, Otton, 138
Ottewell, 138
Ottoway, Otway, 138
Oulton, 335

Outlaw, 258
Outright, 109, 206
Ovens, 163
Over, 51, 347
Overbeck, 51
Overy, 49, 51
Owen, 318
Owensmith, 206
Ower(s), 51
Owles, 267
Owlett, 267
Oxborough, Oxbrow, 42
Oxford, 337
Oxley, 350
Oxman, 199
Oxnard, 177

Pac(e)y, 71
Packman, 196
Packwood, 351
Pacock, 269
Paffard, 248
Pagan, 146
Page, 323
Pagnell, 151
Paillard, 224
Pain, 146
Pairpoint, 73
Pakeman, 196
Pakenham, 350
Palferman, Palframan, 199
Palfre(e)man, Palfreyman, 199, 245, 246 n. 1
Palfrey, 245, 246 n. 1, 261
Palgrave, 335
Palmer, 2
Palphreyman, 199
Panckridge, 144
Pane, 147
Pannaman, 197
Pannell, 147
Panner, 181, 224
Pan(n)ett, 147
Panniers, 58
Pannifer, 224
Pan(s), 224
Panter, Panther, 57
Pantry, 19, 55, 245
Papigay, 270
Papillon, 273
Papworth, 351
Paramor, 289
Pardew, Pardey, Pardoe, 278
Parfitt, 252
Parfrement, 199
Pargeter, Pargiter, 28, 180
Parham, 336
Paris, 28, 37, 61, 144
Parish, 28
Park, 49

396

397

399

408

413